Introduction to Logic

Introduction to Logic

Charles W. Kegley
California State College

Jacquelyn Ann Kegley
California State College

Charles E. Merrill Publishing Company
A Bell & Howell Company
Columbus   Toronto   London   Sydney

Published by
Charles E. Merrill Publishing Company
A Bell & Howell Company
Columbus, Ohio 43216

This book was set in Caledonia.
The Production Editor was Sharon Keck Thomason.
The cover was designed and prepared by Columbus Bank Note Company.

Library of Congress Catalog Card Number: 77–088934
International Standard Book Number: 0–675–08358–3

Printed in the United States of America
1 2 3 4 5 6 7 8 9 10 / 83 82 81 80 79 78

Preface

The *benefit* of a good course in Logic is hardly debatable. However, what constitutes a good course in logic is. This fact is perhaps best exemplified by the abundance
of available introductory texts. So, why have we decided to write another one?
Surely, we have not tried to define the ideal course in logic. Rather we present a
comprehensive treatment of topics that can be utilized by students and instructors in
seeking to define their own courses in logic.

The opening chapter identifies the basic logical concepts (statement(s), argument,
inductive vis-a-vis deductive reasoning, etc.). The remainder of the text is divided
into three main parts, each of which can be studied in relative independence of each
other. Part one deals with logic and language, part two covers deductive logic, both
traditional categorical and modern truth functional as well as quantificational logic.
Part three is devoted to a thorough treatment of inductive logic.

Any definition of a good course in logic would be remiss if the needs of the students
were not taken into consideration. This factor has been of paramount importance in
the development of this program. Several instructional techniques have been employed to facilitate these considerations.

One concept is presented at a time. Discussions of the concepts make abundant
use of examples, drawn from a broad range of disciplines and interests (political
science, business, philosophy, sports, science, etc.) to show the relevance of logic to
every human endeavor. Exercises immediately follow each discussion to test the
student's mastery of the concept. The answers to the odd-numbered problems are
provided in the back of the book for immediate reinforcement. Each chapter concludes with a summary outline for easy recall of the main points. Throughout the text,

great care has been taken to present the material in a style that will be conducive to the students' understanding and retention.

Finally, in addition to these instructional features, we have developed a set of seven cassette tapes which parallel the coverage of the text. These tapes provide answers and explanations to a series of optional exercises presented in the text. For easy identification, these optional exercises appear in the shaded areas of the text— just as this sentence does. Any time a student sees questions in a shaded area, he/she should listen to the tapes for the correct response. After answering the questions stated in the text, the tapes then *ask* one or two additional questions, followed by the correct response.

These tapes can be used at the discretion of either the instructor or the student. They can be utilized as an integral part of the course or merely used as additional practice is needed.

We believe this program has sufficient flexibility and breadth to allow the instructor to develop what he or she considers to be an ideal course in logic. We would appreciate any suggestions you might have, for the question "How do you teach people to think clearly?" has no easy answer.

Contents

Chapter 7 Truth-Functional Statements 219

Chapter 8 The Method of Deduction 271

Chapter 9 Quantification Theory 299

Part III: Induction   333

Chapter 10 Inductive Generalization and Analogy   335

Chapter 11 Necessary and Sufficient Conditions, Causal Relations, and Mill's Methods   367

Chapter 12 The Hypo-Deductive Method of Reasoning   395

Chapter 13 Decision Making   429

Introduction to Logic

Part I
Language

1

INTRODUCTION

1.1 WHY LOGIC?

Clear beginnings are important to any undertaking. Thus, it is wise to begin this text by answering two obvious and very important questions: What is logic? and Why take a course in logic? A brief answer to the first question is that logic is the study of reasoning, of how to think clearly, how to reason validly, how to argue soundly. It deals with the methods and principles by which one distinguishes good from bad reasoning.

Why should we be concerned to study the nature of reasoning, good or bad? First of all, we cannot escape engaging in reasoning. From the time we wake up in the morning and try to decide what we want for breakfast or what clothes we will wear until we go to sleep for the night, we are facing choices, making decisions, trying to solve problems of one sort or another. In making decisions and in solving problems, we presumably appeal, in one way or another, to reasons for doing what we do and for choosing the solutions we choose. Many of these decisions of everyday life may be trivial; others may be highly significant. Many of our acts and solutions may be habitual and unconscious; others will be deliberate and conscious acts. Whichever is the case, if we are rational, we are committed to the ultimate support of our decisions and even of our habits by reasons. If we are rational, we seek to develop warranted habits and warranted decisions, that is, habits and decisions for which good reasons can be produced. And, logic is concerned with the justification of conclusions, that is, with providing good reasons for what is asserted in our conclusions.

At a deeper level, a level underlying our decisions and habits, there are our beliefs of various kinds; that is, those things we accept as being true or probably true. For example, we believe that a college or university education will advance us vocationally, that a certain career is suited to us, and that this or that person will make the best wife or husband. These kinds of beliefs guide our daily acts and decision making. But beliefs, too, must be based on *reasons* of some sort. These range from the unexamined assumptions most of us employ, on the one hand, to the evidence we have carefully considered on the other hand. But, once again, being rational human beings we *demand* and *want* to know explicitly the reasons for our beliefs and for the beliefs of others. Further, we know that not all reasons are equally good reasons and that some are not good at all. For example, wishing the term paper were written is no reason for believing it has been written. But, to raise the question of good or bad reasons for beliefs is to make a logical appraisal. Logic is primarily concerned with the *relation* between reasons and beliefs, or, more specifically, between evidence and a conclusion. Logic asks the question: "Are these beliefs (conclusions) justified by their evidence (reasons)?" Thus, because we as human beings operate in worlds of various kinds of beliefs, our own and the beliefs of others, we cannot escape reasoning. And, if we are *thinking* human beings, who are concerned about the evidence that justifies beliefs, we cannot escape logic.

Further, we live in an age when there are many hidden persuaders that attempt to mold and shape our beliefs, our buying habits, our political decisions, our social behavior. Witness such books as *The Making of the President* or the constant concern of Ralph Nader on behalf of the consumer. In order to escape being taken and being molded, many times unconsciously, we need to have the ability to cut through flowery rhetoric, subtle and beguiling advertising, flattery and threats to the heart of the matter—exactly what is being offered or said and *why?* Are the reasons, the evidence, adequate to support the assertions being made? Thus, logic, the art of thinking, ultimately is a highly practical matter. The study of logic should make us aware of the differences between persuasion through various psychological techniques, and persuasion based on rational argument and supporting evidence.

Still further, there is Socrates' belief that "the unexamined life is not worth living." The human being is a rational animal and to live a full and meaningful life our reason, not just our appetites and emotions, must be utilized and developed. We should live at a higher level than that of opinion which is unclarified and usually unjustified. Often opinions are held merely because someone else holds the same opinion or a large number of people have such a belief. Each human being, argued Socrates, should try to think through his beliefs and the reasons why they are held, and should searchingly probe the beliefs governing basic institutions in society. Further, the ability to think soundly has traditionally been a characteristic of the educated person. The educated person is the individual capable of utilizing and dealing with all the many good and bad things life has to offer, capable of adapting, adjusting and being in control of life rather than controlled by it. Although, the term 'educated person' is not used as often today in common discourse, some of its meaning, at least as far as logical thinking is concerned, is captured in the requirement on many university and college campuses that logic be considered a basic subject. Such schools require that all undergraduates take the course because it provides the skills and tools necessary for dealing with and benefiting from one's educational experiences in the humanities, the social and natural sciences, and in professional training. Logic, then, is considered an eminently practical subject area, a basic subject.

Why logic is considered basic can further be seen by considering the following. First of all, a course in logic requires us to reflect on the nature of thought—something we rarely take time to do in life or even in our educational career. In logic we gain increased insight into the principles of reasoning, and thus learn what it means to *prove* a claim rather than just to assert it or state it in an eloquent language. Second, in logic we become acquainted with traditional fallacies and errors in reasoning. Knowing the kinds of mistakes we can make is to take a first step toward avoiding them in our own reasoning. Third, in studying logic we learn certain easily applied techniques for detecting the correctness and incorrectness of various kinds of reasoning so that errors may be avoided and we may not be misled by other's errors or by their sheer power of persuasion. Fourth, the ability to reason correctly is not something automatically and magically acquired. Rather, it is more like an artistic skill requiring actual practice. Application and practice under guided supervision is a key part of a course in logic; it is not usually specifically available elsewhere. Fifth, two operating ideals of logic, in addition to adequacy of proof are clarity and economy of expression. One area of logical analysis is the area of language itself, particularly its misuses and its misleadings due to ambiguity and vagueness. Clarity of expression and clarity of meaning are sought as well as clarity of argument. In learning to abstract from nuances of expressions to reveal the structures and skeletons of logical connections, we learn more about how language itself operates. Sixth, our age is one in which scientific method is a paramount tool for dealing with the world. Hence an important feature of a logic course is that it gives a general introduction to scientific method—to inductive generalization, analogy, the developing and testing of hypotheses, causal reasoning, and probability reasoning. These tools are important in all areas of life—business, law, medicine—as well as to all fields of science and technology. Finally, a course in logic equips us with valuable critical thinking skills applicable to all the other courses of study in the entire academic endeavor.

1.2   WHAT IS LOGIC?

The basic aim of logic is to teach us to reason correctly. *Reasoning* is the activity or process of adducing and collecting reasons, weighing them, and drawing conclusions based upon these reasons. *Correct reasoning* is finding reasons and/or evidence which do in fact support and/or prove our conclusions.

This means that logic concerns the *justification* of ideas and statements and not thinking processes as such. Thinking processes themselves are the subject matter of psychology. Psychology is concerned to ask *how* a person came to think of this idea or to make this claim. It would be interested in the fact that the chemist Kekule discovered the model for representing the benzene molecule while dreaming. Logic, on the other hand, asks *what reasons* are there for accepting Kekule's model as adequate. Psychology studies *how* people actually *do* think; logic is interested in how people should think if they want to think clearly and reason validly.

Logic, then, is interested in *justification* of ideas and assertions. It is interested in proof and in establishing claims. It is concerned with the solidity of the grounds we produce to support our claims.

1.3 STATEMENTS, PROPOSITIONS, AND SENTENCES

Because it is concerned with justified assertions, logic deals with statements or with propositions, written or oral. Although statement and proposition do not have exactly the same meaning, their meaning in logic is so nearly the same that for our purposes we can and shall use them interchangeably, giving preference to the term *statement*.

What, then, is a statement or a proposition? A statement is an assertion or denial: something is said to be or not to be the case. For example, the sentence, "Thomas Jefferson was the first Vice-President of the United States" asserts something to be the case, whereas, the sentence, "Thomas Jefferson was not the first Vice-President of the United States" denies something to be the case. Propositions are also assertions or denials, but in Aristotelian logic they are assertions or denials of class relationships. For instance, the sentence "All whales are mammals" asserts a relationship between the class of whales and the class of mammals. You might think of propositions as a kind of categorical statement that relates two categories or classes. A statement is an assertion, and assertions make a claim on our attention and to our belief. A statement is something to be taken seriously. When a statement is made we can ask about its truth or falsity and can demand grounds or reasons for making the assertion.

Statements are usually made by means of oral or written sentences. However, sentences and statements must be carefully distinguished. A sentence is a grammatically constructed expression in some language. The following are all sentences:

1. Who was the first President of the United States?
2. Will you please be quiet.
3. Stand up!

Sentence one is a question, sentence two is a request, and sentence three is a command. None of these sentences is used to assert something to be or not be the case. Further, we would not normally raise the question of the truth or falsity of these sentences. Thus, a sentence may be used to make a statement, but not all sentences are statements.

The relationship between sentences and statements is a complex one, and further illustration is needed. For instance, two different sentences can express the same statement. "Jane loves cats" and "Jane is a cat-lover," though different sentences, make the same statement. Their grammatical structure is different, but they assert the same thing to be the case. Further, a sentence is always a form of language, but statements are not restricted to any one language nor even necessarily tied to language. Thus, the following sentences, though written in different languages all make the same statement.

Love makes the world go round.

El amor anima el universo. L'amour anime l'univers.

Liebe macht die Welt rundherum gehen.

Further, sentences are not the only vehicles for making statements. In suitable circumstances a shrug or a nod, a gesture, or a silence will do the job— sometimes very effectively!

It must also be noted that it is not solely declarative sentences that constitute statements. In the first place, not every occasion when a declarative sentence is spoken, written, or even presented in code is an occasion when a statement is being made. What is at issue is intention; for example, the sentence might have been used as part of a poem or song, written to practice spelling, or coded to see if one understands the code. It is not proper to ask of such sentences: "Are they true or false?" In other words, context is also important in determining whether an assertion is being made and thus when a sentence is a statement.

Further, although questions, commands, exclamations, requests, and performative utterances are not usually used to make statements, they might *imply* or *contain* statements. For example, negative questions can *include* statements. The questions "Doesn't life have a meaning?" and "Doesn't George look silly?" can be taken to make the following statements, "Life presumably does have a meaning," and "George looks silly."

Statements are identified by asking: "Is an assertion or denial being made?" We can ask of a statement: "Is it true or false?" This does not mean that you always do know or could know if it is true or false. Something, however, is claimed or purported to be true or false.

Tape Exercises

Now, examine each of the following sentences and decide whether the sentence expresses a statement, command, question, exclamation, or performative utterance. Give reasons for your decision. [When you have made your choices, turn to Tape 1, band 1.]

1. The house was set far back in the woods and lay in a deep shadow—a fortunate fact in light of its state of disrepair.
2. We find the defendant guilty of first degree murder as charged.

3. How can anyone possibly decide between the two candidates?
4. Will you please quit clicking your transistor radio on and off.
5. It is obvious that the overload caused the power failure.

Exercises for § 1.3

A. In everyday contexts, which of the following sentences are most likely to express a statement, command, question, exclamation, or performative utterance?

1. The play *No Exit* was written by the French existentialist, Jean-Paul Sartre.
2. Good heavens, what a mess!
3. What scientist first used the telescope to make important astronomical studies?
4. Take this memorandum over to the student records office.
5. The defendant was declared not guilty.
6. How long will this inflation last?
7. There is some doubt concerning the authorship of the Shakesperian plays.
8. What speed!
9. I declare the meeting adjourned.
10. Abraham Lincoln was a great debater.
11. Alice claims that she was with John at a movie during the time of the break-in.
12. Ah, that Spring should vanish with the Rose!
13. Come here, my child.
14. The symptoms are very much like those of yellow fever.
15. Please quit talking.

B. In what contexts could the following sentences *express* statements? Write out the implied statement in each case.

1. Do you really believe in witches?
2. What a terrible waste of time!
3. How can you possibly believe this man to be innocent?
4. Vote for the right party! Vote Republican!
5. Don't tell me Galileo wasn't a coward in giving in to the Church!
6. How long can we tolerate the incompetency of this administration?
7. Oh, Wilderness were Paradise now!
8. How could you have made such a mistake?
9. Will this meeting never end!
10. You mean you're not taking me to the dance, as you promised?

1.4 ARGUMENTS

Logic, then, is interested in statements. It is, however, primarily interested in statements in relationship to each other; it is interested in argument. An argument is more than an assertion or statement. An argument is the use of one or more statements to support a conclusion.

An *argument* is a set of statements in which one, called a *conclusion*, is claimed to be the consequence of or to be justified by the others, called variously *evidence*, *reasons*, *grounds*, or *premises*. Thus, every argument consists of two parts: (1) one or more statements called *premises* that cite evidence or reasons; (2) a statement called the *conclusion*, which is claimed either to follow from the premises or to be supported by the evidence.

An argument may also be thought of as the implicit or explicit formulation of an *inference*. Inference is the act of drawing a conclusion from one or more facts, or data. The points from which the inference proceeds are the data and the points to which the inference proceeds is the conclusion. Thus, from the fact that we enjoyed the movie *Airport*, we might infer that we would enjoy the movie *Airport* '75. From the fact that the sun has risen so many times we might infer that it will continue to do so. From the fact that a figure is a rectangle, we might infer that its diagonals will bisect each other. From the fact that we received A's on all three previous logic tests, we might infer that we will receive an A on the next logic test. There is no limit to the range and variety of facts that may be used as data for an inference.

An inference, then, is the process of moving from data to conclusion. Whenever an inference is expressed or formulated, there is an argument. Thus, our inference about *Airport* '75 might be formulated into an argument as follows:

Data		*Conclusion*
I liked *Airport*.	_____	So, probably, I will like *Airport* '75.

Because

Airport '75 is very much like *Airport* only even more exciting. [Reason]

The inferences about the sun and the rectangle would look like this:

Data		*Conclusion*
The sun rose today	_____	So, probably, the sun will rise tomorrow

Because

The sun has always risen in the past

Data	*Conclusion*
This figure is a rectangle _____	So, the diagonals of this figure will bisect each other

Because

The diagonals of rectangular figures bisect each other

Each one of these arguments represents a different field of discourse. The first is in the area of psychology or common sense, the second scientific, and the third mathematical; yet each argument follows the same form: Data⟶ Warrant/Reason⟶ Conclusion. In specifically writing out the argument, the data, of course, becomes a premise also. So, our three arguments would have the following form:

Premise:	I liked the movie, *Airport*.
Premise:	*Airport* '75 is very much like *Airport* and I hear, even more exciting.
Conclusion:	So, probably I will like *Airport* '75.

Premise:	The sun has always risen in the past.
Premise:	The sun rose today.
Conclusion:	So, probably the sun will rise tomorrow.

Premise:	The diagonals of rectangular figures bisect each other.
Premise:	This figure is a rectangle.
Conclusion:	So, the diagonals of this figure will bisect each other.

Argument, then, is *discourse containing inference*. It should never be confused with the popular use of the term *argument* as meaning *dispute*. It is true that many inferences concern matters about which we have deep feelings, but the emotional aspects of a discourse do not make it an argument. The most heated argument, in the sense of dispute, may always be analyzed into one or more facts that A wants B to admit and to use as the basis for an inference, or some conclusion that he insists may be inferred from facts accepted by him and B.

In order to understand better the notion of an argument, we can also note its relationship to the concept of proof. Proof consists of connecting one or more admitted facts with one or more other facts that call for proof. In law, for example, to *prove* means to connect a number of facts, called *evidence*, in such a way that they converge on the statement which is to be established, e.g., "John Smith is guilty of negligence." The proof takes this form: *if these facts are admitted, then this conclusion must be admitted.* It is the same in philosophy, theology, and the natural, social, and historical sciences. *You admit this and this and this and this; therefore you should admit that.* The reasoning is: If we admit these facts, then we must accept this generalization. A similar movement of thought is found in mathematics, though the language is changed. Instead of evidence, statements, and generalizations, we hear of axioms, postulates, definitions, and theorems. But proving a theorem in mathematics, like proving an accusation before a judge or a generalization in the laboratory, consists in connecting sets of ideas by the *if-then* relation. *If these axioms and definitions are granted, argues the mathematician, then these theorems must be granted.* It is the same in any universe of discourse. Proof, in any context is argument, is discourse connecting facts as data and conclusions.

1.5   LOGICAL ANALYSIS

Logic is concerned to do two things with arguments, analyze them and criticize them. Logical analysis means identification of those facts that are being used as data (premises) and separation of them from those that are to be inferred as conclusion. Analysis, which involves clearly stating an argument, must precede criticism. It is generally unwise and sometimes fatal to criticize an argument you do not understand.

The first logical step in dealing with an argument, then, is to identify its structure. Arguments may be very complex, but all can be put into two basic and simple forms:

A.   This is true, *therefore*, that is true. (If this is true, then, that is true.)

B.   This is true *because* this is true. (This is true, *if* this is true.)

Translated into logical terms, the forms are:

A.   Premises (evidence, grounds, reasons), therefore, conclusion.

B.   Conclusion because of premises.

The following are simple examples of these forms:

A.   Because George went to the movie last night with his girlfriend, therefore Betsy, who is George's girlfriend, went to the movie also.

B.   All freshmen are intelligent because all undergraduates are intelligent and all freshmen are undergraduates.

C.   Because litmus paper when put into acid turns red and I put this litmus paper into acid, then it will turn red.

D.   George is probably guilty of the murder because he had a motive, he was near the scene of the crime, and one of his special Turkish cigarettes was found in the apartment.

Although arguments can be reduced to these simple forms, their form is not always easy to identify. This is so for a number of obvious reasons. (1)

Arguments are rarely given to us in these simplified textbook forms. Rather, they are embedded in complex patterns of discourse, along with all sorts of rhetoric, irrelevancies, and subtle connections with other arguments. (2) It is not often that we find premises arranged in logical order, leading clearly and concisely to their intended conclusion. Premises and conclusions can be found in any number of orders. They can be separated by all kinds of irrelevant and repetitious statements. Still worse, premises and/or conclusions are often only suggested rather than clearly stated. In these cases, we have to supply the missing items. (3) Language itself adds to the difficulty of recognizing arguments. As indicated above, we have to be able to know exactly what is being said as well as to distinguish between statements and nonstatements. Recognizing arguments is no easy matter. It is an *art* we must develop, and it requires practice. There is no magic formula, no simple technique. There are, however, some clues and aids.

There are *linguistic clues to recognizing arguments*, certain words that usually indicate premises and those that usually indicate conclusions. *Premise-indicating words* are: *because, for, since, in view of, as shown by, inasmuch as, for the reason that, may be inferred from, is substantiated by.* *Conclusion-indicating words* are: *thus, hence, so, therefore, accordingly, consequently, proves that, it follows that, we may infer.* Premises always indicate data and grounds for the conclusion. The conclusion is the *main* assertion or claim being made. In trying to identify arguments it is usually wise to look for the conclusion first. Ask "What is the main point, the overall claim?" To find premises, ask for the reasons for the claim.

Consider the following example.

> Absolute equality of opportunity is clearly incompatible with any positive solidarity of the family. . . . Where married women are employed outside the home, it is, for the great majority, in occupations which are not in direct competition for status with those of men of their own class. Women's interests, and the standard of judgment applied to them, run, in our society, far more in the direction of personal adornment. . . . It is suggested that this difference is functionally related to maintaining family solidarity in our class structure.[1]

The main point of the paragraph is the first sentence, and thus this is the conclusion. The other three sentences in the paragraph are meant as premises or reasons. Thus, the argument can be constructed as follows:

Premise I: Where married women are employed outside the home, it is, for the great majority, in occupations which are not in direct competition for status with those of men of their own class.

---

[1] T. S. Parsons, "An Analytical Approach to the Theory of Social Stratification," in *Essays in Sociological Theory*, rev. ed. (New York: Free Press, 1965) pp. 79–80.

Premise II: Women's interests, and the standards of judgment applied to them, run, in our society, far more in the direction of personal adornment.

Premise III: It is suggested that this difference is functionally related to maintaining family solidarity in our class structure.

Conclusion: Therefore, absolute equality of opportunity [for women] is clearly incompatible with any positive solidarity of the family.

Tape Exercises

Construct arguments for the following examples. [Turn to Tape 1, band 2 to check your answers.]

1. The functioning of our democratic system depends on an educated citizenry and on participation of citizens in governing by the vote. Hence, if we want a strong democratic system, we should support education and the vote.

2. If one wants to be a good teacher, one needs not only to know the material and how to communicate its contents, but also how to make it exciting and interesting to others. Being a good teacher, therefore, requires study, imagination, and practice.

3. Once in the classroom, women will discover that instructors and textbook writers in every field, consciously or unconsciously, join hands to 'keep women in their place.' Introductory sociology texts, which are required reading for over a hundred thousand students a year, mention women only in chapters on the family. Further, in these chapters, women are described in their 'traditional' roles as full-time homemakers and mothers unlinked to the economic and political world. Many of these chapters on the family do not even touch some of the major problems of the modern family.

4. The question in a case involving obscenity, just as in every case involving an attempted restriction upon free speech, is whether the words or pictures used in such circumstances are of such a nature as to create a clear and present danger that they will bring about a substantial evil that the state has a right to prevent. . . . We believe that under the current state of knowledge there, is grossly insufficient evidence to show that obscenity brings about any substantial evil.[2]

Before continuing with our analysis of argument, we must indicate that statements can be used to do things other than argue and thus we must be able to distinguish between nonarguments and arguments. One very simple distinction must be made between a conditional statement and an argument. A conditional statement is an if-then statement, such as:

If litmus paper is put into acid, then it turns red.

---

[2] *Obscenity and Censorship* (American Civil Liberties Union) New York: 1963, p. 7.

A conditional statement merely asserts that two circumstances are dependently related, that is, that if one occurs, the other must occur and if one doesn't occur, the other cannot occur. A conditional statement does not present an argument as such; it does not provide evidence for a conclusion. It is not an argument, but, of course, it can serve, as can any statement, as a premise or as the conclusion of an argument. Thus,

> If Litmus paper is put into acid, it turns red. This litmus paper was put into acid; therefore, it will turn red.

Statements may also be used to describe a scene, a situation, an event, that is, to give one a picture of it, but not to draw any conclusions about it. Consider the following:

> The house stood far back in the shadows of the enormous trees lining the driveway and entryway. It had fallen into a state of ill-repair, with broken shutters, shattered windows, missing tiles, chipped bricks and splintered wood. It must have once been an elegant house.

In this passage no conclusion is drawn, but rather, the statements are used to paint a picture in our mind's eye. Contrast the above with the following passage.

> One can only conclude that it is indeed a shame that this house has fallen into such a state of ill-repair. Afterall, once it was an elegant house; one which anyone would be proud to own. Now, in its condition, it has little economic or aesthetic value to anyone. Any decrease in value is to be decried.

The statements in this passage are clearly being used to draw a conclusion. The argument is as follows:

Premise I: The house was once an elegant house, one which anyone would be proud to own.
Premise II: Now, in its condition, it has little economic or aesthetic value to anyone.
Premise III: Any decrease in value is to be decried.
_____
Conclusion: It is indeed a shame that this house has fallen into such a state of ill-repair.

A passage, though containing statements, can thus be a description rather than an argument. An argument is only present when one of the statements is claimed, either explicitly through conclusion-indicating words or implicitly, to follow from the other statements, which then serve as grounds for, or reasons for believing the conclusion. Consider the following:

This thread broke because a weight exceeding one pound was suspended from it.

The slush on the sidewalk remained liquid during the frost because it had been sprinkled with salt and salt lowers the freezing point of water.

Senator Slugh was not reelected because of his stand on school busing.

Each of these above examples can be put into the form 'Q because P,' but though they share this form with arguments, they are not *intended* to be arguments, but rather are offered as explanations. Rather than asserting a logical connection between statements, that is, that one statement can be inferred from the others, they each use 'because' to indicate a causal connection between events. These passages intend to explain events by citing causes. Why did the thread break? Because too much weight was suspended from it? Why didn't the slush freeze? Because of the salt? Why wasn't the Senator reelected? Because of his stand on busing. In each of these cases the intent is to explain why Q is the case—Q is the case because of P. When the main intention is argument, we are interested in establishing the truth of Q, and P is offered as evidence for it. If P is true, then Q is true.

Because we are dealing with passages containing statements, we must be concerned to identify nonarguments. Context, of course, is extremely important in this regard because it may help clarify the intention of the writer or speaker. Argument is present when the purpose is to establish the truth of one or more statements on the basis of the truth of other statements. Explanations answer the question *why*. It should be noted, however, that even explanations can be cast in argument form, though they still remain explanations rather than arguments because of their function. This aspect of explanation will be discussed in more detail in chapter 10.

Tape Exercises

Identify the following as arguments, descriptions or explanations. [The answers are given on Tape 1, band 2.]

1. World War I began because an Austrian Count was murdered by a Serbian radical.

2. Let us not waste time in sterile litanies and nauseating mimicry. Leave this Europe where they have never done talking of man, yet murder men everywhere they find them, at the corner of every one of their own streets, in all the corners of the globe. For centuries they have stifled almost the whole of humanity in the name of a spiritual experience. Look at them today, swaying between atomic and spiritual disintegration.   [Frantz Fanon]

3. There is already enough misery in the world; therefore, love your neighbor.

4. This is a scholarly book that uses traditional disciplines and concrete data to document the status of women and assess the effects of sexism.

5. A society in which debts are repaid is a better society than one in which they are not repaid, for repaying debts maximizes pleasure and maximizing pleasure is the highest good of all.

Exercises for § 1.5

Determine whether or not the following are arguments. If they are arguments, indicate premises and conclusions. Do not ask whether they are good or bad premises or conclusions, but merely ask what is intended as premises and conclusions.

1. Tom will not be able to play basketball this season because he is on academic probation and he wants to stay in school.

2. If one creates the proper pressure, he can make an iron needle float.

3. Given the victim's broken watch which stopped at 1 A.M. and the coroner's testimony that time of death was between midnight and 3 A.M., we can infer that the murder occurred at 1 A.M.

4. Since this is a red wine, it cannot be a Chablis.

5. The pipes broke because of the sub-freezing temperatures.

6. If inflation continues and unemployment increases, then fewer young people will be able to attend college. The inflation probably will continue and unemployment will increase. Therefore, fewer young people will be attending college this year.

7. The Vietnam War was a futile tragedy because finally South Vietnam fell into the hands of the Communists.

8. Because he had the motive of revenge and access to the keys and the house, there is little doubt that Hans committed the murder.

9. The statement "All Thebians lie" cannot be true because it was made by Cornelius, who is a Thebian.

10. Whales are not fish because fish are cold-blooded and whales are warm-blooded.

11. Since John Boy went away to school, and he has always been involved in unusual and exciting things, there is thus little of excitement occurring at the farm.

12. Logic is a good subject for everyone to take because it enables one to think more clearly and read more correctly.

13. Young children learn by imitation of the actions of others, consequently parents and older children should be careful of their behavior and the things they say.

14. Because the team has played all the tough teams and won, they probably will finish the season with a 100 percent victory record.

15. What a rotten T.V. season! We ought to abolish commercial T.V. and have only public T.V. as they have done in Great Britain; then we would have better programs.

16. Marry him (her)? Not on your life!

17. While formerly leukemia and cancer were infrequent among children, now they are quite common. Our chemically processed foods of today lack the mineral vitamins, hormones, and ferments of the unrefined natural foods of yesterday.

18. A child's reaction to its environment can be only instinctive, animal-like; it is, therefore, from the point of view of evolution, regressive.

1.6 ANALYZING ARGUMENTS

There are five helpful steps in analyzing arguments.

1. Read or listen to "get the point." Find the conclusions or the main conclusion first. What is the chief thing being said? What is being argued? What is the thesis? What is the claim?

2. Once you have located the conclusion(s) or main conclusion, find the statement offered to support it. What are the reasons, the evidence for this thesis? What data is being offered in support of the conclusion?

3. Rule out repetitious statements or those that are obviously irrelevant to the conclusion. Rule out statements that are for emotional effect alone. Rule out phrases or statements that are for literary effect or for mere rhetoric.

4. If there are missing premises, supply them. Follow the principle of adding whatever is needed to make the argument *a good one*. Ask: What additional evidence is needed for support? What must be assumed for the conclusion to follow? If conclusions are missing or only implied, state them.

5. Further, look for any subsidiary arguments within one main argument. Draw them out and set them in the proper order.

With these steps in mind, let us consider the following paragraph.

> Natural men, without divine grace suffer either from pride or from despair. For if they know the excellence of man, they are ignorant of his corruption, so that they easily avoid sloth but fall into pride. And if they recognize the infirmity of nature, they are ignorant of its dignity, so that they easily avoid vanity but fall into despair.   [Pascal (paraphrased)]

In looking for a conclusion in this paragraph, we discover two uses of the word 'so', which is a conclusion-indicating word. There are, then, at least two conclusions. But, in fact, the very first sentence of the paragraph is the main point of the passage and is intended as the main conclusion. This is indicated by the use of 'for' immediately after this sentence, which implies that what follows are premises. The passage can thus be set out as follows:

First Argument

Premise:	If natural men, [*this is the meaning of 'they' in the second sentence*], without divine grace, know the excellence of man, they are ignorant of corruption.
Conclusion:	So, they easily avoid sloth but fall into pride.

Second Argument

Premise:	If natural men, [*they*], without divine grace, recognize the infirmity of nature, they are ignorant of its dignity.
Conclusion:	So, they easily avoid vanity but fall into despair.
Implied Premise:	Natural men, [*they*], without divine grace, either know the excellence of men and are ignorant of this corruption or recognize the infirmity of nature and are ignorant of its dignity.
Final Conclusion:	Thus, natural men, without divine grace, suffer either from pride or despair.

A difficult aspect of analyzing arguments occurs when premises and/or conclusions are only implied rather than stated, as in the argument above. In order to reach the final conclusion one must assume that natural men fall into one or the other of the two categories set out in the two subarguments. Otherwise one cannot draw the either-or conclusion. Arguments that are not fully stated are called *enthymemes*. Usually what is unstated is made clear in the context of the argument, though not always. In looking for missing parts ask: Do the premises adequately support the conclusion or do we need another to link the premises and conclusion? Consider the following:

This philosophy book will not be a best seller, because it is too intellectual.

The person offering this argument assumes the truth of the following: "Books which are too intellectual are not best sellers!" Consider another example:

No person has told me about a personal shortcoming. Therefore, I have no personal shortcomings.

The person offering this argument is assuming as unstated the premise: "People always tell you of your shortcomings if you have any."

Sometimes in analyzing arguments we discover that a conclusion is missing rather than a premise. If a series of statements clearly leads toward a certain conclusion, without ever stating that conclusion, the conclusion can be assumed to be implicitly stated and one is justified in adding it to complete the argument. Consider the following:

An economy that is based on excessive taxation is fundamentally an unsound economy. Every government, of course, has the right to tax both individuals and corporations, inasmuch as taxation is the only means that a government has of maintaining itself. When, however, taxes are so high that they are prejudicial to a free economy, a situation has developed in which the government is no longer serving the interests of the citizenry at large. Is there any doubt that we are now in a situation of excessive taxation?

This argument is a rather complex one and needs to be analyzed step by step. Taking the first sentence "An economy that is based on excessive taxation is fundamentally an unsound economy," we see that it has no premise or conclusion indicating terms, but it does have the force of a rather strong assertion. We set it down then as a possible conclusion. The second sentence about the right of government to tax, in light of the first sentence, appears somewhat apologetic and therefore might be a reason or premise. Yet, if we examine the sentence closely, we see it is a miniargument because it speaks both about the right to tax and why a government has the right to tax. Thus, we set out the second sentence as follows:

Premise: (Inasmuch as) taxation is the only means that a government has of maintaining itself.
Conclusion: (Therefore) government has the right to tax both individuals and corporations.

Turning to the third sentence of the passage, we see that it is a counter to the assumption of government's right to tax because it states an exception to this right and also a criteria to judge when government taxation is proper, namely, when it serves the citizenery at large. This sentence should be combined with sentence one of the passage to give the following:

Premise: When taxes are too high they are prejudicial to a free economy.
Premise: An economy which is not free is fundamentally an unsound economy.

Conclusion: Therefore, an economy based on excessive taxation is fundamentally an unsound economy.

Premise:	An economy based on excessive taxation is fundamentally an unsound economy.
Premise:	An unsound economy is one which no longer serves the citizenry at large.

Conclusion:	Therefore, excessive taxation by the government does not serve the citizenry at large.

This helps us continue the argument, namely,

Premise:	Excessive taxation by the government does not serve the citizenry at large.
Premise:	There is now excessive taxation.

Therefore:	The government is not now serving the citizenry at large.

Now, consider the following arguments in which one or more premises are missing. In seeking to supply missing parts for an argument, we should ask, "What would make the argument as good as possible?" This is sometimes called *The Principle of Charity*, namely, you should make another's argument the best possible.

A fellow jury member says to you, "His testimony is truthworthy because he has access to the facts." How can you make his argument stronger? First, you note the hidden premise or assumption needed to make this argument more complete, namely, "Accessibility to the facts is a prime characteristic of a trustworthy testimony." The argument would be even stronger, however, if it was reconstructed as follows:

He has access to the facts.
He considered the facts and assessed them correctly.
　　(Careful consideration and assessment of the facts is a prime char-
　　acteristic of a trustworthy testimony.)

Therefore, his testimony is trustworthy.

Consider next this argument:

Leisure is nonproblematic, and thus leisure is essential for the development of thought.

In order for the conclusion to follow, a missing premise must be supplied, namely, "The development of thought occurs in nonproblematic situations." However, even with the addition of this premise, the argument remains rather weak because the phrase 'unproblematic' is unclear in meaning. Does it mean that the person is not faced with such struggle-for-survival problems as food, clothing, shelter and therefore has time to engage in pure thought? Surely, it would be a very weak argument indeed if one eliminated all mental problems, for how could thought then develop at all? We shall be discussing meaning and definition and their importance to argument in the next chapter.

Knowledge is also often important to filling in an argument. Consider the following:

> Skinner is a determinist, and I believe in moral responsiblity, therefore, I cannot agree with Skinner's conclusions.

In order to reconstruct this argument, you would have to know that a determinist is one who believes that all our actions are completely determined by our previous actions and that therefore in choosing a course of action we do not really have free choice between alternatives. Rather, given the circumstances and all our previous learning and background, we had to make the choice we did. Our choice was already determined by the circumstances. You would also need to know that denying that there is free choice in actions amounts to saying we have no choice at all and also implies that we cannot raise the question of moral responsiblity. If you had no choice, then you cannot be held responsible. Thus, the argument would be reconstructed as follows:

> Skinner is a determinist.
> A determinist holds that all our actions are completely determined by circumstances and that in choosing a course of action we do not have free choice among alternatives.
> If there is no free choice among alternatives, there can be no judgment about moral responsibility.
> Skinner thus denies judgment about moral responsibility as legitimate.
> I believe in moral responsibility.
> _____
> Therefore, I disagree with Skinner's conclusions.

Recognizing arguments, then, is a complex affair, requiring much practice. Consider one more example, an argument about pornography.

> I think there ought to be no rules whatever prohibiting improper publications. . . . I think prohibitions immensely increase people's interest in pornography as in anything else. Thus, for example, during Prohibition in America there was far more drunkenness than there was before. Consider also the child who is told not to do something. He always has an increased interest in doing exactly that thing and will persist in trying to do it. [Paraphrased from *Bertrand Russell Speaks His Mind* (New York: Bard Books, 1960), p. 60.]

The main point and conclusion of this argument is that there should be no prohibition on publishing pornography. It is supported by a series of arguments and implied premises. The argument may be set out as follows:

First Argument

Prohibition of drinking in America led to more drunkenness than before.

Prohibition of an action leads a child to have an increased interest in doing that action.

C.I   Therefore, Prohibitions of anything lead to an increased interest in that which is prohibited.

Second Argument

Prohibitions of anything lead to an increased interest in that which is prohibited.

C.II   Therefore, Prohibition of pornography would lead to an increased interest in pornography.

Third Argument

Prohibition of pornography would lead to an increased interest in pornography.

An increased interest in pornography would be undesirable. [*Implied*]

C.III   Therefore, Prohibitions on pornography would be undesirable.

Fourth Argument

Prohibition on pornography would be undesirable.

We should avoid that which is undesirable. [*Implied*]

C.IV   Therefore, there should be no prohibition on publishing Pornography.

Tape Exercises

Supply the premises for the following arguments. [Turn to Tape 1, band 3, to check your answers.]

1. John is an egotist, for he is always boasting about his achievements.

2. If there were spirits or souls, we could not know them, for all our knowledge is based on sensation.

3. Municipal parks should never be used for political meetings because they are the property of the general public.

4. Kant held that all proofs for the existence of God are fallacious. Therefore, he was an atheist.

Because the main concern of logic is with argumentation, we must be absolutely clear about what an argument is before we proceed to the rules for identifying good and bad arguments. Obviously, not just any group of statements constitutes an argument. What identifies an argument, as indicated above, is that *some statements (the premises) are put forth in support of another statement (the conclusion)*. Wherever this is the case, no matter how complex or disordered the situation, *we have an argument*. The art of identifying premises and conclusions can be cultivated only through practice on real, everyday examples—from newspapers, political speeches, magazine articles, editorials, text books, advertising materials, lectures, sermons, and the like. Thus, any exercises offered in the context of this book should be considered only beginnings in the art of recognizing argumentation. Real expertise should be tested out on materials taken from everyday life.

Exercises for § 1.6

A. Supply the missing parts in the following arguments. When the missing parts are added, are all the arguments good ones? If not, why not?

1. A college education does not pay, for most wealthy people have succeeded without it.

2. War can no longer be tolerated. It upsets economies, disrupts trade, and makes for lopsided distribution. Wars are also tragic in the cost of human life and human suffering.

3. Jane must be a citizen, for she is able to vote.

4. Animal life cannot subsist without a supply of water. Therefore there can be no life on the moon.

5. Computers cannot be used in humanities subjects because the humanities are not quantitative. Further, the humanities are interested in human beings and their creative activities. (More than one part missing.)

6. This film probably will not be an economic success because it is too intellectual.

7. Because this child does not know how to spell, there is no reason for thinking that he is unintelligent.

8. Juvenile delinquents should not be treated as criminals because they are too young to be criminals.

9. Being a barber, you are no doubt a good conversationalist.

10. Some entertainment is educational; sitting through geometry is anything but entertaining.

11. Nutrition experts urge us to start the day with a good breakfast. Therefore, I am going to have coffee and a donut every morning.

12. You are being unreasonable in questioning the facts in this case. Therefore, I will not listen to you.

13. Genuine metaphor is the work of genius, for the power of making a good metaphor is the power of recognizing important resemblances.

14. John will do well in college because he studies hard and is very conscientious.

15. Mary won't make a good scientist because she generalizes too quickly and impulsively. Further, she has far too much imagination. (More than one missing part.)

16. Some rules admit of exceptions. This rule admits of exceptions. Therefore, it is not a principle.

17. They are not true friends because they didn't support me in the election.

18. Shan is a Hindu; therefore, he must believe in reincarnation.

19. "God must have loved the plain people. He made so many of them." [Abraham Lincoln.]

20. "Women and foxes, being weak, are distinguished by superior tact." [Ambrose Bierce.]

B. Trying to construct arguments from discourse written informally and for everyday use is often very difficult. Test your skill on the following. Set forth the premises and conclusions and supply any missing premises or conclusions. [Tape 1, band 3.]

1. Writing a term paper is no easy task. It's difficult enough to write a good English composition. But ordinarily it isn't necessary in writing a composition to do research. Writing a term paper, however, is a task that involves plenty of research work. This means going to the library to find the books you need, locating the passages that relate to your topic, and knowing how to interpret them. If you ever have had the experience of writing a term paper, I'm sure you've found out for yourself that term paper writing is no easy task. Nothing that involves research is easy.

2. Shopping today for groceries is not an enjoyable experience. Shopping for basic grocery items in a modern supermart is a distressing experience because it gets a person all confused. Suppose you want to buy a carton of cottage cheese—just plain cottage cheese. What you find is cottage cheese mixed with all sorts of flavorings from pineapple to chives. Suppose, too, you want to buy some cereal—for humans, I mean. What you find is an infinite variety of foods for dogs, cats, and canaries! This, I say, is a distressing experience, because it gets you all confused.

3. I can't think of anything more futile than worrying about the past. Did you ever meet anybody who could change the course of past events? Of course not; past events are entirely outside of human control. Think of all the people who continually worry about their past lives, as if worrying made a difference. I'm sure that if these people would devote as much time and energy to present opportunities as they spend mulling over the past, they would be far better off. I repeat, it's futile to worry about the past, because the past is something that can't be controlled.

4. Academic achievement is losing its meaning. In the past ten years the American educational system has been wracked by declining student achievement and rampant inflation of grades and an overall lowering of academic standards. The number of basic classes have been reduced; graduation requirements have been weakened; and electives, which are less demanding, are emphasized.

5. The notion that life is sacrosanct is actually a Hindu idea, although Hindus practice things like suttee. It is not Christian or biblical. If it were, all heroism and martyrdom would be wrong, to say nothing of carnivorous diet, capital punishment and warfare. The sanctity (what makes it precious) is not in life itself, intrinsically, it is only extrinsic and good by accident according to the situation. "Death is not always an enemy: it can sometimes be a friend and servant.

   . . . When life is not good it deserves neither protection nor preservation. Our present laws about 'elective' death are not civilized." Let law favor living, not mere life.   [Joseph Fletcher.]

6. A valuable lesson has been imparted by Japan to the U.S. (*International*, Aug. 9). Justice is only just when the rules pertain to everyone. Kakuei Tanaka, who was the highest elected official in Japan, is accused of making illegal gains by usurping the powers of his office. He was jailed and will stand trial. Nixon, in his own manner, pulled the same stunt—but we all know how that turned out. Japan has withstood the shock admirably. Are we that much weaker in our own convictions?   [Mark J. Burneko]

C. The following passages contain more than one argument. For each, indicate premises and conclusions and the correct order of the argument. Beware of any missing premises. [Tape 1, band 4.]

1. If we wager that God exists and he does then we gain eternal bliss; if he does not, we have lost nothing. If we wager that God does not exist and he does, then eternal misery is our share; if he does not, we gain only lucky true belief. The obvious wager is to bet that God exists. With such a bet we have everything to gain and nothing to lose. This is far superior to a bet where we have little to gain and everything to lose.   [Pascal]

2. The dilemma of the museum is that it takes its aesthetic stand on the basis of art history, which it is helping to liquidate. The blending of painting and sculpture into the decorative media, the adulteration of styles, the mixing of generes in order to create an "environment" for the spectator has completed the erosion of values derived exclusively from the art of the past. What is needed to replace these values is a critical outlook toward history and the part played by creation in contemporary culture, politics and technology. Aesthetics does not exist in a vacuum. The museum seems unaware of how precarious it is to go as far out from art as it has on no other foundation than its simple-minded avantgardism. In the direction it has taken nothing awaits it but transformation into a low-rating mass medium.   [Harold Rosenberg, *The Dedefinition of Art*]

3. Although in highly civilized societies the motives that lead to the accumulation of capital become very complex, yet acquisitiveness, desire for mere possession of goods, remains probably the most fundamental of them, blending and cooperating with all other motives. . . . It might be plausibly maintained that the phenomena with which economic sciences is concerned are in the main the outcome of the operation of this instinct, rather than of the enlightened self-interest of the classical economists. The possession and acquisition of land affords satisfaction to this desire in a very full degree, land being so permanent and indestructible a form of property. And this instinct

has played its part, not only in the building of large private estates . . . but also in the causation of the many wars that have been waged for the possession of territories. Wars of this type are characteristic of autocracies; for the desire to possess is more effective in promoting action when the thing to be acquired is to become the possession of a single individual, than if it is to be shared by all the members of a democratic community. Accordingly, one of the most striking effects of the democratisation of States is the passage away of wars of this worst type.   [William McDougall, *Social Psychology*]

4. Natural selection leads to divergence of character; for the more organic beings diverge in structure, habits, and constitution, by so much the more can a large number be supported on the area—of which we see proof by looking to the inhabitants of any small spot and to the productions naturalized in foreign lands. Therefore, during the modification of the descendants of any one species, and during the incessant struggle of all species to increase in number, the more diversified the descendants become, the better will be their chance of success in the battle for life. Thus the small differences distinguishing varieties of the same species, steadily tend to increase, till they equal the greater differences between species of the same genus, or even of distinct genera.   [Charles Darwin, *The Origin of Species by Means of Natural Selection*]

5. There is always some other factor besides the mere drinking of alcoholic liquors which determines drunkenness. Drunkards are pathological. Normal persons do not become drinkers to excess. Pathological restraint is also bad. Heavy drinkers would otherwise almost certainly be victims of other vices. The D'Abernon Committee and other bodies of experts have found that many benefits come from moderate drinking. Alcohol is often medically useful. Thus, abstinence from alcohol should not be enforced for everyone.

6. The degeneracy of America and American civilization is becoming increasingly noticeable. Literature, journalism, and art have more and more laid stress on the morbid and abnormal. Just look at the crude, puerile and violent sentimentalism of American films. These are surely signs of degeneracy. Further advanced technology has subjected men more and more to machines. This has resulted in populations marked by a mania for gambling and for watching other people playing games which they themselves do not play. These people also have an insatiable desire for something new, which shows itself in the endless buying of vulgar newspapers and the incessant pursuit of machine-made pleasures. Further divorce rates are steadily rising and the birth rate is no longer sufficient to maintain the population. Home life and domestic duties cease to attract women who prefer the excitement of careers and free living.

7. If God did not exist, there would be no objective moral law because moral law must be decreed by some being, a being that is all-good. Furthermore, no objective law depends merely on a human being. But, surely, there are objective moral laws, so God exists.

8. If you study heroin users, you soon discover that a majority of them have used marijuana before using heroin. The percentage of heroin users who have previously used marijuana is much larger than the percentage of nonheroin users who have previously used marijuana. So, there is every reason to

believe that a causal connection exists between the use of marijuana and the use of heroin. Heroin use is intrinsically bad and should be stopped. We can cut down on marijuana use, and therefore on heroin use, by keeping our laws against marijuana.

1.7 DEDUCTION AND INDUCTION

It is customary in logic to classify *all* arguments into two basic kinds: *deductive* arguments and *inductive* arguments. A *deductive argument* is an argument which claims that the premises *necessarily* imply or entail the conclusion. That is, the premises constitute conclusive evidence for the conclusion. An *inductive argument* is an argument which claims only that the premises provide some evidence for the conclusion. That is, the premises make the conclusion *more or less probable*.

One of the basic differences, then, between deductive and inductive argumentation is the strength of the *claim* made for the argument.[3] Consider the following example.

All whales are mammals.
All mammals are warm-blooded creatures.

Therefore: All whales are warm-blooded creatures.

Looking at this argument carefully, we see that anyone who understands the meaning of the words used can see *without appeal to any information except that given in the two premises* that the conclusion is justified. The inference drawn is conclusive: if the premises were true, it would be *impossible* for the conclusion not to be true. Whenever reasons are offered in *complete* justification of a conclusion, we have a case of deduction.

Another way of looking at the conclusive nature of deductive argument is to speak of deductive arguments as *explicative*, that is the conclusion merely spells out what is already *contained* implicitly in the premises. Reflection on the premises tell you necessarily what the conclusion *must* be. In deductive arguments, the conclusion merely sums up the premises; it does not go beyond the evidence in the premises. No additional evidence is needed. *If true*, the evidence provided in the premises of a deductive argument is *conclusive*. Consider the following examples of groups of premises and their relations to the alleged conclusion:

---

[3] Logicians frequently describe the difference between deduction and induction by saying that deduction moves *downward* from a statement which is self-evident or axiomatic to a conclusion whereas induction moves *upward* from observed instances to a tentative conclusion. The oldest example of deduction may well be this: All men are mortal. Socrates is a man; therefore, Socrates is mortal. An example of induction might be: In instances numbers 1, 2, 3, and many more, cigarette smoking has been seen to be injurious to the health of the smoker, so we conclude that, as the Surgeon General of the U.S. expresses it, cigarette smoking is (probably) injurious to one's health. Although this is a way of describing the difference between deduction and induction, we warn that the matter is not simple, particularly, as we shall see, in the philosophy of science.

A. Mercury is heavier than iron.
    Iron is heavier than water.
    _____

    Therefore: Mercury is heavier than water.

B. All men are either husbands or bachelors.
    No bachelor is a husband.
    _____

    Therefore: No man is both a bachelor and a husband.

C. Abraham Lincoln was a president of the United States.
    Abraham Lincoln was assassinated.
    _____

    Therefore: At least one president of the United States was assassinated.

In all three of the above cases, we have or ought to have the feeling that the conclusion is *justified* by the premises. In dealing with arguments such as the above, we commonly use such expressions as "the conclusion *must* be true" or "the conclusion really does *follow* from the premises." Each of these expressions is a way of expressing the type of relationship that holds between the premises and conclusion of a deductive argument, namely, the premises cannot be true without the conclusion being true. Thus, in each of the cases of deductive argument above *it is impossible for the premises to be true without the conclusion also being true.*

Inductive arguments, too, must be identified by the two fundamental characteristics already used to identify deductive arguments—the type of *claim* they make and the relationship between premises and conclusion in terms of information given. Thus, we summarize the central differences between inductive and deductive arguments.

	Deductive	*Inductive*
Claim:	I. If all the premises are true, the conclusion *must* be true.	I. If all of the premises are true the conclusion is *probably true*, but not necessarily true. *Or* it is *improbable* that the conclusion is false given that the premises are all true.
Information Given	II. All of the information or factual content in the conclusion is already contained, at least implicitly, in the premises. Deductive arguments are *explicative.*	II. The conclusion contains information not present, even implicitly, in the premises. Inductive arguments are *ampliative.*

Let us examine some inductive arguments with these two characteristics in mind. Take the following example:

George smokes Burro filters.
Burrow filters were found at the scene of the crime.
_____

So, George *may be* the guilty party.

In a deductive argument we saw that *if* we accepted the premises as true, we were forced to accept the conclusion as true; it followed *necessarily*. However, in the above inductive argument, even if we accept the premises as true, we are *not* thereby required to accept the conclusion as true; the conclusion does not follow *necessarily*. The premises, in this case, provide *some* grounds, but not conclusive grounds, for the conclusion. The *claim* made in this case is a cautious one. Indeed, on the basis of the same premises, we could have drawn a different conclusion from the one drawn, namely, that "George is one of the suspects." An inductive argument, then, only claims that *if* all the premises are true, the conclusion is *probably* true, but not necessarily true.

Another way to look at the distinction between deductive and inductive arguments is to consider deductive arguments as *explicative*, its conclusion providing no additional information than that given in its premises, and inductive arguments as *ampliative*, because the conclusion *goes beyond* the evidence in the premises. The conclusion is not implicitly contained in the premises. Thus, in inductive arguments, the *strength* of the argument varies with the evidence provided in the premises. The argument is *more or less probable* depending on the evidence provided. Additional information, additional premises may make inductive arguments stronger or weaker. Consider the following:

If the premise "George had a motive for the crime" is added to the inductive argument above, the argument is *strengthened*. However, if the premise "glass found at the scene of the crime had lipstick stains on it," is added to that inductive argument, the argument is *weakened*. The conclusion is rendered *less probable*. Amount and type of evidence is extremely important in inductive argument, as we shall see.

In trying to determine whether an argument is deductive or inductive, then, one should ask first about its claim: Does the argument convey the tone *if* you accept these premises you *must* accept the conclusion. If it does, then it is a deductive argument. Second, one asks about the information provided. Is the argument merely explicative of the information given in the premises or does it go beyond that information? Also, remember that you are only assessing the strength of the claim being made (the conclusion necessarily follows) and not the truth or falsity of the premises. The rationale for this will be explained in the next section.

Using our two characteristics, type of claim and information given, we can easily distinguish the following two arguments.

A. 1. All asbestos material is a nonconductor of heat.
   2. This jacket is made of asbestos material.
   _____
   Therefore, this jacket is a nonconductor of heat.

B. All observed asbestos materials are nonconductors of heat.
   This piece of material is asbestos.
   _____
   Therefore, this piece of material will probably be a nonconductor of heat.

Argument *A* is a deductive argument, first of all, because its conclusion is necessarily true *if* its premises are true. It makes a conclusive claim. Second, the argument is merely explicative, for if I understand the full meaning of the premises, then I already know that "this jacket is a nonconductor of heat." Argument *B* is an inductive argument because it makes only a *probable* claim and it does go beyond the information given in the premises—it tells us about an untested piece of asbestos material on the basis of tested or observed pieces of asbestos. And, as any good scientist knows, the unobserved does not necessarily have the same characteristics as the observed. In fact it was discovered that asbestos, at a very low temperature, will conduct heat. If the piece of asbestos talked about in the above argument was at this low temperature, then the conclusion of the argument would be false. Additional evidence is always important and crucial in inductive reasoning.

In talking about the two examples, several things should be apparent. First, inductive and deductive reasoning go hand in hand in many of our thought and reasoning processes. We shall show how this is true when we discuss scientific method and decision making. They need each other. This can be seen from the observation that deduction can only show that *some* statements are true and justified, if *other* statements are true or justified. Second, it must be quite clear that the difference between deductive and inductive argument is not that between a good argument and a bad one. Rather it is between the two sorts of claims that an argument, good or bad, may make about the way in which its conclusion *follows from* its premises.

Tape Exercises

A. Distinguish the premises and conclusions in the following arguments. Determine whether the arguments are deductive or inductive, explitive or ampliative. [The answers are given on Tape 1, band 5.]

1. It is regrettable that the saving in electricity fell so far short of expectations. Under the circumstances, however, it appears that the inconvenience and even dangers of winter daylight saving time outweigh the benefits. Thus, the decision to go back to the previous system is sensible.

2. If the fetus is a human life, then there are only a few circumstances where abortion is justified, and if the fetus is just a mass of cells, then all cases of abortion are justified. Either the fetus is a human life or just a mass of cells. Hence, either there are only a few circumstances where abortion is justified or all cases of abortion are justified.

3. Some students of the witch craze have argued that by the 17th century the witch trials had ended because of the new spirit of science and progress. But the witch craze came before this spirit had really taken hold. It appears more likely that the witch craze ended because the institutions that found it advantageous to persecute witches no longer had the power to do so. The inquisition was dismantled by the monarchs. The local judges involved in witch burning in the Holy Roman Empire could no longer do so because of the centralization of the legal system under the emperor.

4. To deliberately take life is murder. Suicide is the deliberate taking of human life. Therefore, suicide is murder.

Exercises for § 1.7

Examine the following. (a) Specify premises and conclusions. (b) Determine whether they are deductive or inductive arguments. (c) For inductive arguments, indicate how they are *ampliative*. What premises might strengthen and/or weaken the conclusion?

1. Farmer Jones plowed up two plots of ground, applied a coat of lime to one and then planted both with corn. The lime plot yielded ten bushes per acre more than the other. Probably the extra yield was due to the application of lime.

2. Because it is evident that Richard Nixon was involved in the attempt to cover-up an illegal break-in at the Watergate Building and that he authorized certain other dubiously legal activities, he should have been legally prosecuted as would any other citizen.

3. Since the Vietnam War was never legally declared a war by the United States and because it was more a civil war among the Vietnamese people, the United States was wrong to enter militarily into the Vietnam conflict.

4. Traffic accidents among drivers under the age of twenty-one have zoomed up 33 percent since Illinois lowered the legal drinking age for beer and wine from twenty-one to nineteen nearly three years ago. Further, a survey conducted by the *Chicago Tribune* showed an increase in teenage drunken driving arrests and traffic fatalities: the number of drivers under the age of twenty-one who were arrested for driving while intoxicated increased 20 percent between 1972 and 1975. The number of drivers in this age group who were killed in accidents increased 7.15 percent. Surely the lowering of the legal drinking age has been a disaster for the Illinois Highways. [Paraphrased from *The National Enquirer*, August 31, 1976.]

5. Arthur lied when he said that he saw the burglar's face in the reflection of the glass over the Renoir. All the stolen paintings were oils, and oils are never framed under glass. There was no glass to cause a reflection, and thus Arthur could not have seen the burglar's reflection.

6. The governor's commission strongly recommends that use of marijuana continues to be illegal since marijuana leads to the use of heroin. This is evidenced by the fact that 94 percent of 1,000 heroin addicts interviewed reported that they had smoked marijuana before becoming addicted to heroin.

7. One major argument against live televising of criminal trials is that television creates an atmosphere that makes it impossible to conduct a fair trial. This is because the trial judge is forced to devote an unduly large proportion of his time and attention to keeping the situation within manageable bounds. In a recent case, for example, the judge made no less than ten separate rulings on television coverage during the trial. Furthermore, the presence of television cameras and technicians tends to distract and divert witnesses and can have an unpredictable effect on their testimony.

8. The vegetable peddler was an obvious phony. Vegetable peddlers know their vegetables, but this vegetable peddler called the green cucumber ripe, whereas ripe cucumbers are yellow.

9. A new drug, acebutol, already available in Great Britain and now under study here, looks excitingly good for dangerous heart rhythms. At Stanford University not long ago, doctors tried it for a man with a potentially lethal arrhythmia that resisted all the standard antiarrhythmia drugs such as quinidine and procainimide, and had required repeated electrical shocking of his heart. In the eight months he has been on acebutol, he has had no recurrence of arrhythmia.

10. Smith could not have been emerging from the bank opposite the scene of the fight. The fight occurred on May 30, Declaration Day, when all the banks are closed. How can one emerge from a closed bank?

11. Two contrary psychic tendencies exist universally in the father-son relationship, i.e., submission and rebellion, and both derive from the Oedipus complex. Since most patriarchial religions also veer between submission to a paternal figure, and rebellion (both submission and rebellion being sexualized), and every god, like a compulsive super-ego, promises protection on condition of submission, there are many similarities in the manifest picture of compulsive ceremonials and religious rituals, due to the similarity of the underlying conflicts.   [F. Fenichel, *The Psychoanalytic Theory of Neuroses*]

12. One can only conclude that academic achievement is losing its meaning. In the past ten years the American educational system has been wracked by declining student achievement, rampant inflation of grades and an overall lowering of academic standards. The number of basic classes have been reduced, graduation requirements have been weakened, and less demanding electives are emphasized.

13. The professor was reading a book written in Hebrew, which is read from the back to front. Therefore, he would not have turned the pages with his right hand, but with his left.

14. China's population control program stands out as the most extraordinary of all because, as the world's most populous nation with close to 1 billion

people, it apparently has succeeded where India, the second most populous nation with more than 600 million people, has failed. Reports from China indicate that the population has been persuaded to forego premarital sex, to postpone marriage until both husband and wife are in their mid-twenties. No such success reports come from India.

15. Johnson's story was clearly an invention. He said the buck rose first on his forelegs. Unfortunately for him, a deer gets off the ground hind-end first.

16. The results of this experiment seem to run counter to the theory that putting an emotionally upset child in with a group of well-adjusted children will improve the emotional development of the child. Thus, for example, Redl introduced a boy with considerable masochistic tendencies into a group of normal boys who were all friends and members of the same club. In a short time the disturbed boy had stirred up in the others 'more sadistic-pleasure temptations than they could cope with,' and their violent aggressions disrupted the social relations of the entire group.

17. The robbers entered the house either from the front or the rear. Had they entered the house from the front, the line crews would have seen their car. But the linemen did not see their car. If the robbers entered the house from the rear, they must have arrived by boat. This proves that the robbers came by boat.

18. Casual determinism is true, from which it follows that no one has free will, and consequently no one is morally responsible for what he or she does. But if none of us is morally responsible for what we do, then we cannot be obligated to do anything. That is, there is nothing we ought to do; nothing is right and nothing is wrong. Therefore, ethical nihilism is correct.

1.8   LOGIC AND THE QUESTION OF TRUTH

In light of the basic difference in the claims of deductive and inductive arguments, some logicians employ different criteria for judging the correctness or incorrectness of these arguments. Because the deductive argument claims to provide conclusive proof for its conclusion, the key to the notion of a *correct deductive argument* is the characteristic that *if its premises are true, its conclusion must be true.* Such correct deductive arguments are called *valid.* Validity, then, is considered the correct term to apply to deductive arguments. Inductive arguments, however, claim only to provide some evidence for its conclusion. They do not claim to provide conclusive evidence. To find correct inductive arguments we ask: "relevant to the evidence provided in the premises, how probable is the conclusion?" Because of the weaker claim of inductive arguments, some logicians speak of inductive arguments not as valid or invalid, but rather as strong or weak. We shall follow this practice in discussing inductive arguments.

Having understood what an argument is and how to recognize arguments, both deductive and inductive, we are ready to turn to the central task of logic, which is to distinguish correct arguments from incorrect arguments. In appraising arguments there are two basic questions that should always be asked.

The factual scientific question of truth and falsity.   Are the statements in the argument true or are they false?

The logical question of support or justification.   Do the statements making up the premises provide adequate grounds, evidence or reasons for asserting the conclusion?

In logic we shall not ask the first question. Logic, properly speaking, is not concerned with the question of factual truth and falsity. Logic is concerned only with the question of *support and justification.* To understand why this is the case, the following points must be made.

1. Logic's primary concern is with the analysis of arguments and not with each particular statement making up the argument. Arguments never are called true or false. Arguments are valid or invalid, strong or weak. Truth and falsity only can properly be attributed to statements. They alone can be called true or false.

2. Logic is engaged in an if-then kind of endeavor because it asks: If the premises *as given* are true, does the conclusion probably or necessarily follow? Logical analysis is concerned with the relationship between premises and conclusions—with the kind of backing the premises provide for the conclusion. The skill of logical analysis is applicable to every field of endeavor precisely because it deals in if-then and formal relationships and not in substantive questions of the truth and falsity of statements.

3. Further, the kinds of criteria that determine the truth or falsity of statements, or the strength of the warrants and backing offered, depend in part on the context or field in which they occur. For example, the criteria used to determine whether the statement "If x is greater than y, and y is greater than z, then x is greater than z" is different from the criteria used to determine the truth or falsity of the statement "Copper conducts electricity" or the assertion that "All citizens of the U.S., eighteen years or older, are eligible to vote." The former (mathematical statement) is true or false depending solely upon definition and logical rules. The latter statements are verified or falsified by experimentation and the relevant evidence that can be cited. Logic, of course, can lead us to raise questions of truth and falsity, though it does not as such seek to answer them. Suppose I discover, through logical analysis, that the following argument is deductively valid:

> If children are repressed, they will suffer psychologically when they grow up. But either a child is repressed or he is allowed free expression. It follows that if an adult does not suffer psychologically, he must have been allowed free expression as a child.
>
> [Sigmund Freud]

If I know that this argument is deductively valid, I can, of course, go on to accept it as also true on other grounds—on the evidence for or against it. Equally, I might be suspicious of what Freud is saying and thus go on to try to determine whether or not each of his claims are true. If the argument is discovered to be formally invalid, I probably would be led to examine Freudian theory much more critically in terms of the evidence.

Logic, then, is concerned not with the truth or falsity of statements, but with the justification of conclusions, with the relationship between premises or evidence and conclusions.

1.9 VALIDITY AND DEDUCTIVE ARGUMENTS

As indicated earlier, deductive arguments carry the claim of *conclusive proof* of their conclusions. Deductive arguments are called *valid* or *invalid*. A valid argument is one that *if its premises are true, then its conclusion must be true*. A valid deductive argument is one that cannot have true premises and a false conclusion. The conclusion cannot be false in a valid argument provided the premises are true. *Valid arguments preserve truth*.

Validity has to do with the connection between the premises and the conclusion of deductive arguments. The relation between premises and conclusion which we recognize by using the word 'valid' is of fundamental importance to right reasoning. Further, this notion of 'validity' and cases of this relation are constantly recognized in ordinary conversation and thought, even by people who are not students of logic. Thus, we find these common phrases used to refer to this relation.

This statement *follows from those*.

If such and such is true, then so and so *must* be true.

These facts are *conclusive evidence* for what we are trying to prove.

These common phrases, of course, spell out one aspect of deductive argument that we have already discussed—its claim to *conclusiveness*. What perhaps needs more elaboration, however, is the *explicative* nature of deductive argument and its relationship to validity. Here we also need to distinguish between valid arguments and other good types of arguments.

The distinction between valid arguments and other types of good arguments may be seen by asking whether *stated* premises without *appeal to further knowledge* are enough to determine the truth of the conclusion. Max Black, in his excellent text, *Critical Thinking*, cites the following example. Suppose my daughter says to me "Don't go out now, its raining and you will get wet." Putting this in argument form, we get something like the following:

Premise: It is raining now.

Conclusion: If you go out, you will get wet.

Considering this argument just as it is stated, it can be rated as a good argument and would be so rated by almost anyone asked to evaluate it. It is quite reasonable for us to accept the conclusion of this argument without asking for more evidence. However, the argument is not valid. If it were, it should contain *all* the reasons that justify the conclusion, and it does not. It does not, for example, tell us what connection there is between rain and people getting wet. Further, if this were a conversation between ducks, the conclusion would not necessarily follow, for ducks go out in the rain without getting wet because the rain slides off their backs. If we confine ourselves just to the reasons given in the premises of the argument, the conclusion does not necessarily follow though it reasonably follows. The argument would become deductive and valid if it were expanded as follows.

P_1 It is raining now.
P_2 It will still be raining when you go out.
P_3 Rain is wet.
P_4 Persons who go out when something wet is falling get wet.
P_5 You are a person.

Conclusion: Therefore, if you go out, you will get wet.

Thus, an argument may be sufficient for all practical purposes and yet not valid. An argument is valid when the truth of the premises assures the truth of the conclusion *without reference to any further evidence.* Another aspect of validity is what is often referred to as its *formal nature:* A person cannot both admit the truth of the premises of a valid argument such as the expanded one above, and deny the conclusion. If you admit the truth of premises one through five above and deny the conclusion, then you have failed to understand the *meaning of the words used.* As you are pondering the above argument, it is likely not raining at all. Yet, you see that the argument is valid. If those premises were true, the conclusion would necessarily be true even though you do not know all the premises to be true. In other words, the validity of a deductive argument depends on the meaning of the words used and is independent of the actual truth or falsity of the premises.

Another way of getting at the formal nature of an argument is to speak of its form and matter. The matter is the actual content of the argument, the assertions being made. It is these that are called *true* or *false.* The form of the argument is the structure or manner in which it is put together. The important point is that form and matter can be separated. Validity concerns the pattern, structure, or form of an argument and not the truth of falsity of the statements making up the argument. Validity is a formal thing and has nothing to do with what the argument is about, the content or matter. Let us look at some examples of valid arguments.

(1) All birds are feathered.   True
    All crows are birds.   True

    Therefore, all crows are feathered.   True

(2) Dogs are fish.   False
    Fish are warm-blooded.   False

    Therefore, dogs are warm-blooded.   True

(3) Lions are vegetarians.   False
    Vegetarians eat bread.   False

    Lions eat bread.   False

(4) Men are becoming smarter.   ?
    People who are becoming smarter need
      more to read.   ?

    Men need more to read.   ?

All of the above arguments are valid and yet there are a variety of truth values involved. There is no direct relation between the truth and the validity of the conclusion, and moreover, in 4 the conclusion can be seen to be valid even though the truth or falsity of the premises and conclusion is unknown. Truth and falsity of content and validity must be distinguished. Take 1 again as an example.

All birds are feathered.
All crows are birds.

Therefore, all crows are feathered.

The validity of this argument depends on its structure and not on what it is about or on the truth and falsity of its statements. Validity tells us nothing about the actual truth or falsity of the statements. We do know that *if* it is valid, then *if* the premises are true, the conclusion *must* be true. Because validity is formal and depends on structure, we can abstract from the above argument its basic form and symbolize it as follows, using '∴' to stand for 'therefore,' 'A' to stand for 'birds,' 'B' for 'feathered,' and 'C' for 'crows.' Thus, we get:

All A are B.
All C are A.

∴ All C are B.

Any argument that has this pattern is *always valid,* whatever it is about. Thus, for A, B, and C we can substitute anything we want and still we will have a valid argument. Thus,

> All dogs are birds.
> All toads are dogs.
> ─────────────
> ∴ All toads are birds.

Notice, that all the statements in this argument are false, and yet the argument remains valid. Logic *only* says, *if* it is true that "all dogs are birds" and "all toads are dogs," then it *must be* true that "all toads are birds."

> All monkeys are blue-skinned.
> All apes are monkeys.
> ─────────────
> ∴ All apes are blue-skinned.

Here we have a valid argument in which one premise is true, one premise and the conclusion are false. Consider yet another case.

> All dogs are birds.
> All canaries are dogs.
> ─────────────
> ∴ All canaries are birds.

This valid argument has false premises, but a true conclusion. The following instance of our valid argument form has a true conclusion, but one false premise.

> All dogs are warm-blooded.
> All cats are dogs.
> ─────────────
> ∴ All cats are warm-blooded.

In summary, then, validity has to do with the formal structure of arguments and is independent of what the argument is about. It is essentially independent of the truth and falsity of the statements making up the argument. The one connection between validity and truth is that validity *excludes* the possibility that all the premises are true and yet the conclusion is false. A valid argument is one in which *if* the premises are true, the conclusion must be true. In arguments, every combination of validity-invalidity and truth-falsehood can occur except one: *a valid argument with true premises cannot have a false conclusion.* Valid arguments point up what must be true provided that our assumptions are true. Thus, for example, we cannot consistently assert that "all communists are atheists," and yet deny that one communist, Mr. Jones, is not an atheist. The pattern,

All A are B.
X is an A.
∴ X is a B.

is a valid argument form. It makes no difference if *in fact* Mr. Jones is not a Communist. Our valid argument form tells us that *if* Mr. Jones *were* a Communist and *if* all Communists were atheists, then Mr. Jones would have to be an atheist.

Similarly, invalidity is tested by finding an interpretation of the argument form which violates the definition of validity, that is, which has true premises and yet the conclusion is false. Take the case of the following argument.

All communists are atheists.
Mr. Jones is an atheist.
∴ Mr. Jones is a communist.

This argument has the following form.

All A are B.
X is a B.
∴ X is an A.

To show that this is an invalid argument form we need only to find an example of this form which has true premises and a false conclusion. Consider the following example.

All birds are warm-blooded.
Mrs. Smith is warm-blooded.
∴ Mrs. Smith is a bird.

The premises are factually true, but the conclusion is obviously false. The argument form is an invalid one. Validity preserves the truth of the premises in the conclusion; invalidity fails to preserve the truth of the premises in the conclusion. Validity excludes the possibility that all the premises are true and yet the conclusion is false; invalidity does not exclude this possibility. We thus have the following definitions.

Valid Deductive Argument: An argument in which, if the premises are true, then the conclusion must be true.

Valid Deductive Argument Form: An argument form in which we cannot consistently interpret the nonlogical terms to make the premises true and the conclusion false.

Tape Exercises

Determine the validity or invalidity of the following arguments, and also indicate the factual truth or falsity of the premises, if determinable. [The answers are given on Tape 1, band 5.]

1. All criminals are breakers of the law.
   Some neurotics are not breakers of the law.

   Therefore: some neurotics are not criminals.

2. No Pekinese are dogs.
   All collies are dogs.

   No Pekinese are collies.

3. All birds are canaries.
   No canaries are yellow.

   No canaries are birds.

4. All women are unsavory persons.
   No pioneers were unsavory persons.

   No women were pioneers.

5. All Californians are growing taller.
   All people growing taller are drinking more milk.

   All Californians are drinking more milk.

The main question of deductive logic, then, is the question: "Is the conclusion a valid consequent of the premises?" Logicians focus on the connection between the premises and the conclusion rather than on the truth or falsity of the premises and conclusion taken by themselves.

We might put the validity-truth distinction another way—by speaking of two kinds of errors or mistakes we can make in reasoning. We can make a *factual error* or a *logical error.* In putting forth an argument we make two claims: That our premises are true and that if these premises are true, the conclusion should also be true. Thus, in light of these two claims, we can commit two errors in argument. We can commit a *factual* error—our premises may be false. However, this does not mean we have necessarily also committed the second error—the *logical error,* which is that our argument is invalid. The truth of the premises do not really guarantee the truth of the conclusion. This is so because arguments can be valid with false premises. The validity of a deductive argument does not guarantee the truth of its conclusion. Logic does not help us escape the factual error; it concentrates entirely on avoiding the logical mistake of employing an invalid type of argument. Truth and validity, then, are different and one must never speak of arguments as true or false. The ideal of reasoning, however, should be to avoid both mistakes, to reason validity from true assumptions. An argument that achieves this is called a *sound argument.* Thus, a sound argument is an argument that is valid and has true premises and therefore a true conclusion. To call a deductive argument *unsound*, then, is to say that it does not establish the truth of its conclusion. It fails to do so either because it is invalid or because not all of its premises are true.

Having set out the distinctions between truth and validity, it must also be said that in practice we desire our premises to be true and we usually do not describe an argument as a good one if the premises are false. Why, then, you ask, should one be concerned with validity if it is merely a matter of form and does not necessarily guarantee the truth of the conclusion? In answer to this question several points need to be made. First, we must often depend upon arguments whose premises are not known to be true. The scientist who works with hypothesis, seeking to find the correct one to explain the facts with which he is dealing, does not know in advance which one is true. Rather he uses them as premises in order to deduce testable consequences from them. This is indeed the case with most, if not all, problem solving situations in which alternative courses of action are available. Our very purpose in considering various arguments is to decide which alternative premise to make true. Second, formal deductive reasoning does perform the important function of helping us to see what conclusions can and cannot be validly drawn from certain premises. Suppose we are arguing about B. F. Skinner and social control and we have agreed on the following two statements: "Liberty is not compatible with social control," and "The right to voice one's opinion is a form of liberty." What valid conclusion could we draw, if any? Knowing the rules for validity, we would find that a valid conclusion can be drawn from these two premises, namely, "The right to voice one's opinion is not compatible with social control." One could, then, go on to formulate further implications of this conclusion.

In addition, knowing certain basic techniques of compound statement logic, we could supply the unstated conclusion and assess the validity of the argument contained, for example, in the following news story.

KENT, Ohio—A highway Patrol officer denied today that a police helicopter reported spotting a sniper just before Guardsmen killed four students and wounded several others during an anti-war demonstration yesterday.

The National Guard said after the shootings that a sniper spotted by a police helicopter had fired on the Guardsmen first.

But a Highway Patrol official said today, if there had been a sighting, it would have been logged and there is no such entry in the records.

The *valid* conclusion of the above argument is obvious, and it has clear implications for all concerned, namely, "There was no sighting of a sniper by a Highway Patrol helicopter."

Further, *validity* applies only to deductive reasoning. Other criteria come into play with inductive reasoning. These criteria, however, still concern the relation between premises and conclusion and the kind of support given to the conclusion by the premises, and not with the truth or falsity of statements. But knowing whether arguments are valid is really a good half of the battle won, because very often we do not know the truth or falsity of the statements or are not even in a position to determine their truth, but we can attack an argument as fallacious. Further, if the argument is valid, then we are more willing to make the effort to determine the truth of the premises.

One final word is in order. Good arguments should be seen as good by all reasonable people, but some people refuse to be impressed, and our knockdown arguments leave them standing up. What does one say in this case? First of all, logical validity and soundness and the power to persuade simply are not equal. There is no royal road to success in practical argumentation. Some people will remain irrational and will not admit to the most convincing argument. Second, there are many crucial issues in life in which no argument settles the dispute once and for all and beyond the possibility of being reopened. We must keep open the dialectic, though always with our logical facilities at the height of critical awareness. Only then will we know what conclusion we are arguing for and on what grounds.

Exercise for § 1.9

A. Which of the following arguments are examples, one or the other, of the valid argument forms?

A.   All A are B
     All C are A
     ———————
     ∴ All C are B

B.   If A then B
     A
     ———————
     ∴ B

Which of the following are examples of one or the other of the invalid argument forms?

C.   All A are B
     x is a B
     ———————
     ∴ x is an A

D.   If A, then B
     Not A
     ———————
     Not B

1. All persons who knowingly and needlessly endanger their health are irrational persons. All college students who smoke are persons who knowingly and needlessly endanger their health. Therefore, all college students who smoke are irrational.

2. If a whale is a mammal, then it is warm blooded. A whale is a mammal. Therefore, it is warm blooded.

3. All metals conduct electricity. All iron objects are metallic. So, all iron objects are electrical conductors.

4. If you received a scholarship, then you are a full-time student. You did not receive a scholarship. Therefore, you are not a full-time student.

5. All children are illogical. Mary is illogical. Therefore, Mary is a child.

6. All poisonous snakes are dangerous. All rattle-snakes are poisonous snakes. Thus, all rattle-snakes are dangerous.

7. All scientists are creative thinkers. A poet is a creative thinker. Thus, a poet is a scientist.

8. If a university is great, then it has a good library. Ridiculous University is not a great university. Therefore, Ridiculous University does not have a good library.

9. All Malaysians are Moslems. Sam is a Moslem. Therefore, Sam is a Malaysian.

10. If we score another touchdown, then we will win the game. We did not score another touchdown. Therefore, we did not win the game.

B. Each of the following arguments is valid. Which ones of them are also sound?

1. All dogs are carnivores. All carnivores are meat eaters. Therefore, all dogs are meat eaters.

2. No college students are canaries. All freshmen are college students. Therefore, no freshmen are canaries.

3. All mothers are female. No daughters are female. Therefore, no daughters are mothers.

4. No Methodists are Catholics. All Methodists are Protestants. Therefore, some Protestants are not Catholics.

5. No millionaires are poor. Some millionaires are friendly. Thus, some friendly people are not poor.

6. All dogs are fish. No trout are fish. Therefore, no trout are dogs.

7. All triangles are squares. All squares are rectangles. Thus, all rectangles are triangles.

8. All fathers are male. All daddies are fathers. Thus, all daddies are male.

9. All cats are feline. All Persians are cats. Thus, all Persians are feline.

10. All dogs are birds. No birds are carnivorus. Thus, no dogs are carnivorous.

C. Indicate whether the following statements are true or false.

1. An argument can have false premises and a false conclusion and still be valid.

2. One can properly speak of an argument as true or false.

3. If the premises of a valid argument are true, then the conclusion *must* be true.

4. An argument can have true premises and a false conclusion and still be valid.

5. Logic is primarily concerned with establishing the truth or falsity of statements.

6. Any argument which has a valid argument form is valid regardless of context.

7. A deductive argument which has a false premise and a true conclusion can be sound.

8. If the premises of a valid argument are false then the conclusion must be false.

9. Logic is primarily concerned with factual truth and falsity.

D. Answer the following questions.

1. If you know only that the premises of a given argument are true, does this tell you whether the argument is valid?

2. Do all invalid arguments have false premises?

3. If you know only that an argument is invalid, can the truth value of that argument's premises be determined?

4. To describe an argument as valid is to affirm that it is impossible for its premises to be true and its conclusion to be _____.

5. If a valid argument has true premises, then its conclusion must be _____.

6. A valid argument with a false conclusion cannot have _____ premises.

7. If an argument has true premises but a false conclusion that argument cannot possible be _____. (Two answers are possible.)

8. To describe an argument as sound is to affirm that its premises are _____ and its conclusion is _____.

9. If an argument has a false premise it cannot possibly be _____.

10. To describe an invalid argument is to affirm that it is possible for the premises to be true and the conclusion _____.

E. Assuming ordinary context, examine each of the following arguments. Identify the conclusion and premise. Supply a missing premise that would make the argument deductively valid.

1. No dogs are cats because cats are feline.

2. John makes mistakes because he is human.

3. No profiteers are patriots because no good citizens are profiteers.

4. No ducks are graceful. After all, nothing that waddles is graceful.

5. Some greedy creatures cannot fly because pigs are greedy.

6. Gold is not a compound substance, for it is a metal.

7. Every citizen of the United States is eligible for election to this office. Therefore, he is eleigible for election.

8. He deserved to be expelled from school because he cheated on the exams.

9. The President of the United States cannot perform miracles. He is, after all, a man.

10. The power of recognizing important resemblances is the work of genius. Hence the making of genuine metaphors is the work of genius.

1.10 GOOD VERSUS BAD INDUCTIVE ARGUMENTS

Inductive arguments are more difficult and tricky to evaluate than deductive arguments because the premises do not necessarily imply the conclusions and because strength is not determined by formal considerations. As indicated earlier, an inductive argument can be strengthened or weakened by the addition of further premises. This is because it is weak or strong relative to the evidence presented in the premises. Thus, recall our example:

> George smoked Burro Filters.
> Burro filters were found at the scene of the crime.
> _____
> George is guilty of the crime.

If we add the premise—George had a motive for the crime—the argument is strengthened. If we add the premise—George was seen at the scene of the crime about the time of the murder—the conclusion becomes even more likely. If, however, the premises—lipstick stains were found on a glass, fingerprints of another person were found in the apartment, they were not George's fingerprints, and Helen had a motive for the crime—are added, we have considerably weakened the argument. These premises add evidence that is counter to the conclusion, and thus they give far less support to the conclusion.

Because of the ampliative nature of inductive arguments, additional premises make a difference to strength or weakness. It is inappropriate to speak of inductive arguments as valid or invalid because once an argument is found to be valid no thing can make it *more* valid. No enlarged set of premises will make it more valid. Indeed, inductive arguments should not be described in absolute terms. Rather, we say that an inductive argument is stronger or weaker than some other inductive argument. When we do assert that an inductive argument is strong, it should be interpreted as an assertion that *in light of the evidence available* to us this particular argument is the strongest that could be given in support of this conclusion.

In determining whether premises strengthen or weaken an inductive argument, various kinds of criteria apply, depending on the kind of inductive reasoning being used. To help you better understand the nature of inductive argument, it might be helpful to review briefly the kinds of criteria used to test enumerative generalization. The standard form of this type of inductive argument is as follows.

> George is a human being and is mortal.
> Sally is a human being and is mortal.
> Horace is a human being and is mortal.
> Mary is a human being and is mortal.
> _____
> Therefore, probably all human beings are mortal.

Three primary criteria are usually used to test this type of inductive argument. The first is that of *number*. The larger the number of similar and relevant cases provided in support of the conclusion, the stronger the conclusion. Thus, consider the difference in degree of support that the following two premises give to their conclusions.

> I have taken two courses in philosophy and found them interesting. Therefore, I shall find a third course in philosophy interesting.

> I have taken eight courses in philosophy and found them interesting. Therefore, I shall find a tenth course in philosophy interesting.

The second argument is obviously stronger than the first.

Variety is the second important criteria by which we test the strength of inductive arguments. If students are able to say, "We have taken eight courses in philosophy and found them interesting. These courses covered many different areas and concerns—theory of knowledge, philosophy of science, philosophy of art, philosophy of religion, political philosophy, logic, philosophy of history, metaphysics," they have a stronger case for concluding that the ninth course in philosophy will also be interesting than a student whose eight courses all have concerned one area, the area of values. This is true because the more variety involved, the less likely that a student will encounter an unknown factor that will make a difference to strength or weakness. Thus, the student who has taken eight courses on values and found them interesting might find a ninth course on science and knowledge uninteresting. Further, the student who has taken a greater variety of courses probably has had a greater variety of teachers, whereas the student with lesser variety might have had one or two teachers and might find the new teacher of the ninth course incompatible with his or her personality, and thus the course, unpleasant. It should also be observed that number and variety go together—the greater number *and* the greater variety, the more probable the conclusion.

The third criteria relevant to assessing inductive arguments concerns the *scope of the conclusion.* How much does the conclusion claim? How broad an area of application is involved? How far does the conclusion go beyond its premises? Thus, consider the following:

> I have taken eight courses in philosphy in many different areas and with many different teachers and found them all interesting.

Conclusion 1:   I shall find a ninth course in philosophy interesting.
Conclusion 2:   I shall find my next two courses in philosophy interesting.
Conclusion 3:   I shall find my next five courses in philosophy interesting.
Conclusion 4:   I shall find all courses in philosophy interesting.

Each conclusion is broader in scope than the preceding one. The broader the range of application, and so the farther away from the evidence in the premises the conclusion is, the weaker the argument. Variety, number, and scope all work together. Thus, the greater the number and variety involved and the closer the conclusion is to the premises in terms of application, the stronger the argument.

Tape Exercises

In order to test your understanding of inductive argument at this early stage, complete the following problems. Assess the strength or weakness of the conclusion relative to the evidence cited. Indicate why you assess them as you do. Indicate additional evidence that might strengthen or weaken the conclusions. [The problems are analyzed in Tape 1, band 6.]

1. *Sample, Data or Evidence:* A careful tabulation of all the books checked out of the Broder County Aslen Library over a period of two months, which shows that 65 percent of the 10,000 books checked out were nonfiction books on contemporary public figures.

1st Conclusion:	A slight majority of Broder County Aslen residents are interested in the lives of contemporary public figures.
2nd Conclusion:	A majority of Broder County Aslen residents are interested in the lives of contemporary public figures.
3rd Conclusion:	A majority of Broder County residents are interested in the lives of contemporary public figures.
4th Conclusion:	Californians are interested in the lives of contemporary public figures.
5th Conclusion:	People today are interested in the lives of contemporary public figures.

2. *Sample, Data or Evidence:* The careful listening, to and discussion of Beethoven's 9th Symphony, and Beethoven's 5th Symphony, and the consensus by 40 music students that they are of high quality.

1st Conclusion:	All of Beethoven's symphonies will be of high quality.
2nd Conclusion:	All of Beethoven's works will be of high quality.

3. *Data or Evidence:*   All the coins in my pocket are nickels.

1st Conclusion:	The next coin I take out of my pocket will be a nickel.
2nd Conclusion:	The next 10 coins I take out of my pocket will be nickels.
3rd Conclusion:	The next coin that everyone in this room takes out of his pocket will be a nickel.
4th Conclusion:	The next coin that everyone takes out of his pocket will be a nickel.

Exercises for § 1.10

A. Which of the following are true statements and which are false statements?

1. Validity can properly be attributed to inductive arguments.

2. Inductive arguments are ampliative: they allow us to arrive at information that is not logically contained in the premises.

3. One can speak of valid inductive argument forms.

4. The addition of a premise to an inductive argument may change its inductive strength or weakness.

5. All inductive arguments are unreliable because they are inconclusive.

6. Knowledge of the subject matter is of importance in judging the correctness of inductive arguments.

7. If the premises in an inductive argument are true, then the conclusion *must* be true.

8. How many (number) is an important consideration in judging inductive arguments.

9. Inductive strength is always a matter of degree.

10. Inductive arguments may be judged on form alone.

B. Assuming ordinary context, evaluate each of the following inductive arguments. Identify premises and conclusion. Add a premise that will strengthen the argument. Add a premise that will weaken the argument.

1. John has liked all three philosophy classes he has taken. Therefore, he will also like the fourth.

2. All crows observed to date have been black. It is highly probable therefore that all crows observed in the future will be black.

3. I have picked three winners at the races today. Therefore, I am pretty sure I will win in the next four races also.

4. Every opera I have ever attended was a classic bore. I am sure that tonight's performance won't be any better.

5. The political polls predicted that Governor Snorkle will be reelected overwhelmingly. So, I am not going to bother to cast my vote for his opponent.

6. Most Democrats are for an energy bill. Senator Philipps is a Democrat, so he probably will favor the bill.

7. Every time in the past when the interest rates rose, the stock market fell.

8. Quit worrying about yourself. The life expectancy of someone in your occupational category is seventy. You will live to be at least seventy.

9. Our basketball team has won its last five games. It should win tonight's game also.

10. I think your trouble is the fuel pump. My car cut out like that one time and it was the fuel pump.

C. Suppose you have been doing some psychological testing with white rats. A maze has been constructed with a female rat at the end. Four males have been run through the maze and each has found its way to the female.

You, therefore, *conclude* that any male rat will find its way to the female.

Using the three criteria of number, variety and scope of generalization, determine whether your conclusion would be strengthened or weakened by each of the following additional premises or items of information. Indicate *why* you made the choice you did.

1. All four rats had been previously conditioned in the maze.
2. The first two rats had been deprived of food for two days.
3. The first three rats had been isolated from females for one week.
4. The rats were arbitrarily selected from a cage containing seventy-five rats.
5. Only one of the four rats had been previously conditioned in this maze.
6. The conclusion is weakened to read: any white rat will find his way to the female.
7. The rats were each five months old.
8. Seventy-five male rats were run through the maze, and each found its way to the female.
9. The four rats were males who were isolated from females for two weeks.
10. The conclusion is weakened to read: all male rats when suitably conditioned will find their way to the female if they have been isolated from females for one week or longer.

Chapter Outline

A. The basic aim of logic is to teach one to reason correctly: *Correct reasoning* is finding reasons and/or evidence which do support and/or prove one's conclusions.
B. Logic is concerned with *statements*.
   1. A *statement* is an assertion of denial—something is said to be or not be the case. Of a statement it can usually be asked: is it true or false?
   2. A *proposition* is a statement which relates two classes or categories, such as, "All whales are mammals."
   3. Sentences and statements must be distinguished.
      a. A *sentence* is a grammatically constructed expression in some language.
      b. Sentences may be used to make statements, for example, "America is beautiful," but not all sentences are statements, for example, "Who is there?"
      c. Different sentences can make the same statement—"America is a beautiful country," and "A beautiful country is America."
   4. Statements can be identified by asking: "Is an assertion or denial being made?"

C. Logic is interested in *argument:* An argument is a set of statements, in which one, called a *conclusion* is claimed to be the consequence of or to be justified by the others, called variously, *evidence, reasons, grounds,* or *premises.*

1. All arguments, however complex, are analyzable into two basic and simple structural forms.

    a. This is true, therefore, that is true.

    b. This is true, because this is true.

2. Certain words usually indicate premises and others usually indicate conclusions.

    a. *Premise indicating words:* because, for, since, in view of, as shown by, inasmuch as, for the reason that, may be inferred from, is substantiated by.

    b. *Conclusion indicating words:* thus, hence, so, therefore, accordingly, consequently, proves that, it follows from, we may infer.

3. All arguments may be classified into two basic kinds:

    a. *Deductive argument:* An argument in which it is claimed that if the premises are true, the conclusion must necessarily be true. It claims that the promises constitute conclusive proof for the conclusion. Deductive arguments are called valid or invalid.

    b. *Inductive argument:* An argument which claims only that the premises provide some evidence for the conclusion. The premises establish the conclusion as only more or less probable. Inductive arguments are called strong or weak.

4. *Validity* is a characteristic of deductive arguments such that if the premises are true, the conclusion must necessarily be true. *A valid argument with true premises cannot have a false conclusion.*

5. Validity is characteristic of the formal structure of argument. Valid arguments are those which are structured or formed in certain ways. All arguments which have a valid logical form are valid regardless of the content of the argument.

2

DIMENSIONS OF LANGUAGE

2.1 INTRODUCTION

The late British prime minister, Winston Churchill, once said that the most important thing that should be gained from an education is a thorough knowledge and command of one's native language. Language is an immensely rich tool as the great persons of all walks of life have recognized. Yet, to communicate and to understand are immensely difficult tasks.

Logic is concerned with both communication and understanding. It demands that we sort through the various uses and functions of language to concentrate on the actual argument being presented. It forces us to seek clarity and precision—to understand what is being said. Arguments in any usage—everyday, legal, philosophical, etc.—rarely appear in a form that makes formal logical analysis easy, but they must be susceptible to such analysis insofar as they attempt to be rational. Further, in learning to recognize arguments and to assess their strengths, we learn that if we want to argue rationally we need to think out clearly what we intend to say before we say it. Knowing what we intend to say, we then can concentrate on using our language skills to say it well—with wit, irony, transition, flow, style, and persuasive power.

Further, although we may wish it were not the case, language can be used merely to persuade or influence without concern for rational arguments. The appeal in these cases is not to reason, to 'logical cogency'; rather the appeal is psychological, to opinions, prejudices, emotions. Indeed, in many cases the deliberate aim is to create ambiguity rather than clarity. To know, then, whether conclusions really do follow, we must be aware of the various ways language can be used and misused.

In approaching the question of the uses of language, we should recall the distinctions already made between the ways in which sentences can be used. Some sentences can be used to make statements—to assert something to be or not be the case. We can ask about their truth or falsity. Sentences used to make statements are usually declarative sentences like "Water boils at 100°C at sea level" and "It is raining." In addition, there are interrogative sentences that ask a question, exclamatory sentences that express an emotion or attitude, and hortatory sentences that make commands and requests. These do not normally make or imply statements.

Logic, we have emphasized, is exclusively concerned with statements and thus with sentences that assert or deny something.

2.2   USES OF LANGUAGE

The grammatical structure of a sentence is only one way to identify use of language; there are many uses of language. The British philosopher, Ludwig Wittgenstein, in his *Philosophical Investigations* (translated by G. E. M. Anscombe [Oxford: Basil Blackwell, 1967], pp. 11–12) gives the following examples:

Giving orders and obeying them.
Describing the appearance of an object, or giving its measurements.
Constructing an object from a description (a drawing).
Reporting an event.
Speculating about an event.
Forming and testing a hypothesis.
Presenting the results of an experiment in tables and diagrams.
Making up a story; and reading it.
Play-acting.
Singing catches.
Guessing riddles.
Making a joke; telling it.
Solving a problem in practical arithmetic.
Translating from one language into another.

Clearly, language is a very fascinating and flexible tool. And, in spite of the fact that it has so many and varied uses, most of these can be classified under five general categories, or functions.

Cognitive (Informative) Function.   Language may be used to convey information. The following statements are examples of this use of language.

"There are two windows in my room."

"On September 1, 1939, Hitler's armies invaded Poland."

"All material bodies attract in direction proportion to their masses and in inverse proportion to the square of their distances."

It is characteristic of these and all similar statements that they can be spoken of as either true or false. They declare something to be or not be the case. Thus, the criteria of truth and falsity are relevant to every statement that purports to convey information and that exemplifies the cognitive or informative function of language. This does not mean, however, that other criteria are not applicable to statements of information. Statements of information can also be assessed as significant or insignificant and as useful or not useful. Further, although the question of truth or falsity can always be raised about statements of information, it does not follow that determining their truth or falsity is possible or is an easy matter. Whether consistency and coherence, correspondence, or workability is the mark of the true is still an open question. Logic is not concerned in its deductive aspect to establish factual truth or falsity. It asks: Assuming the truth of the premises, do the conclusions follow? Finally, as indicated in chapter 1, statements can be used in contexts other than argument, such as in explanation and description. Consider the following examples.

If rehabilitation and protection of society from unrehabilitated offenders were the only purposes of legal punishment, the death penalty could be abolished because it cannot attain the first end and is not needed for the second.

This series of statements is used cognitively-informatively because we may ask about each of the statements made, Is it true or false? These statements also constitute an argument because the first statement is asserted to follow from the next two statements. Now look at another series of statements.

A convicted man may be found to be innocent; if he is executed, the penalty cannot be reversed. Except for fines, penalties never can be reversed. Time spent in prison cannot be returned. However, a prison sentence may be remitted once the prisoner serving it is found innocent; and he can be compensated for the time served.

These sentences are all statements. All of them purport to inform us of facts, and of all of them we can ask whether they are true or false. However, this series of statements does not constitute an argument, for no one of them is claimed to follow from the others. Rather, they merely describe the situation of convicted persons who are found innocent.

Finally, consider a third passage.

Why did moisture form on the outside of the glass when it was filled with ice yesterday? Because the temperature of the glass after it was filled with ice water was considerably lower than the temperature of the surrounding air; the air contained water vapor and water water in air is in general precipitated as a liquid whenever the air comes into contact with a sufficiently cold surface.

Again, we have a series of statements and language used informatively, but it is used neither to argue or describe but to explain why moisture formed on the outside of the glass. Language may be used informatively, then, to describe, argue, and explain. Logic is concerned primarily with the argumentative use of language.

Expressive   Here language is used to express feelings or attitudes. The following examples may be said to reveal attitudes or feelings.

"Am having a wonderful time."

"What a glorious sunset!"

"The dirty rat."

"Lily-livered boy!"

The important point here is that expressions such as these give no information about the person, object, situation, or condition referred to, but they do indicate the emotions, feelings and attitudes of the speaker; they reveal how the speaker feels about something. These expressive phrases are also often evaluative, that is, they reveal a positive or negative judgment on the part of the speaker. Thus, the phrase, "The dirty rat" expresses the strongly negative judgment of the speaker.

Evocative or Directive   Language may also be used to evoke certain feelings, emotions, and attitudes in others, as well as certain responses or actions. Pleas, requests, commands are evocative as well as shouts of warning and attempts at persuasion. Examples of the evocative function of language are:

"Look out!"

"Squads right!"

"Please close the door."

"See your dentist twice a year."

"Joe Blank for Congress."

These are obviously designed to produce some kind of action or effect. Indeed, in classifying use of language under this category, we are really referring to the use of language from two perspectives: (1) the purpose or purposes of the user of the sentences, and (2) the effect the user of language wishes to have or might have. The same is not generally true of the informative and expressive functions of language, because these usually disclose fairly clearly the purpose(s) of the user. The evocative function, and to a lesser extent, the performative function, have reference both to purpose and to effect.

An important aspect of the use of language in both the expressive and evocative ways is what is often called the *emotive meaning* of words and expressions. Words and phrases, because of certain associations, may have

emotional suggestiveness and thus function to evoke certain emotional responses and attitudes in us. Words can convey negative or positive attitudes
and arouse in us negative or positive emotions and attitudes. Consider the
difference in emotive meaning conveyed by each of the following words which
have the same literal meaning, 'bureaucrat,' 'government official' and 'public
servant.' Or, consider the impact of the phrase 'a foreign midget' as compared
with 'a car made abroad.' The differences in emotive meanings was humorously
illustrated by Bertrand Russell when he wrote "I am firm, you are obstinate, he
is a pig-headed fool."

The important point for logical analysis is to distinguish between the informative function and the evocative function. Logic is interested in what is being
asserted, not in how it is asserted. Emotional appeals are irrelevant to the
logical adequacy of an argument.

Language, of course, would be impoverished if emotive words were eliminated. After all, these kinds of words are the essential tools of poetry, drama,
and literature. Consider lines such as the following:

"How silver-sweet sound lovers' tongues by night,
Like softest music to attending ears."

[Romeo and Juliet]

However, though it is an intriguing question as to precisely how literature,
poetry and drama gives us truth claims, we do not *primarily* ask of literature
that it defend its assertions in a logical manner. What is important to recognize
is that the logician is essentially concerned with neutral words. If emotive
words are used in an argument, we need to reduce them to a relatively neutral
content to analyze properly the structure of the argument. Emotive words tend
to introduce vagueness and ambiguities into an argument, and in many contexts they serve to distract attention from the content of the argument and to
condition one to accept a conclusion on the basis of insufficient evidence.

In dealing with emotive terms, which do have an evaluative dimension, we
must take into consideration the context in which they occur. For example,
though 'motherhood' almost always has a positive emotive force, this clearly is
not the case in the following statement: "Motherhood is the chain whereby
male facist pigs have enslaved women." Further, though the application of 'pig'
to humans generally has negative emotive force, the exclamation in *Charlotte's
Web* about Wilbur, that "He is some pig!" is surely positive. Further, we usually
can order terms, with evaluative dimensions on a continuum from positive,
through neutral, to negative connotations. Consider the following examples:

aroma, fragrance, smell, odor, stench

execute, slay, kill, murder, butcher

trustful, unsuspicious, confiding, credulous, gullible.

Tape Exercises

A. Indicate for each of the following what type of language usage is involved—informative, expressive or evocative—and then turn to **Tape 2, band 1,** for a brief analysis of these.

1. Hatred and happiness are not compatible.
2. Ah, the sheer, breathtaking beauty of this scene!
3. You must make certain beyond a reasonable doubt that the defendant took part in the bank robbery in San Francisco on June 11, 1975.
4. In the 15th century Nicholaus Copernicus proposed that we consider the possibility that the planets revolve around the sun.
5. Believe in me and together we shall make the changes necessary to change this country.

B. Now try ordering the following phrases from most emotive (strongly negative or positive) to least emotive or neutral. Check your answers with the tape.

1. brave, foolhardy, courageous, sensible, afraid, coward.
2. different, bizarre, unusual, strange, unique.
3. benevolent, generous, stingy, careful, magnanimous, fair.

The Evaluative Use of Language   The evaluative use of language involves issues of bewildering complexity discussed in such widely ranging contexts as philosophy of science, law, ethics, aesthetics, and the social sciences. There is still much disagreement about how the evaluative use of language should be characterized. Although in an introductory course we cannot discuss in detail the logic of evaluative judgments, nor specify the various ethical systems that can and do set the context for the many value judgments we all make, we can attempt to clarify the various kinds of value judgments we do make and the various ways they can be characterized. We can also show, though briefly, the role they play in argumentation and decision and the questions that can and should be raised relative to these judgments. As indicated, statements, in their cognitive-informative use, make claims or assertions about 'states of affairs,' about what is or is not the case. About these we can ask Are they true or false? Furthermore, these are assertions about which some kind of universal or general agreement can be attained. For example, "A molecule of water is composed of two atoms of hydrogen and one atom of oxygen." We usually speak of all such assertions as statements of *'fact'*.

Value judgments, on the other hand, are claims or assertions about what is of worth, of value,—what is good, just, beautiful. Another way to talk about the evaluative use of language is to say that it is employed in contexts in which reference is to *values, standards, criteria or rules.* For example, when someone makes the statement "You had an inadequate score on the college entrance examination," he or she is making a value judgment that has indirect reference to some standard used in evaluating college applicants, for example, an S.A.T. score of _____, which is required for admission to college. If someone says, "It is wrong for a judge to preside over a case in which he has a vested interest," he or she is making a value judgment relative to a certain procedure and standard of conduct in the legal profession. The judgment concerns what *ought* or *ought not* to occur. If a scientist says to a student, "You have conducted an improper experiment because you failed to take account of all the variables," the instructor has made a value judgment relative to a rule of scientific procedure.

Thus, value judgments may be made in different areas of life and relative to certain standards—educational, economic, social, political, scientific. These judgments are objective in the sense and to the degree that specific, generally agreed upon standards or criteria can be pointed to in justifying the judgment.

Another type of value judgment is what we call a functional value judgment for it refers to a particular function or purpose performed or served by the thing being judged. Thus, "John is a good basketball player" and "This is a good car" are functional value judgments referring to specific standards of performance.

A more subjective kind of value judgment is that of personal taste—"I like tea better than coffee" and "I prefer menthol cigarettes." These judgments are subjective because personal tastes whether in wine, sex, or song, cannot be disputed.

Value judgments that are even more controversial are illustrated in the following. "The actions of the Watergate people were *wrong*." "Stealing is wrong," and "Truman capote's novels are trash." The first falls into the realm of ethical judgments, and the second states a moral belief, attitude or standard. The third seems to be making an aesthetic judgment about the artistic value of Capote's books, but it may convey an implied moral judgment as well. Let us examine these two kinds of value judgments more closely. Ethical judgments are judgments that claim that a certain action or type of action ought or ought not to be performed, and it passes judgment on the goodness or badness of human conduct or character. Some examples are the statements "Adultery is wrong," "Capital punishment is wrong," "Telling the truth is right." Aesthetic judgments are judgments made in the context of what we consider beautiful or ugly and are used to express the claim that a work of art does or does not possess aesthetic value. They involve references to certain standards and possession of certain qualities, e.g., form, harmony, balance, coherence, expressiveness, or similar attributes.

The *ethical* and *aesthetic* use of language raises two very important questions. First of all, how are these uses of language to be interpreted? Is an ethical statement, such as "Murder is wrong," merely an expressive use of language, translatable into "I do not like murder" or "Murder—ugh!" Is an ethical statement merely a directive type statement, that says "Do not kill!" Finally, is an ethical judgment an assertive-type statement and thus one for which we may be asked to give reasons for its acceptance? If it is the latter, then ethical judgments should be open to logical analysis which is always concerned about reasons and the evidence used to justify claims. This is a controversial issue and cannot be settled here (nor do the three types we have cited exhaust the possibilities). Our discussion should stimulate the interested student to turn to the area of philosophy called metaethics in which the intrepretation of ethical language and the meaning of the content of ethical sentences is discussed. We shall assume that in arguments we need (1) to spell out and specify any value judgments being made, (2) to indicate whether any reasons are given for these value judgments, and (3) to show what role they play in the argument or in the decision-making process. This will be especially important when we discuss agreement-disagreement in the next chapter.

A second major question raised by ethical judgments in particular concerns *standards* or *values*—"What rules or principles, if any, ought we to accept for the guidance of our lives?" This is an extremely important question for anyone seeking to lead a mature and rational life. The difficult task of determining possible moral values we can hold, deciding what sorts of actions are right or wrong, and deciding what sort of way of life we should adopt is a task undertaken by another branch of philosophy called *Normative Ethics.* Likewise the questions of interpretation of *aesthetic value* judgments, the meaning of aesthetic terms such as 'beauty,' 'ugly,' 'sublime,' 'tragic,' and the possible standards and criteria of aesthetic value are wrestled with in the branch of philosophy called *aesthetics.*

Before leaving the evaluative realm of language, we should call attention to a very important type of value judgment—those ought judgments that are hypothetical (sometimes called conditional) but which have to do with the alleged fact(s) of the matter. A hypothetical judgment is a conditional statement, which (you will recall from chapter 1) says that if p is so, then something else, say q, is also so. "If I put litmus paper in acid, then it will turn red." In the evaluative realm, conditional statements relate values and means or values and consequences, for example: "If I want a more efficient and larger supply of energy, then I ought to build nuclear energy plants": "If I want to maintain my health, then I ought to stop smoking"; "If I want a more efficient factory, then I should automate"; "If I want to prevent danger to human lives, I ought to stop production of nuclear power plants." Note that these kinds of ought judgments are hypothetical in the sense that they allow us to make an assumption in the 'if' clause that is followed by the 'then' clause. Thus, certain questions require answers. For example: Will nuclear power plants give us a larger and more efficient supply of energy? Will smoking impair my health? Will automation make my factory more efficient? Will nuclear power plants endanger human lives? Factual evidence can be gathered to help us establish whether or not these implied assumptions are true or false. The ethical dilemma comes when we come to a point at which we have amassed sufficient evidence to show that such and such is in fact the case,—that cigarette smoking *does* impair health. Then we can raise the ethical question: Given this evidence, ought I to continue to smoke cigarettes or not? Indeed, the question may be divided, that is, we may recognize that we are forced to choose between two presumed values, the pleasure of smoking as compared with the danger involved. Here we may have to decide which ethical judgment to support and why—"I ought to maintain my health" and "I ought to be able to enjoy the pleasure of smoking." We are content here to call attention to the nature of the hypothetical as contrasted with value judgments, as the philosopher Kant did, and to identify some of the contexts in which they occur, political and the like.

Tape Exercises

Consider the following. Are evaluative judgments involved? If so, what kind? [For an analysis of these six sentences, turn to Tape 2, band 1.]

1. Women ought to stay in their place—in the home.
2. Many Americans think it is wrong to marry within the family.
3. Dante is a greater poet than Edgar Allen Guest.
4. Banana splits are better than fudge sundaes.
5. This is a good motorcycle.
6. Cannibalism is wrong.

Performative   Another usage of language is the performative. Included under this use of language are expressions commonly used in the context of social relations. Performative expressions usually perform a social function. They are characteristically first person present and are neither true nor false. "I apologize" is to apologize; it performs its function even if the apology is insincere. Other examples of the performative function of language are:

"I baptize thee. . . ."

"I pronounce you man and wife."

"I declare the meeting adjourned."

The performative use of language is evaluated on the basis of its appropriateness rather than on the basis of its truth or falsity.

Very often in ordinary discourse multiple functions of language are at work in a single sentence. For example, consider the sentence "Murder is a horrible crime." It could be taken to be performing three linguistic functions. It expresses an attitude and evaluation on the part of the speaker; it evokes a response in us, perhaps keeping us from committing such an act; and it is saying something about murders: it is declaring something to be the case.

Exercises for § 2.2

A. For each of the following, (1) indicate what primary language function is being expressed—informative, expressive, evocative, evaluative, or performative.

Briefly explain why you classify it as you do. (2) If you think that several functions are involved, identify and explain them. Point out: what is being asserted, what attitude is being expressed, and what attitude it tries to evoke. (3) Which are the emotive words? Classify them as negative, neutral, or positive. [Turn to Tape 2, band 1, for an analysis of the shaded items.]

1. The new relief cuts are not working any hardship on families getting public assistance.

2. Women of the world unite! You have nothing to lose but your chains.

3. What an absolutely stupid thing to do!

4. I extend my hand in fellowship to you the new member of Delta Crum.

5. Hit a home run, Rocky!

6. Electromagnetic theory, which was largely developed a generation before Einstein, is the only classical theory which stands unchanged in the face of relativity.

7. Many companies have not really answered the question: Who is responsible for MIS design, planning and development? Why is there a leadership vacuum?   [Donald F. Cox and Robert E. Gould, "How to Build a Marketing Information System."]

8. What possible objection can you have to the proposal? It takes in everyone's suggestions.

9. When I walked in Adolf Hitler's salon in the Kaiserhoff Hotel I was convinced that I was meeting the future dictator of Germany. In something less than fifty seconds I was quite sure I was not. He is inconsequent and voluble, ill-poised, insecure, the very prototype of the Little Man.   [Interview with Adolf Hitler, by Dorothy Thompson. *Cosmopolitan Magazine*, March, 1932.]

10. What the cigarette companies do primarily, then, is to counteract anti-cigarette publicity by saying that medical evidence does not support the adverse conclusions reached, by establishing research councils and codes to promote their good will and get anti-cigarette forces from pressuring them, and, at the same time, by inundating the market with new brands and filters in the hope that people will continue to smoke more and more as the cancer scare dies.   [Keith Hansen, "The Cancer Scare: Did It Hurt the Cigarette Industry?"]

11. The buffalo, the passenger pigeon, the health hen, and the plains antelope were early victims of the frontier men's indifference—either totally exterminated or so severely reduced in number that they survived only as protected remnants. The list of endangered species continues to grow. Today, encroachment upon habitats and the indiscriminate use of pesticides have brought new candidates to the point of extinction. . . .   [Lawrence G. Hines, *Environmental Issues* (W. W. Norton, 1973), p. 4.]

12. Education is fatal to anyone with a spark of artistic feeling. Education should be confined to clerks, and even then it drives to drink. Will the world learn that we never learn anything that we did not know before.   [George Moor, *Confessions of a Young Man*]

13. A journalist is a grumbler, a censurer, a giver of advice, a regent of sovereigns, a tutor of nations. Four hostile newspapers are more to be feared than a thousand bayonets.   [Napoleon]

14. If ever this free people—if this government itself is ever utterly demoralized, it will come from this incessant human wriggle and struggle for office, which is but a way to live without work.   [Abraham Lincoln]

15. In the intercourse of the world people should not take words as so much genuine coin of standard metal, but merely as counters that people play with.   [Jerrold]

16. Language is a solemn thing—it grows out of life—out of its agonies and ecstasies, its wants and its weariness—every language is a temple in which the soul of those who speak it is enshrined.   [O. W. Holmes]

17. A country man between two lawyers is like a fish between two cats. [Franklin]

18. Laws grind the poor and the rich men rule the law.   [Goldsmith]

19. Laws are the very bulwarks of liberty; they define every man's rights, and defend the individual liberties of all men.   [J. G. Holland]

20. Money is an article which may be used as a universal passport to everywhere except Heaven, and as a universal provider of everything except happiness.   [*Wall Street Journal*]

21. Money is the life blood of the nation.   [Swift]

22. Money does all things; for it gives and it takes away, it makes honest men and knaves, fools and philosophers; and so on to the end of the chapter. [*L'Estrange*]

23. Imagination rules the world.   [Napoleon]

24. The lunatic, the lover and the poet are of imagination all compact. [Shakespeare]

25. I believe that war is at present productive of good more than of evil.   [John Ruskin]

26. War, which society draws upon itself, is but organized barbarism, an inheritance of the savage state, however disguised or ornamented.   [Napoleon]

27. It [monogamy] was not in any way the fruit of individual sex-love, with which it had nothing to do. It was the first form of the family to be based, not on natural, but on economic conditions—on the victory of private property over primitive, natural communal property.   [Friedrich Engels]

28. The ethical aspect of monogamous marriage consists in the parties' consciousness of this unity as their substantive aim, and so in their love, trust, and common sharing of their entire existence as individuals. . . . The family as the immediate substantiality of mind, is specifically characterized by love, which is mind's feeling of its own unity.   [Hegel]

29. The principle which regulates the existing social relations between the two sexes—the legal subordination of one sex to the other—is wrong in itself, and now one of the chief hindrances to human improvement.   [J. S. Mill]

B. For each italicized word or phrase in the following sentences, rate the emotive force of this word or phrase [for the speaker] on a continuum ranging from strongly, moderately, or slightly positive, through relatively neutral to slightly, moderately, or strongly negative. Consider the context of the statement.

1. [One businessman to another] Jones is a *fool*. I wouldn't do business with him if I were you.
2. [Physiologist to class] *Smell* is one of the five senses of the body by which a substance is perceived through the chemical stimulation of nerves.
3. [History professor to class] A *fool* was a man kept in the household of a nobleman or king to entertain by joking and clowning.
4. [Man to wife] She is your *mother* and my mother-in-law.
5. [Boy to friend] The *smell* of cookies baking!
6. [Women's liberationist to lady at cocktail party] No, I certainly am not a *mother!*
7. [Son to friend] My parents have given me a *free* hand in this matter.
8. [Advisor to U.S. Ambassador to India] This proposal by the Ambassador from Russia is obviously nothing but a *Red* plot!
9. [One man to another] We want only *red-blooded* Americans in our club.
10. I can't stand the sight of *blood!*
11. [One little old lady to another] Don't you know they believe in *free* sex!
12. All that I am my *mother* made me.   [John Quincy Adams]
13. [Thompson commenting on Hitler] "He is the very prototype of the *Little Man.*"
14. [One researcher to another] That is a *fantastic* ideal.
15. [Jesus to disciples] "Let the *little* ones come unto me."
16. [Father to son] All that you propose sounds to me like *fantastic* nonsense.
17. [One solicitor to another] With all this wealth, he gave so *little*.
18. [Man to woman] Shall we trip the light *fantastic?*
19. [Painter to pupils] *White* is a most flexible and yet beautifully simple color.
20. [One senator to another] It sounds like the *White* House is trying to *white*wash this whole business.

C. For each of the following indicate whether or not a value judgment is being made and if so, what type of value(s) are involved—ethical, aesthetic, social, personal taste, functional. [Check Tape 2, band 2, analysis of shaded items.]

1. City slums are ugly.
2. His betrayal of his friends was morally reprehensible.
3. Her second marriage was a disaster.
4. The quantity of his poems is more impressive than their quality.
5. Hitler was a reprehensible man.
6. I like blueberry pie better than pumpkin pie.
7. This is a fine piece of machinery.
8. These eggs are bad.

9. One ought to keep one's promises.

10. Jerry does not like Schoenberg's music.

11. If one wants to have efficient cities, one ought to turn them over to management experts rather than politicians.

12. In order to achieve the ideal state we would need control of the population through education, eugenics, and occupational assignments.

13. Michelangelo's David is a masterpiece of sculpture.

14. Monogamous marriage is a unique and socially valuable institution.

15. Many Catholics oppose abortion laws.

2.3 LOGICAL VERSUS NON-LOGICAL MATERIAL

Because of the complexities of language, it becomes obvious that one essential part of analyzing arguments in ordinary use is to separate logical from nonlogical material. Logic is concerned with language used informatively, with what is being asserted. This means that logical analysis requires one (1) to clearly distinguish language usage, (2) to translate emotive content into neutral content whenever possible, and (3) to distinguish between *factual assertion* and *expression of an attitude* toward what is being asserted.

Consider the following two assertions:

a. Jackie makes up fantastic stories.

b. Jackie tells little fibs.

The two sentences, declare the same thing to be the case—"Jackie tells fictions." They disagree in the attitude expressed. Sentence *a* is more likely to be used by someone with an approving attitude, and sentence *b* by someone with the opposite attitude. It is the statement being asserted that logic asks about, not the *expressed attitudes*. Incidentally, statements of beliefs should be considered cases of the cognitive use of language. For example, the sentence "I believe monogamous marriage to be an institution that hinders the development of real interpersonal relations" asserts a statement. We can ask: Is this statement true or false, and on what grounds do you hold this belief? A statement of belief requires a person to give some reasons for a belief, to specify those statements he can offer in defense of that belief. The expression of an attitude, on the other hand, indicates a positive, negative, or neutral evaluative stance toward something or someone. Consider the following statement from a newspaper editorial:

A fabulously rich playboy who got tired of his ponies, got the idea that he would like to repudiate the free enterprise that privileged his grandfather to endow him with so many million dollars he could never hope to count them.   [Quoted by Max Black in *Critical Thinking*, p. 157]

What is it, if anything, that is being asserted in this sentence? Is there any kernal of hard fact separate from the expression of an obviously negative attitude toward the person and his action? In order to fix upon a neutral kernel, one must first identify all the emotively ladened phrases and try to neutralize them. Proceeding in this fashion, we get first the emotive phrases and their suggested implications:

Emotive Phrases	X	*Conveyed Message*
"playboy tired of his ponies"	(the man in question is)	idler, waster of time in either trivial activities like polo or in race-track gambling
"fabulously rich" "so many million dollars he could never hope to count them"		excessively wealthy has more money that he can use
"got tired of" "got the idea" "privileged" "endow"		easily bored, or irrational and irresponsible—doesn't make decisions based on good reasons
"would like to repudiate the free enterprise"		X has received special and unearned favors
		here X is accused of trying to negate something positive—free enterprise
		further, it is implied that 'he is biting the hand that fed him'—repudiating that which gave him all he had.

Having set out the emotive aspects of the sentence, it helps first to restate these emotive overtones more explicitly in order to see their full intent. Explicitly, the statement can be rendered as follows:

An idle playboy, who has far more money than he deserves, is now irresponsibly attacking the system which gave him the fortune he had but never earned.

The next step is to try to neutralize the statement as follows:

A very wealthy sportsman has decided to oppose the system of unregulated enterprise that enabled his grandfather to leave him his large fortune.

Thus, the kernel of fact, the assertion being made in the original emotively-laden sentence, is something like: "This rich man is for federal control of industry." Even here, we might ask whether these last two statements differ. Translating into neutral terms is a very difficult matter, and we must use as much caution as we can to avoid our own emotive bents to sneak into the picture.

In order further to summarize and illustrate the kind of material that is the subject matter of logic as opposed to that which is not, consider the following two statements. The first is from Jerome K. Jerome's *Three Men in a Boat:*

> We got to Waterloo Station at eleven, and asked where the 11:05 started from. Of course, nobody knew; nobody at Waterloo ever does know where a train is going to start from, or where the train when it does start is going to come or anything about it. The porter who took our things thought it would go from #2 platform, while another porter with whom he discussed the question, had heard a rumor that it would go from #1. The stationmaster, on the other hand, was convinced that it would start from the local.
>
> To put an end to the matter we went upstairs and asked the traffic superintendent and he told us that he had just met a man who said he had seen it at #3 platform. He went to #3 but the authorities there said that they rather thought that that train was the Southhampton Express or else the Windsor Lou. But they were sure it wasn't the Kingston train, though why they were sure it wasn't they couldn't say.
>
> Then our porter said he thought it must be on a high-level platform; said he knew the train. So we went to the high-level platform, and saw the engine driver and asked him if he were going to Kingston. He said he couldn't say for certain, of course, but rather thought he was. Anyhow, if he wasn't the 11:05 for Kingston, he said he was pretty confident he was the 9:32 for Virginia Water or the 10 A.M. express for the Isle of Wight or somewhere in that direction, and we should all know when we got there. We slipped a half crown into his hand and begged him to be the 11:05 for Kingston.
>
> "Nobody will ever know, on this line," we said, "what you are or where you're going. You know the way. You slip off quietly and go to Kingston."
>
> "Well, I don't know, gents," replied the noble fellow, "but I suppose some train's got to go to Kingston, and I'll do it. Give me the half crown."
>
> Thus we got to Kingston by the London and Southwestern Railway.
>
> We learned afterwards that the train we had come by was really the Exeter Mail, and that they had spent hours at Waterloo looking for it and nobody knew what had become of it.[1]

Now consider a second statement by the famous German philosopher, Leibnitz.

[1] Jerome K. Jerome, *Three Men in a Boat*, (London: J. M. Dent & Sons Ltd., 1971) pp. 49-50. Reprinted by permission of the publisher.

The human soul is a thing whose activity is thinking. A thing whose activity is thinking is one whose activity is immediately apprehended, and without any representation of parts therein is a thing whose activity does not contain parts. A thing whose activity does not contain parts is one whose activity is not motion. A thing whose activity is not motion is not a body. What is not a body is not in space. What is not in space is insusceptible of motion. What is insusceptible of motion is indissoluble. (For disillusion is a movement of parts.) What is indissoluble is incorruptible. What is incorruptible is immortal. Therefore, the human soul is immortal.

Observe about these twelve remarkable sentences the following: First, there is something to be proved, namely, the immortality of the soul. Second, there is a clearly defined aim to the whole paragraph. Nothing is there which is extraneous to the aim—though the language used is technical and difficult. Third, there is a necessary connection between every sentence and between all of the sentences, all twelve of the sentences as a whole. This is a prime example of inference, that is, of drawing a conclusion from premises. Leibnitz believes that if you grant that the human soul is a thing whose activity is thinking you will be led by irresistible reasoning to the conclusion that the human soul is immortal. If you accept the first premise as true, you are drawn by his logic to accept the conclusion as true.

The point of our illustration is to show that the highly entertaining statement of Jerome's is historical, expressive, and evocative of amusement in its readers or hearers. It is not a candidate for logical analysis, and it is not an argument. The second is not only an argument but a very tight deductive argument and one which asks us to show any conceivable reason why it does not prove its point.

Tape Exercises

Consider the following passages. Are all of them possible candidates for logical analysis or does one or more of them count as strictly nonlogical material? Why? If some of them are candidates for logical analysis, do they also contain nonlogical material such as emotive phrases? Can you point them out? Can they be neutralized to make straight-forward assertions? [Turn to Tape 2, band 2, for an analysis of these passages.]

1. Magnified one thousand times, the insect
   Looks farically human; laugh if you will!
   Bald head, stage-fairy wings, blear eyes,
   A caved-in chest, hairy black mandibles,
   Long spindly thighs.[2]

2. What the cigarette companies do primarily, then is to *counteract anti-cigarette publicity* by saying that medical evidence does not support the *adverse conclusions* reached, by establishing research councils and codes to promote

[2] Robert Graves, "Blue Fly," in *Collected Poems* (New York: Collins-Knowlton-Wing Inc., 1961).

their goodwill and get anti-cigarette forces from *pressuring them* and, at the same time, by *inundating* the market with new brands and filters in the hope that people will continue to *smoke, and smoke more as the cancer scare* dies. All of the above, of course, are reflected in the industry's publicity and advertising.

The companies do not mention anything about health claims, as they did in the forties and early fifties. Thus, P. Lorillard, maker of Old Gold, dropped the medical *claim gimmick* during the 1953-54 scare and used the slogan "No doggone medical claims . . . Old Gold is man's best friend for a treat instead of a treatment." The companies now use ads implying rather than stating that cigarette smoking brought such things as social success, sex appeal and a youthful, healthful, robust physical constitution to the cigarette smoker. Under the Industry Code cigarette advertising is not supposed to depict cigarette smoking "as essential to social prominence, distinction, success or sexual attraction." Nevertheless cigarette ads still depict healthy and good looking young people in meadow scenes with streams running by. This action by cigarette companies is an evasive maneuver against the government agencies that are attempting to curb cigarette smoking.[3]

Exercises for § 2.3

Analyze the following editorial by doing the following: (1) Specify the use of emotive words and phrases and the meanings they imply; (2) determine what neutral facts or claims, if any, are stated; (3) indicate the attitude of the editorial; (4) indicate what effect you think the editorial might be trying to produce.

Not the Man

The Post-Dispatch's state political correspondent, Curtis A. Betts, has made a thorough analysis of the background of Circuit Judge Ray G. Cowan of Kansas City. It shows that the Judge who impaneled the state grand jury to investigate the Binaggio-Gargotta murders and the tie-up between crime and politics is himself a product of the Pendergast school of boss rule.

No wonder Judge Cowan tossed off the federal grand jury report on violation of state laws. No wonder he asked the state grand jury to "go slow." No wonder he is such a contrast to Federal Judge Reeves, who 12 years ago in the historic vote fraud inquiry, told federal grand jurors to "move on them!"

In view of his own background, Judge Cowan should have disqualified himself. He should step out and permit the investigation to be under a judge who believes in vigorous inquiry.   [*St. Louis Post-Dispatch*]

2.4 KINDS OF DISAGREEMENT

Given the complexity of language as well as its usage in emotive and evocative ways, it should be fairly obvious that any consideration of argumentation in

[3] From Keith A. Hansen, "The Cancer Scare: Did It Hurt the Cigarette Industry?" in *New Consumerism*, ed. by William T. Kelley (Columbus, Ohio: *Grid Inc.*, 1973), p. 324.

everyday discourse would often require us to deal with arguments in the context of disagreement between individuals—disagreement that can be very emotional. Certainly, the first thing that must be done in situations of such controversy is to agree on what the argument is about. The first question is: What, exactly, is the issue at hand? The second step is to set out as clearly and fairly as possible the positions of the disputants. So the second question is: What exactly are the disputants' claims and what is the evidence or reason offered in support of their claims? To specify positions in this kind of situation involves distinguishing *assertion of fact from expression of attitudes*. Let's examine this distinction.

First of all, assertion of facts or beliefs involves statements about which we can ask, "Are they true or false?" Thus, the sentences "The planets in our solar system revolve around the sun" and "The planets and sun in our solar system revolve around the earth" make two different statements and involve two contradictory beliefs. Both cannot be true, and thus there is genuine disagreement in belief. The two sentences "My little girl tells highly imaginative stories" and "My little girl tells fibs" make essentially the same statement; they assert that my little girl makes up stories. However, they express two different attitudes: the first sentence expresses a more positive attitude; the second sentence expresses a somewhat negative judgment about the girl's practice. Similarly, the sentences "This exam is difficult" and "This exam is challenging" make substantially the same assertion—that the exam is hard. But, they express different attitudes toward the facts. This is a case of disagreement in attitude but not in belief.

Another situation of disagreement, and probably the one that is most common, is disagreement *in both belief and attitude*. Consider the following:

Women have a strong inborn feeling for all that is beautiful, elegant and decorated.   [Immanuel Kant]

Instead of calling them beautiful, there would be more warrant for describing women as the unaesthetic sex.   [Arthur Schopenhauer]

Kant's statement asserts women to have a natural feeling for the beautiful, and it expresses a positive attitude toward women. Schopenhauer's statement on the other hand, by calling women unaesthetic, implies that women have no feeling for the beautiful. He also expresses a general negative attitude toward women. Here is disagreement both in belief and in attitude.

In discussing disagreement in belief, however, we must note two kinds of disagreement over belief that can occur: (1) *real* disagreement, and (2) *apparent* disagreement. The statements of Kant and Schopenhauer are in real disagreement because it is logically impossible that they both could be true at the same time. Kant says "Women have a feeling for the beautiful," and Schopenhauer says "Not so! Women do not have a feeling for the beautiful." He says they are "unaesthetic." These two statements are logically inconsistent— they cannot both be true at the same time. A *real disagreement*, then, is one in which the statements of the disputants' positions are logically inconsistent: they cannot both be true at the same time.

An *apparent* disagreement is one in which the statements of the disputants' positions are not logically inconsistent—it is possible for both of them to be true at the same time. Consider the following example:

John Doe is a Conservative.

John Doe is a Republican.

A person can be considered by many to be a Conservative in his political ideas and actions, but he can also be a member of the Republican party. In other words, both assertions can be true. What is not stated is that Conservative and Republican are not necessarily identical. So called liberal Republicans might consider someone very conservative, indeed more conservative than being a Republican warrants, whereas the person involved has a different perception of the matter. Here is disagreement which needs to be and can be clarified.

However, apparent disagreement can be much more complex and tricky than this. For example, how is one to assess disagreement between Al and Bob in the following interchange?

Al: John Larkin has a nasty, negative attitude toward everything.

Bob: That's not true. John Larkin is a nice guy and not at all negative.

Al: Well, he is critical about everything and everybody.

Bob: He is not critical about everything and everybody.
        He does have strong views on things and voices his views forthrightly.

Al: Well, he has been negative about student government and about all its activities.

Bob: He is opposed to student government because he thinks most of the members of our student body can't afford the fees and most of its activities have been social and not of any real benefit.

Al: He also is critical of fraternities and has made some nasty cracks about my fraternity friends.

Bob: John is opposed to fraternities on a number of grounds and he considers many of their activities silly. Incidentally, he thinks the activities of your Drama Club are excellent.

Al: Does he really? I didn't know that.

Bob: John also supports your efforts to get financial aid for the band.

Al: Maybe John isn't such a bad guy after all.

Bob: I told you he was a nice guy and not at all negative.

The point brought out by this dialogue is that disputes in everyday life can seem to be real disagreements in the sense that the positions of the disputants often appear to be over inconsistencies and really be opposing positions as do the positions of Al and Bob at the beginning. However, the dispute is about each person's perceptions of another person and of his behavior. Our perceptions of objects, of situations and events, or of persons are always to some degree limited by our perspective, among other things. We may not have the whole picture. A particular object may look oblong to us rather than round because we are viewing it from a certain angle. The dispute between Al and Bob is an *apparent,* not necessarily a real disagreement because it is potentially resolvable. In fact, it is resolved to a degree. That it could be resolved at least to a degree could be seen if the two disputants' positions had been stated as follows:

Al: I perceive John Larkin's behavior as having a nasty and negative attitude toward everything.

Bob: I perceive John Larkin as a nice guy and not at all negative.

Apparent disagreement, then, does not involve positions that are logically inconsistent; on the contrary, they are potentially resolvable. However, this does not mean that there are not genuine elements of disagreement involved nor that the disagreement can always be resolved. Al does find John's criticisms of student government and fraternities offensive, though he might be persuaded later to agree with him. Further, there is a hint that John might speak out a little too forthrightly and thus be seen by others as excessively negative. Further, though limited perspectives hopefully can be broadened by further insight and dialogue, there are cases in which the fundamental beliefs which form part of people's perspective are not changeable, or at least not easily changed. Thus, the little ducks prayed to God:

> Dear God,
> Give us a flood of water.
> Let it rain tomorrow and always.
> Give us plenty of little slugs
> and other luscious things to eat.
> Protect all people who quack
> and everyone who knows how to swim.
> Amen   [Carmen de Gasztold]

It is a basic fact of the history of politics that the measures and actions of different statesmen are viewed and judged differently depending on the perspective of the judger. One person might regard certain acts of legislation as dangerous innovations and radical departures from established order. Another person might regard the same acts as fair, democratic and moderate. The most important points to remember in approaching any disagreement, then, are (1) to be sure the position of each disputant is clearly set out (this includes specifying any points of agreement there may be between the disputants as well as their areas of disagreement), (2) to separate the disagreements of belief and attitude, (3) to restate the dispute, especially if it involves perspectival viewpoints on behavior and situations in order to see if the disagreement is genuinely real or only apparent and so possibly resolvable.

One other type of disagreement that can occur and can be an obstacle to any form of resolution is a merely verbal disagreement, namely, a dispute in which a key word or phrase is being used with different meanings. William James in his famous essay "What Pragmatism Means" describes a classic example of such a dispute:

> Some years ago, being with a camping party in the mountains, I returned from a solitary ramble to find everyone engaged in a ferocious metaphysical dispute. The *corpus* of the dispute was a squirrel—a live squirrel supposed to be clinging to one side of a tree-trunk; while over against the tree's opposite side a human being was imagined to stand. This human witness tries to get sight of the squirrel by moving rapidly round the tree, but no matter how fast he goes, the squirrel moves as fast in the opposite direction, and always keeps the tree between himself and the man, so that never a glimpse of him is caught. The resultant metaphysical problem now is this: *Does the man go round the squirrel or not?* He goes round the tree, sure enough, and the squirrel is on the tree; but does he go round the squirrel?

James' friends deadlocked in a tie, with the numbers on both sides of the dispute, even, appealed to him for an answer. The answer he gave was as follows:

> 'Which party is right,' I said, 'depends on what you *practically mean* by going round the squirrel. If you mean passing from the north of him to the east, then to the south, then to the west, and then to the north of him again, obviously the man does go round him, for he occupies these successive positions. But if on the contrary you mean being first in front of him, then on the right of him, then behind him, then on his left, and finally in front again, it is quite obvious that the man fails to go round him, for by the compensating movements the squirrel makes, he keeps his belly turned towards the man all the times, and his back turned away. Make the distinction, and there is no occasion for any further dispute. You are both right and both wrong according as you conceive the verb 'to go round.'

James wishes to imply that it makes no practical or important difference which interpretation of "to go round" is taken as correct. Therefore, the whole dispute is an idle and merely verbal one—only an apparent disagreement. Some disagreements may be of this sort, and time can be saved if clarification of meaning is made. Further, clarification of the meaning of terms in the debate can help to resolve some disagreement and move the disputants to more substantive issues. However, the resolution or recognition of a verbal dispute may lead to a dispute over the meanings themselves. In this case the verbal disagreement is a genuine one. This can happen especially if the meaning of the words does have a practical effect. Take the example of the word "poor." It could be defined to mean "receiving less than the median income" or "receiving less than $1,000 per person per year." If the dispute were over who should receive certain aid, the decision on the meaning of "poor" could be a very important one. Another example of a dispute over words which might turn into a more substantial disagreement over what meaning to adopt is the interpretation of a phrase such as "all students with demonstrable need are eligible for fellowships." The phrase "demonstrable need" is a tricky one. More will be said about meaning in our chapter on definitions. We conclude here by noting that all logical analysis, and more particularly, analysis of disagreement, should make sure that the words are being used with the same meaning by both sides.

Finally, being able to deal with agreement-disagreement is a very important skill to develop and for several reasons: First, in voting on candidates, referendum, issues, it is imperative to our voting intelligently to know exactly where candidates agree and disagree, exactly what points are for and against an issue and where there are areas of agreement between supporters of seemingly opposite positions. Second, if we are in business or a profession and need to make certain decisions, we consult experts or a committee for recommendations. Often, however, there may be disagreement between the experts or among the committee members. A decision maker will need to clarify areas of agreement and disagreement and possible resolutions. Finally as a student, you should find your skill at sorting out agreement-disagreement valuable in writing essays or papers in which you are asked to compare and contrast various views on a single issue or question.

Tape Exercises

Consider, for example, the following quotations. Where are the speakers in agreement or in disagreement, and what type or types of disagreement is involved? [Turn to Tape 2, band 3, for an analysis of the quotations.]

1. a. Our country in her intercourse with foreign nations may she always be in the right; but our country, right or wrong." [Stephen Decatur]
   b. "Our country, right or wrong. When right, to be kept right; when wrong, to be put right. [Carl Schurz]

2. a. I like peppermint candy ice cream better than anything in the world.
   b. I like chocolate chip ice cream the best.

3. a. This strikes me as a situation in which someone is trying to stir up a lot of trouble.
   b. This is a situation of well-intentioned but misguided action.

4. a. The art of winning in business is in working hard. [Elbert Hubbard]
   b. The best mental effort in the game of business is concentrated on the major problem of securing the consumer's dollar before the other fellow gets it. [Stuart Chase]

5. a. Character is higher than intellect—A great soul will be strong to live as well as to think. [Emerson]
   b. Every man, as to character, is the creature of the age in which he lives—very few are able to raise themselves above the ideas of their times. [Voltaire]

6. a. The progress of democracy seems irresistible, because it is the most uniform, the most ancient, and the most permanent tendency which is to be found in history.   [De Tocqueville]
   b. Democracy is ever eager for rapid progress, and the only progress which can be rapid is progress down hill.   [Sir James Jeans]

7. a. Science is always wrong. It never solves a problem without creating ten more.   [George Bernard Shaw]
   b. The sciences are beneficent. They prevent men from thinking.   [Anatole France]
   c. In the scientific world I find just that disinterested devotion to great ends that I hope will spread at last through the entire range of human activity.   [H. G. Wells]
   d. Science is but the statement of truth found out.   [Coley]
   e. What are the sciences but maps of universal laws; and universal laws but the channels of universal power; and universal power but the outgoings of a universal mind.   [E. Thompson]
   f. Science surpasses the old miracles of mythology.   [Emerson]
   g. Science ever has been and ever must be the safeguard of religion.   [Sir David Brewster]
   h. Human science is an uncertain guess.   [Prior]
   i. When men seized the loadstone of science, the loadstar of superstition vanished in the clouds.   [W. R. Alger]
   j. Godless science reads nature only as Milton's daughter did Hebrew, rightly syllabling the sentences, but utterly ignorant of the meaning.   [Coley]

Exercises for § 2.4

A. Identify the kinds of agreement or disagreement exhibited by the following pairs. Indicate why you think these are the kinds of disagreement involved by answering the following questions. Do they agree or disagree in attitude? Do they agree or disagree in belief? Is it real disagreement—if one position is true, the other must be false? It is apparent disagreement—the positions are not inconsistent, both may be true? Is there verbal disagreement—they interpret words or phrases differently?

1. a. Harry Truman was a foul-mouthed haberdasher who should have stayed in Missouri.
   b. Harry Truman was a man of the people who made a good President because he had plain common sense.

2. a. Mr. Strong's contribution of $1,000 was completely adequate.
   b. Mr. Strong gave a mere $1,000.

3. a. The government troops ruthlessly routed the rebel forces.
   b. The rebel forces have suffered a momentary setback.

4. a. Jerry has a good executive job with the oil firm and makes good money.
   b. Jerry is a low-level yes-man to a bunch of oil executives.

5. a. Ann's advertising layouts are a bit unusual.
   b. Ann's layouts are too far-out.

6. a. Mr. Chad is quite a conversationalist.
   b. Mr. Chad carries on an incessant monologue.

7. a. George is a superficial person who never gets close to anyone.
   b. George is a shy but very deep person.

8. a. Beauty is but a vain and doubtful good; a shining glass that fadeth suddenly.   [Shakespeare]
   b. To cultivate the sense of the beautiful is one of the most effectual ways of cultivating an appreciation of the divine goodness.   [Bovee]

9. a. There is no book so bad but something valuable may be derived from it.   [Pliny]
   b. A book may be compared to your neighbor: if it be good, it cannot last too long; if bad you cannot get rid of it too early.   [Brooke]

10. a. At the bottom of not a little of the bravery that appears in the world, there lurks a miserable cowardice. Men will face powder and steel because they have not the courage to face public opinion.   [E. H. Chapin]
    b. The best hearts are ever the bravest.   [Sterne]

11. a. The musician, the painter, the poet are, in a large sense no greater artists than the man of commerce.   [W. S. Maverick]
    b. The lawyer and the doctor and other professional men have often a touch of civilization. The banker and the merchant seldom.   [Jim Tully]

12. a. He that is over-cautious will accomplish but a little.   [Schiller]
    b. When using a needle you move your fingers delicately and with a wise caution—Use the same precaution with life.   [Rance]

13. a. To dispense with ceremony is the most delicate form of conferring a compliment.   [Bulwer]
    b. If we use no ceremony toward others, we shall be treated without any.   [Hazlitt]

14. a. Chance is always powerful—Let your hook be always cast; in the pool where you least expect it, there will be a fish.   [Ovid]
    b. Chance is a word void of sense; nothing can exist without a cause.   [Voltaire]

15. a. The origin of civilization is man's determination to do nothing for himself which he can get done for him.   [H. C. Bailey]
    b. It is the triumph of civilization that at last communities have obtained such a mastery over natural laws that they drive and control them.   [H. W. Beecher]

16. a. Every product of genius must be the production of enthusiasm.   [Disraeli]
    b. Enthusiasm is an evil much less to be dreaded than superstition. . . . The former grows inveterate by time; the latter is cured by it.   [Robert Hall]

17. a. All men are by nature equal, made all of the same earth by the same Creator.
    b. It is not true that equality is a law of nature—Nature has no equality—Its sovereign law is subordination and dependence.   [Vauvenargues]

18. a. Equality is the share of everyone at their advent upon earth.   [Enclos]
    b. Men are by nature unequal—It is vain, therefore, to treat them as if they were equal.   [Froude]

19. a. Half the truth will very often amount to absolute falsehood.   [Whately]
    b. No tempting form of error is without some latent charm derived from truth.   [Keith]

20. a. Experience is the shroud of illusions.   [Finod]
    b. Experience is a jewel and it had need be, for it is often purchased at an infinite rate.   [Shakespeare]

21. a. Those who dispise fame seldom deserve it. We are apt to under value what we cannot reach.   [Jeremie Collier]
    b. It is an indiscreet and troublesome ambition that cares so much about fame . . . to be always shouting to hear the echoes of our own voices. [Longfellow]

22. a. Of all the noblest possessions of this life fame is the noblest: when the body has sunk into the dust the great name still lives.   [Schiller]
    b. Fame—a few words upon a tombstone and the truth of those not to be depended upon.   [Bovee]

23. a. To have freedom is only to have what is absolutely necessary to enable us to be what we ought to be and to possess what we ought to possess. [Rahel]
    b. The only freedom which deserves the name is that of pursuing our own good in our own way, so long as we do not attempt to deprive others of theirs, or impede their efforts to obtain.   [J. S. Mill]

24. a. Two persons cannot long be friends if they cannot forgive each other's little failings.   [Bruyere]
    b. Never contract friendship with a man that is not better than thyself.   [Confucius]

25. a. Frugality is a fair fortune and habits of industry a good estate. [Franklin]
    b. Frugality is good if liberality be joined with it. The first, without the last, begats covetousness, the last without the first begats prodrigality. [Penn]

B. Compare and contrast the following. Indicate those in real disagreement, those only in apparent disagreement and those in attitude disagreement.

1. a. The principal foundation of all states is in good laws and good arms. [Machiavelli]
   b. The best of all governments is that which teaches us to govern ourselves.   [Goethe]
   c. It is better for a city to be governed by a good man than even by good laws.   [Aristotle]
   d. The less government the better, if society be kept in peace and prosperity.   [Channing]

2. a. Habit is the deepest law of human nature.   [Carlyle]
   b. Habits are the petrification of feelings.   [L. E. Landon]
   c. Good habits are the best magistrates.   [G. B. Cheever]

3. a. It is better to desire the things we have than to have the things we desire.   [Henry Van Dyke]
   b. Happiness consists in the attainment of our desires and in our having right desires.   [Augustine]
   c. To be happy is not the purpose of our being, but to deserve happiness.   [Fichte]
   d. Happiness is not the end of life; character is.   [H. W. Beecher]
   e. Happiness is the supreme object of existence.   [J. Gilchrist Lawson]
   f. The happiest life is that which constantly exercises and educates what is best in us.   [Hamerton]

4. a. Politics is a profession; a serious, complicated and, in its true sense, a noble one.   [Dwight D. Eisenhower]
   b. Most statesmen have long noses. But I suppose that is very lucky, because most of them cannot see further than the length of them.   [Paul Claudell]
   c. A politician is like quick-silver; if you try to put your finger on him, you find nothing under it.   [Austin O'Malley]
   d. Politics I conceive to be nothing more than the science of ordered progress of society along the lines of greatest usefulness and convenience to itself.   [Woodrow Wilson]
   e. Politics is the most practical of arts. It is most concerned with 'hard facts,' for what facts are harder than the facts of human interest and passion. [William Ernest Hocking]
   f. There is no gambling like politics.   [Disraeli]
   g. Government—The Santa Claus of something-for-nothing and something-for-everybody.   [B. Goldwater]

C. Discuss each of the following disputes. If it is merely verbal, resolve it by explaining the different senses attached by the disputes to the key word or phrase that is used differently. If it is an apparently verbal dispute that is really genuine, locate the difference in meaning and explain the real disagreement involved.

1. a. The only freedom which deserves the name is that of pursuing our own good, in our own way, so long as we do not attempt to deprive others of theirs, or impede their efforts to obtain it.   [J. S. Mill]
   b. Real freedom comes from the mastery, through knowledge of historic conditions and race character which makes possible the intelligent use of experience for the purpose of progress.   [Hamilton Wright Mabie]
2. a. Mr. Thompson is a just man. He always follows the letter of the law.
   b. Mr. Thompson is a tyrant who does know how to be fair and impartial.
3. a. The computer is a good thing. It is efficient and time-saving and saves man many laborious hours.
   b. The computer is useful, but not necessarily good. It can be used in bad or evil ways, as in military operations.
4. a. This idea of reincarnation is entirely new to me.
   b. Its not a new idea at all, but has been in existence for thousands of years.
5. a. John is extremely intelligent. His I.Q. is far above average.
   b. Then why is he doing so poorly in his classwork and written work?

6. a. Equality is and should be the share of everyone at their advent on earth; and equality is also theirs when placed beneath it.
   b. Some must follow and some must command, though all are made of clay.   [Longfellow]
7. a. Gordan Manypockets is a very poor man, not one friend can he count among his acquaintances.
   b. On the contrary, Gordan has more wealth than he can count or keep track of.
8. a. Mrs. Smootch has very poor taste, serving that kind of food when Jews and Hindus were to be present.
   b. But Mrs. Smootch is known as a gourmet with excellent taste in foods.
9. a. Dr. Trolly has been a very creative scholar. Look at all the new ideas and discoveries he has stimulated in his students.
   b. Dr. Trolly never created any discoveries or produced any books of his own. How can you call him creative.
10. a. Faith is to believe on the word of God, what we do not see and cannot prove.   [Augustine]
    b. Faith affirms many things respecting which the senses are silent, but nothing which they deny.   [Pascal]

Chapter Outline

A. Language may be used to do various things. It can perform basically five functions:
   1. *Cognitive*—conveys information and asserts or denies something to be the case.
   2. *Expressive*—expresses feelings or attitude.
   3. *Evocative-Directive*—evokes responses of feeling, attitude, action.
   4. *Evaluative*—makes claims about what is of worth or of values, e.g., what is good, just, beautiful. They are different types of value judgments.
      a. *Value judgments relative to specific standards*, e.g., educational, social, economic, scientific.
      b. *Value judgments referring to certain required standard of performance*—as a professional, as an applicant, as a machine, etc. These refer to a particular function to be performed.
      c. *Value judgments of personal taste*, e.g., I like tea. About these there can be no dispute.
      d. *Ethical* judgments which claim that a certain action or type of action ought or ought not to be performed or a certain standard ought to be adopted.
      e. *Aesthetic judgments* about what we consider to be beautiful or ugly.
   5. *Performative*—performs a social function.
      All or any of these functions can be at work in a single sentence, e.g., "Abortion is the murder of innocent beings."
B. One aspect of the expressive and evocative usages of language is what is often called the *emotive meaning* of words and expressions. Words can convey

negative and positive attitudes, can arouse in us negative and positive attitudes and emotions.

C. Logical Analysis must be concerned to distinguish logical from non-logical material. One important part of this analysis is to neutralize emotively laden assertions so that one can be sure exactly what claim is being made.

D. An important area of everyday discourse where logical analysis is a necessary tool is disagreement or dispute. Three basic kinds of disagreement must be distinguished:

1. Disagreement *in attitude*—disagreement about the way in which the facts, events, people are viewed or valued.

2. Disagreement *in belief*—disagreement about what is being claimed or asserted. This can be sub-distinguished into two kinds:

   a. *Real* disagreement—one in which the statements of the disputants are logically inconsistent; both cannot be true at the same time.

   b. *Apparent* disagreement—one in which the statements of the disputants' positions are not logically inconsistent. Rather, both can be true at the same time. The disagreement is potentially resolvable.

3. *Verbal disagreement*—key words or phrases are not being used with the same meaning by both sides. This kind of disagreement can be *only apparent or more genuine* depending on the practical effects the adoption of a particular meaning will have.

3

MEANING AND DEFINITION

3.1 SIGNS AND SYMBOLS

In order to understand how words may be used and be misused, it is helpful to understand the nature of *signs* and *symbols* and how to distinguish between the two. A clear distinction between sign and symbol—and one that will always hold—probably cannot be framed. However, most philosophers agree on the following.

A *sign* is an object or an event signifying some meaning. It calls for action or reaction here and now. Signs are *natural* or *conventional*. Natural signs refer and "point to" by being associated with an object in its physical environment. They do so apart from any linguistic developments in a given language community. A ripple in fast moving water may be a natural sign indicating an obstruction close to the surface. A track mark is a natural sign signifying the proximity of a deer. Smoke is a natural sign of fire. Conventional signs refer to particular objects or classes of objects by being associated with them via a social community. The meaning of conventional signs is based on social convention and is characterized by an arbitrary element. There is no natural, or intrinsic relationship between the conventional sign and the thing signified. An example of a conventional sign is a red traffic light.

Signs are *one-dimensional*. They are designed to elicit a particular and immediate mental or physical reaction, and they have a single meaning. Symbols, on the other hand, are *multi-dimensional;* they point beyond themselves in a special and unusual way. They are not as particularly and directly connected with their objects as signs are.

The symbol leads the hearer to conceive or imagine an object, an event, or a meaning. It is not concerned primarily with direct action but with thought and imagination which, to be sure, may lead to action. Psychologists tell us that animals can deal with (react to) signs. Examples of this ability are found in Pavlov's experiments with dogs or observation of the fox who so shrewdly reacts to natural sign objects and events. Man alone, however, uses symbols. Indeed, some philosophers consider man's symbol-producing and using ability as one of his distinctively human characteristics. Psychology, philosophy, sociology, and religious studies are fields in which symbolism performs important functions.

The importance of symbols to logic becomes readily apparent when we recognize that words are the symbols of language. Words refer to particular objects or classes of objects by the meaning associated with them in a language community. Thus, words have meaning in a language community, and as a consequence this meaning is arbitrary and subject to change. There is the important but humorous saying, "A rose by any other name smells as sweet." That is, there is nothing about the letters R-O-S-E that compels us to name that particular flower by that name. Any proper name such as 'John' or any class name such as 'rose' and any other meaningful word is a linguistic symbol and a conventional sign. No necessary connection holds between a linguistic symbol and its meaning.

That words are the results of conventions and agreements can be seen from the procedure of conferring proper or personal names on children. Two parents decide to call their son, John. This is an arbitrary act because he could have been called by any other name. There may have been reasons for the name, such as choosing it to honor a grandfather, but these are wholly external to the naming activity. The fact that a new planet is called 'Pluto' rather than 'Mickey Mouse', or a hurricane 'Mabel' rather than 'Mary' is a matter of custom. Similarly, it is customary to give planets the names of Greek gods. Failure to recognize that words are arbitrary, conventional symbols results in two kinds of errors. Magical power may be attributed to words, in which case they are held to be sacred and unique. Thus, the Hebrews did not pronounce the word 'Jaweh' when they read the Old Testament because it stood for God and they thought the term so holy that it should not be taken on the lips of sinful men. However noteworthy this reverence may be, it must be seen that any attribution of magic to words, whether it be Ali Baba and the cave or Cinderella's fairy godmother, fails to recognize that words have no intrinsic connection with their meanings. The connection is given by a language or social-religious community. Paul Tillich, the philosopher-theologian, thus speaks of symbols as living or dying—they may have vital and powerful meaning for the community or they may lose that meaning and become empty or dead.

A second kind of error resulting from failure to recall the arbitrary nature of linguistic symbols is *reification*. The use of a name, whether it be a proper name like 'George Washington,' 'Santa Claus,' or a general term or title like 'Secretary of State,' does not provide any assurance that the proposed thing named has any actual existence. Both kinds of names may be empty. To insist on the existence of a proposed object merely because it has a name is to *reify* the object. The *fallacy of reification* is an argument that attributes existence to an object proposed by a name on the basis of no evidence other than the name itself. To claim that 'ghost' must refer to an existing object involves the fallacy of reification. Any removal of a name far from its referent invites trouble, for example 'the State' without the people, 'the Presidency,' without the man.

That which is intended by the meaning of a symbol is called the *referent*. The referent of the linguistic symbol 'Washington, D.C.' is the city that has this name. The referent of the linguistic symbol 'green' is a color. The point made above is that it cannot be assumed that any given symbol always has a referent. Bertrand Russell's famous example was 'The Present King of France.' There is no king in France today, so this phrase has no referent. The phrase, however, does make sense. Take the two phrases, 'Morning Star' and 'Evening Star'; the phrases differ in meaning, in *sense*, but they happen to have the same referent, the planet Venus.

This example also makes it necessary to distinguish between 'word' and 'term.' In actual language usage, it is often necessary to employ several words combined in a 'phrase,' a linguistic expression designating one intended referent. Although 'the Declaration of Independence,' 'the woman next door,' 'the book on the table' consist of several words, they designate specifically unique referents. They function as single words, as units of thought and meaning. A *term is any word, or group of words, which through its unitary meanings designates a referent, refers to, or identifies some object, class, condition, event, relation, or situation, and, is the linguistic symbol thereof*. The following, then, are all properly called terms.

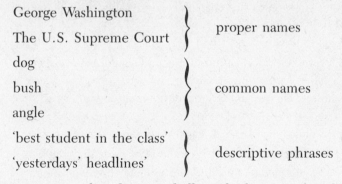

George Washington
The U.S. Supreme Court } proper names

dog
bush } common names
angle

'best student in the class'
'yesterdays' headlines' } descriptive phrases

From now on, therefore, we shall speak of terms rather than symbols or words.

One final point: Although for most purposes signs and symbols can be distinguished, in practice the distinction sometimes breaks down. A humorous and then a serious example will make clear what we mean. The sign over the bathroom in a public building may say 'Men' or 'Women' or it may contain a picture symbolizing a man or a woman. Or again, what is a Latin cross—is it a sign, or a symbol, or both? We speak of making 'the sign of the cross,' but surely the cross on top of a church, as contrasted with the Islamic star and crescent, is primarily a symbol rather than a sign. In spite of these mixed or borderline instances, the distinctions made earlier hold generally and merit careful use.

Tape Exercises

A. Indicate the referent, if any, of the following terms. If there is none, tell why it does not have a referent.

1. The United States of America
2. You
3. Triangle
4. Red Planet
5. The tallest man on the football squad
6. My husband
7. Adlai Stevenson
8. Brother
9. Blue
10. The present Emperor of Germany

B. Consider the following examples. Do any of them commit the fallacy of magical power or the fallacy of reification? If so, why?

1. Knowing the complete and true name of a thing gives us complete control over it.
2. The meaning of the word 'mass' has changed considerably throughout the history of western thought.
3. Keep saying "I'm going to win," and I will.
4. The Presidency is a complete and beautiful thing and cannot be tarnished by any man.
5. Certain words are able to change and influence the inner and outer reality of those saying them.
6. But Mamma, Snow White must be real; I just read about her in a book.
7. Language is a powerful tool and poetry the method of changing reality.
8. Language can be badly misused by unscrupulous people who shape and bend common meanings.

C. Identify the terms in the following sentences as proper names, common names, or descriptive phrases. [Analysis of these problems can be found on Tape 3, band 1.]

1. John Paul Jones is an American naval hero.
2. Some guaranteed merchandise is shoddy.

3. The color of her eyes was blue.
4. Every student has a social security number.
5. Green is my favorite color.
6. If one has good vision, sunspots can occasionally be seen by the naked eye.
7. All of Barbara's brothers attended college.
8. Every American citizen may vote when they attain the proper age.
9. My house is built of stone.
10. The smartest student in the class is George.

3.2   DENOTION AND CONNOTATION

Related to the notions of sense and reference are the notions, connotation and denotation, intension and extension. The *connotation* or intension of a term refers to the common set of properties, characteristics, qualities shared by the term in question. The *denotation,* or extension of a term refers to the specific individuals included in the meaning of the term, that is, to those specific individuals to which the term can be applied. Thus, the denotation of the term 'dog' is all the things to which this term can properly be applied. The denotation of the term 'planet' are the referents Mercury, Venus, Earth, Mars, whatever planets exist.

In its primary sense the connotation of a term is its meaning or interpretation with respect to attributes or qualities in general. The denotation of a term concerns the individuals possessing certain attributes or qualities. Thus, the denotation of 'automobile' is every particular object to which this term applies. The connotation of the term 'automobile' are all the properties shared by these objects—'self-propelled vehicle,' 'vehicles that are used for carrying passengers,' and the like.

Denotation and connotation are related to each other in an inverse way. As the connotation increases, the denotation (extension) decreases, and vice-versa. The term 'man' has a broad denotation and is widely applicable, but the term 'living man over twenty years old' has a decreased denotation—it applies to fewer individuals. The following is a series of increasing intension and decreasing extension, 'King,' 'good King,' 'good King of France,' 'the present good King of France.'

When we speak of the meaning of a term we can refer either to its denotative meaning or its connotative meaning or to both. Connotation may also be distinguished as subjective and objective connotations.

Subjective Connotation   The subjective connotation of a word refers to the properties or characteristics that any particular person believes that that word has, or, to put it differently, the object, phenomena, or events that they think are connoted or meant by that word. Recall the term 'dog'. Subjectively (to a particular person) this word may connote a four-legged animal, a very poor automobile or suit of clothes, a bad experience as when we say, "what a rotten day I've had, not fit for a dog," and the like. Another good example for illustrating connotative definition and range of meaning is the word 'red'. In an average classroom, as one writes the word 'red' on the chalkboard and asks college or university students what it connotes, it soon becomes clear that the range of meaning is very wide, including the following meanings: blood, Communism, Marxism, house of ill repute, a liturgical color in the church for specific seasons, and many more. Connotation, in its subjective sense, thus is often popularly used to indicate the emotive meanings an individual or a group may associate with a term. Obviously, subjective connotation depends much more on context and on place and time of the utterance than does objective connotation. Consider the difference in the word 'statesman' as compared with the word 'politician.' Clearly, in the contexts of advertising and propaganda, for example, connotation plays a very important role.

Objective Connotation   The objective connotation of a word is quite a different matter. This refers to what is sometimes called the intention of the term or the total set of characteristics common to all the objects that make up the term's extension. Objective connotation is the publicly agreed upon meaning of terms and should not vary substantially with context, time, and place. Consider, for example, the words 'ball' and 'box.' The objective connotation of these words points to the shared characteristics of every instance in existence of the word 'ball' or 'box.' It is plain that this connotation is extremely wide, but it is nevertheless limited to the properties common to all objects that are balls or boxes. And there would be little, if any, disagreement among people about those objects that can properly be called 'balls' or 'boxes.'

However, there are several reservations that may be noted. First, some terms such as 'game' and 'art' just do not have a particular set of properties shared by all their denota. These terms point to what are called 'family resemblances' rather than a specified set of properties. It would be difficult to claim that all games share these specific properties. Further, it is not always easy to answer the question as to what properties are connoted by a term. This is true because terms can have more than one meaning or connotation. The term 'temperature' connotes one thing to the average person, another thing to the doctor, and still another thing to the physicist. All of these meanings, however, would be objective rather than subjective connotations because there would be common agreement among the average person, the doctor, and the scientist that 'temperature' connotes the degree of hotness or coldness or something whether it be water, air, or the human body. The differences would occur when specification of the method of measurement of temperature or further specification of the notions of hot and cold was required. Connotations, because they concern the meaning of a term, change and shift. The terms 'person,' 'cool,' or 'garble' have gone through, and are still undergoing, so many changes that it is difficult to identify the connotation. Because of these considerations, some logicians wish to give up all talk of connotation. Yet, given context, time, and place we can usually agree upon the connotation of a term. The above notions may be summarized in the following diagram.

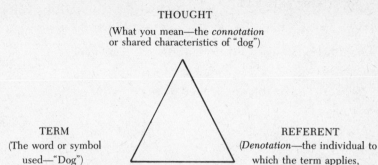

THOUGHT
(What you mean—the *connotation*
or shared characteristics of "dog")

TERM
(The word or symbol
used—"Dog")

REFERENT
(*Denotation*—the individual to
which the term applies,
e.g. "Fido")

Arbitrary, man-made relation

Before going on, a review of the essentials of connotation-denotation and their relation to sense-referent may be helpful. Consider first the notion of the referent of a term. A referent of a term is any object to which that term refers or applies.

Tape Exercises

A. Which of the following are referents of the terms indicated, and which are not? Briefly explain in each case why you answer as you do. [Check your answers with Tape 3, band 2.]

1. City
    a. New York City
    b. The capital of Michigan
    c. The Emerald City
    d. Arizona
    e. Carthage—destroyed by the Romans in the Punic Wars

2. Singer
    a. Bing Crosby
    b. Elvis Presley
    c. Santa Claus
    d. The tenor in the church choir
    e. Enrico Caruso

3. The President of the United States during the 1960s
    a. John F. Kennedy
    b. Abraham Lincoln
    c. John Wayne
    d. Lyndon Johnson
    e. The second eldest son of the Joseph Kennedy family

B. Which of the following terms have sense, but not a referent? Why?

1. Ghost

2. Buffalo Bill

3. The current King of England

4. Unicorn

C. Which of the following two items have the same referent?

1. The angry planet

2. The youngest President of the United States

3. The red planet

4. The first Roman Catholic President of the United States

5. The Babe

6. The great crab

7. The sign of the zodiac for mid-June through mid-July

8. The great home run hitter

D. For each of the following terms, indicate whether the characteristics listed below the term are part of the connotation of the term, part of the denotation or neither.

1. *Pentagon*
    a. Plane figure
    b. Blue in color
    c. Bounded by five straight lines
    d. Containing five angles
    e. The ground plan of the Department of Defense Building in Washington, D.C.

2. *Iceberg*
    a. A mass of ice of at least two tons
    b. Floating in the water
    c. Made of fresh water
    d. Green
    e. In the northern hemisphere
    f. Has been detached from a glacier
    g. That which sunk the Titanic

3.3 AMBIGUITY-VAGUENESS

Related to the above distinctions are two more important notions, *ambiguity* and *vagueness*. Words can have multiple meanings. Thus, for example, the term 'light' may mean 'fire,' 'illumination,' 'radiant energy,' 'frivolous,' 'unimportant,' 'understanding,' 'settled on,' as in:

'Give me a light.'

'Put a light in the window.'

'Light is both waves and particles.'

'He is a light, vain person.'

'It is a light matter.'

'The bird is going to light.'

'As I pondered, light dawned on me.'

Sometimes, multiple meaning is intended and relevant to the context. This is especially true in literature. In the following piece of poetry, for example, the word *sun* has multiple meanings as does *light*.

"It is the East and Juliet is the sun.
   Sun brings light
   promise of new life
   indescribably wonderful."

Indeed, we must be very careful to distinguish between multiple meanings and ambiguity. When we have multiple meanings, we have at least two senses in mind, but we do not have to choose. Indeed, we are invited to take in all the meanings at once as in many jokes. With ambiguity, we have at least two senses, but we need to make a choice, and the context does not indicate to us which choice is correct. However, in terms of logical analysis, we must be able to pin-point exactly what is being said. Ambiguity must be avoided. A term is ambiguous when it can be interpreted as having two or more meanings in a given context. Consider "All freshmen are not required to take math courses." At least two interpretations of the sentence are possible. It could mean: "No freshman are required to take courses in math" or "Some freshmen are not required to take courses in math." If we are to set up arguments, we need to know which statement to take as part of our argument. Only thus can ambiguity be avoided. Often in actual practice a person will resort to ambiguity to avoid certain issues. One may argue: "The government should not establish minimum standards regarding wages and hours of work of employees, because such regulations violate the freedom of the employer to run his own affairs." This argument is ambiguous. Does it mean to argue for complete freedom with no government interference, no regulations regarding health and sanitation and performance of contractural obligations? Or does it mean to argue for opportunity to make decisions? To understand the real argument, ambiguities have to be clarified. A good case of ambiguity that evades the issue is the letter of recommendation that states: "When you come to know this person as well as I know him, you will have the same regard for him as I do."

Terms, as we have discovered, have ranges of applicability—denotations. If these are left indefinite, and undetermined, they are called *vague*. For example, when is the term 'bald' applicable—one hair, three hairs, no hairs? What is 'poverty?' Does 'poor' mean 'having less than $3,000 annual income' or 'belonging to the bottom fifth of the income distribution,' or what?

Logic is interested in specificity and clarity, and so it is interested in remedying ambiguity and vagueness. This brings us to the realm of definition.

Exercises for § 3.3

A. Indicate whether the kind of sign referred to in each of the following statements is a natural or conventional sign.

1. A red flashing light means come to a full stop and then proceed with caution.
2. His eye infection is a sign of some other trouble.
3. A solid yellow line means do not pass.
4. This track is a sign that a bear was here very recently.
5. The skull and bones on the bottle means poison.
6. The wedge sign ('v') means 'either . . . or . . . .'
7. That star on the hood is the sign of the Mercedes-Benz.
8. The shaky handwriting is a sign of feebleness.
9. To most kids the big *M* is a sign for MacDonald's hamburgers.
10. His posture is a sign of military experience.

B. Indicate whether each of the following is a term or a sentence.

1. The oldest of the Walton children.
2. Refreshments were provided by the host.
3. Morning Star.
4. The student sitting in the farthest right hand corner.
5. This is red.
6. That red flag.
7. They finally reached the top of the hill.
8. The light of the moon.
9. This is the White House.
10. The Capitol.
11. How much is 8 x 8?
12. 8 x 8.
13. The Voice of Free Europe.
14. There is a free press in the U.S.
15. George.

C. Order the following set of terms to increasing connotation and decreasing denotation.

1. dog, thing, animal, organic substance, mammal, bulldog, Boston bulldog, four-legged mammal.
2. Treasure Island, literature, adventure novel, English Literature, novel, pirate adventure novel.

3. light white wine, beverage, liquid, wine, Chablis, alcoholic beverage, white wine.

4. American teenage girl, female, human being, thing, woman, animate substance, teenage girl.

5. Logic class, college class, philosophy class, class.

D. Indicate for each property or thing whether it is denoted or connoted by the given term.

1. man
     animal
     Abraham Lincoln
     erect stance
     Mohammed Ali
     rationality
     Neanderthal
     makes symbols

2. dog
     four legged
     Bulldog
     man's best friend
     barks
     Lassie

3. medical doctor
     practices medicine
     healing
     dentist
     give medical treatment
     osteopath

4. scientist
     engaged in research
     Einstein
     collecting of data
     experimentation
     physicist

5. schizophrenia
     mental disorder
     split personality
     Doctor Jekyll and Mr. Hyde
     bizarre behavior

E. For each of the following terms indicate whether the connotations are objective or subjective.

1. Socialism
    a. government ownership of instruments of production
    b. anitindividual
    c. the socioeconomic organization of Sweden
    d. police state
    e. slavery.

2. Yankee
   a. one who lives in the northern part of the United States
   b. meddler
   c. ingenuity
   d. a Union soldier in the Civil War.

3. politician
   a. crookedness
   b. compromiser
   c. one who seeks public office
   d. one actively engaged in party politics
   e. scheming opportunist.

4. capitalism
   a. large concentrations of wealth
   b. ruthless and aggressive
   c. an economic system in which all or most of the means of production are privately owned and operated for a profit
   d. 'Big Business'
   e. imperialism.

5. Yellow
   a. cowardly
   b. a color lying between orange and green in the color spectrum
   c. gold
   d. jaundice
   e. hot.

F. For each of the following terms indicate at least three meanings that each can have.

1. sound
2. grace
3. good
4. right
5. free.

G. For the following sentences underscore those terms that are vague and require more precision.

1. ". . . nor shall private property be taken for public use, without just compensation."   [*Constitution of the United States*, Amendment V]

2. "The right of the people to be secure in their persons, houses, papers and effects, against unreasonable searches and seizures, shall not be violated."   [Ibid., Amendment IV]

3. "Excessive bail shall not be required, no excessive fines imposed, nor cruel and unusual punishments inflicted."   [Ibid., Amendment VIII]

4. "Congress shall have the power to enforce this article by appropriate legislation."   [Ibid., Amendment XIII, Sec. 2]

5. "Treason against the United States, shall consist only in levying war against them, or in adhering to their enemies, giving them aid and comfort." [Ibid., Article III, Sec. 2]

3.4 KINDS OF DEFINITION AND THEIR USES

Satisfactory communication and the determination of the truth and falsity of a statement requires understanding the kinds of objects, ideas or processes to which the words in a sentence apply. Definition comes from the Latin word *de-finis*, meaning concerning the boundaries. Definitions should clarify the meaning of terms, sometimes by restricting and circumscribing the meaning, in other cases by expanding the meaning. This can be done in a number of different ways and to serve different purposes. Definitions can be classed into different types depending on the defining method employed. We shall follow the general practice of identifying several so-called kinds of definition even though all of these, except definition by genus and differentia, fall short of what is really desired.

Functional   Functional definitions are attempts to state the meaning of a word by reference to the use or function of the referent in question. 'Wrench' might be defined as 'a tool used for tightening and loosening bolts.' If we asked, "What is a chair?" we might be told that it is something to sit on, and this surely is one of a chair's functions. A better definition would be a seat having a back and intended for one person to sit on.

It is clear that great care must be taken when defining a word via its function. One reason is that other things may be able to perform the same function. A stool may perform the same function as a chair. Second, the referent itself may have other significant functions. For example, both 'knife' and 'sword' could be defined as 'an instrument with a handle and a thin blade used for cutting.' We do not, however, use the words 'knife' and 'sword' interchangeably. Still a third difficulty is that defining in terms of function is irrelevant and incompetent to deal with terms or concepts having no discernable function. It would be difficult to give a functional definition of art, cold, glorious, and many other words.

Tape Exercises

Give a functional definition for the following: tool, table. [Check your answers on Tape 3, band 2.]

Operational   Operational definitions state a series of operations that exemplify the meaning of a word as it is applicable to a particular object or occasion. An operational definition of 'acid' would state the procedures for determining whether a solution is an acid; for example, 'an acid is a solution in which litmus paper turns red.' Operational and functional definitions are sometimes confused, but they are distinct types of definitions. A functional definition defines by pointing to the way in which the thing being defined can be used or to the functions the thing performs, for example, "A bridge is a thing that provides connections between two things." An operational definition helps us to apply a term correctly and thus to learn its meaning by asking us to do something, to perform an operation or an experiment. This is why operational definitions play an important role in science. They provide the bridges by which theory can be systematically connected with experience or observation. They help make possible the systematic testing of scientific theories in the laboratory. Operational definitions, however, also have weaknesses and indeed they have been the subject of much discussion in philosophy of science.

One weakness of operational definitions is that we often can use different operations to identify the same concept. We can operationally define 'current strength' either in terms of the amount of deflection of a magnetized needle or of the amount of some element such as copper that is deposited per unit time in an electrolytic plating process. Each of these operations involve us in different theoretic frameworks, and operational definitions must be judged adequate relative to these frameworks. For that matter, a broker may use 'current strength' to refer to something totally different from the above—to the strength or weakness of present-day market prices, stock offerings, and the like.

A more serious objection is that there is a sense in which operational definitions are not truly definitions. An operation helps us identify something as being properly called an 'acid,' only words really *define*—" 'acid' means 'an electrolyte which furnishes a hydrogen ion,' "—not operations. Concepts define; operations do not.

Tape Exercises

Give an operational definition for the following: magnetic, electric. [Check your answers on Tape 3, band 2.]

Synonymous   Synonymous definitions use a term with what is presumed to be the same or similar meaning as the word(s) being defined.

'Vagrant' means 'vagabond.'

'Abdominous' means 'big-bellied.'

These kinds of definitions are most helpful in two contexts: (a) bilingual situations—'Logic' means the same thing as the Spanish word *logica*, and (b) contexts in which we wish to increase our vocabulary or to develop the ability to make clear, even subtle distinctions. This is illustrated in the statement in *Gone with the Wind* that "Scarlett was incensed by Rhett's lack of consideration." If asked, "What does 'incensed' mean?" we probably would reply that Scarlett was angered, offended, enraged, irritated, provoked. Each is in a sense correct and helps the person who knows what 'angry' etc., means but who has no idea what 'incensed' means. However, what if they don't know what angry, offended, etc., mean? Further, as illustrated in the above answer to "What does 'incensed' mean?" each of the presumed synonyms is inadequate and misleading precisely because each of the terms has a different meaning, even a shade of meaning which is difficult to fix upon.

Another objection, as suggested above, is that such definitions are not helpful if the synonym is also unknown. They do not enlarge our knowledge. Still further, they do not handle the problems of ambiguity and vagueness. They seek to define a word simply by offering another term which may be familiar.

Tape Exercises

In order further to understand synonymous definition and its problems, give synonymous definitions of the following: apprehend, emergent. [Check your answers with Tape 3, band 3.]

Stipulative   The notion of stipulation arose in the field of law and economics in which it means to specify, promise, guarantee. For logic it means in effect: I (we) propose to mean by x the following . . . it is a decision to assign a new meaning to a term, usually in a given context. We may choose a symbol to represent some notion, such as " '$A^{12} = B$' means '$A \times A \times A \times A \times A \times A \times A \times A \times A \times A \times A \times A = B$' ". We may coin a new term—Horace Walpole coined the word 'serendipity' to refer to 'the faculty of finding what one did not seek.' Stipulative definitions are appraised as useful or misleading, clear or obscure, but not as true or false. Stipulative definitions should facilitate the communication of ideas and should be used consistently in the context in which they are proposed. A good example of the use of a stipulative definition to gain clarity was Alexander Fleming's decision to replace the phrase 'mold broth filtrate' with the word 'penicillin.'

A dangerous employment of stipulative definition occurs when one out of a number of possible meanings is assigned to a word. (Recall: to stipulate means to propose or decide to use a term with a certain meaning.) So, for example, in political discussion the author may stipulate that 'democracy' means 'majority rule but with no minority rights,' or that 'good' means 'that which affords pleasure.' The danger here is that although the proposal is legitimate and honestly made, it is likely to lead to confusion. Why? (1) Because it diverges from dictionary or the widely used meanings of the given term. (2) Readers or listeners are likely to forget that a special and arbitrary meaning has been assigned for purposes of using it in a given context.

Tape Exercises

Think briefly about some of the problems and dangers involved in the following stipulative definitions. [Check your answers with Tape 3, band 3.]

1. For the purposes of student government elections, I shall stipulate that 'student' shall be defined as 'all those registered for a full fifteen hours of credit'.

2. From now on in this country, all those who have broken any state, city, or county laws shall be designated a 'criminal'.

Lexical, Dictionary, Ordinary Language   A lexical definition states the traditional or conventional meaning of a word that is already in use. A lexical definition may be understood to be saying something of the form, "A traditional usage of the word '*x*' is '*y*.' " For example, 'automobile' means a self-propelled vehicle for use on streets or roadways. Because a lexical definition *reports the usage of a word,* it may be judged as true or false, reliable, or accurate.

There is so much confusion in almost all expositions of lexical definition that we are tempted to omit consideration of it altogether. Yet, we dare not ignore it because it is one customary way of assigning meaning; also, the difficulties need to be identified so that they may be avoided.

The first point to clarify is this: unlike stipulative definitions, which usually are proposed for terms which have little or no meaning, or for which a new and often debatable definition is being proposed, lexical definitions aim at eliminating ambiguity (recall the distinction between ambiguity and vagueness) or at recording a widely accepted meaning of a term. For example, someone says to you that he or she played a hoax on you and you ask, "What does that mean? What's a *hoax*?" Now your quick answer may be that they were taking advantage of your credulity or your naïveté. But a better answer is to quote the dictionary. *Hoax* means to deceive by an amusing fabrication or fiction. That, you reply, is what people mean by hoax, and what they have meant for 300 years or more. Or again, 'lamp' means: "a vessel containing oil, which is burnt at a wick, for purposes of illumination." Notice: we do not say this is what *I* mean by 'lamp,' or what 'lamp' will mean in the following discussion. Rather we say, "This is what the word *really* means; it is the way it is properly used." These, then, are two dictionary, lexical, ordinary language definitions or, more loosely, agreed upon statements of the meaning of a term.

We would be fortunate if the solution to the problem of definition was to consult the dictionary, see how the term is used, but it is not. The following difficulties must be identified and possible confusions avoided if this kind of definition is to be used effectively.

First, we said earlier that statements may be either true or false, and so most logicians say that lexical definitions—which are or involve statements—may be either true or false. In a superficial and somewhat misleading sense this is correct. For we may ask: Is this a true report of how 'lamp' or 'hoax' is used by English speaking people, or of how its meaning is given in a standard dictionary? The answer is yes, but it refers merely to the report, not strictly to whether the *definition* as such is true or false.

Second, closely related to the above is the practice of logicians of speaking of 'real' definitions, as if the lexical, dictionary or ordinary usage were real, correct, true as contrasted with fanciful and arbitrary definitions. But this is misleading because 'real' does not mean that what is defined is a real, existing object, process, experience, or whatever. No space-time existence is inferred in real definition, whether the term be 'horse' or 'mermaid.'

Third, for many people dictionary definitions are circular and often very exasperating. Who, for example, has not looked up a word in the dictionary only to find that (a) it is defined in other terms, the meaning of which we don't know, so the chain of inquiry seems endless and one feels more frustrated than informed; or (b) the dictionary fails to indicate all the shades and nuances of the term and hence conveys far less than the full meaning of the word? Our earlier reference to *Gone with the Wind* illustrates the second point.

Fourth, as linguists and academicians know so well, dictionaries, like authorities, frequently disagree with each other. Still further, unless they are unabridged and encyclopedic in their exhaustiveness, they rarely can keep up-to-date. A page-long list of words could be made up, for example, of New Testament terms employed in the King James version, the meaning of which is either totally lost or so changed that the meaning is lost.

Fifth, and finally, definition by ordinary language, by established usage runs into a variety of difficulties. One is the problem of discovering the usage of a term. If, for example, the word is 'democracy,' how do we sort out the bewildering diversity of meanings given the term by the ordinary person, by political scientists, philosophers, historians as well as by authors with wildly conflicting political persuasions? The more widely the criteria of usage employed, the more difficult it becomes to fix upon even a variety of meanings. Another problem is raised by the quest for ordinary language and established usage. What, for example, is the ordinary usage of the word 'god'? What peoples? What culture? How many make a usage ordinary rather than extraordinary? Again, when is a usage established? The expressions "That's real good" or "It ain't necessarily so" are presumably well established and certainly, to the grammarians or ordinary language experts, established in the worst sense. But how clear is their meaning? As Robert H. Ennis wrote, ". . . if the group is a large one, and exhausts a particular culture, then we have a sufficient condition for elevating a usage to the status of *a* meaning or *the* meaning. The minimum size of the group and the extent of usage in a culture that turn the necessary condition into a sufficient condition are not matters that can be specified."[1]

---

[1] Robert H. Ennis, *Logic In Teaching*. (Englewood Cliffs: Prentice-Hall, 1969), p. 171. This is a particularly fine discussion not only of dictionary and so-called established usage, but of definition in general, pp. 123–91.

Precising   A precising definition seeks to eliminate vagueness by helping to
decide where to draw the boundaries of application. A great many legal
decisions involve precising definitions in which certain statutory terms are
specified so that they include or exclude the case at issue. Everyone is familiar
with a government agency that issues licenses for cars, usually called the
Department of Motor Vehicles. But what is a vehicle? Does the term include
trucks, house trailers, trailers attached to or detached from an automobile?
Does it include the increasing variety of teenage or even children's soap box
cars that clearly are motor driven and carry a passenger? What is required is not
a dictionary definition but one that will reduce, and if possible eliminate,
vagueness. It should be a definition in the use of which we can agree that *this* is
a motor vehicle or *that* is not a motor vehicle. To cite other common examples,
what does 'bald' mean? We can agree easily enough that Yul Bryner is bald, but
how much or how little hair requires us to describe a person as bald? When is a
person 'sexy'? In attitude? In acts? How does one define these, or is it
impossible?

The aim of precising definitions is to help us to eleminate vagueness and to
make a decision in borderline cases. If many of these seem trivial (as one of our
examples suggests), many others are serious, as the faltering efforts of the
United States Supreme Court to define 'obscenity' demonstrate.

Two additional points should be made. One is that precising definitions are in
principle different from stipulative definitions even though at first glance they
seem to be the same. For in attempting to reduce vagueness, we are dealing
with a term that has a dictionary meaning and that usually is well-embedded in
ordinary language ('vehicle' and 'bald'). We would be confused and incorrect to
propose a radically new meaning for familiar terms whose weakness is their
vagueness. The other point is that, as with other kinds of definition, it is not
proper to speak of their truth or falsity. Rather, they are useful or useless,
convenient or troublesome.

Theoretical   Theoretical definitions state a formal or technical meaning of a
word for use by specialists in a given field. In physics words such as 'mass,'

'field,' 'stress,' and 'strain,' are defined within the terminology of particular theories and can only be understood in the context of theories and subject areas. Another example of a theoretical definition is "Enzymes are special kinds of protein that control the different steps in the synthesis or breakdown of an organic molecule." Theoretical definitions are often of no more or less value than the theories of which they are a part. Many times they are used as much to achieve acceptance of a theory as to shed light on it. Finally, because theories are always subject to revision and replacement, they may soon become obsolete. Terms such as 'gravitation,' 'light,' and 'heat' illustrate the point in the sciences. But the changes are no less radical in other fields. With changes in the understanding of human nature, such terms as 'soul' and 'mind' become centers of intense controversy concerning what, if anything, they mean. Theoretical definitions are an important part of our lives today because of the prominence of science.

Tape Exercises

Guess the theoretical definition of the common term 'ego'. [Check Tape 3, band 3, for an answer.]

Exercises for § 3.4

A. For each of the following, indicate the kind of definition that is being given: functional, operational, synonymous, stipulative, precising, theoretical, denotative by example.

1. A body is to be called electric if it is 'capable of attracting small bodies when rubbed.'

2. A plane is a carpenter's tool for shaving a wood surface in order to make it smooth.

3. An athete is a connoisseur.

4. A boat is a watercraft such as a canoe, row boat, speed boat, sail boat, ocean liner.

5. A juvenile delinquent is to be considered a youth of not more than 18 years of age who commits an act in violation of the law.

6. The electric volume-density at a given point in space is the limiting ratio of the quantity of electricity within a sphere whose center is the given point to the volume of the sphere, when its radius is diminished without limit.

7. From now on, any substance that is reddish, has the melting point 1083°C, and the atomic number 29 shall be called copper.

8. A mineral is any of certain inorganic elements, as iron, and phosphorous.

9. A bar of iron or steel is called a magnet if iron filings are attracted by its ends and cling to them.

10. A saw is a cutting tool with a series of sharp teeth.

B. Discuss the inadequacies of each of the following definitions in terms of the limitations of the kind of definitions they represent.

1. A saw is a cutting tool with a series of sharp teeth.

2. An object is said to be harder than another if drawing a sharp point of that object upon the surface of the other object produces a scratch on that object.

3. Grace is charm.

4. I stipulate that in this discussion *communism* shall be used to mean a hypothetical stage of socialism, as formulated by Marx, to be characterized by a classless and stateless society and by the equal distribution of economic goods.

5. For the purposes of this law a vehicle will be understood to be any device or contrivance for carrying or conveying people or objects on land.

6. An electron orbit is any one for which the angular momentum of the electron is a whole multiple of $h12\pi$ and there is no radiant energy while the electron is in orbit.

7. An existentialist is a philosopher such as Kierkegaard, Tillich, Sartre and Jaspers.

C. Look up the following words in a standard dictionary and discuss in each case the inadequacies of the lexical definitions given.

1. philosopher
2. logician
3. lower class
4. life
5. mind

3.5 CONNOTATIVE AND DENOTATIVE DEFINITIONS

Recalling the earlier discussion of connotation and denotation, we can anticipate what connotative and denotative definitions would be like. Connotative definitions may, broadly speaking, be said to be of two types. The first and looser kind attempts to capture the meanings suggested by a term. What, for example, is the meaning of 'dictator'? Clearly its connotation is very wide. Comedian Charlie Chaplain did a masterful job of describing *The Dictator* in a film by that name. The term *dictator* is drab and colorless if it is defined simply as a ruler or governor whose word is law, or as the absolute ruler of a state. The point is not that these do not give us the established, dictionary meaning of the term; they do, but the meaning is far richer in connotation. It often includes the notion of one invested with absolute authority in times of emergency. It also includes the notion of *arbitrary* rule, the image generated by Nero fiddling while Rome burns, of Hitler condemning thousands of Jews to horrible death. Consider the meaning of 'die' and 'death'. The connotation is enormously rich. The dictionary's typical phrase, 'to lose life' says little or nothing. Biological death is now defined not in terms of consciousness or heart beat but of brain waves. But we speak of the pains of death, or suffering spiritual death, or of 'perishing everlastingly,' or more. In short, this first kind of connotative definition is fascinating and useful, but it is the special tool of the poet, the philosopher, the explorer of language in its widest uses.

   The second type of connotative definition that logicians employ seeks to state the essential characteristics, qualities, or properties of the term being defined. Thus *bachelor* is defined as an adult male who is unmarried. This type of connotative definition is the traditional kind of definition, that is, by *genus* and *differentia;* a type of definition usually considered the real and only genuine type of definition and a type of definition going all the way back to the Greek philosopher, Aristotle. This type of definition seeks to define by first specifying the general class to which the item belongs and then seeks to specify further and distinguish the meaning of the term from that of other terms also in that class. Thus, for example, 'chair' belongs to the general class, or 'genus,' of 'furniture,' and it, in turn, is distinguished in its meaning from that of other terms denoting other kinds of furniture—'table,' 'sofa,'—by a *specific difference* that separates 'chair' from 'table' within the class or genus 'furniture'. The specific difference that distinguishes chair from other pieces of furniture is that it has a seat for one person, usually has four legs and a back, and is normally movable. 'Bachelor,' for example, is defined as 'a man (genus) who is unmarried (difference)'. Definition by genus and difference is an important and, perhaps the only proper, kind of definition, for so many terms share common characteristics and belong to similar classes, and good definition seek to show both the commonalities and differences.

Tape Exercises

Consider the following list. Define the terms by use of *genus* and *differentia*. [Check Tape 3, band 3, for the specification of these terms.]

doe	filly
buck	stallion
fawn	husband
mare	wife
colt	daughter

   Turning to the denotative definitions, we recall that the denotation of a term is the set or class of individuals to which the term applies. Thus, the denotation of 'human' is the class of men and women. To give a denotative definition, then, is to specify the things falling under the term. We could give a denotative definition of 'university' by naming individual instances to which the term is correctly applied, for example, "A university is the kind of school of higher education you find at Princeton, Harvard, Yale, Brown, Columbia, and the like." Denotative definitions may be said to be of the following types.

Enumerative   An enumerative definition specifies the denotation of a term by listing *all* the individuals to which the term applies. These definitions are not really practical for most terms because it would be impossible to list all the numbers of objects denoted by the term. For example, how could you list all the objects called 'star'?

Denotative Definition by Example   Because of the impracticality of enumeration, we usually indicate denotation by listing a few examples. We can roughly specify what 'spice' means by saying that pepper, nutmeg, cloves, and cinnamon are examples of 'spice' or 'seasoning.' What is a skyscraper? The Empire State Building, the Chrysler Building, and so on.

Ostensive or Demonstrative   We may give examples of things to which a term applies without using words. A demonstrative or ostensive definition defines a term by pointing to or otherwise indicating one or more *instances* of its denotation. To define 'chair,' we might point to various examples. Ostensive definitions, of course, are limited geographically and are time consuming. Also, they are limited to physical, visual objects.

Denotative definitions, in fact have three basic weaknesses or limitations. First of all, they cannot handle terms with empty extensions (terms whose referents have no existence)—'centaur,' 'mermaid,' or 'the present King of France'. Second, we usually cannot completely enumerate. As a result, they may be dangerously misleading. For example, are we to conclude from the above examples that all skyscrapers are in the United States? Or, if you reply that 'bird' means crow, swallow, blue jay, robin, does 'bird' mean only animals that fly over land? Finally, individual instances may fit under many different terms; the Empire State Building fits under both 'building' and 'skyscraper.'

Exercises for § 3.5

A. Give denotative definitions-by-example of the following:

1. skyscraper
2. planet
3. bird
4. disease
5. city

B. For the following connotative definitions indicate those terms that represent the *genus* and those that represent the *differentia*.

1. A *window* is an opening for admitting light and air, usually having pane or panes of glass, generally movable for opening or shutting.
2. A *pencil* is a pointed, rod-shaped instrument of wood or metal with a center core of graphite or crayon, used for marking, writing and drawing.
3. A *house* is a building for human beings to live in.

4. A *fever* is a state of abnormally increased body temperature.

5. A *bicycle* is a vehicle consisting of two wheels, one behind the other, equipped with handle bars and a saddle-like seat and propelled by the feet.

6. A *religion* is a social institution concerned with man's relationship with the supernatural.

7. A *university* is an institution of higher learning qualified to award the Ph. D. degree.

8. An *engine* is any machine that uses energy to develop more power.

9. A *lie* is a false statement made with the intent to deceive.

10. A *contract* is an agreement enforceable by law.

3.6 RULES FOR FORMING AND CRITICIZING DEFINITIONS

In discussing the various kinds of definitions above, we have been concerned to point to weaknesses which all of these face. We have also indicated that traditionally the most proper and complete kind of definition has been considered to be that of definition by *genus* and *differentia*. Why this has been the case will be evident shortly. First, we should recall at this point the reason why logicians are interested in definitions. It is precisely this: logicians are interested in knowing most clearly and concisely what is being asserted and what is being concluded. More often than perhaps we can imagine, arguments contain explicit or implicit definitions that are crucial to the argument. Further, verbal disagreement is a frequent kind of contention, and here definition plays a key role. Finally, as rational persons we want to set out arguments, theories, proposals and essays that are clear and cogent, and definitions will often be required. Thus, as part of our logical skills, we need the facility in identifying, criticizing, and formulating definitions. We turn to the traditional rules for formulating definitions, which are applicable primarily to definition by genus and differentia. They are also applicable in limited and important senses to other types of definition. Further, the other types of definition perform their functions well in specified contexts.

RULE 1: A definition should state the essential characteristics of the term being defined. Thus, a definition of 'man' as 'the animal that laughs' fails to state the essentials of the usual meaning of the word 'man'. A definition of 'man' as 'an animal having a power of speech and reason' is more adequate. This rule tells us to concentrate on the general class to which the item being defined belongs and to specify as far as possible that which differentiates it from other members of the class.

Clearly, however, this is a rule that in many instances is difficult to apply. As Wittgenstein and other philosophers have pointed out, it is nearly impossible in some cases to decide precisely what the essential characteristics are. Is 'man' no longer to be classified as man if he does not possess the characteristics of reason? of speech? of capacity for laughter? This difficulty applies to nearly all general terms such as 'art,' 'religion,' and 'living organism'.

Tape Exercises

To test your grasp of this rule, indicate which of the following definitions violate Rule 1, and which do not. In each case, briefly explain why you answer as you do. [Turn to Tape 3, band 4, to check your answers.]

1. A house is a building used as a sheltered place of habitation for animals or people.
2. A rectangle is a parallelogram all of whose interior angles are right angles.
3. A politician is a person who makes a business of seeking and holding public government office.

Rule 2:   The definition must not be too broad nor too narrow.   It should carefully set out the limits of applicability. That it should not be *too broad* means that it should not include cases to which it does not refer. That it should not be *too narrow* means that it should not exclude cases to which it does refer. For example, the definition: "A sensation is an elementary state of consciousness" is much too broad because there are many elementary states of consciousness that are not sensations, states such as affection, thinking, desiring and the like. On the other hand, the definition "Government is an institution created by the people to protect their rights" is clearly too narrow. It identifies one of the functions of government, but certainly government is not limited to protection of rights. A definition can be both too narrow and too broad, for example, "A novel is a narrative story." It is too broad in the sense that some narrative stories are not novels. It is too narrow because some novels are not adequately characterized as "a narrative story."

Tape Exercises

Proceeding to the next rule, see if you can indicate which of the following definitions violate Rule 2 and which do not and why.   [Check your answers with Tape 3, band 4.]

1. An automobile is a four-wheeled vehicle.
2. A square is a four-sided figure.
3. A pet is a cat or dog.

Rule 3: Noncircularity. A definition should not contain the term to be defined or any term merely synonymous with it. If it does, it is circular. The classic example occurs in the Platonic dialogues when the question, "What is justice?" arose. We gain no insight if we are told that "justice is the way of acting justly." Other examples of circular definitions are: "A cat is a feline creature" and "A scientist is one who engages in scientific activity."

Tape Exercises

Look at the following definitions. Which do and which do not violate the Rule of Noncircularity? Why? [The answers are on Tape 3, band 4.]

1. A snake is an offspring of a snake.
2. An awkward situation is a very clumsy situation.
3. A desk is any piece of furniture used as a desk.

Rule 4: Clarity. A definition should be stated in clear, precise, and, if possible, literal language. It should not be stated in vague, obscure, poetic, figurative, facetious, sarcastic, or cynical language. The purpose of definition is to set out the meaning of a term, to define its boundaries. Thus, clarity is essential to the heart of its task. Further, the definer should seek to express his or her definition in a language that the intended hearer or reader can be expected to understand. Highly theoretical and highly figurative and metaphorical language should be avoided, the latter because it is open to varied interpretations and meanings. We do not learn much by being told that "A headlight is a form of nocturnal illumination," and that "Life is neither the wick nor the wax of a candle, but the burning." Definitions like these may be suggestive, but not advisable for purposes of clarification and precision.

This is not to deny that there may be cases in which a metaphor or figure of speech is used with unusual power to shed light on the meaning of a term. In the older logic texts an often-recurring example was this: "architecture is frozen music." This highly suggestive definition can lead an imaginative mind to speculate on the important respects in which architecture, which deals with objects in space and time, is related to music, with its temporal and juxtaposed elements. The Taj Majal is a form of music and poetry even though it is cold, static marble and precious stones and constitutes a building. The trouble is that all such figurative and metaphorical definitions, no matter how suggestive and imaginative, do not meet the requirement of offering a clear, precise, unambiguous meaning of a term.

Tape Exercises

Which of these violate Rule 4 and why? [These are analyzed on Tape 3, band 5.]

1. Money is the root of all evil.
2. The devil is the prince of darkness.
3. A college is a gateway to opportunity.

Rule 5: Not Negative. A definition should, if possible, be positive and not negative. It should state what the term is or implies, not what the term is not or does not imply. When we ask, for instance, what a spiritual being is, it does not help very much to be told that a spiritual being is not a material being. Defining negatively usually does not get at essential characteristics and thus also violates the first rule. It should be noted, however, that negative definitions can have their place and, in fact, often can not be avoided. Thus, it does make sense to speak of 'baldness' as 'lacking hair on the head,' or of 'odd-numbers' as 'the set of numbers that are not even,' or even of 'bachelor' as 'an *un*married man.'

Tape Exercises

Note the negative tone of each of the following definitions. How might they be improved? [These are analyzed on Tape 3, band 5.]

1. A negative reply is one that is not positive.
2. A liberal is not a conservative.
3. A sick person is not healthy.

Rule 6: Neutrality. A definition should be stated in as neutral terms as possible. That is, we should avoid as far as possible engaging in *persuasive* definitions. Persuasive definitions are those whose purpose is to *influence attitudes on conduct*. Thus, the following definitions express attitudes and seak to influence attitudes.

"A conservative is a person who wishes to preserve the best of the past for future generations."

"Abortion is the murdering of defenseless human beings."

Tape Exercises

Indicate why the following violate Rule 6. [The answers are on Tape 3, band 5.]

1. A liberal is a person foolhardy enough to be open-minded to ideas that challenge tradition and naïve enough to favor reform in politics and education.
2. A male chauvinist is an oversexed egoist.
3. A mother is a slave who serves her children for twenty years or more.

Sometimes *persuasive* definitions are not seriously offered as definitions but rather as epigrams or editorial comments or as a mere expression of belief. Thus, Oscar Wilde defined foxhunting as "the unspeakable in pursuit of the inedible," and Ezra Pound spoke of a philosopher as "just a guy too damned lazy to work in a laboratory." These men were not seriously proposing definitions, nor were they intending to deceive us by using them. Some persuasive definitions are deliberately designed to be misleading. They seek to pass as legitimate definitions while they are phrased to appeal to prejudices and emotions and to influence behavior. Thus, for example, "A Catholic is a person who is obedient and subservient to the Pope," or "A woman is the passive and inferior sex."

Some logicians make a distinction between persuasive and loaded definitions. A loaded definition is said to undertake to actually define the term, but it does so in a prejudicial way. A humorous example of this is offered by Samuel Johnson in his *Dictionary* published in the 18th Century.

"oats: A grain which in England is generally given to horses, but in Scotland supports the people."

Johnson's definition does tell us that 'oats' is a grain and is usually fed to horses, but it also conveys a low opinion of the people of Scotland who eat the same food as horses do. Another example of a *loaded definition* is offered by Ronald Munson in his *The Way of Words*.[2]

"An integrationist is a person committed to the foolish and dangerous doctrine that the races of man ought to have equal rights and should form one society."

This definition does tell us what an integrationist is, but it also contains a value judgment, namely, that this point of view is foolish and dangerous.

For our purposes, we do not find it necessary to distinguish loaded and persuasive definitions, but merely to state our Rule 6.

In sum, then, definitions should provide meanings that make communication simpler, make understanding of ideas or points of view more readily attainable; and illuminate rather than obscure meaning. In dealing with the validity of arguments, we must seek above all clarity and precision. We must not allow ambiguity, vagueness, persuasive definition, and the like to hinder us from understanding exactly what is being argued. We can also question the misuse of definitions to win arguments.

Exercises for § 3.6

A. For each of the following definitions indicate the violations of rules for a good definition.

Rules:

1. Rule of essential characteristics.
2. Rule of limits of applicability: not too narrow and not too broad.
3. Rule of noncircularity.

---

[2] (Boston: Houghton Mifflin Co., 1976).

4. Rule of clarity.

5. Rule of affirmative instances.

6. Rule of neutrality.

Definitions:

1. Sleep is an unconscious state.

2. Science is organized knowledge.

3. "Adultery is an act done under cover of darkness and secrecy and in which the parties are seldom surprised."   [Maryland Court of Appeals, 1931]

4. Biology is a science which studies the biological nature of living things.

5. Man is an ape with possibilities.

6. Education is the liberation, organization and direction of power and intelligence, with the development of taste and culture.   [Abraham Flexner]

7. A conservative is a person characterized by the tendency to conserve things as they are.

8. Psychology is the science of human behavior.

9. A conservative is a man who is too cowardly to fight and too fat to run. [E. Hubbard]

10. An accomplice is one associated with another in crime, having guilty knowledge and complicity.

11. Alimony is matrimonial insurance for women paid by the men for having poor judgment.

12. A mineral is any substance that is neither vegetable nor animal.

13. Competition is an economic struggle for survival among businessmen in which the consumer benefits the most.

14. A clock is an instrument for keeping time.

15. The dog is man's best friend
He has a tail on one end.
Up in front he has teeth
And four legs underneath.   [Ogden Nash]

16. An atheist is the opposite of a theist.

17. A democracy is a form of government in which all, even the fool have a voice.

18. A kiss is a lipservice to love.   [Warren Goldberg]

19. Divorce is a legal separation of two persons of the opposite sex who desire to respect and honor each other.

20. An accident is an event happening unexpectedly and without fault.

B. Definitions are often used and misused in arguments. For each of the following, point out premises and conclusions, point out definitions and criticize each of the definitions, using the six rules discussed above. [Turn to Tape 3, band 6. analysis of problem 2.]

1. A team of researchers from the University of Colorado has found that religious people who are drawn to the mystical qualities of life make the safest drivers.

According to their report,the subjects of their study was 264 airmen at Lowry Air Force Base in Denver, whose accident records were known. According to Vernon Allport's definition, the religious man is one who is concerned with the supernatural meaning of all existence and particularly his place in it. Subjects who belonged to this type according to the test had collision accident scores lower than those of the non-religious type. The study concluded that this non-religious type (The Theoretic and Aesthetic) had higher scores because of a general tendency to be less conventional, psychologically more complex and conflicted, and more ready to resort to complex defense operations as a protection against anxiety.

2. The development of leisure in a civilization permits time for the development of the arts, philosophy, history and the sciences. When these areas of human endeavor become developed, then the civilization can truly be said to be a 'high' civilization. Thus, the test of the quality of a civilization is the quality of its leisure. What then about leisure in America? In America we have a great deal of time, but we do not truly have leisure. Because leisure is indeed an affair of mood and atmosphere rather than simply of the clock. Leisure is not a chronological occurence but a spiritual state. It is unhurried pleasurable living among one's native enthusiasms. Leisure is those pauses in our lives when experience is a fusion of stimulation and repose. Genuine leisure yields at once a feeling of vividness and a sense of peace. In America we have plenty of time to kill, but we do not have leisure.

3. Little imagination is necessary to see that socialized medicine is a completely wrong thing. Medicare is socialized medicine, and it has brought nothing but disillusionment to the patients and headaches to the doctors. Further, socialism is the takeover by the government of everything traditionally re-served for the individual. Indeed, to talk about medical care which is free is a contradiction in terms, for freedom means *no* control, *no* regulation, *no* restraint. Socialized medicine is against democracy which is the control of everything by the people. Therefore, we should vote down this bill which proposes to socialize medical care in the U.S.

4. One must protect against the pacifist babbler who in reality is a crudely made-up egoist. He trespasses against the natural laws of development, for these laws are upheld by the individual's willingness to sacrifice himself in favor of the community and not by the cowardly-know-it-alls who oppose the use of force under any circumstances. The patriot has true natural instinct and unconsciously obeys the deeper necessity of the preservation of the species, if necessary, at the expense of the individual.

5. There is nothing wrong in including fantasy stories in a collection labeled *Science Fiction*. After all, science fiction is a form of fantasy and furthermore, the type of reader who enjoys science fiction is really the type of person who believes in the fantastic rather than in science anyhow.

6. "Whoever kills a tyrant kills not a man but a beast disguised as a man. For, being deprived of all natural love for their fellow creatures, it follows that

tyrants are without human sympathies, and hence are not men but wild animals. Thus, it is clear that whoever kills a tyrant is not committing homicide, since he kills a monster and not a man."[3]

3.7 CLASSIFICATION AND DIVISION

Closely related to many of the issues discussed in this chapter are questions concerning the nature of classification and division. These are matters that occur both in deductive logic, which after all is a logic of classes and of their relations, and in inductive logic which, for example, is concerned not merely with the observation of innumerable facts but with classifying facts for a useful purpose. Indeed, all description—which is at the heart of the sciences—is, in a sense, classification.

We can begin by learning that classification and division are reverse processes. In classifying, we observe that individuals are similar in certain respects, and so they form a class: nails, automobiles, human beings, blonds brunettes, and redheads. (The last example was deliberately cited to show that both individuals *and* classes may share one or more characteristics, and so two or more classes make up other classes.) Because this process may be repeated, we may subsume one class or group of classes under a wider class and so ascend to an ever increasing generality.

The same process operates in reverse in *division*. In this case we descend from a wider class to a narrower class. The subclasses reach their limit only when we arrive at the smallest unit or even the single member of a subclass.

A familiar illustration of classification and division are the books in a library. Assuming that your own library or that of one's college or university is not a mere collection, willy-nilly, of hundreds of thousands of books, obviously some principle or principles of organization is employed. Presumably we will not choose to divide them according to the size or color of the books; we probably will divide them according to subject matter. This will provide sections or classes for the sciences, subclasses for the physical, biological, and social sciences, another section for the arts, and so forth. What soon becomes apparent is that we should be aware of the logical principles involved so that our classification or division will be rational and expeditious. There are three such rules.

The first is to choose *one* principle and to stay with it without exception. What that principle is depends solely on our interests and needs. For example, Lineaus the Swedish botanist classified flowers according to physical, external characteristics. The same is true of the classification of insects, the reason being that although internal characteristics might disclose important differences, these characteristics are very difficult to determine. Again, the manager of a shoe or hardware store may select anyone of several principles of

---

[3] Michelangelo, in *Great Conversations*, Louis Biancolli, ed. (New York: Simon and Schuster, 1948, p. 28.

classification—size, function of the items, sales price, and the like—but his logic course serves him well in advising him to choose a single principle and stay with it.

A second principle is to seek *mutual exclusion* of classes and subclasses. The point is that when we divide a class into several species, no case should occur in which an individual could be a member of more than one subclass. This is a difficult principle to employ for obvious reasons. Recalling our task of organizing a library, where shall we place the books on the history of science or the philosophy of religion? They cannot be put both into the history and science sections and into the philosophy and religion sections. We are forced to put the books, as a matter of convenience or personal preference, in one section or the other.

Third, the system of classification should be *exhaustive*. This means that it must be able to accommodate all the instances or subclasses to be classified. We would be in an odd situation, for example, if our library did not have a place for books on engraving, etching, or lithographing. This rule is one of the bases for the logicians' objection to such expressions as 'etc.,' 'miscellaneous,' 'and the like.' Too often these mean that we are throwing together a lot of embarrassing items that do not fit into our established classes.

Observing these three rules will save us from major confusion and difficulties, but admittedly there will be cases in which we shall be hard put to apply them.

Some of the difficulties of classification, particularly in the area of science, can be seen from a historical study of the classification of chemical compounds. Before the seventeenth and eighteenth centuries, classification of chemical compounds was based on a few physical properties such as color, taste, smell, consistency, solubility and method of preparation. Thus, for example, magnesium carbonate and maganese dixoide were distinguished by color and called white magnesium [*magnesia alba*] and black magnesium [*magnesia nigra*].[4] Likewise, if two different methods of preparation were used, the two substances were distinguished as separate compounds. For example, there was *spirit of nitre* and *aqua fortis*, which today are both called *nitric acid*.[5] However, in the latter part of the nineteenth century, with the work of Bergman and Lavoisier, the chemical composition of compounds became a more important principle of classification, and color, taste, and so on were generally treated as mere indicators of chemical composition. Today such things as boiling point and atomic weight are important.[6]

Speaking of classification in science, it should be noted once again that classification is directed to a specific purpose or end. Objects are classified in order to increase our knowledge of them, to give further insight into their

[4] Maurice P. Crosland, *Historical Studies in the Language of Chemistry* (Cambridge, Mass.: Harvard, 1962), p. 86.

[5] Ibid., p. 90.

[6] For a thorough discussion of the problems of definition and classification in science see: Peter Achinstein, *Concepts of Science* (Baltimore: The John Hopkins Press, 1968).

properties, their similarities and differences and their interrelations. The scientist seeks ever increasing universality, that is, general laws and theories interrelating large segments of phenomena. Thus, a classification scheme contributing to this interest is considered better than another, from the scientist's point of view. The scientist will concentrate on characteristics of things, organisms, processes, which are more likely to be connected to other characteristics and which thus may lead to the formulation of general laws and explanatory hypotheses. It is these characteristics that will be considered important. Further, the scientist's judgment about what are important characteristics will change as theory in science changes and grows. Early in science, whether in chemistry or biology, external physical characteristics of chemical compounds and organisms were considered important. Later, after Newton, it might be weight or mass. Today, in light of subatomic physics, atomic weight and internal gene construction are considered important. As knowledge in science grows, it is quite reasonable to expect earlier classification schemes to be rejected in favor of newer ones based upon what are considered more important characteristics.

Exercises for § 3.7

A. For each of the following items, discuss various ways in which they might be classified. Indicate the principle used and division into subclasses. [Number 2 is analyzed on Tape 3, band 6.]
1. vehicles
2. dogs
3. horses
4. airplanes
5. vegetables
6. educational institutions
7. books
8. works of art
9. religions
10. colleges

Chapter Outline

A. Words are linguistic symbols based on social convention. Thus, no necessary connection holds between a linguistic symbol and its meaning.
B. Failure to remember the conventional nature of words can lead to two errors.
   1. *Reification:* This error consists in assuming that because something has a name it actually exists. This error is also committed when one removes a name too far from that to which it refers.
   2. Another error which results from forgetting that words are conventional symbols is attributing magical power to words.

C. The word 'term' is used to refer to any word or group of words that have a single meaning.

D. The meaning of a term may be spoken of in two senses: *intentional* and *extensional* meaning.
  1. The *denotation* of a term is its *extensional* meaning and refers to the specific individuals to which the term may be applied, for example, 'dog'—Rover, Fido, Lassie.
  2. The *connotation* of a term is its *intensional* meaning and is the totality of those characteristics which anything must possess in order that the term correctly applies to it. For example, the connotation of the term "automobile" is "self-propelled vehicle that is used to carry passengers."

E. Related to connotative and denotative meaning are the notions, *ambiguity* and *vagueness*.
  1. *Ambiguity* results when a term can be interpreted as having two or more meanings *in a given context*. It must be distinguished from *multiple meaning* in which different senses are intended and no choice need be made between them.
  2. *Vagueness* results when the range of application of a term is undetermined or left indefinite. When a term is vague, we do not always know to what individuals it is properly applied.

F. Definition is concerned with clarifying the meaning of terms by restricting, circumscribing or expanding their meaning. There are different types of definition. Connotative definitions can be—
  1. *Functional* definitions, which state the meaning of a term by reference to its use or function;
  2. *Operational* definitions, which state the meaning of a word as it is applicable to a particular object or occasion;
  3. *Synonymous* definitions, which use a term with the same or similar meaning as the term being defined;
  4. A *stipulative* definition, which is a decision to assign a new meaning to a word, usually in a given context;
  5. A *lexical* definition, which states the traditional or conventional meaning of a term;
  6. A *precising* definition, which specifies the application of a term;
  7. *Theoretical* definitions, which state a formal or technical meaning of a word used in a given special field;
  8. *Essential Connotative* definitions, which attempt to state the essential characteristics, qualities, or properties that characterizes a term. A traditional method for achieving such essential definitions is by stating *genus* and *species*.

G. *Denotative* definitions specify the things to which the term applies. Types of denotative definition are—
  1. *Enumerative* definition, which lists *all* the individuals to which the term applies;
  2. *Denotative definition by example*, which cites examples of the individuals to which the term applies;
  3. *Ostensive or Demonstrative definition*, which points or indicates examples of things to which the term applies;

H. The rules for framing good definitions are—
1. The definition should state the essential characteristics of the term being defined;
2. A definition should carefully set out the limits of applicability and be not too narrow or too broad;
3. A definition should not contain the term to be defined or any term synonymous with it;
4. A definition should be stated in clear, precise, nonfigurative language;
5. A definition should be affirmative if possible;
6. A definition should be stated in as neutral terms as possible.

4

THE INFORMAL FALLACIES

We have dealt with the various uses of language and the ways in which language can be used to express and convey our thoughts and also how it can mislead us and others. We turn now to argumentation as it is encountered in everyday speech—newspapers, magazines, TV programs, addresses, lectures, sermons, bull sessions, family arguments —"the lot" as the British say. We shall be concerned in this chapter with what are traditionally called "informal fallacies."

A *fallacy* is an argument that provides inadequate support for its conclusion. A fallacious argument is one in which the premises, even if true, would never entail nor justify the conclusion that is drawn. Parallel to our distinction between two types of arguments, namely deductive and inductive, there are two kinds of fallacies: *formal* and *informal* (nonformal). A *formal fallacy* is an invalid form of deductive argument. It violates one or more of the rules of deductive reasoning (see chapter 1, section 1.9). For example, consider this argument.

All *A* are *B*.
X is a *B*.
∴ *X* is an *A*.

An invalid form, it will be recalled, is one in which it is possible to have true premises and a false conclusion. Thus, the above argument can be shown to be invalid by finding an interpretation of it that has true premises and a false conclusion, for example:

All whales are mammals.
Mrs. Jones is a mammal.
_____
∴ Mrs. Jones is a whale.

In formal fallacies, the operating criterion is *validity*. We shall explain formal fallacies in detail in chapter 5 and 6, and 7 and 8, which are concerned with the form of deductive argumentation.

The notion of a fallacy is broader than the notion of validity. Thus, an argument can be valid and still be fallacious. This is the case because, as we learned earlier, to call an argument *valid* is merely to say that it has a certain form or structure such that, if the premises are true, the conclusion necessarily could not be false. Invalidity is sufficient to make arguments fallacious, but arguments can be fallacious in other than this formal way.

An argument is fallacious when the premises fail to establish, prove, its conclusion. Of course, invalid arguments fail to do this, but valid arguments also can fail to prove the conclusion drawn. Fallacious valid arguments can occur in two types of circumstances. The first is when the argument fails to meet the requirement of consistency, namely, that it should not be impossible for all the premises to be all true. The fallacy of inconsistency occurs when one argues from premises that are contradictory. Two statements that are contradictory have opposite truth-values. If one is true, the other is false and vice versa. The statements, "John is fat" and "John is not fat," are contradictory. Thus, if the two premises are contradictories, one of them must be false. If one of them must, by logical necessity, be false, then the argument fails to be consistent. In such cases it is impossible for all the premises to be true.

Arguments with contradictory premises are fallacious because any critical thinker would consider inconsistent, contradictory premises rather doubtful evidence for a conclusion. However, arguments with contradictory premises may be *formally valid*. They are valid because they fulfill the condition of validity, namely, that it should be impossible for an argument to have true premises and a false conclusion. Clearly, it is impossible for an argument whose premises are inconsistent to have all true premises and a false conclusion, because it is impossible for this kind of argument to have all true premises. Thus, the property of being fallacious is broader in scope than the characteristic of validity. So we repeat, *a valid argument can be fallacious*.

The other circumstance in which the valid argument can be fallacious is the case of *begging the question,* which will be discussed shortly. In cases of begging the question the truth of the conclusion is already assumed in the premises. This is the case because the premises express the conclusion in some usually obvious way. If the conclusion is already given in the premises, we cannot properly speak of the premises proving or establishing the conclusion. Arguments that beg the question, then, are fallacious. They are also, however, valid, because they meet the requirement that it should be impossible to have true premises and a false conclusion. They meet this requirement because they assume the truth of the conclusion in the premises.

The fallacy of inconsistency and two forms of the fallacies of begging the question will be discussed in more detail shortly. The point to be made here is that logical validity is formal and that it does not guarantee that an argument is not fallacious. Furthermore, an argument may be fallacious in more than one way. Hence for an argument to escape being fallacious it must meet three requirements: (1) It must be consistent; (2) It must not beg the question; and (3) It must be valid, that is, if the premises are true, the conclusion must be true.

Informal fallacies are fallacies, then, that necessarily involve considerations other than validity. They are the fallacies or errors in reasoning committed constantly in everyday discourse. In dealing with these, we shall not be dealing with deductive arguments as such. Further, we shall also go beyond the scope of inductive argumentation in its proper sense, though some inductive fallacies will be considered.

We can summarize the three points to keep in mind concerning informal fallacies as follows. First, as indicated earlier, we are not concerned in logic with the truth or falsity of the assertions making up arguments—whether, *in fact*, all children are selfish, all politicians are rotten. Rather, we are concerned with the correctness of the arguments leading to conclusions. Logic asks the question: Do the premises warrant or entail the conclusion? Second, we are concerned with incorrect argument and reserve the term "fallacy" for arguments that violate some canon of reason. A fallacy is an argument in which the premises fail to support its conclusion. Third, fallacies in arguments may be deliberate, or they may be inadvertent and accidental. For example, a person may be quite well aware of the fact that she is committing a fallacy, but nonetheless deliberately do so in order to win an argument. This occurs constantly (and, alas, effectively) as in a law court, a political debate, or in popular advertising. We shall supply ample illustrations of these occurences in the exercises and tapes. In all these cases, persuasion is the over-riding criterion, and not logical argument. On the other hand, fallacies may be due to our own confusion, in that we think we are arguing validly, when as a matter of fact on examination we find that our argument violates one or more rules of valid reasoning.

If anyone doubts the practicality of logic in everyday life, all that is required to see its usefulness is to deal with the kind of errors in reasoning we study in this chapter. Incidentally, although each of these fallacies has a technical name, and although it is helpful to learn to identify them by name, it is much more valuable to be able to state *why* a given argument is fallacious than it is to give it the proper label.

The informal fallacies do not lend themselves to any neat classification. Logicians have come up with various suggestions. Generally, however, they can be classed as fallacies of relevance, fallacies of neglected aspect, fallacies of ambiguity, or misuse of language. *Fallacies of irrelevance* deal primarily with specific ways in which the premises of an argument may be irrelevant to the conclusion. *Fallacies of neglected aspect* are concerned with ways in which premise fail to give or neglect all of the evidence or grounds for the conclusion. Both of these general type of fallacies historically have been called *material fallacies* because each concerns the relevance or adequacy of the material (facts or reasons) mentioned in the premises. *Linguistic fallacies*, on the other hand, are concerned with bad arguments that result from the incorrect or improper use of language. We shall present the fallacy of inconsistency and the fallacy of begging the question, including its interrogative form, *complex question*, as a separate class of fallacies, namely, *valid but fallacious*. In discussing the fallacies, we shall try to point out both what makes them *invalid* and what makes them *seem* valid. No attempt will be made to cover all the informal fallacies, only the most common ones.

4.2   THE FALLACIES OF INCONSISTENCY AND BEGGING THE QUESTION

We begin with a type of fallacy that is strictly logical, and although it is less dramatic and entertaining than others, it is of crucial importance in thinking clearly.

The fallacy of inconsistency   The fallacy of inconsistency occurs when one argues from contradictory premises, from premises that necessarily could not all be true. Contradictory statements must have opposite truth values and thus, if premises are contradictory, one of them must be false. To base a conclusion on contradictory premises is, of course, to argue fallaciously, because such premises cannot prove the conclusion. Contradictory premises make two contradictory assertions; both cannot be true. For example, we do not at the same time argue that the earth is rotating in orbit and that it is not rotating in orbit. Nor does anyone usually argue that "Horace is fat;" "Horace is not fat;" therefore, "Horace needs to go on a diet."

Inconsistency, however, is usually far more subtle; we often unwittingly contradict ourselves. Suppose I say "Jane, like other people, is a unique person." This is a self-contradictory statement because 'unique' means 'only one of a kind.' Thus the sentence is saying 'Jane is like other people' and 'Jane is not like other people.'

Inconsistent arguments are likewise not always easy to detect because usually they have underlying and unexamined assumptions that prove to be inconsistent. For example, the candidate who promises the voters at the same time to reduce taxes and to improve schools, pave highways, build new parks, provide old-age pensions, inaugurate a program to relieve unemployment, and build new hospitals will more than likely end up committing the fallacy of inconsistency. This is so because while promising to reduce taxes the politician would find that in order to keep other promises he or she would either have to raise taxes or, at a minimum, not reduce taxes. Likewise, the person who takes as his campaign slogan the statement that 'I shall treat all citizens alike' and then also argues for 'an increased pension for veterans' is engaged in arguing inconsistently. This is so because to say 'all citizens will be treated alike' and 'some will receive special treatment and so will not be treated equally' is to contradict oneself. To guard against contradictory assumptions, promises should be thought out in advance to see if all of what is promised is consistent.

A classic example of inconsistency is pointed out by William James in the following passage:

> Our determinism leads us to call our judgments of regret wrong because they are pessimistic in implying that what is impossible ought to be. But, then how about the judgments of regret themselves? If they are wrong, other judgments, judgments of approval presumably, ought to be in their place. But as they are necessitated, nothing else *can* be in their place; and the universe is just what it was before—namely, a place in which what ought to be appears impossible.[1]

Before analyzing this argument, we need to know that *determinism* is the thesis that every event in the world is totally conditioned by its cause or sequence of causes. This means that every human act is explained by and is a result of one's total past up to the time of one's act. In still other words, my choice could not have been otherwise than what it is, given the summary of events, beliefs, character, and so on, present at the time of any act. However, if my act was completely determined, then I am not really responsible for it. I should have no regrets because I could not have done otherwise. Judgments of regret are wrong because they imply that the act could have been otherwise, and this is impossible if determinism is true. Thus, James' argument against determinism can be stated as follows:

If determinism is true, judgments of regret are wrong.
Determinism is true.

∴ Judgments of regret are wrong.

If judgments of regret are wrong, then they should be replaced by judgments of approval.
Judgments of regret are wrong.

∴ Judgments of regret should be replaced by judgments of approval.

If determinism is true, judgments of regret are necessitated [could not be otherwise].
Determinism is true.

∴ Judgments of regret are necessitated.

---

[1] William James, "The Dilemma of Determinism," from *The Will to Believe and Other Essays in Popular Philosophy* (New York: Longmans, Green, 1897), p. 183.

If judgments of regret are necessitated, then they cannot be replaced by judgments of approval.
Judgments of regret are necessitated.
_____
∴ judgments of regret cannot be replaced by judgments of approval.

If judgments of regret are wrong, then they should be replaced by judgments of approval.
Judgments of regret cannot be replaced by judgments of approval.
_____
∴ judgments of regret are not wrong.

Thus, James believes he has shown that if we accept determinism as true we end up accepting two sets of contradictions.

(1) Judgments of regret are wrong.
Judgments of regret are not wrong.

(2) Judgments of regret should be replaced by judgments of approval.
Judgments of regret cannot be replaced by judgments of approval.

The fallacy of inconsistency is also committed when we say one thing at a particular time and place and something quite different at another time and place *without either explaining the change or retracting the former statement.* We sometimes speak of this as 'talking out of both sides of one's mouth.' Suppose a person at one time and place says that she favors a comprehensive national health insurance plan and then, on another occasion, that a national health insurance plan is a threat to free, and 'good' medical service. If that person does not explain—if she can—why she has changed her mind on the issue of national health insurance, she has committed *the fallacy of inconsistency.*

Politicians are notorious for committing the fallacy of inconsistency. For example, while campaigning for Republican candidates in 1966, Richard Nixon stated:

He [President Johnson] owes it to the people to come clean and tell them exactly what the plans [about the Vietnam War] are; the people should be told now, and not after the elections.[2]

However, on March 10, 1968, now a candidate for President of the United States, Mr. Nixon stated:

No one with this responsibility who is seeking office should give away any of his bargaining position in advance. . . . Under no circumstances should any man say what he would do next January.[3]

_____
[2] William G. Effros, *Quotations: Vietnam 1945–1970* (New York: Random House, 1970).
[3] Ibid.

One cannot be consistently for and against openness *without explaining the change in position* or *retracting one of the statements.*

Politicians usually commit the fallacy of inconsistency because they are trying to represent different constituencies with different viewpoints. Thus, if one wishes to speak to the poor, the older, and the retired, one might feel the need to favor a compulsory national health plan. But if one is speaking to the American Medical Association, one would not find it expedient to support such legislation. The point, however, is that citizens can demand to know exactly where their representatives stand, and an inconsistent position is no stand at all.

In dealing with any pronouncements, platforms, proposals, then, it behooves every rational person to ask if the pronouncements are *consistent.* Have they said two contradictory things at the same time and/or at different times without explaining the contradiction as a change of mind and without evidence to support the change? Further, different spokesmen for a single institution may make contradictory and inconsistent statements. Suppose, for example, the advertising for a major oil company says that the company is, in all of its projects, primarily in favor of ecology and good use of the land. It would be inconsistent of the company, then, to have its president say in the stock holders report that ecology cannot be a major concern of the company because profit has a higher priority.

Inconsistency occurs, then, when contradictory statements are made by (a) a person or group at the same time, (b) by one (group) at different times, and (c) by different spokesmen of an institution or position. The fallacy of inconsistency is not committed when a person either retracts one of the contradictory statements or explains with supporting evidence that he (she) has changed his (her) mind.

Tape Exercise

[These questions are discussed on Tape 4, band 1, for chapter 4.]

A. It is said of St. Augustine—unfairly and inaccurately, one hopes —that he was heard to pray "Oh Lord, deliver me from evil—tomorrow morning." Assuming his was not an attempt at humor, wherein does the inconsistency lie?

B. In the Proceedings of the Aristotelian Society of England, the statement of the proverbial Irishman is quoted: "Mike and Ike are very much alike—especially Mike." What is the inconsistency?

C. Some people consider "What is the sound of one hand clapping?" very profound What is the inconsistency?

Petitio principii (begging the question)   The fallacy of begging the question is one in which the conclusion is assumed or stated in another form in the premises. Or, the conclusion repeats in some form its first premise. It is for this reason that the fallacy of begging the question can also be called *circular argument.* As indicated earlier, such arguments are formally valid, but fallacious. The label "begging the question" comes from the Greek notion of *disputa-tion* in which a person, setting out to argue a case, may ask to be granted (beg) certain premises on which to build. The fallacy—much more serious—consists in asking to be granted *the question at issue*, which is precisely what one is required to prove. This fallacy has three basic patterns.

First, it may be a simple restatement of the premise in the conclusion.

There are good reasons for these requirements, therefore, these require-ments are justified.

This argument really says, "These requirements are justified because these requirements are justified." Or, schematically,

$$\frac{P \text{ is true.}}{\therefore P \text{ is true.}}$$

A more complex form of this occurs when the conclusion and the initial assumption are separated by another statement.

If men are to survive, they must be fit—indeed, only the fittest survive. And we can verify this by simply looking around and seeing who has survived. Obviously, they have survived because they are fit.

This argument schematically looks like this:

Because	P is true	(men survive)
	Q is true	(they are fit)
Because	Q is true	(they are fit)
	P is true	(men survive)

A third form of the fallacy of begging the question is one in which a number of premises occur in the argument,but the conclusion repeats the first premise. It generally takes the following form, though the length of the chain of arguments can vary:

P is true because Q is true.
And Q is true because R is true.
And R is true because P is true.

An example of this type of circular argument is:

What do we mean by democracy? Democracy is the preservation of human rights. What do we mean by rights? By rights we mean those privileges God grants to all of us, man's inherent privileges. Privileges such as liberty. By liberty we mean religious and political freedom such as we enjoy under democracy.

This argument begins and ends with democracy.

Question-begging arguments are, in one sense, correct arguments. They are valid because they assume the conclusion in the premise. They give a ground(s) for affirming *P*, *P* itself. What goes wrong with these arguments is this: such arguments do *not* really give reasons for believing the conclusion, because *P* in and of itself does not give us grounds for saying *P* is true.

Tape Exercises

Consider each of the following: Show why they are examples of the fallacy of begging the question. [Check your answers with Tape 4, band 1.]

1. Opium has sleep-giving power because the drug possesses dormative virtue.
2. To allow every man unbounded freedom of speech must always be on the whole advantageous to the state: for it is highly conducive to the interests of the community that each individual should enjoy a liberty perfectly unlimited of expressing his sentiments.

Complex question   In the fallacy of a complex question, we are dealing with question-begging in an interrogative form. A complex question is one in which two questions are really involved and in which an answer is already presumed. For example, "When are you going to stop beating your wife?" really comprises two questions: "Do you beat your wife?" and "When are you going to stop beating your wife?" This complex question presumes that you have already answered yes to the first. The fallacy of complex question, however, only occurs when a complex question is used in an argument in such a way that it commits us to a certain presupposition and uses that committal in supporting the conclusion. In other words, a question is posed in such a way that *any* answer must take for granted the conclusion that ought to be proved. Consider the following example.

Why has the union not sought legal help rather than playing into the hands of the administration? It is clear that joining the union is not going to help a faculty member.

In this argument we find two questions: "Why has the union not sought legal help?" and "Why has it played into the hands of the administration?" The appropriate response demanded by the first question is probably "I don't know." But, the second question commits us to the presupposition that the union *has* played into the administration's hands, and this commitment, in turn, supports the conclusion.

Tape Exercises

Consider the following examples of complex questions. [The examples are discussed on Tape 4, band 1.]

1. An excellent example of a complex question is the question: the prosecuting attorney asks the defendant "Why did you wipe the fingerprints from the gun?" What are the two questions the attorney really asked?

2. What would you say to your employer if he or she asked you "When are you going to stop stealing things from the company?"

Exercises for § 4.2

A. Analyze the following, pointing out any contradictory assumptions or implications that might be involved.

1. A speaker who advocates a society almost completely planned and administered by a central government says: "Let the government manage your affairs so that you may have more time to enjoy liberty and freedom to do as you wish."

2. When a federal judge in Texas instructed a jury to return a verdict of innocent in a horse theft case, the jury foreman dutifully announced: "We find the gentleman that stole the horse not guilty, Your Honor."

3. Young lady defending her fiancee, "Yes, he's prejudiced, but in an unbiased sort of way."

4. Candidate for office: I agree with you, sir, strict regulation of competition is needed between these oil companies. Then there will truly be free enterprise.

5. Governor to press: I have stood all along for academic freedom and free interchange of ideas in the educational community. I merely think professors should get back to basic subjects and quit teaching irrelevant and dangerous courses.

6. Consider two well-worn problems in theology. (a) God is omniscient, he knows from all eternity everything that happens. Man, however, is free and responsible, so he chooses to perform good or evil acts. (b) God is both all good and all powerful. Evil, however, is an indisputable fact of life. How can both of these judgments be held at the same time?

B. For each of the following arguments identify whether they commit the fallacy of begging the question or the fallacy of the complex question.

1. Newsman to coach before the game, "By what score will your team lose?"

2. Centralization of government is bad because it centers power on a few individuals. It is bad to center power on a few individuals because it gives them too much control over their fellows. It is bad when a few individuals can control their fellows, for then centralization of government is inevitable.

3. Did you embezzle the funds to pay your debts?

4. This argument is fallacious. I know it is fallacious because it is not valid. It is not valid because it contains a fallacy.

5. A good scholar is one who publishes many articles in the professional journals. For the articles in the professional journals are what good scholarship consists of.

6. You do believe that murdering a unborn child is a bad thing, don't you Mrs. Jones?

7. This is the right thing to do. It is the right thing to do because it is morally obligatory. And anything morally obligatory is the right thing to do.

8. When did you decide that witchcraft was nonsense?

9. The best students are those who come to college well equipped. Being well equipped enables one to survive four years of college. Those who survive four years of college are well equipped.

10. Is it really necessary to examine the issue farther?

4.3 FALLACIES OF IRRELEVANCE

The meaning of the term 'relevance' applies to arguments in which the premises are irrelevant in some way to the conclusion that they claim is true. More cautiously stated, the premises either are not *sufficiently* relevant or are not relevant *in the appropriate way* to the conclusion. The irrelevance is logical because the argument is incorrect. The premises do not support the conclusion, though there is a pretense that a successful and valid argument has been presented. To repeat, what is irrelevant is the premises in relationship to the conclusion. Fallacies of irrelevance may be identified as follows.

Appeal to force (argumentum ad baculum)   Appeal to force is the kind of argument that threatens those who do not accept the conclusion. The person who blackmails illustrates this fallacy perfectly. In the movie *The Godfather*, on two different occasions the head of the family says, "We'll make him an offer he can't refuse." When his colleague says, "But how can he possibly accept this kind of offer; it's no good?" the reply is given, "Never mind, he will understand, and he will accept"—meaning that he will be forced to accept because he will have no alternative. The appeal to force is not always as brutal as that of the Mafia. It may be employed in terms of threats, of retaliations, of punishment, of boycott. Unfortunately, many parents use this kind of argument in getting their children to obey or to get them to do what they want, as when they say, "Willie, you'd better be a good boy, or Santa Claus won't bring you your sled for Christmas." The reason for being good ought not to be based on threat or reward. The appeal to force is an appeal to consequences and takes the following form: *Accept the conclusion; otherwise unfortunate consequences will result.*

Some would question whether the fallacy of appeal to force is strictly a fallacy. They do so on the grounds that fear is not likely to lead us to any conclusions. That is, though we might *say* that the conclusion was true, we would not *believe* or *conclude* it was true. In other words, fallacies of appeal to force are not fallacies at all because we are not really taken in by the 'argument,' but only appear to be so duped because we are afraid. Rather than involve ourselves in the controversy over whether the appeal to force is or is not a logical fallacy, it is important to realize that such an appeal is an often employed technique of persuasion. The main point with regard to this fallacy is to recognize it for what it is. We should always ask exactly what are the reasons offered for the conclusion? *Why* are we asked to take a certain action? Even the child has the right to ask for a good reason why he should put his toys away.

Further, a distinction must be made between pointing out the dire consequences that will follow from a particular action on the one hand, and threatening to use force if that action is taken, on the other hand. Thus, we do not commit the fallacy if we point out that very undesirable consequences will follow the passing of a certain congressional or Senate bill. We do commit this fallacy if we go on to say, "and if you don't agree to vote against it, I and my colleagues will oppose any bills you present. To cite another example, a supporter of the cause of the blacks may say, "If you don't improve the lot of the blacks and meet their demands, there will be riots," and a spokesman for whites may say, "If you surrender to black extremists' demands, there will be a white backlash." These statements warn and predict the results of certain actions, and they certainly are relevant to the evaluation of these courses of action. However, appeal to dire consequences (and thus indirectly appeal to fear) should not cloud our reason and lead us to neglect relevant questions and considerations. We would want to know both the pros and cons for improving the lot of blacks regardless of a possible white backlash. A good example of appeal to fear that tended to keep people from asking for other relevant factors was used against Barry Goldwater in his 1964 presidential campaign. A brief film of a child playing followed by film of the explosion of an atomic bomb raised the fear of Goldwater as a militarist. Many did not go on to ask precisely what Goldwater stood for and whether atomic war was a predictable consequence of Goldwater's views.

The psychological attitude of the person or group appealing to force or to the threat of force almost always reveals that the arguers recognize that the evidence, or the reasons offered for their conclusion is weak if not worthless. Whenever, even for a good cause, one argues, "Speak quietly but carry a big stick," he or she is admitting that the final appeal will be to force. This has no greater logical value when uttered by the president of a great nation than when voiced by the godfather of a mob.

The appeal to pity (argumentum ad misericordiam)   Another argument that appeals to consequences is the appeal to pity. Here the premises offer the avoidance of unpleasant consequences as a reason for accepting the conclusion. This argument appeals to pity or to sympathy rather than to evidence or to reasons. In a famous trial, Clarence Darrow, arguing in defense of Thomas I. Kidd who was charged with criminal conspiracy, appealed to the sympathies of the jury by dwelling on the long hours of the working miner, the lack of unions, the fact that Kidd was working hard for better conditions for miners, and the like. All of this, of course, was irrelevant to the question, What evidence is there to support or refute the charge of conspiracy? The form of the appeal to pity argument is "For mercy's sake, accept this conclusion." Thus, we might argue as follows:

Susan's parents have sacrificed to send her to college.
If Susan receives a low grade, she will not graduate.

.∴. Susan should get a C in English.

What is relevant to a grade in a course is the performance of the person and not his or her economic or other circumstances. The appeal to pity usually involves the use of emotive words, but they are not essential. A situation can be manipulated to play on sympathy without words. All of us have seen appeals for aid effectively carried out by a single photograph of a starving child or by a beggar prominently displaying his or her blind eyes or twisted limbs to the pity of passers-by. Sympathy is, of course, a noble human emotion and should probably motivate many actions, but it should never be allowed to take the place of logical analysis when that is required or to obscure or replace the relevant facts.

Students of philosophy may recall the classic example of Socrates who, on trial for his life, refused to employ the standard practice of his day and appeal to the court on grounds of pity and sympathy, such as his age, his dependent wife and three children. The point is not that he might not have saved his life by doing so; it rather is that he had spent his life teaching people how to search for the truth and to reason clearly and honestly. So doing, he set an example for all ages.

Appeal to the People (argumentum ad populum)   This argument seeks to win support for its conclusion by appealing, in the premises, to popular prejudices, loyalties, hopes, and sympathies. Rather than provide rational support and good evidence for its conclusion, it appeals to such things as superpatriotism, sympathy for the underdog, virtue, motherhood—any and every notion approved by people generally. This type of argument involves a transfer technique: it tries to associate the conclusion it wants accepted with what most people approve, and the conclusion it wants rejected with that which most people disapprove. Highly emotive terms are often used: positive ones like 'our founding fathers,' 'the American flag,' 'our noble heritage,' and 'God'; and negative ones like ' communist,' 'Red,' 'reactionary,' 'revolutionary,' and Franklin D. Roosevelt's famous 'economic royalists'. Similarly, television commercials use sex appeal to sell soap, shampoo, mouthwash, deodorants. Vance Packard, in his book, *The Hidden Persuaders*, wrote: "The women are buying a promise. . . . The cosmetic manufacturers are not selling lanolin, they are selling hope. . . . We no longer buy oranges, we buy vitality. We do not buy an auto, we buy prestige."[4] The appeal-to-the-people argument is widely used by politicians who quote the Bible, Lincoln, and the Constitution and who seek to identify themselves with the audience, whatever its makeup—whether teachers, farmers, plumbers, auto workers, organized labor, the clergy. A common type of argument by appeal-to-the-people is, in fact, the appeal to 'plain folks,' for example:

> I am a farm boy myself. My folks were farmers, and I spent some of the happiest years of my life on our farm in Wisconsin. You can be assured that as a Senator, I shall have your best interests at heart.

The main point is that the premises contain little of relevance in assessing the qualifications of the person running for Senator to represent all the people. The appeal is to emotions, rather than reason; the relevant objective evidence, so essential to sound thinking, is ignored.

Appeal to the people thus involves the technique of 'attitude fitting'. Candidates for public office tend to color their proposals so that they vary directly as attitudes vary from region to region and group to group. When speaking in coastal regions, a candidate may stress such things as state's rights or ownership of tidelands. While in areas heavily populated by organized labor he or she might talk about collective bargaining and state regulation of industry. Because of its appeal to our likes and dislikes, the argumentum ad populum is especially hard to guard against. The best defense is to be more suspicious of ideas and attitudes that are pleasing and match our own—to ask if they are sincerely expressed or merely 'fitted' to us for effect.

Another common form of the appeal-to-the-people argument is known as the *bandwagon*. In this kind of argument, we are asked to accept a conclusion because the majority accepts that conclusion—"Millions of Americans are switching to Hotsuns, why don't you?" Mere numbers constitute a kind of pseudoauthority. However, even unanimity is far from infallible. The majority can be wrong, and because a large number of people accept a conclusion is not necessarily a cogent reason (or any reason at all) for us to accept a conclusion. The majority of people at one time thought the earth was flat and that the earth was at the center of the solar system. John Stuart Mill, in a classic essay on freedom, warned against the subtle tyranny of the majority. To be free is to make one's own judgments.

Subtle uses of appeal-to-the-people occur with deplorable frequency in the political realm. Rightwing groups argue a political position by associating themselves with an emotion-laden symbol of patriotism, the American flag. Another example of appeal-to-the-people arguments is the use of a phrase such as "Everybody knows that high tariff walls are economically sound." In the heat of the Vietnam war debate, a group of opponents of the war called themselves the 'peace movement'. This label itself did two things. First, it implied that all of the opposition was against peace. Second, it played on the fact that everyone is for peace. But peace is an end that can be achieved by many different means.

---

[4] Vance Packard, *The Hidden Persuaders* (New York: Pocket Books, 1963), p. 60.

Tape Exercises

Consider the following. Indicate why they commit the fallacies of appeal to force, appeal to pity or appeal to people. [Check your answers with Tape 4, band 1.]

1. In a recent series of primaries in which candidates for the Presidency of the United States were seeking the nomination, endless news reports and statements by candidates were made about how well they had done in certain states and how they would perform in forthcoming elections. Granted, "everybody applauds a winner," and likes to identify with a winner. But what was this worth logically?

2. You ought to vote for representation by a union in all dealings with the plant managers because if you don't we shall see to it that you lose your job.

3. You should give Miss Brown as much benefit of the doubt as you can in your grading. After all, she had a very difficult time in her youth, coming from a poor family and losing her parents at a young age.

4. If you elect me to this office, I promise to be faithful to the principles on which George Washington founded this great Republic and to the causes for which our sons fought so nobly in battle.

5. A successful man does not act in an ordinary way. Nor does he dress in an ordinary fashion. He wears a suit that reflects his innovative thinking and sound judgment. Thus, when you buy, buy from the corporate collection for the innovative, the influential and the individual.

6. Any measure that might lead to war should not be taken since no mother wishes her son to be killed fighting in a foreign land.

7. If you aren't worth the best, who is? Buy Roguefort the great eating cheese—the connoisseur's choice.

Argument against the man (argumentum ad hominem)   Argument against the man is directed not to the point at issue but to the person. It claims to attack a person's *assertion*, but in fact it attacks the *person*. It can take three basic forms. The first two forms are the most common: (a) *abuse*; (b) *circumstantial*; and (c) *'you're another'—tu quoque*.

Some glaring examples of the abusive form of the argument are the following: "We cannot believe the testimony of this witness, after all, he is an ex-con." "One cannot accept Doctor Smith's view on Medicare, for he is a known woman hater." "How can the proposals of that group be taken seriously? They're a bunch of hippies." The *abusive* form of the argument against the man takes the following logical form:

X says P
X is bad
_____

$\therefore P$ (what he or she says) is false.

Thus: who can believe anything Professor Smith teaches? He is a known communist.

The second form of the argument against the man discredits a person's claims by arguing that because of special circumstances he or she is prejudiced or biased. Consider the following: "In reply to the gentleman's claim that his program is designed to help the poor, I need only point out that he himself counts the most influential men on Wall Street as his friends, that he has never been hungry in his life, that only recently he inherited six million dollars, and that his children attend private schools in England." Here a Senator is accused of being insincere and prejudiced against the poor because of his own wealthy circumstances.

A more simple example is: "Getty's argument for oil depletion can be immediately dismissed in light of the fact that he is an oil billionaire." The *circumstantial argument* thus takes the following form:

> X says P.
> X is, because of special circumstances, prejudiced.
> _____
> $\therefore P$ (what X says) is false.

A more complicated example of this form is the following:

> The Administration appointed and the Senate approved the nomination of Jane Brown to the Civil Rights Commission. The Civil Rights Commission exercises a quasijudicial function. It decides whether something is wrong and makes recommendations to the Justice Department, which then prosecutes. It also makes recommendations for 'civil rights' laws. Brown has long been an active member and one of the chief protagonists of the Southern Civil Rights Association, and the appointment of Brown is the same thing as making the SCRA an arm of the Justice Department and of making a judge out of a party to a suit. There can be no unbiased findings, and no true justice under such an arrangement.

The argument is that because Brown is an active member and chief protagonist of the SCRA, therefore her findings will be biased and her decisions unjust. Her *special circumstances* will make her biased. Now, her membership in SCRA might be a reason to be more skeptical of her findings and decisions, but it is not a reason to conclude she will be biased. She might, in fact, be more cautious and more just precisely because of her sensitivity to justice and injustice.

Another way to look at the circumstantial argument against the person is in terms of what is sometimes considered a separate fallacy—the fallacy of *Damning the Origin,* or *Source.* Here the arguer seeks to reject an opinion or argument by pointing to its undesirable source. For example, a local paper printed the following response to an article in the letter column of the paper, "This town should resist the assault on its boundaries by lobbyists for the real estate developers who are trying to line their own pockets and are interested only in their own economic advantage." Now, it is true that we should take into account the reliability of a person before adopting his or her view or believing without warrant something that person tells us. It is also true that if a plan or argument is backed by a source that stands to gain economically, we should beware of possible bias on the issue. However, anticipating bias does not justify dismissal of a proposal or argument without inquiry into its merits. An argument should always be heard and judged valid or invalid, good or bad and not dismissed on the grounds of its source. Where the argument originates is irrelevant to the questions, "Does the conclusion follow from the premises?" "Are the statements true and worth merit?" In other words, the fallacy of damning the source really is another form of the circumstantial argument against the person, for it attacks the arguer and not the argument.

A third form of the argument against the man is called *tu quoque* or *"You're another."* This fallacy is committed when one tries to reply to a charge made by an opponent by making the same or a similar charge against the opponent. The underlying assumption of the *tu quoque* argument is that one who complains of wrong-doing should have clean hands. The arguer seeks to turn attention from charges that are difficult to answer by showing that the accuser is guilty of misconduct. This device can be very effective because it often deflects attention from the original grievance and creates sympathy for the accused party. Examples of the *tu quoque* argument are:

> You ask why do we treat our native population this way? I reply, "Who was it that killed most of the American Indians?"

> I have been accused of being a supporter of Big Oil. In reply, let me point out that most of the money for my opponent's campaign came from Ajax Oil.

The *tu quoque* clearly is one more form of *ad hominem* argument. In *tu quoque* A argues that *what* B *says is false* (the charge against A) *because* B *is guilty of the same or similar things.* The argument is redirected against the person. Further, even when countercharges may be deserved, all that is demonstrated by a *tu quoque* argument is that *neither* side is right. In fact, both are wrong. What is demanded by reason is not condoning or excusing of wrongs, but clarification and substantiation of allegations. To answer an allegation of wrong-doing by citing the accuser's misdemeanors is only to confuse issues.

Arguments that avoid the real issue by attacking persons commit the fallacy of *ad hominem.* However, it should not be overlooked that not all arguments criticizing a person are fallacious. Consider the following fictitious argument:

> President Blue, while in office, has accepted immense bribes, imprisoned his political opponents, taken vast sums of money from the U.S. Treasury and put it into foreign banks, and has made plans to declare himself king. Therefore, we should impeach him.

The premises do attack the President's character, but if they are true, they are both relevant to the conclusion and constitute good grounds for accepting the

conclusion. Further, personal considerations are relevant for judging the reliability of a person, specifically, his or her willingness to tell the truth. Thus, we
should keep in mind the following statement by British logician Horace W. B.
Joseph:

> A barrister [lawyer] who meets the testimony of a hostile witness by proving that
> the witness is a notorious thief, though he does less well than if he could disprove
> his evidence directly, may reasonably be considered to have shaken it, for a man's
> character bears on his credibility. And sometimes we may be content to prove
> against those who attack us, not that our conduct is right, but that it accords with
> the principles they profess or act upon.[5]

Appeal to authority (argumentum ad verecundiam)   In our age of increasing specialization and ever-expanding knowledge, all of us must rely at different times and places on authorities in fields of technical information. In
argument and in everyday matters, it is proper and inevitable we make
reference to authorities and to specialists. However, source material derived
from authorities is not always used correctly and fairly. An argument that
appeals to authority says that a view is correct because of the authority that
supports it. It takes the form "X says P, X is an authority, therefore P is true."
The authority may be a person, a book, an institution—whatever is appealed to
as unquestionably true. Such an argument is fallacious especially when it
misuses the source material or cites an authority who is not properly an
authority. To be a valid appeal to authority, the authoriative source must be
qualified as an expert in the field in which he or she is cited. The authority
should be clearly identified so that the qualification can be examined. The
authority should have professional standing, that is, be judged qualified by
fellow experts, and he or she should be a current authority. The growth of
knowledge is so rapid today that even a year can render an opinion obsolete.

An argument that appeals to authority can be fallacious for the following
reasons.

(1) The so-called authority frequently has only the appeal of prestige or
popularity, but no special competence in any field of learning. This is characteristic of testimonials of movie stars, of athletes and the like. Marsha
Superstar calls Milk-Plus shampoo the best. What evidence is there that she
knows more about shampoo than physicians or chemists?

(2) An authority may be quoted in an area outside his or her field of
competence. This constitutes a misuse of so-called expertise. To quote Einstein
on the existence of God is to cite a specialist in the area of physics on an issue in
religion about which he may know very little.

(3) The authority may be misquoted or misinterpreted. This does not in itself
constitute a logical fallacy, but is a case of an argument with a false premise. For
example, Albert Einstein is sometimes quoted to support the theory that there
is no such thing as right or wrong, except as it is relative to a particular culture.

---

[5] *An Introduction to Logic*, 2nd rev. ed. (Oxford: Claredon, 1916) p. 591.

It is claimed that Einstein proved everything is relative. In fact, Einstein expounded an important *physical* theory of relativity, but his theory had nothing whatever to say about cultural or ethical standards. The use of Einstein as an authority in the above instance is a case of misinterpretation of the statements of an authority, for he was writing in another field and is misinterpreted even in the field in which he did write.

(4) Authorities who are equally competent frequently disagree. The only sensible conclusion to draw is that if there is a disagreement between authorities we should ask *why* we should accept *any* of them. Thus we are driven back to the quest for objective evidence on which any authority or specialist is supposed to base his or her judgment.

The main point here is that what we want in an argument are the reasons or evidence for the conclusion. Even if we are asking for testimony from a specialist we expect to be given evidence that is relevant to the question, and evidence clear enough to convince us of the conclusion that is drawn. Anyone who reasons clearly wants to know the grounds of authority and what it is that warrants the conclusion. No truly rational person accepts an argument that says "This is so because we say it is so, and that's the end of the matter."

The fallacy of argument by appeal to authority, then, takes the following form:

> A asserts P
> A is an authority (where A is not an authority or where statements of type P
>   lie outside A's area of competence)
> _____
> ∴ P is true.

Just because A asserts P, it does not follow that P is true. However, if A is a reliable specialist concerning P, then the fact that A asserts P is good grounds for concluding that P is true. In other words, the following is a correct argument pattern:

> A is a reliable authority on facts of type T.
> A said S, which is of type T.
> _____
> ∴ S is true.

We must determine that A is a reliable expert, noting all the qualifications made above. The specialist is ready to cite evidence and given reasons for his or her judgment, the typical authoritarian is not.

Tape Exercises

If you are inclined to laugh at anyone who says we know how many teeth there are in a horse's mouth and then quotes Aristotle in proof; if you are likely to sneer at anyone who says they know what personal survival after death is like and then quotes the *Koran*, the *Mahabharata*, or the Bible, what are the *grounds*, the *justification* for your laughter or sneer? Are they sound? Consider the following examples. [Further discussion is included in Tape 4, band 2.]

1. Friedrich Nietzche said God is dead, but this need not be taken seriously because Nietzche was a degenerate with syphilis who eventually went insane.
2. How can the Democrats keep a straight face when they mention Watergate? What about those iceboxes and fur coats during the Truman administration?
3. I am going to increase my dosage of vitamin C because the noted physicist Linus Pauling says it not only prevents cold but it prevents cancer.
4. We cannot trust Dr. Technuck's views on the safety of nuclear energy plants. After all, he is employed by Con Edison.

Irrelevant Conclusion (Ignoratio Elenchi)   This occurs whenever an argument appears to justify a particular conclusion, but actually establishes another conclusion than the one argued. The conclusion just does not follow from the premises given because these premises cite irrelevant evidence. A humorous example of this fallacy is cited as the following:

We charge the present administration with having betrayed the American farmer, and we shall make this charge stick. We all know that the farmer is indispensable to our national life. He produces the very food we eat and makes it possible for us to continue our life's work. He provides social and economic stability in the Nation, which is torn by industrial strife, and he provides the inexhaustible human resources which make our large cities possible. To betray the farmer, therefore, is to strike at the very heart of the Nation, and that is what the present administration is doing.

What we need to ask here is what conclusion is drawn, and what reasons are given for drawing it. The conclusion is that the present administration is betraying the farmer and striking at the very heart of our nation. But no reasons have been given for this conclusion. All of the clichés and truisms about the farmers' important work are irrelevant to the conclusion that is drawn, and that is how this fallacy gets its name. The conclusion simply does not follow from these premises. In all arguments, we must ask, "What is the conclusion that is being drawn?" and "On what grounds is it argued?" We shall not likely fall prey to the fallacy of irrelevant conclusion—or any other fallacy—if we keep our critical faculties sharp.

We can easily identify an irrelevant conclusion argument if there is an apparent shift in the *kinds* of things talked about in the premises and those things talked about in the conclusion. Consider the following argument about the Vietnam War.

Because,   (1) There was no stable government in Vietnam.
            (2) Guerilla tactics were difficult to cope with.
            (3) We were risking nuclear war with Red China.

∴ We had no moral right to be in Vietnam.

This argument shifts from talking, in the premises, about the difficulties and risks involved in the war to talking about moral right in the conclusion. A better conclusion for this argument would be:

The Vietnam war was costly and dangerous.

Another example of an irrelevant conclusion is:

The increase in the cost of living is inevitable in an expanding economy.

∴ increase in the cost of living is a good thing for the economy.

This conclusion shifts from inevitability to goodness. What is inevitable is not necessarily good. Other examples of the fallacy of irrelevant conclusion are the prosecuting counsel in a murder case arguing that murder is a horrible crime; an educator arguing that a liberal education is not practical because it does not result in a cash dividend.

'*Red Herring' or 'Pettifogging*'   A fallacy closely related to irrelevant con-clusion is that technique called *red herring* or *pettifogging,* which essentially is to dwell on irrelevancies in order to avoid the main issue. The *red herring* is the false issue that is used to draw attention away from the real issues. This kind of technique is employed often by political figures who wish to avoid answering a charge or taking a clear stand on an issue. Thus, a candidate who was asked to take a stand on the question of increasing taxes for the improvement of schools drew a red herring across the trail by dwelling on the reasons why he was opposed to progressive education. By the time he had finished discussing this issue, the original question about taxes was forgotten.

Adolf Hitler often used the red herring technique in his speeches. A good example is found in a speech he made before the Industry Club in Dusseldorf a year before the Nazi Revolution. A main concern for many of the industrial leaders in the audience was the Nazi resort to violence in order to establish a dictatorship. Hitler began his speech by referring briefly to the question of violence. Then, with the use of several jokes, he diverted the attention of the audience from this issue. Next he drew a red herring across the path by introducing the issue of pacificism, which was an unpopular minority idea. He indicated that the composition of the government coalition was half pacifist.

. . . The other fifty percent have formed a coalition on the basis of pacifism; they reject war on principle; they demand that freedom of conscience should be inviolate; and they declare this to be the highest, the sole good which we possess today.

The attention of the audience was successfully diverted to the issue of pacifism, and Hitler continued his speech without ever taking up the charge of the violent overthrow of democracy. The best defense against diversionary techniques such as the red herring is to concentrate on the main issue and to return to it again and again.

In an excellent discussion of fallacies and of the use and abuse of language, Ronald Munson, in *The Way of Words* pointed out that most of the fallacies in informal logic can be used as clever but illogical techniques for winning an argument.[6] Most of them employ precisely the fallacy we are discussing, red herring. Thus it is easy to make a straw man out of one or more of the premises, to raise trivial objections to a proposal, to appeal to popular prejudices either to support or oppose a motion, to argue against the person rather than "Talk to the point," and the like.

Tape Exercises

If you were involved in a heated argument against capital punishment or against the legalization of abortion, what fallacies in reasoning would you expect to encounter? We'll discuss some of these on Tape 4, band 2.]

Also consider the following. Indicate why either the fallacy of irrelevant conclusion or the fallacy of the red herring is committed. [Check your answers with the tape.]

1. Reporter to Senator: "How do you feel about the right to life issue?" Senator's reply: "I know how I voted on the right to die issue,which may be at the other end of the spectrum but essentially the same thing."

2. Of course socialism is desirable. Why? Because we are well on our way to socialism now. Its complete triumph is inevitable.

3. Student in audience: "Are you going to propose a national health insurance program?" Political candidate: "We now spend on health care far more than any other nation in the world per capita—$50 for every American. My belief is that the net cost above that figure would be minimal."

Argumentum ad ignorantiam   Another fallacy of irrelevance is that known as the fallacy of the argument from ignorance. This is not to be understood as meaning that the person engaged in the argument is ignorant. Rather, it consists in arguing from the *absence* of evidence or of relevant reasons that the conclusion reasonably follows. Evidence that we do not have can hardly be considered a relevant argument. The assumption in this type of argument is that the failure to prove one side establishes the opposite side. An example of this is:

---

[6] *The Way of Words* (Boston: Houghton-Mifflin Co., 1976).

Mental telepathy may be accepted as a fact, because nobody can prove it is impossible.

This clearly is no proof at all. If a person believes that mental telepathy—communication with those at a distance or those who are dead—is a fact, *he or she* must prove it. It is not the responsibility of the opponent to *disprove* it.

The arguments called *ad ignorantiam* fallacies may have two forms:

a. There is no proof (or you have not proved) that P is false.

   ∴ P is true.

b. There is no proof (you have not proved) that P is true.

   ∴ P is false.

Absence of proof is never the same as proof. Only evidence can constitute proof or disproof. The inability to prove that Hitler died in a bunker in Berlin does not prove that he is living. To show that he still lives we need concrete evidence. A vicious use of the argument *ad ignorantiam* took place during the McCarthy era and his famous series of charges of communism leveled against American citizens. For example, one Methodist Bishop, G. Bromley Oxnam, was charged with being a communist. In this case, no evidence was presented to show that Bishop Oxnam was a communist, or even that he advocated the communist methods. The public was left in ignorance, but with the insinuation that he was a communist, and the appeal was made to ignorance of any disproof. The point was that he did not need to prove that he was not a communist. That a certain proposition or theory cannot be demonstrated to be true is not in itself sufficient proof that a contradictory or a contrary proposition or theory is true. The inability to verify a given idea is irrelevant to the truth or falsity of some other idea. Always ask of an argument: "What have you proved?" Never be trapped into concluding: this is so because you cannot disprove it.

It should be noted, however, that there are two presumed forms of the *argumentum ad ignorantiam* that are not fallacious. In a law court, if it is not proved that A is guilty, it *follows* that A is not guilty. But this is not a fallacious argument only because an additional premise is added to the argument, namely, the principle that a person is presumed innocent until proved guilty. Thus, the argument really is:

It has not been proved that A is guilty.
If a person is not proved guilty, then he is assumed innocent.

∴ he is innocent.

Another interesting class of arguments is exemplified by considering the basis of the failure to turn up required evidence *for* a scientific statement. Such an argument, however, also has an added premise, thus:

> It has not been proved that P is true.
> If evidence were available, scientists would have found it.
>
> ∴ P is false.

In this latter case, it should be noted that evidence could turn up later because scientists just may not have had adequate instrumentation, may not have been looking for the correct thing, or may, later, see that their whole problem needed to be recast in a different form. The minor premise falsely appeals to the presumed lack of evidence, but in fact we do not know what, if anything, the evidence proves.

Exercises for § 4.3

Using the following list, identify the fallacy of irrelevance most conspicuously committed in each of the following arguments. The fallacies are:

1. Appeal to force
2. Appeal to pity
3. Appeal to people
4. Argument against the man
   a. abusive
   b. circumstantial
   c. you, too
5. Appeal to authority
6. Irrelevant conclusion
7. Red herring
8. Appeal to ignorance

1. John tried for three hours to prove a theorem in his text, but he could not prove it. He concluded, therefore, that the theorem, as stated in the text, must be wrong.

2. One should not take too seriously John Locke's defense of constitutional monarchy because Locke was an apologist for the reign of William and Mary, the constitutional monarchs who ascended the throne in 1689.

3. Eminent minds have come to the conclusion that in our civilized world, the evil in man prevails over the good. As Hobbes put it, "The life of man is solitary, poor, nasty, brutish, and short. If I am accused of pessimism, all I can say is that I have lots of company and famous company too."

4. A wholesaler sued a retailer for $200, claiming that he had shipped that amount in goods to the defendant and had not been paid. The retailer claimed that he had paid the bill. The wholesaler plaintiff stated that he had no record of the payment. The retailer defendant then said that the court should dismiss the case because the plaintiff could not disprove his claim that he had paid the bill.

5. An ad in the *New Yorker* magazine shows a photo of two very stately mansions next door to each other with two men standing in the door of one of the houses. The caption reads "I was wondering if I could possibly borrow a cup of Johnnie Walker Black Label."

6. A railroad spokesman said, "The Union's spokesman accuses us of speaking the language of railroads. We wouldn't dream of suggesting that he speaks the language of unions."

7. A foreman is fired by ABC Steel Company. He gives a newspaper interview charging unfair labor practices in the company. A company official declares: "The foreman is sore about being fired. He is a troublemaker and was once convicted of embezzlement."

8. An ad in the *New Yorker:* "The Pilikan 120: The fountain pen that never went out of style. Classics never go out of style. The Pelikan 120 is the great classic fountain pen, long a favorite of European pen purists."   [January 1976]

9. We cannot explain electricity, sunlight or life. In a like manner, we cannot explain mental telepathy. The lack of explanation should not hinder but rather lead us to accept mental telepathy as a fact.

10. *President:* "Just how would you suggest improving the performance of our sales force?"
Sales Manager: "I'll simply tell them that the returns for next month will have to be up by 14 percent. Any employee failing to show improvement will be dismissed at once."

11. *Paul:* "Liberty U.S.S.R. style is a travesty on individual freedom. Free speech does not exist, voting is a farcical ratification of official candidates, the slightest opposition is dealt with by the secret police and the mental hospitals."
Peter: "I don't think it behooves us to criticize other nations in view of our racial discrimination and the new findings on CIA spying.

12. The invention of the atom bomb was a good thing. Given the coinciding of the smashing of the atom, the development of nuclear physics, and World War II, its development was inevitable.

13. Advertisement: "You'll love these blankets. They cuddle close to you and comfort you just like mother used to do when you were a child. Soft, warm, good to touch—you'll put them first on your list of friends for life."

14. In the past, America has prospered without price-wage control. There is therefore no reason why we should start control now.

15. Your arguments for the new bill on collective bargaining are without merit because you are a member of the UPC, which is part of the Teamster's Union.

16. Political candidate: "You ask if I supported increased funding for colleges and universities? Let me tell you that I am gravely concerned about the status of education today. Just look at the appalling reports about the inability of students to read, write, and think. We need a whole rethinking of what we are about in higher education.

17. Mark Anthony's speech at Caesar's funeral—paraphrased: Look at how pitiful Caesar's wounds are to behold. And Brutus, how dearly Caesar loved him and

yet he plucked his cursed steel away. How Caesar loved you for he remembered you in his will! How can anyone think Caesar aspired to be a dictator?

18. Woman reacting to Schopenhauer's *Essay on Women:* "It is only a man whose intellect is clouded by his sexual impulses, who was a disappointed lover and an unhappy child that could speak of women as 'that undersized, narrow-shouldered, broad-hipped and short-legged race.' "

19. Mother crab to offspring: "Son, don't walk sideways like that, it's very awkward. Walk straight forward. That's the way to have an elegant appearance." Young crab: "But mother, *you* walk sideways."

20. Every slip of the tongue is significant in that it reveals some unconscious and suppressed desire. There can be no question of the truth of this principle because it was put forth by Sigmund Freud, the founder of psychoanalysis.

4.4 FALLACIES OF NEGLECTED ASPECT

Another important group of fallacies are those of neglected aspect. We commit a fallacy of neglected aspect whenever we fail to take into account some important factor or omit some important part of the truth. A humorous story is told about the testimony of a trainman at a trial following a disastrous wreck at a railway crossing. The trainman testified that he had signaled vigorously by waving a latern. He even demonstrated to the jury the way in which he had waved it. When he was later congratulated on his testimony by the railroad's attorney, he was heard to say, "I was terribly afraid that the other lawyer would ask me if I had the latern lighted." In this case the neglected factor was not only relevant, but it probably would have changed the conclusion reached. The moral of the story is that before deciding any issue, take care that you have taken into account all relevant factors and considerations. Fallacies of neglected aspect occur frequently and in a number of different varieties. We turn now to discussion of seven such fallacies.

Hasty generalization   A generalization is a conclusion made about a group of instances when not all of the instances have been observed. For example, if an instructor with a class of thirty students finds that the first three students he questions have not read the assigned essay, and on this basis concludes, "The students in this class have not read the assignment," then his conclusion is a generalization because it includes not only the students he has questioned, but the others as well. The reliability of his generalization depends upon two conditions: (1) an adequate number of instances and (2) the extent to which the sample instances are like the other instances. If the samples are too few, or if they are unlike the others, we may say that the instructor has committed the fallacy of *hasty generalization*—that he has jumped to a conclusion. A sampling of three students hardly seems a sufficient ground on which to draw a conclusion about the whole class of thirty. Further, if by chance the three questioned were among the weakest, then his sample would be unrepresentative, and his generalization would be even less reliable.

The fallacy of *hasty generalization* can be subdivided into two kinds, though both errors often are committed in the same instance.

The fallacy of insufficient statistics or small sample consists in making an inductive generalization on the grounds of an insufficiently large or quantitatively unrepresentative sample. Examples are:

> Women drivers should be relieved of their licenses. I was nearly run into twice by women this morning while on my way to work. Women just can't drive.

> Joe has taken his lucky rabbit's foot on his four previous fishing trips and had tremendous luck. He has his lucky foot this time, so he should return with lots of fish.

> Look at the terrible civil strife and mess in Ireland. All Irish must be hot-tempered troublemakers.

Two encounters with women drivers, three fishing trips, and even the incidents in Ireland are not sufficient grounds to draw an 'all' type conclusion.

Another form of the *fallacy of hasty generalization* is that called *the fallacy of biased statistics*. This consists in basing an inductive generalization upon a sample that is known to be unrepresentative or one for which there is good reason to believe that it may be unrepresentative. In generalizing, we are concerned not only with numbers, but also how well a sample represents the total group. Thus, if a buyer wants to determine the quality of a farmer's wheat, she does not take a handful just from the top of the load. Rather, she takes a portion from the front of the load, a portion from the back, one halfway down and two on each side of the bottom. She might then dump all of this in a sack, shake it, and take a handful. In this case, the inference "This handful of wheat is of quality x, therefore, the whole load is of quality x," is a good one. This form of the fallacy of *hasty generalization* is easy to fall into because frequently our prejudices induce us to select or be content with instances that are not typical. There seems to be an impulse in many of us to suppress the counter-instances. We look exclusively for evidence to support an idea. This selection process can be very subtle because no actual case may be suppressed, but the sample is chosen to avoid damaging cases. For example, an investigation of the effectiveness of television advertising could be made to yield decidedly different results, depending on whether the survey was made near a college campus or in an underprivileged part of town. People who engage often in polling techniques know the influence of regional and occupational differences. A classic example of a fallacy of biased statistics, cited in many logic texts, is the prediction in 1936 by *The Literary Digest* that Franklin Roosevelt with his New Deal would be defeated by Alfred Landon. Landon ran on the slogan, "Save the American Way of Life." However, Roosevelt won by a landslide with 60.7 percent of the popular vote and 523 presidential electors out of 531. The *Digest* based its prediction on 2.25 million sample ballots, a large enough sample. Its mistake was to send its ballots only to telephone subscribers and automobile owners. In 1936, there were 9 million unemployed who had neither telephone nor automobile. Further, it was precisely those on relief who were strongly in favor of Roosevelt and his New Deal. *The Literary Digest* was the victim of the fallacy of biased statistics in more ways than one: after the election, it folded.

In seeking to avoid the fallacy of hasty generalization, we should be on guard against stacking the evidence in our favor. We should try to think of possible counter-instances rather than just to avoid them. Further, we should not let our sense of the dramatic lead us into sweeping statements instead of cautious ones. Statements with qualifiers might not be as colorful, but at least they are more likely to be true. Finally, in the realm of inductive generalizations, it seldom pays to take the easy way out, such as sampling three instances rather than thirty or examining any number indiscriminately rather than being sure we sample typical cases.

Tape Exercises

What day passes without encountering these and similar statements, spoken as if they were unquestionable truths: "Artists are a sloppy and immoral bunch." "The only way to succeed is to have 'pull.'" "Don't you know that every person has a price." "Everybody knows that wars are started because of economic rivalry." What is the proper reply to these generalizations? We discuss this on the tape for chapter 4 as well as other examples of this type of fallacy. Tape 4, band 3.]

False cause [*post hoc ergo propter hoc*]   Causal reasoning is a part of our everyday life as well as of scientific investigation. However, as another type of inductive reasoning, it too involves pitfalls similar to those of hasty generalization. The fallacy of false cause is to think something is the cause of a given effect or event, when it is not the cause at all. The Latin phrase *post hoc ergo propter hoc* means "after this, therefore because of this." It refers to the error of assuming that, merely because two events occur together or in immediate sequence, one event is *cause* and the other is the effect. Two events that appear to be causally related may not be so related at all for two reasons: (1) the relationship may be merely coincidental; and (2) both may be the effects of an undetermined cause. Further, an effect may be produced by different kinds of cause or have multiple causes. The following is a humorous example of coincidental relationship and the fallacy of false cause.

Because industrious and hard-working people all own cars, the way to make people industrious and hard-working is to give them cars.

A case in which presumed cause and effect are both effects of an undetermined cause is that in which one argues that this patient had an upset stomach and then a high fever and therefore the upset stomach is the cause of the high fever. But the high fever and upset stomach are effects of an undetermined cause, probably a virus.

Take another case. Suppose Lynn, who has chronic hayfever caused usually by goldenrod, takes a drive in the country with her family. Suddenly, she begins to sneeze and cough badly and concludes that, though it seems unlikely, the goldenrod must have bloomed early this year. She thus turns the car back toward home. However, given that it was rather early for goldenrod, Lynn probably has committed the fallacy of false cause. Other things may cause the symptoms of hayfever, and people allergic to one thing are often allergic to other things.

Finally, events may have multiple causes. Take the following example:

> If, after the First World War, America had joined the League of Nations, the policies of European statesmen would have been such as to make Hitler's rise to power impossible, and the Second World War would not have started. The United States did not, however, join the League of Nations at that time, and is, therefore, responsible for the Second World War.

Why is this fallacy of false cause? Because it assumed that America's failure to join the League of Nations in 1919 was the sole cause of World War II. As a matter of fact, the Second World War might or might not have been avoided if we had joined the League of Nations at that time. To regard our joining or not joining as the sole cause is to commit this fallacy.

Thus, we must be very cautious about asserting causal relationships. Lack of caution often underlies much superstition. For example, if someone says that the witch doctor went through his rites and incantations and the patient recovered shortly thereafter, therefore the patient was cured by these rites and incantations, he is committing the fallacy of false cause. What has to be shown is that the rites and incantations effected the cure.

Tape Exercises

How many superstitions can you name, whose base lie in this fallacy? Dozens, without doubt—the unlucky thirteenth floor or the thirteen who came to dinner. How would you deal logically with someone who confronted you with these well-worn maxims? [After considering your reply, listen to the tape. Other examples of false cause will also be discussed. Tape 4, band 3.]

Accident   The fallacy of accident occurs when we misapply a general rule to a specific case. Stated differently, we commit the fallacy of accident when we accept a generalization as if it were true universally and without exception, when, as a matter of fact, exceptions can and do occur. This is an *inductive fallacy* because it concerns the amount and kind of evidence cited. It overlooks the fact that most generalizations apply within certain specified boundaries (e.g., at sea level, in a vacuum). When these limitations are ignored, generalization can be false or nonapplicable. These qualifications or reservations are generally understood but usually are not spelled out. As a consequence, whether intentionally or unintentionally, we commit the fallacy of accident when we apply a generalization to 'accidental' cases to which it was never intended to apply. Thus, to argue that

Man is a rational animal, therefore Joe Snort is rational

is to ignore the accidental circumstances—Joe is dead drunk—which render the generalization inapplicable. Again, to conclude that water will boil at 212 degrees Fahrenheit at 10,000 feet above sea level is to ignore the relevant qualification to the formula, '212 degrees Fahrenheit is the boiling point of water,' namely, that it does so *only at sea level.*

The philosopher Plato cites a good example of the fallacy of accident in his *Republic.* In talking with Cephalus about what is just, Cephalus postulates that justice is defined as "telling the truth and paying back anything we may have received." Socrates raises doubts about Cephalus' definition by this reply, "Suppose, for example, a friend who had lent us a weapon were to go mad and then ask for it back, surely anyone would say we ought not to return it. It would not be 'right' to do so; nor yet to tell the truth without reserve to a madman." In other words, Socrates has pointed to cases to which Cephalus' definition is inapplicable.

Tape Exercises

To avoid the fallacy of accident, we should be aware that most generalizations and even scientific laws apply only in specified areas and under specified conditions for example, the law of gravity. Be sure the generalization really applies to the case. Consider the following: indicate why they commit either the fallacy of hasty generalization, the fallacy of false cause or the fallacy of accident. (Turn to **Tape** 4, band 4, for an analysis of these examples.)

1. Legalized abortion is a bad thing. One need only look at the number of unmarried women listed in the abortion statistics of states where abortion has been legalized to see that legalizing abortion has caused increased sexual activity outside of marriage.

2. The juvenile delinquents that I know all come from broken homes. It's obvious that a broken home is a breeding place for delinquency.

3. Anyone who commits a crime should be punished. Thus, John who sold heroin while working as an undercover agent, should be punished.

4. The new president must be prejudiced against Catholics and Jews. His first three appointments were all Protestants.

5. There has been a war during every Democratic regime. Once Carter goes into the White House we can tool up for another war.

Black-or-white fallacy (false dilemma)   Everyone probably has had experience with a true dilemma, that is, a situation in which we are forced to choose between undesirable alternatives. For example, a surgical operation is dangerous, but to delay is to risk grave illness or even death. To study tonight is to give up the party, but not to study is to risk flunking the final exam. However, there are also dilemmas that are not true dilemmas—there are more than two alternatives or intermediate positions between two extremes. To pose a false dilemma one represents a situation as offering a choice between two undesirable alternatives when, in fact, other choices are possible. To assume false alternatives is to commit the Black-or White Fallacy. Alternatives are erroneously reduced to two.

This is sometimes also called the "all or nothing" fallacy. It treats things as contradictories that are only contraries. Contradictories are statements that have opposite truth values. If one is true, the other must be false. Thus, the statements "John is rich" and "John is not rich" are contradictories. If one is true, the other is false, and vice versa. The statements "John is rich" and "John is poor," however, are only contraries. If "John is rich" is true, then "John is poor" is false. However, John doesn't necessarily have to be either rich or poor. The reason this fallacy is called the black and white fallacy is that 'black' and 'white' are not strictly contradictory predicates. If a thing is black all over, it cannot be white all over; but it might be neither black nor white. An example of the fallacy under discussion is the following argument:

If I work, I pay the government money.
If I don't work, they pay the money.
I'd rather receive money than put it out, so I won't work.

This argument sounds legitimate on the surface, but the alternatives are not genuine contradictories. One can work and not pay the government money and one can not work and not receive money.

Another example of this fallacy is the following:

Either the Soviet Union is ahead of the United States in the race for superior nuclear war power, or
The United States is ahead of the Soviet Union.

∴ they refuse to work jointly for fear that one or the other would be giving up its advantage.

The argument overlooks the possibility that both countries are equal in the race.

Tape Exercises

In the field of ethics, religion, and politics, we are cursed with the frequency with which we encounter this fallacy of black or white. How ought we to reply to the person who throws alternatives such as the following at us and assumes that we are stupid or evil if we do not answer as expected? "Damn this detante talk: you are either for or against Communism"; "What do you mean, 'you don't know if [Judaism, Christianity, Islam, etc.] is true or not—it's either true or false"; "We are for law and order; don't you know whether you are or not?" [Compare your answers with the discussion on Tape 4, band 4.]

Fallacy of the beard   A fallacy related to that of the black-or-white fallacy is the fallacy of the beard. In failing to admit the possibility of a middle ground between extremes, we commit the black-or-white fallacy. We fall into the fallacy of the beard when we use the middle ground or the fact of continuous and gradual shading between extremes, to raise doubt about the existence of real differences between such opposites as strong and weak, good and bad, and white and black. But because we cannot determine the exact point at which white ceases to be white does not prove that there is no difference between white and black. Further, by raising doubt about pinpointing real differences, we may be led to ignore significant differences even in cases where one extreme shades gradually into another.

This fallacy derives its name from the ancient quandry over "How many hairs constitute a beard?" The fallacy, then, consists in arguing from the *vagueness* of distinctions to the absence of *any* meaningful distinctions. Because we cannot draw a precise line between a beard and nonbeard (say, 5,000 hairs), it does not follow that there are no clear cases in which we can say that this is a beard. The inability to draw sharp distinctions in certain contexts does not mean that no distinction at all can be made. Consider the following arguments:

I'm against the two-thirds rule in voting. If you require a two-thirds rule, why not a three-fourths rule, or a 99 percent rule? Indeed, why not go all the way as in totalitarian countries and require everyone to vote 'yes'?

If we provide medical care for the aged, we may as well go ahead and provide it for the whole population. In fact, the state may as well go ahead and guarantee food and lodging for everyone.

In both cases, the argument goes from one extreme to the other, claiming that there is no difference between the two extremes because "It's all a matter of degree." But this assumes that differences of degree are not genuine differences. It assumes that there are no important differences between contraries connected on a continuum. In black and white thinking, boundaries are drawn too sharply, while the fallacy of the beard results in blurring significant distinctions. This fallacy is also sometimes called *slippery slope* because it assumes that once you begin something, you have to go all the way—you cannot have a little bit of socialism, a little bit of health care; rather, you slide all the way into the water.

Tape Exercises

Consider the following. Are they examples of either the black-white fallacy or the fallacy of the beard? [Check your answers with Tape 4, band 4.]

1. There are two ways to buy your next T V Trust your luck or trust the facts. The facts are more dependable than your luck, so buy Quasar.

2. Long Beach has just introduced pay tennis. But if you use the "users argument" as a base for the charging of fees for the use of selected facilities, you could then apply that argument to any other public facility like a branch library or a stretch of beach. Where would be the end? Who would establish the limit?

3. We will never have an ideal president. If presidents are ambitious, they will be willing to sacrifice the good of the people for their own private advantage. If they are not ambitious, then they will be ineffectual.

4. No, I'm not going to buy you an electric saw. If I did, then you would want a circular saw, and then a power drill, and soon you would want a whole workshop. We can't afford all this, and besides we haven't got room for all that.

Exercises for § 4.4

For each of the following statements, identify the fallacy committed.

    a. Hasty Generalization
    b. False Cause
    c. Accident
    d. Black-or-White
    e. Beard

1. The type of service one can expect doctors to give under socialized medicine is shown by the English physician who boasted of examining eighty patients in three hours.

2. If the children are provided with a TV set, they will become spectators at the expense of healthful out-door play, and if they do not have a set, they will miss part of the culture of contemporary times.

3. The West must make up its mind about Angola. Shall we write Angola off and let the Russians have a free hand, or shall we support Angola and come to terms with the costs? Our answer will determine whether Angola will be on the side of freedom or go the way of Russia.

4. The amount of destruction from tornados has been increasing in the past years. It must be the result of atomic testing, which has upset the climate.

5. I have had several blacks in my Freshmen composition classes, and they just didn't perform up to standards. The whole idea of getting more blacks in college is doomed, too, because they lack the ability.

6. Disloyalty is always wrong. Therefore, Congresswoman Stone was wrong to uncover corruption in her party.

7. There cannot be any real difference between science and art because their methods gradually shade into one another.

8. If we are going to buy a car, we must either get a good one or a cheap one. We can't afford a good one, and we don't want a cheap one; so we will just have to do without one.

9. In England 31.5 percent of 966 boys between the ages of seven and fifteen were juvenile delinquents from broken homes. We can conclude, therefore, that a broken home is a breeding place for delinquency.

10. There is no such thing as a bad boy. Boys are in varying degrees maladjusted and cannot ever be considered really evil.

4.5 FALLACIES OF AMBIGUITY OR MISUSES OF LANGUAGE

We are on the last stage of our study of fallacies, and are now facing a set of fallacies that is extremely interesting and often entertaining. Before examining these fallacies of ambiguity, we should review what ambiguity is and distinguish it from vagueness. When we say that a term is *ambiguous*, we mean that it has two or more meanings and that we cannot tell by context or by any other way which meaning, if any, is intended. When we say that a term is *vague*, we mean something quite different. We mean that we cannot determine the boundaries of the term as far as its meaning is concerned. To put the same point differently, it is difficult or impossible, when a term is vague, to know whether the term applies or not in a given context. We shall give examples of ambiguity of many different sorts presently. An example of vagueness is the term 'living' or the term 'religion.' Whether, for example, a cell or a fetus is a 'living being' or not gets people quite excited when they argue about the legalization of abortion. Unfortunately, the argument is confused because no agreement can be reached on what we mean by 'living.' If agreement is reached and every cell is considered living, then the argument is lost. Of course, the argument is more complex than this because 'living being' is here equated with living person, potential or actual. A more humorous example is to ask, "When is a person bald?" Clearly, you cannot do this by counting the number of hairs on one's head, so we have a vague notion of baldness. We know that a person who has *no* hair on his head is bald, but is the person with three hairs on his head bald? Yul Bryner, the actor, is certainly bald, and that person with an afro-hair-do is not bald. But what about our friend who has lost half the hair on his head?

Equivocation   The first fallacy of ambiguity is *equivocation*. This occurs when a term or concept is used with two different meanings and results in a fallacy because we do not know which of these two legitimate meanings is intended. The trouble is that often both of them are intended.

> Partisans are not to be trusted.
> Democrats are partisans.
> _____
> ∴ Democrats, are not to be trusted.

The point to see here is that the term 'partisans' can be used in two quite different senses. On one hand, it refers to people who are biased and prejudiced. On the other hand, it refers merely to the members of a political party. Another favorite example is the following:

> All laws should be respected and obeyed.
> The formula $R = E/I$ is a law.
> _____
> ∴ The formula $R = E/I$ should be respected and obeyed.

A moment's thought would show that the term 'law' is used in one sense to describe that which exists in positive law in a community or in a state, whereas in the other sense it is used to describe the observable principles in physical nature. We cannot ever establish the conclusion that is desired here by using the term 'law' in two entirely different senses.

One question to ask in any argument is this: "Is there a term here that is being used in two different senses?" If there is, we are likely to have a fallacious conclusion and shall be guilty of committing this fallacy of ambiguity.

Cases of equivocation often hinge on the fact that many terms have more than one meaning, depending on the context. These are sometimes called *relative terms* because their meaning is decided relative to the way in which they are used. Consider "good." We may argue about whether Lincoln was a good man, a good president, a good mediator. We speak of a good safecracker or spy, a good hammer or towel, and the like. Clearly, "good" is being used in the latter context as synonymous with efficient, effective, good-of-its kind. In the former context it refers to the ethical qualities of a person, as in "Jesus was a good man."

The fallacy of amphiboly (syntactical ambiguity)   A sentence can have different meanings because of its syntactical structure, that is, the meaning of a sentence can be ambiguous because the awkward or ungrammatical way in which it is expressed makes it difficult for us to know how to interpret its meaning.

One amusing example is: "Clean and Decent Dancing Every Night Except Sunday." Is one to conclude that the dancing on Sunday night is not clean and decent?

Another example is: "The shooting of the hunters is terrible." This can mean that the hunters are terrible at shooting, that it is terrible that the hunters are being shot, or that the fact that the hunters are shooting at all is terrible. Sentences that are ambiguous because of awkward construction are called *amphibolous sentences*.

When an amphibolous sentence is used with two different meanings in an argument and the correctness of the argument depends upon the sentence maintaining a constant meaning throughout the argument, the *fallacy of amphiboly* occurs. For example:

> My companion said, "The shooting of the hunters is terrible." If he believes that the shooting of the hunters is terrible, then he must be against the killing of wildlife.
>
> ∴ My companion is an animal lover.

The fallacy of amphiboly occurs in this line of reasoning if an erroneous conclusion is drawn because of a misinterpretation of the sentence, "The shooting of the hunters is terrible." If, in the first premise, the sentence means that the hunters are terrible at shooting, then the meaning has shifted in the second premise and the conclusion is wrong.

A classic example of drawing a wrong conclusion because of an amphibolous statement is that of Croesus, King of Lydia who, in contemplating waging war on Persia, consulted the Delphic Oracle. Croesus' reasoning was as follows:

> The oracle said, "If war is waged, a great kingdom will fall."
> This means the kingdom of Persia will fall.
>
> ∴ I will wage war.

A great kingdom did fall, that of Croesus, who was defeated by Cyrus of Persia. Another humorous example of the fallacy of amphiboly is the following:

> "There must be lots of jobs available in physical education, because the bulletin announces that the dean will give a talk to graduating seniors about their employment opportunities in the college gymnasium."

Accent   The meaning of sentences can also be changed by accenting or emphasizing some word or phrase. Consider the statement by a book reviewer: "I cannot recommend this book too highly." Depending upon where we place the emphasis, this could mean either that the book was so fine that she could not find words sufficient to praise it, or that she did not want to regard it as very important at all. If the reader drew an erroneous conclusion because of misplaced emphasis, then the fallacy of accent would have occurred:

> The reviewer said, "I cannot recommend this book too highly."
>
> ∴ We shall not publish it.

Another example of the fallacy of accent is:

> The Bible says, "Thou shalt not bear false witness against your neighbor. John Jones is not my neighbor.
> _____
> ∴ I can lie about him if I want.

This also might be called a fallacy of equivocation; 'neighbor' in the first sentence means 'any person we encounter' and in the second sentence 'any person living next door.'

A more insidious form of the fallacy of accent consists in quoting out of context. To quote out of context is, in a way, to accent some sentence or sentences by neglecting the sentences that surround them. The fallacy of quoting out of context, then, consists in omitting significant portions of an entire statement and thus conveying a meaning not intended by the person quoted. Thus, for example, a movie critic might write: "The scintillating dialogue of the play from which this movie is made is completely gone, and the overall effect is about as richly rewarding as getting knocked down by a truck." A promoter of the film, however, might advertise the film by saying,

> "A movie critic described the movie with such phrases as 'scintillating dialogue' and 'richly rewarding.'
> _____
> ∴ It is a movie not to be missed."

A more complex example of quoting out of context occurred in the 1960s when many newspapers demanded that direct action be taken to remove Castro's communist government in Cuba *because* the Monroe Doctrine provided that "an interposition by a European power in the Western Hemisphere would be the manifestation of an unfriendly disposition toward the United States." What was left out of this argument was the fact that the warning to Europe to keep its hands off the Western Hemisphere was set in the context of our assurance not to meddle in the affairs of Europe.

Students frequently have trouble identifying the particular kind of fallacy exhibited in an argument. They often confuse equivocation, accent, and amphiboly because they fail to fix upon the precise fault in the reasoning they are encountering. Yet rarely will a single statement or argument embody two or more of the above fallacies.

Tape Exercises

What is the source of confusion in the following? [Check your answers with Tape 4, band 5.]

1. How much is twice four and six?
2. As he dreamed on, he realized that this was a picture of the most sexy girl he had ever seen in the men's locker room.

3. Believe me, nothing is too good for my wife.

4. Now you must agree with me; every right ought to be enforced by law. Voting is a precious right, so it must be enforced by law.

5. Even at ninety my granny don't use glasses. She drinks right out of the bottle.

6. Figure Class I: A studio course working directly with the human figure. Anyone wishing to take advantage of the model without instruction may do so.

7. Attractive young woman to personnel director, "What do you mean exactly when you say I can expect frequent advances?"

8. Sons and daughters of members under sixteen will be admitted free.

Composition   Composition and division are two fallacies that are the converse of one another, and we must see these as opposite sides of the same coin. The problem with composition is it leads us to conclude that what is true of the constituent parts of something is also true of the *whole* itself. Stated from another point of view, it is a fallacy to argue that what is true of individual members of a collection taken separately is true of the collection as a whole. The classic illustration of this would be in the argument that because every single part of a typewriting machine is light in weight, the machine as a whole is light in weight. This is not only nonsense, but it attributes to the whole what is true only of the parts.

Another very good example of composition is to argue for higher prices of farm produce, and automobiles, and all other products on the grounds that higher prices produce more profit for the farmer, the automobile manufacturer, and the like, and therefore are good for all people. The fallacy of the argument clearly is that what any particular group may derive as a profit may disappear when the result of the application of this to everyone and to all is concerned. Obviously, the higher price disappears if the goods are increased in price proportionately to everyone; a general increase in all prices eliminates all the benefits of high prices for each particular group, yet many people are taken in by this argument.

Beware of *all!* The main problem with the fallacies of composition and division is that the word *all* is ambiguous. It may be taken, construed, or understood *distributively* or *collectively*. This simply means that we may take 'all' to mean each and every instance of a group, or to mean the collection of a group as a whole.

Perhaps the best example is from mathematics. Recall the following: "All angles of a Euclidean triangle" means all of them taken collectively. But we may also assert that all the angles of a Euclidean triangle are less than two right angles. In this case, 'all angles of the triangle' means each and every angle is taken separately, and each angle is less than 180°.

The fallacy of composition and the fallacy of hasty generalization should be carefully distinguished. A generalization is reasoning from *some* to a *greater number,* and it is a hasty generalization when the *some* are either too few or not typical. Composition is reasoning from *each* to *an organized whole*. That is, it involves false reasoning that says if *each* member of a group has a certain characteristic, then the group, as an organized whole, has that characteristic. The latter fallacy ignores the fact of organization, which makes for an interaction and an interrelationship of parts, which produce changes that could hardly be predicted from knowledge of the separate parts.

Division   The fallacy of division, as we said above, is the reverse of the fallacy of composition. This means that we argue incorrectly that what is true of the whole must be true of the members of and parts of that whole. Consider a humorous example of this:

> Carrier pigeons are practically extinct.
> This bird is a carrier pigeon.
> ∴ It is practically extinct.

Consider one more example:

> You can trust the majority to do what is right in the long run.
> John Brown is a member of the majority.
> ∴ He can be trusted to do what is right in the long run.

(It should be as plain as day that John Brown may be the one person in the group who cannot be trusted to do anything that is right.)
   One thing should be kept in mind when dealing with the fallacies of composition and division: sometimes when one reasons from what is true of each part and vice versa, no error is committed. Consider the following:

> All parts of this chair are red.
> ∴ This chair is red.

Or,

> The car is brand new, so
> the parts of the car are brand new.

The fallacies of division and composition are fallacies of ambiguity because the distributive and collective meanings of 'all' or the verb 'to be' are confused. In the sentence, "Hotsuns are low-priced," the verb 'to be' is used *distributively,* for we are saying that each and every Hotsun is low-priced. However, in "Hotsuns are plentiful," we are using the verb 'to be' *collectively,* for we are saying that Hotsuns as a class or group are plentiful, not each and every car in the group. Keeping this in mind, we see that in the *fallacy of composition*, the *premises* are using the *distributive sense* of the verb 'to be,' referring to each and every, and shifting in the *conclusion* to the *collective sense* of the group as a whole. For example:

> Alex Jones, John Henry, and Bob Green are All-Star players.
>
> ∴ We can easily have an All-Star team and win the pennant.

In the premises, the reference is distributive, referring to each and every member, whereas the conclusion shifts to the collective sense of the team as All-Star.

In the fallacy of division, the shift is from the *collective* to the *distributive*. For example:

> McGovern was decisively rejected by the voters.
> John Jones was a voter.
>
> ∴ John Jones decisively rejected McGovern.

The premises say that McGovern was rejected by the voters as a group. The conclusion is erroneous and does not follow because it shifts to the distributive sense, in saying each and every voter rejected McGovern.

Tape Exercises

Have you ever gotten into an argument with a friend about who may be expected to win the annual game between the All-Stars and a particular baseball team from the opposite, that is National or American, league? If you have, did you argue that the All-Star Team must win because everyone of its players is a super-player and an expert in his field? Whether this was your answer or not, listen to the tape and see if you agree. Or to consider another example, how would you react to the comedian who said to you "Dogs are widely distributed over the United States, and my collie is a dog; therefore, my collie is widely distributed over the United States." [Further discussion of these questions are included in the tape for Tape 4, band 5.]

Exercises for § 4.5

A. Identify each of the numbered statements as one of the following fallacies of ambiguity:

> a. Equivocation
> b. Amphiboly
> c. Accent
> d. Composition
> e. Division

1. Water extinguishes fire, and oxygen is a component of water. Therefore, oxygen will extinguish fire.

2. If only we have an all-star cast, then the play would be a matchless performance.

3. Peanuts must be a basic necessity in our diet, and we should be sure to eat them regularly, for they are listed by the Department of Agriculture, along with rice, corn, cotton, wheat and tobacco, as 'basic crops.'

4. Since the gossips say that her first husband was a very upright man, her present husband must *not* be a very upright man.

5. Will you give aid and comfort to the enemies of the U.S. government or the government of Alabama?" "Do I have to make a choice?"

6. I understand Farnsworth is a practicing attorney. I don't want to put my case into the hands of a lawyer who still has to practice. I want a lawyer who knows law well enough that she no longer needs to practice.

7. I have read this essay very carefully and say that it is well written and excellently constructed. I base this judgment on the fact that every sentence in the essay was well written and well put together.

8. Nothing is better than filet mignon. But tripe is better than nothing. Therefore, tripe is better than filet mignon.

9. The natives here must be barbarians because John heard one of them say that as they were eating a friend, the nephew of the chief came in.

10. My friend took part in the last Gallup Poll. But it expressed a pretty conservative view on things. Therefore, my friend must have conservative views.

B. From the total list of fallacies, identify the fallacies committed in the following.

1. A number of thinkers have thought belief in a separate mind or soul to be an unfounded idea, with little base in reality. Therefore, one should not hold to belief in such an idea.

2. The dope trade is an economic drain on the underprivileged classes and on other users. Further, most of the profit from the drug traffic goes to the Mafia. Therefore, it is immoral to support the sale of illegal drugs in any form.

3. You cannot possibly hold Smothers responsible for embezzling that money. After all, he has had nothing but troubles this past year—his daughter running away, the son being arrested, and then the divorce.

4. One should never betray friends. Thus, Jim should not tell the police that Tim took the money.

5. If you give my husband an inch, he takes a yard. First, it was a new lawnmower, then a metal stepladder. Before you know it, we won't have room in the garage for the car.

6. No matter how much evidence you provide, you cannot prove that we have communication with beings in outer space. One therefore must conclude that belief in such communication is mere science fiction.

7. Gerald you may have faith in your plan, but I'm telling you that if you persist, you will find yourself without any place to work on your inventions.

8. You ask my views on nuclear energy plants. Well, this whole business of threats by those Arab oil countries is just uncalled for. If I were in charge, I would take a firm stand with those countries. The western nations need to take a firm stand.

9. One had better think carefully about appointing Warren to the environmental resources commission. After all, he is a employee of an oil company and would have economic interest in exploiting the environment.

10. I have visited three Arab countries and I tell you they are all out to get rich.

11. You say that I have avoided the issue of energy control. I tell you that my opponent is an expert at evasion. Has she ever given an answer to the question about the support of her campaign by the oil companies?

12. When did you stop thinking about this issue?

13. Have you noticed that since we have tremendously increased air travel and experimented with the supersonic planes, the weather changes have been so erratic. We had better cut down on air travel or our whole climate will be changed.

14. Jane wrote on the application that she was fair. But I find her a very unfair person. I have never seen her treat anyone equally.

15. Chrotia-5 is the most effective pain reliver on the market. It is the best reliever because it is used by more people than any other product. It is used by more people than any other product because it is recommended by more doctors. More doctors recommend it because it is the most effective pain reliever on the market.

16. I won't depend on Walter to support such a progressive idea. After all, he is a member of the school board, and it has a reputation of being very conservative.

17. My fellow laborers, I am glad to be with you all tonight where the air is open and forthright and not full of intrigue. Those who work hard for their bread know the meaning of the dollar, and that's why, my friends, I, who have toiled with my hands as you have, can fight in congress to give you every bit of your dollar back that is possible.

18. Each molecule in this atom is moving very rapidly. Therefore, the whole atom is moving rapidly.

19. We must make a choice in this situation. Either stop the aggression in Angola now or Russia will dominate Africa.

20. Look at all the Americans who smoke Xaxi. That many people can't be wrong.

C. Identify the fallacies committed in the following essay.

The Seaweed Caper

1. How can you possibly be against the processing of seaweed?

2. John Bum used to eat seaweed, but he was an old derelict sailor anyhow.

3. Hans Meer, the noted nuclear physicist, says seaweed processing is the wave of the future. Therefore, it must be the thing to do.

4. Look, if you go into this seaweed business in my territory, you will be collecting seaweed between your toes.

5. I have a right to my own taste. And if I have a right, it is right to process seaweed.

6. If you start processing seaweed, pretty soon you will be serving grass, and twigs, and briar bushes in the best restaurants.

7. We have to get in on this seaweed market now or the Russians will be cleaning up the market with their caviar. It's your choice.

8. Think of all the poor underwater creatures. If we take the seaweed, we will be making their neighborhoods less desirable.

9. You talk about the poor sea creatures. Look what you have done to the chicken population.

10. You cannot prove that seaweed processing will be profitable, therefore, I conclude that your venture will be a flop.

11. Thirteen of my friends find seaweed delicious and healthy. I conclude that all people will find it delicious and healthy.

12. Your friends are not only an unlucky lot, but they eat twigs. Thus, you cannot trust their opinion.

13. Seaweed is such as all-American phenomena. It conjures up pictures of old Cape Cod or Monterey and Carmel. How could I lose?

14. Seaweed is expensive to obtain and difficult to process. It is immoral to support this eat-seaweed campaign.

15. Seaweed is an excellent source of food. It is an excellent source of food because ocean creatures have survived on it for centuries. And ocean creatures have survived on it for centuries because it is an excellent source of food.

16. Joan Jerky is a member of the seaweed eating club, and she has the intelligence of a clam. Thus, the whole club is a bunch of clams.

17. My dear sir, you are abusive to sea creatures and all ocean fare. No person who loves clam chowder ought to believe you.

18. Further, why are you persecuting the poor seaweed?

Chapter Outline

This chapter is primarily concerned with fallacies committed in the informal argumentation of everyday discourse.

A. A fallacy is an argument that provides inadequate support for its conclusion. It fails to *prove* its conclusion.
   1. A *formal fallacy* is an invalid form of deductive argument. An argument is formally fallacious because it fails to meet the criteria of *validity*, namely, that it be impossible to have true premises and a false conclusion.
   2. An *informal* fallacy is committed when the premises fail to prove the conclusion for *reasons other than formal invalidity*.

B. An argument can be *valid* and *fallacious* in two kinds of circumstances:
   1. A valid argument can be fallacious because it fails to meet the requirement of *consistency*, namely, that it should not be impossible for all the premises to be all true.
      a. The *fallacy of inconsistency* occurs when one argues from premises that are *contradictory*. If two premises are contradictory, one of them must be false and thus the argument does not meet the requirement of consistency that it not be impossible for all the premises to be true.
      b. Inconsistent arguments with contradictory premises *are fallacious* because such premises provide doubtful evidence for the conclusion.
      c. Arguments with contradictory premises, though fallacious, are *formally valid*. It cannot be invalid—have all true premises and a false conclusion—because it is impossible for this kind of argument to have all true premises.
   2. A valid argument can be fallacious if it is a case of *begging the question*.
      a. In cases of *begging the question* the conclusion is already expressed in the premises and thus, one cannot properly speak of the premises *proving* the conclusion.
      b. Arguments that beg the question, though fallacious, are valid. They cannot have true premises and a false conclusion because they assume the truth of the conclusion in the premises.
C. Informal fallacies can be classified as follows:

GENERAL TYPE	SPECIFIC FORMS
I. *Fallacies that are Valid*	*Inconsistency:* Use of contradictory premises to support a conclusion or contradictory arguments at different places and times, without explanation or retraction.
	Begging the Question: This fallacy unjustifiably assumes the truth of the conclusion in the premises. The conclusion is in fact already stated in the premises. It asks one to grant the conclusion rather than proving it.
	Complex Question: This is a form of begging the question because it consists of posing a question in such a way that any answer must take for granted the conclusion that ought to be proved.
II. *Fallacies of Irrelevance* The premises are not sufficiently relevant or relevant in the appropriate way to the conclusion, and thus they fail to prove the conclusion.	*Appeal to Force:* This fallacy argues accept this conclusion otherwise unfortunate consequences will result.
	Appeal to Pity: The form of this fallacious argument is, accept this conclusion, for pity's sake. It is emotive appeal.
	Appeal to the People: This argument fallaciously appeals to popular prejudice, majority opinions, etc., to support a conclusion.
	Against the Man: This attacks the arguer rather than the argument. X says Y. X is bad. ∴ Y is false.

Abusive: Attacks moral character.

Circumstantial: Judges a man by the company he keeps.

Tu quoque: You too! Answers a charge by accusing the person making a charge of the same or a similar thing.

Appeal to Authority: Argues for a conclusion on the grounds that an authority supports it. It is a fallacy when the authority is not a specialist in the field.

Irrelevant Conclusion: In this fallacious argument the premises are *entirely irrelevant* to the conclusion; they, in fact, establish a different conclusion.

Red Herring: This is to use a false issue to divert attention from the real issues.

From Ignorance: This fallacy draws a conclusion on the grounds of *absence of evidence*. It falsely assumes that if there is no proof, then this proves something either true or false.

III. *Fallacies of Neglected Aspect*
These fallacies fail to take into account some important part of the truth.

Hasty Generalization: Use of relevant, but insufficient evidence to reach a conclusion. It is a fallacy because relevant evidence is omitted.

Insufficient statistics: The conclusion is based on too little evidence (too small a sample).

Biased statistics: The conclusion is based on unrepresentative evidence. Relevant and significant factors have been omitted.

False Cause: Labeling something as the cause of something else when, in fact, it is not the cause or only one of the causes.

Accident: This involves the misapplication of a general rule to a specific case. Certain relevant qualifications to the general rule are ignored.

Black and White: This fallacy involves the assumption of false alternates. It is the erroneous reduction of alternatives or possibilities to just two.

The Beard: The fallacy involves falsely assuming that because distinctions are vague, no distinctions can be made. It tries to falsely blur all distinctions.

IV. *Fallacies of Ambiguity*
These fallacies result when one is misled by *language* to believe that a conclusion follows when it actually does not follow.

Equivocation: This fallacy occurs when a term or concept is used with two different meanings and because of this ambiguity the premises fail to support the conclusion.

Amphiboly: In this fallacy, a phrase or term is wrongly interpreted because of *awkward grammatical* construction and a misleading conclusion is drawn.

Accent: In this fallacy misinterpretation occurs because a phrase or word is falsely accented or emphasized.

The premises usually involve ambiguities—phrases or words are used in two different senses.

Composition: This fallacy and its converse result from the ambiguous use of the word, 'all' which may refer either to a group as a whole, e.g., "The team has spirit." or to each and every member of the group, e.g., "All members of the team have spirit."

In the *fallacy of composition*, one concludes that because individual members of a group have certain characteristics the group as a whole has these characteristics.

Division: This fallacy occurs when one argues that what must be true of the group as a whole must be true of each member or part of that group.

Part II
Deduction

5

CATEGORICAL PROPOSITIONS

5.1 QUANTITY AND QUALITY

In *categorical deductive logic*, which is the traditional logic originated by Aristotle in his *Organon,* we shall be dealing with certain kinds of arguments called *syllogisms.* Syllogisms, however, are made up of propositions or statements of specific kinds, and these sustain certain relations to each other. So, whether you choose to master, treat lightly, or even ignore the syllogistic form of argument, you would be well advised to master the identification of statements and their logical relations. Our first task is to explain the building blocks of the syllogism, the simplest one of which is the *categorical proposition* or *statement.* Categorical statements derive their name from the fact that they relate, by means of their subject and predicate terms, two categories or classes of things. For example, the statement "All men are mortal," asserts some type of relationship between the class of *men* (human beings) and the class of *mortals.* It says, in effect, that *all members of the class of men are also members of the class of mortals.* It says that the class of men is included in, or subsumed under the class of mortals. Using two circles to represent each of the classes, we can represent the statement "All men are mortal" as in figure 2. But not all statements are simple, universal affirmatives, as in: All iron is heavy. We soon discover that there are four, and only four, kinds of categorical propositions:

1. *Universal affirmative:* "All men are mortal." This may be translated into the **A** statement form, "All *S* are *P.* ("*S*" standing for subject term, "*P*" for predicate term.)

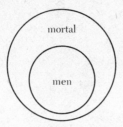

FIGURE 2

2. *Universal negative:*   "No men are mortal,"—**E** form: "No *S* are *P.*"
3. *Particular affirmative:*   "Some men are mortal,"—**I** form: "Some *S* are *P.*"
4. *Particular negative:*   "Some men are not mortal,"—**O** form: "Some *S* are not *P.*"

The letters *S* and *P* in such schematic statements as "All *S* are *P*" and "No *S* are *P,*" are placeholders for terms that specify sets or classes of things. These sets or classes can be any sort of entity or collection—the set of squares or rectangles or metals or dishonest persons. We shall examine these in greater detail shortly. First, we wish to stress the nature of the four elements or components of any and every proposition. These are:

1. *quantifier:*   the words "All," "No" or "None," and "Some." They tell us *how many* or what *quantity* of a given term is involved. So: all, no, none, or some baseball players are wealthy, healthy, or whatever.

2. *subject term:*   indicates a class, such as, men, mortals, congressmen. The subject term often includes more than the subject of the sentence—Some [golden-haired, sexy film stars (subject term)] are unhappy individuals.

3. *copula:*   some form of the verb "to be" such as "is," "are." This, and this alone, indicates a *relationship* between the subject term class and the predicate term class.

4. *predicate term:*   asserted or denied of the subject term, as in all grapes (subject term) are fruit (predicate term). Similarly, a predicate term, as a subject term, may be very complex—Religions are [social institutions which are concerned about man's salvation (predicate term)].

Now we are in a position to examine each of the four kinds of categorical propositions more closely.

A: *The universal affirmative*   First, observe that the word *all* in the **A** form should be taken in the strict sense of *each* and *every.* "All *S* are *P*" is false if there exists one instance, element, member of the class of *S*'s that are *not P.* For example, "All the students at Siwash Subnormal are Americans" is false if there is one student there who is not American.

Second, we need to distinguish between class *inclusion* or class membership, on the one hand, and class *identity,* on the other hand. In the former case, the **A** proposition is asserting *total class inclusion* of its subject class in its

predicate class. It means to say that *all* (every) member of the class S is also a
member of the class P. However, the **A** proposition does not say anything about
all the members of the class P. It only tells us what is shown in figure 3.

Every S is a P

Every S is identical with some P

Thus:

FIGURE 3

In the second form of the **A**, universal affirmative proposition, we are dealing
with class identity. This is illustrated in the statement, "All (circles) are (closed
plane curves with an equal radii at all points or such that all the points on the
curve are equidistant from the center"). Our parentheses serve to identify the
subject and the predicate term. Again: "Washington, D.C. is the capitol of the
United States of America." In both statements the subject and predicate classes
are identical, neither is larger or smaller than the other.

If we could diagram this it would show two circles, one on top of the other,
that is, both the same size and with the same center.

I: *Particular affirmative propositions*   The **I** form is "Some S is P."

What is affirmed by the statement "Some prizefighters are millionaires" is
that of all possible prizefighters, at least one or possibly several or even many,
but not all prizefighters are millionaires. Does it affirm that some prizefighters
are *not* millionaires? No, it does not. It may be taken to imply this, but it cannot
logically be construed that way. It literally says, *some S* is *P* —some
prizefighters are millionaires (a statement which, in the fourth quarter of the
20th century happens to be true).

Further, "some," as used in the **I**, particular affirmative proposition, is not
definite. This we indicated above but need to emphasize here again. If it is
asserted that some peaches in this basket are edible and ripe, we know that at
least one, maybe many, but certainly not all are edible and ripe. In figure 4, we
show the classes of peaches and edible and ripe things intersecting or overlapping and sharing at least one member in common.

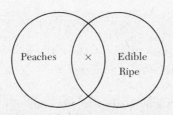

FIGURE 4

E: *The universal negative proposition*   The E proposition is the clearest and cleanest of all the four kinds. It flatly denies that even a single member of the subject class is a member of the predicate class. Some examples are, No horses are able to fly, No gold is cheap, No Christians are Buddhists. The diagram in figure 5 is clear: the two classes are absolutely distinct. There is no overlap or intersection.

FIGURE 5

O: *Particular negative proposition*   The **O** proposition is a tricky one and causes more trouble and confusion than any of the preceding three. On the face of it, what is said seems clear:

Some (*S*) is not (*P*).

Logically this means that at least *one* of the class *S* is not a member of the class *P*. It does not say whether there is one or two or many that are not, but it clearly excludes *at least one* of the members of class *S* from class *P*. Dozens of logicians have tried to construct illustrations that would make this **O** particular negative proposition clear and almost none have succeeded. A near approach was achieved by the oddly worded example of a first-rate logician, Herbert L. Searles, who wrote:

> "Suppose you are playing tennis and lose some of your tennis balls. You suspect they are in a nearby field. In order to convince yourself that they are *not in the field,* what part of the field would have to be covered in order to be able to assert, 'Some of my tennis balls are not in the field?' It is obvious that the whole field would have to be covered."[1]

Thus, visually, the *S*, represented by a single *X*, is completely outside the circle representing the nearby field.

Tape Exercises

Identify the subject and predicate terms of the following statements. [Check your answers with Tape 5, band 1.]

---

[1] Herbert Searles, *Logic and Scientific Method: An Introductory Course,* 2d ed. (New York: The Roland Press, 1956), p. 78.

1. Applications for passports executed before any other official than an agent of the Department of State are not acceptable.
2. Persons who can't distinguish right from wrong are legally insane.
3. Ratios of volumes of gases used and produced in a chemical reaction are represented by small, whole numbers.
4. Black cows give white milk.

Exercises for § 5.1

What are the subject and predicate terms of each of the following?
What is the form of each—**A, I, E,** or **O**?

1. Some professors are good scholars but terribly boring lecturers.
2. No persons who have not been told that they have a terminal disease are able to imagine how terrifying that news can be.
3. All nuclear power plants are so constructed that we need not worry about their possible danger to the environment.
4. Some members of our basketball team are not all-around athletes.
5. Some pieces of sculpture that have won prizes and sell for a high price are not the kind of things I would want in my living room.
6. No people who are unwilling to work are citizens who should receive government help.
7. Some members of the Senate are not persons of unquestioned moral character.
8. All the cars in parking lot *C* are owned by students.
9. No term papers, like women's skirts, which are not long enough to cover the subject but short enough to be interesting, are papers worth grading.
10. Some union managers are more concerned to line their own pockets than to help the union members.

5.2 QUALITY AND QUANTITY AND DISTRIBUTION

In describing the four kinds of propositions employed in deductive logic (**A, I, E,** and **O**), we have already discovered that each one of these must *affirm* (as in **A** and **I** propositions) or *deny* (as in **E** and **O** propositions) the relationship between the subject term and the predicate term. These determine the *quality* of a proposition—that each one must affirm or deny a relationship. It may help our memory to associate **A** and **I** with *affi*rm and **E** and **O** with *ne*go, Latin for deny.

The quality of propositions is clear and simple enough: the quantity of the subject and predicate terms is not always as clear. In fact, it is clear enough in the universal negative proposition, **E,** for it is as plain as can be that in this universal negative, both subject and predicate terms are distributed. No S is P means that no instance of S is an instance of P. Thus, 'no dogs are things that can fly' refers to every member of the class 'dogs' and to every member of the class 'things that can fly.' This is precisely what *distribution* means, that the term refers to or denotes *every* member of that class,—all or no or none. Thus, if we encounter the proposition "No communists are democratic," we know that the subject term, 'communists' refers to every member of that class, and the predicate term, 'democratic' to every member of that class. The two classes are totally excluded. Alas, the other three kinds of propositions are not as clear, but we must make the distribution of terms in them as clear as possible.

As we turn to propositions **A, I** and **O,** recall that *distribution concerns the quantity or number of members of the class being referred to by the term.* So, a term is distributed in a categorical statement if, by virtue of the form of the statement, it refers to *every* thing or kind of thing that is denoted by that term. Now, how is it with a universal affirmative proposition? Clearly, the subject term in this proposition is distributed because it reads, '*All S is P.*' What about the predicate term? It is undistributed because we do not know about all but only some of the members of the predicate term unless they are cases of class identity. Consider: "All snakes are creepy crawly things." The subject term, 'snakes,' is obviously distributed, but the predicate term is *not* distributed because it does not affirm something about every instance of 'creepy, crawly things.' For shorthand, we write it so:

All S^d is P^u.

How about the particular affirmative, I, proposition, Some S is P? Obviously the subject term is *un*distributed because it states that only some, not all of the subject term is designated. So, 'Some (cars)^u are (economical)^u.' But watch! Neither does it affirm anything about *all* economical things. There may be economical motorcycles, airplanes, lawn mowers, etc. So, in the **I** proposition both the subject and the predicate terms are undistributed.

What about the particular negative, **O,** proposition? The subject term is clear because the phrase 'Some S' shows that the subject term is undistributed. But what about the predicate term, P? It is distributed because if something is excluded from P it must be excluded from all P. As we said before, if I can say "Some of my tennis balls are not in the parking lot," we know about some (undistributed) of the subject but about all (distributed) of the predicate term, the parking lot.

The distribution of terms may be diagramed in several ways. Examine the two charts in figure 6 and table 1.

Exercises for § 5.2

In each of the following, what is its quantity and quality? Are the subject and predicate terms distributed or undistributed?

PREDICATE TERMS

	Undistributed	Distributed
Distributed	A d u All S is P	E d d No S is P
Undistributed	I u Some S is P u	O u Some S is not P d

(left margin label: SUBJECT TERMS)

FIGURE 6

1. All democracies with a large number of political parties are likely to have weak governments.

2. Some barber colleges are doomed to go out of business because men are wearing long hair.

3. No pornography that embodies sadism and violence is fit to be circulated.

4. Some people are certain to be angry with the Supreme Court decision on capital punishment.

5. All fat people are supposed to be happy people.

6. Some members of the Mafia are not gangsters and lawbreakers.

7. No tennis balls used in ten games are fit to be played with again.

8. Some dietetic candies are attractive to look at but tasteless to eat.

9. All totalitarian regimes are likely to suppress one or more of the "four freedoms."

10. Some of Shakespeare's plays are inferior to the plays of Aeschelus.

5.3 TRANSLATING STATEMENTS INTO STANDARD FORM

If the statements we encounter in arguments in everyday life were expressed in the neat, clear forms we have deliberately thus far employed, much confusion would be avoided. But of course they are not. For a variety of reasons, we come upon statements in political, social, religious and other discourse that require identification and clarification. In short, they require what amounts to translation from the ambiguous form in which they are stated into one of the four kinds of propositions we have described as necessary for purposes of clear reasoning. In what follows, we shall examine cases of the kinds of ambiguity that most frequently occur.

TABLE 1

	Distribution	Diagram
A: *All* S *is* P Universal Affirmative Every *S* is *P*. An *S* is *P*. *S*'s are *P*'s. Whatever is *S* is *P*. If anything is an *S*, then it is a *P*.	*Every* S *Some* P is identical with D U	 Figure 7
E: *No* S *is* P Universal Negative None of *S* is *P*. Not any *S* is *P*. An *S* is not a *P*. *S*'s are not *P*'s. Nothing that is *S* is *P*. There are no *SP*'s.	*Every* S *Every* P is distinct from D D	 Figure 8
I: *Some* S *is* P Particular Affirmative A few *S* are *P*. Many *S* are *P*. Most *S* are *P*. There are *SP*. Some things are both *S* and *P*.	*Some* S *Some* P is U U	 Figure 9
O: *Some* S *is not* P Particular Negative A few *S* are not *P* Many *S* are not *P* Most *S* are not *P* There are *S* which are not *P* All that is *S* is not *P* Not everything *S* is *P* Not all *S* is *P*	*Some* S *Every* P is distinct from U D	 Figure 10

We would think that any statement beginning with the word 'all' would be so clear that no confusion could occur. After all, we saw that any subject term preceded by the quantifier, 'all' is distributed, for example, All soldiers are brave. But 'all' can be understood collectively or distributively. What, for instance, does the sign in the bookstore say when it reads "All the books on this table $10"? Are you warranted in putting all of them in a bag and paying $10 for them? You probably could win the legal argument, because the bookstore manager should not have used the ambiguous word 'all' if what he or she meant was 'any' or 'each' book costs $10. The point is, in logic 'all' must be taken to mean *each and every member of a class taken separately,* not all as a collective whole, as in "All the coins in my pocket." But we are able to handle both senses of 'all' in logic if we specify our meaning. Consider "All the angles of a triangle are equal to two right angles" versus "All the angles of a triangle are less than two right angles." In the first case we mean all the angles collectively; in the second case we mean each and every one taken separately.

Tape Exercises

What are we to understand by the report, "All of the floats in the parade made the parade a stunning affair"? [Turn to Tape 5, band 1, for a discussion of this and similar questions.]

Even the quantifier 'some,' which again sounds clear enough, can get us into trouble. Does it mean 'only some,' as in, "Some of the gang escaped"? This appears to mean 'some but not all.' Or does it mean 'at least some' and *perhaps all?* For example, "Some of the oranges in this basket are spoiled." Can we conclude that some are not spoiled? Again, we shall consider on the tapes the ambiguities of 'a few,' 'hardly any,' 'many,' 'several,' 'most.' For logical purposes, the word 'some' must always be understood to mean at least *one* but definitely not *every one*. The 'some' of an **I** proposition, therefore, means anything from one to one less than 'all'.

Tape Exercises

In everyday speech, we constantly encounter statements with no quantifier. "Bureaucrats are parasites on the public." "Tax collectors are an abomination in the eyes of the Lord." With all these, what we must do for the sake of rational discussion is agree on the intended meaning. Does the speaker really mean 'all' bureaucrats, 'all' tax collectors or does he or she mean 'most,' 'some'? [Turn to Tape 5, band 2, for further discussion.]

We constantly come upon sentences which have no copula, no verb form 'to be,' 'are,' and the like. "Our friends really messed things up at last night's party"; "Franco's Spain tolerated no opposition"; "But John is younger than Ann." Awkward though it sounds, we should restate these in clear logical form: "Our friends" (subject term) are "people who messed . . ." (predicate term); "Franco's Spain is a state that tolerated no opposition"; "John is a person who is older than Ann." The point is to identify clean-cut subject and predicate terms and then further identify them concerning quantity and quality.

Much the same is required with statements that employ an adjective rather than a noun. They talk about attributes or about qualities rather than about objects and things: "All submarines are beautiful"; "Some stars are self-luminous"; "This staging of the play is magnificent." What is needed, even though it may sound awkward, is to cast these in terms of nouns, for example, "All submarines are beautiful objects."

Another type of ambiguity occurs with statements using the words 'only,' 'none but,' and the like. These are especially misleading and are called by logicians 'exclusive' propositions. What is meant by the statement "Man alone laughs" or by the poet's observation—an ambiguity favored for illustrative purposes by almost all logicians—"Only the brave deserve the fair"? We can say that such sentences do not mean what most students assume that they mean; for instance, that "All men are creatures that laugh." On the contrary, they can all be rendered as **A** propositions if we first reverse the subject and predicate terms. So, what the first sentence means is "All creatures capable of laughing are men." The original can also be cast in the form of an **E** proposition if we negate the subject term, namely, "No nonmen (nonhuman beings) are creatures that laugh." The ambiguity of the poet's statement can be clarified by stating it either as an **A** proposition—"All who deserve the fair are brave"—or as an **E** proposition—"No nonbrave person deserves the fair."

Tape Exercises

Translate the statement "Only philosophers are wise." [Consult Tape 5, band 2, for further discussion.]

What are we to do with so-called *exceptive* propositions, as in "All but persons with criminal records are eligible," or "All the shoes except those on the shelves are on sale"? Again, two translations are possible. They can be construed as **A** propositions and read, "All persons with no criminal records are eligible" and, "All the shoes not on the shelves are on sale." They can also be translated as **E** propositions, namely, "No persons with criminal records are eligible," and "No shoes on the shelves are on sale."

Tape Exercises

Translate the following: "All students will be admitted unless they are without shoes and shirts and pants;" "All but union organizers will be allowed to lobby." [Turn to Tape 5, band 2, for further discussion.]

Finally, what do 'all are not' sentences mean logically? If the registrar asks the professor about the grades on a final examination and the latter replies, "All of the students did not pass," what is the registrar to conclude? Aside from the chastisement for ambiguity, which the professor deserves in this case, the registrar may correctly say, "Well, I assume you are not saying that 'None of the students passed.' " What is involved is that 'all are not' means 'not all' and this means 'some are not.' So, we have an **O** proposition, "Some of the students did not pass." What does the familiar expression "All is not gold that glitters" really say? It means "Some things that glitter are not gold."

To further understand why "all are not" is equivalent to "some are not," we need to recall that the 'all' A statement is always universal and affirmative and thus the combination of 'all' and 'not' is clearly illegitimate. Further, 'not' works on the verb turning it from affirmative quality to negative quality. Thus a negative statement is required. Clearly, total exclusion is not intended by the statement "Not all desserts are fattening," but rather a particular statement— "Some desserts are not fattening."

Tape Exercises

Translate the following into standard categorical form. [Check your answers with Tape 5, band 3.]

1. It is only the ignorant who despise education.
2. Not all dividends of corporations are subject to the dividend exclusion.
3. To see is to believe.
4. Not any of the components is defective.
5. No person except a natural-born citizens or a citizen at the time of the adoption of this constitution should be eligible for the office of president.
6. There are no deductions allowed for gambling losses that exceed gambling gains.
7. All persons are competent to make a will except infants, persons of unsound mind, and idiots.
8. There is no wheat without chaff.
9. Whenever one is angry, one's adrenalin production increases.
10. Fools walk where angels fear to tread.

Exercises for § 5.3

State the following in standard form propositions and identify them as **A, I, E** or **O**. [The shaded items are analyzed on Tape 5, band 3.]

1. All the mail arrived on time.
2. Every book he has is here.
3. A whale is a mammal.
4. Socrates is mortal.
5. Anything that is expensive is good.
6. He always arrives late.
7. He who hesistates is lost.
8. Only visitors will be admitted.
9. None but the courageous deserve the Congressional Medal of Honor.

10. None of the mail arrives on time.

11. Each person is not liable.

12. A bat is not a bird.

13. Nothing that is a vegetable is a mineral.

14. Not anything that is pleasurable is free.

15. Nowhere he goes, will I go.

16. There are no innocent coeds.

17. Most coeds are innocent.

18. Many Russians are not Bolsheviks.

19. All that glitters is not gold.

20. Not everything that is expensive is well made.

21. Most kittens are loveable.

22. Almost 60 percent of the student body are over twenty years of age.

23. All the students except graduates may sing in the choir.

24. "Except ye be born again ye cannot enter the Kingdom of Heaven."

25. The sincere alone are to be respected.

5.4   VENN DIAGRAM REPRESENTATION OF CATEGORICAL STATEMENTS

Categorical statements, as we have indicated, express relationships between the class of things represented by the subject term and the class corresponding to the predicate term. We also indicated that classes may be related in several ways:

Identity   Two classes may be said to be identical only when they have the same or synonymous members. We test for identity of two classes, S and P, by asking: *Is every element that is a member of* S *also a member of* P? Is every element in P also in S? (See figure 11.)

FIGURE 11. *All* S *is* P: *All squares are equilateral parallelograms having four right angles. All of class* S *is identical with the class of* P.

Inclusion   A class S is said to be included in a class P if *all* the members of S are also members of P. (See figure 12.)

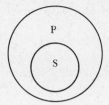

FIGURE 12. *All* S *is* P: *All dictators are undemocratic. All of the class* S *falls within the larger class* P.

Exclusion   In exclusion, the class S is entirely excluded from the predicate class P. They have no members in common. (See figure 13.)

FIGURE 13. *No* S *is* P: *No dictators are modest.*

Partial Inclusion   Some members of S are also members of P. (See figure 14.)

FIGURE 14. *Some* S *is* P: *Some dictators are undemocratic.*

Partial Exclusion   Some members of S are excluded from every part of P. The predicate class P, is denied universally of the class S. (See figure 15.)

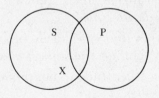

FIGURE 15

The type of visual circle representation of the categorical statements used in figures above are called Euler diagrams. However, a nineteenth-century logician, John Venn, proposed another way to symbolize the categorical propositions, and his way has advantages over the Eulerian circles. In the Venn diagrams, we begin with two intersecting circles, one representing the subject class and the other the predicate class. (See figure 16.)

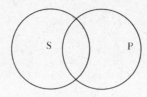

FIGURE 16

We then adopt three kinds of markings:

(1)   A *shaded area* indicates that there are *no members* in the class represented by that area; (2) An *X* in an area segment indicates that the class
represented by that area has *at least one member.* (3) A line over a term, *p*,
indicates the complement of the term, or not-p. Then we consider that all
categorical statements have two terms, a subject term and a predicate term.
Each term has, as its extension, a class of objects—the first, a subject class; the
second, a predicate class. Given any two such classes, say *S* and *P*, every object
in the world must fall into one of four class SP, $S\bar{P}$, $\bar{S}P$, $\bar{S}\bar{P}$. Schematically, this is
represented in figure 17.

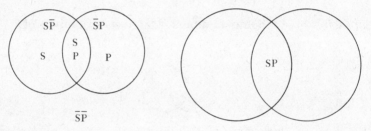

FIGURE 17

Thus, taking the categorical statement, "All students are proud," we get:

1. SP: The students that are proud beings. These students are members
   of *both classes.*
2. $S\bar{P}$:   The students that are not proud. They are members of the *subject
   class,* but *not the predicate class.*
3. $\bar{S}P$:   Beings that are not students and are proud. These are members
   of the *predicate class,* but *not* the *subject class.*
4. $\bar{S}\bar{P}$:   Beings that are neither students nor proud. These are beings that
   are *not members of either class.*

Applying these to the diagram in figure 17, we have the diagram shown in
figure 18. Each of the categorical statements can thus be visually represented
by Venn diagrams.

A. *All S is* P: "All students are proud"—means that there are no students
who are not proud, that is, no members of the class of *S* outside of *P*. In other
words, "$S\bar{P} = 0$." The class of "students who are not proud" is empty, has no
members. Therefore, we shade out that area in figure 19.

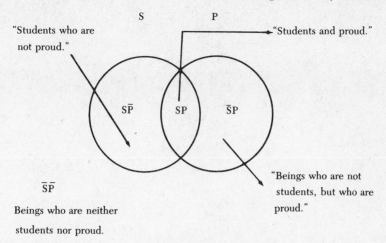

"Students who are not proud."

S   P

"Students and proud."

S̄P̄   SP   S̄P

S̄P̄

Beings who are neither students nor proud.

"Beings who are not students, but who are proud."

FIGURE 18

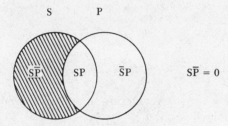

S   P

S̄P̄   SP   S̄P

SP̄ = 0

FIGURE 19

E. *No S is* P: "No students are proud"—means total class exclusion, no members in common. In other words, there are no beings who are *both* students and proud. The class of "proud students" is empty, has no members: SP ≠ 0. Thus, in figure 20 we shade out the area representing that class.

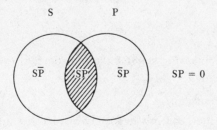

S   P

SP̄   SP   S̄P

SP = 0

FIGURE 20

I. *Some S is* P: "Some students are proud" is interpreted as "There is at least one member of the class of students who are proud." The class is not empty: SP = 0. In this case we place an X in that area in figure 21.

O. *Some S is not* P: "Some students are not proud is interpreted to mean "The class of students who are not proud has at least one member. It is not empty: SP̄ ≠ 0. (See figure 22.)

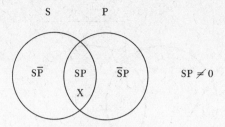

FIGURE 21

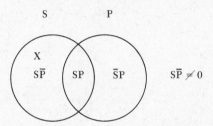

FIGURE 22

Tape Exercises

Translate the following into standard form, and construct a Venn diagram. [Check your answers with Tape 5, band 4.]

1. A wise traveler never despises his or her country.
2. All but the guilty shall be punished.
3. Black cows give white milk.
4. All professors are not lovers.
5. There are beautiful and intelligent women.

Exercises for § 5.4

Translate each of the following statements into standard categorical form, and construct a Venn Diagram.

1. All love is not friendship.
2. Many of the so-called controls in society involve rewards.
3. All people are familiar with the constant babbling of the small child from babyhood onward.
4. Acculturation does not always produce inhibited, warped personalities.
5. Only slaves and women were denied the rights of citizenship.
6. Not all who sow shall reap.
7. Eligible bachelors are scarce.
8. No one has the power to change the changeless.

9. There are no ghosts.

10. Some who lose come back again and again.

5.5 The Square of Opposition and Existential Import

In this section we shall be concerned with four possible relationships, known as *opposition*, which can hold between categorical statements having the same subject and predicate terms. Two statements of this sort may be related as *contradictories, contraries, subcontraries* and *alterns*. The *opposition* relationships are such that given the *truth value* (truth or falsity) of any *one* of the four categorical statements, **A, E, I** and **O**, each remaining statement can be established as true, false, or undetermined.

Existence   There is a controversy among logicians today about whether or not all opposition relationships are always valid inferences. In traditional Aristotelian logic, the four opposition relationships, presented in the Square of Opposition, are held to be valid.

The question of the invalidity of the *opposition* relationships arose as a new and higher form of logic—quantification predicate logic—was developed. Predicate logic interprets all particular categorical statements (**I** and **O** forms) as implying the existence of things to which the subject term applies. Thus, the categorical statements, "Some cats are finicky" and "Some cats are not finicky" are restated in conjunctive form as "There exists at least one thing x such that x is a cat and x is finicky," and "There exists at least one thing x such that x is a cat and x is not finicky." In this interpretation, particular categorical statements whose subject term denote nonexistent things (for example, "Some unicorns are blue" and "Some unicorns are not blue") are false statements. In predicate logic, the only opposition relationship that validly holds is the *contradictory* relationship. In conjunction with this, we have the so-called Boolean Square of Opposition shown in figure 23.

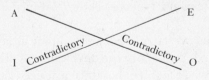

FIGURE 23

In light of the presumed difficulties raised for the traditional Square of Opposition by the existence question, many logicians proposed that we continue working with the opposition relationships, but assume they are valid *only* if we *make the existential assumption* we *presuppose the existence of things denoted by the subject term.*

There are others, however, who think the whole existence controversy is a pseudo issue. They ask us to look at categorical statements as explaining the meaning of the *class relationships* of exclusion-inclusion, partial inclusion, and partial exclusion in the abstract, apart from actual things that can be members of classes. Consider this series of statements:

All unicorns are one horned.

Some unicorns are one horned.

No unicorns are one horned.

Some unicorns are not one horned.

The point is that we are asking what is being said about the various kinds of class relationships, regardless of whether they are classes *having existing members or not*. To talk of existence seems to confuse truth and validity.

For example, the **A** statement means to talk of the total inclusion of the subject class in the predicate class—the class of unicorns is included in the class of one-horned beings. It would be false to this meaning to say "No unicorns are one horned" and "Some unicorns are not one horned." Surely if we assert "*All* unicorns are one horned," we are also committed to asserting "*Some* unicorns are one horned." Further, if the statement "No unicorns are one horned" intends to assert total class exclusion, it is false to that *meaning* to talk of any kind of inclusion; **A** or **I** and partial exclusion of **O** is included in the meaning of **E**.

Turning to the **I** and **O** statements, if we assert an **I** statement, we intend to say that two classes are in a relationship of partial inclusion—they overlap in membership. Such an assertion definitely rules out total exclusion, **E**, but does not commit us either to total inclusion, **A**, or partial exclusion, **O**. Similarly, with an **O** statement of partial exclusion, it is false to such an assertion to talk of total inclusion. But an **O** statement leaves open (does not involve any commitment about) total exclusion, **E**, or partial inclusion, **I**.

In the interpretation that categorical statements are concerned exclusively with the *meanings* of certain types of class relationships, all the opposition relationships hold.

It is this position that we favor, and we hope for a day when the existence problem will be resolved, perhaps in the development of a value-free logic. For the present purposes, we recognize that the existence issue is part and parcel of predicate logic and that reference is made by some to the *existential assumption*. We shall indicate, as each opposition relation is discussed, why 'existence' seems to make difficulties. It is suggested, therefore, that we use the *opposition relationships* to understand the full meaning of the categorical statements, and if we talk about unicorns, beware that they *might not exist*.

Contradiction   The first opposition relationship is contradiction. *Two statements are contradictory if they must have opposite truth values, that is, both cannot be true and both cannot be false at the same time.* Contradictory statements are "mutually exclusive:" if one is true, the other must be false and vice-versa. For example, "John is rich" and "John is not rich." We must concentrate on "mutually exclusive." Consider the **A** form, All *S* is *P*. We said that this is false if there is an *S* that is not a *P*. Thus, the contradictory of the **A** statement is the **O** statement, "Some *S* is not *P*," and vice-versa. They are "mutually exclusive." All that is needed to falsify the statement, "All men are mortal," is *one* case of a man who is *not* mortal. And, if we assert that there is a man who is not mortal, this can only be falsified by proving that all men *are* mortal. Similarly, the **E** statement, "No man is immortal," is falsified by producing one case of a man who is immortal. Thus, the **E** statements and the **I** statements are contradictories. "No ballet dancers are fat" and "Some ballet dancers are fat" are mutually exclusive. The *contradictories*, then, are **A** and **O**, and **E** and **I**.

Contraries   A second kind of relationship that can hold between statements is contrary. When we explain the black and white fallacy, we indicate that *contraries* may be defined as follows: *Two statements are contraries if both cannot be true at the same time but both may be false.*

Thus, the statements, "This rug is black all over" and "This rug is white all over," provided they are about the same rug at the same time, cannot both be true. However, they can both be false, as when the rug in question is yellow. Contraries are not mutually exclusive. Turning to the categorical statements, it can be seen that **A** and **E** are contraries. "All distinguished men drink Old Mule Sweat," and "No distinguished men drink Old Mule Sweat" cannot both be true statements. However, they both may be false. Distinguished men may drink Young Crow or 1000 other kinds of booze. Thus, in dealing with contraries, we assume that if one is true, the other is false. If "All men are mortal" is true, then "No men are mortal" is taken to be false. But notice: if one is false, we are told nothing about the truth value of the other. If "All men enjoy pornography" is false, it does not follow that "No men enjoy pornography." The second statement is *undetermined.* The *contraries*, then, are **A** and **E,** if either one of them is true, the other is false. If either of them is known to be false, the truth value of the other is left undetermined.

The following summarizes the contrary relationship. Using ~ to abbreviate "it is not the case that" and → to stand for "it follows that," we can say

A → ~ E   From the truth of one, we
E → ~ A   can infer the falsity of the
                 other.

The following inferences do not hold:

~ A → E   We cannot validly infer
~ E → A   from the falsity of one to
                 the truth of the other.

That these inferences do not hold can best be seen by considering the fact that some false statements, such as "All flowers are dogs," have true contraries, and some, such as "All flowers are blue," have false contraries. The main point for logic is that we cannot tell from the form alone which is which.

Again, as already indicated, many logicians argue that this relationship of contraries fails to hold if the subject term of the categorical statement refers to a null class, that is, a class that has no members. Consider the categorical statements: "All unicorns are one horned" and "No unicorns are one horned." These are contrary statements: both *cannot* be true at the same time. However, if we interpret particular categorical statements as asserting the existence of at least one member of the subject class, then, the categorical statements "Some unicorns are not one horned" and "Some unicorns are one horned" *are both false,* because no unicorns exist. These **I** and **O** statements are both *false,* and their *contradictories,* **E** and **A,** must both be true. Contradictories have opposite truth values. But, if **A** and **E** are *both true,* they are *not* truly contraries. Because of these technical problems, many logicians speak of adopting the *existential assumption,* namely, that with all categorical statements, we *can assume that no subject term represents an empty set.* On this assumption, the contrary relationship always holds.

Subcontraries.   The relationship between **I** and **O** has traditionally been called that of subcontraries. Subcontraries may be defined as follows: *Two statements are subcontraries if both cannot be false, but both can be true.* Thus, we can easily see why both "Some football players are professionals" and "Some football players are not professionals" can be true. But why cannot both be false? If both are false, then *both* their contradictories, "No football players are professionals" and "All football players are professionals" must *both be true.* As we have already seen, this cannot be the case. [Once again, it must be noted, **I** and **O** can both be false if the subject class is empty, for example, "Some round squares are round" and "Some round squares are not round" are both false.] Granting the existential assumption, then, the logical relationships between subcontraries may be summarized:

$\sim$ I $\rightarrow$ O

From Falsity to Truth

$\sim$ O $\rightarrow$ I

These are *one way* inferences. The following do not hold: I $\rightarrow$ $-$ O and O $\rightarrow$ $-$ I. We cannot infer from the truth of one subcontrary to the falsity of the other. Once again the fact that these inferences do not hold can best be seen by examples. Thus, from the truth of "Some cats are yellow," we cannot infer the falsity of "Some cats are not yellow." And, from the truth of "Some cats are not yellow," we cannot infer the falsity of "Some cats are yellow."

Alterns   A final case of relationships between the categorical statements is subalternation, or the logical relationships between universal and particular statements. Thus, for example, if "All the cars on this lot are Chevrolets" is true, then the truth of "Some cars on this lot. . . ." is also implied. Once again, however, existential import is usually assumed, for "Some unicorns are blue" does not follow from "All unicorns are blue " *if* it is understood to assert that unicorns exist. Provided, therefore, that existential import is assumed, the following summarizes the subaltern relationship:

A → I

E → O

The Square of Opposition.   All of the logical relationships shown in figure 24 between the categorical statements have been traditionally schematized by the *Square of Opposition* (assuming existential import).

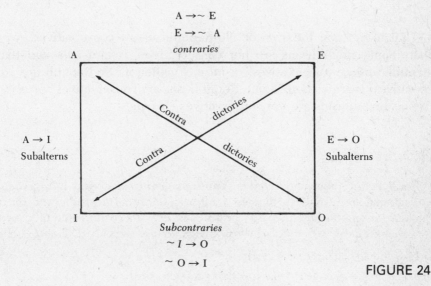

FIGURE 24

We can move around the square making certain conclusions as we move along. Thus, if we begin with *A* as true, we get the following:

A → ~ E

~ E → I

For example, if we assume "All Republicans are conservatives" as true, then we know that "No Republicans are conservatives" is false. If "No Republicans are conservatives" is false, then "Some Republicans are Conservatives" must be *true*.

   If we start with *A* again, we can get the following:

A → I

I → ~ E

If we know that "All Republicans are conservatives" is *true*, then we know that "Some Republicans are conservatives" is *true* and "Some Republicans are not conservatives" is *false*.

If we start with *E*, we can get:

E → O

O → ~ A

or:

E → ~ I

~ I → O

Thus, if we know the *truth* of "No Republicans are conservatives," we know that "Some Republicans are not conservatives" is also *true* and that "All Republicans are conservatives," is *false*. Further, if "No Republicans are conservatives" is *true*, then "Some Republicans are conservatives" is *false* while "Some Republicans are not conservatives" is *true*.

Tape Exercises

Translate the following statements into standard categorical form. Then (1) diagram them; (2) indicate their contradictory, their contrary and/or subcontrary; and assuming the statements to be true, (3) give the truth value of their contradictories, contraries and alterns. [Check your answers with Tape 5, band 4.]

1. A few logicians are not mad.
2. There are chemical processes that produce light.
3. A rolling stone gathers no moss.
4. Comparison is not proof.
5. A baited cat may grow as fierce as a lion.

Exercises for § 5.5

A. Match the opposition relationships listed on the left to the descriptions on the right. They may have more than one answer.

Oppositions	Descriptions
Contradictories	1. Both cannot be false._____
Contraries	2. Both cannot be true._____
Subcontraries	3. They have opposite truth values.
	_____

Oppositions	Descriptions
Alterns	4. Truth moves downward, falsity moves upward.

_____

5. Can both be false._____
6. Can both be true._____

B. Complete the blanks in the following:

1. Given, "All concepts are definable" as *false*, then "No concepts are defina-ble" is _____, "Some concepts are not definable" is _____, and "Some concepts are definable" is _____.

2. Given, "Some dogs are collies" as *true*, then "All dogs are collies" is _____, "No dogs are collies" is _____, and "Some dogs are not collies" is _____.

3. Given, "Some persons are not shy" as *true*, then "All persons are shy" is _____, "No persons are shy" is _____, and "Some persons are shy" is _____.

4. Given, "No persons are sheep" as *true*, then "All persons are sheep" is _____, "Some persons are sheep" is _____, and "Some persons are not sheep" is _____.

5. Given, "Some persons are not shy" as *false*, then "All persons are shy" is _____, "No persons are shy" is _____, and "Some persons are shy" is _____.

C. What is the *contrary* of the following propositions?

1. All redheads are hot tempered.
2. Some bankers are dull conversationalists.
3. No members of the Mafia are good sports.
4. Some TV shows are insults to a low-level ape.

D. What is the *contradictory* of the following propositions?

1. All politicians are dishonest.
2. Some gentlemen prefer blonds.
3. No Marxist is a supporter of free elections.
4. Some Republicans are not conservatives.

E. What logical propositions may be inferred from each of the following?

1. All football players are rough and tough.
2. No Democrats are economic conservatives.
3. All American-made automobiles are expensive.
4. No American-made automobiles are expensive.

5.6   IMMEDIATE INFERENCES: CONVERSION, OBVERSION, AND CONTRAPOSITION

Three additional kinds of immediate inferences can be carried out with categorical statements. These involve categorical statements that have exactly the same subject and predicate terms. They are *conversion, obversion* and *contraposition*. These are accomplished by a purely verbal transformation of categorical statements, namely, transformations accomplished by simple operations on the terms of the statements. Thus, for example we may interchange the subject and predicate terms of the statement, "No dogs are six-legged animals," and get, "No six-legged animals are dogs."

Using these operations or transformations, we can get grammatically different, but *logically equivalent* forms of categorical statements. *Equivalent statements* are those that can take each other's place without changing the context within which the substitution is made. Expressed differently, *equivalent statements are those which necessarily have the same truth value.* If one of the propositions is true, the other must also be true; and if one is false then the other must be false, for example, "All who deserve the fair are brave" and "No person who is not brave deserves the fair."

Thus, the three kinds of immediate inferences, because they produce equivalent statements, may be thought of as eduction. *Eduction* is a process of making explicit in a second proposition a meaning that is virtually contained in the original from which it is derived. That is, these inferences are really methods of drawing out the implied meanings of a given statement. They do not produce new truths, but give us the same truths from a different point of view. They further our understanding of the four kinds of categorical statements.

Conversion   Conversion is the operation of interchanging the subject and predicate terms in a categorical statement. "No *S* is *P*" becomes "No *P* is *S.*" However, two important rules need to be stated in dealing with conversion: (1) The *quality* of the converse must be the same as the original; if the original is affirmative, the converse must be affirmative; if negative, it must be negative. (2) No term may be overextended, that is, it's *quantity* must not be increased. A particular term (undistributed) cannot be changed to a universal term (distributed). Another way of stating this second rule is that when subject and predicate terms are *alike* as regards distribution (either both distributed or both undistributed) then the conversion is valid, but when they differ as regards distribution, then conversion is invalid. This rule must be especially observed in converting an **A** and **O** statement. Let us see how conversion works.

   A *Proposition.*   Because of rule 2, an **A** proposition cannot be converted into an **A** proposition. From "All scientific knowledge is organized knowledge" we cannot infer "All organized knowledge is scientific knowledge."

Nor, from "All communists are atheists" can we infer "All atheists are communists." To make these fallacious inferences is to ignore that the predicate term of the **A** statement is undistributed. The **A** statement does not say anything about *all* members of the *P* class. All of the subject class is included in the predicate class, but not vice-versa. To infer 'All *P* are *S*' from 'All *S* are *P*' is to commit the fallacy of illicit conversion. An **A** proposition properly converts into an **I** proposition.

> **A:** All scientific knowledge is organized knowledge.
> *Converse* **I:** Some organized knowledge is scientific knowledge.

> This conversion is called *conversion by limitation*.

E *Statement*   Because both subject and predicate term of the **E** are universal—distributed—there is no chance of overextension. Thus, "No scientist is an ignorant person," converts to, "No ignorant person is a scientist." These are equivalent statements and maintain the meaning of the **E** statement, namely, total class exclusion.

I *Proposition*   Similarly, because the subject and predicate terms of the **I** statement are both particular and undistributed, conversion does not violate the rule of overextension. Thus, "Some ignorant people are prejudiced people," converts to, "Some prejudiced people are ignorant people." The conversion maintains the meaning of the **I** proposition, namely, overlapping membership of classes or partial inclusion of two classes in each other.

O *Statements*   **O** statements, in fact *do not convert*, and any attempt to convert one of these propositions is a *fallacy of illicit conversion*. Thus, from "Some detectives are not policemen," *it does not follow* that "Some policemen are not detectives"; and from "Some dogs are not collies," it cannot be inferred that "Some collies are not dogs." This is so because in the original statement, the predicate term is *distributed*, it totally excludes the predicate class—*these are members of the subject class totally outside the predicate class*. This is all the **O** statement tells us; it does not tell us anything about the membership of the predicate class. Thus, we are not entitled to also infer that some *P* are not *S*.

Conversion may be summarized as follows:

A: All *S* is *P* converts to Some *P* is *S*.
E: No *S* is *P* converts to No *P* is *S*.
I: Some *S* is *P* converts to Some *P* is *S*.
O: Some *S* is not *P* does not convert.

Obversion   The obversion of a statement, in effect, changes the *quality* of the original. In spite of the change of quality, what is produced is an *equivalent statement*, one essentially alike in meaning to the original. If the original is true, the obverse is necessarily true. Obversion draws out further meanings of each of the four categorical statements.

There are two essential rules of procedure in obversion. (1) *Negate the copula:* Make an affirmative negative—*is* to *is not*—or make a negative affirmative—*is not* to *is*. (2) *Contradict the predicate term:* Give its complement. Replace a predicate term *P* by replacing it with non-*P*. Take care in producing complements to be sure they are true contradictories—truly mutually exclusive. Language can trip us up here, and we can confuse contradictories and contraries. In order to avoid misleading terms, which are not really complements, it is advisable to attach the prefix *non* to the original predicate term, as a means of contradicting it. Thus, the complements of *moral, responsible, valuable* and *flammable* are correctly rendered as nonmoral, nonresponsible, nonvaluable and nonflammable.

In schematic form, obversion proceeds as follows:

Original	Obverse
A: All *S* are *P*.	**E:** No *S* are non-*P*.
E: No *S* are *P*.	**A:** All *S* are non-*P*.
I: Some *S* are *P*.	**O:** Some *S* are not non-*P*.
O: Some *S* are not *P*.	**I:** Some *S* are non-*P*.

Consider this in more detail.

1. **A** *statements obvert to* **E**
   (**A**) Every virtuous person is happy.
   obverse (**E**) No virtuous person is non-happy.
   This does maintain the meaning of the **A** proposition, namely that there is *no S who is not also a* P.

2. **E** *statements obvert to* **A**
   (**E**) No just act is rewarded.
   obverse (**A**) *Every* (un)just act *is* (non)rewarded.
   Once again, this draws out the meaning of the **E,** namely, there is no case of an *S* which is also a *P*.

3. **I** *statements obvert to* **O**
   (**I**) Some people *are* talkative.
   obverse (**O**) Some people *are* not non-talkative.
   This keeps true to the joint partial overlapping of the two classes.

4. **O** *statements obvert to* **I**
   (**O**) Some workers are not union members.
   obverse (**I**) Some workers are non-union members.
   Once again the meaning of the **O** is further spelled out.

Contraposition   A third type of immediate inference is contraposition, which consists of (1) taking the complement of both subject and predicate term and (2) interchanging these complemented terms. We negate the subject and predicate terms individually and then transpose them. We do *not* change the quality or quantity of the sentence. Thus, the contrapositive of "All members are voters" is "All non-voters are nonmembers," and the contrapositive of "Some students are not idealists" is "Some nonidealists are not nonstudents." Contraposition of the **I** and **E** do not produce equivalent statements and therefore are not valid. Because contraposition does not add in any significant way to our understanding of the categorical statements, we shall say no more about it.

The immediate inferences are summarized in table 2.

Table 2

Rules of Inference	All *S* is *P*	No *S* is *P*	Some *S* is *P*	Some *S* is not *P*
Conversion: Transpose *S* and *P*	Some *P* is *S*	No *P* is *S*	Some *P* is *S*	Invalid
Obversion: Change quality and replace *P* by non-*P*	No *S* is non-*P*	All *S* is non-*P*	Some *S* is not non-*P*	Some *S* is non-*P*
Contraposition: Interchange *S* and *P* and replace *S* by non-*S* and *P* by non-*P*	All non-*P* is non-*S*	Invalid	Invalid	Some non-*P* is not non-*S*

In section 5.6 we have discussed four possible relationships, known as *oppositions*, which can hold between categorical statements having the same subject and predicate terms. They are summarized in table 3.

TABLE 3

Categorical Form	Opposition Relation	*Definition of the Relation*

1. **A:** All *S* are *P*
   O: Some *S* are not *P*
 	
   E: No *S* are *P*
   I: Some *S* are *P*
	Contradictory	Both *cannot* be true and both cannot be false.
		Have opposite truth value.

2. **A:** All *S* are *P* **E:** No *S* are *P*	*Contrary*	Both *cannot* be true, but both can be false.
3. **I:** Some *S* are *P* **O:** Some *S* are not *P*	*Subcontrary*	Both can be true, but both *cannot* be false.

4. **A:** All *S* are *P*
   I: Some *S* are *P*
 	
   E: No *S* are *P*
   O: Some *S* are not *P*
	Alterns	If the universal is true, the particular is true; if the particular is false, the universal must be false. Otherwise undetermined.

Exercises for § 5.6

A. Convert and obvert the following propositions.
  1. No unstable person is a good lieutenant.
  2. All dope peddlers are criminals.
  3. Some wealthy people are snobs.
  4. All enemy captured must be put in jail.

B. Give the contrapositive of the following.
  1. Honest politicians alone are to be trusted.
  2. No lovers of truth are braggarts.
  3. Only union members are eligible.
  4. All educated people are wealthy.
  5. No lawyers are clergymen.

Chapter Outline

A. In traditional logic the basic type of statement with which we are concerned is the *categorical statement*.
  1. A categorical statement makes a claim about relations between two classes. (A class is a collection or group of entities which have a common property or properties, e.g., lakes, rocks, dogs, thin ladies.)
  2. Each categorical statement has five essential aspects.
      a. *Quantifier:* Words "No" and "Some" that indicate *how many* (quantity) of a given term is involved.
      b. Subject term that describes or characterizes the class referred to by the subject term.
      c. *Copula:* Some form of the verb "to be" that indicates a relationship between the subject term class and the predicate term class.
      d. *Predicate term:* Indicates or describes the predicate class.
  3. Each categorical statement has quality and quantity.
      a. *Quantity:* It is *universal*, referring to the total class, "All" or "No"; or *particular*, referring only to some, but not all members of the class.
      b. *Quality:* The statement *affirms* or *denies*.
B. There are *four* forms of categorical statements. Using S and P to represent subject and predicate terms, we may depict the four forms of categorical statements as follows:

  A: All S are P   Universal Affirmative
  E: No S are P   Universal Negative
  I: Some S are P   Particular Affirmative
  O: Some S are not P   Particular Negative

C. *Distribution:* An important aspect of categorical statement is the distribution of its terms.
  1. A term is distributed if it refers to *every* kind of thing that is denoted by that term; otherwise, it is undistributed.
  2. The rules of distribution are:
      a. Universal statements distribute their subject terms.
      b. Negative statements distribute their predicate terms.

3. Distribution may be summarized as follows:

Categorical Form	Subject Term	Predicate Term
A	Distributed	Undistributed
E	Distributed	Distributed
I	Undistributed	Undistributed
O	Undistributed	Distributed

D. All statements, in order to be used in testing of the validity of syllogisms, must be translated into standard form categorical statements.

Special problem cases for translation are:

a. *Exceptives:* Reverse the order of subject and predicate terms.
   None but S is P = All P are S.
   Only S are P =All P are S.

b. *Negatives*
   Not all S is P = Some S is not P.
   All S are not P = Some S is not P.
   Not everything S is P = Some S is not P.

c. *Reference to time and place:*
   He always arrives late = All times he arrives are times he arrives late.
   Wherever he goes, I go = All places he goes are places I go.

6

THE SYLLOGISM

6.1 THE CATEGORICAL SYLLOGISM

The heart of traditional logic, the syllogism, is a special form of argument in which a categorical statement is inferred from two categorical premises. *A categorical syllogism is an argument consisting of three categorical statements that together involve three terms, each term appearing just twice.*

We should translate all arguments into standard form before we can ask the question of validity. The standard form categorical syllogism has the following features.

(1) It contains three terms and *only three terms. The major term* is the predicate term of the conclusion—*P* is the major term. The *minor term* is the subject term of the conclusion—*S* is the minor term. The *middle term* is the third term that appears in the premises.

(2) In a standard form syllogism, the premises must come in a certain order. The premise containing the major term (the predicate term of the conclusion) must come first. It is called the *major premise*. The premise containing the minor term (the subject term of the conclusion) comes second and is called the *minor premise*. The conclusion comes last. For example, the argument, "All people are rational, Americans are people, therefore, all Americans are rational," can be translated into standard form as follows:

$$\begin{array}{cc} \text{M} & \text{P} \end{array}$$

Major premise: All people are *rational beings*.

$$\text{S}$$

Minor premise: All Americans are people.

∴ All Americans are rational beings.

S–Minor term   P–Major term   people–Middle term

Syllogisms are named or classified according to their *mood* and *figure*. Mood is determined simply by naming, in consecutive order, the kinds of categorical statements used in the syllogism. Thus, the mood of the above syllogism is *AAA* because it is composed of three universal affirmative statements. Obviously, it could be composed of any combination of **A, I, E** and **O**.

The figure of a syllogism is determined by the position of the middle term. The middle term can occupy four different positions: subject term of the major premise and predicate term of the minor premise; predicate term of both premises; subject term of both premises; and predicate term of the major premise and subject term of the minor premise. These four figures can be represented as follows:

First Figure   Second Figure   Third Figure   Fourth Figure

First Figure	Second Figure	Third Figure	Fourth Figure
M P	P M	M P	P M
S M	S M	M S	M S
S P	S P	S P	S P

These are easy to remember because of their symmetry—the middle terms form the front of a shirt collar. The figure of the *AAA* syllogism above, then, is the First Figure. This was traditionally called the syllogism "Barbara" (because there are three *A*'s in the name).

By specifying the mood and figure of a syllogism, its *form* is fully given. Indeed, mood and figure constitute the form of the syllogism. For example, *AEE–4* means that the major premise is an **A** statement, and the minor premise and the conclusion are **E** statements. The syllogism is in the fourth figure.

A   All P is M
E   No M is S

∴ **E**   No S is P

In putting syllogisms into standard form, we follow four steps: (1) Translate each statement into its categorical form. (2) Find the conclusion, and locate the subject and predicate terms so that the major and minor premises can be determined. (3) List the major premise first, then the minor. (4) Determine mood and figure. Consider the following:

Every drink containing alcohol is an intoxicant, and each drink that contains alcohol is a stimulant, so intoxicants are stimulants.

This translates into:

All drinks containing alcohol are intoxicants;
All drinks containing alcohol are stimulants;
So, all intoxicants are stimulants.

Then, taking the next three steps we get:

A   All drinks containing alcohol are stimulants;
A–3 All drinks containing alcohol are intoxicants;

A   All intoxicants are stimulants.

In straight argument form, we have

All M are P
All M are S

All S are P

Or, using letters more appropriate to the actual subject and predicate terms, we have:

All D are S
All D are I

All I are S

<hr>

Tape Exercises

Consider the following. How might they be translated into syllogisitic form? Tape 6, band 1.]

1. Every successful businessman is concerned with making a profit; but no person who devalues money is concerned with making a profit, and thus no persons who devalue money are successful businessmen.
2. Some people are not profiters because some people are concerned with selling quality products and no profiters are concerned with selling quality products.

Exercises for § 6.1

1. Everything fattening should be avoided, but some cakes are fattening and therefore should be avoided.
2. Only atheists deny God's existence, for only skeptics are atheists, and all who deny God's existence are skeptics.

3. A broad education is indispensable for a writer. Studies in the liberal arts and the sciences are part of a broad education and thus are indispensable for a writer.

4. Some plants are petunias because all blue flowers are plants and some petunias are blue flowers.

5. Not all fish are sharks because all sharks are dangerous and not all fish are dangerous.

6. Nothing that is invincible is subject to defeat. All nations are subject to defeat and so no nations are invincible.

7. Some women have no morals, but women who have no morals are unhappy. Therefore some women are unhappy.

8. Not all children are lovable, but lovable people are fun to be with. Therefore some children are not fun to be with.

9. No ghosts are observable, for all visible objects are observable and ghosts are not visible.

10. All capitalists are supporters of tax deductions, but internal revenue people are not supporters of tax deductions. Thus, we may conclude that no internal revenue people are capitalists.

6.2 WAYS OF DETERMINING VALIDITY: RULES AND DIAGRAMS

Validity, we recall, is a matter of form, of the *structure* of the argument. If a syllogism having a given form is *valid,* then all syllogisms having that form are valid. If a syllogism having a given form is *invalid,* then all syllogisms having that form are *invalid.*

A traditional way of determining the validity of syllogisms is by means of six rules, two concerning the quality of the statements making up the argument and two concerning quantity or distribution. (Later we shall add two more rules that are less frequently used.)

Rules of Quantity

1. **The middle term must be distributed at least once.**
2. **No term can be distributed in the conclusion that is not distributed in the premises.**

Rules of Quality

3. **It is impossible to have two negative premises.**
4. **If there is a negative premise, there must be a negative conclusion, and if there is a negative conclusion there must be a negative premise.**

We shall consider each rule in turn so that we may understand why they correctly indicate validity/invalidity. But in doing so, we shall also introduce another method of testing validity of the syllogistic forms, the Venn diagrams. We work both with rules and with diagrams together because they help to make each other understandable and because both work together in testing validity.

To diagram a syllogism, three overlapping circles are required, one for each term. In overlapping the circles, seven class areas are formed. (See figure 25.)

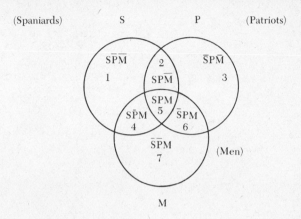

FIGURE 25

Using the Barbara syllogism *AAA–1* to illustrate

> All men (human beings) are patriotic.
> All Spaniards are men.
> _____
> All Spaniards are patriotic.

the areas are as follows:

1. $S\bar{P}\bar{M}$—The class of Spaniards (the minor term class); individuals who are Spaniards, but *not* patriotic and men.
2. $SP\bar{M}$—Individuals who are both S and P, but not men (patriotic Spaniards, but not men).
3. $\bar{S}P\bar{M}$—The class of patriotic beings (the major term class); individuals who are patriotic beings, but neither Spaniards or men.
4. $S\bar{P}M$—Individuals who are both S and M, but not P (Spaniards and men, but not patriotic).
5. SPM—Individuals who are patriotic Spaniards, and men.
6. $\bar{S}PM$—Individuals who are both P and M, but not S (individuals who are patriotic and men, but not Spaniards).
7. $\bar{S}\bar{P}M$—The middle term class, the class of men (individuals who are men, but neither Spaniards nor patriotic).

In diagramming syllogisms, we shade out to indicate empty classes and use x to indicate there is at least one member of the class. We shall find that in some cases there is not enough information in the premises to tell us exactly where to put the x, for example:

Some *M* are not *P*.
Some *S* are not *M*.

Some *S* are not *P*.

Figure 26 shows the diagram for this syllogism.[1]

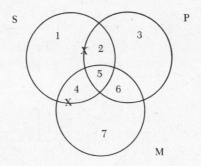

FIGURE 26

The first premise does not tell us which area of *M*—4 or 7—to put the *x* in, so we put it on the line in between 4 and 7. Similarly, the second premise does not tell us what area of *S* to put the *x* in—1 or 2—so we put it on the line between the two. Where there is an *x* on the line, the syllogism is usually invalid.

We diagram only the premises and always the universal premises first, if there are any. Once the premises are diagrammed, if the syllogism is valid, we can read the conclusion from the diagram. If invalid, the conclusion is not represented by the diagram.

Taking our example,

All *M* are *P*.   All men are rational.
All *S* are *M*.   All philosophers are men.

All *S* are *P*.   All philosophers are rational.

We diagram the premises as shown in figure 27.

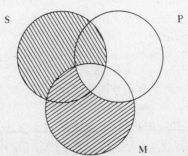

FIGURE 27

[1] In succeeding diagrams we will refer to diagram sections as they are numbered in figure 26.

The major premise, "All M are , means that "*Every* man is identical with some P, or "All of the class M is included in the class P." Therefore, there are *no* M *which are not* P. We thus shade out all of circle M outside circle P. The classes S$\bar{P}$M and $\bar{S}\bar{P}$M are empty—areas 4 and 7. In regular language, "All men are rational" means that the classes, "Human philosophers who are not rational" (S$\bar{P}$M) and "Humans who are not philosophers or rational" ($\bar{S}\bar{P}$M) is empty. The minor premise, "All S are M" means that "Every S is identical with some M" or "All of the class S is included in the class M." Therefore, there *are no* S *that are not* M. We thus shade out all of the circle S outside the circle M—areas 1 and 2. The classes S$\bar{P}\bar{M}$ and SP$\bar{M}$ are empty. In other words, "All philosophers are men" means that the classes "Philosophers who are not rational or men" and "Philosophers who are rational, but not men" are empty.

Once the premises are diagrammed, we check to see if we can read the conclusion from the diagram. The conclusion is "All S are P," which means that there is no S that is outside of P. All of the circle S outside of circle P must be shaded—areas 1 and 4. Classes S$\bar{P}\bar{M}$ and S$\bar{P}$M must be empty. These areas are shaded out on the diagram, and thus, the syllogism is valid.

Tape Exercises

Translate the following arguments into syllogistic form and test them for validity using the Venn diagrams. [The answers are given on Tape 6, band 1.]

1. This college has team spirit because colleges that have football teams have team spirit and this college has a football team.

2. Some types of alcoholic liquor are harmful to the body because some stimulants are harmful to the body and all alcoholic liquors are stimulants.

Now consider a syllogism of the form **AAA–2:**

All P is M.
All S is M.

All S is P

An example of this form is:

All communists are atheists.
All philosophers are atheists.

All philosophers are communists.

Recalling distribution of the **A** statement, we translate it as follows:

D–U   *Every P is identical with some M.*
D–U   *Every S is identical with some M.*

D–U   *Every S is identical with some P.*

The major premise tells us that the class of communists is included in the class of atheists. The minor premise tells us that the class of philosophers is also included in the class of atheists. However, there is nothing to assure us that the *M*'s in the two premises are the *same M*'s. There is nothing to guarantee that the atheists who are communists are the same atheists who are philosophers. The middle term is supposed to function as a link between the subject and predicate term, to be a relating bridge. Here, there is *no* link, no assurance that *S*'s have anything whatever to do with *P*'s. This is also indicated by the diagram of the syllogism shown in figure 28. Shading out all of *P* outside of *M*—2 and 3, and all of *S* outside of *M*—area 1 and 2 we discover that area 4 remains unshaded. But the conclusion "All *S* is *P*" would require that both areas 1 and 4 be shaded. The syllogism is invalid. It commits *the fallacy of the undistributed middle*.

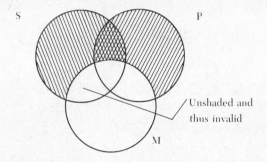

FIGURE 28

Consider a syllogism that does not violate the rule of the distributed middle.

No *P* is *M*.
Some *S* is *M*.

Some *S* is not *P*.

Every *P* is distinct from every *M*.
Some *S* is identical with some *M*.

Some *S* is distinct from every *P*.

Here the middle term does link *S* and *P* because every *M* is distinct from every *P* and, thus, that *S* which is identical with some *M* will also be distinct from every *P*. This is easily seen in the diagram in figure 29. "No *P* is *M*" requires that all overlapping areas between *P* and *M* be shaded out—areas 5 and 6. The classes *SPM* and *S̄PM* are empty. "Some *S* is *M*" requires that an *x* be in an area where S and M overlap. Because area 5 is already shaded, the x must go in area 4. (This is why universal propositions should be shaded first. It indicates what areas are out). The conclusion would require that there be an x in either 1 or 4. There is one in area 4, and; thus, the conclusion is valid. There is a member in the class $SM\overline{P}$.

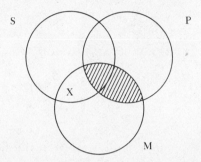

FIGURE 29

Next, consider the following argument in which a term, the major term P, is undistributed in the premises but distributed in the conclusion.

All mothers are parents.	All M are P	A
No fathers are mothers.	No S are M.	**E–1**
No fathers are parents.	No S are P.	**E**

or

M
Every mother is identical with <u>*some* parent.</u>
Every father is distinct from *every* mother.

Every father is distinct from <u>*every* parent.</u>

The error here is that we have asserted that what is true of *some* parents (in the premises) is true of *every* parent (in the conclusion). The major premise tells us that for every mother (M) some parent (P) is identical with her. This is true of all and *only* those parents who are mothers. The minor premise says that every father is distinct from every mother. Taken together, they do imply that every mother parent is distinct from every father parent, but the conclusion says too much, namely that *every* father is distinct from every parent, including the nonfather parents (of which it is true) and the father-parents (of which it is patently false). What is true of some (nonfather) parents is not true of every parent. Thus, the *fallacy of illicit major* is committed when the major term is distributed in the conclusion, but not in the premises. The diagram of the syllogism in figure 30 easily shows why this is a fallacy.

"All mothers are parents" requires the shading of areas 4 and 7. "No father is a mother," requires the shading of areas 4 and 5. The conclusion, "No father is a parent," however, requires the shading of both areas 2 and 5. Area 2, the class of "Fathers who are parents," remains *unshaded*. The syllogism is invalid.

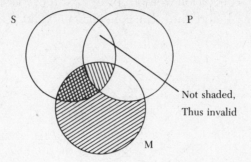

Not shaded,
Thus invalid

FIGURE 30

The fallacy of the illicit minor is illustrated in the following syllogism.

> Some spaniels are not good hunters.
> All spaniels are gentle dogs.
> ———————————————————
> ∴ No gentle dogs are good hunters.

or

O	Some *M* is not *P*.	*Some M is distinct from every P.*
A–3	All *M* are *S*.	*Every M is identical with some S.*
E	No *S* is *P*.	*Every S is distinct from every P.*

The argument moves from some *S* to a conclusion about every *S*. That this is a fallacy can be seen in the diagram shown in figure 31.

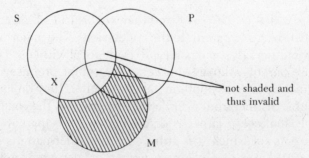

not shaded and
thus invalid

FIGURE 31

"All *M* is *S*" requires the shading of areas 6 and 7. "Some *M* is not *P*" requires an *X* in either 4 or 7, and must in this case be placed in 4. The conclusion, "No *S* is *P*," however, requires that areas 2 and 5 be shaded, and neither is shaded. It is *invalid*.

Look at the following. Translate them into syllogistic form and show why they commit either the fallacy of undistributed middle or the fallacies of illicit major or illicit minor. [Tape 6, band 2.]

1. All young ladies are sensitive creatures and all ballerinas are sensitive creatures. Thus, all ballerinas are young ladies.
2. All Hindus are vegetarians. No Methodists are Hindus, and therefore no Methodists are vegetarians.

Turning to the rules concerning quality, we see that **Rule 3** states that in a valid syllogism it is impossible to have two negative premises. Consider:

No wars are moral.	No P is M.
No murders are moral.	No S is M.
No murders are wars.	No S is P.

Knowing that every P is distinct from every M and that every S is distinct from every M is *no* reason to suppose that S's are distinct from P's. It is possible that every S is P, some S is P, or that some S is not P. In fact, *no* conclusion is entailed by two negative premises. This is easily seen in the syllogisms and their diagrams shown in figures 32 and 33.

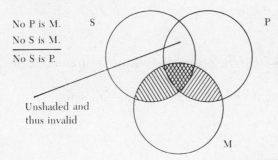

No P is M.
No S is M.

No S is P.

Unshaded and thus invalid

FIGURE 32

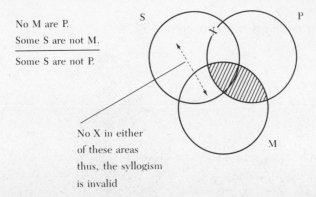

No M are P.
Some S are not M.

Some S are not P.

No X in either
of these areas
thus, the syllogism
is invalid

FIGURE 33

In figure 33, we do not know where to put the *X*. We put it on the line, which tells us nothing. This syllogism also violates rule three.

Our fourth rule (the second rule about quality) asserts that if a syllogism is to be valid and have a negative premise, then its conclusion must be negative; and if its conclusion is negative, then it must have a negative premise. Consider the following.

No *M* are *P*.
Some *S* are *M*.
———————
Some *S* are *P*.

Here the major premise excludes all *M*'s from *P*'s. The minor premise affirms that some *S*'s are *M*'s. The conclusion "Some *S* are *P*" just does not follow. Consider the diagram shown in figure 34.

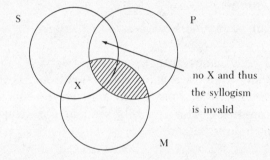

FIGURE 34

What *does* follow from the premises and the diagram in figure 34 is, Some *S* is not *P*.

Another case that violates **Rule 4** is the following:

All *P* is *M*.
All *M* is *S*.
———————
Some *S* is not *P*.

This argument is diagrammed in figure 35.

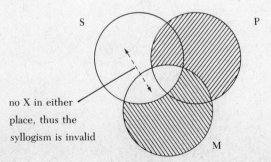

FIGURE 35

The conclusion certainly cannot be read from the diagram.

There are two additional rules for valid syllogisms that are not used quite as often as the first four.

Rule 5: No valid standard form categorical syllogism should have two universal premises and a particular conclusion.

Rule 6: A valid standard form categorical syllogism must have exactly three terms used with the same meaning throughout.

Rule 5 concerns the matter of existential import discussed in chapter 5. In the modern Boolean interpretation of categorical deductive logic, the universal statements, **A** and **E,** do not have existential import. They do not assert that the classes they refer to have actual existent members. For example, the statement 'All ghosts are invisible' says nothing about whether or not ghosts exist, but rather is interpreted to mean 'If anything is a ghost, it is invisible.' Likewise, the statement, 'No unicorns are blue' says nothing about the existence or nonexistence of unicorns, but rather asserts that 'If anything is a unicorn, then it is not blue.' Further, the particular statements do have existential import. The statement 'Some collies are black and white' says 'There are (existing) collies who are black and white'. The statement 'Some cats are not black' says 'There *are* some cats who are not black.' Thus, if a syllogism concludes from universal premises to a particular conclusion, it makes the illegal move from premises that have no existential import (which say nothing about existence or nonexistence) to a statement that does have existential import (which does make assertions about existence). Syllogisms that make the illegal move from universal premises to a particular conclusion thus commit *the existential fallacy.*

That these types of syllogisms are invalid can easily be seen from use of the Venn diagram. Consider the following example:

All ghosts are invisible.
No men are invisible.
_____
Therefore some men are not ghosts.

If we try to diagram this syllogism, we see an immediate problem. (See figure 36.) First we set out our three circles; then we diagram the major premise shading out all *P* outside of *M*; then we diagram the minor premise, shading out the overlap between *S* and *M.* But, the conclusion 'Some *S* are not *P*' cannot possibly be read from the diagram since we have no *X.* However, we do see what conclusion would make the syllogism valid. That conclusion is 'No S are P,' or 'No men are ghosts.'

Our sixth rule requires three terms and *only* three terms. It has to do with the essential character of a valid syllogism, namely that it is valid because the relation that the conclusion asserts to hold between two terms does, *in fact,*

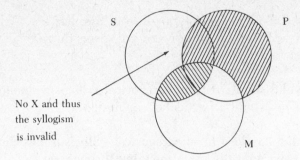

No X and thus
the syllogism
is invalid

FIGURE 36

hold. But this can be true only if the premises assert a relationship of the major and minor terms (the two terms in the conclusion) to a third term (the middle term). The middle term is the bridge connecting the other two terms. When it really does its job, the syllogism is valid. A valid syllogism, then, must have three terms and *only* three terms.

The problem arises with a tendency among people to equivocate (to use a single term in two different senses) while assuming they have the same meaning. We have already dealt with this fallacious form of arguing in chapter 4 on informal fallacies, but some readers may not have dealt with that yet and it never hurts to review. Let us take the classical example of equivocation:

All nature has laws. Laws require a lawgiver.
Therefore, nature has a lawgiver.

In this case, the word *law* is used equivocally. In the premise, "All nature has laws," 'laws' is used in the sense of 'laws of nature'—'descriptions of the uniform behavior of natural events.' In the second premise, "Laws require a lawgiver," 'laws' refer to 'commands issued by a governing body' or 'civil laws'. 'Civil laws' are prescriptions or commands and require a lawgiver, whereas 'natural laws' are purely descriptive and have no relation to commands; they thus do not need a lawgiver. In this syllogism, because the middle term is used in two different senses, no bridge could be built between the major and minor terms, and thus the syllogism couldn't possibly be valid. It commits *the fallacy of four terms*. In fact, an argument with four terms cannot really be called a syllogism because a syllogism is defined as having three terms and only three terms. Thus, this last rule really tells us to be sure we have a syllogism in the argument being appraised.

Tape Exercises

Identify the formal fallacies committed by the following arguments. [Check your answers against Tape 6, band 2.]

1. Whatever goes up must come down.
   Prices have gone up.

   Thus, prices will go down.

2. No misers are happy men.
   Some happy men are not artists.

   Some artists are not misers.

3. All unicorns are one-horned animals.
   No dogs are one-horned animals.

   Some dogs are not unicorns.

Using the rules and the diagrams, then, we can test the validity of syllogisms. We can also determine what conclusions, if any, can be drawn from a set of premises. Consider the following set of premises:

Christianity asserts the existence of a transcendent God.

Theistic religions assert the existence of a transcendent God.

These can be translated into two **A** statements:

All (Christianity) are (religions asserting the existence of a transcendent God.)

All (theistic religions) are (religions asserting the existence of a transcendent God.)

The conclusion would have to be affirmative because the two premises are affirmative. But closer examination reveals that no valid conclusion can be drawn from these premises because the middle term (religions asserting existence of a transcendent God) is undistributed in both cases.
Consider another set of premises:

"Some women make good legislators;
no good legislator is irresponsible."

We know, by **Rule 4,** that the conclusion *must be negative.* The middle term (good legislators) is distributed at least once; the term 'women' is undistributed and therefore, must be undistributed in the conclusion. 'Irresponsible people' is distributed and can be either distributed or nondistributed in the conclusion. Because a negative conclusion is required and the term 'women' must be undistributed, then the conclusion has to be an **O** statement with 'women' as its subject.

No M are P.   No (good legislators) are (irresponsible people).

Some S are M.   Some (women) are (good legislators).

Some S are not P.   Some women are not irresponsible people.

Our diagram also gives us the conclusion shown in figure 37.

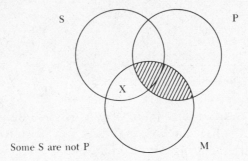

Some S are not P

FIGURE 37

Exercises for § 6.2

A. Cast each of the following syllogisms into Venn diagrams.

1. All of the college's cars are Chevrolets.
   All of the cars in the parking lot are Chevrolets.
   ∴ All the cars in the parking lot are the college's cars.

2. All who are advocates of civil disobedience are radicals.
   Jones is not a believer in civil disobedience.
   ∴ Jones is not a radical.

3. No good plan calls for building an outdoor swimming pool in Alaska.
   This plan calls for building an outdoor swimming pool in Alaska.
   ∴ This is not a good plan.

4. Some attractive paintings are expensive.
   Some Picasso's are attractive.
   ∴ Some Picasso paintings are expensive.

5. All Class A runners are eligible to enter the Olympics.
   No freshmen are Class A runners.
   ∴ Some freshmen are not eligible to enter the Olympics.

B. For each of the following syllogisms indicate any rule which has been violated.
   Classify each syllogism as valid or invalid.

1. All Occidentals are haughty persons
   Some haughty persons are crooks.

   ∴ Some crooks are Occidentals.

2. No intuitive thinkers are creative intellects.
   All intuitive thinkers are illogical reasoners.

   ∴ No illogical reasoners are creative intellects.

3. All good people are concerned with human welfare.
   All virtuous people are good people.
   _____
   ∴ All virtuous people are concerned with human welfare.

4. Some politicians are tiresome people.
   All bores are tiresome people.
   _____
   ∴ All bores are politicians.

5. Some dishes are fragile things.
   No fragile things are iron things.
   _____
   ∴ Some dishes are not iron things.

6. All scholars are idealists.
   Some empiricists are idealists.
   _____
   ∴ No empiricists are scholars.

7. Some athletes are fat persons.
   No fat persons are ballet dancers.
   _____
   ∴ Some athletes are not ballet dancers.

8. All poets are creative thinkers.
   Some scientists are not poets.
   _____
   ∴ No scientists are creative thinkers.

9. No tragic actors are happy people.
   Some comedians are not happy people.
   _____
   ∴ Some comedians are not tragic actors.

10. All kings are vain men.
    No kings are humble men.
    _____
    No vain men are humble men.

11. No clowns are poets.
    No poets are logicians.
    _____
    ∴ No logicians are clowns.

12. All beautiful women are vain creatures.
    Some coeds are not beautiful women.
    _____
    ∴ Some coeds are not vain creatures.

C. Test the validity of the following syllogisms by Venn diagrams. Indicate whether each syllogism is valid or invalid and why.

1. **IAI–2**

2. **AAA–2**

3. **OAI–3**

4. **AEE–1**

5. **OAO–4**

6. **EIO–2**

7. **EIO–4**

8. **EAE–4**
9. **AOO–3**
10. **AAA–1**

6.3   TESTING FOR VALIDITY BY LOGICAL ANALOGY

There is a third method for testing the validity of syllogisms, namely, the method of 'logical analogy.' This method is, in some ways, a little harder to apply because rather than being purely mechanical, it requires a little imaginative reconstruction on our part. This method, however, does point to and emphasize the fact that the validity or invalidity of a syllogism depends exclusively upon the form of the argument and not on the specific content. Recall our example from chapter 1.

All communists are atheists.
Mr. Parkins is an atheist.
_____

Therefore, Mr. Parkins is a communist.

Symbolically this syllogism has the form: **AAA–2.**

All P are M.
All S are M.
_____

All S are P.

Recall now that if a syllogism is valid, *any other syllogism of the same form is valid*, and, if a syllogism is invalid, any other syllogism of the same form will also be invalid. Recall further our definition of invalidity, namely, that a deductive argument is invalid if it is possible for it to have true premises and a false conclusion. Putting these together we have the foundation for the method of *logical analogy*, which is to show the fallaciousness of deductive argument by constructing an argument with the same form, but whose invalidity is immediately visible. That is, *we construct an argument with the same form, which has premises known to be true and a conclusion known to be false*. Thus, taking our example above which has the form,

All P are M.
All S are M.
_____

All S are P.

we substitute 'dogs' for P, 'animals' for M and 'cats' for S and we have the following obviously invalid syllogism:

All dogs are animals.
All cats are animals.
_____
All cats are dogs.

Because if a syllogism is invalid, any other syllogism of the same form will be invalid, our original syllogism

All communists are atheists.
Mr. Parkins is an atheist.
_____
Therefore, Mr. Parkins is a communist.

is also invalid.

The method of logical analogy, then, is a good way of showing an argument fallacious, and it serves again to emphasize that validity of syllogisms is a formal matter. This method, however, has its limitations, as indicated, for it requires our ability to be able to think up a logical analogy. If we are unable to come up with a logical analogy with true premises and a false conclusion, it does not mean that the syllogism as such is invalid, but rather may mean our imaginative and thinking ability is limited.

Tape Exercises

Test the validity of the following arguments using logical analogy. [Check your answers against Tape 6, band 3.]

1. In the book of Job in the Bible the friends of Job present the following argument: Job is a sinner because all sinners suffer affliction and Job is suffering affliction. Using logical analogy, show that their argument is fallacious.

2. In the heat of a political debate, your friend argues that Senator Camron is an economic conservative because all economic conservatives believe in strict budgetary controls and the Senator is arguing for strict budgetary controls. Check the validity of his argument by logical analogy.

3. You are a doctor, and you have applied for membership in an exclusive tennis club. You are told that you are ineligible. When you ask for the reason you are given the following argument: Only those with an income over $150,000 are allowed to apply for membership, and business executives are the only people with incomes over $150,000. Thus, the only people eligible to apply for membership are business executives. Is the argument valid?

Exercises for §6.3

Show that the following arguments are invalid by the method of constructing logical analogies.

1. All of the state cars are Plymouths, and all of the cars in this garage are Plymouths. Thus, all of the cars in this garage must be state cars.

2. It is true that all careful readers are good students and are good thinkers. Therefore, some good students are good thinkers.

3. No introverts are good teachers because no shy and retiring persons are good teachers and some introverts are shy and retiring persons.

4. All male models are handsome men, and all tall and thin men are handsome men. Therefore, all male models are tall and thin men.

5. All blue chip securities are safe and dependable investments. No speculative stocks are blue chip securities. Therefore, no speculative stocks are safe and dependable investments.

6. None but true yogis are qualified for the highest mystical experiences, and only true yogis are saints. Therefore, only saints are qualified for the highest mystical experiences.

7. No professors are vain because all ignorant people are vain and no professors are ignorant.

8. All students majoring in business will have a good chance for employment, but no English majors are students majoring in business. Therefore, no English majors will have a good chance for employment.

9. Only those interested in progress voted the Democratic ticket in this election. All those who voted the Democratic ticket in this election voted for the new blood and imaginative thinking of Jane Doe. Thus, all those who voted for the new blood and imaginative thinking of Jane Doe are people interested in progress.

6.4   THE ENTHYMEME

In chapter 1 we discussed elliptical arguments in which one premise or the conclusion is unexpressed because it is deliberately left out or is only implied. These arguments with missing parts are known as *enthymemes*, which means 'to hold in mind' (some part of the argument is not directly expressed). In the context of categorical deductive logic, then, an *enthymeme* would be an incompletely stated syllogism.

Enthymemes are quite prevalent in everyday discourse for several reasons. One such reason is that the missing parts are often obviously implied and to state that premise or conclusion would be to belabor the obvious. At other times the person stating the enthymeme may be deliberately leaving something unstated because the unstated assertion may be clearly false or it may constitute an unjustified assumption. To make these assumptions explicit would enable us to examine them critically. Completing an enthymeme, then, is the first stage to critical analysis.

Traditionally, in discussion of enthymemes in categorical logic, three different types are usually mentioned: (1) An enthymeme of the *first order* is one in which the first or major premise is missing; (2) an enthymeme of a *second order* is one that omits the minor premise; and (3) an enthymeme of the *third order* is one that has an unstated conclusion. In Anthony's oration over the body of Caesar we find an example of a *first order* enthymeme.

He would not take the crown.
Therefore 'tis certain he was not ambitious.

Remembering the *principle of charity* discussed in the first chapter, we should always reconstruct the argument in its best possible form. In the case of syllogisms, this means we should try to make the syllogism *valid*. The conclusion of our enthymeme, 'tis certain he was not ambitious,' can be translated into an **E** statement, 'No Caesar(s) are persons who are ambitious'. This establishes 'Caesars' as the minor term and 'persons who are ambitious' as the major term. Further, recalling the rule that if a term is distributed in the conclusion it must be distributed in the premises, we must set up the syllogism so that both 'S' and 'P' are distributed in the premises if we want it to be valid. Still further, because our other premise 'He would not take the crown' translates into an 'E' as 'No Caesars are persons who will take the crown,' and recalling the rule that there can be only one negative premise in a valid syllogism, we know our premise must be an affirmative one, either **I** or **A**. But an **I** statement would not distribute the major term, and we said that if both 'S' and 'P' are distributed in the conclusion, they must be distributed in the premises. Our enthymeme can thus be spelled out as a *valid* syllogism of the form **AEE–2**.

All persons who are ambitious are persons who will take the crown.
No Caesars are persons who will take the crown.
_____
Therefore, no Caesars are persons who are ambitious.

Symbolically, it has the **AEE–2 form:**

All P are M
No S are M
_____
No S are P

The valid Venn diagram is shown in figure 38.

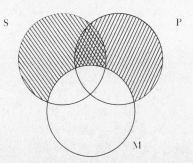

FIGURE 38

The second order enthymemes are those that omit the minor premise. Consider the following: 'Some smokers are foolish because none but foolish people needlessly destroy forests'. In this case we have an **I** statement for a conclusion, 'Some smokers are foolish,' and an **A** statement for the major premise, 'All who needlessly destroy forests are foolish people.' 'None but' translates to all with the term following 'but' as the predicate term. In order to turn this enthymeme into a valid syllogism, we need an affirmative premise, either an **A** or an **I**. It cannot be an **A** statement because one of our rules tells us that a syllogism is invalid if it has two universal premises and a particular conclusion. Thus, we can construct a valid syllogism as follows:

> All who needlessly destroy forests are foolish people.
> Some smokers are people who needlessly destroy forests.
> _____
> Therefore, some smokers are foolish people.

This has the **AII–1** form and affords a valid Venn diagram as shown in figure 39.

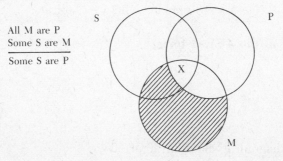

All M are P
Some S are M
_____
Some S are P

FIGURE 39

2. No angels are human beings because all human beings are mortal.
3. All sweet and gentle beings are lovable.
   Thus, all babies are lovable.

Our third order form of the enthymeme is the case in which the actual conclusion is missing. Look at the following: "No kite fliers are afraid of uncontrollable forces, but all children are afraid of uncontrollable forces." The conclusion here is unstated, but because we have a negative premise, we know that we must have a negative conclusion and that it must be universal, for both premises are universal. Further, since it must be an 'E' statement, it must be stated so that 'S' and 'P' remain distributed in the premises. We can construct our syllogism as follows:

All children are afraid of uncontrollable forces.
No kite fliers are afraid of uncontrollable forces.

No kite fliers are children.

Because 'No kite fliers are children' has as its converse and equivalent, 'No children are kite fliers,' the syllogism could have been constructed as follows:

No kite fliers are afraid of uncontrollable forces.
All children are afraid of uncontrollable forces.

No children are kite fliers.

Tape Exercises

All of the following are also examples of enthymemes of the third order. Provide the proper conclusions for these enthymemes. [Check your answers with Tape 6, band 5.]

1. Liberty is not compatible with social control, and the right to voice one's opinions is a form of liberty.
2. Some women make good legislators, and no good legislator is irresponsible.
3. No spider bites show only one puncture, and all the bites on Stephen's arm show only one puncture.

Exercises for § 6.4

A. Complete the following enthymemes, rendering them as valid syllogisms:

1. No children are responsible beings because no children are rational beings.
2. No men are fickle and some fickle people are women.
3. Some artistic people are versatile because all musicians are versatile.

4. No profiters are patriots because no good citizens are profiters.

5. All radicals are crazy and no sensible people are crazy.

B. Using the rules and Venn diagrams, determine what conclusions, if any, follow from the following premise sets:

1. Determinism agrees that all events including human actions are completely determined by past events. Spinoza's philosophy argues that all events including human actions are completely determined by past events.

2. All totalitarian governments are restrictive. There are totalitarian governments which have been overthrown.

3. Not all existentialist philosophers are theistic. Sartre is not a theist.

4. Attempts to enforce morals always restricts someone's freedom, but some things restricting someone's freedom are necessary.

5. There are philosophers who not concerned with ethical judgments and there are scientists who are.

6. Monogamous marriage is an important part of the American way of life. However, things which are an important part of the American way of life are not always perfect.

7. No critical thinker makes logical errors. Those who read superficially make logical errors.

8. Sometimes political expediency leads to moral error, but moral error is never justified.

C. State any two premises that will validly lead to the following conclusions:

1. No logical exercises are too easy.

2. All students are people who want to remold things nearer to their heart's desire.

3. All sensitive creatures are dissatisfied people.

4. All big corporations are monopolistic.

5. All rational men are opposed to dictators.

6.5   FURTHER HELP

We have now discussed the major elements of deductive reasoning, and more particularly, the traditional expression deduction takes in the syllogism. Further, we should be able to analyze the syllogism—determining its mood and figure—and to test a syllogism for validity. One problem remains, namely, the need to translate or render the arguments that we encounter in ordinary language in syllogistic form should that be possible and desirable. For both in everyday life and in discussions of a technical nature, we come upon arguments that puzzle us and lead us to try to analyze and evaluate them in terms of syllogistic reasoning. There are two general kinds of problems, one concerned with the very careful rendering of the propositions—the building blocks of the syllogism—the other with the possibility of expressing the propositions, once they are correctly identified, in proper syllogistic form.

We dealt with the first kind of difficulty in the chapter on propositions. It may be wise to reread section 5.3 again to cultivate skill in translating such problematic words and phrases as 'none but,' 'all except,' and the like, plus those that do not refer to *classes* of objects, events, or processes but to qualities, relations and the like, as in "Babe Ruth always hit home runs." The second kind of trouble arises with arguments that have the ring of a proper syllogism but in which, for example, the conclusion is stated first and the premises or reasons are given after the conclusion. These difficulties are combined and augmented when we are presented with an argument that calls for translation in both these respects. They abound in everyday life. Consider two examples, abortion and capital punishment.

Much of the excited and heated argument for or against abortion hinges on a premise that can be clearly stated. It runs something like this:

> All killing is evil.
> Performing an abortion, at any stage of pregnancy, is killing.
> Therefore, performing an abortion is evil.

The debate is not over. On the contrary, it may have just begun because, for instance, several questions are sure to arise concerning the definition of 'killing'. But an important service will have been performed: one of the main issues will have been identified.

As this is being written, the United States Supreme Court handed down the decision that a girl who is a minor need not have parental consent to have an abortion. Reading the opinions of the members of the Court will probably allow us to construct in syllogistic form the argument that was advanced. It might read: All female citizens of the United States, regardless of age, are eligible for an abortion in a state in which abortions are legal. New York is a state in which abortions are legal. Hence, all female citizens of New York are eligible for an abortion.

Turning to another example, the heated debate over capital punishment usually hinges on the answer to a very few basic questions. One of them is, "Does capital punishment deter?" So, considerable progress has been made if this aspect of the argument at least is clearly stated, as

> All cases of capital punishment are cases of failure to deter serious crimes.
> All crimes so serious as to warrant capital punishment are cases in which the punishment deters potential criminals.
> Capital punishment is not capable of detering serious crimes.
> Therefore, capital punishment is not warranted.

How would you analyze in syllogistic form an argument advanced by a president for sending United States troops into another country on the grounds of the principle of national self-interest?

Exercises for § 6.5

A. Translate the following into standard syllogistic form and test for validity by rules and Venn diagrams.

1. Only a lawyer as clever as Clarence Darrow could have won an acquittal in this case. Attorney Jones won an acquittal. Therefore, Attorney Jones is as clever as Clarence Darrow.

2. No present day rock and roll groups are groups having the class of the Beatles of the 1960s. The Yollers, who are a present day rock and roll group, don't have the class of the Beatles of the 1960s.

3. This 200 year old nation of ours is going to the dogs. Any nation that has lost its moral values is going to the dogs. Thus, our nation is losing its moral values.

4. Art is always the expression of economic interests. American painting, being an art, reflects our capitalistic economic interests.

5. Only the fittest survive, for there is a universal struggle for existence, in which no one that is not fit can survive.

6. Avoid everything intoxicating. Ravel's "Bolero" and other similar pieces of music are intoxicating. Therefore, all such music should be avoided.

7. Christianity hasn't failed; it hasn't been tried.

8. The gypsies believe the bear to be the brother to man because he has the same body beneath his hide, because he drinks beer, because he enjoys music, and because he likes to dance. So also believe the Indians. Are the Indians then gypsies? (Hemingway, *For Whom the Bell Tolls,* thanks to W. R. Werkmeister.)

9. "You can get an education in college if you try. But you must bring three things with you: a certain minimum intellectual equipment, habits of work, and an interest in getting an education. Without them you can still get into college and stay there for four years. You can have a good time; you can keep out of trouble; you can get a degree and become a full-fledged alumnus with a proprietary interest in all subsequent football scores; but you cannot get an education." (Robert M. Hutchins, quoted in Herbert L. Searles, *Logic & Scientific Methods,* 2d ed. New York: The Ronald Press, 1956.)

10. Make no mistake about it: it's the federal government that really is responsible for full employment and it alone is able to organize, integrate, yet compel the economic powers of private industry and of government to work together to produce full employment, and if necessary the government will have to pick up the bill to guarantee full employment.

Chapter Outline

A. A categorical syllogism is an argument consisting of three categorical statements, two of which are premises and one a conclusion. The three categorical statements contain three different terms in all, each term appearing in
exactly two different statements. The three terms are:
  1. The *major term,* which is the predicate term of the conclusion.
  2. The *minor term,* which is the subject term of the conclusion.
  3. The *middle term,* which is the third term appearing in the premises but
  not in the conclusion.
B. Thus, in order to identify the terms of a syllogism, it is necessary first to
identify the *conclusion* of the syllogism.
  1. The *major* premise is the premise containing the major term and should
  be written first.
  2. The *minor* premise is the premise containing the minor term and should
  be written second.
  3. The principle involved in Venn diagrams is that *in valid syllogisms* we
  need no further information than that already contained in the premises;
  to know that the conclusion is true and does follow.
C. The *mood* of a syllogism is the categorical form of each statement in the
syllogism, named in consecutive order, e.g., **AAA.**
D. The *figure* of the syllogism is how the terms of the syllogism are arranged
within the statements in which they occur. Figure is primarily determined
by the position of the *middle term.* The four possible figures of the syllogism
are:

I	II	III	IV
M P	P M	M P	P M
S M	S M	M S	M S
S P	S P	S P	S P

E. There are three methods of determining the validity of a given syllogism: *by
consulting the rules of the syllogism, by using Venn diagrams,* and *by logical
analogy.*
F. The *rules of the syllogism* are:
  1. In a valid syllogism, the middle term must be distributed *at least* once.
  Any syllogism violating this rule commits *the fallacy of the undistributed
  middle term.*
  2. In a valid syllogism, no term (either the major or minor term) can be
  distributed in the conclusion unless it is also distributed in a premise. A
  syllogism which violates this rule commits one or the other of two fallacies: *the fallacy of the illicit major or the fallacy of the illicit minor.*
  3. No valid syllogism can have two negative premises.
  4. Any valid syllogism has one negative premise if and only if it has a
  negative conclusion.
  5. No valid standard form syllogism can have two universal premises and a
  particular conclusion.

6. Any valid syllogism must have three terms and three terms only, each maintaining the same meaning throughout.

G. Venn diagrams are a device for depicting logical relations spatially by drawing three intersecting circles corresponding to the three terms of the syllogism. *Shading* is used to indicate what regions within the intersecting circles are said to be empty of members. An *X* is used to indicate what regions are being said to contain members.

1. Venn diagrams show a syllogism to be *valid* when, in diagramming the premises, we "automatically" diagram the conclusion also.

2. The syllogism is shown to be *invalid* when the premises have been correctly diagrammed and the conclusion is not thus automatically diagrammed or depicted.

3. In using the Venn diagrams, one diagrams *only* the premises and *never* the conclusion.

7

TRUTH-FUNCTIONAL
STATEMENTS

7.1 SIMPLE AND COMPOUND STATEMENTS

In this chapter we turn to another kind of deductive logic, one that involves very basic and familiar types of statements, statements that are key pins upon which much reasoning turns. This kind of deductive logic is variously called *propositional logic, sentential logic* and *truth-functional logic* because the basic building blocks for arguments in this logic are propositions or truth-functional compound statements rather than 'terms' such as in categorical deductive logic.

To begin to understand truth-functional compound statements we need to distinguish between simple and compound statements. A *simple* statement is one that does not contain any other statement as a component part; for example, men are rational beings. Every *compound* statement does contain one or more statements as component parts. For example, if all men are rational beings, then the world ought to be able to live in peace. In analogy with chemical analysis, some logicians speak of atomic statements rather than simple statements and compound statements as molecular statements. This is particularly apt because molecules can be built up of any number and kinds of atoms and just so compound statements can be made up of any number of simple statements. Some examples of simple or atomic statements are:

Jack went to the movies.

More stringent antipollution measures will be enacted.

There will be a third world war.

The moon is made of blue cheese.

An *old maid* is an unmarried woman.

Castor and Pollux were twins.

Examples of compound statements or molecular statements are:

It is not true that Jack went to the movies.

More stringent antipollution measures will be enacted, and the quality of our air will be improved.

Either the United Nations will be strengthened or there will be a third world war.

If the moon is made of blue cheese, then the astronauts would have eaten it.

An *old maid* is an unmarried woman, and Elsie is unmarried, and thus she is an "old maid."

Castor and Pollux were twins if and only if they had the same mother.

Tape Exercises

Consider the following statements. Are they compound—molecular or simple—atomic statements? [Check your answers with Tape 7, band 1.]

1. It is hardly likely that George left the house without leaving a message.
2. Carol married Tim, and Helen married George.
3. The situation in Lebanon gets worse all the time.
4. If riots continue in Rhodesia, then the government may have to do something about apartheid.
5. Either George will take the assignment on or Carter will have to find another person for the position.

In ordinary language, many words and phrases can be attached to simple statements to change them into statements that mean something else and thus into compound statements. For instance, the statement "Washington crossed the Delaware" can be changed drastically by attaching various phrases and words to it:

Nobody seriously believes that Washington crossed the Delaware.

Maybe Washington crossed the Delaware.

It is likely that Washington crossed the Delaware.

I am certain that Washington crossed the Delaware.

It is false that Washington crossed the Delaware.

Washington crossed the Delaware and the U.S. defeated the British.

Either Washington crossed the Delaware or the historians are wrong.

If Washington crossed the Delaware, then there will be evidence to show that he did.

Washington crossed the Delaware if and only if he had a boat.

The expressions, 'nobody seriously believes,' 'it is likely,' 'I am certain,' do transform the original statement by embedding it in a longer statement that usually has a different meaning from the embedded statement. However, these phrases do not essentially touch the original statement in terms of its truth-value. If it is true that Washington crossed the Delaware, these four phrases do not alter the truth-value of the statement asserting that fact. It is true whether believed or not. Sentences involving expressions like 'nobody seriously believes,' 'it is likely,' 'I am certain' are compound statements, but *not* truth-functional compounds.

Phrases like 'It is false that,' and, 'either or,' 'if . . . then' and 'if and only if' do transform or operate on the original statements in a crucial way. The truth-value of the compound statement formed by these phrases is *absolutely determined* by the truth-value of the component parts. That is, the truth-value of the compound statement is a *function* of the truth-values of its component parts. All statements whose truth-values are dependent on the truth-values of its components are called *truth-functional statements,* and the phrases that form these truth-functional compounds are called *truth-functors.* Logic which deals with truth-functional compounds then, is also called *truth-functional logic.* The five truth-functional compound statements that will be studied are:

1. *Negation,* which is usually indicated by the word *not,* and such a phrase as *it is false that* (Washington was not killed in the Revolution).

2. *Conjunction,* which is usually indicated by the word *and,* but other words like *but, while* and *likewise* also indicate it (Washington was the first U.S. President and John Adams was the second President.)

3. *Disjunction,* which is usually indicated by the words *either . . . or* (Either nations will cooperate or all will perish).

4. *Material implication,* which is usually indicated by the phrase 'if . . . then,' but is also indicated by the phrase 'only if' and the word *if* alone (If prices continue to rise, then the unions will ask for higher wages).

5. *Material equivalence,* which is usually indicated by the phrase 'if and only if' (We can preserve our democracy if and only if we preserve freedom of speech).

7.2 TRUTH-FUNCTORS AND TRUTH-VALUE

Crucial to truth-functional logic is the notion that statements are usually either true or false. If you say "Nixon resigned the presidency," you have said something true. If you say "Nixon did not resign the presidency," you have said something false. We call a sentence *true* if the statement it is normally used to make is true, false if that statement is false. Further, we need to distinguish clearly between saying that a statement may have either of two truth-values and saying which of these two truth-values the statement may, *in fact,* have. It is not the business of logic to establish factual truth or falsity. In truth-functional logic we assume that statements have one or the other of the *two* truth values, but *not both*. Thus, truth-functional logic is referred to as a *two-valued* logic, in contrast to other statement logics in which statements may take on any of three or more truth-values.

In truth-functional logic, then, our concern is with the *truth-value* of truth-functional compound statements. In order to determine this value, we need to know only (1) the truth-value of its component statements, and (2) the rule that specifies the way in which the truth-value of the compound statement is dependent on the truth-values of its component statements. The rules are specifically tied to the definitions of each of the five truth-functional connectives. We shall turn to these in a moment. First, however, a further look at truth-functional logic.

It is the job of truth-functional logic to point out that *if* it is true to say

Tom stole it

then it is equally true to say

Tom stole it or Dick stole it.

Or if it is true that

Tom stole it

then it is false that

Tom did not steal it.

Tape Exercises

Consider the following: If it is true that Washington crossed the Delaware and false that Lincoln was president during the American Revolution, what might be the truth-value of the following statements? [The answers are in Tape 7, band 1.]

1. Washington did not cross the Delaware.
2. Abraham Lincoln was not president during the American Revolution.
3. Washington crossed the Delaware and Lincoln was president during the American Revolution.
4. Washington crossed the Delaware and Lincoln was not president during the American Revolution.
5. If Lincoln did not live until the 1860s, then he was not President during the American Revolution.

7.3 SYMBOLIZATION: STATEMENT
FORMS AND ARGUMENT FORMS

Truth-functional logic is also called 'symbolic logic,' for in developing this type of logic in the late 1800s, and early 1900s, logicians found it convenient to set up an *artificial symbolic language* that would be free from the many defects of everyday language—vagueness and ambiguity, equivocation and amphiboly—and that would enable them to clearly exhibit the logical structures of statements and arguments. In developing symbolization, logicians have three main concerns: (1) to analyze clearly and concisely the *forms* of the particular type of statements of the logic with which it is dealing, (2) to develop a specific criterion for the *validity* of the arguments built up of these statements, and (3) to apply the most economical *procedures* for deciding which of these arguments meet the criterion and are *valid*. This last concern with economical procedures has a paradoxical consequence. By means of symbolization, we can analyze arguments almost *mechanically* nearly leaving behind conscious reasoning processes. We almost quit thinking! However, to say this is misleading, for in mastering the symbolization and their deeper meanings, what we do is make highly complex reasoning processes habitual and unconscious, just as highly technical mathematical reasoning becomes everyday habit for many.

Although the truth-functors (the truth-functional connectives) are named for the specific linguisitic acts of negating, conjoining, disjuncting, implying, and equivalenting, we will define them abstractly so that we can use them without relating them to particular words, objects, or real things. In order to deal with the truth-functional connectives in a purely formal way, we must do two things: (1) designate symbolic notation for each of these connectives, and (2) give each of the connectives a formal definition. We must also have a way to set up statement forms and argument forms.

Before we can define the connectives, we must have a way of designating statements abstractly. We do this by taking lower-case letters such as p and q as statement markers, that is, as symbols that mark the position of statements. Next we need symbols for each of the truth-functional connectives. We shall adopt the notation of the *Principia Mathematica*. Combining these with statement markers, we get the following abstract representation of each of the truth-functional compounds; alternative notation is also indicated.[1]

TABLE 4

	Principia Mathematica	Hilbert	Polish
negation	$\sim p$	$\bar{p}$	N
conjunction	$p \cdot q$	$p \mathbin{\&} q$	K
disjunction	$p \vee q$	$p \quad q$	Apq
material implication	$p \supset q$	$p \rightarrow q$	Cpq
material equivalence	$p \equiv q$	$p \leftrightarrow q$	Epq

---

[1] Many logic texts follow the symbolization developed by Whitehead and Russell in the *Principia*, but the symbols used by the logician Hilbert are used more often by mathematicians. The Polish notation, developed by logicians in Poland, is considered by some to be most easily understood, but it is not as frequently used.

We now have all the ingredients for statement forms. A *statement-form* is an expression that consists exclusively of logical symbols and statement variables, such as

$$p \cdot (q \lor r)$$

The *statement-form* of a given statement is produced as follows: (a) If the statement is simple, replace it with a single statement-marker; (b) if the statement is compound, then replace each simple statement therein with a statement-marker, using p for the first statement and for any subsequent occurrence of it. Use q for all occurrences of the second statement, and so on. Then add the appropriate logical symbols and parentheses, for example.

The statement-form of "if George is a liar then either he is stupid or he is crazy" is: $p \supset (q \lor r)$.

A *substitution instance* of a statement-form is any statement that has that form. A substitution instance of a given statement-form may be rendered as follows: "It is false that Nixon resigned the presidency" is a substitution-instance of $\sim p$. "Nixon resigned the presidency and Gerald Ford became president" is a substitution instance of $p \cdot q$. Replace all occurrences of p in the form with a single simple statement; replace all occurrences of q with another simple statement (always use the same letter to replace the same statement) and so on for r, s, etc. Then, replace the logical symbols with English equivalents, and punctuate where necessary to prevent ambiguity.

Statement-forms in and of themselves are not called true or false; only substitution-instances of statement-forms can be true or false. Thus, knowing that the statement "Nixon resigned" is true, we know that the statement "It is false that Nixon resigned" is false. Knowing that the statements "Nixon resigned" and "Gerald Ford became president" are both true, we know, as we shall see, that the conjunctive statement is true.

Exercises for § 7.3

For each of the following compound statements identify the constituent statements and the 'truth-functors' involved. Then, using the truth-functor symbols and 'p,' 'q,' 'r' as statement variables, put each statement into its symbolic statement form. The sentence, "We can both buy a new car and go to Hawaii for the summer," can be analyzed as follows:

constituent statements:	We can buy a new car.
	We can go to Hawaii for the summer.
truth-functor:	and
statement form:	p and q

[The shaded items are analyzed on Tape 7, band 1.]

1. If the market does not rise, then we will sell all the Waterville Railway stock.

2. You can't eat your cake and have it too.

3. If something isn't done soon about the pollution in Lake Erie, then it may be irredeemably lost to safe swimming.

4. It is true that no treatments are yet in sight for many hereditary diseases and that persons with diabetes or hemophilia will still transmit these genes to their offspring.

5. If you fire the gun too rapidly, then it jams.

6. Either John will choose to stay in school or he will take a semester off to go back-packing.

7. Jane will graduate if and only if she passes logic.

8. It is false that the Secretary of State will resign after a new president is elected.

9. Jerry was not at the party last night.

10. There was an exploratory operation, but nothing came of it.

11. Either we sell out our oil stock or we invest in some insurance stock.

12. If 75 percent of the employees subscribe; the group insurance plan will go through.

13. Either the college will supplement the research funds or outside sources will be sought.

14. The building can be used as a residence hall if and only if two fire escapes are constructed.

15. Logic involves both thought and practice.

7.4 THE TRUTH-TABLE

To define our truth-functors abstractly, we shall use a device known as a *truth-table*. It is an array that shows the truth-values of a statement. For instance, letting the letter p serve as a marker for any statement, and the letter T stand for the truth-value *true*, and the letter F stand for the truth-value false, we can show that any statement has two truth-values as follows:

$$
\begin{array}{c}
p \\
\hline
T \\
F
\end{array}
$$

In dealing with truth-functionally compound statements, we see that given any *two* statements, p and q, there are just four possible sets of truth-values they can have:

$$
\begin{array}{cc}
p & q \\
\hline
T & T \\
F & T \\
T & F \\
F & F
\end{array}
$$

If we had a truth-functor that combined three different statements, three statement-markers or statement-variables would be needed and the truth-table would have eight lines. The number of lines a truth-table has is two raised to the power that is equal to the number of different statement-variables involved. Mathematically, this is written

2^n, where n equals the number of statement-variables in the table.

So, a truth-table with one statement-variable has $2^1 = 2$ lines; a table with two different statement-variables has $2^2 = 4$ lines; a table with three different statement-variables has $2^3 = 8$ lines; a table with four different statement-variables has $2^4 = 16$ lines; and so on. We shall indicate later on how specifically to build a truth-table.

We turn now to the definitions of our truth-functors.

7.5 NEGATION

The word *negate* comes from the Latin root *negare* which means to say no or deny, and the truth-functor negation accordingly denies the statement on which it operates. Thus, the statement "It is not the case that lead is heavier than gold" is the negation or (denial or contradictory) of its single component statement, "Lead is heavier than gold."

We have introduced the symbol $\sim$ called a *curl* (or a *tilde*) to symbolize negation. Where p is any statement whatever, its negation is written $\sim p$. Because the negation of a true statement is false and the negation of a false statement is true, we can take the following truth-table to define the truth-functor negation symbolized by the curl.

p	$\sim p$		Lead is heavier than gold	It is not the case that lead is heavier than gold
T	F	or	T	F
F	T		F	T

We deny or negate sentences in English in various ways. For example, all of the following are equivalent ways of expressing the negation of the statement, "Eleven is an even number."

1. Eleven is not even.
2. Eleven is uneven.
3. It is not the case that eleven is even.
4. It is false that eleven is even.
5. Eleven is odd.

But, for formal purposes, negation is best expressed by the phrase "*It is not the case that,*" taken in the sense of an operator on statements *that reverses their truth-value*. If the original statement is true, the negated statement is false; if the original statement is false, the negated statement is true. In the above examples the negated statements are all true by virtue of the fact that "Eleven is even" is false. Using *p* to represent "Eleven is even," all of the above negation statements are represented by *the statement-form or formula* $\sim p$. The expression $\sim p$ is the logical form of all the examples of negated statements: it represents a simple statement being denied.

Although the statement-forms *p* and $\sim p$ cannot be said to be either true or false until a substitution for *p* is made, a relation between the two in terms of truth and falsity can be precisely defined: corresponding substitution instances of *p* and $\sim p$ cannot be true simultaneously and both cannot be false simultaneously. If one is true, the other must be false, and if one is false the other must be true. *The negation of a statement is the contradictory of the original statement.* To repeat, then, in dealing with negation and with the truth-functor "It is not the case that," represented by the *tilde* ($\sim$), we are dealing with *contradictories*.

This understanding of the symbol $\sim$ corresponds to most English variants of "not." It does not conform exactly, however, for $\sim$ *always* means contradictory, whereas, *not* does not. Thus, the statement, "Some coeds do not smoke cigarettes" does *not deny* that some coeds *do* smoke cigarettes. "Some coeds do smoke cigarettes" and "Some coeds *do not* smoke cigarettes" may both be true. The *not* here does not function as a contradictory.

There can also be more than one negation involved. Consider the following:

"It is false that it is not the case that Mary is not short."

Given, *p* as representative of the statement, "Mary is short," we see that we have three negations represented as $\sim\sim\sim p$. Using the rule: *an even number of negations leaves the truth value unchanged, and odd number reverses the truth value*, we solve $\sim\sim\sim p$ by means of the following truth table.

p	$\sim p$	$\sim\sim p$	$\sim\sim\sim p$
T	F	T	F
F	T	F	T

We see from this table that negation applied twice brings us back to the original statement.

Tape Exercises

Consider the following statements. Are they all examples of negations? If so, put them into symbolic form, using the italicized letters for statement variables. [Check your answers with Tape 7, band 2.]

1. Stephen is not ill.
2. It is not the case that Washington did not cross the Delaware.
3. The number two is not an odd number.
4. There will not be a run-off election.
5. It is false that the plane is in bad shape.

7.6   CONJUNCTION

A statement consisting of two constituent statements joined by the truth-functor *and* is called a *conjunction*. The component statements are termed *conjuncts*; they may be simple or compound statements. A simple conjunction is "Picasso was a painter and he was also a sculptor." The symbol · (dot) is used for logical conjunction and may be read as the English *and*. Using p and q as statement-variables for "Picasso was a painter" and "He was also a sculptor", we symbolize conjunction in the following statement-form: $p \cdot q$.

There are a number of ways in English to express conjunction. Thus, all of the following statements are conjunctive statements.

Matthew stays *but* Jane leaves.

Matthew stays, *however* Jane leaves.

Matthew stays, *moreover* Jane leaves.

Matthew stays *although* Jane leaves.

Matthew stays *yet* Jane leaves.

Matthew stays *even though* Jane leaves.

Each of these statements can be symbolized as $p \cdot q$. Though in English these expressions are not entirely synonymous, there is a common factor in their meanings which justifies the use of the ·. The common factor represented by the · is that a person who asserts a compound statement connected by any of these English terms automatically commits himself to *accepting both of the constituent statements*. Thus, a conjunction may be defined as follows: If a substitution instance of p is true and another of q is true, then the corresponding substitution instance of $p \cdot q$ is true. Otherwise, it is false. This may be represented graphically by the truth table.

p	q	$p \cdot q$		Matthew Stays	Jane Leaves	$p \cdot q$
T	T	T		T	T	T
F	T	F	or	F	T	F
T	F	F		T	F	F
F	F	F		F	F	F

A conjunction is true only if its component statements are true.

Caution must be used in translating statements into conjunctive form. For example, what shall we do with statements like the following?

1. Dante's *Inferno* is artistic and philosophical.
2. MacArthur and his troops returned to the Philippines.
3. Jane and Michael met one day and got married the next.

Statement one above could be rendered as: "Dante's *Inferno* is artistic and Dante's *Inferno* is philosophical.

Statement two does not correctly translate into "MacArthur returned to the Philippines and his troops returned to the Philippines" because it does not capture the sense that they did this *together* or at the same time. The truth table definition of ·, however, cannot account for this. Substitution instances of $p \cdot q$ are true whenever corresponding substitution instances of p are true and q are true—regardless of some special connection between p and q. Thus, the *truth* of the conjunction $p \cdot q$ is independent of the order of the compounds. *The statement forms,* p · q *and* q · p *are logically equivalent.*

This is why "Jane and Michael met one day and got married the next" cannot be handled in truth-functional logic. It expresses temporal order, it means 'and then,' and its truth or falsity would be drastically affected by reversal of the components. These kinds of statements can, however, be handled in higher forms of logic.

Thus, once again, the logician does not seek to *represent* in detail ordinary language, but rather to analyze some of the most prominent logical features of the language. The dot · effectively does this by giving the *minimum content* of the sense of logical conjunction.

Tape Exercises

Consider the following statements. Can they all be translated into conjunctions without loss of meaning? If not, why not? Check your answers with Tape 7, band 2.]

1. The operation was very serious, but his recovery was spectacular.
2. Although Tom liked Jane, he also liked Betty.
3. Running for political office is a grueling affair, however, it has many rewards.
4. John and Mary got married and had three children.
5. It is noon, and I am hungry.

To repeat, the conjunction is true only when its conjuncts are true. Reflecting on this tells us that certain simple inferences follow from this definition alone. If we are committed to the truth of a statement symbolized by p and committed to the truth of another statement symbolized by q, then we are committed to the truth of p and q. Thus, the argument form known as *conjunction* is obviously valid. We also recall from chapter 1 that once an argument form is *valid*, it is always and everywhere valid. Any argument having the form of conjunction, then, will be valid. Thus, knowing the truth of the statement, "Nixon resigned the presidency," and the truth of "Gerald Ford became president," we also know the truth of the statement "Nixon resigned the presidency and Gerald Ford became president."

$$\frac{\begin{array}{c} p \\ q \end{array}}{\therefore p \cdot q}$$

Moving in the other direction, if a conjunction is true, then each conjunct is true by itself. Thus, we have two more *valid inference schemata*, or *argument forms* called *simplification*.

$$\frac{p \cdot q}{\therefore p} \qquad \frac{p \cdot q}{\therefore q}$$

So, if we know the statement "Nixon resigned the presidency and Gerald Ford became president" is true, we know that the statement "Nixon resigned the presidency" and the statement "Gerald Ford became president" are true.

We have already discussed argument-forms in chapter 1 and again in chapter 6, but a brief review may be in order. An argument form is a sequence of statement-forms (in this case, truth-functional statement-forms) such that, when we uniformly replace distinct statement markers (p, q, r) with distinct true-false statements and uniformly replace connective symbols with their ordinary language counterparts, the result is a valid or invalid deductive argument. Thus,

> Tom is distraught.
> Jane is angry.
> _____
> Thus, Tom is distraught and Jane is angry.

is a substitution instance of the valid argument-form called conjunction.

Exercises for § 7.6

A. Put the following statements into symbolic form. Then, assuming: "Civil War continues in Lebanon"; "Syria moves into to stop the conflict in Lebanon"; and "Israel remains neutral" as true and "The U.S. pledges support to the Christian Lebanese"; "Russia pledges support to Lebanese Moslems"; and "The U.N. steps into the Lebanese conflict" as false, determine the truth-value of each of the compound statements. (Parentheses should be placed around smaller units.)

1. Civil War continues in Lebanon, but Syria will move into stop the conflict in Lebanon.
2. It is likely that Israel will remain neutral while Civil War will continue in Lebanon and the U.N. will step into the Lebanese conflict.
3. It is false that Russia will pledge support to Lebanese Moslems.

4. It is not true that Israel will remain neutral,and it is the case both that Civil War will continue in Lebanon and Syria will move in to stop the conflict in Lebanon.

5. It is false that the U.S. did not pledge support to the Christian Lebanese.

6. The U.N. stepped into the Lebanese conflict although Russia did not support the Lebanese Moslems, but Israel remained neutral.

7. It is false both that Russia pledged support to the Lebanese Moslems and the U.S. pledged support to the Christian Lebanese.

8. Although Civil War will continue in Lebanon, the United States will not pledge support to the Christian Lebanese, and Russia will not pledge support to the Lebanese Moslems.

9. It is not the case that Civil War will continue in Lebanon and Syria will move in to stop the conflict in Lebanon.

10. Israel will remain neutral while Syria will move in to stop the conflict in Lebanon, but Russia will pledge support to the Lebanese Moslems and the United Nations will step in to stop the conflict.

B. Identify the following arguments as examples of either the argument form known as Conjunction or that known as Simplification.

1. Jimmy Carter was elected president. Mondale was elected vice-president. Thus: Jimmy Carter was elected president and Mondale was elected vice-president.

2. The tennis courts were crowded, but Charles and John managed to find partners for tennis. This is the case because Charles and John managed to find partners for tennis and the tennis courts were crowded.

3. I am free on Monday at ten,and I will take French 20 because I am free on Monday. Also, I will take French 20.

4. All giants are over ten feet tall,and giants make good basketball players. All giants are over ten feet tall. Thus, giants make good basketball players.

C. Construct truth tables for the following statements, using the italicized letters for statement variables.

1. Dollar *a*larm clocks do not keep perfect time.

2. It is not the case that something is both a *s*olid and a *l*iquid.

3. Water at room temperature is not a *s*olid, but water at room temperature is a *l*iquid.

4. *R*obins fly and *t*rout swim.

5. It is false that water at room temperature is not a *l*iquid.

7.7   DISJUNCTION

A statement consisting of two constituent statements joined by the truth functor *or* is called a *disjunction;* the component statements are called *dis-*

juncts. An example of a disjunction is: "Either the dog is scratching at the door, or someone is trying to get in." Using the *wedge* (v) as an abbreviation for the truth-functor *or*, and statement variables *p* and *q* respectively for the statement "The dog is scratching at the door" and "Someone is trying to get in." We symbolize this disjunction as:

$$p \vee q$$

In asserting a disjunction, we intend to put forth *alternatives*. We can state alternatives, however, in two senses: *inclusive* and *exclusive*. The inclusive sense of *or* is the case in which we intend to admit the possibility that both disjuncts are true. Thus, in asserting the disjunction "School is automatically closed on foggy days or on holidays," we suggest that school is closed on foggy days, that it is closed on holidays, *and* that it is closed on foggy holidays. In its inclusive sense, then, the disjunction means

p <u>or</u> q <u>or both</u>
p <u>and/or</u> q

This inclusive sense of disjunction is represented by truth-table.

p	q	p v q
T	T	T
T	F	T
F	T	T
F	F	F

The only case in which the inclusive disjunction, symbolized as pvq *is false is when both disjuncts are false.*

The exclusive sense of disjunction is the case in which we intend to rule out both disjuncts as true. One disjunct excludes the other, as in the following example:

John is at the play, or he is studying in the library.

There is no mistaking the sense of *or* here: John cannot be in both places at once. The exclusive sense of disjunction says

p <u>or</u> q <u>but not both</u>

This sense of the disjunctive, however, is not used in truth-functional logic and is partially captured in the inclusive disjunctive. That is, the two types of disjunctions share a common meaning, namely, that *at least one disjunct must be true.*

An interesting case of disjunction is the negative case, namely, "Neither Israel will remain neutral not will Syria go into Lebanon to stop the conflict."

This particular form of the disjunction may be written in two ways. The first way is as a negation of the disjunction. $\sim(p \lor q)$. The second is as a conjunction with two negative conjuncts: $(\sim p \cdot \sim q)$. That these two forms are equivalent can be seen by doing a truth table for each and noting that they are exactly the same. Thus:

p	q	$p \lor q$	$\sim(p \lor q)$
T	T	T	F
F	T	T	F
T	F	T	F
F	F	F	T

p	q	$\sim p$	$\sim q$	$\sim p \cdot \sim q$
T	T	F	F	F
T	T	T	F	F
T	F	F	T	F
F	F	T	T	T

Tape Exercises

Consider the following statements. Are they intended as inclusive or exclusive disjunctions? [Check your answers with Tape 7, band 2.]

1. Either chimpanzees are intelligent or psychologists are mistaken.
2. Either Jim will go fishing or Jack will go skiing.
3. Either it is noon or my watch is wrong.
4. Either cobalt is a solid or it is a liquid.
5. Either Jane will take ballet or she will take ice skating lessons.

The definition of the disjunction, as that of conjunction, also produces some valid argument forms. Given the definition of the disjunctive as *false when both disjuncts are false; otherwise it is true*, we see that the following two argument forms as symbolized are valid. (These are called the *disjunctive syllogism*, using *syllogism* to mean a deductive argument consisting of two premises and a conclusion.)

$$p \lor q \qquad\qquad p \lor q$$
$$\underline{\quad \sim p \quad} \qquad\qquad \underline{\quad \sim q \quad}$$
$$\therefore q \qquad\qquad\qquad \therefore p$$

If we are asserting a disjunctive statement as *true*, we are saying that either one or both of its disjuncts are true. This is seen by looking at the truth-table for the disjunctive.

p	q	$p \lor q$
T	T	T
T	F	T
F	T	T
F	F	F

Thus, if we assert a disjunction as true and at the same time assert *one* of its disjuncts to be false, then we can *validly* conclude that the other disjunct is true. The disjunctive syllogism is valid on either interpretation of the disjunction, that is, whether an inclusive or exclusive disjunction is intended. Thus:

> Either the dog is scratching at the door or someone is trying to get in.
> The dog is not scratching at the door.
> ──────────────────────────────────────
> ∴ Someone is trying to get in.

However, we can only validly conclude from the falsity of a disjunct, never from the truth of the disjunct. Because we know a disjunctive statement to be true and also that one of its disjuncts is true, we cannot *validly* conclude that the other disjunct is false. The disjunctive is defined as false only when both disjuncts are false. Consider the following.

> Either the dog is scratching at the door or someone is trying to get in.
> The dog is scratching at the door.
> ──────────────────────────────────────
> ∴ There is no one trying to get in.

> Either the dog is scratching at the door or someone is trying to get in.
> Someone is trying to get in.
> ──────────────────────────────────────
> ∴ The dog is not scratching at the door.

It is obvious that it could be true that *both* the dog is scratching at the door and someone is trying to get in. This is shown by the truth-table for the disjunctive.

p	q	$p \lor q$
T	T	T
T	F	T
F	T	T
F	F	F

The following, then, are *invalid* disjunctive argument forms.

$$p \lor q$$
$$\underline{p }$$
$$\sim q$$

$$p \lor q$$
$$\underline{ q}$$
$$\sim p$$

Exercises for § 7.7

A. Consider the following arguments. Put them in symbolic form, using the italicized letter as statement variables. Which are valid forms of the disjunctive argument and which are invalid?

1. Either Jane will take *b*allet or Jane will take ice skating lessons. Jane will take *b*allet. Therefore, she will not take ice skating lessons.

2. Either *I*srael will remain neutral or *S*yria will go into Lebanon. *Syria* will not go into Lebanon. Thus, *I*srael will remain neutral.

3. Either the Mid-East *c*onflict will come to a *h*alt or there will be *t*rouble in Africa. The Mid-East *c*onflict did come to a halt. Therefore, there will be trouble in Africa.

4. The Democrats will *w*in the vote on their bill because either the Republicans will *o*ppose the proposal of the Cocker committee or the Democrats will *w*in the vote on their bill and the Republicans did not *o*ppose the proposal of the Crocker committee.

B. Put the following into symbolic form. Given that "The students will approve a student fee," "The college will support the student newspaper," and "Outside funds will be raised for the student center" are *true* and "The students will vote for a student center," "The college opposes student fees," and "The college will launch a football team" are *false*, determine the truth-value of each of the following truth-functional compound statements.

1. Either the students will approve a student fee or the college will launch a football team.

2. Either the college will not oppose student fees or the college will not launch a football team.

3. Either the students will vote for a student center or the college will oppose student fees.

4. It is not the case that either the college will support the student newspaper or that outside funds will be raised for the student center.

5. Either the college will oppose student fees and the college will launch a football team or the students will approve a student center, but it is not true that outside funds will be raised for a student center.

6. Either it is not true that the college will oppose student fees or the college will not launch a football team.

7. It is the case both that either the college will support the student newspaper or outside funds will be raised for the student center and either the students will approve student fees or the college will launch a football team.

8. Neither will the college support a student newspaper nor will outside funds be raised for a student center.

C. Complete the following disjunctive major premises in such a way as to get *two* valid syllogisms in each case.

1. Either you are lazy or you are inefficient.

2. Either you dislike me or I have offended you.

3. Either Ford or Carter.

D. Is the following argument valid or invalid?

Either it is raining or it is not raining.
It is raining.
_____

Therefore, it is not raining.

7.8   CONDITIONAL STATEMENTS AND
MATERIAL IMPLICATION

A statement composed of two constituent statements and the truth functor *if
. . . then*, is called a conditional statement. It also is called a *hypothetical*
statement or an implication. The component statement that precedes *then* is
called the *antecedent* (meaning 'that which precedes'), and the component
following *then* is termed the *consequent* ('that which follows'). The antecedent
and the consequent may be either simple or compound. A sample conditional
is as follows:

If the fan belt *b*reaks, then the generator will *s*top turning.

Using the symbol $\supset$ (the horse shoe) to represent the *if . . . then*, the above
conditional can be symbolized as follows:

$$p \supset q$$

The statement connective *if . . . then* is defined in truth functional logic as
follows: If a substitution instance of p is true and a substitution instance of q is
false, then a substitution instance of $p \supset q$ is false; for all other substitutions of
p and q, the corresponding substitutions of $p \supset q$ are true. In other words, a
conditional statement is false if its antecedent is true and its consequent false.
This is graphically represented by the following truth table:

p	q	$p \supset q$
T	T	T
T	F	F
F	T	T
F	F	T

Thus, $p \supset q$ is tantamount to saying it is not the case that p can be true and q
can be false, i.e., it *denies* the conjunction of its antecedent with the negation of
its consequent. The following two statement-forms are *logically equivalent*;
that is, they have the same truth-values.

$$(p \supset q) \text{ and } \sim(p \cdot \sim q)$$

(Being logically equivalent, these statement-forms have the same truth-values, the same truth-tables). Thus,

p	q	$\sim(p \cdot \sim q)$	$p \supset q$
T	T	T	T
T	F	F	F
F	T	T	T
F	F	T	T

It should also be noted that unlike conjunction and disjunction, the order of statements in a conditional makes a truth-functional difference. We obviously cannot reverse the order of the statements in a conditional. Thus:

If the fan belt breaks, then the generator will stop turning.
If the generator stops turning, then the fan belt will break.

The falsifying conditions for the two statements are different; $p \supset q$ is false when $p = T$ and $q = F$, but $q \supset p$ is false when $p = F$ and $q = T$. Thus, they have different truth-tables.

p	q	$p \supset q$	$q \supset p$
T	T	T	T
T	F	F	T
F	T	T	F
F	F	T	T

In order to make quite clear the meaning of the conditional in truth-functional logic, we shall examine it from two other aspects—first, from the point of view of *implication* and then via the concepts of *necessary and sufficient conditions*. First, the notion of *implication*. The conditional statement asserts that the antecedent implies the consequent, that is, *if* the antecedent is true, then its consequent is true. Being hypothetical, the conditional statement does not say anything about the truth of either of its component statements; it only says *if* the antecedent is true, then the consequent must be true. It does not, for example, assert *causal implication*, for example, that when blue litmus paper is placed in acid, the litmus paper will turn red. This kind of implication is discovered empirically, as indicated in our chapter on Mill's Methods. It does, however, capture some of the meaning of causal implication, for the statement, 'If blue litmus paper is placed in this solution, then the litmus paper will turn red,' asserts that if the litmus paper is put into acid, it will turn red. The statement is falsified if in fact the litmus paper is put into acid and does not turn red.

Nor is the *implication* of the conditional statement *logical implication*, namely, of the sort that a valid deductive argument has. For example, All men are mortal; Socrates is a man; thus, "Socrates is mortal." The premises imply the conclusion; it necessarily follows. The truth-functional conditional does, however, capture the core of meaning of logical implication. *Invalidity* is defined as permitting true premises and a false conclusion. Thus, lack of implication is parallel to the falsifying case of the conditional. And to say premises logically imply their conclusion is to say *if* the premises are true, the conclusion must be true.

Turning back briefly to causal implication, it is usual to speak of causal implication in terms of necessary and sufficient conditions. A sufficient condition is one in whose presence the consequent or effect *must* occur. The rock hitting the glass with sufficient impact causes the shattering of the glass. A necessary condition is one in whose *absence* the consequent event cannot occur. If there is no mother, there is no child (at least until test-tube babies become a reality). Further, other conditions may be sufficient to cause the same effect—shattered glass. So, presence of the effect does not require presence of that particular sufficient condition, in this case, the rock. And a necessary condition (oxygen) can be present without producing the effect (combustion). We can now understand the conditional statement in terms of necessary and sufficient conditions, for it asserts the antecedent, p, as a sufficient condition for the consequent, q, and q, as a necessary condition for p. This makes good sense in light of the truth-table definition of the conditional. Thus, it can be summarized as in table 5.

TABLE 5

p q	$p \supset p$	
T $\supset$ T	T	p as sufficient condition for q; when present, q is present.
T $\supset$ F	F	p as sufficient condition: if present, q must be present and isn't, therefore, it is **F**.
		q as necessary condition for p: if absent (**F**), p should also be absent. In this case, it is not. Therefore, conditional is false.
F $\supset$ T	T	p as sufficient condition: may be absent (**F**) and q present.
		q as necessary condition: may be present and **p** absent, e.g., oxygen, combustion.
F $\supset$ F	T	q as necessary condition of p, when absent (**F**) p must be absent.

Thus, the statement

   Oxygen is a necessary condition for combustion

can be expressed

   Combustion occurs *only* if there is oxygen present

and as

   If combustion occurs then oxygen is present.

Tape Exercises

Consider the following statements. How would you express them in conditional statement form? [Check your answers with Tape 7, band 2.]

1. Continuing rising prices is a sufficient condition for the union to demand a wage increase.
2. A necessary condition for voting is citizenship.
3. That some men are capable of perfection implies that some should have attained it.
4. We can preserve our democracy only if we have freedom of speech.
5. Provided the weather stays stable, the crop should be excellent.

The conditional, as defined in truth functional logic, seeks only to set out a minimal common meaning for all uses of the *if . . . then* in English—that the consequent cannot be false when the antecedent is true. Because it seeks a minimal condition, the definition of the conditional only partially corresponds to all uses of *if . . . then* in English just as the disjunction corresponds only partially to all the meanings of *or* in English.

Thus, the implication relationship symbolized by the ⊃ is called *material implication,* and its special name indicates that it is a special notion not to be confused with other more usual kinds of implication. Although most conditional statements assert more than merely material implication between antecedent and consequent, we now propose to symbolize *any* occurrence of *if-then* by the truth-functor ⊃. Such symbolizing does abstract from and ignore part of the meaning of most conditional statements. But the proposal can be justified on the grounds that the validity of valid arguments involving conditionals is preserved when the conditionals are regarded as asserting material implications only.

Further, we can accomplish much with the ⊃ symbol in formal logic. For example, from the definition of the ⊃ symbol we get a valid argument form known as *Modus Ponens.* If we assert a conditional along with a separate assertion of the antecedent, the consequent follows validly because we have the definition of the conditional, which states that the consequent cannot be false when the antecedent is true. The pattern for *Modus Ponens* is

$$p \supset q$$
$$\underline{\quad p \quad}$$
$$\therefore q$$

Consider the following example.

If we have desegregation we will have some busing.
We have desegregation.
_____
∴ We will have some busing.

Another valid argument pattern that follows from the definition of ⊃ is known as *Modus Tollens*. Given the definition of $p \supset q$ as $\sim(p \cdot \sim q)$, (It is not true that p can be true and q can be false) we see that if we assert a conditional and the denial of its consequent, we can validly infer the denial of its antecedent. The form of *Modus Tollens* is

$$p \supset q$$
$$\underline{\sim q}$$
$$\therefore \sim p$$

Consider the following example.

If the paper burns, there is sufficient oxygen present.
There is not sufficient oxygen present.
_____

∴ The paper does not burn.

Parellel to the two valid conditional argument statement forms are two fallacies or invalid conditional statement argument form. The first is called the *Fallacy of Affirming the Consequent*. It has the following form:

$$p \supset q$$
$$\underline{q}$$
$$\therefore p$$

It is obviously a fallacy because our definition of the conditional *only* says the consequent cannot be false when the antecedent *is* true. It does not tell us anything about the reverse, namely, when the consequent is true. Recalling the truth-table for the conditional, we see that the conditional is still considered true even when the antecedent is false and the consequent true, for example,

p	q	$p \supset q$
T	T	T
T	F	F
F	T	T
F	F	T

Consider an example:

If Nixon resigns, Gerald Ford will become president.
Gerald Ford became president.
_____

∴ Nixon resigned.

The only relationship the conditional asserts between its antecedent and its consequent is that when the antecedent is true, the consequent must be true.

In our example, we can see that the statement "Gerald Ford became president" could be true and "Nixon resigned" could be false *because* "Nixon was impeached" and "Nixon died" could equally be the condition which brought Ford to office.

Another invalid conditional argument form is called *Fallacy of Denying the Antecedent*. It has the following form:

$$p \supset q$$
$$\frac{\sim p}{\sim q}$$

This is obviously a fallacy because our definition of the conditional, *only*, says the consequent cannot be false when the antecedent is true. It doesn't tell us anything about what follows from the falsity of the antecedent. Thus, the truth-table for the conditional tells us that the conditional is still considered true even when the consequent is false.

p	q	$p \supset q$
T	T	T
T	F	T
F	T	T
F	F	T

Consider our example again:

> If Nixon resigns, Gerald Ford will become president.
> Nixon did not resign.
> _____
> ∴ Gerald Ford did not become president.

It can quickly be seen that it could be false that Nixon resigned and still true that Gerald Ford became president.

Two of these conditional argument-forms play a key role in science and in other types of reasoning concerned with the assessment of evidence such as law. Thus, the *fallacy of affirming the consequent* is common in science because it is committed whenever *confirmation*, which may be taken as an affirmation of a consequent, is believed to be proof (or certainty) rather than only probability. Thus, for example, the following commits the fallacy of affirming the consequent.

> If Newton's law of gravitation is true, this stone, when released, will fall to the ground.
> This stone, when released, will fall to the ground.
> _____
> Therefore, Newton's law of gravitation is true.

Newton's law of gravitation holds in this case and many others and thus it is probable, but not certain or true. The *fallacy of affirming the consequent* also occurs frequently in courts of law whenever a person is convicted of a crime on circumstantial evidence.

> If Hauptmann is the kidnapper, then some of the ransom money will be found in his house.
> Some of the ransom money was found in his house.
> ___
> Therefore, Hauptmann is the kidnapper.

Finally, *Modus Tollens* is very important in science because it is the mode of disconfirmation, and many scientists believe disconfirmation is far more important to the advancement of scientific knowledge than confirmation.

> If this substance is an acid, then it will donate a proton to another substance.
> This does not donate a proton to another substance.
> ___
> Therefore, this substance is not an acid.

Even in law, *Modus Tollens* can be valuable to establishing innocence.

> If James is the murderer, then we will be able to establish a motive for the crime.
> We cannot establish a motive for the crime.
> ___
> Therefore, James is not the murderer.

The conditional statement as defined, then, does capture and important aspect of the *if . . . then* in English and also performs an important function in formal logic.

Before leaving the conditional, it should be noted that it has several variations. All of the following are forms of the $p \supset q$.

1. If Susie studies, she will pass—if p then q.
2. Susie will pass if she studies—q if p.
3. Susie will pass provided that she studies hard—q provided that p.
4. Susie will pass *on the condition* that she studies hard—q on the condition that p.
5. Susie will graduate *in case that* she studies hard—q in case that p.
6. Paper burns *only if* there is oxygen—p only if q.
7. Provided that the paper burns, there is oxygen—provided that p, q.
8. On the condition that the paper burns, there is oxygen—on the condition that p, q.

9. In case the paper burns, there is oxygen—in case *p, q*. (Note that the phrases, if, provided that, on condition that, and in case that determine the antecedent, regardless of sentence order. Only *if* is the sign of the consequent.)

10. An unusual form of the conditional is an exceptive statement involving *unless*—'No wills are legal unless witnessed by two persons.' This is translated into: 'If wills are not witnessed by two persons, then they are illegal'. Or, 'He is a general unless he is a colonel,' becomes 'If he is *not* a colonel, then he is a general'. Thus, '*p* unless *q*' becomes 'If not *q*, then *p*' or '~*q* ⊃ *p*.'

Exercises for § 7.8

A. Express the following statements symbolically, using the italicized letters, then reduce each to the equivalent negation of a conjunction.

Example:	Provided the *m*arket will rise, we will *s*ell all our railroad stock.
Translates to:	If the *m*arket will rise, then we will *s*ell all our railroad stock.
Symbolically expressed:	(*M* ⊃ *S*)
Negation of a conjunction:	(*M* · ~*S*)

1. If anything is an *a*tom, then it is a system of *e*nergy.

2. Although we had not *i*ntended to, we went to the *b*each over the weekend.

3. The *f*oundation will make a $100,000 grant provided it is *m*atched by private funds.

4. Unless *y*ou are here by 7:30, *I* shall leave.

5. The *P*ost Office is responsible for the package only if it is *i*nsured.

6. *T*aking a basic subjects course is necessary if one wishes to *g*raduate.

7. If we permit the student government to *c*arry on without coordinated planning, the *i*nevitable result is chaos.

8. Jerry will *t*ake French Literature if he *p*asses French 3.

9. On the condition that Brains would help him with math, Jim agreed to undertake the dangerous mission.

10. *T*aking an Introduction to Philosophy course is sufficient for taking an *a*dvanced philosophy course.

B. Given: 'the *m*arket rises,' '*s*ell our railway stock' and 'invest in *o*il stock' as *true* and '*p*ut our money in the bank,' 'invest in *i*nsurance stock' and '*b*uy commodities' as *false*, determine the truth-value of each of the following compound statements. Put the statements into symbolic form first. [The shaded items are analyzed on Tape 7, band 3.]

1. If the market rises, then we will sell all our railway stock and invest in oil stock.

2. If the market rises, then we will sell all our railway stock, but we will not put our money in the bank.

3. If the market does not rise, then either we will sell all our railway stock or put our money in the bank.

4. Either we will invest in oil stock, or if the market rises, then we will sell our railway stock.

5. If the market rises and we sell our railway stock, then we will not invest in commodities.

6. We will buy oil stock only if the market rises.

7. We will invest in commodities if we sell railway stock.

8. It is not the case that if the market rises then we will sell our railway stock and buy commodities.

9. If either the market rises or we will sell our railway stock, then we will buy commodities.

10. Whenever the market rises, we will buy oil stock.

11. The market rising is a necessary condition for our selling our railway stock.

12. If the market does not rise, then neither will we sell our railway stock nor will we buy commodities.

13. Either we will put our money in the bank or if the market does not rise, then we will sell our railway stock.

14. That the market does not rise is a sufficient condition for our buying oil stock.

15. It is not the case that if the market rises, then we will buy insurance stock and we will not buy oil stock.

16. Neither will we buy commodities nor will we buy oil stock, but if the market rises, then we will sell our railway stock.

17. Unless the market rises, then we will not sell the railway stock.

18. If the market rises, then if we do not put the money in the bank, then we will invest in oil stock.

19. If either we buy commodities or invest in oil stock, then we will sell our railway stock.

20. Provided the market rises, then we will sell all our railway stock and we will invest in oil stock.

C. Put each of the following arguments into symbolic form and determine whether they are examples of the valid Modus Ponens and Modus Tollens argument forms or examples of the fallacies of denying the antecedent and affirming the consequent. For review, here are each of those argument forms.

Valid	Invalid
Modus Ponens	Denying the Antecedent

Valid

Modus Ponens

$p \supset q$

p

$\therefore q$

Modus Tollens

$p \supset q$

$\sim q$

$\therefore \sim p$

Invalid

Denying the Antecedent

$p \supset q$

$\sim p$

$\therefore \sim q$

Affirming the Consequent

$p \supset q$

q

$\therefore p$

1. If war has its duties, then peace has its responsibilities. War has its duties. Therefore, peace has its responsibilities.

2. If a man swallows potassium cynanide, he will die. This man died. Therefore, he swallowed potassium cynanide.

3. If this number is even, then it is divisible by two. The number seven is not divisible by two. Therefore, the number seven is not even.

4. If people are sentient beings, then they experience pleasure and pain. People are sentient beings. Thus, they experience pleasure and pain.

5. If Darwin's Theory of evolution is correct, then we should find fossils that reveal sequential changes throughout the ages. We do find fossils which reveal sequential changes throughout the ages. Therefore, Darwin's Theory of evolution is correct.

6. This theory must be true, for it has been confirmed by our experiments, and we know that if a theory is true, it will be confirmed by our experiments.

7. This substance is not sodium because it burns with a green flame, which it would not do if it were sodium.

8. Inasmuch as the defendant's footprints were found at the scene of the murder and we know that they were certain to be found there if he were the murderer, we may conclude that the defendant is the murderer.

9. Neither will the instructor give Harry a make-up test nor give him a zero on the test missed. However, if the instructor will not either give him a make-up test nor give him a zero on the one missed, then Harry will fail the course. Thus, Harry will fail the course.

10. If men are not wise, then they will show reverence for those matters that are beyond their understanding. In my classes in the social sciences and philosophy, I have noted the instructors often confess to an inability to explain some things, and yet they do not show reverence for those matters. Is this not sufficient to show that they are not wise?

7.9 BICONDITIONALS

A statement consisting of two constituent statements joined by the truth-functor 'if and only if' is called a *biconditional*. The constituents themselves may be either simple or compound. A sample biconditional is as follows:

Charles will continue college if and only if he receives a scholarship.

Using the (triple bar) ≡ to symbolize the connective if and only if, we get

$$p \equiv q$$

A biconditional is equivalent to the conjunction of a pair of conditionals. Thus, the biconditional statement above is logically equivalent to the following statement.

Charles will continue college only if he gets a fellowship, and he will continue college if he gets a fellowship.

This statement may be symbolized as follows:

$$(p \text{ only if } q) \cdot (p \text{ if } q)$$

or

$$(p \supset q) \cdot (q \supset p)$$

If we see the biconditional as a conjunction of these two conditionals, we also see that p and q are each necessary and sufficient conditions for each other. This means that if p is true, (present), q must be true and vice-versa, and if p is false (absent), then q must be false and absent and vice-versa. This leads to the definition of the biconditional which is *defined as true if and only if the component statements agree in truth-value*. This is represented in the truth-table as follows:

p	q	$p \equiv q$	$(p \supset q)$	$\cdot$	$(q \supset p)$
T	T	T	T	T	T
T	F	F	F	F	T
F	T	F	T	F	F
F	F	T	T	T	T

The biconditional plays an important role in the notion of equivalence of statements as we shall see shortly.

Exercises for § 7.9

Translate the following statements into symbolic form, using the italicized letters.

1. The college will *l*aunch a football program if and only if sufficient non-state *f*unds are raised.

2. The student government will *v*ote student fees only if the college will *l*aunch a football program, and the student government will *v*ote students' fees if the college will *l*aunch a football program.

3. John's *v*iolating the rules is a necessary and sufficient condition for his being *d*isqualified.

4. If and only if the city votes a *p*ay raise for the fire fighters will the teacher's union *e*nd their strike.

5. Only if the furnace is *r*evamped will the building be declared *s*afe, and if the furnace is revamped, then the building will be declared safe.

7.10 LOGICAL PUNCTUATION AND CONSTRUCTING TRUTH TABLES

Before moving on to testing truth-functional arguments for validity, a few words need to be said both about putting complex arguments into symbolic form and constructing truth-tables. First, the artificial logic of truth-functional logic, with its statement variables p, q, r, and its logical connectives $\sim$, $\cdot$, v, , and $\equiv$, also needs punctuation in order to express complicated arrangement of symbols. Suppose for example, we have the statement: 'Jane will marry Tom or she will finish her last quarter and graduate.' If we write only:

$$p \text{ v } q \cdot r$$

the statement can have two interpretations:

p v $(q \cdot r)$ Jane will marry Tom, or she will finish her last quarter and graduate.

$(p \text{ v } q) \cdot r$ Jane will marry Tom or she will finish her last quarter, and she will graduate.

Only one of the two can be a correct reading or interpretation because they are not logically equivalent. This is shown by substituting the *same* truth-values for the variables and getting conflicting results:

$$p = T, q = T \text{ and } r = F$$

p v $(q \cdot r)$	$(q$ v $q) \cdot r$
T v $(T \cdot F)$	T v $T \cdot F$
T v $\quad F$	$T \cdot F$
T	F

To resolve ambiguities of this sort, we use parentheses, brackets and braces. For example, the following statement

If it doesn't continue to rain and the dam holds up, then the city will be safe and the rescue will not be needed.

can be symbolized as follows:

(it doesn't continue to rain · the damn holds up)
(the city will be safe · the rescue will not be needed)

or

$$(p \cdot q) \quad (r \cdot \sim s)$$

A more complicated example is as follows:

Argentina mobilizes and Brazil declares an embargo, or it is not the case that both Cuba continues to send arms into South America and the Dominican Republic appeals to the U.N.

Thus,

p q

Argentina mobilizes · Brazil declares an embargo

r

v ~(Cuba continues to send arms into South America ·

s

the Dominican Republic appeals to the U.N.)

Thus,

$$(p \cdot q) \text{ v} \sim(r \cdot s)$$

Developing the ability properly to symbolize truth-functional statements is very important to our utilization of this type of logic. A further technique to be mastered is the construction of truth-tables.

We have seen earlier that truth tables enable us to represent graphically and *define* the connectives. But given these definitions, they also enable us to represent graphically the truth-values of all possible truth-functional compounds under all possible interpretations. For example, the truth-functional compound 'José will or Betsy will not run' becomes the statement-form p v $\sim q$.

This compound has a determined truth-value for each interpretation of its constituent parts. As indicated earlier, given two variables, there are mathematically four and only four truth-values combinations possible. It can be represented thus:

p	q	p	v	$\sim q$
T	T	T	T	F
T	F	T	T	T
F	T	F	F	F
F	F	F	T	T

The following steps should be followed in building truth-tables.

Step 1. *List all possible truth-value assignments for the different statement variables in the compound.* This tells us how many rows we need.

  a. The number of rows is 2^n where n is the number of different statement letters that occur in the compound:

    1 letter $2^1 = 2$ rows
    2 letters $2^2 = 4$ rows
    3 letters $2^3 = 8$ rows
    4 letters $2^4 = 16$ rows
    5 letters $2^5 = 32$ rows

  b. Listing possible truth value assignments systematically may be done by these rules.

    (1) List under first variable T's and F's equal to half of the rows needed:
        3 variables ½ of 2^3 = ½ of = 4
        4 variables ½ of 2^4 = ½ of = 8

    (2) Under second variable, alternate T's and F's in pairs.

    (3) Under third variable, alternate T's and F's.

p	q	r
T	T	T
T	T	F
T	F	T
T	F	F
F	T	T
F	T	F
F	F	T
F	F	F

    (4) For four variables
      (a) Write eight T's and eight F's under first variable.
      (b) Alternate T's and F's by fours under second variable.
      (c) Alternate T's and F's by 2's under 2nd.
      (d) Alternate T's and F's under 4th.

Step 2. *Substitute truth-values.* After the possible combinations are set up, moves to determine the truth-values for the smallest components, using the definitions of the connectives. Thus, in the example given above of $p \ v \ {\sim}q$, first determine the truth values for p, merely by rewriting the original p column under p, and for ${\sim}q$ (recalling the meaning of negation—a statement and its negation have opposite truth values) by reversing the truth values in the original q column. Thus,

p	q	p	v	${\sim}q$
T	T	T		F
T	F	T		T
F	T	F		F
F	F	F		T
		Step 1		Step 2

(columns labeled: Step 1 under p, Step 2 under p-rewrite, Step 2 under ~q)

Step 3. Having dealt with the smallest components, *move to the next larger component(s), repeating* **Step 2** *until you reach the main truth-functional connective.* In our example, the main connective is the next largest component. Here we apply the definition of disjunction: a disjunction is false if and only if both disjuncts are false.

p	q	p	v	${\sim}q$
T	T	T	T	F
T	F	T	T	T
F	T	F	F	F
F	F	F	T	T
Step 1		Step 2	Step 3	Step 2

Again, the steps for determining the truth-value of any compound are:

1. Enumerate all the combinations of truth and falsity for its variables, using the formula 2^n, where n represents the number of variables.

2. Determine the truth-values for the smallest compound.

3. Continue to determine truth-values for each next largest constituent of the compound until the main connective is reached.

Following these three steps, we can deal with very complex compound statements, such as, 'Either Sam will go only if Mike goes and if Mike doesn't go then Sam won't go or Sam will go if and only if Mike goes.' Reading 'Sam goes' as p and 'Mike goes' as q we get:

$$[(p \supset q) \cdot ({\sim}q \supset {\sim}p)] \ v \ (p \equiv q)$$

The truth table for this compound is as follows:

p	q	[(p ⊃ q)	·	(~q ⊃ ~p)]	v	(p ≡ q)
T	T	T	T F T	F T	T	T
T	F	F	F T F	F F	F	F
F	T	T	T F T	T T	T	F
F	F	T	T T T	T T	T	T
Steps 1	1	5	6 3 4	3 7		2

Step 1: Set out possible combinations.

2: Determine truth value of the smallest constituent component $(p \equiv q)$.

3-6: Next largest component is the left disjunct, which is a conjunct. This breaks down into two conditionals. Thus, we have to determine the values of each of these conjunct-conditionals. To do this we:

(a) determine truth values of the negations in the right conjunct-conditional—3

(b) determine the truth-value of the right-hand conjunct-conditional—4

(c) determine the truth-value of the left-hand conjunct-conditional—5

(d) determine the truth-value of the total conjunction—6

7: Finally we are ready to determine the truth-value of the main connective, the disjunction using the results obtained in steps 6 and 2—7

7.11 TESTING ARGUMENTS

Truth-tables are important because they are one method for establishing the validity or invalidity of compound statement arguments. A valid argument is one in which it is *impossible* for the premises to be true and the conclusion false. Using this definition we shall adopt the following principle:

An argument is invalid if and only if there is one or more rows on its truth-table where all the premises are true and the conclusion is false.

Consider this argument:

If desegregation is instituted, busing will be necessary.
Desegregation is instituted.

∴ Busing will be necessary.

It is an instance of *Modus Ponens*.

$$p \supset q$$
$$\underline{p }$$
$$\therefore q$$

Its truth table is as follows:

			Premise 1	Premise 2	Conclusion
	p	q	$p \supset q$	p	q
1	T	T	T	T	T
2	T	F	F	T	F
3	F	T	T	F	T
4	F	F	T	F	F
Steps		1	3	2	2

The only time that both premises are true is at line 1. But, when this occurs, the conclusion too *must* be true, and it is. Thus, the argument *is valid*.

Consider next an invalid argument:

If Mike is a runner, he has good lungs.
He has good lungs.
_____

∴ Mike is a runner.

Its form is:

$$p \supset q$$
$$\underline{q }$$
$$\therefore p$$

Its truth table is as follows:

			Premise 1	Premise 2	Conclusion
	p	q	$p \supset q$	q	p
1	T	T	T	T	T
2	T	F	F	F	T
3	F	T	T	T	F
4	F	F	T	F	F

On line 1 the premises are both true and the conclusion is true. But this proves nothing, because this can happen in both valid and invalid arguments. What we are looking for is a case where the premises are true and the conclusion is false. This we have on line 3. Thus, the argument is invalid. It is known as the *Fallacy of Affirming the Consequent.*

Our final example will be a more complex argument.

If four is less than six and every number less than six is prime, then four is prime. It follows that if four is less than six, it is a prime number.

Using *p, q,* and *r* to represent respectively, 'four is less than six,' 'every number less than six is prime'; and 'four is prime,' the argument may be symbolized as follows:

	p	q	r	Premise $(p \cdot q) \supset r$		Conclusion $p \supset r$
1	T	T	T	T	T	T
2	T	T	F	T	F	F
3	T	F	T	F	T	T
4	T	F	F	F	T	F
5	F	T	T	F	T	T
6	F	T	F	F	T	T
7	F	F	T	F	T	T
8	F	F	F	F	T	T

There is one case in which the premise is true and the conclusion false, namely, on line 4, but that is enough to make the argument invalid.

Shortened truth-table   The truth-table method may be considerably shortened by concentrating on the invalidating case, namely, that in which the premises are true and the conclusion false. Thus, the shortened method consists in: *Beginning with truth value assignments that falsify the conclusion, check whether the premises can all be made true consistently with the truth value assignments that falsify the conclusion.*

Take the following argument:

If God had made man, then man would have been endowed with an *essence.* However, because God did not make man, man has no essence.

Using *p* and *q* to represent 'God has made man' and 'man has an essence,' the argument may be symbolized as follows:

$$p \supset q$$
$$\frac{\sim p}{\therefore \sim q}$$

The only truth-value that would make q false is T, because q is a negation which reverses substitution of the truth value of the original. In our realm of possibilities this can occur twice, for example, lines 1 and 3. We then check out these two possibilities to see if the premises are both true—

	p	q	$p \supset q$	$\sim p$	$\sim q$
1	T	T		F	F
2	T	F			
3	F	T	T	T	F
4	F	F			

We do find such a case, namely, line 3. The argument is valid. Line 1 is no problem because one premise is already false, and the only case we are interested in is that of true premises and a false conclusion.

Tape Exercises

Before turning to the exercises, test your skill at truth-tables by trying to prove the validity of the following argument forms. [Check your answers with Tape 7, band 4.]

1. $(p \supset q) \cdot (p \supset r)$
   $\sim q \lor \sim r$
   _____
   $\therefore \sim p$

2. $p \supset q$
   $q \supset r$
   _____
   $\therefore p \supset r$

3. p
   $\therefore p \supset q$

Exercises for § 7.11

A. Use truth-tables to prove the validity or invalidity of the following argument forms:

1. $p \supset q$
   $\therefore \sim p \supset \sim q$

2. $p \supset q$
   $\therefore p \supset (p \cdot q)$

3. p
   $\therefore p \lor q$

4. $(p \lor q) \supset (p \cdot q)$
   _____
   $\therefore (p \supset q) \cdot (q \supset p)$

5. $p \supset q$
   $q \supset r$
   _____
   $\therefore r \supset p$

6. $\sim p \lor (q \cdot p)$
   $\sim q$
   _____
   $\therefore \sim p$

7. ~(p · q) v r
   ~(r · p)
   _____
   ∴ q v ~r

8. ~p v (q · ~r)
   r v ~p
   _____
   ∴ ~p v q

9. p ⊃ (q ⊃ r)
   p ⊃ q
   _____
   ∴ p ⊃ r

10. (p ⊃ q) ⊃ (p ⊃ r)
    (p ⊃ q) · (q ⊃ p)
    _____
    ∴ p ⊃ r

11. p · (p ⊃ q)
    ~p v q
    _____
    ∴ q

12. p v q
    ~p v ~q
    _____
    ∴ (p · ~q) v (~p · q)

13. p ⊃ (q ⊃ r)
    (q ⊃ r) ⊃ s
    ∴ p ⊃ s

14. (p ⊃ q) ⊃ (p · q)
    p v q
    _____
    ∴ p · q

15. p ⊃ (q v r)
    (q · r) ⊃ ~p
    ∴ ~p

16. (p ⊃ q) · [(p · q) ⊃ r]
    p ⊃ (r ⊃ s)
    ∴ p ⊃ s

17. p ⊃ (q v r)
    ~q
    _____
    ∴ ~r ⊃ ~p

18. p ≡ (q · r)
    ~r v q
    _____
    ∴ p ⊃ q

19. ~p v (q · r)
    ~q v ~r
    _____
    ∴ ~p

20. ~p v (q · r)
    ~p
    _____
    ∴ ~q v ~r

21. p ⊃ (q v r)
    (q · r) ⊃ s
    _____
    ∴ p ⊃ s

22. (p v q) ⊃ r
    r ⊃ (p · q)
    ∴ (p v q) ⊃ (p · q)

23. (p ⊃ q) ⊃ (p ⊃ r)
    p ⊃ q
    q ⊃ p
    _____
    ∴ p ⊃ r

24. (p v q) ⊃ (p · ~q)
    ~q ⊃ r
    _____
    ∴ p ⊃ r

25. (p · q) ⊃ r
    p ⊃ s
    _____
    ∴ (s · q) ⊃ r

26. (p ⊃ q) ⊃ r
    s ⊃ p
    _____
    ∴ (s · q) ⊃ r

B. Use truth-tables to test the validity or invalidity of the following arguments. In putting these arguments in symbolic form, use the suggested letters in parentheses.

1. The producer is the obedient servant of the consumer in a market economy only if there is free competition. Either there is not free competition or the producer cannot control prices. Therefore, it is not the case that the pro-

ducer is both the obedient servant of the consumer and is able to control prices. [S, F, C]

2. If we do not include Red China in the conference, these problems will not be settled. If we do not recognize Red China as the bona fide government of China, we will not include her in the conference. Therefore, if these problems will be settled, we will recognize Red China as the bona fide government of China. [I, S, R]

3. There is no right or wrong if there is no God. For, if there is no God, there is no moral law and there is no right or wrong unless there is moral law. [R, G, L]

4. You will have to follow either the B.A. or the B.S. curriculum. If you follow the B.A. curriculum, you will have to take only one course in mathematics, and if you follow the B.S. curriculum, you have to take at least three courses in mathematics. Anyhow, you will take either one course in mathematics or three courses in mathematics. [A, S, O, T]

5. If the Democrats carry on a good campaign, then either they will win the White House or they will win a majority in the Congress. They won the White House and a majority in Congress. Thus, they campaigned well. [C, W, M]

6. Unless there is a higher moral law, the positive law of a country is founded merely upon power, and if the positive law of a country is founded merely upon power, there is no reason why one with sufficient power to violate it should not do so. Therefore, only if there is not a higher moral law is there no reason why one with sufficient power to violate the positive law of a country should not do so. [H, P, V]

7. Thomas will be reappointed if and only if his dissertation is accepted and completed. If he completes his dissertation, it will be accepted. Thus, Thomas will be reappointed. [R, A, C]

8. If student fees are voted on favorably, then the student government will have funds to carry on many activities. But if student fees are voted on favorably, then the student government will have to contribute to the football program. Thus, if student fees are voted on favorably, then either the student government will have funds to carry on many activities or the student government will have to contribute to the football program. [V, F, C]

9. If Barker went on academic probation and became ineligible for football, then Moore would be the starting quarterback. But Moore is not the starting quarterback. Thus, Barker did not go on academic probation and was not ineligible for football. [B, I, M]

10. If I legally force the contractor to build the house at the contract price, then either he will give me poor construction or I will have to eliminate some of the special features of the house and it will not be attractive. But, I will not eliminate the special features. Thus, I will not legally force the contractor to build the house at contract price and the house will be attractive. [L, P, E, A]

11. If Jim marries Tanya, then either Betty will be angry or Caroline will be heartsick. If Betty will be angry and Caroline will be heartsick, then the

wedding will be a sad affair. Then, if Jim marries Tanya, the wedding will be a sad affair. [*J*, *B*, *C*, *S*]

12. If Keene double-crossed Evelyn, then either the jewels were in the piece of sculpture or in Lowell's suitcase. If the jewels were in the piece of sculpture and in Lowell's suitcase, then Keene did not doublecross Evelyn. Thus, Keene did not double-cross Evelyn. [*K*, *S*, *L*]

7.12   TAUTOLOGIES, CONTRADICTIONS, AND CONTINGENCIES

Truth-tables may also be used to place statement-forms into one of three exhaustive and exclusive categories: tautologies, contradictions, and contingencies.

Tautology: A statement form is a tautology *if it is true under all possible interpretations of its variables.* Any statement that is a substitution instance of a tautologous statement form is true in virtue of its form and is itself said to be a tautology. Such a statement is also called a *logical truth.* Obviously, a statement-form is a tautology if and only if the final column of its truth-table has only *T*'s, showing that all of its substitution instances are true. Thus, the following may be seen to be tautologies from their truth-tables.

p	v	$\sim q$
T	T	F
F	T	T

p	q
T	T
T	F
F	T
F	F

		$[(p \supset q) \cdot$	$p] \supset q$	
T	T	T		
F	F	T		
T	F	T		
T	F	T		

p	$\supset$	q
T	T	T
F	T	F

Tautologies have several interesting features: First, because they are logically true, they can tell us nothing about the universe we live in. Take the case of p v $\sim p$, 'It is cold or it is not cold'. Such a statement is necessarily true, but it is noninformative about the weather. You will not know whether to wear a coat or to dress coolly.

Second, because tautologies are logically true and not factually true, we can determine their truth value *a priori* or independently of the evidence. We do not need to consult the weather to know whether 'It is cold or it is not cold,' is true. It is true, whatever happens.

Now suppose you read the following statement in the newspaper:

It is and it is not cold.

Obviously, this statement is false. We do not need to know anything about the weather to know that this statement is false. It is false as a matter of logic: its truth is impossible.

Statements whose truth is logically impossible are called *contradictories*. A statement-form is a contradiction if it is false under all possible interpretations of its variables. Any statement such as 'It is and it is not cold,' which is a substitution instance of a self-contradictory statement form, is false by virtue of its form and is itself, thus, a contradiction. The following statement forms may be seen to be contradictions by their truth tables.

$p \cdot \sim p$			$\sim(p \lor \sim p)$				p	q	$(p \supset q) \cdot (p \cdot \sim q)$			
T	F	F	F	T	T	F	T	T	T	F	F	F
F	F	T	F	F	T	T	T	F	F	F	T	T
							F	T	T	F	F	F
							F	F	T	F	F	T

A statement-form that has both true and false statements among its substitution instances is called a *contingent* statement-form and any statement whose specific form is contingent such as, 'Either it will rain or it will be windy,' is called *a contingent statement*. It should be obvious that any statement form is *contingent* if its truth-table contains at least one T and at least one F under its major connective. Further, contingent statements like 'Either it will rain or it will be windy' and 'If it rains then the picnic will be cancelled,' are contingent precisely because their truth values are dependent or contingent on their contents rather than on their forms alone.

Finally, tautologous and contradictory statements are not always as obvious as the simple statements we have cited above. Thus, the statement-form $[p \lor (q \lor r)] \supset [q \lor (p \lor r)]$ would not at a superficial glance be thought tautologous, but, indeed, it is tautologous as its truth-table demonstrates.

p	q	r	$[p \lor (q \lor r)]$		$\supset$	$[q \lor (p \lor r)]$	
T	T	T	T	T	T	T	T
T	T	F	T	T	T	T	T
T	F	T	T	T	T	T	T
T	F	F	T	F	T	T	T
F	T	T	T	T	T	T	T
F	T	F	T	T	T	T	F
F	F	T	T	T	T	T	T
F	F	F	F	F	T	F	F

Indeed this statement form is a postulate of truth-functional logic and as we shall see shortly, all principles of logic are tautologies.

Exercises for § 7.12

A. Use truth-tables to determine whether the following statement forms are tautologous, self-contradictory, or contingent. [The shaded items are analyzed on Tape 7, band 4.]

1. $(p \cdot q) \supset (p \vee q)$
2. $p \supset [(p \supset q) \supset q]$
3. $(p \cdot q) \cdot (p \supset \sim q)$
4. $(p \vee q) \cdot (p \cdot q)$
5. $(\sim p \cdot p) \cdot (p \supset \sim p)$
6. $p \supset (q \supset p)$
7. $p \supset [p \supset (q \cdot \sim q)]$
8. $\sim (p \cdot q) \cdot (p \vee q)$
9. $[p \supset (q \supset p)] \supset [(q \supset q) \supset \sim (v \supset v)]$
10. $\sim [p \cdot \sim (p \vee q)] \supset [q \cdot \sim (q \vee p)]$
11. $\{[(p \supset q) \cdot (r \supset s)] \cdot (q \vee s)\} \supset (p \vee r)$
12. $\sim (\{[(\sim p \vee r) \vee \sim r] \cdot [(\sim q \vee \sim r) \vee r]\} \cdot \sim r)$

B. Use truth-tables to determine whether the following statements are tautologous, self-contradictory or contingent:

1. I like eggs and adore bacon only if either I like eggs or I adore bacon.
2. If it rains and is windy then either it rains or it is windy.
3. If Jack marries Jane then if Tom marries Helen then Jack marries Jane.
4. Logic is fun and math is tedious, but if logic is fun then math is not tedious.
5. It is not the case that if student fees will be voted in and neither student fees will be voted in nor football will be inaugurated then football will be inaugurated and neither football will be inaugurated nor student fees voted in.

7.13   TAUTOLOGY, VALIDITY AND LOGICAL IMPLICATION

Tautology plays a fundamental role in truth-functional logic because it enables us to state a criterion of validity for truth-functional arguments and argument-forms. In establishing this criterion of validity, we must first formulate the concept of conditionalizing arguments and argument forms. For every argument and argument form, there is a corresponding conditional statement whose antecedent is the conjunction of the argument's premises and whose consequent is the argument's conclusion. Thus to any argument of the form

$$p \supset q$$
$$\underline{\sim q}$$
$$\therefore \sim p$$

there corresponds the conditional statement of the form

$$[(p \supset q) \cdot \sim q] \supset \sim p$$

The validity criterion for argument and argument forms can be stated as follows: *A truth-functional argument form is valid if and only if its correspond-ing conditional is a tautology.* Now let us see how the criterion operates. Is the following statement form valid?

$$p \supset q$$
$$\underline{\sim q}$$
$$\therefore \sim p$$

First we construct its corresponding conditional.

$$[(p \supset q) \cdot \sim q] \supset \sim p$$

Next we construct its truth table to see whether it is a tautology.

p	q	$[(p \supset q) \cdot \sim q] \supset \sim p$				
T	T	T	F	F	T	F
T	F	F	F	T	T	F
F	T	T	F	F	T	T
F	F	T	T	T	T	T

The truth-table contains only *T*'s under the major connective, and thus it is a tautology.

Thus, if we want to find out whether an argument is valid, we first determine whether it is a truth-functional argument. Then we write down its argument form and construct a corresponding conditional of the argument form. Finally, using a truth-table we test the conditional to see if it is a tautology. If the conditional is a tautology, the argument is valid. If not, it is invalid. Consider the following argument.

True capitalism is found only where there is free and open competition. In the case of big monopolies there is hardly free and open competition. The conclusion is obvious.

This argument can be restated into a clearly truth-functional argument as follows:

If true capitalism is found, then there is free and open competition. There is no free and open competition in cases of big monopolies.

Therefore, true capitalism is not found in cases of big monopolies.

The form of this argument is:

$$p \supset q$$
$$\underline{\sim q}$$
$$\therefore \sim p$$

We have already proved above that its corresponding conditional $[(p \supset q) \cdot {\sim}q] \supset {\sim}p$ is a tautology, and thus the argument is valid. Our criterion of validity for truth-functional arguments then is: *A truth-functional argument is valid if and only if its corresponding conditional is a substitution instance of a tautology.*

Further, because we have already identified substitution instances of tautologies as logical truths, we can also state our validity criterion as follows: *A truth-functional argument is valid if and only if its corresponding conditional is logically true.* These explications of validity fit well with our intuitive sense of validity, namely, that in a valid argument, it must be impossible for the premises all to be true and the conclusion false. If an argument is valid, its corresponding conditional is a substitution instance of a tautology, and thus it is impossible for the antecedent of the conditional (the conjunction of the argument's premises) to have the truth value T while the consequent (the conclusion) takes the value F. No valid argument then will have true premises and a false conclusion. Further, all substitution instances of tautologies are true; thus the corresponding conditional of a valid truth-functional argument must be true; thus in no case will its antecedent—the conjunction of the premises—be true while the consequent—the conclusion—is false.

Finally, if a truth functional argument form is valid, for example,

$$p \supset q$$
$$\underline{\quad {\sim}q \quad}$$
$$\therefore {\sim}p$$

we shall express that fact by saying either $[(p \supset q) \cdot {\sim}q]$ *logically implies* ${\sim}p$, or $[(p \supset q) \cdot {\sim}q] \supset {\sim}p$ is a tautology. In other words, *logical implication* is expressed in terms of tautology.

7.14   CONSISTENCY AND VALIDITY

As indicated, to call an argument valid is to say that the premises entail the conclusion, that is, it is impossible for the premise set to be true and the conclusion false. But this is equivalent to saying that the *conjunction* of the premise set with the *negation* of the conclusion is a contradiction. That is, one cannot consistently (without self-contradiction) affirm the premises *and* deny the conclusion, or one cannot simultaneously hold the premises to be true *and* the conclusion false. Consider the following:

Either I am not lost or I will find my way.
I will not find my way, or I am not lost.
Therefore, I am not lost.

Taking *p* and *q* to represent respectively, 'I am lost' and 'I will find my way,' it may be symbolized as follows:

~*p* ∨ *q*
~*q* ∨ ~*p*
―――――――
∴ ~*p*

To test the argument for validity we conjoin the premises with the *negation* of the conclusion to see if a contradiction results.

p	*q*			[(~*p* ∨ *q*)	·	(~*q* ∨ ~*p*)]	·	*p*		
T	T	F	T	T F F	F	F F T				
T	F	F	F	F F T	T	F F T				
F	T	T	T	T T F	T	T F F				
F	F	T	T	F T T	T	T F F				

It is a contradiction, and thus the statements are inconsistent, and thus the original argument is valid.

Two things should be noted about consistency. First, inconsistency, logically speaking, is always bad, for as we have noted, it is the same as asserting a contradiction. Second, it is a logical fact that *from inconsistent premises, we can prove anything whatever.* But if everything follows from inconsistent premises, then *nothing is proved.* The moral is evident: *avoid inconsistent premises.*

7.15 LOGICAL EQUIVALENCE, TAUTOLOGY, AND SOME LAWS OF LOGIC

We can also use tautology to define logical equivalence. *One statement is logically equivalent to another if and only if there is no row on the truth table where one statement is true and the other false.* If one statement is logically equivalent to another, the two statements they make have the same claim. Thus, consider the following:

If the water freezes the pipe will expand.

Either the water will not freeze or the pipe will expand.

These can be seen to be equivalent by the following truth-table:

p	q	$p \supset q$	$\sim p \vee q$
T	T	T	F T T
T	F	F	F F F
F	T	T	T T T
F	F	T	T T F

Another way of looking at logical equivalence is: *two statements are logically equivalent if and only if the biconditional formed from them is logically true* (is a tautology). Thus:

p	q	$(p \supset q) \equiv (\sim p \vee q)$
T	T	T T F T
T	F	F T F F
F	T	T T T T
F	F	T T T T

Some very important laws of logic are logically equivalent or tautologous; for example, laws about the interrelations of conjunction, disjunction and negation. For example, the Law of Double Negation: $p \equiv \sim\sim p$ can easily be proven tautologous by the following truth-table.

p	$\sim p$	$\sim\sim p$	$p \equiv \sim\sim p$
T	F	T	T
F	T	F	T

The laws concerning the relations between disjunction and conjunction are called De Morgan's Laws because they were rediscovered by Augustus De Morgan [1806–1871]. In English they are:

The negation of the [disjunction/conjunction] of two statements is logically equivalent to the [conjunction/disjunction] of the negations of the two statements.

It will be recalled that a disjunction is falsified if *both* of its disjuncts are false. Thus asserting the negation of a disjunct $p \vee q$ is logically equivalent to asserting the conjunction of the negations of p and q. In symbolic form we have:

$$\sim(p \vee q) \equiv (\sim p \cdot \sim q)$$

Similarly, the conjunction asserts that *both* conjuncts are *true*. To contradict it, then, is to assert that at *least one* is *false*, which is equivalent to the disjunction of the negation of p and q. In symbolic form, we have the equivalence:

$$\sim(p \cdot q) \equiv (\sim p \lor \sim q)$$

Exercises for § 7.15

A. Show that the following arguments are valid or invalid by putting them into argument form, constructing a corresponding conditional and determining whether they are or are not a tautology. Shaded items are on Tape 7, band 5.]

1. If Governor Thomas supports the candidates, then Senator Jones will also give his support. But if Senator Jones gives his support, then Mayor Smith will leave the party. If Mayor Smith leaves the party, then Governor Thomas will not support the candidate. Therefore Thomas will not support the candidate.

2. If Johnson gets the contract, then he will be made a partner, and he did get the contract. Therefore he will be made a partner.

3. If I sell this house, then I will be able to pay cash for the land. If I will be able to pay cash for this land, then I will sell this house. Therefore, either I will sell this house or I will pay cash for the land.

4. If Carl knows who murdered Jack and if he values his life, then he will seek police protection. There is no doubt that Carl values his life. Thus, Carl knows who murdered Jack only if he values his life.

5. If Tom is playing golf, then Harvey went to the auction and Sally went to the beauty salon. Harvey did not go to the auction. Thus Tom is not playing golf.

6. If either Carol is elected president or David is elected treasurer, then both Carol is elected president and David is elected treasurer. But it is not the case that both Carol is elected president and David is elected treasurer. Therefore, neither Carol was elected president nor David was elected treasurer.

7. This house may accept this resolution or it may reject it. But if you turn it down, you may expect a resolution to set up another investigating committee, and such a resolution will carry by an overwhelming majority of this body. Therefore, the house should accept the resolution.

8. There can be no democracy unless the voters are able to know the truth. But they can never know the truth if but one side of any fact or set of facts finds expression. We need, therefore, freedom of the press.

9. If your husband leaves you, then either he was never a good marital risk or you have failed him in some aspect of your life together. Your husband left you. Therefore either he was never a good marital risk or you failed him in some aspect.

10. If there is to be a president who truly represents the interests of the people, the voters must understand where each candidate stands on issues and they must vote. But the voters don't understand where the candidates stand on

the issues. Therefore, there will not be a president who truly represents the people.

B. Use truth tables to decide which of the following biconditionals are tautologies:

1. $(p \equiv q) \equiv (q \equiv p)$
2. $\sim(p \vee q) \equiv (\sim p \cdot \sim q)$
3. $p \equiv [p \vee (p \cdot q)]$
4. $p \equiv [p \cdot (p \vee q)]$
5. $(p \supset q) \equiv \sim(p \cdot \sim q)$
6. $(p \supset q) \equiv (\sim p \supset \sim q)$
7. $[(p \supset q) \supset r] \equiv [(q \supset p) \supset r)]$
8. $[(p \vee q) \supset r] \equiv [(p \supset r) \cdot (q \supset r)]$
9. $(p \supset q) \equiv [(p \vee q) \equiv q]$
10. $[\sim(p \cdot q) \cdot q] \supset \sim p$

7.16   THE THREE LAWS OF THOUGHT

Traditionally, it has been held that there are three basic laws of thought that are necessary and sufficient conditions for correct thinking. These laws have been formulated in two different ways, one for the logic of classes and the other for the logic of statements. They are:

1. *The Law of Identity:*
   a. 'A is A' or "Anything is itself."
   b. *If a statement is true*, then it is true—asserts that every statement of the form $p \supset p$ is true, that is, it is a tautology.
2. *The Law of Excluded Middle:*
   a. Anything is either A or not A.
   b. *Any statement is either true or false*—asserts that every statement of the form $p \vee \sim p$ is true, it is a tautology.
3. *The Law of Contradiction:*
   a. Nothing can both be A and not A.
   b. *No statement can be both true and false*—asserts that every statement of the form $p \cdot \sim p$ is false (self-contradictory).

Objections have been made to these laws, and we need briefly to discuss these in order further to explicate the meaning and significance of these laws. A group of writers called the 'General Semanticists' hold that the Law of Identity is false and vicious because it is not true for a world that is in constant change. If things are in constant flux, nothing is ever the same from moment to moment. When we say that "a table is a table," we ignore the fact that the table *now* is different from what it was a while ago. S. I. Hayakawa, in his *Language in Action*, asserts that "no word ever has the same meaning twice" on the grounds that the thing referred to has changed in the meantime.

These criticisms can be answered as follows. First of all, one must not confuse physical identity and logical identity. The statement "X has changed" requires that 'X' retain its identity throughout the series of changes, for otherwise; it would be impossible to say that "X has changed." There is constant physical change in the world, but there is also identity. Further, there is constancy of referent throughout a given unit of discourse, an identity in our meanings. Otherwise, we could not communicate. The physical characteristics of a particular table may have changed, but there has been identity of meaning. When we speak of a table, we mean a table, for a table is itself and not some other thing.

Another criticism of the Law of Identity concerns statements whose truth-values change with time, for example, "America's bicentennial birthday was celebrated today." This statement may be true for July 4, 1976 but not for July 4, 1977. However, "America's bicentennial birthday was celebrated today" is an incomplete statement of the speaker's meaning. The full statement would be "America's bicentennial birthday was celebrated today, July 4, 1976." If this was true on July 4, 1976, it will be true everywhere and at all times. Logic is concerned with *complete* or *nonelliptical* statements, and when dealing with these, the Principle of Identity is perfectly sound.

The Principle of Excluded Middle has been the object of attacks also. One such attack is that it fosters false 'either-or' thinking, representing a 'two-valued orientation' toward a world which, in fact, requires a miltivalued orientation. Examples of this black-or-white type of thinking are expressed by those who hold that all people are either good or evil and the patriot who argues: "The U.S. is always right" against the critic who says "The U.S. is always wrong." As we indicated in our discussion of the Black-White fallacy, there not only are usually other alternatives (people are sometimes good and sometimes evil; the U.S. is sometimes right and sometimes wrong), but there are degrees as well as mixtures of right and wrong. Thus, this criticism of the Law of the Excluded Middle confuses contrary and contradictory. The law says anything is *A* or it is contradictory. Thus, a person is either rich or not rich; the U.S. is always right or not always right. It does not assert that a person is either rich or poor, that the U.S. is right or wrong.

What is required when dealing with statements and the Law of Excluded Middle is precision. If a statement is precise, then we can determine that it is either true or false. Take "Either the lawn has been mowed or it has not been mowed." Suppose only part of the lawn has been mowed? Does this mean that the statement is both true and false? No, not if the statement is made sufficiently clear. If by 'lawn' we mean 'parts of the lawn,' then the statement is true. If by 'lawn' we mean *all* of the lawn, then the statement is false.

Finally, the Law of Contradiction asserts that nothing can be both *A* and not *A*. A thing cannot both be white and not-white *at the same time* and *in the same respect*. A statement cannot be both true and false, in the same context. Some have attempted to counter the Law of Contradiction by citing Einstein's law of relativity, which tells us that for one person two events are simultaneous while for another they occur successively. This, however, misses the point that for one frame of reference the events are simultaneous and for another they are successive. *But, for any given frame of reference, the events are not both simultaneous and successive.*

These three laws of thought are fundamental and privileged; they have played an important role in our discussion of truth-functional logic. In filling in and utilizing truth-tables, we assume all three, assigning the same truth-values for the same variable, and assigning one or the other truth-value.

Exercises for § 7.16

A. Analyze and discuss the following in terms of the Three Laws of Thought.

1. A person must be either sane or insane, and an insane person is absolutely incapable of reasonable thought and this is a dangerous kind of thinking.

2. All the cells in my body have changed completely since the day I was born, and thus I am not John Ivan as I was named at my birth.

3. "I am happy" is both true and not true.

4. The people before Copernicus thought the earth was at the center of the universe, and now they don't. The truth value of this statement has changed.

5. Light appears to be both corpuscular and not corpuscular. This defies the Law of Contradiction.

Chapter Outline

A. In truth-functional logic we are concerned with deductive arguments whose premises and conclusions include statements of a kind different from categorical statements, namely, *truth functional statements.*

  1. *Truth-functional statements* are compound statements whose truth-value is completely determined by the truth-value of their component parts.

  2. Truth-functional statements are formed by phrases like *It is false that, and, either or, if . . . then,* and *if and only if,* which are called *truth-functors.* These truth-functors operate on statements to form truth-functional statements. Given the definitions of each of these truth-functors, we know the truth-value of all truth-functional statement, given the truth-value of each of the component statements.

B. The truth-functors are defined as follows:

  1. *Negation:* Negation is the operation or result of prefixing the phrase "*It is not the case that,*" and its equivalents to a statement. This operation *reverses the truth-value* of the original statement. If the original statement was true, its negation is false and vice-versa. In other words, the negation of a statement is the *contradictory* of the original statement. Negation is indicated by the curl symbol ($\sim$). Thus, the negation of a statement p is $\sim p$.

2. *Conjunction:* Conjunction is the operation or result of linking together two or more statements by 'and' or its equivalent. The result of such an operation is that *a conjunction is true if and only if its components are true;* otherwise it is false. Conjunction is indicated by the dot symbol ($\cdot$), e.g., $p \cdot q$.

3. *Disjunction:* Disjunction is the operation or result of linking together two statements by the phrase 'either . . . or . . .' or its equivalent. The results of such an operation is that the *disjunction is false* when *both disjuncts are false;* otherwise it is true. Disjunction is indicated by the wedge symbol "v" and thus the disjunction of the statements p and q is symbolized as $p \text{ v } q$.

4. *Conditional:* A conditional statement is a statement consisting of two simpler statements linked by the words *if . . . then . . .* or their equivalent. The part that follows the *if* is called the *antecedent* and the part that follows the *then* is called the *consequent.* The conditional statement, in truth-functional logic, is interpreted as *material implication,* namely, that a conditional statement is false if its antecedent is true and its consequent false. Otherwise, the conditional statement is true. The phrase 'if . . . then . . .' and its equivalents are symbolized by the horse shoe ($\supset$) and thus, the conditional statement is symbolized as $p \supset q$.

5. *Biconditional:* A biconditional statement links two simpler statements by the words 'If . . . then,' or their equivalent. The result of this operation is that the *biconditional is true "if and only if" the component statements agree in truth-value.* Otherwise, it is false. The phrase "If and only if" is symbolized by the triple bar ($\equiv$), and thus the biconditional formed from two statements, p and q, is symbolized as $p \equiv q$.
   A biconditional is logically equivalent to the conjunction of a pair of conditionals. Thus, the biconditional may also be represented symbolically as $(p \supset q) \cdot (q \supset p)$.

C. The Truth-Table:
   1. A truth-table is a schematic device for representing graphically the truth-values of all possible truth-functional compounds under all possible interpretations. The truth-table also enables us to see all possibilities of truth and falsehood of premises and conclusions of truth-functional arguments and thus to determine the validity of these arguments. Truth-tables also tell us what truth-functional statements are *tautologies* and *contradictions,* and what statements are *logically equivalent.*
   2. The principle used in judging the validity of truth-functional arguments is: *An argument is invalid if and only if there is one or more rows on its truth-table where all the premises are true and the conclusion is false.*
   3. A shortened truth-table method consists in taking all cases of truth-value assignments that falsify the conclusion of an argument, checking whether the premises can all be made true by the truth-value assignments that falsify the conclusion. *If so, the argument is invalid.*

D. One can speak of truth-functional statements-forms as *tautologies, contradictions, contingencies,* and *logically equivalent.*
   1. A truth-functional statement form is a *tautology if it is true under all possible interpretations of its variables.* That is, a truth-functional statement is a tautology if it is true whether its component statements are true or false.

2. A truth-functional statement form is a *contradiction if it is false under all possible interpretations of its variables,* false whether its component statements are true or false.
3. A truth-functional statement is *logically equivalent* to another if and only if their truth-tables are exactly the same or if the biconditional formed from the two statements is a tautology.

E. Corresponding to the various kinds of truth-functional statements are familiar patterns of argument, some of which are valid and some of which are *fallacies*—invalid argument forms.

TABLE 6. Valid Truth-Functional Argument Forms

Name	Pattern(s)	Example
Double negation	Not (not p) $\therefore p$	It is not the case that George did not study his logic.
	$\sim\sim p$ $\therefore p$	$\therefore$ George studies his logic.
Conjunctive argument	p q $\therefore p \cdot q$	George studies his logic. George passed the test. $\therefore$ George studies his logic and George passed his test.
Simplification	$p \cdot q$ $\therefore p$	George studied his logic and George passed the test. $\therefore$ George studied his logic.
	$p \cdot q$ $\therefore q$	George studied his logic and George passed his test. $\therefore$ George passed his test.
Disjunctive argument	$p \vee q$ $\sim p$ $\therefore q$	Either John will marry Ellen or he will continue to date Louise. John will not marry Ellen. $\therefore$ John will continue to date Louise.
	$p \vee q$ $\sim q$ $\therefore p$	Either John will marry Ellen or he will continue to date Louise. He will not continue to date Louise. $\therefore$ John will marry Ellen.
Conditional Arguments a. *Modus Ponens* (Affirming the antecedent)	$p \supset q$ p $\therefore q$	If it rains, then the picnic will be cancelled. It is raining. $\therefore$ The picnic will be cancelled.
b. *Modus Tollens* (Denying the consequent)	$p \supset q$ $\sim q$ $\therefore \sim p$	If it rains, the picnic will be cancelled. The picnic was not cancelled. $\therefore$ It did not rain.

TABLE 7. *Invalid Argument Forms:* An argument can be shown to be invalid if it has a pattern corresponding to an invalid argument form.

Name	Pattern(s)	Example
Invalid disjunctive argument	$p \lor q$ p _____ $\therefore \sim q$	John will come or write a letter. John came. _____ $\therefore$ John did not write a letter.
	$p \lor q$ q _____ $\sim p$	John will come or write a letter. John wrote a letter. _____ $\therefore$ John will not come.
Invalid conditional arguments a. Fallacy of affirming the consequent	$p \supset q$ q _____ $\therefore p$	If it rains, then the game will be cancelled. The game was cancelled. _____ $\therefore$ It rained.
b. Fallacy of denying the antecedent	$p \supset q$ $\sim p$ _____ $\sim q$	If it rains, the game will be cancelled. It did not rain. _____ $\therefore$ The game was not cancelled.

THE METHOD OF DEDUCTION

8.1 INFERENCE RULES

Truth tables are adequate to test the validity of any truth-functional argument, but they do become impractical as the number of statement markers increases because truth columns grow at the rate of 2^n. Thus, with four variables truth columns are sixteen rows long. Calculations on truth tables, though possible in principle, are far too cumbersome. In such cases deduction is easier. The method of deduction shows an argument form to be valid if it is possible to deduce its conclusion from its premises by a sequence of elementary arguments that have already been shown to be valid by means of the truth tables. The elementary arguments, in essence, are a set of rules, called *transformation rules*, for they specify which truth-functional statement forms may be inferred from which others. The transformation rules are then subdivided into *inference* rules and *substitution* rules. Systems made up of such sets of rules are called *natural deduction systems*. The selection of the rules in these systems is relatively arbitrary; any set will do so long as it is complete.

There are two basic groups of rules. The first group of rules consists of those that permit us to infer one truth-functional statement form from one or more other truth-functional statement forms. We have already used these elementary argument forms and have established their validity by means of truth-tables. For example, there is *Modus Ponens*

$$p \supset q$$
$$\underline{p}$$
$$\therefore q$$

As an inference rule, this elementary valid argument form tells us that from $p \supset q$ and p, we can infer q. Similarly the valid argument form *Modus Tollens*

$$p \supset q$$
$$\underline{\sim q}$$
$$\therefore \sim p$$

as an inference rule tells us that from $p \supset q$ and $\sim q$ we can infer $\sim p$. The basic inference rules we will use are eight in number.

Rules of Inference

1. *Modus Ponens* (M.P.)
$$p \supset q$$
$$\underline{p}$$
$$\therefore q$$

2. *Modus Tollens* (M.T.)
$$p \supset q$$
$$\underline{\sim q}$$
$$\therefore \sim p$$

3. *Hypothetical Syllogism* (H.S.)
$$p \supset q$$
$$\underline{q \supset r}$$
$$\therefore p \supset r$$

4. *Disjunctive Syllogism* (D.S.)
$$p \vee q$$
$$\underline{\sim q}$$
$$\therefore p$$

5. *Constructive Dilemma* (C.D.)
$$(p \supset q) \cdot (r \supset s)$$
$$\underline{p \vee r}$$
$$\therefore q \vee s$$

6. *Addition* (Add)
$$\underline{p}$$
$$\therefore p \vee q$$

7. *Simplification* (Simp.)
$$\underline{p \cdot q}$$
$$\therefore p$$

8. *Conjunction* (Conj.)
$$p$$
$$\underline{q}$$
$$\therefore p \cdot q$$

Rules 7 and 8 both deal with conjunction. *Simplification* is called an *and-elimination* rule and *conjunction* is called an *and-introduction* rule because they enable us to eliminate or introduce a conjunction. Rule 6, Addition, is called an *or-introduction* rule because it allows us to introduce a disjunction.

Before moving on to the second group of rules, we shall first deal with the notion of proof, using only these eight inference rules. Consider the following argument.

Either the Democratic victory will be a landslide, or the Republicans will lose by a slim margin and the Democrats will carry the House and will have a majority in the Senate.

The Democratic victory will not be a landslide. Therefore either the Republicans will lose by a slim margin or the Independent Party will have a sizable portion of the vote.

If we put this argument into symbolic form, we get the following translation:

$$L \vee [R \cdot (H \cdot S)]$$
$$\sim L$$
$$\overline{}$$
$$\therefore R \vee I$$

To establish the validity of this argument by means of a truth-table would be bothersome because the five component statements would require thirty-two rows. However, the argument can be proved valid by deducing its conclusion from its premises by means of only three rules of inference and a sequence of three steps. The first step in setting out this deduction is to assume the two premises.

1. $L \vee [R \cdot (H \cdot S)]$
2. $\sim L$

From these two premises, we can validity infer

3. $R \cdot (H \cdot S)$

by the inference rule *Disjunctive Syllogism*, for example, from $p \vee q$ and $\sim p$, infer q. Now from

4. $R \cdot (H \cdot S)$

we can infer by the inference rule *Simplification* $(p \cdot q / \therefore p)$

5. R

Finally from 4 we can infer

6. $R \vee I$

by means of the inference rule, *Addition* $(p / \therefore p \vee q)$.

The deduction or chain of inferences was set out as follows:

$$L \vee [R \cdot (H \cdot S)]$$
$$\sim L$$
$$\overline{}$$
$$R \cdot (H \cdot S)$$
$$R$$
$$R \vee I$$

In formally setting out our proof of validity, however, it is customary to write the premises and the statements deduced from them in a single column and to set off in another column to the right of each statement its *justification*, that is, the inference rule used along with the steps used and in the order used. All the premises are usually listed first with the conclusion written directly after the last premise from which it is separated by a slash and the traditional three dots ∴ (or 'therefore') indicating the conclusion. Usually the statements are numbered and the justification for each statement indicates the numbers of the preceding statements from which it is inferred and the abbreviation for the rule of inference by which it follows from them. Thus, our formal proof for the validity of the above argument is written

1. $L \vee [R \cdot (H \cdot S)]$
2. $\sim L \, / \, \therefore R \vee I$
3. $R \cdot (H \cdot S)$ 1, 2. D.S.
4. R 3. Simp.
5. $R \vee I$ 5. Add.

We now have a new criterion for validity, namely: *A truth-functional argument is valid if and only if there is a derivation by means of the inference rules of elementary valid arguments of its conclusion from its premises.* An elementary valid argument, of course, is a substitution instance of an elementary valid argument form. For example,

$$L \vee [R \cdot (H \cdot S)]$$
$$\underline{\sim L \qquad\qquad}$$
$$\therefore R \cdot (H \cdot S)$$

is an elementary valid argument used in the above proof; it is such a valid argument because it is a substitution instance of the elementary valid argument form *Disjunctive Syllogism* (D.S.). It results from

$$p \vee q$$
$$\underline{\sim p \quad}$$
$$\therefore p$$

by substituting 'L' for 'p' and $[R \cdot (H \cdot S)]$ for 'q'.

Exercises for § 8.1

A. Of which elementary valid argument forms are the following abbreviated arguments substitution instances? [The shaded items are on Tape 8, band 1.]

1. $(P \supset Q) \vee (T \cdot S)$
   $\underline{\sim(P \supset Q) \qquad}$
   $(T \cdot S)$

2. $(R \vee S) \supset (T \cdot U)$
   $\underline{\qquad (R \vee S) \qquad}$
   $\therefore (T \cdot U)$

3. $N \supset (O \vee P)$
   $\underline{\sim O \vee P \qquad}$
   $\therefore \sim N$

4. $[(H \cdot \sim 1) \vee C] \cdot [(I \cdot \sim H) \vee D]$
   $\therefore [(H \cdot \sim 1) \vee C]$

5. $[(O \supset P) \supset Q]$
 $\therefore [(O \supset P) \supset Q] \vee [(C \vee D) \supset E]$

6. $(C \vee D) \supset (J \vee K)$
 $(J \vee K) \supset (L \supset M)$

 $\therefore (C \vee D) \supset (L \supset M)$

7. $[(O \cdot P) \supset Q] \supset \sim(C \vee D)$
 $[(O \supset P) \supset Q]$

 $\therefore \sim(C \vee D)$

8. $[(J \cdot K) \supset (L \cdot M)] \cdot [(O \cdot P)$
 $\supset (R \cdot S)]$
 $(J \supset K) \vee (O \cdot P)$

 $\therefore (L \supset M) \vee (R \cdot S)$

9. $[N \supset (O \cdot P)] \cdot [Q \supset (O \cdot R)]$
 $N \vee Q$

 $\therefore (O \cdot P) \vee (O \cdot R)$

B. Make up a substitution instance—either an abbreviated argument such as A, B, $\therefore (A \cdot B)$, or an unabbreviated argument in English—for each of the following inference rules.
  1. conjunction
  2. simplification
  3. modus tollens
  4. hypothetical syllogism
  5. disjunctive syllogism
  6. addition

C. For each of the following arguments state the Rule of Inference by which its conclusion follows from its premise or premises:

1. $(H \cdot I) \vee (J \supset K)$
 $\sim(H \cdot I)$

 $\therefore (J \supset K)$

2. $[A \vee B) \cdot C] \supset (D \vee E)$
 $\sim(D \vee E)$

 $\therefore \sim[(A \vee B) \cdot C]$

3. $[L \supset (M \supset N] \cdot [(O \supset P) \supset Q]$
 $\therefore [L \supset (M \supset N)]$

4. $(S \equiv T)$
 $(U \cdot V)$

 $\therefore (S \equiv T) \cdot (U \cdot V)$

5. $[P \supset (O \cdot Q)] \cdot [R \supset (S \vee T)]$
 $P \vee R$

 $\therefore (O \cdot Q) \vee (S \vee T)$

6. $[(S \supset T) \supset (U \vee V)]$
 $\therefore [(S \supset T) > (U \vee V)] \vee$
 $[(W \vee X) \cdot (Y \vee Z)]$

7. $(J \equiv K) \supset (L \equiv M)$
 $(L \equiv M) \supset (N \equiv O)$

 $\therefore (J \equiv K) \supset (N \equiv O)$

8. $[C \supset (F \equiv G)] \vee (H \vee I)$
 $\sim[C \supset (F \equiv G)]$

 $\therefore H \vee I$

9. $[(H \cdot \sim I) \supset C] \cdot (I \cdot \sim H) \supset D]$
 $(H \sim I) \vee (I \sim H)$

 $\therefore C \vee D$

10. $(M \supset O) \cdot (O \supset P)$
 $Q \supset R$

 $\therefore [(M \supset O) \cdot (O \supset P)] \cdot (Q \supset R)$

11. $(A \lor B) \supset \sim(C \cdot \sim A)$
     $\sim\sim(C \cdot \sim A)$
     _____
     $\therefore \sim(A \lor B)$

12. $(X \cdot \sim Y) \equiv (Y \supset Z)$
     $\therefore [(X \cdot \sim Y) \equiv (Y \supset Z)]$
     $\lor (X \equiv \sim Z)$

13. $(E \lor F) \supset [(A \supset B) \supset C]$
     $[(A \supset B) \supset C] \supset \sim(E \lor F)$
     _____
     $\therefore (E \lor F) \supset \sim(E \lor F)$

14. $(A \lor B) \supset [(D \lor E) \supset (D \cdot E)]$
     $\sim[(D \lor E) \supset (D \cdot E)]$
     _____
     $\therefore \sim(A \lor B)$

15. $[(J \supset K) \supset (S \supset L)] \cdot [(X \supset Y)$
     $(Z \supset W)]$
     $(J \supset K) \lor (X \supset Y)$
     _____
     $\therefore (S \supset L) \lor (Z \supset W)$

16. $[(O \supset P) \supset Q] \supset \sim(C \lor D)$
     $\sim[L \supset (M \supset N)]$
     _____
     $\therefore \{[(O \supset P) \supset Q] \supset$
     $\sim(C \lor D)\} \cdot \sim[L \supset (M \supset N)]$

17. $[(C \equiv W) \lor (D \equiv X)] \cdot [(E \equiv Y)$
     $\lor (F \equiv Z)]$
     $\therefore [(C \equiv W) \lor (D \equiv X)]$

18. $(F \equiv F) \supset \sim(G \cdot \sim F)$
     $(F \equiv G)$
     _____
     $\therefore \sim(G \cdot \sim F)$

19. $[\sim(H \cdot \sim I) \supset (H \supset I)]$
     $\supset [(I \equiv H) \supset \sim(H \cdot \sim I)]$
     $\sim[(I \equiv H) \supset \sim(H \cdot \sim I)]$
     _____
     $\therefore [\sim(H \cdot \sim I) \supset (H \supset I)]$

20. $\sim[L \supset (M \supset N)] \supset \sim(O \lor P)$
     $\sim[L \supset (M \supset N)]$
     _____
     $\therefore \sim(O \lor P)$

D. Each of the following is a formal proof of validity for the given argument. Indicate the justification for each statement that is not a premise. [The shaded items are analyzed on the tapes.]

1. 1) $A \supset B$
    2) $B \supset C$
    3) $A \lor \sim D$
    4) $\sim C \:/\therefore \sim D$
    5) $A \supset C$
    6) $\sim A$
    7) $\sim D$

2. 1) $P \cdot Q$
    2) $[(P \lor R) \supset S] \therefore P \cdot S$
    3) P
    4) $P \lor R$
    5) S
    6) $P \cdot S$

3. 1) $J \supset K$
    2) $J \sim K$
    3) $J \:/\therefore \sim J$
    4) K
    5) $\sim K$
    6) $\sim J$

4. 1) $A \supset B$
    2) $B \supset C$
    3) $A \:/\therefore C$
    4) B
    5) C

5. 1) $M \supset N$
    2) $N \supset O$
    3) $P \supset Q$
    4) $M \lor P \therefore O \lor Q$
    5) $M \supset O$
    6) $(M \supset O) \cdot (P \supset Q)$
    7) $O \lor Q$

6. 1) $J \supset K$
    2) $J \lor L$
    3) $\wedge K \:/\therefore L$
    4) $\sim J$
    5) L

7. 1) $(A \supset B) \cdot (C \supset D)$
   2) $(E \supset F) \cdot (G \supset H)$
   3) $A \vee E$ / $\therefore B \vee F$
   4) $A \supset B$
   5) $E \supset F$
   6) $(A \supset B) \cdot (E \supset F)$
   7) $B \vee F$

8. 1) $A \supset B$
   2) $B \supset C$
   3) $C \supset D$
   4) $\sim D$ / $\therefore \sim A$
   5) $A \supset C$
   6) $A \supset D$
   7) $\sim A$

9. 1) $J \supset K$
   2) $\sim L \supset (M \supset N)$
   3) $L \vee (J \vee M)$
   4) $\sim L$ / $\therefore (K \vee N)$
   5) $(M \supset N)$
   6) $(J \supset K) \cdot (M \supset N)$
   7) $J \vee M$
   8) $(K \vee N)$

10. 1) $A \supset B$
   2) $B \supset C$
   3) $D \supset E$
   4) $A \vee D$ / $\therefore C \vee E$
   5) $A \supset C$
   6) $(A \supset C) \cdot (D \cdot E)$
   7) $C \vee E$

E. Construct a formal proof of validity for each of the following arguments. [The shaded items are analyzed on the tapes.]

1. 1) $(G \vee H) \supset (J \cdot K)$
   2) G / $\therefore J$

2. 1) $(P \supset Q)$
   2) $(R \supset S)$
   3) $(P \vee R)$ / $\therefore Q \vee S$

3. 1) $A \cdot B$
   2) $(A \vee C) \supset (D \vee E)$ /
     $\therefore A \cdot (D \vee E)$

4. 1) $T \supset (C \cdot D)$
   2) $T \cdot B$
   3) $F \vee W$
   4) $(C \vee D) \supset \sim W$ / $\therefore F$

5. 1) $J \supset K$
   2) $L \supset M$
   3) $\sim N \vee (J \vee L)$
   4) $\sim\sim N$ / $K \vee M$

6. 1) $\sim A \supset \sim B$
   2) $\sim A \supset (C \equiv \sim B)$
   3) $(\sim D \vee \sim C) \supset \sim\sim B$
   4) $\sim D \vee \sim C$ / $\therefore C \equiv \sim B$

7. 1) $M \supset (B \supset P)$
   2) $M \supset (P \supset S)$
   3) M / $\therefore B \supset S$

8. 1) $(P \vee Q) \supset R$
   2) $R \supset \sim S$
   3) $\sim S \supset T$
   4) $P \cdot S$ / $\therefore T$

9. 1) $(A \vee B) \supset C$
   2) $(C \vee D) \supset E$
   3) $D \vee A$
   4) $\sim D$ / $\therefore E$

10. 1) $(D \supset F) \cdot (C \supset D)$
   2) $D \vee C$
   3) $(F \vee D) \supset E$
   4) $E \supset G$ $\therefore G$

F. Construct proofs for the following arguments. Use the suggested capital letters as abbreviations for simple statements in symbolizing the arguments. [The shaded items are analyzed on the tapes.]

1. If God is loving, then if he condemns sinners to eternal damnation, God is unjust. But God is loving. He is not unjust. Therefore he does not condemn sinners to eternal damnation. [G, S, U]

2. Either Peter went to Chicago or if he stayed home, then he played in the tennis tournament. But Peter did not go to Chicago, and he stayed home. Therefore, he played in the tennis tournament. [C, H, T]

3. If David won the election, then he made Edward chairman of the investigating committee. But either Frank was made chairman of the finance committee or Edward was not made chairman of the investigating committee. Frank was not made chairman of the finance committee. Therefore, David did not win the election. [D, E, F]

4. Perkins has invested in the development and Quakenbush will provide the building materials. But, if either Perkins invests in the development or Quakenbush provides the building materials, then either Smith will build the ponds or Thomas will do the ground work. Therefore Perkins invested in the development and either Smith will build the ponds or Thomas will do the ground work. [P, Q, S, T]

5. If Jane gets an A in logic, then she will not have to give up the scholarship. But if Jane does not get an A in logic, then she will stay in the Honors Club if and only if she will not have to give up the scholarship. But if either Jane will not be an A student or she will not stay in Honors Club, then it is not the case that she will not have to give up the scholarship. Either Jane will not be an A student or she will not stay in Honors Club. Therefore she will stay in Honors Club if and only if she will not have to give up the scholarship. [L, S, H, A]

6. If football is inaugurated, then there will be money for an olympic pool. If there will be money for an olympic pool, there will be money for hockey. Either football will be inaugurated or there will be money for tennis. There will not be money for hockey. Therefore, there will be money for tennis. [F, O, H. T]

7. If Allison marries Tom, she will be unhappy if their marriage is not romantic. But Allison will marry Tom even though their marriage will be good but not romantic. Therefore Allison will be unhappy. [M, U, R]

8. If Arthur becomes president of the club, then the club's social prestige will rise; and if Bert becomes treasurer, then he will make the club's financial position more secure. Either Arthur will become president or Bert will become treasurer. If the club's social prestige rises, then Bert will become treasurer; and if the club's financial position becomes more secure, then Walter will join. Therefore either Bert will become treasurer or Walter will join. [A, S, B, F, W]

9. If either Nolan or Olsen are guilty, then Paul will know. If either Paul knows or Quiller is innocent, then Rankin is on the right track. Either Quiller is innocent or Nolan is guilty. But Quiller is not innocent. Therefore Rankin is on the right track. [N, O, P. Q, R]

10. If Senator Carlson is engaged in immoral activities, then the Senate Committee should investigate only if Senator Dawson comes forth with his testimony and other Senators receive the same treatment. If Senator Dawson comes forth with his testimony and other Senators receive the same treatment, then resignation should be demanded if and only if guilt is proved beyond a doubt. But it is false that resignation should be

demanded if and only if guilt is proved beyond a doubt. Therefore it is not the case that if Senator Carlson is involved in immoral activities, then the Senate committee should investigate. [*C, I, D, T, R, G*]

8.2   RULES OF REPLACEMENT

Our eight Rules of Inference enable us to prove the validity of a fair number of truth-functional arguments, but there are many other valid truth-functional arguments whose validity cannot be proven by means of these rules alone. Thus, in this section we introduce a set of eleven rules determined by a set of valid biconditionals. We have already dealt with some of these biconditionals in the last section on tautology, namely those two valid biconditionals called De Morgan's Theorems:

$$\sim(p \cdot q) \equiv (\sim p \vee \sim q)$$
$$\sim(p \vee q) \equiv (\sim p \cdot \sim q)$$

These biconditionals functioning as rules can be stated as follows:

1. The negation of a conjunction can be replaced with a disjunction by dropping the negation sign, replacing the conjunction with a disjunction, and negating each of the resulting disjuncts.
2. The negation of a disjunction can be replaced with a conjunction by dropping the negation sign, replacing the disjunction with a conjunction and negating each of the resulting conjuncts.

Another valid biconditional we introduced early in chapter 7 is that known as Double Negation:

$$p \equiv \sim p$$

This biconditional, when it serves as a rule, may be stated as follows:

Any statement can be replaced with its double negation, and any double negated statement can be replaced with the statement.

The set of rules determined by valid biconditionals perform a different function from our eight Rules of Inference; they allow us to replace any statement form or part of a statement form with a statement form or part of a statement form that is logically equivalent to what was replaced. The replacement rules can work inside statement forms while the rules of inference must cover the whole line, that is, they work only from whole step to whole step. Our eleven rules are called Rules of Replacement and are as follows:

Rules of Replacement

Any of the following logically equivalent expressions may replace each other wherever they occur.

9. *Absorption* (Absp.)
$(p \supset q) \equiv p \supset (p \cdot q)$

10. *Double Negation* (D.N.)
$p \equiv \sim\sim p$

11. *De Morgan's Theorems* (DeM)
$\sim(p \lor q) \equiv (\sim p \cdot \sim q)$
$\sim(p \cdot q) \equiv (\sim p \lor \sim q)$

12. *Commutation* (Comm.)
$(p \lor q) \equiv (q \lor p)$
$(p \cdot q) \equiv (q \cdot p)$

13. *Association* (Assoc.)
$[(p \lor q) \lor r] \equiv [p \lor (q \lor r)]$
$[p \cdot q \cdot r] \equiv [p \cdot (q \cdot r)]$

14. *Distribution* (Dist.)
$[p \lor (q \cdot r) \equiv [(p \lor q) \cdot (p \lor r)]$
$[p \cdot (q \lor r)] \equiv [(p \cdot q) \lor (p \cdot r)]$

15. *Transposition* (Trans.)
also called *Contraposition*
$(p \supset q) \equiv (\sim q \supset \sim p)$

16. *Material Implication* (Impl.)
$(p \supset q) \equiv (\sim p \lor q)$

17. *Material Equivalence* (Equiv.)
$(p \equiv q) \equiv [(p \supset q) \cdot (q \supset p)]$
$(p \equiv q) \equiv [(p \cdot q) \lor (\sim p \cdot \sim q)]$

18. *Exportation* (Exp.)
$[(p \cdot q) \supset r] \equiv [p \supset (q \supset r)]$

19. *Tautology* (Taut.)
$p \equiv (p \lor p)$
$p \equiv (p \cdot p)$

Consider now how some of these rules can be used in combination with our Rules of Inference to provide a proof for an argument. Let us take the following argument:

$$P \supset Q, \sim(\sim R \cdot \sim P), \sim R \therefore Q$$

1. $P \supset Q$
2. $\sim(\sim R \cdot \sim P)$
3. $\sim R \; /\!/ \therefore Q$
4. $\sim\sim R \lor \sim\sim P$ 2. De Morgan's Theorem
5. $R \lor \sim\sim p$ 4. Double Negation
6. $R \lor P$ 5. Double Negation
7. P 6, 3 D.S.
8. Q 1, 7 M.P.

It should be noted that the eight Inference Rules and eleven Rules of Replacement constitute a *complete* system of truth-functional logic in the sense that the construction of a formal proof of validity for *any* valid truth-functional argument is possible. However, some of the rules are redundant. Thus, for example, *Modus Tollens* is redundant because every instance in which *Modus*

Tollens is used the Principle of *Transposition* and *Modus Ponens* can function equally well. *Disjunctive Syllogism* could also be replaced. But these two argument forms are easy to grasp and the use of all nineteen rules makes proofs considerably easier.

There are also two important differences between the method of deduction and that of truth-tables. First, the use of truth-tables is completely mechanical. It requires little thinking, but merely carefully following rules of procedure. But there are no mechanical rules for the construction of formal proofs. We must think out where to begin and how to proceed. (We shall try to give some hints about proof construction in a moment.) Another important difference between the method of deduction and truth-tables is that the method of deduction is method of *proof*, but not a method of disproof. In demonstrating that a conclusion follows by means of a chain of inference from its premises, you have proved *validity*, but in doing so you have not proved invalidity. If you cannot prove that a conclusion follows from its premises, it may only mean that you have not been clever enough to stumble on the right sequence. With truth-tables you can determine both validity and invalidity.

Before discussing some rules of thumb that are useful in constructing proofs, an important difference between the Rules of Inference and the Rules of Replacement must be reemphasized. The Rules of Inference apply only to whole lines of a proof. Thus, in a formal proof, S can be inferred from $S \cdot O$ only if $S \cdot O$ constitutes a whole line. It would be incorrect to use Simplification to infer $P \supset S$ from $P \supset (S \cdot O)$. The rules of Replacement on the other hand, can be applied to whole lines or parts of lines because logically equivalent expressions can replace each other wherever they occur even if they do not constitute whole lines of a proof. Consider the following examples of lines of proofs.

1. $p \vee (\sim q \supset r)$
2. $(q \cdot r) \cdot (\sim p \vee \sim p)$

The following actions can be carried out on these.

(a) Turning to line one and the statement form $p \vee (\sim q \supset r)$, we can work with just part of the disjunction, namely, its second disjunct, $(\sim q \supset r)$, which can be changed by means of Tranposition, to $(\sim r \supset \sim\sim q)$. Thus, we would take the following steps:

1. $p \vee (\sim\sim q \supset r)$
2. $p \vee (\sim r \supset \sim\sim q)$ 1. Transp.

(b) Working with example two, $q \cdot [r \cdot (\sim p \vee \sim p)]$, we can work on the second conjunct, $(\sim p \vee \sim p)$ by using tautology and changing it to $\sim p$. Thus, we would take the following steps:

2. $(q \cdot r) \cdot (\sim p \vee \sim p)$
3. $(q \cdot r) \cdot \sim p$ 2. Taut.

Here our Rules of Replacement have been applied to parts of lines. They can also be applied to a whole line. Thus from $(A \cdot B) \supset C$ we can infer the statement $A \supset (B \supset C)$ by Exportation.

Now we are ready to discuss a few Rules of Thumb to follow in constructing formal proofs. A good rule to follow in dealing with truth-functional arguments in general is to concentrate on the general form of the statements and not to be overwhelmed by the complexity of statements or a large number of statement letters. Consider the following argument:

$$(A \lor D) \supset [(C \lor D) \supset (C \cdot D)]$$
$$\sim[(C \lor D) \supset (C \cdot D)]$$
$$\therefore \sim(A \lor D)$$

Looking at the first premise, though it has four letters and is rather complex, it has as its basic connective a conditional and thus it is the form $p \supset q$. Next, the second premise has as its major connective a negation and thus it takes the form $\sim q$. Looking at the argument more carefully, we see that it is a substitution instance of *Modus Tollens*.

$$p \supset q$$
$$\frac{\sim q}{\therefore \sim p}$$

Another good rule of thumb is to be alert for statements that occur in the premises but not in conclusion. These statements may not be necessary to the derivation of the conclusion. Any clearly excess baggage should be ignored or eliminated. Further, we often want to free parts of statements or join them. Our Rules provide many procedures both for eliminating and freeing statements and for connecting them. Some of these are:

1. *Simplification* allows the dropping of a right hand conjunct.
2. *Modus Ponens* allows elimination of a conditional and liberation of the consequent.
3. *Hypothetical syllogism* allows marriage of an antecedent with a different consequent.
4. *Double Negation* helps us eliminate double negation.
5. *Conjunction* allows us to join two statements.
6. *Addition* allows us to add a statement.

Some students seem reluctant to use Addition because they mistakenly believe it is cheating to be able to add statements simply at will. However, as others have pointed out, not only is Addition valid, but it is a weakening type of assertion rather than a strengthening kind. Consider the statements "Logic is useful," and "Logic is useful or logic is fun." If we accept the single statement, "Logic is useful" as true, then we must also accept the statement "Either logic is useful or logic is fun," because the fact that logic is useful makes the disjunction true whether logic is fun or not. But the single statement "Logic is useful" is stronger than the statement "Logic is useful or logic is fun" because from the disjunction we can infer neither that logic is fun nor logic is useful, but only the much weaker conclusion that one or the other is true of logic. The moral of the story is: Do not hesitate to use Addition.

Another good procedure for constructing proofs is to break down the compound statements that occur in the premises because, in general, a statement alone on a line is very useful in obtaining a conclusion. Once again our elimination techniques come into play, namely, Simplification and *Modus Ponens*. Consider the following argument:

1. $\sim(P \lor Q)$
2. $\sim P \supset R \, / \therefore R$

The conclusion, in this case, is a single statement represented by R. R is connected in premise number two to $\sim P$. A possible way of obtaining our conclusion is to separate or obtain a $\sim P$ on a single line so that *Modus Ponens* could be used on two to obtain R. Looking at premise one, we see that it can be replaced by a conjunction with two negative conjuncts, thus giving us a $\sim P$. The Rule of Replacement applicable is De Morgan's Theorem. Thus,

3. $\sim P \cdot \sim Q$ 1. *De M.*

Now Simplification can be used to obtain $\sim P$ as follows:

4. $\sim P$ 3. *Simp.*

Now we can use *Modus Ponens* to infer our conclusion

5. R *M.P.*

A final rule of procedure that is helpful in doing proofs is to work backward from the conclusion looking for a statement or statements from which it can be deduced. Indeed, this rule of procedure is probably the most important of all. We employed this procedure in the above proof. Sometimes it is necessary when there are no obvious statements in the premises from which the conclusion could be derived to transform the conclusion by using replacement rules.

The following argument is often cited to illustrate this procedure.

1. $A \supset B$
2. $C \supset B \, / \therefore (A \lor C) \supset B$

The conclusion can be transformed as follows:

1. $(A \lor C) \supset B$ the conclusion
2. $\sim(A \lor C) \lor B$ 1. Impl.
3. $(\sim A \cdot \sim C) \lor B$ 2. De M.
4. $B \lor (\sim A \cdot \sim C)$ 3. Comm.
5. $(B \lor A) \cdot (B \lor \sim C)$ 4. Dist.

Now we can solve the proof by working *forward* from the premises toward this intermediate statement $(B \lor \sim A) \cdot (B \lor \sim C)$. Our proof thus can be constructed as follows:

1. $A \supset B$
2. $C \supset B / \therefore (A \lor C) \supset B$
3. $\sim A \lor B$ 1. Impl.
4. $B \lor \sim A$ 3. Comm.
5. $\sim C \lor B$ 2. Impl.
6. $B \lor \sim C$ 5. Commt.
7. $(B \lor \sim A) \cdot (B \lor \sim C)$ 4, 6. Conj.

Now we reverse the process of working backwards from the conclusion as follows:

8. $B \lor (\sim A \cdot \sim C)$ 7. Dist.
9. $(\sim A \cdot \sim C) \lor B$ 8. Comm.
10. $\sim (A \lor C) \lor B$ 9. De M.
11. $(A \lor C) \sim B$ 10. Impl.

Thus, our rules of thumb help us in constructing proof, but we do need to develop our own thinking ability and there is no substitute for practice as a method of acquiring facility in formal proof construction.

Exercises for § 8.2

A. For each of the following arguments state which of the rules, those of Inference or Replacement, by which its conclusion follows from its premises. [The shaded items are analyzed on Tape 8, band 2.]

1. $(A \supset B) \lor (C \supset D)$
$\therefore (C \supset D) \lor (A \supset B)$

2. $(A \lor B) \supset C$
$\therefore \sim (A \lor B) \lor C$

3. $C \supset (D \supset E)$
$\therefore (C \cdot D) \supset E$

4. $(\sim A \cdot \sim B) \lor C$
$\therefore C \lor (\sim A \cdot B)$

5. $p \supset (q \cdot r)$
$\therefore [(p \supset q) \cdot (p \supset r)]$

6. $\sim A \lor (B \lor C)$
$\therefore (\sim A \lor B) \lor C$

7. $(A \cdot B) \supset (C \cdot D)$
$\therefore [(A \cdot B) \supset C] \cdot [(A \cdot B) \supset D]$

8. $(\sim\sim J \lor K) \supset K$
$\therefore (J \lor K) \supset K$

9. $(\sim A \lor A) \lor B$
$\therefore \sim A \lor (A \lor B)$

10. $A \supset [(B \supset C) \cdot (C \supset B)]$
$\therefore A \supset (B \equiv C)$

11. $(\sim P \cdot Q) \cdot (R \lor S) \lor [\sim(\sim P \cdot Q)$
$\cdot \sim(R \lor S)]$
$\therefore (\sim P \cdot Q) \equiv (R \lor S)$

12. $[V \supset \sim(W \lor X)] \supset (V \lor Z)$
$\therefore \sim(V \lor Z) \supset \sim[V \sim(W \lor X)]$

13. $[(A \lor B) \cdot (C \supset D)] \supset [(A \cdot B) \supset (C \lor D)]$
$\therefore \sim[(A \lor B) \cdot (C \supset D)] \lor [(A \cdot B) \supset (C \lor D)]$

14. $[A \cdot (B \lor C)] \lor [A \cdot (D \sim E)]$
$\therefore A \cdot [(B \lor C) \lor (D \sim E)]$

15. $\sim(R \lor S) \supset (\sim R \lor \sim S)$
$\therefore \sim(\sim R \lor \sim S) \supset \sim\sim(R \lor S)$

16. $[\sim(Q \cdot R) \supset \sim P] \cdot [\sim P \supset \sim(Q \cdot R)]$
$\therefore \sim\sim\{[\sim(Q \cdot R) \supset \sim P] \cdot [\sim P \supset \sim(Q \cdot R)]\}$

17. $[(Q \lor \sim R) \supset \sim P] \lor [\sim P \supset (\sim Q \lor \cdot R)]$
$\therefore [\sim P \supset (\sim Q \lor \cdot R)] \lor [(Q \lor \sim R) \supset \sim P]$

18. $[P \cdot (Q \lor R)] \lor [\sim(Q \cdot R) \cdot \sim P]$
$[P \cdot (Q \lor R)] \lor [\sim P \cdot \sim(Q \cdot R)]$

19. $[A \cdot (D \cdot \sim E)] \cdot [(B \cdot D) \cdot \sim E]$
$\therefore [(A \cdot D) \cdot \sim E] \cdot [(B \cdot D) \cdot \sim E]$

20. $[(A \supset C) \supset (B \lor E)] \cdot [(B \lor E) \supset (A \cdot C)]$
$\therefore [A \supset C) \equiv (B \lor E)]$

B. For each of the following proofs of validity state the justification for each line which is not a premise. [The shaded items are analyzed on the tape.]

1. 1) $\sim(P \lor M) \lor (S \cdot R)$
2) $\sim S / \therefore \sim M$
3) $\sim S \lor \sim R$
4) $\sim(S \cdot R)$
5) $(P \lor M) \supset (S \cdot R)$
6) $\sim(P \lor M)$
7) $\sim P \cdot \sim M$
8) $\sim M \cdot \sim P$
9) $\sim M$

2. 1) $A \supset B$
2) $\sim(B \lor C) / \therefore \sim A$
3) $\sim B \cdot \sim C$
4) $\sim B$
5) $\sim A$

3. 1) $(D \lor \sim E) \lor F$
2) $(D \lor \sim E) \lor F / \therefore E \supset F$
3) $(\sim D \lor E) \cdot (\sim D \lor \sim D)$
4) $(\sim D \lor \sim D) \cdot (\sim D \lor E)$
5) $(\sim D \lor \sim D)$
6) $\sim D$
7) $D \lor (\sim E \lor F)$
8) $\sim E \lor F$
9) $E \supset F$

4. 1) $(J \cdot K) \supset L$
2) $\sim(K \supset L) / \therefore J \supset M$
3) $J \supset (K \supset L)$
4) $\sim J \lor (K \supset L)$
5) $\sim J$
6) $\sim J \lor M$
7) $J \supset M$

5. 1) $(P \supset Q) \supset Q / \therefore P \lor Q$
2) $(\sim P \lor Q) \supset Q$
3) $\sim(\sim P \lor Q) \lor Q$
4) $(\sim\sim P \cdot \sim Q) \lor Q$
5) $(P \cdot \sim Q) \lor Q$
6) $Q \lor (P \cdot \sim Q)$
7) $(Q \lor P) \cdot (Q \lor \sim Q)$
8) $Q \lor P$
9) $P \lor Q$

6. 1) $A \cdot B$
2) $(A \lor C) \supset D / \therefore (A \cdot D)$
3) A
4) $A \lor C$
5) D
6) $(A \cdot D)$

7. 1) $Q \supset \sim P$
    2) $\sim P \supset (Q \supset \sim R)$
    3) $(\sim S \vee \sim R) \supset \sim\sim Q$
    4) $\sim S / \therefore \sim R$
    5) $\sim S \vee \sim R$
    6) $\sim\sim Q$
    7) Q
    8) $\sim P$
    9) $(Q \supset \sim R)$
    10) $\sim R$

8. 1) $\sim F \vee [(G \cdot H) \vee (\sim G \cdot \sim H)]$
    2) $F / \therefore H \equiv G$
    3) $F \supset [(G \cdot H) \vee (\sim G \cdot \sim H)]$
    4) $F \supset (G \equiv H)$
    5) $G \equiv H$
    6) $(G \supset H) \cdot (H \supset G)$
    7) $(H \supset G) \cdot (G \supset H)$
    8) $H \equiv G$

9. 1) $(J \vee K) \supset L$
    2) $(L \vee K) \supset \{J \supset [(M \supset N)$
       $(N \supset M)]\}$
    3) $(J \cdot N) / \therefore M \equiv N$
    4) J
    5) $J \vee K$
    6) L
    7) $L \vee K$
    8) $J \supset [(M \supset N) \cdot (N \supset M)]$
    9) $(M \supset N) \cdot (N \supset M)$
    10) $(M \equiv N)$

10. 1) $(P \cdot Q) \supset \sim R$
    2) $R \vee (S \cdot T)$
    3) $P \equiv Q / \therefore P \supset S$
    4) $(P \supset Q) \cdot (Q \supset P)$
    5) $P \supset Q$
    6) $P \supset (P \cdot Q)$
    7) $P \supset \sim R$
    8) $(R \vee S) \cdot (S \vee T)$
    9) $R \vee S$
    10) $\sim\sim R \vee S$
    11) $\sim R \supset S$
    12) $P \supset S$

C. Construct a formal proof of validity for each of the following arguments. [Shaded items will be analyzed on the tape.]

1. 1) $N \supset (P \cdot R)$
    2) $R \supset P$
    3) $\sim P / \therefore \sim N$

2. 1) $(A \supset B) \supset D$
    2) $\sim (C \vee D) / \therefore A$

3. 1) $\sim (A \vee \sim B) / \therefore B$

4. 1) $A \supset U$
    2) $\sim I$
    3) $U \supset I / \therefore \sim U$

5. 1) $L \vee M$
    2) $\sim M / \therefore \sim M \cdot L$

6. 1) $F \supset W / \therefore W \vee \sim F$

7. 1) $(L \cdot E) \supset C$
    2) $(E \supset C) \supset P$
    3) $L / \therefore P$

8. 1) $(C \supset D) \cdot (A \supset B)$
    2) $C \cdot A / \therefore B \vee D$

9. 1) $A \supset B$
    2) $(\sim C \cdot \sim A)$
    3) $\sim\sim C / \therefore \sim A$

10. 1) $(P \supset Q) \supset R$
    2) $(S \vee T) \supset (P \cdot Q)$
    3) $S / \therefore R$

11. 1) $\sim E \vee (\sim W \vee \sim A)$
    2) $(W \cdot A) \vee (\sim W \cdot \sim A)$
       $/ \therefore \sim E \vee (\sim W \cdot \sim A)$

12. 1) $(P \vee Q) \vee \sim R$
    2) $(P \vee Q) \supset (S \cdot \sim Q)$
    3) $R / \therefore P \cdot R$

13. 1) $(C \supset H) \cdot (A \supset L)$
    2) $O \supset (\sim H \cdot L)$
    3) $O / \therefore (C \supset A) \cdot (H \supset M)$

14. 1) $J \supset (K \supset L)$
    2) $\sim M \vee J$
    3) $(K \supset L) \supset (N \cdot P)$
    4) $M / \therefore P \vee A$

15. 1) $M \supset \sim C$
    2) $\sim C \supset \sim A$
    3) $D \vee A / \therefore \sim M \vee A$

D. Using the suggested notation for symbolization, construct a formal proof of validity for the following arguments. [The shaded items are analyzed on Tape 8, band 3.]

1. If both Arthur and Bob lend their support to Gordan, then the campaign will be a success. Arthur will lend his support. Therefore, if Bob lends his support, the campaign will be a success. (A, B, C)

2. It is false that the roadway is not needed, but true that the state will assess the city for its construction. Thus, either the roadway is needed or the people who are against it have lied. (N, A, L)

3. If the solution is not acid, then the litmus paper will not turn red. The litmus paper turned red. Hence, the solution is acid. (R, A)

4. Either money was not the issue or nepotism was the more serious problem. But if it was not reelection that was sought, then nepotism was not the more serious problem. Therefore if money were the issue, then reelection was what was sought. (M, N, R)

5. Terry will be called to testify if and only if John is witness for the defense. John is not witness for the defense. Therefore Terry will not be called to testify. (T, W)

6. If there was foul play in this case, then a special investigation will be undertaken. But it is not true both that Harvey will be put on the case and that a special investigation was undertaken. Yet I am told that Harvey will be put on the case. However, it must be concluded that there was no foul play in this case. (F, I, H)

7. Either it is the case that if Roberts makes the lowest bid on the project, then Smithers will be suspicious or Thomas will get the contract. It is not the case that either Smithers is suspicious or Thomas got the contract. Therefore either Roberts did make the lowest bid on the project or Quiller did not give a fair appraisal of the bids. (R, S, T, Q)

8. Money is worth having if and only if wealth is happiness. Thus, either wealth is not happiness or money is worth having. (M, H)

9. If love makes the world go round then if people turn it themselves, human relations are genuine. Love does make the world go round. People do turn the world themselves. Therefore, human relations are genuine. (L, P, G)

10. Harry will not both read Husserl and swim in the ocean or he will go to Los Angeles. Either Harry will not go to Los Angeles or he will answer his mail. Harry did swim in the ocean, but he did not answer his mail. Therefore, he will not read Husserl. (R, S, G, A)

11. John has a job or he is living off his girlfriend and his mother is angry. If John has a job, then he is wasting his money. If he is wasting his money, then his mother is angry. Thus his mother is angry. (J, L, A, W)

12. Arthur is egotistical and Betty is rich and lonely. If Betty is rich and Arthur is egotistical, then either Betty will marry Arthur or she will ignore him or have arguments with him. Betty did not marry Arthur, but they are neither friends nor does Betty have arguments with him. Therefore, Betty just ignores him. (E, R, L, M, I, A, F)

13. If the quarterback does not pass and the end advances, then either the fullback is blocked or the halfback is tackled. If the quarterback does not pass then if the fullback is blocked, then there was a stalemate. Either the quarterback passes or if the halfback is tackled then the play is lost. The quarterback does not pass and the end advances. Therefore, either there is a stalemate or the play is lost. (*P, A, B, T, S, L*)

14. Either fees are increased or if expenditures rise, then the debt ceiling is raised. If fees are increased then students will be lost. If expenditures rise, the college will borrow more money, then if the debt ceiling is raised then interest charges will rise. If fees are not increased and students are not lost then if the debt ceiling is raised the college still will borrow more money. The students are not lost. Either interest charges did not rise or the college did not borrow more money. Therefore, either the debt ceiling is not raised or expenditures did not rise. (*F, E, D, L, B, C*)

8.3   CONDITIONAL PROOF

In working with proofs of validity thus far, we have seen that, except for premises, every line in a given proof is a logical consequence of some previous line in that proof and hence a logical consequence of one or more of the premises. However, we often do reason to a conclusion from assumptions not stated as premises of that argument. In fact making our proofs of validity could be easier if we could make use of assumed statements. Thus, for example, take an argument that appears in several current logic texts:

If the set or prime numbers is finite, then the set of prime numbers has a smallest number and a largest number. Therefore, if the set of prime numbers is finite, then it has a largest number.

This can be symbolized as:

$$F \supset (S \cdot L) / \therefore F \supset L$$

If I could assume '*F*' that is, that the set of prime numbers is finite, '*S* · *L*' then follows from my assumption of '*F*' and premise one by *Modus Ponens*. Then the Commutation and Simplification give me '*L*,' the consequent of the conclusion.

Let us set out the argument in proof form. The first step was to assume '*F*,' which cannot be deduced from the first premise. To make clear that '*F*' is an assumed premise we write *Assumed Premise* (A P) beside it and point an arrow at it from the left.

    1. $F \supset (S \cdot L)$ $/ \therefore F \supset L$
→2. F *Assumed Premise* (AP)

From premise one and our assumption two, we obtain

   3. $S \cdot L$ 1, 2 MP

To make clear that 3 has only been deduced with the help of our assumption (2), we let the tail of the arrow marking the assumption to run down beside it.

   1. $F \supset (S \cdot L)$ / $\therefore F \supset L$
  2. F *Assumed Premises* (AP)
   3. $S \cdot L$ 1, 2 MP

So long as we continue to make deductions with the help of our assumption rather than from our premise alone, we continue the arrow alongside the lines we deduce:

   1. $F \supset (S \cdot L)$ / $\therefore F \supset L$
  2. F *Assumed Premise* (AP)
   3. $S \cdot L$ 1, 2 MP
   4. $L \cdot S$ 3. Comm.
   5. L 4. Simp.

Given premise 1, we have now shown that *if* 2 is true, then 5 must be true as well. We have established the conditional '$F \supset L$' by deducing its consequence from its antecedent with the help of our premise. To show that '$F \supset L$' follows from the premise alone and that our assumption can now be discarded, we *close off* the assumption by extending the tail of the arrow horizontally under 5 and writing '$F \supset L$' beneath it. This indicates that the assumption made at line 2 is no longer operative. Beside line 6, we write '2–5 CP,' for the justification permitting 6 must refer to all the steps in the subordinate deduction. The rule permitting the whole move is the *Rule of Conditional Proof* (CP). Thus, our total proof is as follows:

   1. $F \supset (S \cdot L)$ / $\therefore F \supset L$
  2. F *Assumed Premise* (AP)
   3. $S \cdot L$ 1, 2 MP
   4. $L \cdot S$ 3. Comm.
   5. L 4. Simp.

   6. $F \supset L$ 2–5 CP

In the case of the above argument, we could have deduced six from one by our known rules in the same number of steps, but this is not usually the case. It is either impossible or makes the proof much longer and more difficult.

A conditional proof of the validity of any argument whose conclusion is a conditional statement is constructed by assuming the antecedent of its conclu-

sion as an additional premise and then deducing the consequent of its conclu-
sion by a sequence of elementary valid arguments, our nineteen Rules of
Inference.

However, our rule of conditional Proof is more versatile than this statement
would indicate. In our example above, only one assumed premise was used but
any number of premises can be introduced into a proof on the condition that
every one of the assumed premises is eventually discharged so that the conclusion of the argument depends only on the given premises. Further an assumption need not be the antecedent of the conclusion. Any assumption may be
made provided that before we finish the deduction we construct a conditional
with the added premise as antecedent and whatever was deduced with its help
as the consequent. Consider the following example:

1. $\sim A \supset \sim B$
2. $C \cdot D \supset E$
3. $(C \vee B) \cdot D$ $/ \therefore \sim A \supset E$
4. $\sim A$
5. $\sim B$ 1, 4 M.P.
6. $\sim B \vee \sim D$ 5. Add
7. $\sim (B \cdot D)$ 6. De M.
8. $C \cdot D \vee B \cdot D$ 3. Dist.
9. $B \cdot D \vee C \cdot D$ 8. Comm.
10. $C \cdot D$ 7, 9 D.S.
11. E 2, 10 M.P.
12. $\sim A \supset E$ 4, 11 C.P.

The added premise $\sim A$ enabled us to readily deduce E, and we end with the
conditional.

The following is an example of a proof with more than one assumed premise.

1. $(A \vee B) \supset C$ $/ \therefore [(C \vee D) \supset E] \supset (A \supset E)$
2. $(C \vee D) \supset E$ AP
3. A AP
4. $A \vee B$ 3. Add
5. C 1, 4 MP
6. $C \vee D$ 5. Add
7. E 2, 6 MP
8. $A \supset E$ 3, 7 CP
9. $[(C \vee D) \supset E] \supset (A \supset E)$ 2, 8 CP

The technique of *Conditional Proof* greatly facilitates proving validity, and
speed and ease of proof is provided.

Exercises for § 8.3

Using CP, prove the following arguments valid. [The shaded item is analyzed on Tape 8, band 3.]

1. 1) $(R \supset Q) \supset P$
   2) $T \vee S$
   3) $\sim(R \cdot T)$
   4) $\sim Q \supset \sim S \ / \therefore P$

2. 1) $(P \supset E) \cdot (A \supset L) \ / \therefore$
      $(P \vee A) \supset (E \vee L)$

3. 1) $P \supset Q$
   2) $Q \supset R$
   3) $\sim P \supset (S \vee T) \ / \therefore \sim R \ (S \vee T)$

4. 1) $(P \vee Q) \supset R$
   2) $(S \vee T) \supset [(A \vee B) \supset P]$
      $/ \therefore S \supset (A \supset R)$

5. 1) $A \supset B$
   2) $C \vee \sim A \ / \therefore A \supset (B \cdot C)$

6. 1) $(A \cdot B) \equiv C$
   2) $\sim C \supset (\sim A \supset D)$
   3) $A \ / \therefore \sim D \supset (A \vee B)$

7. 1) $F \supset (S \cdot L) \therefore F \supset L$

8. 1) $\sim A \supset \sim B$
   2) $A \supset C$
   3) $B \vee D$
   4) $D \supset E \ / \therefore E \vee C$

9. 1) $(A \vee B) \supset (C \cdot D)$
   2) $(D \vee E) \supset F \ / \therefore A \supset F$

10. 1) $\sim D \supset \sim(A \vee M)$
    2) $\sim(A \cdot \sim F \ / \therefore \sim A \vee (F \cdot D)$

8.4   THE REDUCTIO AD ABSURDUM

Another powerful technique of proof is that known as *Reductio ad Absurdum* or *Indirect Proof.* The technique is as follows: Assume the contradictory of the conclusion as an added premise and try to deduce a contradiction. The logic of the proof depends on the notions that you cannot derive false statements from true ones and on the feature of entailment discussed earlier, namely if P entails Q, then $P \cdot \sim Q$ is a contradiction. If the premises entail the conclusion and are true, then the conclusion must be true, and the contradictory must be false. Thus to assume premises to be true, and yet to assume a premise that is the contradictory of the conclusion, is to contradict oneself. Consider the following argument:

1. $\sim(P \cdot Q) \supset R$
2. $Q \vee \sim R \ / \therefore Q$
3. $\sim Q$ AP
4. $\sim R$ 2, 3 DS
5. $P \cdot Q$ 1, 4 MT, DN
6. $Q \cdot P$ 5. Comm.
7. Q 6. Simp.
8. $\sim Q \cdot Q$ 3, 7 *Reductio ad Absurdum*

Thus we have obtained a contradiction. Obviously, if premises 1 and 2 are true, then the added premise 3, $\sim Q$, is false. And if $\sim Q$ if false, then Q is true. Hence we have shown the argument valid. Note that we have marked our arrow and line as in conditional proof. Indeed *Indirect Proof* may be considered a special kind of conditional proof. Thus we could set up the above argument as follows:

1. $\sim(P \cdot Q) \supset R$	
2. $Q \text{ v} \sim R \ / \therefore Q$	
3. $\sim Q$	AP
4. $\sim R$	2, 3 DS
5. $P \cdot Q$	1, 4 MT DN
6. $Q \cdot P$	5. Comm.
7. Q	6. Simp.
8. $\sim Q \supset Q$	3, 7 CP
9. $Q \text{ v } Q$	8. Implic.
10. Q	9. Taut.

Exercises for § 8.4

Construct *Reductio ad Absurdum* proofs of the following. [The shaded items are analyzed on Tape 8, band 4.]

1. 1) $H \supset (A \supset B)$
   2) $\sim C \supset (H \text{ v } B)$
   3) $H \supset A \ / \therefore C \text{ v } B$

2. 1) $\sim A \supset (B \cdot C)$
   2) $\sim C \ / \therefore A$

3. 1) $A \supset B$
   2) $\sim(B \text{ v } C) \ / \therefore \sim A$

4. 1) $(B \cdot D) \text{ v } (E \cdot C)$
   2) $\sim B \ / \therefore E$

5. 1) $[A \supset (B \text{ v } C] \supset (D \supset A)$
   2) $\sim A \ / \therefore \sim D$

6. 1) $[(A \cdot B) \text{ v } C] \supset (D \text{ v } E)$
   2) $D \supset \sim(B \text{ v } C)$
   3) $E \supset D \ / \therefore \sim C$

8.5   PROOF OF INVALIDITY

As indicated earlier, we cannot construct formal proofs for invalidity. Further, failure to prove an argument invalid does not mean no such proof can be constructed; it might mean instead that we lack ingenuity. We can, however, prove an argument invalid by finding a substitution instance of it that has true premises and a false conclusion. This is essentially also what the truth table does when it shows a row in which truth values are assigned in such a way that the premises are made true and the conclusion false. In such a case the argument is invalid. Consider the following argument:

$A \supset B$
$B \supset C$
———————
$\therefore C \supset A$

What assignment of truth values would be required to make the conclusion false? Obviously, if C is T and A is F, the conclusion, $C \supset A$ is also false since a conditional is false when its antecedent is true and its consequent false. But what about the premises? We have yet to assign a truth-value to B. In order for the premises to be true we could assign either T or F to B, because in both cases they would be true, for example:

I. $\mathbf{F \supset T \quad \} \quad T}$ II. $\mathbf{F \supset F \quad \} \quad T}$
  $\mathbf{T \supset T \quad \} \quad T}$ $\mathbf{F \supset T \quad \} \quad T}$
  —————————   —————————
  $\mathbf{T \supset F \quad \} \quad F}$ $\mathbf{T \supset F \quad \} \quad F}$

The argument is thus proven invalid.

This method of proving invalidity, is of course, closely related to the truth table method of proof because, in effect, what we did above is construct one row of the given argument's truth-table. This can be seen if we write out I horizontally as

A	B	C	$A \supset B$	$B \supset C$	$C \supset A$
$\mathbf{F}$	$\mathbf{T}$	$\mathbf{T}$	$\mathbf{T}$	$\mathbf{T}$	$\mathbf{F}$

An argument is proven invalid if there is at least one row of its truth table in which all the premises are true but its conclusion is false. The method of proving invalidity discussed here then is a method of constructing such a row. Of course, with very complex arguments such a construction might not be so easy and a certain amount of trial and error will be necessary.

Exercises for § 8.5

Prove the invalidity of the following arguments by the method of assigning truth-values. [Shaded item analyzed on Tape 8, band 4.]

1. 1) $(S \supset C)$
   2) $C \supset (R \lor O \lor Y)$
   3) $R \ /\therefore S$

2. 1) $[(X \cdot Y) \cdot Z] \supset A$
   2) $(Z \supset A) \supset (B \supset C)$
   3) B
   4) $\therefore X \supset C$

3. 1) $P \supset Q$
   2) $R \supset S$
   3) $R \lor O \ /\therefore P \lor S$

4. 1) $A \lor B$
   2) $C \lor B$
   3) $A \ /\therefore \sim B$

5. 1) $F \supset T$
   2) $T \ /\therefore F$

6. 1) $(I \cdot S) \supset (G \cdot P)$
   2) $[(S \cdot \sim I) \supset A] \cdot (A \supset P)$
   3) $I \supset S \ /\therefore P$

8.6 INCONSISTENCY

An *inconsistent* argument is one in which the conclusion contradicts the premises and thus one in which the negation of the conclusion can be deduced. We can show that a set of premises is inconsistent (and that, therefore, at least one premise is false) in two ways:

1. We show by truth table analysis that the conjunction of the premises is a contradiction.
2. We show by using our rules of inference that a contradiction follow from the premises.

Consider the following proof.

1. $A \lor B$
2. $\sim B \lor \sim A$
3. A $/\therefore B$
4. $\sim\sim A$ 3. DN
5. B 1, 4 DS
6. $\sim B$ 2, 4 DS
7. $B \cdot \sim B$ 5, 6 Conj.

Using our rules we have derived a contradiction from the premises and thus we have proven the argument to have inconsistent premises. The method of proving that an argument has inconsistent premises, then, is to use our rules to derive a contradiction from the premises. Thus, we can prove the following argument has inconsistent premises.

1. $P \supset Q$
2. $\sim P \supset R$
3. $\sim(Q \lor R)$ $/\therefore S$
4. $\sim Q \cdot \sim R$ 3. De M.
5. $\sim Q$ 4. Simp.
6. $\sim P$ 1, 5 MT
7. R 2, 6 MP
8. $\sim R \cdot \sim Q$ 4. Comm.
9. $\sim R$ 8. Simp.
10. $R \cdot \sim R$ 7, 9 Conj.

Exercises for § 8.6

Construct a proof to show that the following sets of premises are inconsistent. [Shaded item analyzed on Tape 8, band 4.]

1. 1) $P \supset Q$
   2) $P \cdot \sim Q$

2. 1) $\sim A \vee B$
   2) $\sim B \vee \sim A$
   3) A

3. 1) $A \equiv B$
   2) $B \cdot \sim A$

4. 1) $A \equiv B$
   2) $B \supset C$
   3) $\sim(C \vee \sim A)$

5. 1) $A \supset (B \vee C)$
   2) $\sim(\sim A \vee C)$
   3) $\sim B$

6. 1) $(A \vee B) \equiv (C \supset D)$
   2) $\sim(\sim D \vee B)$
   3) $\sim A$

7. 1) $(A \vee B) \supset C$
   2) $B \cdot D$
   3) $\sim(C \vee \sim A)$

8. 1) $\sim C \vee (A \supset B)$
   2) $C \supset \sim B$
   3) $A \cdot C$

Chapter Outline

A. A truth-functional argument may be proved valid by deducing the conclusion from its premises by a sequence of elementary valid arguments. Such a method of proving validity is called the *method of deduction*.

B. The elementary argument forms are called *inference* or *transformation* rules because they specify which truth-functional statement forms may be inferred from which others.

C. A second set of rules, called *Replacement Rules*, determined by valid biconditionals, allow us to replace any statement form or part of a statement form with a statement form or part of a statement that is logically equivalent to what was replaced.

D. The rules are as follows:

Rules of Inference

1. *Modus Ponens* (M.P.)

   $p \supset q$

   p

   $\therefore q$

2. *Modus Tollens* (M.T.)

   $p \supset q$

   $\sim q$

   $\therefore \sim p$

3. *Hypothetical Syllogism* (H.S.)

   $p \supset q$

   $q \supset r$

   $\therefore p \supset r$

4. *Disjunctive Syllogism* (D.S.)

   $p \vee q$

   $\sim q$

   $\therefore p$

5. *Constructive Dilemma* (C.D.)

   $(P \supset q) \cdot (r \supset s)$

   $p \vee r$

   $\therefore q \vee s$

6. *Addition* (Add.)

   p

   $\therefore p \vee q$

7. *Simplification*

   $p \cdot q$

   $\therefore p$

8. *Conjunction* (Conj.)

   p

   q

   $\therefore p \cdot q$

Rules of Replacement

9. *Absorption* (Absp.): $(p \supset q) \equiv p \ (p \cdot q)$
10. *Double Negation* (D.N.): $p \equiv \sim\sim p$
11. *DeMorgan's Theorems* (DeM.): $\sim(p \lor q) \equiv (\sim p \cdot \sim q)$
                                   $\sim(p \cdot q) \equiv (\sim p \lor \sim q)$
12. *Commutation* (Comm.): $(p \lor q) \equiv (q \lor p)$
                                   $(p \cdot q) \equiv (q \cdot p)$
13. *Association* (Assoc.): $[(p \lor q) \lor r] \equiv [p \lor (q \lor r)]$
                                   $[(p \cdot q) \cdot r] \equiv [p \cdot (q \cdot r)]$
14. *Distribution* (Dist.): $[p \lor (q \cdot r)] \equiv [(p \lor q) \cdot (p \lor r)]$
                                   $[p \cdot (q \lor r)] \equiv [(p \cdot q) \lor (p \cdot r)]$
15. *Transposition* (Trans.): $(p \supset q) \equiv (\sim q \supset \sim p)$
16. *Material Implication* (Impl.): $(p \supset q) \equiv (\sim p \lor q)$
17. *Material Equivalence* (Equiv.): $(p \equiv q) \equiv [(p \supset q) \cdot (q \supset p)]$
                                    $(p \equiv q) \equiv [(p \cdot q) \lor (\sim p \cdot \sim q)]$
18. *Exportation* (Exp.): $[(p \cdot q) \supset r] \equiv [p \supset (q \supset r)]$
19. *Tautology* (Taut.): $p \equiv (p \lor p)$
                                   $p \equiv (p \cdot p)$

E. The Method of Deduction, unlike the Truth Table Method, is only a method of proof, that is, it can only prove validity and not invalidity.

F. The Rules of Inference can be applied only to whole lines while the Rules of Replacement may be applied both to whole lines and parts of lines.

G. The Method of Deduction is not purely mechanical as are the truth tables, but rather requires thought and ingenuity. There are, however, a few rules of thumb to follow in constructing proofs.
   1. Always concentrate on the general form of statements however complex they may be.
   2. Statements that occur in the premises but not in the conclusion should be ignored or eliminated.
   3. Use Addition to introduce statements that occur in the conclusion but not in the premises.
   4. Break down compound statements.
   5. Work backward from the conclusion transforming it, if necessary, by replacement rules.

H. The *Rule of Conditional Proof:* If from *Pr*, the conjunction of the premises of an argument, plus some assumed premises p one can infer q, then one can infer p$\supset$q from *Pr* alone. Any number of premises may be introduced into a proof on the condition that every one of the assumed premises is eventually discharged so that the conclusion of the argument depends only on the given premises.

I. The *Reduction ad Absurdum* technique proves validity by adding the contradictory of the conclusion as a premise and deducing a contradiction. This technique is based on two notions:
   1. You cannot derive false statements from true ones.
   2. If P entails Q, then $P \cdot \sim Q$ is a contradiction.

J. A truth-functional argument can be proven invalid by finding a substitution instance of it which has true premises and a false conclusion. This is similar to finding a row of an argument's truth-table in which truth values are assigned in such a way that the premises are made true and the conclusion false.

K. An *inconsistent* argument is one in which at least one of the premises must be false because the premises are contradictory.

    1. Such an argument is formally valid because there could be no case in which both premises could be true.

    2. An argument can be proven inconsistent by deriving a contradiction from its premises.

9

QUANTIFICATION THEORY

9.1 SINGULAR STATEMENTS

In this chapter we are concerned to discuss another type of deductive logic—
predicate logic. It is a logic that combines the term or predicate analysis of
traditional categorical logic with the statement analysis of truth-functional logic
and can thus handle both truth-functional arguments and categorical syllogisms
as well as many other types of argument. For example, truth-functional logic
cannot handle this standard valid **AAA** syllogism.

All humans are mortal.
Socrates is human.
_____
Therefore Socrates is mortal.

Each of the statements in this argument are simple statements, and thus this
syllogism would be symbolized, in truth-functional logic, as the invalid form.

A
B /∴ C

What is needed, then, is a logic that can handle categorical statements and
that, unlike Aristotelian logic, can also handle compound statements.

Consider the statement 'Socrates is human'. This statement is called a
singular statement. It asserts that a particular property, 'being human,' belongs to a particular individual, 'Socrates'. Traditional logic and grammar

specify 'Socrates' as the *subject* term and 'human' as the *predicate* term. If we let the capital letter *H* denote the property of being human and the small letter *s* name the individual, Socrates, we can symbolize the statement 'Socrates is human' as *Hs*. Similarly, the statements 'Beethoven is human' and 'Carol is human' can be symbolized as *Hb* and *Hc*. All of these statements have the same general structure, and they each ascribe a *property* to some *individual entity*. Further, in logic it makes a difference whether the predicate term that specified the property is an adjective, a noun, or even a verb, though, as we learned earlier, clarity calls for a noun. The following statements are grammatically different, but they take on the same logical form in symbolization: 'Saul Bellow is a writer'; 'Pat Boone likes to sing a lot'; 'Julie London fascinates most men'. They can be symbolized as: *Wa; Sa; Ba*.

We shall now introduce some notational conventions. *Capital letters* will be used to denote predicate expressions true or false of things such as "is a philosopher," "is human." Small letters *a–w* will be used to denote individual objects, things—any things that can have properties ascribed to them. They are called *individual constants*. Now that we have specified our two groups of symbols, we note that writing a predicate symbol immediately to the left of an individual symbol gives us the symbolic formulation of a singular proposition asserting that the individual named has the property specified, for example, 'Horace is tall' becomes *Ha*. Further, the letters *xyz* will be used as *individual variables*, that is, as place markers to be replaced by individual constants. These do not designate specific individuals; rather they range indiscriminately over all individuals. Thus, expressions like '*x* is a human' and *Hx* are neither true or false because no particular individual is designated by *x:* Such expressions will be called *open sentences*. Any singular statement is a *substitution instance* of an open sentence, obtained by substituting an individual constant for the individual variable. Thus, replacing the variable *x* in *Hx* with the constant *a*, we get the statement *Ha*. Singular statements, *Ha, Hb, Hc, Hd*, and soon, are either true or false, but the *open sentence Hx* is neither true or false but is true or false of things. The following are examples of statement forms and some of their substitution instances.

Open Sentences	Statement
1. *HX*	*Hb*
2. *Bx · Cy*	*Bb · Ca*
3. *(Bx · Cy) ⊃ Dz*	*(Ba · Cb) ⊃ Dc*

9.2 QUANTIFIERS

Predicates also are used in statements other than singular statements that refer to particular individuals. Consider the two general statements 'All things move' and 'Something is beautiful'. The first statement may be reformulated as 'Given anything whatever, it moves'. In order to symbolize this in our predicate logic, we need to introduce the *universal quantifier* (x), which is used to assert that *all* entities have some property or properties. The statement form 'it moves' can be symbolized as Mx, and thus we obtain the symbolism of our first general statement 'All things move' as:

$(x)Mx$

This is usually read as:

Given any x, x moves.

Turning to our second general statement, 'Something is beautiful,' we can use the same procedure. This statement can be restated as

There is at least one thing that is beautiful.

Substituting our individual variable x for 'things,' we get

There is at least one x such that x is beautiful.

'X is beautiful' can, of course, be symbolized as Bx. Now we introduce the *Existential Quantifier*, symbolized by $(\exists x)$, which asserts that at least one entity has a given property. Thus, our second general statement can be symbolized as

$(\exists x)\ Bx$

Having introduced the quantifiers, several other concepts need to be specified, namely, that of *bound* and *free variables*. The expressions Mx and Bx, or 'x moves' and 'x is beautiful,' as already indicated, are called *open sentences*. They are open because 'x' is indefinite; we do not know to what it refers. Though these sentences are not statements, they are true or false of certain things. Thus 'x moves' is true of all things that move and 'x is beautiful' is true of all things that are beautiful. Further open sentences can become part of quantified statements. Though open sentences are not statements, they always make a statement when they are quantified. Thus, the *open sentence*:

'x moves'

becomes the statement:

$(x)\ (x\ \text{moves})$

Though this statement does not say what particular thing moves, it does say that 'All things move' and this is either true or false. Similarly, the *open sentence*

'x is beautiful'

becomes the statement:

(∃x) (x is beautiful)

which asserts that something is beautiful and this is either true or false—either something is beautiful or nothing is beautiful.

Open sentences contain *free variables*, namely those that are unquantified. The *x* in 'x is beautiful' is free because it does not fall within the scope of any quantifier. The *x* in '(∃x) (x is beautiful),' however, is a *bound variable* because it is quantified. In dealing with free and bound variables, we need take care of the *scope* of the quantifiers. In general, the scope of the quantifier is the extent of the expression *bound* by that quantifier and is usually indicated by parentheses, brackets, or braces. Thus, we have the following definitions.

1. An occurrence of an individual variable is *bound* if and only if it either is a part of a quantifier or else lies within the scope of a quantifier containing an occurrence of that same variable.
2. An occurrence of an individual variable is *free* if and only if it is not bound.

Having introduced scope of quantification, we can also see that the notation of predicate logic can be used to symbolize statements more complex than the ones so far considered. Consider the following sentences:

1. Arthur is honorable.
2. Betsy is beautiful.
3. Either Arthur is honorable or Betsy is beautiful.
4. If Betsy is beautiful, then she had better also be wise.
5. Arthur is honorable if an only if he is also trustworthy.
6. Betsy is not beautiful.

Each of these may be symbolized as follows.

1. *Ha*
2. *Bb*
3. *Aa* v *Bb*
4. *Bb* ⊃ *Wb*
5. *Ha* ≡ *Ta*
6. ~*Bb*

Now consider the following two statements.

1. Something is square and round.
2. Something is square and something is round.

These two statements can be symbolized as follows:

1. $(\exists x)(Sx \cdot Rx)$
2. $(\exists x)(Sx) \cdot (\exists x)(Rx)$

In the first case, the scope of the existential quantifier is the total conjunctive expression, whereas in the second case we have two separate quantified statements. The two examples above have different meanings and different truth-values. Case one is blatantly false because nothing can be both square and round.

Finally, in dealing with free and bound variables, it should be noted that *to be bound, a variable must be within the scope of a quantifier using the same letter*. Thus, the y in $(x)(Hy \supset Bx)$ is not bound, although it is within the scope of the (x) quantifier.

Tape Exercises

To test your comprehension of quantification and its symbolism, symbolize the following sentences. [Check your answers with Tape 9, band 1.]

1. x is a lemon.
2. x is sweet and red.
3. Something is a triangle.
4. Something is a square and something has four sides.
5. x flies.

9.3 THE TRADITIONAL CATEGORICAL STATEMENTS

It should be clear by now that our predicate logic notation can handle the four traditional categorical statements studied in chapter 5:

A (Universal Affirmation)—All humans are mortal.

E (Universal Negative)—No humans are mortal.

I (Particular Affirmative)—Some humans are mortal.

G (Particular Negative)—Some humans are not mortal.

For review and for those who did not study categorical statements, the meanings of each of these statements can be briefly specified. The **A** statement,

"All humans are mortal," means to assert the total inclusion of the subject class in the predicate class—there are no humans who are not mortal. The **E** statement, "No humans are mortal," means that the two classes are totally exclusive of one another; they have no overlapping members. If it is true, it means there are no human mortals. The **I** statement, "Some humans are mortal," means there is at least one human who is mortal. The **O** statement, "Some humans are not mortal," means there is at least one human who is not mortal.

Turning now to the predicate logic version of a Universal Affirmative, we see that it can be paraphrased as:

For all things x, if it is human then it is mortal.

The universal affirmative categorical statement is rendered as a hypothetical because it is not taken to make any claim about the existence of members of the classes to which it refers. Thus "All unicorns are black," can be rendered as "For all things x, if x is a unicorn, then x is black," or $(x) (Ux \supset Bx)$. Using our individual variable x for 'it,' our truth-functional notation for if-then, and the universal quantifier (x) for 'Given any individual entity,' we get:

$(x) (Hx \supset Mx)$

The parentheses in $(x)(Hx \supset Mx)$ indicate that the universal quantifier (x) has as its scope the entire conditional statement form $Hx \supset Mx$. $(x) (Hx \supset Mx)$ thus becomes the symbolic formula for All H's and M's and any sentences that take this form such as: 'Every H is M,' 'Each H is M,' 'An H is M,' 'Only M's are H's,' 'None but M's are H's' and 'No H's are not M.' Thus 'Whales are mammals' is correctly symbolized as $(x) (Wx \supset Mx)$ and 'None but the brave are fair' is symbolized as $(x) (Fx \supset Bx)$.

The traditional **E** statement "No humans are mortal" likewise is taken not to assert anything about existing members of the classes to which it refers. It may be paraphrased as:

For all things x, if it is human then it is not mortal.

Thus, it is symbolized as:

$(x) (Hx \supset \sim Mx)$

This symbolization captures the essential meaning of the **E** statement, namely, that "H's are never M's."

Turning to the particular statements, these can easily be handled with the existential quantifier and a conjunction statement form. The particular categorical statement, **I,** unlike the **A** and **E** universal statements, is taken to assert the existence of at least one individual who is a member of both classes. Thus, "Some humans are mortal" is paraphrased as:

There is at least one thing that is human and mortal.

It is symbolized as:

$(\exists x)(Hx \cdot Mx)$

The **O** statement "Some humans are not mortal" likewise asserts that there is at least one individual who is a member of the subject class but not of the predicate class. It is paraphrased as:

There is at least one thing that is human but not mortal.

It is symbolized as:

$(\exists x) Hx \cdot {\sim}Mx$

It should be noted that the symbolization of the two particular categorical statements is in keeping with the traditional understanding that 'some' asserts existence. Further, **A** and **O** are contradictories and also are **E** and **I**. The four categorical statements can, thus, be represented in a square array as:

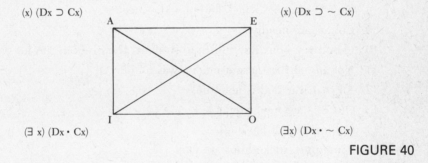

FIGURE 40

Further, if the contradictory relations hold, we can see that ${\sim}(x)(Hx {\supset} Mx)$ can be rendered as $(\exists x)(Hx \cdot {\sim}Mx)$ and ${\sim}(x)Hx {\supset} {\sim}Mx$ can be rendered as $(\exists x)$ $(Hx \cdot Mx)$.

Though contradictory relations hold, other of the traditional relations do not. For further discussion of the Square of Opposition see chapter 5.

Tape Exercises

Translating English sentences into our new logical symbolism is important to the easy use of predicate logic. Translate the following. [Turn to Tape 9, band 1, to check your answers.]

1. Everything is either hot or cold.
2. Nothing is movable.

3. Blondes are beautiful.

4. Not all wines are good.

5. There are white whales.

6. Men are foolish.

7. It is not the case that all men fear death.

8. Some metals are not precious.

9. Only citizens can vote.

10. There are honest men.

Exercises for § 9.3

A. Translate each of following into quantification symbolization.

1. Snakes are reptiles.
2. Some flowers are roses.
3. Ladies are always proper.
4. Not every applicant was hired.
5. Boy scouts are always helpful.
6. Politicians are not honest.
7. Every politician is ambitious.
8. Only those qualifying can enter the race.
9. Cobras are deadly.
10. If Bob is a bona fide full-time student, then he can run for office.
11. Not any of the ransom money was found.
12. All that was said is not true.
13. Old cars are never reliable.
14. Collies are not lap dogs.
15. Sometimes snake bites are fatal.
16. Every obstacle can be overcome.
17. Each car was defective.
18. Not all bankers are dignified.
19. None but the hardy can survive.
20. Not every defective car was recalled.

B. Using the contradictory relationships between the four traditional categorical statements, restate each of the following to make it begin with a quantifier instead of a negation sign:

1. $\sim [(x)\,(Wx \cdot Mx)]$
2. $\sim [(x)\,(Cx \supset Bx)]$
3. $\sim [(\exists x)\,(Cx \cdot \sim Bx)]$
4. $\sim [(x)\,(Cx \supset Dx)]$

C. Translate each of the following taking care to give proper scope to the quantifier.

1. Everything is difficult and everything is easy.
2. Things are both difficult and easy.
3. Some blondes are beautiful and some blondes are dumb.
4. There are black cats.
5. No things are both square and round.

D. In the sentences listed below Cx stands for 'x is a collie' and Dx represents 'x is a dog'. For each sentence, indicate whether it is (a) a statement; (b) a singular statement; (c) an existentially quantified statement; (d) a universally quantified statement; (e) it contains any free variables; (f) it contains any constants; and (g) it is a truth-functional compound of quantified statements.

1. $Cx \supset Dy$ 6. $Ca \supset Da$
2. $(\exists x)(Cx \cdot Cx)$ 7. $(x)(Cy \supset Dx)$
3. $(x) Cx \supset (\exists x) Dx$ 8. $(x)(Cx \supset Dx)$
4. $Ca \cdot Da$ 9. Dx
5. $(\exists x)(Cx \cdot Da)$ 10. $(\exists x)(Cx \cdot dx$

9.4 RELATIONS BETWEEN THE QUANTIFIERS

There are certain basic relations between the quantifiers. Thus the universal general statement "Everything is mortal" symbolized by $(x) Mx$ is denied by the existential general statement, 'Something is not mortal,' symbolized by $(\exists x) \sim Mx$. Because each is the denial of the other, the following biconditions are logically true.

$$[\sim(x) \sim Mx] \equiv [(\exists x) Mx]$$
$$[(x) \sim Mx] \equiv [\sim(\exists x) Mx]$$

Further, $(\exists x) Ax$ says "There are A" or "A exists." If we deny this, we get $\sim(\exists x)$ or "It is not the case that there are A," which is the same thing as saying everything is non-A. Thus, we have another logically true bi-conditional:

$$\sim(\exists x) Ax \equiv (x) \sim Ax$$

Further, to deny $(x) Ax$ is to say "It is not the case that everything is A" or "There are x's that are not A." Hence we establish another equivalence:

$$\sim(x) Ax \equiv (\exists x) \sim Ax$$

Using the Greek letter *phi* to represent any predicate whatsoever, the equivalent relations between universal and existential quantification can be set down as follows:

$$[(x)\phi x] \equiv [\sim(\exists x)\sim\phi x]$$
$$[(\exists x)\phi x] \equiv [\sim(x)\sim\phi x]$$
$$[(x)\sim\phi x] \equiv [\sim(\exists x)\phi x]$$
$$[(\exists x)\sim\phi x] \equiv [\sim(x)\phi x]$$

The general connections between universal and existential quantification can also be described in terms of the traditional Square of Opposition:

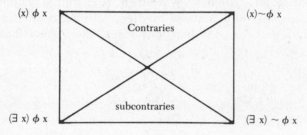

FIGURE 41

Assuming the existence of at least one individual, $(x)\phi x$, which says, "Everything is ϕ and $(x)\phi x$ which says 'Nothing is ϕ' are *contraries*, that is, both might be false, but both cannot be true. $(\exists x)\phi x$, which says, 'There are ϕ' and $(\exists x)\sim\phi x$, which says 'There are non-ϕ' are *subcontraries*, that is, they can both be true, but both cannot be false. The statements at opposite ends of the diagonal are *contradictories*, of which one must be true and the other false. Finally, on each side, the truth of the top statement implies the truth of the lower statement.

There is another aspect of quantified statements that needs to be spelled out. In our preceding discussion, we have construed quantifiers as stating *quantity*, that is, *how many*. However, quantified statements can also be construed as condensed versions of much longer statements. Suppose we decide to limit the universe to only four individual entities. What, then, would the quantified statement $(x)Ax$ assert in such a universe? It asserts that Aa and Ab and Ac and Ad. In other words, it expands into a conjunction $(Aa \cdot Ab) \cdot (Ac \cdot Ad)$. Thus, in a limited universe, the symbolization $(x)Fx$ would be shorthand for $(Aa \cdot Ab) \cdot (Ac \cdot Ad)$, called the *expansion* of $(x)Ax$ with respect to that limited universe. Similarly, the existential quantification $(\exists x)Ax$, in a limited universe of four objects would say either 'a is an A' or 'b is an A' or 'c is an A' or 'd is an A'. The expansion of the existential statement $(\exists x)Ax$, in our limited universe is $[(Aa \vee Ab) \vee (Ac \vee Ad)]$.

If we wanted to limit our universe in this manner, we could eliminate quantifiers and say everything in our expanded form as truth-functions. Thus, in such a limited universe, our **A** categorical statement, $(x)\,(Ax \supset Bx)$ would be equivalent to:

$[(Aa \supset Ba) \cdot (Ab \supset Bb)] \cdot [(Ac \supset Bc) \cdot (Ad \supset Bd)]$

Other expansions are as follows:

Quantified Symbolization	*Expansion*
1. $(\exists x)(Ax \cdot Bx)$	1. $[(Aa \cdot Ba) \lor (Ab \cdot Bb)] \lor$ $[(Ac \cdot Bc) \lor (Ad \cdot Bd)]$
2. $\sim(\exists x)Ax$	2. $\sim[(Aa \lor Ab) \lor (Ac \lor Ad)]$
3. $(x)(Ax \supset \sim(Bx \cdot Cx)]$	3. $[Aa \supset \sim(Ba \cdot Ca)] \cdot$ $[Ab \supset \sim(Bb \cdot Cb)] \cdot$ $[Ac \supset \sim(Bc \cdot Cc)] \cdot$ $[Ad \supset \sim(Bd \cdot Cd)]$

A final word of caution. Quantification logic does apply to the real universe, but there probably are not a finite number of entities in the real universe, and we do not have a name in our language for every entity. Thus, in a universally applicable logic, we cannot construe universally quantified statements as *equivalent* to any very long conjunction we might construct nor an existentially quantified statement as shorthand for a very long disjunction. Such a construal of quantified statements does, however, help further clarify their nature.

Exercises for § 9.4

Assume a universe limited to two entities and construct expansions for the following statements:

1. $(\exists x)(Ax \lor Bx)$

2. $\sim(x)(Ax \supset Bx)$

3. $(\exists x)Ax \cdot (x)Bx$

4. $(x)[Ax \supset \sim(Bx \cdot Cx]$

5. $(x)[(Ax \cdot Bx) \supset \sim Cx]$

6. $(\exists x)(Ax \cdot \sim Bx)$

7. $(\exists x)(Ax \lor Bx)$

8. $(x)\sim(Ax \supset Bx)$

9. $(x)\sim(\sim Ax \cdot \sim Bx)$

10. $(x)[Ax \supset (Bx \equiv Cx)]$

9.5   COMPLEX SYMBOLIZATION

In order to feel more comfortable with quantification logic, we need to discuss further rendering of English statements into quantified statements and vice versa. Thus, for example, how would you render the statement "Little girls who are either mean or inconsiderate are not loved by their mommies." This becomes (x) {[x is a girl $\cdot$ x is mean $\lor$ x is inconsiderate] $\supset$ [$\sim x$ is loved by her mommy]} or $(x)[Gx \cdot (Mx \lor Ix)] \supset \sim(Lx)$.

Further, the statement "Some people who love cars don't take good care of them" becomes

(∃x) [x loves cars · ∼(x takes good care of them)] or
(∃x) (Lx · ∼Cx)

In order to help you become thoroughly familiar with quantificational symbolization, the following chart is provided.

Statement	Symbolizations
Everything is either hot or cold.	(x) (Hx v Cx)
It is not the case that everything is sour.	∼(x) Sx
Nothing that is hot is cold.	(x) (Hx ⊃ ∼Cx)
Some things are hot or cold.	(∃x) (Hx v Cx)
Some things are not cold.	(∃x) ∼Cx
It is not true that some things are cold.	∼(∃x) Cx
Some mortal humans are cold.	(∃x) [(Hx · Mx) · Cx]
Everything is either hot and cold or neither hot nor cold.	(x) [(Hx · Cx) v ∼(Hx v Cx)]

Tape Exercises

Symbolize the following statements. [The answers are on Tape 9, band 2.]

1. If some ice creams are cold, then this strawberry ice cream is cold.
2. There is something such that if it is placed in water, then it will dissolve.
3. Nothing that is sour is a lemon.
4. Not everything that is sour is a lemon.
5. Nothing is sour.

Exercises for § 9.5

1. Anything that makes the world go round is good, lovable, and powerful.
2. A few logicians are not cold-hearted.
3. Either all lemons are sour or most people are crazy.
4. There are no political candidates who are coy, who are silent, or who are happy.
5. Every boy loves a slimy, wet toad.
6. Philosophers are cloud-walkers and logicians are ground-stompers.
7. A woman with blond hair, beautiful legs, and deep blue eyes does not make a good secretary.

8. A figure is a square if and only if it has four sides and four right angles.

9. There are people who are honest, but they are hard to find.

10. All days are either happy or carefree.

9.6 PROVING VALIDITY

The method of proof of truth-functional logic including the nineteen inferences rules plus *CP* and *IP* is incorporated into predicate logic intact. In proving the validity of quantified arguments, we will use this method or proof plus the quantification equivalences listed on page 308 and some special quantification rules which we shall introduce.

The Rule of Universal Instantation
In setting out our first rule, we recall that an *instance* of the universally quantified formula $(x) Ax$ is a sentence like Fa. Further, because the universal quantification of a statement form is true if and only if its substitution instances are true, from the truth of $(x) Fx$ we can infer the truth of each of its instances. Thus, if $(x) (Hx \supset Mx)$ is interpreted as true, then $Ha \supset Ma$ and $Hb \supset Mb$ are true. This gives us the rule of *universal instantation,* namely, *that from any universally quantified formula we may infer any instance of it.* Using the Greek letter nu to represent any individual symbol whatever, the new rule is stated as:

UI: $(x) \phi x$
$\therefore \phi \nu$

This rule *UI* allows us to drop a universal quantifier and thus, for example, would facilitate the proof of our classical syllogism: "All humans are mortal. Socrates is human. Therefore Socrates is mortal." It is symbolized as:

1. $(x) (Hx \supset Mx)$
2. Hs $1 \therefore MS$

The proof would be:

3. $HS \supset Mx$ 1, U.I.
4. Ms 3, 2, M.P.

There are several restrictions on the use of this rule. First, when the universal quantifier is dropped, the variables thus found in ϕx must be replaced throughout ϕu with but one name or variable. If they are not, we will get an erroneous proof. Thus, the following would be a misuse of *UI:*

1. $(x) (Hx \supset Mx)$
2. HS $1 \therefore MS$
3. $Hs \supset Mt$ 1, U.I.

Further, a universal quantifier must quantify a *whole line* in a proof to be dropped by *UI*. Thus *UI* is misused in the following:

1. $(X) Ax \supset (\exists x) Bx$
2. $Aa \supset (\exists x) Bx$ 1, U I

UI is misused in this case because $(x) Ax \supset (\exists x) Bx$ is not a universally quantified formula but a compound whose parts are quantified. Similarly, *UI* cannot be used to obtain $\sim(Aa \supset Ba)$ from $\sim(x) (Ax \supset Bx)$ because the quantifier (x) does not quantify the negation sign and thus does not quantify the whole line.

Tape Exercises

Consider the following proofs and determine whether they are examples of the correct use of *UI*. Check your answers against Tape 9, band 2.]

1. a) $x [(Ax \cdot Bx) \supset Cx]$
   b) $(Ay \cdot By) \supset Cy$ 1, UI

2. a) $\sim(x) [(Ax \cdot Bx) \supset Cx]$
   b) $(Aa \cdot Ba) \supset Ca$ 1, UI

3. a) $(x) Fx \supset (x)Gx$
   b) $Fa \supset Ga$ 1, UI

4. a) $(x) (Ax \supset Bx)$
   b) $Ac \supset Bc$ 1, UI

5. a) $(x) (Ax \supset \sim Bx)$
   b) $Aa \supset \sim Ba$ 1, UI

The Rule of Universal Generalization

Now consider another standard form syllogism. "All humans are mortal. All Americans are human. Therefore, All Americans are mortal." This argument is symbolized as:

1. $(x) (Hx \supset Mx)$
2. $(x) (Ax \supset Hx)$ $/ \therefore (x) (Ax \supset Mx)$

Using our *UI* rule, we can begin a proof for this argument as follows, using the small letter *y* to denote any *arbitrarily selected* individual.

3. $Hy \supset My$ 1, UI
4. $Ay \supset Hy$ 2, UI
5. $Ay \supset My$ 4, 3 H S

Having dropped our quantifiers in order to use the implication rules of truth-functional logic and having derived line 5, we now need to add a quantifier to obtain the conclusion. We can legitimately do so because the deduced statement $Ay \supset My$, in effect, having y denote 'any arbitrarily selected individual,' asserts the truth of any substitution instance of $Ax \supset Mx$. And, because *any* substitution instance is true, all substitution instances must be true. Thus the universal quantified statement $(x)\,(Ax \supset Mx)$ must also be true. This kind of reasoning is used in geometry all the time. Thus, one can prove that *all* triangles have a particular property by proving that a given triangle has that property, provided that the given triangle is *arbitrarily selected,* that is, as long as what is established does not depend on some special characteristics of the triangle in question, such as that it is isoceles. Thus, we have a valid rule, *Universal Generalization* that can be applied in cases in which the actual letters employed are arbitrarily selected and any other letters could have been selected with the same result. *Universal Generalization* may be stated as follows:

$UG = \phi y$
   $\therefore (x)\,\phi x$ [where y denotes "any arbitrarily selected individual]

Thus, the full proof of our syllogism is:

1. $(x)\,(H \supset Mx)$
2. $(x)\,(Ax \supset Hx)$ $/\therefore (x)\,(Ax \supset Mx)$
3. $Hy \supset My$ 1, UI
4. $Ay \supset Hy$ 2, UI
5. $Ay \supset My$ 4, 3 HS
6. $(x)\,(Ax \supset Mx)$ 5, UG

The Rule of Existential Instantiation
Consider now arguments involving existential quantification. Take as our example the argument: "All mothers are women. Some Mothers are harried. Therefore, some women are harried." Symbolized, this argument becomes:

1. $(x)\,(Mx \supset Wx)$
2. $(\exists x)\,(Mx \cdot Hx)$ $/\therefore (\exists x)\,(Wx \cdot Hx)$

In order to provide a proof for this argument, we need an additional rule to help us eliminate existential quantifiers. Now, the existential quantification $(\exists x)\,Ax$ is true if and only if it has at least one true substitution instance. Thus $(\exists x)\,Ax$ asserts that there is at least one individual that has the property A. There is no assurance that every instance is true, nor do we know which is true. Thus, we use the *Rule of Existential Instantial,* which is stated as follows:

EI: $(\exists x)\,\phi x$ (Where ν is any individual constant other than y having no
   $\therefore \phi x$ previous occurrence in the context.)

Now consider the proof of our argument.

1. $(x) (Mx \supset Wx)$
2. $(\exists x) (Mx \cdot Hx)$ /∴ $(\exists x) (Wx \cdot Hx)$
3. $Ma \cdot Ha$ 2, EI
4. Ma 3, Simpl.
5. $Ma \supset Wa$ 1, UI
6. Wa 5, 4 MP
7. $Ha \cdot Ma$ 3, Comm.
8. Ha 7, Simpl.
9. $Wa \cdot Ha$ 8, 6 Conj.

Having deduced $Wa \cdot Ha$, what we need now is a rule to permit us to add an existential quantifier. Because an existential quantification is true if and only if it has at least one true substitution instance, we add to our list of rules a fourth rule, the *Rule of Existential Generalization*, which says that from any true substitution of a statement form we may validly infer its existential quantification. We symbolize the rule *EG* as follows:

$EG \cdot \phi v$ (where v is any individual symbol)
∴ $(\exists v) \phi v$

Thus the final line of our above proof may be written as:

10. $(\exists x) (Ha \cdot Wa)$

In using *EI*, as in using *UI*, when the existential quantifier $(\exists x)$ is dropped, the variables freed in ϕx are to be replaced by identical variables in ϕv. Otherwise, an erroneous proof will occur. Thus, the following is a misuse of *EI*.

1. $(\exists x) (Hx \cdot Wx)$
2. $Ha \cdot Wb$ 1, EI *Erroneous*

Further, we must carefully heed the restriction on *EI* that the substitution instance inferred can contain only an individual symbol (other than y) having no previous occurrence in the context. To demonstrate how this can mislead if not heeded, we shall give a proof of validity for the obviously invalid argument "Some cats are black. Some dogs are black. Therefore, some cats are dogs." The proof is as follows.

1. $(\exists x) (Cx \cdot Bx)$
2. $(\exists x) (Dx \cdot Bx)$ / ∴ $(\exists x) (Cx \cdot Dx)$
3. $Ca \cdot Ba$ 1, EI
4. $Da \cdot Ba$ 2, EI *Erroneous*
5. Ca 3, Simp.
6. Da 4, Simp.

7. $Ca \cdot Da$ 5, 6, Conj.
8. $(\exists x)(Cx \cdot Dx)$ 7, EG

Before going on, some restrictions to our four rules must be noted.

Several important aspects of existential instantiation must be pointed out. First of all, though we can infer from an existential quantifier any one of its instances, once we have selected one as true (e.g., '$Fb \cdot Gb$') we cannot say what is the truth-value of the others: they may or may not be true. The only assurance we have is that at least *one* is true and we have selected one instance. Thus, in a deduction once we have selected our instance, say '$Fb \cdot Gb$,' we are stuck with it. Consider the following argument.

There are men who smoke. There are men who do not smoke.
Hence, there are men who both smoke and who do not.

This is symbolized as:

1. $(\exists x)(Mx \cdot Sx)$ / ∴ $(\exists x)(Mx \cdot Sx \cdot \sim Sx)$
2. $(\exists x)(Mx \cdot \sim Sx)$

Suppose I had carried on a proof of this argument as follows:

3. $Mx \cdot Sx$ 1, E.I.
4. $Mx \cdot \sim Sx$ 2, E.I. *Erroneous*
5. $\sim Sx$ 4, Simpl.
6. $(Mx \cdot Sx \cdot \sim Sx)$ 3, 5, Conj.
7. $(\exists x)(Mx \cdot Sx \cdot \sim Sx)$ 6, E.G.

This proof is erroneous in line 4 because in line 3 we deduced from premise one that some particular man, say Steve, smokes. But in line 4, we deduced that some particular man does not smoke, and we illicitly assumed that the same man (e.g., Steve) is an instance of both premises. The premises do not entitle us to infer this; because we named "the man who smokes," 'x,' we cannot name the "man who does not smoke," 'x'.

It should also be clear that when we use E.I. and U.I. together in a proof we should use E.I. before we use U.I. U.I. is perfectly general, referring to any arbitrarily selected individual, y, whereas once we have chosen an instance of E.I. we must stick with it. Consider the following proof:

1. $(x)(Gx \supset Ax)$
2. $(\exists x)(Gx \cdot Fx)$ / ∴ $(\exists x)(Fx \cdot Ax)$
3. $Ga \cdot Fa$ 2, E.I.
4. Ga 3, Simpl.
5. $Ga \supset Aa$ 1, U.I.
6. Aa 4, 5, M.P.
7. Fa 3, Simpl.
8. $Fa \cdot Aa$ 6, 7 Conj.
9. $(\exists x)(Fx \cdot Ax)$ 8, E.G.

E.I. is used first on line 3, and in so using instantiation we have named a particular instance, *a*, of $Gx \cdot Fx$. Thus, U.I. then can be used on line 5 since it is perfectly general. Further, line 8 asserts that there is something named '*a*' that is both *F* and *A*. The existential generalization of line 9 makes this explicit.

Turning to universal generalization, it must be pointed out that U.G., like E.I., is not perfectly general. It can be validly employed only when something has been established about an arbitrary object. This means that universal generalization cannot be inferred from any statement that names a particular individual. Thus from *Ra* we cannot infer $(x) (Rx)$. This would be to wrongly infer that 'Everything is red' from 'This ball is red'. Similarly, universal generalization cannot be used on any line that has been obtained from E.I. or has been deduced from $(\exists x) (Fx)$.

Thus, the following is an erroneous use of U.G.:

1. $(\exists x) (Cs \cdot Bx)$
2. $Ca \cdot Ba$ 1, E.I.
3. $(x) (Cx \cdot Bx)$ 2, U.G.

We now summarize our four quantificational rules of inference.

1. *Universal Instantiation* (U.I.): From any universal quantification we may infer any of its instances.

2. *Existential Generalization* (E.G.): From any open sentence we may infer its existential quantification.

3. *Universal Generalization* (U.G.): From a formula we may infer its universal quantification provided it does not name some particular individual.

4. *Existential Instantiation* (E.I.): From an existential quantification we may infer any instance of it, provided that the individual constant being introduced is new to the deduction.

Exercises for § 9.6

A. Construct a formal proof of validity for each of the following arguments. [The shaded items are analyzed on Tape 9, band 2.]

1. 1) $(x) (Ax \supset Bx)$
   2) $(\exists x) Ax$ / $\therefore (\exists x) Bx$

2. 1) $(x) (Bx \supset Sx)$
   2) $(\exists x) (Bx \cdot Ux)$ / $\therefore (\exists x) (Sx \cdot Ux)$

3. 1) $(\exists x) (Ax \cdot Bx)$
   2) $(x) Ax \supset Cx$ / $\therefore (\exists x) (Cx \cdot Bx)$

4. 1) $(x) (Fx \supset Gx)$
   2) $(x) (Gx \supset Hx)$ / $\therefore (x) (Fx \supset Hx)$

5. 1) $(x) (Cx \supset Dx)$
   2) $(\exists x) (Cx \cdot Ex)$ / ∴ $(\exists x) (Ex \cdot Dx)$

6. 1) $(x) (Qx \supset Dx)$
   2) $(\exists x) (Ex \cdot Qx)$ / ∴ $(\exists x) (Ex \cdot Dx)$

7. 1) $(\exists x) (Nx \cdot \sim Px)$
   2) $(x) (Cx \supset Px)$ /∴ $(\exists x) (Nx \cdot \sim Cx)$

8. 1) $(x) (Cx \supset Ux)$
   2) $(x) (Px \supset \sim Ux)$ / ∴ $(x) (Cx \supset \sim Px)$

9. 1) $(x) (Wx \supset \sim Lx)$
   2) $(x) (Px \supset Wx)$ / ∴ $(x) (Lx \supset \sim Px)$

10. 1) $(x) (Wx \supset \sim Tx)$
    2) $(x) (Lx \supset Tx)$ / ∴ $(x) (Wx \supset \sim Lx)$

11. 1) $(x) (Sx \supset \sim Tx)$
    2) $(\exists x) (Sx \cdot Ux)$ / ∴ $(\exists x) (Ux \cdot \sim Tx)$

12. 1) $(\exists x) (Px \cdot \sim Qx)$
    2) $(x) (Px \supset Rx)$ / ∴ $(\exists x) (Rx \cdot \sim Qx)$

B. Construct a formal proof of validity for the following argument using the suggested notation.

1. All military men are natural leaders. There are some military men who are overweight. Therefore, some overweight people are natural leaders. [Mx, Nx, Ox]

2. No neurotics are happy. Some children are happy. Therefore, some children are not neurotics. [Nx, Hx, Cx]

3. None but the brave deserve the fair. Only heroes are brave. Therefore, only heroes deserve the fair. [Dx, Bx, Hx]

4. Some blue chip stocks are stocks that pay good dividends. All blue chips securities are safe investments. Thus, Some stocks that pay good dividends are safe investments. [Bx, Px, Sx]

5. All true lovers are loyal liberals. Some philosophers are true lovers. So some loyal liberals are philosophers. [Tx, Lx, Px]

6. No medicines purchased without a doctor's prescription are habit forming drugs, but some narcotics can be purchased without a doctor's prescription. Thus, some narcotics are not habit-forming drugs. [Px, Hx, Nx]

7. All security police are armed. Some women are security police. Therefore, some women are armed. [Px, Ax, Wx]

8. No poisonous plants are edible. All cultivated mushrooms are edible. Thus, no cultivated mushrooms are poisonous plants. [Px, Ex, Mx]

9. To be a saint is to be a person of great character. None but the deserving are persons of great character. Therefore, saints are always deserving. [Sx, Px, Dx]

10. No cowards are boxers. There are some cowards who are debonair. Thus, some debonair people are not boxers. [Bx, Cx, Dx]

9.7 PROVING INVALIDITY

In our previous chapters on deductive logic, we proved the invalidity of deductive arguments by means of the method of *refutation by logical analogy*. Thus, we proved the following syllogism invalid: "No college students are persons having an IQ of less than 70. All persons having an IQ of less than 70 are morons. Thus, no college students are morons." We proved its invalidity by providing the invalid analogy "No dogs are cats. All cats are mammals. Thus, no dogs are mammals." A similar method can be employed with arguments containing quantified statements. But in the cases of our quantified statements, instead of interpreting terms, we interpret open sentences such as Cx, Px. Consider the following argument:

All Birchers are conservative. No liberals are Birchers.
Therefore, no liberals are conservative.

Symbolized, this becomes:

1. $(x)\ (Bx \supset Cx)$
2. $(x)\ (Lx \supset \sim Bx)$
3. $\therefore\ (x)\ (Lx \supset \sim Cx)$

Can we interpret Bx, Cx and Lx so as to make the premises true and the conclusion false? If we read Bx as 'x is square,' Cx as 'x has shape' and 'Lx' as 'x is round,' and put these interpretations back into our quantified statements, we get:

1. (x) [x is square $\supset$ x has shape]
2. (x) [x is round $\supset$ it is not true that x is square]
   —————————————————————————
   $\therefore$ [x is round $\supset$ it is not the case that x has shape.]

The first two premises are clearly true and the conclusion is blatantly false. Thus, by logical analogy we have shown the syllogism to be invalid.

There is also another way to prove invalidity that involves a different sense of what it means to interpret. This second method is similar to the method of proving invalidity for compound statements by truth value assignments. Thus, instead of providing open sentence interpretations for $(x)Ax$, we restrict the universe to a finite set of objects and give singular sentences as interpretations. Thus if the universe had only one member, $(x)Ax$ would be equivalent to Aa. If it had two members, $(x)Ax \equiv (Aa \cdot Ab)$. Similarly the following equivalencies would hold:

$(\exists x)Ax \equiv Aa$
$(\exists x)Ax \equiv (Aa \vee Ab)$

Further, arguments using quantifiers are valid *if and only if* they are valid no matter how many objects there are in the universe, provided there is at least one. We can prove an argument involving quantifiers invalid if we can provide a universe or *model* with at least one member in which the premises of the argument are true and the conclusion false. Consider the argument: "All birds fly. No elephants are birds. Therefore, no elephants fly." This may be symbolized as:

$(x) [Bx \supset Fx]$
$(x) [Ex \supset {\sim}Bx]$
$\therefore (x) [Ex \supset {\sim}Fx]$

If there is exactly one individual in the universe, the argument then becomes

$Ba \supset Fa$
$Ea \supset {\sim}Ba$
$\therefore Ea \supset {\sim}Fa$

Now since Ba, Fa, and Ea can be treated as p, g, r, and so on, we may use our shortened truth table method to prove it invalid. Thus, when we assign the truth value *true* to Ea and Fa and *false* to Ba, we see that we have a case in which the premises are true and the conclusion is false, and thus the argument is invalid.

One difficulty with this method of disproof is that some arguments may be valid in a one-member universe, or even a two or more member universe. We then go on to try more members, and if the argument is indeed invalid *some* definite universe will be found that will prove invalidity. Consider the following argument: "All babies are lovable. Some babies are girls. Therefore, all girls are lovable." Symbolized, this argument becomes:

$(x) [Bx \supset Lx]$
$(\exists x) [Bx \cdot Gx]$
$\therefore (x) [Gx \supset Lx]$

In a universe of one individual it is logically equivalent to:

$Ba \supset La$
$Ba \cdot Ga$
$\therefore Ga \supset La$

But this argument is valid: it is impossible for its premises to be true and its conclusion false.

We need, then, to find a universe in which it can be proved invalid. Fortunately in this case a two member universe will do. In such a universe the argument is logically equivalent to:

$(Ba \supset La) \cdot (Bb \supset Lb)$
$(Ba \cdot Ga) \vee (Bb \cdot Gb)$
$\therefore (Ga \supset La) \cdot (Gb \supset Lb)$

If we assign the truth value *true* to Ba, La, Ga, Gb and *falsehood* to Bb and Lb, we find a case of true premises and false conclusion. Hence the argument is not valid for a model containing exactly two individuals and is therefore *invalid*. In utilizing more than a one individual model, recall that a universal quantification expands as a *conjunction* and an existential quantification as a *disjunction*.

Exercises for § 9.7

A. Prove the invalidity of the following arguments. Assume a finite universe, expand and use truth-functional methods. For the following no more than three elements will be required. The shaded items are analyzed on Tape 9, band 3.]

1. $(x) (Cx \supset \sim Bx)$
   $(\exists x) (Cx \cdot \sim Dx)$
   $\therefore (\exists x) (Bx \cdot \sim Dx)$

2. $(x [Ax \supset Bx]$
   $(x) [Ax \supset Cx]$
   $\therefore (x) [Cx \supset Bx]$

3. $(\exists x) (Ix \cdot Jx)$
   $(\exists) (Jx \cdot Kx)$
   $\therefore (\exists x) [Ix \cdot Kx]$

4. $(\exists x) [Gx \cdot Hx]$
   $(\exists x) [Ix \cdot Hx]$
   $\therefore (x) [Ix \supset \sim Gx]$

5. $\sim(x) \sim Ax$
   $(x) (Bx \supset Ax)$
   $\therefore (\exists x) Bx$

6. $(x) [Ax \supset \sim Bx]$
   $(x) [Bx \supset Cx]$
   $\therefore (x) [Cx \supset \sim Ax]$

7. $(\exists x) [Ax \cdot \sim Bx]$
   $(\exists x) [Bx \cdot \sim Cx]$
   $\therefore [Cx \cdot \sim Ax]$

8. $(x) [Fx \supset \sim Gx]$
   $(x) [Gx \supset Gx]$
   $\therefore (\exists x) (Hx \cdot \sim Fx]$

9. $(\exists x) [Px \cdot Qx]$
   $(\exists x) [Rx \cdot Qx]$
   $\therefore (\exists x) [Rx \cdot \sim Px]$

10. $(x) [Ax \supset \sim Bx]$
    $(x) [Ax \supset \sim Cx]$
    $\therefore (x) [Cx \supset \sim Bx]$

B. Prove the invalidity of the following arguments, using the suggested notation.

1. No silly girls are successful students, but some intellectuals are silly girls. Therefore, no intellectuals are successful students. [Gx, Sx, Ix]

2. No volkswagons are large cars, yet all limousines are large cars. It follows that no volkswagons are limousines. [Vx, Gx, Lx]

3. Not all teachers are scholars, but all brilliant people are scholars. Thus some brilliant people are not teachers. [Tx, Sx, Mx]

4. Not all the brave are foolhardy. No cowards are brave. Thus some foolhardy persons are not cowards. [Bx, Fx, Cx]

5. Some politicians are orators. Some orators are not dishonest. Therefore, dishonest people are not politicians. [Px, Ox, Dx]

6. Some women are beautiful. Some people are not beautiful. Therefore, no people are women. [Wx, Bx, Px]

7. Only officers are members. Only members are admitted. Therefore, all officers are admitted. [Ox, Mx, Ax]

8. All philosophers are deep thinkers. Some women are deep thinkers. Therefore, some women are philosophers. [Px, Dx, Wx]

9. If anything is glass, it is breakable. There are breakable bottles. Therefore some glass objects are bottles. [Gx, Kx, Bx]

10. Some objects are invisible. Not all invisible things have been seen. Therefore, some objects have not been seen. [Ox, Ix, Sx]

9.8   ASYLLOGISTIC ARGUMENTS

In the preceding sections the arguments cited have primarily been of the traditional categorial syllogistic form. We turn now to an analysis of arguments with a more complicated internal structure. Consider the following argument: "Some sincere and intelligent people are teachers. Every handsome and exciting person is a teacher. So there are exciting people who are intelligent!"

This argument cannot be rendered into the traditional syllogistic form without obscuring its complex internal structure. Rather the argument should be symbolized as follows:

$(\exists x) [(Sx \cdot Ix) \cdot Tx]$
$(x) [(Hx \cdot Ex) \supset Tx]$
$\therefore (\exists x) (Ex \cdot Ix)$

Consider another argument: "Philosophers are both thoughtful and wise. Some philosophers are obscure. Therefore some thoughtful people are obscure." Symbolized this becomes.

$(x) [Px \supset (Tx \cdot Wx)]$
$(\exists x) [Px \cdot Ox]$
$\therefore (\exists x) [Tx \cdot Ox]$

The proof of its validity is as follows:

1. $(x) [Px \supset (Tx \cdot Wx)]$
2. $(\exists x) (Px \cdot Ox]$ / $\therefore (\exists x) [Tx \cdot Ox]$
3. $Px \cdot Ox$ 2, E.I.

4. $Px \supset (Tx \cdot Wx)$ 1, U.I.

5. Px 3, Simp.

6. $Tx \cdot Wx$ 4, 5 MP

7. Tx 6, Simp.

8. $Ox \cdot Px$ 3, Comm.

9. Gx 8, Simp.

10. $Tx \cdot Ox$ 7, 9 Conj.

11. $(\exists x) [Tx \cdot Ox]$ 10, E.G.

In translating from English, care must be taken to be sure the exact meaning of the English sentence is captured. Thus, for example, the sentence "Heroin and marijuana are drugs" should *not* be symbolized as:

$(x) [Hx \cdot Mx) \supset Dx]$

Rather, it says "Heroin is a drug, and Marijuana is a drug," which is properly symbolized as a conjunction of two general statements, for example,

$(x) (Hx \supset Dx) \cdot (x) (Mx \supset Dx)$

However, it can be symbolized as a single noncompound statement, but in this case the word *and* is symbolized not by a dot, but by the v. Thus, it is symbolized as:

$(x) Hx \quad v Mx) \supset Bx$

Another type of statement that is difficult to symbolize is the *exceptive* statement, for example, "All but employees are included." Statements of this form can be translated in two ways. One translation is as a conjunction of two general statements. Thus,

$(x) (Ex \supset \sim Ix) \cdot (x) (\sim Ex \supset Ix)$

They can also be translated as general statements with a biconditional. Thus, the above can be rendered in English as: "Anyone is included if and only if he is not an employee." Symbolically, it becomes:

$(x) (Ex \equiv \sim Ix)$

Other ways of expressing an exceptive statement are: "All except employees are included," and "Employees alone are not included."

We have seen above that all the Rules of Inference used to prove the validity of quantified categorical syllogisms can be used to prove the validity of asyllogistic arguments involving quantifiers. Similarly our method of proving invalidity applies to these types of arguments.

Exercises for § 9.8

A. Translate the following statements into logical symbolism. [The shaded items are analyzed on Tape 9, band 3.]

1. Babies and puppies are lovable and cute.
2. Unhappy babies are either ill-fed or ill-loved.
3. Not all philosophers are either friendly or good.
4. All crows are black only if there are crows and they are black.
5. All except logicians are members.
6. If all men need food and shelter, then so does John.
7. Liberals and Democrats support labor laws and agricultural subsidies.
8. There are souls and there are minds only if there are invisible things.
9. Any model is attractive if she is tall and thin.
10. No one achieves success unless he works hard.

B. Construct a formal proof of validity for each of the following arguments. [The shaded items are analyzed on the tape.]

1. 1) $(x) (Ax \equiv Bx)$
   2) $(x) (Bx \supset \sim Cx)$ / $\therefore$ $(x) (Ax \supset \sim Cx)$

2. 1) $(x) [(Px \lor Qx) \supset (Rx \cdot Sx)]$
       / $\therefore$ $(x) [Ox \supset Rx]$

3. 1) $(x) (Ax \supset Bx)$
   2) $(x) [(Bx \cdot Ax) \supset Cx]$ / $\therefore$ $(x) [Ax \supset (Ax \cdot Cx)]$

4. 1) $(x) [Ax \supset (Tx \lor Dx)]$
   2) $(x) (Tx \supset Wx)$
   3) $(x) (Dx \supset Bx)$ / $\therefore$ $(x) [Ax \supset (Wx \lor Bx)]$

5. 1) $(x) [Gx \supset (Fx \lor Hx)]$
   2) $(\exists x) (Gx \cdot \sim Hx)$ / $\therefore$ $(\exists x) (Fx \cdot Hx)$

6. 1) $(x) [(Ax \lor Bx) \supset (Cx \cdot Dx)]$ / $\therefore$ $(x) (Ax \supset Dx)$

7. 1) $(x) [(Fx \lor Gx) \supset (Hx \cdot Ix)]$ / $\therefore$ $(x) (Fx \supset Hx)$

8. 1) $(x) [Gx \supset (Fx \lor Hx)]$
   2) $(x) (Gx \cdot \sim Hx)$ / $\therefore$ $(\exists x) (Fx \cdot \sim Hx)$

9. 1) $(x) [Ax \supset (Bx \cdot Cx)]$
   2) Aa / $\therefore$ Ba

10. 1) $(x) [Px \cdot (Qx \lor \sim Rx)]$
    2) Ra / $\therefore$ $(Pa \cdot Qa)$

C. Prove or disprove each of the following:

1. Everything is either mental or material. Stones are not mental. So stones are material. [mental—Ax, Material—Bx]

2. Some things are human or gods. It is not the case that some things are gods. It is not the case that some things are human. Thus it follows that some things are human. [Hx, Gx]

3. Philosophers are either brilliant or dull. Some philosophers are not dull. Thus, some brilliant people are not dull. [Px, Bx, Dx]

4. Anything is a snake if and only if it is a reptile. There is something that is either a snake or a reptile. If anything is a snake and a reptile, then it tricked Eve. Therefore, there is something that tricked Eve. [Sx, Rx, Tx]

5. Either fattening foods are not healthy or they are unnecessary. A cake is a fattening food. But all things that are made of carrots are healthy, and there are cakes that are made of carrots. Therefore, there are cakes that are unnecessary. [Fx, Hx, Nx, Cx, Mx]

6. If anyone is either boastful or ungrateful, then he will have few friends. Therefore, if anyone is boastful, then if he is both ruthless and ungrateful, he will have friends. [Bx, Ux, Fx, Rx]

7. All nutritious and delicious things are not poisonous. This thing is delicious and poisonous. Therefore, it is not nutritious. [Nx, Dx, Px]

8. Gods must be either just or merciful. Bali gods are not just. Hence if anyone is a god, then if he is Bali he is merciful. [Gx, Jx, Mx, Bx]

9. If a person has either drive or ambition, then he will succeed. If anyone succeeds, then he will either become happy and content or miserly. If anyone is miserly, then he will have few friends. Were anyone to have a proper childhood, then he would have drive. If a person was nice, then he would have had a proper childhood. Paul is nice and he is not happy. Therefore, Paul does not have many friends. [Dx, Ax, Sx, Hx, Cx, Mx, Fx, Nx, Px]

9.9 RELATIONAL PREDICATES AND MULTIPLE QUANTIFIER

Our logical tools can also be applied to arguments containing *relational predicates*, that is, predicates such as 'x is taller than y' or 'x is a friend of y,' which hold between two or more entities. Thus, for example, the sentence 'Jane is taller than Bob,' can be expressed as 'Tjb' and the predicate in question is called a *two-place*, or *dyadic*, relational predicate. There are also three and four place relational predicates, such as the *triadic* predicate of being 'between.' An example is "The blue ball is between the white and the red ball," expressed as 'Bbwr.'

Moreover, we can also have statements that involve more than one quantifier. Thus, for example, "Everyone loves someone," becomes:

$(x)\ (\exists y)\ (Lxy)$

"Everything is larger than everything," would become:

$(x) \, (y) \, Lxy$

In both cases, the order of the quantifier is irrelevant. In the following two cases, however, the order of quantifiers is highly relevant.

1. Something is soluble in everything.
2. For each thing, something is soluble in it.

Statement 1 says there is some one thing that is such that it is soluble in everything. It should be symbolized as

1. $(\exists x) \, (y) \, Sxy$

Statement 2, however, says for anything you pick, e.g. water, nitric and etc., then there is something which is soluble in it, e.g., sugar. It should be symbolized as

2. $(y) \, (\exists x) \, Sxy$

That these two statements are different can be seen by expanding them. Thus, the first statement is an existential quantifier with another quantifier within its scope— $(\exists x) \, [(y) \, Sxy]$. In expanding it, then, we first eliminate the existential quantifier to get:

$(y) \, (Say) \, \text{v} \, (y) \, Sby$

Then we further expand it to get:

$(Saa \cdot Sab) \, \text{v} \, (Sba \cdot Sbb)$

By contrast, $(y) \, [(\exists x) \, Sxy]$ expands as:

$(Saa \, \text{v} \, Sba) \cdot (Sab \, \text{v} \, Sbb)$

These two statements, then, are not equivalent and care must be given to the scope of multiple quantifiers.

We should also exercise care in dealing with negation and multiple quantifiers. Thus, for example, the sentence "Not everyone loves everyone," becomes:

$\sim(x) \, (y) \, Lxy$

which expands as:

$\sim(Laa \cdot Lab \cdot (Lba \cdot Lbb)]$

Whereas "No one loves any one" becomes:

$(x)\ (y)\ {\sim}Lxy$

and expands as:

$({\sim}Laa\ \cdot\ {\sim}Lab)\ \cdot\ ({\sim}Lba\ \cdot\ {\sim}Lbb)$

"There is someone whom no one loves" becomes

$(\exists x)\ (y)\ {\sim}Lyx$

and expands as:

$({\sim}Laa\ \cdot\ {\sim}Lba)\ \text{v}\ ({\sim}Lab\ \cdot\ {\sim}Lbb)$

Obviously, with relations and several quantifiers involved, it is not always easy to put English sentences into proper symbolization. In dealing with complex sentences, it is always best to set out the quantifiers first and then to try to complete the internal structure of the sentence. Consider, for example, the sentence, "If someone is rude, then everyone present will be offended." We partially symbolize this statement as

$(\exists x)\ (x \text{ is rude}) \supset (y)\ (y \text{ is present} \supset y \text{ will be annoyed})$

We complete our symbolization as follows:

$(\exists x)\ (Rx) \supset (y)\ (Py \supset Ay)$

Now consider a more complex example: "If any human suffers, then some person ought to comfort him." First, we set out our quantifiers as follows:

$(x)\ [(x \text{ is human} \cdot x \text{ suffers}) \supset (\exists y)\ (y \text{ is a person} \cdot y \text{ ought to comfort } x)]$

Now, we can finish our symbolization as:

$(x)\ [(Hx\ \cdot\ Sx) \supset (\exists y)\ (Py\ \cdot\ Cyx)]$

Consider the use of more than two quantifiers for the sentence, "Everyone owes something to someone." This is set out first as:

$(x)\ [x \text{ is a person} \supset (\exists y)\ (\exists x)\ (y \text{ is a person} \cdot x \text{ owes } z \text{ to } y)]$

Finally, this becomes

$(x\ [Px \supset (\exists y)\ (\exists x)\ (Py\ \cdot\ Oxzy)]$

Exercises for § 9.9

A. Limit the universe to two members and expand the following:

1. $(\exists x)\ (\exists y)\ Lxy$ 2. $(x)\ (y)\ {\sim}Lxy$
3. $(x)\ (y)\ Lxy$ 4. $(\exists y)\ (x)\ Lxy$
5. $(\exists x)\ (Fx\ \cdot\ (y)\ Gxy)$

B. Interpreting 'Bxy' as "x belongs to y," put the following into plain English.

1. $(\exists x)\ (y)\ Bxy$ 2. $(x)\ (\exists y)Bxy$

3. $(\exists x)\,(y)\,\sim\!Bxy$ 4. $(\exists x)\,(y)\,(Bxy \equiv Bxy)$
5. $\sim\!(\exists x)\,(\exists y)\,Bxy$

C. Using quantifiers and relational predicates, put the following into symbols. [The shaded items are analyzed on Tape 9, band 4.]

1. Humans are frail.
2. Not all humans are frail.
3. Someone knows someone.
4. Only the brave deserve the fair.
5. Nothing logical is obscure.
6. Everyone belongs to someone.
7. Not all men fear death.
8. If any student fails, then he deserves to fail.
9. Some beautiful people are boring.
10. Ladies and children are excused.
11. God only helps those who help themselves.
12. Anyone who throws stones at glass houses is a fool.
13. You can fool some of the people all of the time, and all of the people some of the time, but you can't fool all of the people all of the time.
14. Every misfortune causes some unhappiness.
15. Some people are happy only when they are alone .
16. All those without sin are allowed to throw stones at those who have sinned.
17. No one borrows money from a friend.
18. If everyone helps someone, then all will benefit.
19. If everyone loved their enemies, there would be no strife.
20. Barbers who don't shave themselves are shaved by someone who is a barber.

9.10 PROOFS INVOLVING RELATIONS

In order to prove arguments involving relations, we need to further limit our quantification rules. The first limitation concerns existential instantiation.

1. *When E.I. is used, the variables thus freed by dropping the existential quantifier cannot be replaced by individual constants, but rather must be replaced by individual variables.*

Thus, one cannot validly infer Fa from $(\exists x)\,(Hx)$. This would be like inferring that this particular animal, Russ, is a fox from the statement that there is at least one entity that has the property Fox. The existential quantifier tells us only that there is at least one thing that is a Fox, but it does not allow us to name any particular thing as a Fox.

A second restriction that must be imposed on existential instantiation is as follows:

2. *Existential instantiation may be used provided that a variable introduced into a proof by E.I. must not occur free previously in the proof.*

Consider the following proof.

1. $(\exists x)\, Fx$
2. $(\exists x)\, Tx$ $/ \therefore (\exists x)\, (Fx \cdot Tx)$
3. Fx 1. E.I.
4. Tx 2. E.I.—*Erroneous*
5. $Fx \cdot Tx$ 3, 4. Conj.
6. $(\exists x)\, (Fx \cdot Tx)$ 5. E.G.

The proof is wrong at line 4 because the same free variable used on line 4 already occurred free on line 3. It leads to a blantantly invalid conclusion. Premise one aserts that something is F, say Fat, which is true, and Premise two asserts that something is T, or thin, which is true. However, it is not true, as the conclusion asserts, that something is both fat and thin. The problem comes with the use of x, on line 4, already freed on line 3. Line 3 only says some entity is fat: it doesn't say that the entity which is fat is thin. In other words, a variable introduced free into a proof by E.I. must *not* occur free previously in the proof.

There are also some restrictions to be placed on universal generalization. First, universal generalization cannot be used on an *individual constant*. One cannot go from Fa to $(x)\, (Fx)$ because it would require us to move from a true statement letting $Fx =$ "Arthur is Foxy" to a false statement, "Everything is Foxy." Similarly, one cannot use U.G. on a variable introduced free into a proof by E.I. or on a variable free in a line obtained by E.I. Thus the following is an invalid use of U.G.:

1. $(\exists x)\, Fx$ $/ \therefore (x)\, Fx$
2. Fy 1. E.I.
3. $(x)\, Fx$ 2. U.G.—*Invalid*

Once again if we take $Fx =$ "x is Foxy," sentence 1 asserts that *something* is Foxy, while 3 asserts that *everything* is Foxy. We cannot use U.G. to allow the passage from "some" to "all."

With regard to U.G., we find that within the scope of an assumed premise we cannot use U.G. on a variable free in that assumed premise. Consider the following proof:

1. Fy $Ap / \therefore (x)\, [Fz \supset (x)\, Fx]$
2. $(x)\, Fx$ 1. U.G.—*Invalid*
3. $Fy \supset (x)\, Fx$ 1, 2 CP
4. $(x)\, [Fz \supset (x)\, Fx]$ 3, U.G.

Once again we can go in this proof from the true premises to a false conclusion. Given $Fy =$ "y is Foxy," the conclusion is the false statement, "If anything is Foxy, then everything is Foxy." U.G. has been misused on line two. U.G. must not be used on a variable free in an assumed premise.

Turning to limitations on U.I., it must be remembered that in using U.I., as in using E.I., the primary aim is to drop a quantifier and free the variables that it bound. Thus, U.I. and E.I. must not be used so that the variable that is supposed to be freed ends up bound.

Universal instantiation, then, must be limited as follows:

1. *UI may be used provided a variable that occurs free in φx occurs free in φv. That is, no instantiated variable may be captured.*

Thus, the following is an erroneous use of UI.

1. $(x) (y) Lxy$
2. $(y) Lyy$ U.I.

In $(y) Lxy$, x is a free variable; only y is bound. Thus, the U.I. has been misused.

A restriction on existential generalization is as follows:

2. *Existential generalization may be used provided that every variable free in φx is free in φv.*

Consider the following proof:

1. $(x) (\exists y) Lxy$
2. $(\exists y) Lxy$ 1. U.I.
3. Lxy 2. E.I.
4. $(\exists x) (Fxx)$ 3. E.G.—*Erroneous*

This proof is wrong because E.G. caught both y and the free x of line 3, which is free in $(\exists y) Lxy$.

9.11 QUANTIFIER NEGATION

Proofs of validity containing relational properties can be greatly facilitated by adding four related equivalence rules:

$$\sim(v) \, \phi \equiv (\exists v) \sim\!\phi v)$$
$$(v) \sim\!\phi \, v \equiv \sim(\exists x) \, \phi v$$
$$\sim(v) \sim\!\phi \, v \equiv (\exists x) \, \phi v$$
$$(v) \, \phi \, v \equiv \sim(\exists v) \sim\!\phi v$$

The rule *quantifier negation* permits the assertion of one side of these equivalence argument forms once the other side has been obtained in a proof.

Consider the following proofs. Note how the rule of quantifier negation facilitates the proof of validity.

A. 1. $\sim(\exists x) Fx$ / ∴ $Fa \supset Ga$
    2. $(x) \sim\!Fx$ 1. Q.N.
    3. $\sim\!Fa$ 2. U.I.

    4. ~Fa v Ga   3. Add
    5. Fa ⊃ Ga   4. Impl.

  B. 1. (x) (Ax ⊃ Hx)
      2. (∃x) Ax ⊃ ~(∃y) Gy   / ∴ (x) (∃y) (Ay ⊃ ~Gx)
    ┌─►3. (∃y) Ay   A.P.
    │ 4. Ay   3, E.I.
    │ 5. (∃x) Ax   4, E.G.
    │ 6. ~(∃y) Gy   2, 5 M.P.
    │ 7. (y) ~Gy   6, Q.N.
    │ 8. ~Gx   7, U.I.
    └──9. (∃y) Ay ⊃ ~Gx   3, 8 C.P.
      10. (x) (∃y) Ay ⊃ ~Gx   9, U.G.

The following are examples of correct proofs of arguments using relational properties.

  A. 1. (x) Sxx   / ∴ (y) (∃x) Sxy
      2. Saa   1, U.I.
      3. (∃x) Sxa   2, E.G.
      4. (y) (∃x) Sxy   3, U.G.

  B. 1. (∃x) [Ax · (y) (By ⊃ Cxy)]   / ∴ (Fx) [Ax (Ba ⊃ Cxa)]
      2. Ax · (y) (By ⊃ Cxv)   1, E.I.
      3. Ax   2, Simp.
      4. (y) (By ⊃ Csy)   3, Simp.
      5. Ba ⊃ Cxa   4, U.I.
      6. Ax · (Ba ⊃ Cxa)   3, 5 Conj.
      7. (∃x) [Ax · (Ba ⊃ Cxa)   6, E.G.

  C. 1. (x) (∃y) (Py · Qxy) ⊃ Rx]
      2. (∃y) [Sy · (∃x) [(Tx · Ux) · Qyx]
      3. (x) (Ux ⊃ Px)   / ∴ (∃x) (Rx · Sx)
      4. Sz · (∃x) [Tx · Ux) · Qyx]   2, E.I.
      5. (∃x) [(Tx · Ux) · Qyx]   4 Simp.
      6. (Tw · Uw) · Qzw   5, E.I.
      7. Tw · Uw   6 Simp.
      8. Uw   7, Simp.
      9. Uw ⊃ Pw   3, U.I.
      10. Pw   8, 9 M.P.
      11. (∃y) (Py · Qzy) ⊃ Rz   1, U.I.
      12. Qzw   6, Simp.

13. $Pw \cdot Qzw$	10, 12, Conj.
14. $(\exists y)(Py \cdot Qzy)$	13, E.G.
15. Rz	11, 14, M.P.
16. Sz	4, Simp.
17. $Rz \cdot Sz$	15, 16 Conj.
18. $(\exists x)(Rx \cdot Sx)$	17, E.G.

Exercises for § 9.11

A. Provide a proof for each of the following. [Shaded items are analyzed on Tape 9, band 4.]

1. 1) $(x)(\exists y) Lxy$ / ∴ $(\exists y)(\exists x) Lxy$
2. 1) $(\exists x)(\exists y)(Ax \cdot Bxy)$ / ∴ $(\exists x) Ax$
3. 1) $(x)(y)(Lxy \supset Hxy)$ / ∴ $(\exists x)(y) Lxy \supset (\exists x)$
                                                  $(\exists y) Hxy$
4. 1) $(x)(Ax \supset Bx)$
   2) $(x)(\exists y)(Cxy \supset Ax)$
   3) $\sim(\exists x) Bx$ / ∴ $(\exists x)(\exists y) \sim Cxy$
5. 1) $(\exists x)[Fx \cdot (y) Gxy]$ / ∴ $(Fx)[Fx \cdot (\exists z)(\exists y) Gzy]$

B. Symbolize each of the following arguments and then prove their validity.

1. There is something that everyone loves. Hence everyone loves something.
2. It is just not true that everyone loves everyone. Thus, there is someone who does not love someone else.
3. All loving is good. Thus, whatever produces loving produces good.
4. Everyone loves himself/herself. Therefore, everyone loves someone.
5. All butterflies are beautiful. Thus, everyone who draws butterflies draws beautiful things.
6. Everyone who loves is happy. All people who care for someone are loving. It is not true that there are happy people. Therefore, someone does not care for someone else.
7. Some people buy anything that is shiny. No people buy cheap, dull things. Hence, dull things that are cheap are not shiny.
8. If one person harms another, then he or she must pay some compensation to the other. When Samantha hit George, she harmed George, so she paid George some compensation. (Px—x is a person; Hxy—x harms y; Cxy—x pays a penalty to y; s—Samantha; g—George)

Chapter Outline

   A. *Predicate logic* combines the predicate analysis of traditional categorical logic with the statement analysis of truth-functional logic.
   B. *Singular* statements assert that a particular predicate belongs to a particular individual, e.g., "Socrates is human," which is symbolized 'Hs.'

C. The *universal quantifier* (x) is used to assert that *all* entities have some predicate or predicates e.g., "All things move," is symbolized as (x) Mx.

D. The existential quantifier (∃x) is used to assert that at least one entity has a given predicate. Thus, "There are beautiful things" is symbolized (∃x) Bx.

E. 'X is beautiful' and 'x moves' are *open sentences*. When they are quantified they become statements.

F. *Free* variables are those that are unquantified; *bound* variables are those that are quantified.

G. The four traditional categorical statements may be symbolized in predicate logic as follows:

    1. All humans are mortal   : (x) (Hx ⊃ Mx)
    2. No humans are mortal   : (x) (Hx ⊃ ~Mx)
    3. Some humans are mortal   : (∃x) (Hx · Mx)
    4. Some humans are not mortal : (∃x) (Hx · ~Mx)

H. The following equivalent relations hold between universal and existential quantification:

    (x) φ x   ≡ ~(∃x) ~ φx
    (∃x) φx   ≡ ~(x) ~φx
    (x) ~φx   ≡ ~(∃x) φx
    (∃x) ~φx ≡ ~(x) φx

I. By limiting our universe of discourse to a finite number of members we can see our existential and universal quantification as equivalent to expanded compound statements. Thus, in a universe of four entities the following equivalencies hold:

    (x) Ax ≡ [(Aa · Ab) · (Ac · Ad)]
    (∃x) Ax ≡ [(Aa v Ab) v (Ac v Ad)]

J. To prove arguments containing quantified statements, we need to add the following quantification rules to our rules of inference:

    1. U.I.: (x) φx ∴ φv 'From any universally quantified formula we may infer any instance of it. *Restriction:* U.I. may be used provided that a variable that occurs free in φx occurs free in φv.

    2. U.G. φy ∴ (x) φx Where y is any arbitrarily selected individual, from any instance of it, we may infer a universally quantified formula. *Restriction:* U.G. may be used provided that (1) y is a free variable; (2) y is not flagged on any previous line; (3) y is not free in an assumed premise within whose scope φy occurs, and (4) y is not free in a line obtainable by E.I.

    3. E.I.: (∃x) φx ∴ φv—Where v is any individual constant other than y and having no previous occurrence in the context, from any existentially quantified formula, we may infer any instance of it. *Restriction:* E.I. may be used provided that (1) v is a constant that does not occur in any previous line, and (2) v occurs free in φv in all places where v occurs free in φ.

    4. E.G.: φv ∴ (∃v) φx—From any true substitution instance of a statement form we may infer its existential quantification. *Restriction:* E.G. may be used provided that every variable free in φx is free in φv.

K. Invalidity may be proven by restricting the universe to a finite set of objects and giving singular statements as interpretations of quantified statements. If a case of true premises and false conclusion is found, then the argument is invalid.

L. Statements containing *relationship predicates,* those predicates holding between two or more individuals, can also be handled in predicate logic.

Part III
Induction

10

INDUCTIVE
GENERALIZATION
AND ANALOGY

10.1   INDUCTIVE AND DEDUCTIVE
SIMILARITIES

In turning now to inductive reasoning, we recall the basic distinction made
earlier between deductive and inductive arguments. We have seen that deduction aims at validity and proof. If a conclusion follows validly from the premises,
the argument carries with it logical necessity. The truth of the premises
logically guarantees the truth of the conclusion. Valid arguments also are
always closed arguments. No additional premises will alter validity. The conclusion, in a sense, merely draws out the information already implied in the
premises.

   Inductive arguments, on the other hand, are those in which the evidence
given supports but does *not* guarantee the conclusion. The conclusion of an
inductive argument also "goes beyond" the evidence in the premises—it
always advances from what we already know to make *new* knowledge assertions. Because induction involves this kind of "leap beyond the known,"
inductive arguments remain always *only probable* and always *"open."* The
strength of an inductive argument may be radically altered by the addition of
new evidence. New evidence may show a conclusion thought strong (highly
probable), to be, indeed, weak, if not even false. In induction, then, we are
dealing only with probability. However, we are also dealing with amplification,
an advance beyond the facts contained in the premises. Induction expands the
content of the premises by sacrificing necessity.

10.2   ENUMERATIVE GENERALIZATION

A traditional pattern of induction is generalization from a number of instances or enumerative generalization. The simplest form of inductive generalization is the inference from 'Some S are P' to 'All S are P.' An example is 'Some black-spore mushrooms are edible' to 'All black-spore mushrooms are edible.' Another example is 'Some water freezes below 32 degrees farenheit' to 'All water freezes below 32 degrees farenheit.' This type of inductive generalization is called a *primary* generalization and takes the logical form 'A is always B,' or 'All A's are B's'.

Another form of generalization from instances or *enumerative* generalization is:

n percent of the examined objects having property A also have property B.

n percent of the objects in the class of objects having property A also have property B.

Or, more simply:

n percent of the examined A's are also B's.

n percent of all A's are B's.

For example:

Seventy percent of the examined adult white American males who smoke three packs of cigarettes a day contract cancer of the lung.

Seventy percent of *all* adult American males who smoke three packs of cigarettes a day will contract cancer.

This second type of generalization is the *statistical* or *proportional* generalization. It has the logical form, *a certain percentage of A's are always B's*. For example, 'Thirty percent of the population die before 50 years of age,' 'Two percent of cancer cases are fatal'. Two important points need to be made about these *statistical* generalizations. First, the percentage need not be expressible in precise numerical terms. The statements, 'More men than women die of heart attacks,' and 'More businessmen than university professors are forced to retire at 60,' are just as genuine cases of statistical generalizations as the examples cited above. Second, these statistical generalizations, contrary to popular opinion, are as rigorous, inclusive and absolute, within their own limits, as primary generalizations. Both statistical and primary generalizations exclude exceptions to what they say. 'All crows are black' tells us there are 'no non-black crows' and, likewise, 'More people die from small pox than from chicken pox,' tells us that it cannot be the case that more people die from chicken pox than from smallpox.' In other words, because a generalization refers to percentages of cases rather than to particular cases, it is nonetheless absolute. Both types of generalizations preclude any exceptions to what they say. However, there are specific weaknesses in statistical generalization when used in explanations in science—we shall discuss these in chapter 12.

A third type of generalization takes the form '*A varies with B,*' for example 'Rate of rent varies with density of population.' 'Atmosphereic pressure varies with distance from the earth's surface'. This type of generalization is called a *functional* generalization—to say '*A* varies with *B*' is the same as to say '*A* is a function of *B*.' The term *function,* in this case, comes from mathematics and means that any change in *B* will be accompanied by a change in *A,* as any change in the circumference of a circle would be accompanied by a change in its radius. The circumference of a circle is a *function* of its radius. This type of generalization will be discussed more thoroughly when we discuss *concomitant variation* in chapter 11.

A related type of generalization is a causal generalization of the logical form *A causes B*. This type of generalization will be discussed thoroughly in the next chapter, but essentially such a generalization says 'Whenever A is present, B will be present, and whenever *A* is absent, *B* is absent'. A final type of generalization is an analogical generalization that has the form *A, B, C, B. C* and *A* share certain properties in common, therefore, *C,* like *A* will have property *B*. Analogical generalization will be discussed in the next section of this chapter.

The important point about these kinds of generalizations is that all are generalizations from a *number of instances,* or *enumerative generalization.* The evidence for every primary generalization, *All A's are B's* is: Every observed A is B and no A has ever been observed that was not B. The primary generalization 'All crows are black,' is based on the following evidence: Every observed crow has been black and no crow has ever been observed that was not black. The evidence for every statistical generalization, *A percentage of A's are B's,* is: In every examined group of *A's,* a percentage have been *B's;* and no group of *A's* has been known that did not contain a percentage of *B's.* Similarly, the evidence for any functional generalization, *A varies with B,* is: Every observed variation of *A* has been accompanied or followed by an observed variation of *B.* Thus, the functional generalization 'When the volume remains the same the temperature of gas varies with the pressure of gas' is based on the following evidence: Every observed variation of temperature of gas, with the volume remaining the same, has been accompanied by an observed variation of pressure.

These three types of generalization, then, are fundamentally generalization from instances, or enumerative generalization. A related type of generalization is a causal generalization, which takes the form *A causes B*.

The causal generalization, *A causes B,* has as its evidence base: Whenever *A* was observed to be present, *B* was present, and whenever *A* was observed to be absent, *B* was observed to be absent. We shall also see in the next section that analogical generalization likewise is a variant of induction by enumeration. In other words, all of these types of generalization are fundamentally generalization from instances or enumerative generalization.

What is involved in enumerative generalization is a *sampling process.* Suppose you are a team of researchers for the National Health Foundation and you want to find out the relationship between cigarette smoking and lung cancer. Obviously you cannot examine every smoker in the United States, so you decide to concentrate on American adult males and on heavy smokers. Further, you cannot examine every member of even this class, but rather you take a "representative group" from this class and determine what percentage develops lung cancer. Then, you infer that the same percent of the *total class* will all contract lung cancer.

Similarly, if you were a politician and you wanted to know what percentage of your electorate supports legalized marijuana, you would not question every registered voter in your county or state, but only a relatively small number of voters. Once you had determined what percentage of this group supports legalized marijuana, then you would infer that the *same percentage of all voters* in the state support legalized marijuana.

This *sampling process* procedure therefore is used to determine what percentage of a certain class of objects (e.g., heavy smokers, voters) has a given property (e.g., lung cancer, approving legalized marijuana). In this process, a relatively small number of objects that belong to the class in question are examined. These examined objects are usually called *the sample.* In examining the sample, you determine what percentage has the property in question. Then, you infer—generalize—that the same percentage of all members of that class (usually called the *population*) has the property in question. Thus, as indicated above, this *enumerative generalization* can be represented schematically as follows:

---

n percent of all the examined A's are also B's.

---

n percent of all A's are B's.

The *sample procedure* does follow certain basic rules, as we shall see shortly. But first, a few comments.

In looking more carefully at this type of inductive reasoning, we see that it does, indeed, demonstrate the general characteristics of inductive reasoning indicated earlier. Thus, it is easy to see why enumerative generalizations are *never* deductively valid inferences. The premise of a generalization can be true and the conclusion false. Thus, for example, it could be quite true that 'Forty percent of the polled (sampled) California voters favor legalized marijuana' (premise), but false to conclude that 'Forty percent of all California votes (polled and unpolled) favor legalized marijuana'. All that is required to make the premise true and the conclusion false is (a) that there be some unexamined A's and (b) that the percentage of these A's that are B's *not* be equal to n percent. Thus, for example, if there are some unpolled California voters and if the percentage of these California voters favoring legalized marijuana is any percentage other than the predicted 40 percent, the above conclusion is false.

In order to make an enumerative generalization deductively valid—such that if the premise(s) was true, it would be impossible for the conclusion to be false—*it must meet one or the other of two conditions:* (1) There are no *un*examined *A*'s, or (2) The percentage of unexamined *A*'s that are also *B*'s is the same as the percentage of examined *A*'s that are *B*'s.

Taking condition (1) first, we would require, then, *generalization by complete enumeration*. However, such a requirement poses almost insurmountable problems. First of all, it is *usually impossible in practice* to examine all the *A*'s. For example, it would be far too difficult, expensive, and time consuming to examine all American males who are heavy smokers, or all California voters. It would also require careful additional checks to make sure that we had not missed a single *A*. There are cases in which complete enumeration would be possible, such as apples in a barrel, cards in a deck. But these are usually trivial additions to knowledge. Take a given room with a certain number of people in it and a desire to establish how many of them smoked cigarettes heavily and how many had or showed signs of cancer; presumbly, one could easily examine every member of this population and make a true generalization. However, very little would be established about the relation between lung cancer and smoking.

In addition to practical difficulties with complete enumerations, there are cases in which it is theoretically impossible to establish any conclusion through generalization by complete enumeration. These are cases in which the "population class" is immense and, for all practical purposes, infinitely large. In these cases it is impossible that there could be *no* unexamined *A*'s. Have we examined all cases to which Newton's law of gravity applies? Have we examined all members of very general populations such as human beings, animals, sea life. Generalization by complete enumeration, then, is not really viable.

What, then, about the second possibility for making enumerative generalizations valid—for example, 'The percentage of unexamined *A*'s that are also *B*'s is the same as the percentage of examined *A*'s that are *B*'s'? This requirement asks of an enumerative generalization a guarantee that it be true. But such a guarantee cannot be given because there is always the possibility of the unexamined *A*'s having a different percentage. We have no guarantees about the unexamined. Generalization by enumeration—unless complete and exhaustive—can only be probable.

Thus, we cannot strictly speak of arguments involving generalizations as valid, but only as strong or weak. An inductive argument with a generalization as a conclusion may be called strong if knowledge of the truth of its premise gives us sufficient reason to believe in the truth of its conclusion. Strength comes in degrees: Some sound generalization arguments give good reasons for believing in their conclusions; some give even better reasons. Arguments concluding in generalizations should be called more or less strong, more or less probable. What, then, are the *criteria for judging strength?*

Good and bad samples   Take two different cases of generalizations. Jill Corner who runs a butcher shop in Hollywood, California, makes a point of polling her customers in a given week about the question of legalized marijuana. She finds that 60 percent favor legalized marijuana and thus concludes that 60 percent of the California voters are in favor of legalized marijuana. Senator Block is also interested in the legalized marijuana question, and he hires Well-Done Polling Company to poll California voters on the question. The company polls 5,000 California voters spread throughout the state, young and old, rich and poor, white and black. It discovers that only 20 percent of these California voters favor legalized marijuana. Which generalization is more justified? It should be obvious that the polling company is on surer ground than the butcher. The difference in strength is to be attributed to the fact that the "Well-Done" sample was both larger and more diversified.

The degree of strength of generalizations depends, first of all, on the *size* of the sample and on its *variety* (homogeneity or heterogeneity).

Number or Size of the Sample: What size is large enough?   Size, of course, is relative to the scope of the generalization and to the population class. Generally speaking, of course, as the size of the sample increases, the reasonably possible differences between the percentage of A's in the sample that are also B's and the percentage of A's in the total population that are also B's becomes increasingly smaller. We must always be sure to ask how big was the sample, what proportion of the class population does it represent? If we have polled 5,000 out of 7,000 voters, the 20 percent approval means more than if we are talking about only 1,000 out of 7,000. Ask: *What percentage of how many?*

Further, the need for numbers also depends on whether we are dealing with a more predictable or less predictable class population and what properties are at issue. Thus, the medical scientists, dealing with the question: What probability is there of getting the measles after exposure? is on surer grounds than the political opinion pollster dealing with a question like the legalization of marijuana. The measles question involves far fewer variables (relevant disturbing and/or contributing factors) than the marijuana question, which involves numerous legal, moral, financial, political, and other factors. Number, in other words, is relevant to the *variety* involved. The Hollywood population would more likely be favorable to legalized marijuana than the more conservative Bakersfield population, and thus 1,000 Hollywood voters still might not be any better indicator than 100 Hollywood voters.

Variety-Diversity of the sample   It is a well-known fact that a person's religion, economic class, geographical area, and so on are factors relevant to his or her opinions. Roman Catholics are less likely to favor legalized abortion than Protestants or Jews. A person's geographical location, age, habits are relevant factors in questions concerning such topics as disease and health. A Pennsylvania coal miner may be more likely to get lung cancer than heavy smokers. A "good sample," then, is a diverse one that takes into account the various possible groupings within a population class and gives each a sufficient representation—not just one Republican and 4,000 Democrats, or 4,000 Los Angeles voters and 1,000 spread out over the rest of California.

A *properly varied sample* is one which, for every grouping of members of population A *relevant* (significant) to the question of being a B (having a certain property, opinion, etc.) the percentage of members of the sample that are members of that grouping is the same as the percentage of members of the total population that are members of that group. If 70 percent of California voters are Republican and 30 percent are Democrat, then 70 percent of the sample should be Republican. If 40 percent of the California voters are urban residents, then 40 percent of the sample should be urban residents.

There are two sampling techniques used to achieve a properly varied sample: (1) *sampling by matching* and (2) *random sampling*. In sampling by matching, we take the following steps:

(a) Determine what are the significant (relevant) characteristics of the class of A's for investigating the property B—what characteristics of voters are important to consider in investigating their opinion on legalized marijuana? What are factors that might influence their opinion on this issue (e.g., religious affiliation, economic status, urban-rural, political party, occupation)?

(b) Divide the population class into groupings parallel to these characteristics (e.g., Protestants-Catholics-Jews-nonreligious).

(c) Determine the percentage of the total population that belongs to each of these groupings: (40 percent Protestants, 25 percent Catholics, 30 percent Jews, 5 percent nonreligious).

(d) Pick a sample that has, for each grouping, the same percentage of members as in the total population class.

When this process is successful, we have *matched* the sample to the population class, and we are guaranteed a properly varied sample. However, there are severe practical limitations on the use of this matching procedure: it requires us to know all the significant characteristics and to know, for every relevant grouping, the percentage of the population belonging to this grouping. Such information is often simply not available.

The other approach to choosing a sample is *random sampling*. This does not, of course, mean picking items "at random" or "as they come." On the contrary, it means careful control of the conditions under which the samples are taken so that each grouping of the total class has an equal chance of being included in the sample.

Suppose we wanted to know the opinion of the student body of Northwestern University on the question of legalized marijuana. In order to get a random sample, we would go to the registrar and take every tenth name on an alphabetical listing of all students. Then we would seek the opinion of these randomly selected students. In this way we would be likely to include in our sample all age groupings, class classifications, sex, religion, majors, and so on.

Random sampling or sampling by matching, of course, does not *guarantee* that the conclusion will be 'true'. In inductive reasoning we only deal with degrees of probability. Even if the samples are selected with greatest care, the sample results may still not be clear and concise representations of the class under study. The smaller the sample, the more indefinite is the picture. As the sample increases in size, it tends to be more representative; but, as indicated earlier, it is only a definitive representation of the total when the sample becomes so large as to be identical with the class it represents (exhaustive enumeration). Size and variety go hand in hand in determining the reliability of a sample, but proportional representation of the relevant groupings is much more important than the mere size of the sample. Indeed, in dealing with these significant groupings, great care must be taken to avoid error. It is difficult to know whether we have taken into account all the significant and determining factors. Further, the sampling process may result in error because of inexperienced workers. For example, if public opinion is being sampled in a large city through a house-to-house canvass, inexperienced canvassers who do not make a second call at houses where nobody was home when they first called may collect unreliable data. This is because the chances of finding somebody at home when the families are large are much greater than they are when families are small; but the size of the families may have some bearing upon the question under investigation. Further, bias may be introduced by inept questioning. Questions can be worded in such a way that the subject is led to a certain answer. For example, the question "Do you agree with the minority who favor legalized marijuana?" would lead many to a "no" answer because of the stigma of being part of a minority rather than part of the majority.

Tape Exercises

Consider, for example, the following questions. Which, if any, would be 'good' questions for an unbiased questionnaire or sampling? [Turn to Tape 10, band 1. for a brief analysis of each of these questions.]

1. What do you think of Beethoven?
2. Are you a heavy smoker?
3. Are big cars gas eaters?
4. Do you oppose the government stepping into the medical malpractice problem?
5. Do you think New York City should clean up its own house before asking the Federal Government for money?
6. Do you approve of 'working mothers'?
7. Do you consider yourself a faithful church member?
8. Which is more important in life, a job or education for its own sake?
9. Do you condone euthanasia?
10. What do you think is the major social issue in America today?

To repeat, then, enumerative generalizations are always only probable and never guaranteed to be true. Further, in making generalizations, certain basic criteria must be applied in judging their soundness. They are:

1. *Is there a clear delineation of the class under study?* Are the characteristic, the property, the opinion, etc. being investigated clearly defined? This also means clear definitions of key concepts. For example, what is a California voter—how determined? What is understood by the phrase, "legalized marijuana"? How does the respondent understand "heavy smoking?"

2. *What is the scope of the generalization?* How big is the class under consideration? How big was the sample? What percentage of what? For example, how many California voters are there? How big was the sample?

3. *How representative is the sample?* Were all significant characteristics taken into account? What method was used to obtain the evidence? What classes of voters were polled? How were they polled? What types of questions were they asked?

4. *Does the generalization go too far beyond its evidence?* If only California voters were studied, it would be wrong to conclude that 40 percent of *all* voters were in favor of legalized marijuana.

Let us apply these rules to the following published report of a study done by two psychologists.

"Dr. Brill and Dr. Malzberg studied the records of over 5,000 people who had been released from mental hospitals. Comparing these with an equal number who had never been admitted to a mental hospital and who were divided into similar groups by age, sex, previous arrest records and socio-economic status, they found that arrests for sex crimes were 50 percent higher among the general population than among the former mental patients and that arrests for rape were 1,000 percent higher among the general population than among the former mental patients. They concluded that 'former mental patients were generally more law-abiding than other citizens.'"

This study may be analyzed as follows:

1. Clear delineation of classes and properties being studied—two classes are being compared. The first, "former mental patients," is carefully delineated by the criterion of "actual release from a mental hospital." The term "mental hospital" is not made clear. The second class is "never admitted to a mental hospital." This is a very large and rather vague classification. The properties under consideration are "arrested for sex crimes" and "arrested for rape." No criterion for identifying these characteristics are given, but presumably police records would be the guide here.

2. *Is the scope of the generalization clear?* Five thousand subjects are being studied from both classes, but we do not know what proportion of

either class this represents. It may or may not be a significant number. Further, the class "never admitted to a mental hospital" would be quite large.

3. *How representative is the sample?* Here the report of the study gives very little information. We do see that the groups were divided according to age, sex, arrest records, and socio-economic status. However, surely even more significant than these groupings are "types of mental illness" represented by the former patients and health records of "those never admitted to mental hospitals." Further, the study ignores the fact that fear of being sent back to a mental hospital would probably be a deterring factor for the former mental patients making them more likely to obey the laws; this is not a factor for the other class.

4. *Does the conclusion go beyond the evidence?* Yes, the conclusion is about general "law-abidingness" and the evidence concerns only "sexual law-abidingness."

The moral of this whole story would be clear: Never accept generalizations uncritically; do not be fooled by numbers and percentages; do not be fooled by the façade of a "scientific study."

Tape Exercises

Analyze the following studies. One is from the past, and one is more recent. Using the four criteria of clear delineation, number, variety and scope, rate the study on the strength of its generalizations relative to the evidence provided. [The passages are analyzed on Tape 10, band 2.]

A. Cancer, stomach, and heart specialists have found that habitual smoking of tobacco has destructive effects upon the body. In 1938, Dr. Raymond Pearl of Johns-Hopkins University studied the case histories of over six thousand white males and found that "smoking is associated with a definite impairment of longevity." Toxicologists list some thirty substances taken into the lungs with each inhale of smoke from a cigarette. Twelve of these substances are acids, while the rest are composed of arsenic, alcohol, and ammonia. Nicotine, a potent poison found in cigarettes, has been found to cause detrimental effects to the nervous system, heart, blood vessels and digestive tract. It may cause nervous excitability, tobacco heart, high blood pressure, indigestion, irritations to the mouth and throat. Recently scientists have reported producing cancer in mice by coating their skin with a concentration of tars from cigarette smoke. Dr. William Lieb, author of *Safer Smoking* and research adviser to a major tobacco company for ten years, states, "Tobacco contains as nice a collection of poisons as you will find anywhere in one small package. The least you can do, out of respect for the only body you will ever have, is to use these poisons, if use them you must, in moderation.[1]

[1] Cited in *Essentials of Logic* by Peter T. Manicus and Arthur N. Kruger (New York: American Book Company, 1968) pp. 411–12.

B. In 1964, a committee commissioned by the United States Public Health
Service· made the following statements: 'Cigarette smoking is a health
hazard of sufficient importance in the United States to warrant appropriate
remedial action.' The following was cited as evidence converging toward this
judgment: 'In 1962, over 500,000 people in the United States died of
arterioschlerotic heart disease (principally coronary artery disease). 41,000
died of lung cancer, and 15,000 died of bronchitis and emphysema. Lung
cancer deaths, less than 3,000 in 1930, increased to 18,000 in 1950. In the
short period since 1955, deaths from lung cancer rose from less than 27,000
to the 1962 total of 41,000. This extraordinary rise has not been recorded for
cancer of any other site. From 1950 to 1962, the number of smokers in
America has increased to 70 million, 66 million of whom are cigarette
smokers. From 1940 to 1963, the per capita (18 years and over) consumption
of cigarettes has increased two-fold, from 1.779 to 4.345. The risk of developing lung cancer increases with duration of smoking and the number of
cigarettes smoked per day and is diminished by discontinuing smoking. In
comparison with non-smokers, average male smokers of cigarettes have
approximately a 9 to 10 fold risk of developing lung cancer and heavy
smokers at least a 20-fold risk. Further, cigarette smoking is the most
important of the causes of chronic bronchitis in the United States and
increases the risk of dying from chronic bronchitis and emphysema. There
can be little doubt that cigarette smoking is to be associated with a 70
percent increase in the age-specific death rates of males.

Exercises for § 10.2

A. Which of the following are generalizations? If they are, what type of generalizations are they? Why are the other statements not generalizations?

1. All genuine diamonds are expensive.

2. Many American bachelors read *Penthouse* magazine.

3. Whenever there is increased budgetary deficits, there are inflations.

4. Twenty percent of American husbands remain faithful to their wives.

5. The next coin I take out of my pocket will be a nickel.

6. This movie is very much like the foreign films I have seen and so I probably
will find it boring.

7. My cat can distinguish colors.

8. You happen to turn on the light switch and the fuse blows, and you therefore
conclude that your turning on the light switch caused the fuse to blow.

9. Knowing that 80 percent of all teenagers drink Pepsi Cola, you conclude
that your nephew, Bob, drinks Pepsi Cola.

10. All the planets of our sun have elliptical orbits.

B. Which of the following conclusions, could, *if true,* be established by use of a
generalization by complete enumeration? Why? Which cannot? Why?

1. All of the people in this room drink some form of alcoholic beverage.
2. All of the members of the University of Toto football team are nonsmokers.
3. All of the students in Logic, Section 2, believe that logic is a relevant and interesting subject.
4. All of the planets of our solar system have elliptic orbits.
5. All planets have elliptic orbits.
6. All citizens of Palm Springs, California, favor building-restriction laws.
7. All past American astronauts were male.
8. All American astronauts are male.
9. All planets of our solar system have gravitational fields.
10. All planets have gravitational fields.

C. If you were asked to choose a sample population by matching the following generalizations for testing, from what kinds of groups should you take at least some members of your sample? [For a discussion of the shaded items consult Tape 10, band 3.]

1. Sixty-five percent of Americans favor legalized marijuana.
2. Seventy-five percent of American college students believe job security is the most important value to be sought in a college education.
3. Forty-five percent of the American public oppose the building of nuclear power plants.
4. Sixty-five percent of Roman Catholic believers oppose legalized abortion.
5. Sixty-five percent of employed American females favor legalized abortion.
6. Sixty-five percent of the American police force feel they have a bad public image.
7. Fifty-five percent of the governors of the states of the U.S. believe more Federal support of cities is needed.
8. Fifty-five percent of American men feel women should not seek equal opportunity in the job market.
9. Forty-five percent of the American public favor the establishment of paid television.
10. Forty-five percent of young Americans favor childless marriages.

D. Using the four criteria of clear delineation, number, variety, and scope , analyze the strengths and weaknesses of the generalizations given below relative to their stated samples. [The shaded items are analyzed on Tape 10, band 3.]

1. *Sample:* A poll of over three hundred physicians in California. Seventy-five percent of them expressed strong opposition to government medical insurance.
   Generalization: American physicians strongly oppose government medical insurance.
2. *Sample:* A questionnaire sent to a random selection of English department heads in all of the major colleges and universities on the Eastern coast of the

United States asking what deficiency appears most frequently among college students today. Eighty-five percent answered that the inability to write proper grammatical English was the widespread deficiency among college students today.

Generalization: The most widespread deficiency among college students today is the inability to write proper grammatical English.

3. *Sample:* A questionnaire given out to every fifth person leaving the Foreign Film Theatre in your city over a period of five weeks asking about their level of college education. Sixty-five percent of the questionnaires are returned, and 85 percent of those returned report having completed a college education.

   Generalization: A large number of movie goers today have college educations.

4. *Sample:* Poll conducted of over one thousand executives of various corporations in the United States asking what was one of the major political problems facing the United States today. Sixty-five percent of those polled replied that the energy problem was the major one and particularly the freedom to develop new energy sources.

   Generalization: A major political problem facing the U.S. today is the energy problem.

5. *Sample:* A random telephone poll of people during the day from 9 A.M. to 5 P.M., asking what were their favorite television programs or kind of television programs. Sixty-five percent responded that quiz shows were their favorite kind of television programs.

   Generalization: The most popular type of television program is the quiz show.

6. *Sample:* A questionnaire sent to readers of *Redbook, McCalls* magazines asking 'What is the major social issue facing the United States today?' Seventy-five percent of the questionnaires were returned, and 85 percent of the replies said that 'equal opportunity for women was the major social problem facing the United States today.'

   Generalization: The major social problem facing the United States today is equal opportunity for women.

E. For each of the following passages, do *each* of the following: (1) Point out the generalizations (What type are they?). (2) Cite the evidence offered to support each of the generalizations. What kind of evidence is offered? (3) Using the four criteria of clear delineation, number, variety and scope, assess the generalizations, and evidence.

1. The key to the conduct of many products and services being marketed are substandard, dangerous, and worthless. Advertising and personal selling are major sources of guidances for consumers, yet much advertising and personal selling falls short of informing customers fully and truthfully about the merits of even a single product. The Federal Trade Commission spot-checks advertising in newspapers, magazines, mail order catalogues, and radio and television broadcasts. About 238,000 advertisements examined during the 1970 fiscal year, 8,000 plus appeared to be untruthful. Among the

catalogues of 50 mail order houses, 178 advertisements were marked for investigation. In 1972, the FTC was proceeding against the manufacturers of eight over-the-counter analgesics, asking that they refrain from false advertising and that they spend some of their advertising budget or corrective advertising such as saying. 'That it has not been established that *Bufferin* is more effective than aspirin for the relief of minor pain.'[2]

2. Businessmen take the viewpoint that since consumerism imposes costs on them, it will ultimately be costly to the consumer. Since they have to meet more legal requirements, they have to limit or modify some of their methods for attracting customers. This may mean that consumers will not get all the products and benefits they want and may find business costs passed on to them. But the businessman is wrong in considering consumerism politically motivated and economically unsound. Consumerism rather, in the long run, will be beneficial to business as well as the consumer. It will increase the amount of product information, and greater buying efficiency which will result in surplus purchasing power and thus the buying of more goods in total. Consumerism will lead to limits on promotional expenditures. Consumerism will result in reducing the number of unsafe or unhealthy products which will result in more satisfied, healthier consumers.

3. The U.S. is not on the verge of running out of oil, but future output is not likely to increase greatly, and over the years it is likely to decline. There is a steady decline in oil discovered per foot of drilling in the past 30 year period since 1937, and this is particularly significant in view of the fact that the oil credited with having been discovered during this period represents the cumulative results of all of the advances in the techniques of exploration and production of the oil industry during its entire history up to 1967. This also was the period of the most intensive research and development in exploratory and production techniques in the history of the industry. The observed decline in the rate of discovery during this period is, accordingly, difficult to account for on any other basis than that undiscovered oil is becoming scarce.[3]

4. Martin K. Whyte, A University of Michigan sociologist, says that civilization may have improved the status of mankind, but it lowered the status of women. Women seem to have had more prestige within many primitive hunting and warfare tribes than in the more civilized societies. Professor Whyte's conclusions are based on a four year study of the status of women in 73 cultures, mostly pre-industrial nations ranging from the ancient Roman and Inca empires to a village in 20th century Japan. 50 possible status indicators were used, from the sex of gods and witches to political influence and authority within the home. In primitive societies, women had somewhat more domestic authority and more value was placed on women's lives.

[2] Eugene R. Beem, "The Plight of the Consumer," in William T. Keeley, *New Consumerism: Selected Readings* (Grid, Inc., 1973) pp. 121–41.

[3] M. K. Hubbard, "Energy Resources," in *Resources and Man* (San Francisco: W. H. Freeman & Co., 1969), pp. 157–239.

With more complex agrarian societies, such as ancient Babylon and Rome, women had less domestic authority, fewer property rights and more ritualized fear by men.[4]

5. Controversies over the authorship of the Shakespeare plays have been raging for many years. Many scholars find it unbelievable that William Shakespeare, a man of lowly origins and scant schooling, could have written such plays of genius. Further he never traveled nor visited the courts of Queen Elizabeth, and yet his plays display great knowledge of other countries and of court life. Louis Benezet, in a book, *Shakespeare: Shakespeare and De Vere* [Granite State Press, 1937] argues that the plays of Shakespeare were really written by Edward de Vere, the 17th Earl of Oxford. The following are some reasons presented in favor of this conclusion.

De Vere was an accomplished poet and his extant poetry is written in a style bearing many similarities to the style of Shakespeare's sonnets.

De Vere was well educated, attended several universities on the continent and was a student of the classics. He, like Shakespeare, was closely associated with plays and actors, for he maintained his own group of actors, with whom he performed before the Queen. Further, historians found in 1720 that Elizabeth had commissioned De Vere to write plays depicting the seriousness of the times. De Vere, however, wanted his identity kept secret because he poked fun at almost every member of the court.

De Vere was also skilled in music and versed in law. Many of the facts, relationships, etc., discussed in the plays fit De Vere's personal life. For example, he knew Ann Vavasor whose family had been feuding for generations with another family, a situation described in Romeo and Juliet. His separation from his wife bears similarities to the Othello case.

Further, De Vere's crest was a lion shaking a spear. In the plays attributed to Shakespeare there is always a hyphen between 'shakes' and 'spear'; whereas, William always signed his name 'Shakspear.' In short, says Benezet, De Vere had all the qualities necessary to write plays of genius whereas a mere butcher's son did not.

6. After a lot of parents complained because their children were getting failing marks, Principal Edwin Andersen of the Prosser, Washington high school made a survey, and ventured an answer: an educational mixture too rich in gasoline. His figures: of seniors with A or B grades only 11% own cars or have use of them regularly. Among C grade seniors, 33% have cars and 62% of the C-minus to-failing seniors are motorized. Cars owned by juniors with A or B grades, none; with C grades, 31%; and with C-minus-to-failing marks, 39%. Tabulations did not include youths who had quit school to buy gas, parts, and polish for their cars.

7. The high degree of intellectualization of the modern American college campus is shown by our study of general conditions. According to the

---

[4] Reported in *Intellect* Magazine (February 1976): 347–8.

National Educational Association, the national median salary of full professors is $10,327, whereas that for head football coach is only $8,554. In most colleges, the contents of the library cost more than the athletic equipment. Attendance at class and adequate performance on examinations is still considered indispensable to remaining in college, and fraternities are not allowed to practice disruptive hazing. The number of goldfish swallowed and of panty raids has declined, and the number of paperback books purchased in the bookstore has increased.

10.3   ANALOGICAL GENERALIZATION

Another very important form of inductive reasoning is inductive analogy. Analogy is a form of reasoning according to which one may infer from one set of attributes or similarities another set of attributes or similarities. Put differently, it is based upon a *comparison* between objects, events, persons, processes and the like. Typically, it reasons as follows: Objects and/or processes of one kind are known to be similar in certain respects to other objects and/or processes of other kinds. Objects of the first kind are known to have certain characteristics but it may not be known whether objects of the second kind have the same characteristics or not. Reasoning by analogy, we hypostatize, or may even tentatively conclude, that because objects of the two kinds are alike in *some* respects, they probably are alike in *other* respects as well.

This is the crux of the argument by analogy. A splendid example of this is cited by Wesley Salmon:

A medical researcher makes experiments on rats to determine the effects of a new drug upon human beings. He finds that rats to which the new drug has been administered develop undesirable side effects. By analogy he may argue that since rats and humans are physiologically quite similar the new drug will probably have undesirable side effects if used by human beings.[5]

It should be fairly plain that such reasoning is strong or weak depending principally upon the similarities of the two types of objects and/or processes being compared and upon the degree or proportion to which they agree. The question, for example, arises as to the ways in which rats and human beings are similar and the ways in which they are dissimilar. For instance, if the question is primarily a physiological one, then we may safely draw a conclusion; but even so we may end up with considerable confusion.

Logicians usually point out that analogical arguments derive their strength—insofar as they are strong—from the following considerations.

Number of entities compared.   The first consideration relevant to the appraisal of an analogical argument is *the number of entities between which the analogies are said to hold*. Suppose that you are trying to decide what classes to

---

[5] Wesley C. Salmon, *Logic* (Englewood Cliffs, N.J.: Prentice-Hall, 1963).

register for in the coming term and the concern is whether to take another philosophy course. If you have taken seven philosophy courses and found all of them interesting, you are on stronger ground to argue that the eighth philosophy course will, like the others, be interesting, than if you have had only three philosophy courses and are considering a fourth. Further, if you are basing your conclusion about the new philosophy course on experience with ten philosophy courses, you are on even stronger ground. The analogical argument that because ten philosophy courses have been interesting, an eleventh philosophy course will likewise be interesting is a strong one, but, of course, not conclusive.

Number of similar features   A second consideration in analogical generalization is the *number of ways* in which things being compared are said to be similar or analogous. Consider our decision to take a philosophy course. Our argument is stronger if the new course is similar to the other ten courses in other ways than merely being a philosophy course. Thus, for example, suppose all ten courses already taken were concerned with values, and with social and practical life (ethics, political philosophy, aesthetics, philosophy of religion, etc.), and the new course is also concerned with these kinds of question. Further, the new course, *like the other ten*, is taught by the same teacher, is lecture-discussion, and meets in the afternoon. If all these similarities hold, then, the argument that the new course, like the others, will be interesting, is a stronger one.

Number of dissimilarities   If similarities are important to the strength of analogical arguments, so are dissimilarities. *Dissimilarities tend to weaken an analogical argument*. Again use our example of choosing a class. If the new philosophy course is logic or philosophy of math rather than in the value area, the conclusion that the new course, like the others, will be interesting, will be weakened. It will be further weakened, for instance, if the new course is taught by a different and unknown instructor. The less dissimilar the instances being compared, the stronger the analogical argument is likely to be.

Relevance   A fourth criteria used in appraising analogical arguments is relevance. In asking about dissimilarities and similarities one asks only about relevant ones. For example, the fact that the new course meets in the afternoon rather than in the morning like the others is probably not a relevant dissimilarity unless time affects one's interest or performance. Relevant similarities, in our example, are obviously course content and teacher.

Strength of the conclusion   A fifth consideration to raise about analogical arguments is how strong is the conclusion relative to the premises. How big a leap does the conclusion take from the known to the unknown? In our example, if one concluded that all other philosophy classes will be interesting rather than just the one new one, this conclusion would be incautious and weaker. The conclusion of an analogical argument is stronger when it is more closely related to its evidence. The more incautious a conclusion, the weaker the argument.

Analogical arguments may be illuminating, but they must be judged very critically. The most famous argument from analogy was, of course, the one used for the existence of God on the grounds that as human beings have intelligence and produce objects (houses, sticks and stones, and clothes) so God has intelligence and created the universe, although in His case with infinite power and wisdom. The discerning philosopher, David Hume, pointed out that this is an extremely dangerous argument by analogy. Why? First, it ignores the radical *dissimilarity* between God and human beings. Second, it fails to distinguish between the fact that people make products out of already-given materials, whereas it is held in traditional Judao-Christian theology that God creates *ex nihilo,* that is, out of nothing. Further, it ignores many other dissimilarities between a human maker and a divine maker. For example, a human maker is prone to error; more than one maker may help produce a single object; a human maker may merely copy someone else's design.

In judging an analogical argument, we must carefully set out both the similarities and dissimilarities between the items being compared and decide whether the negative analogy (dissimilarities) is strong enough to render the positive analogy (similarities) on which the conclusion is based ineffectual. Take the following example, of an analogical argument put forth by the physicist Linus Pauling:[6]

> . . . mutations in these carefully selected organisms almost invariably are detrimental. The situation can be suggested by a statement made by Dr. J. B. S. Haldane: My clock is not keeping perfect time. It is conceivable that it will run better if I shoot a bullet through it; but it is much more probable that it will stop altogether. Professor George Beadle . . . has asked, "What is the chance that a typographical error would improve *Hamlet*?"

In this paragraph, Pauling is saying that: a mutation is as detrimental to a living organism as is a bullet to a clock and a typographical error to *Hamlet*. The analogy is a poor one, for the following reasons.

1. A clock is mechanical and not a living organism. A living organism could adapt to a mutation in such a way that it might not be detrimental. A clock cannot repair itself nor readjust.

2. *Hamlet* is not a living organism. It could not readjust itself.

3. A typographical error can be erased; a bullet or mutation is more permanent.

4. A bullet is mechanical, external, and necessarily destructive. A mutation is usually internal, though it may have external stimulus; it is living and not necessarily detrimental.

---

[6] Linus Pauling, *No More War!* (New York: Dodd-Mead and Company, 1958), p. 53.

Tape Exercise

Analyze the following passage containing an analogical argument by doing the following: (1) Indicate the premises and conclusion of the argument. (2) Point out what is being compared—what is alleged to be the common characteristics they share. (3) What relevant and important dissimilarities have been ignored? (4) How strong or weak do you find the argument?
[This passage is analyzed on Tape 10, band 4.]

Photographs that have actually been taken from space reveal in a dramatic way that our planet is very much a spacecraft, turning on its axis while making its endlessly repeated trip around the sun. This comparison allows us to appreciate the importance of keeping the ship in good repair and functioning properly. We are adrift in the limitless sea of space, and there is no port where we can ever expect to put in. All that we shall ever have is aboard. If we destroy our life-support systems—the atmosphere, the lakes, rivers, and oceans, the forests and swamps—then we will eventually destroy ourselves. If we allow the ship to become more crowded than our necessarily limited supplies can support, then we can expect competition, bloodshed and almost endless suffering. Thus, we must put an end to pollution and see that our population is limited if we are to save ourselves and future generations.[7]

EXERCISES FOR § 10.3

A. Each of the following arguments by analogy has six additional premises suggested for it. For *each* of these alternative premises, decide whether its addition would make the resulting argument more or less probable or, whether it is irrelevant to the strength of the conclusion.

1. A psychologist is experimenting with rats to determine the strength of sexual privation in determining rat behavior. He has worked with five albino male rats and one albino female. The male rats were sexually deprived through isolation for one month. When placed in a maze with the female rat as the bait, the five rats found their way through the maze much more quickly than they had under normal conditions. The psychologist now postulates that the next five albino rats, treated similarly, will also run faster through the maze after sexual privation than under normal circumstances.

   a. The first five male rats and the second five male rats were all young rats.

   b. The first five male rats were given all the other comforts—food, shelter, freedom to roam. The second five were kept isolated together in a very small cage.

   c. Instead of using albino rats, the psychologist used ordinary grey rats on the second round.

---

[7] Quoted in *The Way of Words* by Ronald Munson (Boston: Houghton-Mifflin Co., 1976), p. 365.

  d. The second five rats were also deprived of food during the last two days before being placed in the maze.
  e. The color of the maze was changed.
  f. The psychologist decided on the basis of his experiment to conclude that sexual deprivation plays a significant role in determining rat behavior.

2. A democratic form of government in Botania has given maximum freedom and benefits to the people in Botania, and a large majority of Botanians participated in government in one form or another. The foreign minister of Botania concludes that it is probable that a democratic form of government will also work well in Platonia.
  a. Both countries are small in geographical size.
  b. Botania has a long history of democratic government while Platonia has just emerged from a feudal and an ancestral-oriented government.
  c. A small portion of people in Botania are illiterate, whereas a large number of people in Platonia are illiterate.
  d. The average age in Botania is 49.6 whereas in Platonia the average age is 34.7.
  e. The standard of living in Botania is high while the standard of living in Platonia is low.
  f. Education for all the people is a guiding principle in Botania whereas education for the few elite has been the practice in Platonia.

3. Mr. Carpenter has been investing in insurance stocks for over the past 15 years. The over-all value of his stock has increased about 4 percent per year, and the companies have paid a good and steady dividend each year. He concludes that it is now time to buy another 200 shares of insurance stocks and that he will not only increase the value of his purchase but gain modest dividend earnings.
  a. The stock he intends to purchase is stock of one of the companies of which he already owns stock.
  b. He is purchasing stock in a relatively new insurance company: whereas his previous stock has all been stock of old and established insurance companies.
  c. Rather than the usual 4 percent increases in appreciation and the usual 5 percent dividend, his insurance stocks this past year increased in appreciation by 8 percent and passed a 9 percent stock dividend.
  d. The insurance company in which Mr. Carpenter bought the new stock is heavily into providing medical malpractice insurance for physicians, whereas the other insurance companies in which he has invested are primarily in life insurance.
  e. The oil company stocks have recently decreased in value.
  f. Several of the state governments pass laws regulating medical malpractice suits and insurance premium charges for medical malpractice.

4. Mary Jones has read Hermann Hesse's *Siddhartha* and *Steppenwolf* and found them very interesting and stimulating books. She decides to buy

Hesse's *Magister Ludi (The Glass Bead Game)* and is sure that she will
also find this book interesting and stimulating.
  a. *Magister Ludi,* like *Siddhartha* is concerned with spiritual quest.
  b. *Magister Ludi* deals a lot with the question of living in the world
     versus living out of the world, and Mary, a religious studies major, is
     much interested in these kinds of questions.
  c. Mary decides she will also like Thomas Mann's *Doctor Faustus,* which
     like Hesse's novels deals with Freudian and other psychological
     themes as well as World War II and Germany.
  d. Mary finds out that Hesse was divorced.
  e. Mary decides that she will like the novels of all German novelists.

B. For each of the following—(1) determine whether analogy is being used for
   argumentative purposes; (2) if it is an argument, point out premises and
   conclusions; (3) point out the number of relevant properties the things being
   compared hold in common; (4) point out the relevant dissimilarities (Is the
   negative analogy strong enough to weaken the argument?); and (5) assess the
   overall strength or weakness of the argument.

  1. "That the universe was formed by a fortituous concourse of atoms, I will
     no more believe than that the accidental jumbling of the alphabet would
     fall into a most ingenious treatise of philosophy."   [Jonathan Swift]

  2. Indeed, the most compelling similarity between science and myth is the
     drama each derives from living in the twilight zone between fantasy and
     reality. Physics lives there just as assuredly as do the ancient stories of
     gods and goddesses and demons, for physics is never unrestrictedly true.
     It is only temporarily true, and in a broader context, it is always false for
     sometime in the future each of our theories will most likely be disproved
     by a new discovery. . . . Further, like myth, the power of modern science
     is derived from the metaphorical linkage between facts, not by the facts
     themselves. Thus, science, the actor, emerges from the darkened wings
     of the human mind into the bright lights of shared experience, pretending
     in spite of the mask and the costume that he is real, his world is real, and
     that he is more than an actor. Yet all the time he knows that he is only
     pretending and that he will be judged not by the quality of his truth but by
     the quality of his illusion. Truth slips from our hands when we insist that
     science be true.[8]

  3. The success with which our Constitution unified the thirteen original
     colonies is a powerful argument in favor of a United States of Europe.

  4. In a solid, the molecules can be pictured as a crowd of men all doing
     physical exercises—"the daily dozen"—without moving from the spot
     where they stand. . . . In a liquid the molecules can be pictured as a swarm
     of men gathered together in a hall at a crowded reception; they are tightly
     wedged, but each works his way through the others, with many a push

---

[8] Kim Malville, *A Feather for Daedalus* (Menlo Park, Calif.: Cummings Publishing Co.,
Inc., 1975), pp. 37–38.

and apology. . . . For a gas we have to think of a large open space on which men are walking without looking where they are going; each man continues in a straight line until he bumps into someone else, when he abruptly starts off again in a different direction.[9]

5. Nothing is going to happen until we, the poor, can generate our own political and economic power. Such a statement sounds radical to many middle-class Americans, but it should not. Though many of the poor have come to see the affluent middle class as its enemy, that class actually stands between the poor and the real powers in society—the administrative octopus with its head in Washington, and its arms the conglomerates and the military complex. It is like a camel train. The herder way up in front, leads one camel and all the other camels follow. We, the poor, happen to be the last camel, trudging along through the leavings of the whole train. We see only the camel in front of us and make him the target of our anger, but that solves nothing.[10]

6. An electron is no more (and no less) hypothetical than a star. Nowadays, we count electrons one by one in a Geiger counter, as we count the stars one by one on a photographic plate. In what sense can an electron be called more unobservable than a star? I am not sure whether I ought to say that I have seen an electron; but I have just the same doubt whether I have seen a star. If I have seen one, I have seen the other. I have seen a small disc of light surrounded by diffraction rings which have not the least resemblance to what a star is supposed to be; but the name 'star' is given to the object in the physical world which some hundred years ago started a chain of causation which has resulted in this particular light-pattern. Similarly in Wilson expansion chamber I have seen a trail not in the least resembling what an electron is supposed to be; but the name 'electron' is given to the object in the physical world which has caused this trail to appear. How can it possibly be maintained that a hypothesis is introduced in one case and not in the other?[11]

7. College and university teachers should recognize that what they are engaged in is the selling of a product and thus what is taught on campuses should depend entirely on the student. After all, the teacher is the seller and the students are the buyers and buyers should determine what they want to buy. Further, colleges and universities should be more concerned, as are businesses, with the way in which they package and market their goods. We all know that the packaging often plays a more important role in selling than does the contents.

8. Trying to find the cause of cancer is like trying to find a feather in a haystack while the wind is blowing: each time you think you have found it, the whole darn stack shifts its composition and you are back to picking up pieces of straw little by little.

---

[9] E. N. daC. Adrade, *What is the Atom?* (New York: Harper & Bros., 1926) p. 156.

[10] Ceasar Chavez, "Sharing the Wealth," *Playboy*, 17, no. 1 (January, 1970).

[11] Sir Arthur Edington, *New Pathways in Science* (Ann Arbor: University of Michigan, 1959), p. 10.

9. Rabbit blastocysts—the embryo just before it attaches to the uterus (womb)—have already been sexed with complete success by several experimenters and similar methods have been applied, also with success, to mouse blastocysts. It seems reasonable to assume, then, that human blastocysts, could also be sexed by these methods.

10. The city masses are melted and reduced to one identity by differences that have no law, no meaning and no end. The *he's* and *she's* have become *they's*, the *other*, who are *they*—nobody knows.

10.4   ANALOGY, METAPHOR, AND MODEL

Analogy is a very basic form of human reasoning. It is so because it is a fundamental way to assert connections and to build bridges between seeming unconnected areas of discourse and thought. Because of this bridge building capacity, analogy is a useful tool in helping to explain complex and technical situations, to make them more understandable as in the following case.

In the United States, especially, atom-smashing equipment, such as the Van de Graaf's generators and cyclotrons had been constructed. These machines were already capable of accelerating certain particles used as 'projectiles' up to the enormous energy of nine million volts. Nevertheless, even they had only damaged, without breaking into, the protective walls with which nature in her wisdom had encircled the atomic nucleus and the tremendous stores of energy it contained. The idea that neutrons, which carried no electrical charge at all, might have been able to accomplish what could not be done with such heavily charged projectiles, was too fantastic to be credited. It was as though one were to suggest to troops which had been vainly shelling an underground shelter with guns of the heaviest calibre for a long time that they should start trying their luck with ping-pong balls. [12]

In this passage, the author is attempting to explain how fantastic it was to think that the neutrino, which carried no electric charge, could be used to smash the atom, when the heavily charged particles could not. To make this clear he uses the analogue of shelling an enemy bunker with ping pong balls rather than heavy artillery shells. In a similar way, Sir James Jeans attempted to explain the nature of the spectrum of an element like hydrogen when its atoms are heated by comparing the spectrum to the note emitted when a bell is struck. Just as a bell has a characteristic tone at which it resonates, so the atoms of a particular element resonate to certain frequencies of light.

Analogy in bringing out a relation between things, or resemblances that they share, is certainly fundamental to our ability to classify things. Classification

---

[12] Robert Jungk, *Brighter Than a Thousand Stars* (New York: Harcourt, Brace, 1958), p. 62.

involves both finding affinities and pointing out *differentia,* or dissimilarities. Further, analogy is closely tied to metaphor, an exciting and invaluable tool of our language.

Consider the following example. Metaphor helps a writer intensify language and to make a comparison, usually with the hope of broadening our conception of the things being compared.

> Magnified one thousand times, the insect
> Looks farcically human; laugh if you will!
> Bald head, stage-fairy wings, bleary eyes,
> A caved-in chest, hairy-black mandibles,
>   Long spindly thighs.[13]

In this case the blue-fly is being compared to a somewhat comically shaped human. Note the new conception of an insect that is stimulated by the comparison. Analogy, however, is fundamental to metaphor and metaphorical thinking. A recent description of metaphor is as follows: 'In metaphor, the mind sees and expresses an analogy.'[14]

The importance of metaphor to art and literature has long ago been acknowledged. Aristotle, for example, argued that the mark of imaginative genius was the ability to make metaphors, to see and create important resemblances. Even more significant, however, has been the discovery of the importance of analogy and metaphors in science. Thus, in an important treatise in the development both of mathematics and science, *A Treatise on Probability,* J. M. Keynes writes of Bacon, the so-called father of scientific method:

> Bacon's greatest achievement, in the history of logical theory, lay in his being the first logician to recognize the importance of methodological analogy to scientific argument and the dependence upon it of most well-established conclusions. The *Novum Organum* is mainly concerned with explaining methodological ways of increasing what I have termed the Positive and Negative analogies and of avoiding false Analogies.[15]

In this connection, scientists and philosophers of science are increasingly interested in the role of models and analogies in science. In much of the recent literature on models, models are considered as grounded on analogy and there is general agreement with the statement of E. M. Hutten that 'The model works by means of analogy.'[16]

Further, analogy is being closely tied by many scientists and philosophers of science, such as Toulmin, Hanson, and Kuhn, with scientific discovery and

---

[13] From 'Blue Fly' by Robert Graves in *Collected Poems* (Garden City, New York: Doubleday & Company, Inc., 1958), p. 285.

[14] E. Sewell, *The Human Metaphor* (South Bend, Ind.: Notre Dame Press, 1964), p. 42.

[15] J. M. Keynes, *A Treatise on Probability* (London: Macmillan & Co., 1921), p. 268f.

[16] [E. M. Hutten, *The Ideas of Physics* (London: Allen & Unwin, 1967), p. 90.]

creativity in science. Thus, G. K. Gilbert, a noted American geologist, has this to say:

> To explain the origin of hypotheses, I have a hypothesis to present. It is that hypotheses are always suggested through analogy. Consequential relations of nature are infinite in variety and he who is acquainted with the largest number has the broadest basis for the analogic suggestion of hypotheses.[17]

The distinguished modern physicist Robert Oppenheimer, writes:

> Science is an immensely creative enriching experience; and it is full of novelty and exploration; and it is in order to get to these that analogy is an indispensable instrument.[18]

Many other testimonies to the importance of analogy in science could be added. Analogy, then, would seem to be an important kind of reasoning tool, one well worth mastering. Let us take a classical example of the use of analogy in science, that of the Huygens' wave theory of light, which is as follows:

> I call them [light] waves from their resemblance to those which are seen to be formed in water when a stone is thrown into it, and which present a successive spreading as circles, and these arise from another cause, and are only in a flat surface.[19]

Here light is assumed to be wave-like, similar to water, because both exhibit a certain type of movement, when disturbed, namely, presenting a successive spreading as circles. Light waves were also thought similar to soundwaves. Thus, a basic analogy dominating physics during Huygens' time and for a century thereafter was that light, like sound and water, moves and behaves like a wave. The analogy, however, played a fundamental role in the development of the wave theory of light and became what is called 'a theoretical model,' that is, involving a set of assumptions about light and its behavior, about its inner structure, composition and mechanism, so that the various properties exhibited by light might be explained. Thus, because light was thought to be similar to sound and water, it was postulated that it would have the properties of reflection, and of refraction—the bending of a wave of light as it passes obliquely from one medium to another. These properties were verified and laws of refraction were developed. Also on the basis of the analogy with water and sound, it was postulated that light waves, like sound and water waves, must travel through a medium. In order to accommodate the fantastic speed of light this medium, ether, was postulated to be essentially of the same nature as air, the medium of sound, only much rarer and much more elastic. Here, however,

---

[17] G. K. Gilbert, "The Inculcation of Scientific Method by Example," *American Journal of Science*, 3rd Series (March, 1886): 284–88.

[18] R. Oppenheimer, "Analogy in Science," *American Psychologist* 11 (March 1956) 127–35.

[19] Christiaan Huygens, *Treatise on Light*, (Chicago: Encyclopedia Britannica, 1945) p. 4.

is where the analogy and the theoretical model based on it, misled scientists. None of the properties of ether seemed to be discoverable. Finally in 1887 Michelson and Moreley conducted an experiment that should have been able to detect the motion of the earth through the medium of ether. As many times as the experiments were conducted, the only conclusion that could be drawn from them was that the *earth was immobile!* It was Einstein that suggested ether did not exist and who postulated a new theory of light, the photon theory.

Tape Exercises

Another classical example of an analogy that also became a 'theoretical model' was Bohr's theory of the atom. Point out the possible conclusions Bohr might have drawn about the atoms and electrons, based on the analogy with the solar system. How might he have been misled? [Turn to Tape 10, band 4, for an analysis of this analogy.]

The alternative [to a harmonic model of the atom] was to copy the motion of the planets around the sun. The reason the planets do not fall into the sun is that they have reached stable orbits in which the centripetal force required to constrain them in their orbits is exactly the force of gravitation pulling them in. . . . Similarly in the atom, a revolving electron if moving fast enough would not fall into the positively charged nucleus.[20]

Exercises for § 10.4

Examples of models and analogies prevalent in the history of science are the following:

Model₁	is analogous to	Model₂
Bohr-Rutherford atom		Planetary systems
Container of billiard balls in motion		Kinetic theory of gases
Division of a liquid drop		Nuclear fission
Incompressible fluid flowing through tubes of variable section		Electric field
Society		Organism
Malthusian struggle in society		Natural selection
Machine		Animal and human body
Ocean		Atmosphere
Computer		Brain
Vortex		Atom
Fluid		Electric current
Electric forces		Nuclear forces
Biological evolution		Social evolution

---

[20] Roger Rusk, *Introduction to Atomic and Nuclear Physics* (New York, 1958), p. 161.

Below are examples of some of these models. Can you cite which are examples of which? Discuss positive and negative analogies and possible ways the analogies might mislead.

1. [The essence of the modern computer is not to be found in either the term 'electronic' or in 'digital,' but in the fact that they get their amazing results by the performance of a very large number of very simple processing steps.] *This would also appear to be a valid description of the essence of brain function.*

   Thus our argument has finally led us to the conclusion that computers and the brain do not simply display superficial similarities in some of their operational characteristics. Instead, they are mechanisms of the same kind, in the sense that they obtain their similar results by essentially similar means. If this is true, then it is clear that the computer scientist and the brain scientist need one another for the future development of their respective fields.

   There are foreseeable practical consequences of the cross-fertilization of computer and brain research. There is also a philosophic by-product of the first magnitude that may well come out of this kind of activity. The convergence of computer and brain sciences will render untenable the studied avoidance of the phenomenon of consciousness that has characterized the science of the last fifty years.

   Of greatest human significance, therefore, is the probability that our subjective sensations are ruled in a regular and predictable way by the processes of natural law.

   It leads to what may well be the only sound procedure for permanently plugging the hole in the logical structure of the mechanistic philosophy, *to accept the sense of consciousness itself as a natural phenomena suited to being described by and dealt with by the body of laws and methods of the physical sciences.* [21]

2. Benjamin Franklin developed and refined the one fluid theory. Each unelectrified body contains a normal, or equilibrium, amount which produces no observable effects. The process of electrification, he supposed, consists in taking some of the electrical fluid from one body and giving it to another. Thus, the fluid is not created, but is merely transferred. When an unelectrified body is rubbed, it either gains electrical fluid and thus reaches a positive state (plus), or loses some of its natural amount, leaving it in a negative state. In the process of electrification by conduction he assumed that a normal body will receive additional fluid from a positively charged body, and will give up fluid to a negatively charged body. Thus, the 'direction of flow' of electrical fluid is from a positively electrified body to one that is either a normal or negatively electrified body, and from a normal body to one that is negatively electrified. This convention of determining the flow of electricity (electric current) is still in use.

3. "On account of their close packing and strong energy exchange the particles in a heavy nucleus would be expected to move in a collective way which has some resemblance to the movement of a liquid drop. If the movement is

[21] Dean E. Woolridge, "Computers and the Brain," from *The Machinery of the Brain* (New York: McGraw-Hill Book Company, 1963), pp. 238–9.

made sufficiently violent by adding energy, such a drop may divide itself into two drops.[22]

4. Society is to be considered an organism, similar in many ways to a biological organism. A biological organism has as its basic unit, cells, while a social organism has as its basic unit, individual human beings. Thus, when you talk about the structure of a biological organism, you talk about the relations between cells; whereas, when you talk about structure of the social organism, you talk about relations between human beings. If you talk about 'activities' of a biological organism, you speak about relations between cells; if you are concerned about the 'activities' of a social organism, you are concerned with the observed behavior of individual human beings and groups of human beings. Further, just as all biological organisms are concerned with maintenance and adaptation, so also are all social organisms. Thus, it is proper to speak of *functions* in both cases. In the social context, *functions* are 'those observed consequences which make for the adaptations or adjustment of a given system and *dysfunctions* are those observed consequences which lessen the adaptation or adjustment of the system.

5. Thus the nervous system and the automatic machine are fundamentally alike in that they are devices which make decisions on the basis of decisions they have made in the past. The simplest mechanical devices will make decisions between two alternatives, such as the closing or opening of a switch. In the nervous systems, the individual nerve fiber also decides between carrying an impulse or not. In both the machine and the nerve, there is a special apparatus for making future decisions depend on past decisions, and in the nervous system a large part of this task is done at those extremely complicated points called 'synapses' where a number of incoming nerve fibers connect with a single outgoing nerve fiber. In many cases it is possible to state the basis of these decisions as a threshold of action of the synapse, or in other words, by telling how many incoming fibers should fire in order that the outgoing fibers may fire. (Further), the machine, like the living organism is, as I have said, a device which locally and temporarily seems to resist the general tendency for the increase of entropy.[23]

6. In the next chapter, the Struggle for Existence, amongst all organic beings throughout the world, which inevitably follows from their high geometrical powers of increase, will be treated of. This is the doctrine of Malthus, applied to the whole animal and vegetable kingdoms. As many more individuals of each species are born than can possibly survive; and, as consequently, there is frequently recurring struggle for existence, it follows that any being, if it varies, however, slightly in any manner profitable to itself, under the complex and sometimes varying conditions of life, will have a better chance of surviving, and thus be *naturally selected*. From the strong principle of

---

[22] Lise Meitner and O. R. Frisch, "Disintegration of Uranium by Neutrons: A New Type of Nuclear Reaction," *Nature* 143 (1939): 239.

[23] Norbert Wiener, *The Human Use of Human Beings* (New York: Avon, 1950 and 1954), pp. 48–49).

inheritance, any selected variety will tend to propagate its new and modified form.[24]

7. It must be supposed that a gas contains an enormous number of tiny molecules in rapid motion, which like billiard balls exert only contact force on each other and can travel only in a straight line. These are subject to the conservation laws of classical mechanics. Their diameters are small compared to the mean-path of the molecules; they collide elastically with each other and the walls of the container; and the absolute temperature of the gas is a function of the mean kinetic energy of the molecules. [Summary of the Kinetic theory of gases.]

8. The great task of sociology, as Spencer envisioned it, is to chart 'the normal course of social evolution,' to show how it will be affected by any given policy, and to condemn all types of behavior that interferes with it. Social science is a practical instrument in a negative sense. Its purpose is not to guide the conscious control of societal evolution, but rather to show that such control is an absolute impossibility and that the best that organized knowledge can do is to teach men to submit more readily to the dynamic factors in progress.[25]

Chapter Outline

I. *Chief features of inductions*
   A. Conclusions of inductions can only be probable, never certain.
   B. The strength or weakness of an inductive conclusion depends upon the amount, kind and relevance of the evidence provided in the premises. Ideally, all possible known relevant evidence must be taken into account.
   C. Inductive arguments are always context—dependent because their correctness depends on the evidence available at a particular time, place or context.
   D. Inductive arguments are always subject to revision in light of new evidence or new contexts. Thus, additional premises can strengthen or weaken an inductive argument.
II. *Kinds of inductive reasoning*
   A. *Enumerative inductive generalization from instances:* Proceeds from statements (premises) about observed individuals of such a kind to a statement (conclusion) about *all* such individual.
   Pattern: Some cases of S are observed to be P.
                Therefore, all cases of S are P.
                A_1 is an $S + P$
                A_2 is an $S + P$
                A_n is an $S + P$
                Probably all S's are P's.

---

[24] Charles Darwin, *The Origin of the Species*, Introduction (Chicago: Encyclopedia Britannica, 1952), p. 7.

[25] Richard Hofstadter, *Social Darwinism in American Thought*, rev. ed. (New York: George Brazilter, Inc., 1945–55), pp. 43–44.

1. There are four types of inductive generalization by enumeration.
    a. *Primary generalization:* 'All *A*'s are *B*'s,' e.g., 'All ravens are black.'
    b. *Statistical generalization:* 'A certain percentage of *A*'s are always *B*'s, e.g., 30 percent of the population die before 50 years of age.
    c. *Functional generalization:* 'A varies with *B*, e.g., 'Atmospheric pressure varies with distance from the earth's surface.'
    d. *Causal generalizations:* 'A causes *B*,' e.g., 'The virus of the anphoeles mosquito causes yellow fever.'
2. *Criterion for judging generalizations*
    a. Is the population class, the problem and the relevant characteristics clearly delineated and defined?
    b. Is the sample random, i.e., does it take in relevant variations and dissimilarities?
    c. Is the observed sample representative of the group, i.e., it is a good indication of the characteristics of the unobserved members of the population being studied?
    d. Is the scope of the generalization too broad relative to the premises?
3. *Fallacies of generalization* (See: chapter 4.)
    a. *Fallacy of hasty generalization* is to make a generalization on the basis of insufficient and/or carelessly selective evidence, the sample is not quantitatively representative.
    b. *Fallacy of accident:* Application of a generalization to a case that it does not cover because of accidental or exceptional circumstances.
B. *Inductive analogy:* Proceeds from the similarity of two or more things in one or more respects to the similarity of those things in some further respect.
    1. *Pattern:*   Individual *a* has properties *P, Q, R*.
                     Individual *b* has properties *P, Q, R*.
                     Individual *c* has properties *P, Q, R*.
                     Individual *d* has properties *P + Q*.

    ∴ Individual *d* probably has property *R*.

    2. *Criterion for judging*
        a. How many entities are being compared? The greater the number of objects included that have *P, Q, & R*, the stronger the argument.
        b. In how many respects are they similar? The greater the number of relevant properties held in common the stronger the argument.
        c. In how many respects are they dissimilar and are any of these crucially relevant? The greater the number of relevant dissimilarities, the weaker the argument.
        d. How relevant are the similarities indicated?
        e. How broad is the scope of the conclusion relative to the premises?
    3. *Analogy*
        a. Analogy is considered by many to be a fundamental aspect of human thought processes because of its connecting and bridge building capacity.

b. Analogy is the foundation for both metaphor and models.
c. Analogy is considered to play a prominent role in scientific thinking and has been associated by many with the process of creative
discovery.

11

NECESSARY AND SUFFICIENT CONDITIONS, CAUSAL RELATIONS, AND MILL'S METHODS

11.1 SCIENCE AND SCIENTIFIC EXPLANATIONS

Inductive reasoning, which may be roughly equated with scientific method, has explanation as its aim. It seeks to understand, describe, and explain the order of events in experience and in nature.

We might say that scientific inquiry has twin aims, theoretical and practical. The first aim voices the universal and persistent desire to speculate, to understand, to comprehend. Its elemental questions are, *what* is this? *How* does this operate? *Why* do these objects or processes behave as they do?

In a sense, mathematics is the ideal theoretical science, because in mathematics, as Bertrand Russell said, we are playing with symbols at a level at least a half century ahead of any known way in which mathematics can be used in the space-time world. The sheer desire to understand, however, is exhibited in all spheres of inquiry and in all the fields of the sciences. The practical aim of scientific method, on the other hand, obviously has to do not merely with understanding and "explaining" processes in nature, but also with controlling nature. The first expresses that priceless human ingredient, sheer intellectual curiosity. The second exhibits the quest of persons to control, manipulate, and use natural forces and generally to relate in satisfying ways to nature. We are engaged, then, in scientific thinking in two ways: when we "wonder" (in the flattering Kantian sense) at the order and mystery of "the starry heavens above," and when we try to discover how to prevent something from happening (e.g., death by a kidney failure) or to get something to happen (e.g., generate heat and light).

What is common to both these quests, and what is pertinent to the study in this chapter, is the search for causal explanation. Why does a certain event occur? By what means may we cause it to occur or prevent it from occurring again? Simple and clear as the motivation may be, the reasoning or the "logic" of causal explanation is far from simple and clear. We shall examine presently several of the better attempts to account for *causal* explanation; but before doing that, we shall inquire into the meaning of three more general concepts: "explanation" in general, the scientific concept of "law," and the meaning of "theory."

11.2   EXPLANATION: FOUR KINDS

A well known philosopher of science has written: ". . . the distinctive aim of the scientific enterprise is to provide systematic and responsibly supported explanations."[1] Four different kinds of explanation are usually discussed in the scientific context. The first is called *deductive-nomological*, which is explanation of an occurence by *subsuming it under a general law*. For example, suppose someone asks, "Why did that wire holding that mobile break?" A plausible answer is that too heavy a weight was suspended from it. But to offer this kind of explanation really involves us in asserting a generalization or "law" associating these two events (e.g., whenever too heavy a weight is suspended from a wire, it will break). Given this law and the fact that a heavy weight is suspended from it, it does *follow* that the wire breaks. The explanation really, then, has five parts.

1. For every wire of a given structure S (e.g., a certain material, thickness, etc.) there is a characteristic weight W such that the wire will break if a weight exceeding W is suspended from it.
2. For every thread of the kind S, the characteristic weight $W = K$.
3. T is a piece of wire of the kind S.
4. B, which has a weight greater than K, is suspended from T.
5. $\therefore T$ breaks.

One and 2 are lawlike statements; 3 and 4 are relevant factual statements; and 5 is the conclusion. The particular case of the wire breaking is explained by being subsumed *under general laws* covering similar cases. Notice also that the argument is a deductive one, namely, the premises (called *explanans*) offer logically conclusive grounds for expecting the event to be explained. Deductive logic is used throughout science, and thus scientific reasoning is *not* merely inductive, but a subtle combination of deduction and induction.

Another kind of explanation is *inductive-statistical explanation*. In this case an *individual* case is explained by subsumption under a *statistical law* and the

---

[1] Ernest Nagel, *The Structure of Science* (New York: Harcourt, Brace, & World, 1961), p. 15.

premises do not deductively imply the conclusion, but give only *inductive support*. An example of this type of explanation is:

1. Ninety percent of the persons in age group G have heart attacks.
2. Jones is in age group G.

---

3. The probability of Jones having a heart attack is 90 percent.

Notice that the conclusion is not: "Jones will have a heart attack." This conclusion does not logically follow because Jones could be among the 10 percent who do not have heart attacks. All that can be had in the conclusion is probability. We are given only a likelihood.

Two points need to be stressed in connection with inductive statistical explanation. First, it is not the mere presence of statistical generalization that renders an explanatory argument inductive nor the mere absence of statistical generalizations from an argument that renders it deductive. There *are* deductive arguments that contain statistical generalizations. For example,

Six percent of all American cigarette smokers get lung cancer (statistical generalization).
There are 100,000,000 American cigarette smokers (statement of fact).

∴ Necessarily 6,000,000 American cigarette smokers will get lung cancer.

The above argument is deductive because, *given the truth of the premises*, the conclusion must be true. Now, consider the following explanatory argument.

For every x, if x has a certain disease d, then x has a high pulse rate.
For every x, if x has a certain disease d, then x has high blood pressure.
For every x, if x has a certain disease d, then x has severe pains in his respiratory tract.
For every x, if x has a certain disease d, then x has a fever.
Mr. Jones has a high pulse rate, high blood pressure, severe pains in his respiratory tract, and a fever.

∴ Jones *probably* has a certain disease d.

Although the above argument contains no statistical generalizations, it is only *inductive* because given that the premises are true, it is still possible that the conclusion could be false—as any doctor knows. It is also the fallacy of affirming the consequent. An explanatory argument is deductive or inductive depending on the kind of evidence that the premises provide for the conclusion. If the truth of the conclusion follows necessarily from the truth of the premises, then the argument is deductive. If the conclusion still could be false when the premises are true, then it is inductive.

Although the mere presence or absence of statistical generalizations in the premises of an argument is no indicator of inductive or deductive explanations, there is one case in which the explanatory argument is always inductive: namely, *when the argument contains statistical generalizations in the premises and concludes to explain an individual event or case.* As any good insurance company well knows: *one can never* conclude that businessman John Jones, age 50, *will* have a heart attack and die at 55 on the evidence that 90 percent of adult male businessmen have heart attacks and die at 55.

A further point must be made about explanation. It is generally argued that prediction and explanation are closely related. An explanation should be a potential prediction. That is, the premises should afford grounds of prediction of the event or case explained. If the premises adequately explain the event (e.g., why the thread broke, why it is a 90 percent probability that Jones will get a heart attack), they also give the same grounds for *expecting the event* had it not already occurred.

A third type of explanation much discussed in philosophy of science is called *teleological explanation.* Teleological explanation seeks to answer the question "Why?" by reference to some end, goal, purpose, or motive. Thus, for example, Darwin's evolutionary theory appears to answer the question, "Why does this organism have such and such structural or functional characteristics?" with the phrase, "In order to survive."

> Take the following example of a teleological explanation.
> When supplied with water, carbon dioxide, and sunlight, plants produce starch.
> If plants have no chlorophyll, even though they have water, carbon dioxide, and sunlight, they do not produce starch.
> ∴ Plants contain chlorophyll.

The argument can be restated in one sentence: The function of chlorophyll in plants is to enable plants to perform photosynthesis.

Other examples of teleological-type explanations are:

1. The whiteness of the fur of polar bears is due to the fact that, in their natural habitat, this makes it difficult for them to be seen by their prey.

2. The purpose served by an increase of leucocytes in the blood stream during times of infection is that of guarding the body against attack by deleterious invading organisms.

One also finds teleological type explanations in the various social sciences. Consider the following statements.

1. Among the constitutents of any human personality system will be a mechanism such as the propensity to forget material, the conscious remembrance of which would cause great pain. Without a mechanism such as *repression*, for example, the personality system might well give way under the strain of conflicts too painful to be long tolerated.

2. The persistence of type *X* burial customs in society *Y* is explained not by the manifest functions or purposes attributed to them by the members of that society, but rather by their latent function: shoring up the members' feeling of group solidarity and hence improving morale in the face of the terrors death inevitably inspires in most humans.

Teleological explanations are the subject of much controversy in science and the philosophy of science. One reason that objection has been raised to teleological explanation is that it revives the old Aristotelian teleological interpretation of nature, which to many is an erroneous personification projected into natural events (e.g., the "goal" of the acorn is to "become" an oak tree). Further, in referring to *goals* or *ends* or *purposes* to explain events, there seems to be the tendency to identify these goals with certain *future states of affairs* (i.e., with events that have not yet occurred at the time of the behavior, event, etc., that they are thought to explain or cause). This further leads to the paradoxical conclusion that future (i.e., nonexistent) events have causal efficacy. Thus, Aristotle spoke of the *final cause* of things, meaning the goal, end or purpose of things (e.g., the oak tree is the final cause of the acorn).

To escape this type of difficulty, a number of philosophers of science argue that teleological explanations are really translatable into nonteleological explanations without any loss of meaning. Thus, for example, we can translate the examples about the chlorophyll, and the leucocytes, as follows:

1. "A necessary condition for the occurrence of photosynthesis is the presence of chlorophyll."

2. "Unless human blood contains sufficient leucocytes, during the time of infection, the body activity is impaired by attacking organisms."

Both of these statements now refer to causes or conditions and do not make any reference to the future. This is like saying that *X* is the cause or condition of *Y* rather than *Y* is an effect of *X*, with *X* standing somehow in the future. The case of the polar bear can be handled by linking the likelihood of the survival of the species polar bear (in polar environments) with enhanced ability to carry on predatory activities that the white fur contributes, e.g., "unless the polar bear has white fur, it is more open to attack by enemies and has less chance for survival." One point at issue here is that many philosophers of science believe it illegitimate to attribute purposes to inanimate and nonhuman entities, and therefore, they prefer the neutral translation.

However, others would go even further and argue that reference to purposes, goals, and intentions is illegitimate and unscientific even in dealing with human subjects.

This neutral kind of translation, it is argued, can even handle the examples given from the social sciences as well as so-called "motive" explanation.[2] Thus, the following explanation:

---

[2] See Carl Hempel, "The Logic of Functional Analysis," in Llewellyn Gross, ed., *Symposium on Sociological Theory* (New York: Harper & Row, 1959).

Smith chooses a premedical course and studies hard in order to qualify for medical school.

is retranslated:

Because she wants to go to medical school and believes that qualification for medical school is dependent upon taking a premedical course and studying hard, Smith chooses a premedical course and studies hard.

In this translation, we now refer to a *present desire* and a *present belief* rather than a future goal to explain Smith's behavior. There are, however, many who object to the attempt to reduce all teleological explanations to causal ones. They object on several grounds. Consider the above example.

To begin with, the conclusion does *not* follow from the premises. It is obvious, upon reflection, that when a person has a desire for something and believes that a certain course of action will satisfy that desire, it certainly does not follow that he or she *will* take that course of action. Desires, beliefs, motives do not allow us to predict behavior with any degree of accuracy, although they might allow us to explain it *after the fact*.

Second, in the paradigm of causal explanation (i.e., the "deductive-nomological explanation"), we explain (draw conclusions) by subsuming an individual case under a group of generalizations or laws. But what *laws* are there linking motives to actions? There might be rough generalizations, but no *laws*. Thus, two prominent philosophers have written:

The statement that one person did something because, for example, another threatened him, carries no implication or covert assertion that if the circumstances were repeated the same action would follow.[3]

Further, some would even argue that laws linking motives and actions probably cannot be formulated. Donald Davidson has written:

Generalizations connecting reasons (that is, motives) and action are not, and cannot be sharpened into the kind of law on the basis of which accurate predictions can reliably be made. If we reflect on the way reasons determine choice, decision and behavior, it is easy to see why this is so. What emerges, in the *ex post facto* atmosphere of explanation and justification, is that the reason frequently was, to the agent at the time of the action, one consideration among many.[4]

What Davidson emphasized in this passage is that rarely, if ever, does one motive alone enter into a decision. Thus, for example, Smith could be taking a

---

[3] H. L. Hart and A. M. Honoré, *Causation in the Law* (Oxford: University Press, 1959), p. 52.

[4] Donald Davidson, "Actions, Reasons and Causes," *Journal of Philosophy LX* (1963): 697.

premedical course and studying hard because of the desire to please a boy friend, because of parental push, and so on.

Many philosophers maintain that we should distinguish three things:

1. Causal relations such as we have identified earlier (e.g., why has this pot of water come to boil?)

2. Reasons for an action or an event (e.g., what are the reasons why many people were critical of Richard Nixon's role in the Watergate affair? The "reasons" one may cite are not necessarily the same as the "causes" for the critical attitude.)

3. "Motives" (e.g., a person may know that excessive cigarette smoking *causes* emphysema. Further, he or she may have reasons for stopping or continuing to smoke heavily. But even knowing the doctor's warning, and understanding the effects on his or her body, the person may not be motivated to stop smoking. Philosophers have long pointed out that *reason* does not necessarily motivate.)

The controversy over teleological explanation is broad, and we have only briefly touched on a few of the issues involved. What should concern us here are the following points: (1) There are numerous teleological explanations in the sciences, especially in the biological and social sciences—sciences dealing with living organisms. (2) These teleological types of explanation have dangers: They tend misleadingly to refer to mysterious future causes. They imply "purposiveness"—"purposiveness" is apt for human behavior, but how appropriate is it for other living organisms? When referring to "purposes," "goals," and so on, these refer to entities not directly observable. We can get at "purposes" and "motives" only indirectly through behavior or verbal report. Both behavior and verbal report can be misleading. I can be in pain and not show it, as also I can say that I am in pain when I am not. Similarly, I can lie about my motive.

We must ask about teleological and functional explanations: How well do they explain? Do they really account for *why* the event, occurred, or are they after-the-fact rationalizations? How strong is the evidence in the premises? What evidence is there for the conclusion other than reference to purpose or function? For example, what evidence is there that (a) repression performed this function in *this* case; (b) burial customs in the Kawipe society shore up group morale and solidarity? It should be noted that emphasis on function is de-emphasis on disfunction and that the question can always be raised: Does everything have to have a function?

Finally, although philosophers of science and logicians do not agree as to whether or not it is a distinctive method, nor as to its explanatory value, we nonetheless should identify what is called the *genetic* method of explanation. The name is derived, of course, from the term "genesis" or origin(s), and it attempts to explain the existence or nature of something by tracing it from earlier stages out of which it has presumably evolved. Thus, it is alleged that both inanimate objects—mountains and valley, rivers and oceans, even stars

and planets—and animate or living things—plants, animals, human beings—
can be explained as to their nature by tracing their prior stages of evolution. Is
it the case, for example, that the giraffe is the kind of animal we see in our zoos
because of its evolving from prior forms? Is the Greek spoken and written in
twentieth century Athens to be understood in terms of its evolution from
classical Greek? All attempts at genetic explanation assume that such questions
as the above are answerable by describing how the present forms evolved from
earlier forms.

Clearly there are interesting, often fascinating and dramatic cases, in which
attempts have been made to trace the sequence of steps or stages through
which something has evolved. But that this tracing is difficult, often impossible, is also evident. Surely it is impossible, for example, to identify every
stage through which something has passed from its original form. What *was* its
original form? How can *it* be identified? Furthermore, the selecting of specific
stages or steps in the sequence is often made on the assumption or hypothesis
that these steps, and not others, furnish the causal explanation. But that
assumption cannot be demonstrated. How are we to know, without bias or a
preconceived assumption, about the "earliest" and "latest" stages, which intermediate stages are causal (relevant to causal determinates) in the development of what we are trying to explain? We simply do not know, and so we
operate with assumptions and the selection of available evidence, hoping that a
rational development can be traced. The terms we have come to apply to all
scientific, inductive explanation, for example, "tentative" and "probable" apply
with special force to all genetic explanations.

11.3   LAW

The concept of "scientific law" or "law of nature" is a controversial one in
science and philosophy of science. However, a few statements can be made
indicating how the term "scientific law" is generally understood.

First of all, laws are statements that express regularities. They assert certain
things to be regularly associated. They may be of two logical forms. The first
form is the *nonstatistical generalized conditional statement.* An example of this
is, "For any (every, all) object(s) x, if x is such and such, then x is so and so." This
kind of statement is also called a statement of *universal form*, for it asserts that
every object (or event or condition) that has certain properties also has certain
other properties. The second form is the statistical generalization form. It is a
statement to the effect that a certain percentage of cases having feature F will
have feature G.

Two additional criteria traditionally thought to distinguish "law statements"
from other types of generalization statements are: (1) that laws have *empirical
content* and (2) that they be *true*. Both of these criteria, however, have some
difficulties associated with them. The criterion of empirical content is intended
to rule out a statement like "All bachelors are unmarried men" as a law. Such a
statement is an *analytic* statement. It is a statement true by virtue of the

meanings of the words it contains. Such a statement could not function, as a law does, in a genuine explanation without other empirical statements. Consider the following:

All bachelors are unmarried men.
Jones is a bachelor.
∴ Jones is an unmarried man.

No new content or knowledge has been given in such an explanation. Analytic statements are generally ruled out as "laws of nature." Although they are true, they fail to perform the function normally expected of laws—to explain phenomena, to predict events, and to serve as instruments for making inferences in inquiry.

Generally, then, laws have empirical content of some sort. However, we must not overlook two facts: (1) There is controversy over the "analytic-synthetic" distinction, and (2) some principles in science, which are considered laws, border on the "analytic." Thus, Newton's first law of motion (a body under the action of no external force maintains a constant velocity) is considered by many to define what it is to be a body under the action of no external forces.

Laws should also be true. "All swans are white" does not count as a law, because there are black swans, and we cannot explain a particular swan's being white on the basis of the alleged law. But we must be cautious, for many scientific statements commonly regarded as "laws" (e.g., those of classical mechanics) are only approximate as strictly interpreted they are not true. For example, Newton's first law of motion is not true.

Another criterion suggested to distinguish law statements from other generalizations is that law statements support *contrafactual conditionals*. Contrafactual conditionals allow us to speak about potential (as distinct from actual) events in which *should* A *occur*, B *would also occur*. They take the following form:

If A were (had been) the case, then B would be (would have been) the case, where in fact A is not (has not been) the case.

The ability to support contrafactual conditional statements is linked to the *predictive* and hence *explanatory* force that laws have in contrast to non-laws. Consider the following two statements:

1. All the rocks in this box are gold.
2. Any body subject to no external forces maintains a constant velocity.

From the first statement, it does not follow that if a rock were put into the box, it would be gold. It is an accidental generalization about what in fact happens to be the case. The second statement is a law of nature, for it does follow from it that if a body were subject to no external forces, it would maintain a constant velocity.

Even with this criterion, however, there are some difficulties. The contrafactual conditional, for example, cannot be accounted for in truth-functional logic and runs into problems under logical analysis. Further, counterfactual statements can be derived from almost every universal statement.

A final criterion to distinguish law statements from non-law statements is *systematic connection within a larger theoretical framework*. Consider the statement, "All copper wire at minus 270 degrees centigrade temperature is a good conductor of electricity." Regarding such a statement, it should be noted that we may not know that there are in fact any pieces of copper wire at minus 270 degrees C. temperature, and, further, that we have not, therefore, performed any experiments on such wires. Yet we do not balk at accepting this as a law statement. It is accepted as a law statement presumably because it is a consequence of some *other* assumed laws for which there is evidence of some kind. This statement (and others like it, having no positive instances) will be granted law status if it follows from other laws and theories. The question of the status of Newton's first law of motion could also be argued on this ground. Its position in the body of scientific knowledge entitles it to the status of "law," even if it is decided to be "vacuously true."

Place or position in the current body of knowledge is another criterion used to decide whether certain generalizations are to be called *laws*. If a generalization is an isolated assertion which is not part of a theory or which does not have theoretical ramifications, it is generally not granted law status. The statement "every time the morning sky is red, it rains in the afternoon" is an example of a generalization not called a *law*.

11.4   THEORY

A *theory in the context of philosophy of science is a systematically related set of statements* that seeks to give an organized account of a field of knowledge by fitting together into logical relations the statements embodying the knowledge that has been acquired in that field. The type of logical relationship, ideally sought in scientific theories, is *deductive relatedness*. A theory generally has at least two parts, the postulates and the "correspondence rules."

Postulates   The postulates section defines the basic terms, concepts, and properties with which the theory is concerned. Postulates also specify what kinds of relationships hold between these things.

Take three different kinds of theories, all oversimplified for this purpose. The physical theories are usually stated in terms of complex mathematics.

Bohr's Theory of the Atom

Postulate (1) There are "atoms" and each is composed of a relatively heavy nucleus carrying a positive electric charge and a number of negatively charged electrons with a smaller mass moving in approximately elliptic orbits with the nuclei at one of the focii.

(2) The number of electrons varies with the chemical elements.

(3) Only a discrete set of permissible orbits are possible for the electrons.

(4) The diameters of the orbits are proportional to $h^2 n^2$. h is the value of an indivisible quantum of energy. n is an integer.

(5) The electromagnetic energy of an electron depends on the diameter of the orbit. As long as the electron remains in any one orbit, its energy is constant and the atom emits no radiation.

(6) The electron may jump from an orbit with a higher energy level to an orbit with a lower energy level. When it does, it emits electromagnetic radiation whose wave length is a function of these energy differences.

Newton's Theory

Postulate (1) If and only if a net (resultant) force F acts on a particle P, then P accelerates in the direction of F, and the magnitudes of the acceleration equal the ratio of F to the mass of P.

(2) If a particle P exerts a force F on another particle P^1, then P^1 exerts an equal force on P in the opposite direction.

(3) Any two particles exert on each other a force (gravitational attraction) that is directly proportional to the product of their masses and inversely proportional to the square of their distance apart.

(4) Any set of forces that acts either concurrently or successively on an identical particle has the same effect on the particle's acceleration as a single force that is the resultant (vector sum) of all of them.

(5) Every particle has constant mass.

Robert K. Merton's
Theory for Functional Analysis

Postulate (1) The entire range of sociological data can be subjected to functional analysis.

(2) Functions are observed consequences which make for the adaption or adjustment of a given system.

(3) Dysfunctions are observed consequences which lessen the adaptation or adjustment of the system.

(4) Nonfunctional consequences are irrelevant to the system under consideration.

(5) Manifest functions are those objective consequences contributing to the adjustment or adaptation of the system which are intended and recognized by the participants in the system.

(6) Latent functions are those neither intended nor recognized.

Correspondence rules   A second part of theory is that called *correspondence rules*. It connects the postulates with experimentation. In Bohr's theory, for example, the *theoretical notion* of an "electron jump" is linked with the *experimental notion* of a spectral line (e.g., wave length or a light ray emitted by an atom jumping from one orbit to another). In Newtonian theory, the basic laws would be linked with specific procedures of measurement, and so on. In Merton's theory, for example, mechanisms are spelled out through which functions are fulfilled (e.g., role-segmentation, hierarchic ordering of values, social division of labor, ritual, and ceremonial enactments).

Model   The third party of many, if not all, theories is the *model*. A model is a form of analogy. It is a device for relating a theory to something already familiar and understood; it aids in the developing, interpreting, and setting out of a theory. It can be a mathematical model, an actual physical model, or even another theory. Looking at our three examples, we see that the Bohr theory of atom involves the model of the planetary system. He postulated that the movement of electrons is like the movement of planets around the sun; their orbits are elliptic, and so on. The central notion of Newtonian physics is of the inertial system. The model of Merton's functionalism is the biological organism. As in the biological organism we observe cells, structure or relation between cells, behavior of cells and certain basic functions maintaining the organism, similarly, society must be organized with certain structures and certain functions related to its survival.

There is disagreement over the role models play in scientific theorizing. Are they fundamental and indispensable or merely heuristic and dispensable? However we decide that question, it is clear that models have often misled science. The electron does not behave like the planets, and there is no ether through which light travels, as indicated by the model of the wave theory of light.

Finally on the nature of theory, what are the criteria for describing what is a good theory? Three criteria of a good theory are: (1) *consistency* (i.e., that the theory not involve any internal self-contradiction), (2) *coherence* with the total body of knowledge, and (3) ability to *predict* and *explain*.

Much more could be said about scientific theory, but, for our purposes, the following points are the most important.

The first point is, a theory seeks to organize and integrate knowledge. In doing so, it enables knowledge to expand by means of new ranges of predictions.

Second, theory involves abstraction and conjecture, yet it also seeks to connect itself to the laboratory and to experimentation. One of the crucial tests of a good theory is its testability. It must have testable implications. However, testability is complex. Because a theory is a vast deductive complex of statements, it is difficult to know what statements are at fault if test consequences are negative. Further, the model may be misleading. And, even further, a theory sets out and defines such things as terms and patterns of testing. A well-founded theory dominates a field, and scientists must be constantly alert that a theory does not become dogma rather than conjecture.

Karl Popper's statement that the two central characteristics of the process called science are *conjecture* and *falsifiability* is probably correct. Science is the continual putting forth of bold explanations, bold hypotheses, and bold theories, but it is also, or must be, the willingness to subject these to continuous and rigorous test, to the possibility of falsifiability. Knowledge of fact is always only probable, and we can never be sure that total truth has been reached. There must be continual critical examination of hypotheses, theories, laws, terms, and methods of experimentation. There must be willingness to try new conjectures to see if some data are being overlooked or misinterpreted. Being human, however, even scientists tend to cling to what is known and stable—perhaps far too long. But time usually brings revolutions, and a Newton is surpassed by an Einstein. Thomas Kuhn, in *The Structure of Scientific Revolutions*, for example, argued that falsification described not the strategy actually employed by scientists but rather the fact that often long periods of scientific endeavor were spent in creating ingenious hypotheses, etc., to buffer up existing theories under attack. Thus the Ptolemaic astronomers adjusted their theory to fit new facts, and Newtonian physicists ignored the puzzle of Mercury's motion. What this fact means for the so-called *scientific method* is still a subject of controversy, but alertness has always been necessary for critical thinking; it should not be any less so in science.

Scientific reasoning, then, is a continual movement between fact and observation, theory, conjecture, and criticism.

Finally, scientific reasoning, as we have seen, involves both induction and deduction. But induction and deduction are only forms of argument—forms of relationship between premises and conclusion. They do not tell us anything about truth. They only tell us the relationship between our evidence and our conclusion. But knowing this is surely one step toward knowing whether we are at least on the right path toward the truth.

Exercises for § 11.4

Provide an explanation for each of the following. What type of explanation might be the most appropriate: deductive-nomological, functional, teleological, or genetic? [The shaded items are analyzed on Tape 11, band 1.]

1. Why did moisture form on the outside of the glass when it was filled with ice water yesterday?

2. Why does the English language have so many words of Greek and Latin origin?

3. Why do people tend to forget people's names?

4. Why did Cassius plot the death of Caesar?

5. Why is the sum of any number of consecutive odd integers beginning with 1 always a perfect square (e.g., $1 + 3 + 5 + 7 = 16 = 4^2$)?

6. Why do human beings have lungs?

7. Why does ice float on water?

8. Why did a smaller percentage of Roman Catholics commit suicide than did Protestants in European countries during the last quarter of the nineteenth century?

9. Why do religious wars tend to inflame loyalties so much more than other wars?

10. Why did Henry VIII of England seek to annul his marriage to Catherine of Aragon?

11.5 NECESSARY AND SUFFICIENT CONDITIONS

We are now prepared for a fresh and more thorough discussion of causal explanation. Our illustrations are primarily from the fields of the natural and social sciences, including examples of attempted historical explanations.

The basic notion of causation is that events occur in sequence. It is an easy step from this to the distinction between *antecedent* and *consequent* events. If I drank too much last night I should not be surprised when I wake up with a first-class hangover. If I drive 90 miles an hour and suddenly find myself facing the rear end of a huge truck on a one lane highway, I am a fool not to expect trouble. The basis of my lack of surprise and of expecting a hangover or an accident is the assumption, borne out by repeated experience, of the coherence and interdependence of events. Every time the condition of excess drinking occurred, the headache occurred. We conclude that the antecedent condition is sufficient to produce the consequent, the effect.

Sufficient conditions   A first way of interpreting the causal relation is in terms of *sufficient conditions*. This may be stated as follows: a sufficient condition of an event is such that whenever the antecedent (condition) occurs the consequent (condition) also occurs. Our assumption is that event E_2, occurring every time and shortly after event E_1 occurs, allows us to conclude that E_1 is the cause of E_2. We can name many illustrations from daily life. A nail puncturing my tire is sufficient to produce a flat tire; a rock thrown against my window is sufficient to shatter the glass; a staphlococci germ entering my body is sufficient to generate a fever and make me sick. It does not take much imagination to see, however, that whereas each of these antecedent conditions is *sufficient* to produce the consequence indicated, in none of these cases is it *necessary*. I can get a headache from many conditions other than drinking too much; my tire can go flat if the valve leaks; a bullet will shatter my window pane; I can also develop a fever because of "intestinal flu" germs. The rule—a sufficient condition is such that when present the effect follows—is quite different from a similar rule that describes a necessary condition. Conditions are equally sufficient to produce the same effect (e.g., a rock, a shoe, a bat, a bullet, can all shatter a window). Because of this, in the case of a sufficient condition, we can never *with certainty* infer from effect to cause. Given the shattered window, I cannot conclude with certainty that a rock was the cause.

We have chosen our illustrations deliberately in order to make the following point: Logicians have claimed that when we seek the sufficient conditions for an event our aim is to produce some desirable effect. If a chemist is looking for an element that will "cool" our car or house, he or she is satisfied when a chemical is found that produces that effect. Though generally correct, this may be a dangerous simplification. But if the quest is for nothing more complex than for the cause of the flat tire or the headache, the condition we fix upon as sufficient will probably point to the cause.

Sufficient may be taken as meaning "sufficient to produce" a condition *A*, such that when present, consequent *B* almost always occurs.

Necessary condition   What, then, does "*necessary* condition" mean, and how are necessary conditions related to sufficient conditions? Necessary conditions are such that, if absent, the effect will not occur. If the grass seeds we planted are to grow, nourishment is necessary; in its absence the seeds will not grow. If our car is to run, we must have gas in the tank. If there is life on the planet Mars, the presence of oxygen is one necessary condition. Here a very important point emerges: whereas one or more condition(s) may be necessary for a given effect to occur, no one of the necessary conditions is likely to be sufficient. Recall the necessity of nourishment if the seed is to grow. Clearly, other conditions are also necessary (e.g., a certain range of temperature, a quality of ground).

Tape Exercises

What would you say are the necessary conditions for high scholarship in college? Do these include a high IQ? Time for study? Desire to learn? If these are necessary, as we could likely agree they are, have we at the same time named the sufficient conditions for graduating cum laude or summa cum laude? [We shall discuss this on Tape 11, band 2.]

The usual aim in discovering necessary conditions is the opposite or converse of the aim in searching for sufficient conditions. In looking for sufficient conditions, the aim is to produce a desired effect, but the aim in seeking necessary conditions is to eliminate an undesired effect. The realm of medicine illustrates this. The film *Dr. Erich's Magic Bullet* was a superb and dramatic story of the German doctor's life-long quest for the cause of veneral disease. After hundreds of experiments, he finally identified the condition in the absence of which the disease did not occur. For the first time in history he knew what germs had to be destroyed, and he proceeded to devise the way to destroy them. Further, with references to the necessary condition, thanks to Dr. Erlich's brilliant research, scientists can infer with confidence what the cause of the disease is once they diagnose it. So for the first time in human history, it was, at least in principle, possible to eliminate this dread disease.

Finally, what about a joint search for the necessary and sufficient conditions for the occurrence of an event? The answer is that this is what we really seek in a scientific inquiry. We look for conditions such that whenever these are present the effect occurs and in their absence the effect does not occur. To summarize:

1. Condition *A* is causally sufficient for an effect *B* if *B* follows whenever condition *A* is present. (E.g., decapitation is a sufficient condition for death. Death, however, may be caused in other ways.)

2. Condition *A* is causally necessary for *B* when *B* is never present when *A* is not present. (E.g., the presence of oxygen is a necessary condition for combustion.)

If we really seek causal explanation, we want to identify both necessary and sufficient conditions. The necessary conditions will tell us how to reason from cause to effect; the sufficient conditions will tell us how to draw inferences from effect to cause. We want both. We want to explain cause and effect relations. Ideally we want to identify the necessary and sufficient conditions.

Exercises for § 11.5

In each of the following, what are the necessary, sufficient, or necessary *and* sufficient conditions, (or neither) of each of the following? [The shaded items are discussed on Tape 11, band 2.]

1. Becoming President of the United States.
2. Producing a painting that wins the critic's award at the New York City or Paris Museum of Modern Art.
3. Being a (good) mother.
4. Being a (good) father.
5. Making a million dollars on the stock market.

6. Being a Master Chef.
7. Being a member of the Olympic Team.
8. Writing a successful Broadway play.
9. Controlling inflation.
10. Absence of tooth decay.

11.6 CRITIQUE OF "NECESSARY AND SUFFICIENT CONDITIONS"

In our discussion of cause as being identified with necessary and sufficient conditions we must be careful to employ two qualifications. One is the distinction between a simple and a complex cause, the other is the distinction between a single cause as contrasted with a plurality of causes. For example, there may be a single and unique cause for an earthquake, but this is far from saying that the cause is simple. We are frequently given sympathy for living and working so near to the famous San Andreas Fault in California. Geologists are increasingly clear and remarkably capable of explaining the nature of the possible (expected?) earthquake. But the actual cause is unusually complex. The other point is that an effect may very well have what logicians call a *plurality of causes*. A death, an automobile accident, a crop failure, or an international conflict—each one of these almost surely turns out, on inspection, to exhibit a mingling of several causes. This is one objection that John Stuart Mill was shrewd enough to recognize in his brilliant study of methods of experimental inquiry. But still, a certain effect may be produced by one cause in one instance, and by another cause in another instance.

Tape Exercise

Consider the "condition" and "cause" of typhoid fever. [This topic is presented on Tape 11, band 3.]

Were someone to ask, if there is a difference between 'cause' and 'condition,' the provisional and brief answer must be 'yes, there is,' but an adequate treatment of that question would take us into the philosophy of science. That is another course and goes beyond introductory 'logic'. One interpretation of 'cause' is to equate it with the total set or the complex of conditions. But this is an admittedly vague statement. For, it is dangerous to interpret 'total set' too narrowly, and it is practically disasterous to interpret it too widely because then it becomes equivalent to all the preceding events in the universe. Still, in this first way of explaining causation what we are after is clear: Causal explanation is the joint identification of necessary and sufficient conditions.

Tape Exercises

The following examples call for explanation in terms of necessary and/or sufficient conditions. [Turn to Tape 11, band 3, for comments.]

1. A lighted cigarette or match is thrown near a bush by a camper and a major forest fire develops not much later. Was the cigarette or match the 'cause'? In what sense?

2. The citizens of *x* are deeply dissatisfied with their economic, political, and social circumstances. Is this the cause of the revolution that shortly occurs?

3. A building is under construction, and a brick falls from the top and kills a person walking on the street. What was the cause of the person's death?

This brings us to the question of how we might go about the task of identifying causes as invariable antecedents related to invariant consequences. It was John Stuart Mill who addressed himself to this question. His answer was given in terms of five 'methods of experimental inquiry'. We shall identify and illustrate each of these methods and then point out their strengths and weaknesses. The success of the discussion depends in large part on the illustrations employed. Rather than strive for ingenuity, the criterion we employ in choosing illustrations is clarity and forcefulness. Some of the old and well-worn examples are, like old friends, the best.

11.7   MILL'S METHODS OF INDUCTION.

The method of agreement   The method of agreement asks us always to look for what any set of circumstances have *in common* and, if possible, for the *single characteristic* that they have in common, excluding all others. In other words, the ultimate aim is to seek to eliminate all possible causal factors but one.

Nearly every logic text illustrates the Method of Agreement with some contrived version of food poisoning, the cause being the single respect that all the antecedent conditions had in common. For example, if those and only those who became ill ate spoiled crab salad, the consequent food poisoning is the result of eating the crab. This example has the virtues of clarity and simplicity. A more timely illustration of a cause and effect relation is the near epidemic proportion of gonorrhea among college age persons. To simplify an imagined example, suppose eight out of twenty members of XYZ fraternity came to the college physician for treatment. Identifying their disease as the all-too-familiar cases of gonorrhea, the physician probably would question the men to discover what they had in common as antecedent conditions. He suspects and, we shall assume, soon verifies that those eight members had engaged in intercourse with the same woman. Of course, this is not proof, but it is near enough to it to explain the cases of disease. The method of agreement has worked again.

Another example of the use of the method of agreement is the following. Recently a serious problem developed with the unexpected increase in deaths among premature babies. The condition physicians encountered was diagnosed as hyaline membrane disease (now known as "h.m.d." for short). The treatment they came to use was to give oxygen by tubes in the infant nose or by mask, and before long they came to give more and more oxygen, as the case appeared to require. However, a serious side effect now appeared, namely, a disease known as *fribro plasia*. This is the condition in which the retina of the eye becomes fibratic. In the retrolental area fibers appeared instead of the normal and healthy nerve ending. Now the problem was, how to account for this development. It was discovered that the cause was the use of oxygen. This was the one factor common to all cases of the disease *fribro plasia*. Mill's Method served the purpose.

It should be noted that this first of Mill's Methods, like any inductive method, has no built-in guarantees of its successful use. It assumes that we can and have considered all possible causes and all relevant factors. When we ignore relevance, funny things can occur. Thus, Gilbert K. Chesterton and Hilaire Belloc are alleged to have decided not only to conduct inquiry scientifically into the cause of drunkenness, but also to take a crack at science as allegedly superior to philosophy in general and traditional religion in particular. Surely the story is apocryphal. Their experiment consisted in drinking brandy and water and getting drunk. They then drank scotch whiskey and water and got drunk. Still later they drank gin and water and got drunk. Finally, they drank vodka and water and got drunk. What was the one circumstance that these experiences had in common, or the one factor present in them all? Because water was the one factor that was present in each instance, they concluded 'scientifically' that water was the cause of drunkenness.

Undeniably useful as this method can be (and its utility is demonstrated every day) there are troubles with the method of agreement in addition to the one cited above. Thus, we are required to look for the *single* respect in which a set of circumstances agree. And yet, we do not always have convenient data on which to base our conclusions. We are never sure that we have isolated the one and only circumstance that is common to the several instances of the phenomena. In the first example cited, that of the breaking out of typhoid fever, it happened that all of the victims were members of the Jewish faith. What if it had been pointed out that they were all black, or that they were all 5'5" in height? Would this have had any light to throw on what the cause of the typhoid fever is? We are inclined to say "No, don't be silly." But the trouble is, if Mill's method of agreement is taken literally, we find ourselves in the embarrassing position of not knowing for sure which of the ways in which the events agree is the cause, and we cannot isolate one single cause. Third, the method of agreement over-simplifies the case and tends to lead us to overlook the fact that in numerous cases there is not just one cause involved, but multiple causes. Mill was aware of this difficulty.

The method of difference   The method of difference is a very common method of thinking and of experimentation. What it points to is the one instance or respect in which a set of circumstances differ. In that one instance we are inclined to agree we have found the cause. Consider the following examples:

1. Every day we put a kettle of water on the stove to heat for morning coffee, but after our shower we return to find that it has not come to a boil. Why has it not begun to boil? Because, although the water, the kettle, and the kitchen are all the same as we used daily, we forgot to turn on the fire. We conclude that the one respect in which this event is different from all previous is in the failure to apply heat. Therefore the difference of not having heat applied to the water makes the difference in whether it boils or not.

2. A salesperson in a shop for smokers has dozens of lighters in the showcase and pulls a new one of the kind the customer selected. But on attempting to light it, he finds it does not light. The simple and obvious question is, why is this different from the other lighters that we've been experimenting with, all of which lighted? The one difference that appears is that it had no flint or means of igniting. The method of difference has given us the cause of the failure of the lighter to work.

The difficulty with the method of difference is the correlative of the difficulty with the method of agreement, namely, that we can never be sure that we have isolated the one respect in which a series of events or circumstances differ. In everyday experience and in the examples we cited we do not quibble about this. But if we were to follow the rules rigidly, we would be in difficulty, because we are never sure that we have the single respect in which the circumstances differ.

To summarize and at the same time state a very important point: the method of agreement is negative in its results. It seeks to eliminate conditions that are not sufficient and necessary. The second method, of difference, is positive in its results. It seeks to discover what cannot be eliminated and therefore is sufficient and necessary.

Obviously, the methods of agreement and difference, as Mill himself suggested, need to be used to supplement each other. This led to the proposal to use the following method, which is the third to be commended by Mill.

The joint method of agreement and difference   The joint method is a distinct method combining the assets of both of the first two but advancing the case of experimental inquiry because it is both negative and positive. Some logicians (for example, Werkmeister) hold that this method is not a *joint* method at all, but is simply "an extension of the method of agreement so as to include the observation of negative as well as positive instances." Whether it is a joint method or not, the crux of the matter is that it seeks to employ ways of isolating both the factor that the antecedent events had in common and the one respect in which they differ. To the extent that this can be done, it is clearly a superior method and one that can be used with great effect.

Consider a simple example: It is observed that soil of varying kinds and under different conditions of climate develops a vegetable mold. The mold is present when and only when earthworms are present. If the earthworms are absent there is no mold. The single factor common to the positive instances (the presence of mold) and in the negative instance (the absence of mold) is the presence or the absence of earthworms. It seems reasonable to conclude, then, that earthworms are the cause of mold, all other factors being equal. Take another example: The story is told of a lawyer who suffered from extreme fatigue at the end of his work day, fatigue far out of proportion to the work he was doing. Upon medical examination and finding nothing that was wrong with him, he was advised to consult a psychiatrist. Rather than toy with the idea that he might be neurotic or psychotic, the lawyer decided to experiment himself. He changed his diet, took more exercise, and got more sleep. But nothing did any good. Finally it occurred to him to stop smoking his pipe, which he regularly smoked for the greater part of the day and often inhaled. At the end of a month the fatigue symptoms had diminished to the point of disappearing. When, weeks later, he resumed smoking his pipe, the symptoms of fatigue soon returned. Conclusion? His pipe smoking was the principal cause of his fatigue. It was the one respect in which his normal phenomena and way of life differed.

The objection to this 'joint method,' is concealed in the phrase "all other things being equal." Another way of expressing the trouble is that in scientific study today we strive for the use of what are known as 'control groups'. The main point of control groups in science is to set up an experiment in such a way that one and only one factor is varied at a time. The control group and the experimental group differ (ideally) in a single relevant respect. For example, if we wish to demonstrate the relationship between fluoride and less tooth decay we would ideally try to give fluoride directly by means of pill to the experimental group and not to the control group. If the experimental group showed less tooth decay than the control group, a correlation between fluoride and less tooth decay would be established. However, this is the ideal, and it assumes that the two groups differ only in their consumption of fluoride. If diet and tooth brushing habits (obviously relevant consideration) were not the same, the conclusion about fluoride and less tooth decay would be considerably weakened.

The method of residue   The method of residue is quite a different way of conducting experimental inquiry, and it refers not to the circumstances and to the phenomenon, but to antecedents and consequents, that is, what goes before and what follows after. This is an interesting and extremely clever method. A favorite illustration of it is the case of weighing the contents of a truck or a vehicle when empty and then weighing it again when it is loaded. Clearly, the factors that are weighed on the scale are the same except for what has been put in the truck, because the antecedents are the truck and its cargo, not the driver. The residue of the phenomenon, the amount of difference in the scale indicates is the measure of the weight of the truck's contents. Consider two more examples that may be more interesting.

1. When Lt. Hornblower, in the famous British story, fired cannon shots from a frigate at sea, he was puzzled that they fell short of the enemy French ship. He took into consideration wind direction, the elevation of the cannon, and even the conditions of the weather. Finally it occurred to him that the one thing he had not allowed for was the motion of the ship itself. Taking this into consideration, and making the proper corrections, his shots hit their target. The residue, or that which was left over, was what accounted for the discrepancy.

2. A frequently cited example is the discovery of the planet Neptune in 1781. It was thought until that time that Uranus was the outermost planet of our solar system. Its orbit was calculated on the assumption that the motion it exhibited was determined only by the sun and the planets within the orbit of Uranus. But there was a discrepancy—a residue—amounting to two minutes of arc between the orbit plotted on the basis of these calculations and the actually-observed positions of Uranus. Finally, the astronomer Leferrier questioned whether this residue could not be accounted for by hypostatizing the existence of a hitherto unknown planet at some position in space *beyond* Uranus that was influencing its motion. When the position of this hypothetical planet was plotted, a new planet, which came to be named Neptune, was observed, and the difference was within one degree of the pre-dicted space. Clearly, the method of residue had again been dramati-cally employed.

The method of concomitant variation   Concomitant variation is a fascinat-ing and simple method. It is based on the assumption that two events or circumstances may vary in direct relationship, one to the other. Mill's state-ment of this method is sufficiently clear and brief to warrant quoting:

> Whatever phenomenon varies in any manner whenever another phenomenon varies in some particular manner is either a cause or an effect of that phenome-non, or is connected with it through some fact of causation.

Examples of concomitant variation are varied and intriguing. The following will be particularly instructive.

1. Mercury in a thermometer varies directly in its expansion with the heat in the surrounding medium and so it is inferred that the increased heat

causes the mercury to rise. The whole use of thermometers is based on this simple and clear principle.

2. The more tightly one draws the string on the violin or cello, the higher is the pitch when the string is played. So, the tightness of the string is considered the *cause* of the higher pitch. This every musician, amateur or professional, has observed, sometimes to his or her sorrow.

3. A farmer soon discovers that there is some causal relation between the application of manure to his ground and the quality of the crop that the ground yields. He notes that the quality of his crop was higher when the amount of manure used was higher. He concludes that the quality of his crop is directly proportional with the amount of manure used. The amount of manure was the cause of the quality of the crop. Presumably, whether he ever heard of Mill's Methods or not, he did not rush on to assume that an infinite amount of manure would produce a perfect crop.

In concomitant variation, the variation may be of various kinds: one may increase while the other decreases or vice-versa; they may go up together or down together. The method of concomitant variation is a new and important method but it has significance, as logicians have pointed out, beyond those that Mill imagined. One important lesson to learn is that the four preceding methods have all been qualitative, whereas this is the first method that measures quantity. In an age when we are concerned with measuring the quantity of everything from weight to education, this surely is a very important method to employ.

One criticism of the method of concomitant variation is that correlations are often misleading. They are not necessarily causal.

It might be pointed out, for example, that at the same time the consumption of beer increased at Egghead University more of its students received *D*'s and that this occurred three spring terms in a row. Should we conclude that there is a causal relation between beer consumption and the number of *D*'s recorded? Surely not on this evidence alone. Anthropologists produce a large number of observed correlations about primitive peoples that are mistakenly assumed to be causal. The social sciences abound in allegedly causal explanations that are based on questionable or misleading correlations.

Tape Exercises

Consider the following questions. [They are discussed on Tape 11, band 3.]

1. Is low economic status a cause of juvenile delinquency? Can a correlation be established between the two?

2. Is the reading by parents to their children and their encouragement to the children to read a cause of the children's superior performance in school? How could a cause-effect relation be shown?

In spite of the miscalculations and errors, nature abounds in examples of constantly observed concomitant variation: sun and sunburn, moon and tides, rain or drought and vegetation. What this should suggest is, not a hasty generalization, but scientific testing to demonstrate the presence or absence of causal relations. Finally, logicians have long appreciated the value of Mill's method of concomitant variation when negatively employed. That is, it is valuable in eliminating of irrelevant conditions. Thus, if antecedent event, A, *does* vary and so-called consequent event, E, *does not* vary, or vice versa, we may conclude that we are not dealing with a causal relation.

Tape Exercises

How would you evaluate the claim that there is a causal relation between the colors or the presence of quiet, background music in a factory and the amount of work produced? Is this causal? [Compare your answer with Tape 11, band 4.]

11.8   EVALUATION OF MILL'S METHOD

By way of summary we may say that 'Mill's Methods' should neither be overestimated nor underestimated. Surprisingly, even Mill with his brilliance and utter intellectual honesty made the former mistake; and some of his critics, and later logicians, made the latter. Thus, Mill claimed that they were methods of *discovering* cause and effect relations. He thought that these methods exhibited the heart of inductive reasoning, of observation followed by experiment. He further argued that they were demonstrative, that they afforded proof. Both of these judgments need to be carefully evaluated. For in many cases their scrupulous employment has not yielded discovery, and in a technical sense the *methods* do not yield discovery. Rather they may afford ways in which a 'discovery' can be tested. The last point leads to comments on Mill's second claim, concerning demonstration and proof. As philosophers often say, whether that was a sound judgment or not depends on what we mean by 'demonstration' and 'proof'. Clearly they do *not* yield what we have defined in the sections in deduction as 'proof' or 'demonstration,' as in mathematics or in syllogistic reasoning. They have not in fact, they cannot in principle. But we should be cautious: If we distinguish between strong and weak demonstration, we clearly can achieve weak demonstration. We no longer argue about cigarette smoking and lung cancer. The surgeon general's office bases its required statement in cigarette advertising on what it would call demonstration, or proof beyond-further-argument or law suit. The same could be said about the example, repeated in almost every logic text, about Pasteur's demonstration or 'proof,' against the ridicule of his critics, that his vaccine produced immunity from anthrax. And so on and on; what we learn is that a scientist generates a hypothesis and then tests it by methods of experimental inquiry. Properly understood, Mill's methods constitute brilliant, priceless ways of confirming or falsifying a hypothesis. And this is at the heart of the scientific method.

Tape Exercises

Because so many examples of causal explanation are taken from the physical sciences, we will examine cases of cause-effect in the social sciences, in this case history. The question is, what kind of explanation might best be employed, and how would we evaluate the most likely explanation? [We shall discuss this and the following on Tape 11, band 4.]

Pieter Geyl objects to the claim that Dutch prosperity can be explained by saying, for example, that "Holland achieved success because it was challenged by a harsh environment." Geyl exclaims: "Oh land wrung from the waves!" Every Dutch citizen has heard innumerable times the Dutch people's sterling qualities explained from their age-long struggle with the water. And nobody will contest that here is one factor in the building up of our special type of society. But Geyl insists that this is only one among many such factors. He continues:

> Within the Netherlands community the form peculiar to Holland (the Western seaboard province of which Toynbee is obviously thinking) cannot be regarded as original. If one looks a little more closely, one will observe that within the European and even within the Netherlands cultural area the rise of Holland was fairly late, and this no doubt as a result of these very conditions created by sea and rivers. If in the end it overcame these conditions, it was not without the assistance of the surrounding higher forms of civilization (even the Romans and their dyke-building had an important share in making the region habitable). But can even after that initial stage the continued struggle with the water be decisive in explaining the later prosperity and cultural fecundity of the country? Is it not indispensable to mention the excellence of the soil, once it had become possible to make use of it and above all the situation, which promoted the rise of shipping and of a large international commerce? Was the case of Holland then *wholly due* to hard conditions after all? Is it right to isolate that factor from among the multifarious complexity of reality and to suppress the favoring factors?[5]

Exercises for § 11.8

A. Which experimental methods may best be used in each of the following cases? For what specific purpose would the method be employed? [The shaded items are analyzed on Tape 11, band 4.]

1. Determination of the endurance of athletes performing at heights above sea level.

---

[5] Morton White, *Foundations of Historical Knowledge*, (New York: Harper & Row, 1965.), p. 112.

2. The effect of saying a specific prayer(s) a specified number of times on the cure of cancer.

3. The consumption of 1000 mg. of Vitamin C per day and the absence of the common cold.

4. The case of four in a party of twenty-five, who developed ptomaine poisoning after eating dinner at Immaculate Irene's Banquet Hall.

5. The study of the effect of high pitched sounds on the dogs in the Kennel Club.

6. The measurement of the amount of oil allegedly delivered by a one-ton truck to the local filling station.

7. The smoking of marijuana on tension.

8. The claim that the Women's Liberation is the cause of increasing divorce rate.

B. What conditions are sufficient and what conditions are necessary to result in each of the following?

1. A beautiful, healthy green lawn.

2. A prize-winning painting or piece of sculpture or music?

3. Sentient (beings capable of reason and speech) on the planet Mars or Neptune.

4. The success of the next Olympics games.

5. The holding of a successful Senior-Prom.

6. The maintenance of a happy marriage.

7. The discovery of the cause of cancer.

C. Analyze and evaluate each of the following as claims to being explanations.

1. Alexander Stephens claims that the cause of the Civil War was the violation by the North of the South's constitutional rights, the slavery issue was merely the occasion or at most a contributory cause.

2. The American Revolution was caused by the imposition of the Stamp Tax.

3. The Luthern Reformation was caused by Luther's posting of the Ninety-Five Theses on the Church door at Wittenberg.

4. All history is the history of human thoughts, according to R. G. Collingwood. He writes, "When a historian asks, 'Why did Brutus stab Caesar?' he means 'What did Brutus think, which made him decide to stab Caesar.' "(6)

D. Answer the following true-false questions, giving reasons, if necessary, for your answers:

1. It has been claimed by some philosophers of science that the distinctive aim of the scientific enterprise is to provide systematic and responsibly supported explanations.

2. Scientific reasoning is not merely inductive, but also involves deductive logic.

3. a. One type of explanation in science involves subsuming certain factual statements under general law statements.
   b. It is a deductive type of argument.

---

[6] R. G. Collingwood, *The Idea of History* (Oxford University Press, 1946), p. 214.

Chapter Outline

A. Science and Scientific Explanations
   1. Many argue that the distinctive aim of science is to provide systematic and responsibly supported explanations.
   2. Three kinds of explanations are used in the sciences.
      a. *Deductive-nomological explanation.* This explains a particular instance by subsuming it under a general law or laws. This explanation can be put into deductive form, and if the premises are true, they offer logically conclusive grounds for expecting the event to be explained.
      b. *Inductive-statistical explanation.* This involves the use of statistical law statements. It can be deductive, but it always is inductive in the case where a statistical generalization or generalizations are used to explain an individual event or case.
      c. *Teleological explanation* which explains by reference to some end, goal, purpose or motive. Many argue that these can be reduced to other kinds of explanation and they are considered not as "scientific" as the other kinds.
      d. *Genetic explanation.* This attempts to explain the present or later stages of something in terms of its development from original or earlier stages.
   3. Scientific explanation involves the concept of "law" and of "theory." The former has five characteristics (e.g. that they express regularities and that they are "true"); the latter refers to a systematically related set of statements.
B. Necessary and sufficient condition
   1. *Necessary condition:* If this is absent, the event will not occur (e.g., *malaria protozoa* is cause of maleria; if no protozoa present, no disease). If it is a necessary condition, you can legitimately infer cause from effect.
   2. *Sufficient condition:* in whose presence the event must occur (e.g., whenever a rock hits a glass with great force, under ordinary circumstances, the glass will shatter. However, to shatter glass, it is not necessary to hit it with a rock). If cause is a sufficient condition, we cannot infer cause from effect, but we can infer effect from cause. We are interested in sufficient condition when seeking to produce a desirable effect. Ideally seeking conjoining of necessary and sufficient condition: whenever these conditions are present, the effect occurs and in its absence, the effect does not occur.
C. Mills Methods: these are eliminative in intent, namely, to eliminate all but the causal factor.
   1. Agreement:
      a. Look for the one factor common to the cases exhibiting the effect.
      b. Assumption: At least one of the listed factors is a necessary causal condition for *E*.
      c. Fallible: If necessary condition not present. If more than one causal factor.
   2. Difference:
      a. Look for *a* the one instance or respect in which a set of circumstances differ.
      b. Assumption: One of the factor(s) is a sufficient condition.

    c. Assumption: A factor present in a case not exhibiting the effect cannot be a sufficient causal condition for the effect.

3. Joint Method of Difference and Agreement: Seek a factor common to cases exhibiting the effect but absent in cases lacking the effect.

4. Method of Residues: Eliminate as possible causes those antecedent circumstances whose effects have already been established.

5. Method of Concomitant Variation: Correlate degree of an effect with degree of some factor that accompanies the effect.

6. Evaluation of Mill's Methods:

    a. They are not strictly ways of discovering cause and effect relations.

    b. They do not afford proof. Mill thought they did both.

12

THE HYPO-DEDUCTIVE
METHOD OF REASONING

12.1 HYPOTHESIS FORMULATION AND
TESTING

Induction, as we have seen, is generalization from experience, a generalization that goes beyond the facts actually observed, except in those instances of 'perfect' induction where we have examined all the cases. Induction, then, except in these perfect and usually trivial cases (e.g., 'All the coins I have in my pocket are nickels') is always only probable. All our generalizations, descriptions, explanations are hypothetical. They are provisional suppositions or conjectures put forth to account for known facts, and they serve as starting points for further investigation by which they may be proved or disproved. We approach life and experience with tentative assumptions, expectations and anticipations. When these anticipations are fulfilled, we have at least partially verified them, but when not fulfilled, we usually discard them. If our expectations are continuously met and our assumptions continuously verified, we call our hypotheses 'laws'.

Hypotheses are data and problem oriented. There is some problem, 'mystery,' data to be accounted for (e.g., the car won't start). Further, our hypotheses must be capable of accounting for the problem; they must be relevant (e.g., the car is out of gas or the battery is dead). It will not do to say, 'the car is moody this morning and does not want to go anywhere.' However, our hypotheses are always relevant to and determined by knowledge and past experience, our interests and our prejudices. My hypothesis about the car would probably vary from that of a mechanic or a physicist and certainly from the innocent native's assumption that the 'car is moody'. 'That green muck in the pool' may mean something quite different to the owner of the pool, the caretaker of the pool, and a chemist, and each might offer a different explanatory hypothesis to deal with the situation.

Coming to grips with hypotheses formulation and testing is essentially to come to grips with a fundamental type of activity—problem solving and decision making—which involves us in both inductive and deductive reasoning. These are essentially the same process, but we may distinguish the two by limiting problem solving to science and decision making to those practical areas of life that involve some kind of value judgments. We shall discuss decision making in chapter 13.

Problem solving, or the method of hypothesis formulating and testing, has a schematic pattern that proceeds somewhat as follows.

1. Problem
2. Formulation of Relevant Tentative Hypothesis
3. Elaborating the Implications of these Hypotheses
4. Gathering of More Evidence and Testing of Hypotheses
5. Elimination and Refinement of Hypotheses
6. Confirmation and Solution of the Problem

The first step is to formulate and articulate the problem. This is not always as simple as it seems. All of us are familiar with people who go through life never seeing any problems. To recognize problems is an important ability whether it be in science, psychology, or daily life. The good detective, for example, is the person who smells 'a rat,' who knows something is not quite right. The good doctor is one who spots the symptom; the good teacher is one who spots a problem child or problem situation. One obvious requirement is alertness; another is familiarity with what should be—'a car should start; a car should start in a certain way.' A dead person is explainable only in so many ways; recall the classic case of the man discovered dead in a turkish bath of a dagger wound, yet no weapon was found. What exactly are the relevant facts and what are not?

A classical example of recognizing a problem is that described by Issac Newton in a paper to the Royal Society in 1672. According to Newton's account, he was toying with a prism and a circular beam of sunlight let in through a hole in a shutter when something peculiar caught his attention. The refraction of the beam of light through the prism had, *as expected,* cast a rainbow-hued spectrum of colored light on the far wall. What was peculiar was the *shape* of the spectrum. Newton describes his reaction as follows: ". . . I became surprised to see them in an *oblong* form which, according to the received laws of refraction, I expected should have been circular."[1]

---

[1] *Issac Newton's Papers and Letters on Natural Philosophy,* ed. by I. B. Cohen (Cambridge: Harvard University Press, 1958), p. 48.

The received Laws of Refraction that Newton referred to are the law of the rectinlinear propagation of light and Descartes' version of Snell's Law, namely that the rays of sunlight in the circular beam should be refracted equally by the prism and thus they should remain parallel to one another all the way to the wall. Assuming that this occurs, the image of the spectrum should have a shape geometrically similar to the shape of the hole admitting the light, namely, the shape of the spectrum on the wall should be circular rather than as it was, elongated. To explain this anomaly was the problem.

In attempting to deal with the problem, Newton undertook the second, third, and fourth stages in our hypothesis formulation and testing scheme. He formulated certain relevant and tentative hypotheses and certain implications these would have. Then he proceeded to test these hypotheses and then to eliminate some. Newton proposed Hypothesis one: that refracted light might have a non-rectilinear path (some rays on the edge of the beam might be induced to travel along a curved trajectory). He proceeded to test this hypothesis and discovered that rays drawn from opposite sides of the sun's disc would not diverge sufficiently far on refraction to produce the observed, elongated effect. He thus eliminated hypothesis one. He then tried another hypothesis—that the texture and homogeneity of the glass might have been defective thus causing the elongated effect. However, in testing out this supposition, Newton could detect no significant inhomogeneity in the glass. Newton also dealt with hypotheses concerning the position of the prism with respect to the hole through which the light beam passed, the apparent angular width of the sun's disc and the position of the prism with respect to the dark region inside the room and the sunny region outside. None of these factors, on experimentation, seemed the cause of the elongated shape.

Up to this point Newton's hypotheses fit squarely into the traditional theory of light then dominant in physics. As indicated earlier, what hypotheses we believe to be relevant to our problem depend on our background and knowledge. Richard Kuhn, in his book *The Structure of Scientific Revolutions*, has argued that the scientific community is very much influenced by background and interests in dealing with problems or anomalies in science. When a problem appears in science, the tendency is to formulate explanatory hypotheses in terms of the dominant theory, or paradigm, in the particular field of science. Thus, when Michelson and Morley could not find an ether drag, one explanation within the context of the dominant theory was the Lorentz Transformation Equations. A radical solution was that of Einstein—no ether drag! Scientists, like all people, tend to be bound to tradition and their own background and perspective and often with good reason—it has met the test of experience and time. However, time does move on and the ability to be imaginative and flexible is important. It is not likely that 'the car is moody,' but if all my possible, reasonable, hypotheses fail me, I may need to come up with a new one. New solutions to problems can be better than old ones and they often include advanced knowledge.

The ability to formulate the relevant and possible hypotheses is important. Maybe even more important is the ability to say, this would be explainable, if this *new* hypothesis were true. Turning back to our Newtonian example, after having eliminated a number of relevant hypotheses, Newton next decided to postulate a hypothesis that would require a modification or negation of a traditional law: for example, the Snell Law which says that rays of light are refracted equally. Newton hypothesized that light rays are refracted differently and he set up an experiment to test the hypothesis. In this experiment light rays were passed first through prism A onto screen I and then from screen I to screen II and then through prism B to the far wall. By rotating prism A slightly, light from different parts of the spectrum cast on screen II were supplied to prism B. The result was that the spot of light cast on the wall simultaneously changed color and moved up and down the wall *without* prism B being moved at all. The evidence produced by the experiment is unambiguous: Different portions of the beam emerging from Prism A are refracted differently at Prism B. Newton summarized his results as follows:

> And so the true cause of the length of the Image was detected to be no other than that *Light* consists of Rays differently refrangible, which without respect to a difference in their incidence, were, according to their degrees of refrangibility, transmitted toward diverse parts of the wall.[2]

To summarize briefly, then, inquiry begins with a problem, and what constitutes a "problem" will vary from place to place and from time to time. It will depend very much on context. In every day circumstances a problem is usually generated by some unpleasant circumstance—lack of money, illness, car breakdown, murder, theft. John Dewey went so far as to claim that every case of thinking occurs when a person's ongoing activity is blocked. In academic studies it is usually some unresolved question: Did Shakespeare or Marlowe write the plays? How is freedom to be adequately defined? What events lead to the Watergate scandal? In science, the "problem" almost always occurs within the context of a theory, either in seeking to expand and extend the theory or in dealing with certain data unaccounted for (e.g., measuring the speed of light, the molding of bread, the inability to find an ether drag). The data that cannot be accounted for by present theories become 'anomalies'.

Further, without hypotheses there could be no inquiry because they direct inquiry. They tell us where to begin and what to look for. Facts are not gathered indiscriminately but relative to a proposed solution to a problem. We do not answer the question about the car's failure to start by gathering data on baseball scores or the position of the moon. We are interested only in *relevant facts*. To rule out certain data as irrelevant is to *presuppose* a hypothesis as to what is relevant. As Charles Darwin put it, "observation must be for or against some view, if it is to be of any service."

---

[2] Cohen, *Newton's Papers*, p. 51.

Tape Exercises

A. The following is an account of the discovery of the cause of pellagra as set out in *Hunger Fighter* by Paul de Kriff. Analyze this account in terms of the six step schema of hypothesis formulation and testing outlined above, including both the discarded hypothesis and the confirmed one. Point out the problem or data to be explained, the hypothesis offered, the hypotheses eliminated, and the solution to the problem. [Turn to Tape 12, band 1, for analysis.]

In the second decade of the twentieth century a disease called "pellagra" had become epidemic in the southern states. The disease was also endemic (i.e., its occurrence was confined to some localities and did not occur in others). One village might be affected; a neighboring one not. Pellagra is characterized by gastric disturbances, skin eruptions, and nervous derangement. It was the opinion of the world of medicine that the disease was caused by an unknown microbe. The U.S. Public Health Service decided to send Dr. Joseph Goldberger to Mississippi to try to find a way of eliminating the disease.

In tackling his problem of the cause of pellagara, Goldberg observed the fact that the sufferers were always in contact with other victims. Since this is the consequence that would be expected if the disease were caused by microbes, he adopted the tentative hypothesis that the disease was caused in this manner. He then reasoned that if microbes were the cause, persons in close contact with the victims should catch the disease. But in the first hospital he visited, he found that the orderlies, nurses, and doctors who were in close contact with the victims never caught the disease. This led him to discard the hypothesis that the disease was caused by microbes. He now needed another hypothesis, so he continued his observations. He found that only the poor suffered from the disease. He also noted that the victims' diet consisted of corn-meal mush, hominy grits, and similar foods, but practically no milk or fresh meat. On one occasion, while visiting an orphanage, he found that only the children in the six to twelve age group had the disease. In investigating this further, he found that the children under six were given milk and the children over twelve were fed meat. The orphanagee's funds were limited, so they skimped on the food of the six to twelve year old group, who were too young to work (and so did not "deserve" meat) and who were beyond the "baby" stage, the stage when milk was regarded as essential. This fact suggested to Goldberger the hypothesis that a diet lacking in milk and fresh meat was the cause of the disease. He then reasoned out the consequences of this hypothesis, namely, that remedying these deficiencies in diet would cure the disease. He secured a sufficient amount of milk and fresh meat for the children at the orphanage. The result: All cases of pellagra disappeared. The cause of pellagara had been found.

B. Now consider the following passage from a 1916 paper of Albert Einstein, in which he reduces his problem to a metaphor involving a train and the observation of bolts of lightning striking at two different places. The lightning is detected by two observers, one on the moving train and one alongside the track. Mirrors help the observers to see both points. Einstein describes it as follows:

> If we say that the bolts of lightning are simultaneous with regard to the tracks, this now means: the rays of light coming from two equidistant points meet simultaneously at the mirrors of the man on the track. But if the place of my moving mirrors coincides with his mirrors at the moment the lightning strikes, the rays will not meet exactly simultaneously in my mirrors because of my movement. (Einstein is on a moving train.)
>
> Events which are simultaneous in relation to the track are not simultaneous in relation to the train, and vice versa. Each frame of reference, each system of coordinates therefore has its special time; a statement about a time has real meaning only when the frame of reference is stated, to which the assertion of time refers.
>
> Similarly, with the concept of simultaneity. The concept really exists for the physicist only when in a concrete case there is some possibility of deciding whether the concept is or is not applicable. Such a definition of simultaneity is required, therefore, as would provide a method of deciding. As long as this requirement is not fulfilled, I am deluding myself as a physicist (to be sure, as a non-physicist, too!) if I believe that the assertion of simultaneity has a real meaning. (Until you have truly agreed to this, dear reader, do not read any further.) "After some deliberation you may make the following proposal to prove whether the two shafts of lightning struck simultaneously. Put a set of two mirrors, at an angle of 90° to each other, at the exact halfway mark between the two light effects, station yourself in front of them, and observe whether or not the light effects strike the mirrors simultaneously.[3]

Exercises for § 12.1

A. Pinpoint the problem. [The shaded item is analyzed on Tape 12, band 1.]

1. Pick an interpersonal problem that you presently face. Write a concise statement of the problem as seen by each party involved. If possible, show the statements to the corresponding parties and see if they agree with your interpretation of their perception of the problem.

2. Suppose that you are in your late thirties, your children are well into school, your husband is establishing a name for himself in his profession, you are not employed, and you are bored. List at least three possible delineations of the problem and answers you might come up with in each case.

3. Suppose you are in your late twenties; you have served in the Vietnam War; you are in school and taking an Accounting Major, but somehow you

---

[3] Albert Einstein, 1916, quoted in Aaron Levenstein *Use Your Head* (New York: Macmillan, 1965) p. 164.

just do not feel satisfied. List at least three possible delineations of the problem and answers you might come up with in each case.

4. Consider the following two paragraphs. What problems, if any, are delineated? How might you set out the problem, and what possible answers might be proposed for its solution?

Society seems to be in an uproar. People are unhappy with their lives. Families are breaking down; violence is on the increase; people seem to feel that the world is cruel and headed for destruction. Karl Marx pointed out that people's social attitudes arise from their work lives. The main feature of contemporary work is the high degree of impersonalism.

If people are making a living doing jobs that are not creative, they may feel powerless to control their own existence. It's a dangerous situation because these feelings could lead to extreme political behavior, such as violence, or total submission to leaders with crazy political ideas.[4]

5. What problem is set out in the following? What solutions if any are offered?

Look around you at the upper and middle class neighborhoods. There are increased pranks, outright vicious vandalism and even petty things— tire marks on lawns, smoke-bombs at doors, wrecked mailboxes, broken windows and stolen lights, tools, toys. These things are not done by outsiders, but by bored kids who have everything but the time and love of their parents. There is no sense of property value or rights. There is nothing creative to do or else they are incapable of being creative.

6. How would you account for the following hypotheses that were once regarded as satisfactory? [Shaded item is analyzed on Tape 12, band 2.]
   a. The rise and fall of the Nile is due to the action of the sun.
   b. The earth is at the center of a series of spheres containing the planets and sun, which revolve around the earth, and a sphere of fixed stars.
   c. Light travels through the medium of ether.
   d. Spontaneous generation is responsible for the presence of macro-organisms.
   e. There are no vacuums in the world.
   f. Space is a container for all that is.
   g. Electricity is a man-made phenomenon caused by rubbing and friction.
   h. An arrow shot from the bow does not fall immediately to the ground because a flow of air between the bow and arrow give the arrow impetus.

B. For each of the following passages point out the six steps involved in hypothesis formulation and testing.[5]

---

[4] Kenneth B. Hoover, *The Elements of Social Scientific Thinking* (New York: St. Martin's Press, 1976), p. 13.

[5] Items 1–4 are from Alburey Castell, *A College Logic* (New York: Macmillan, 1938).

1. Benjamin Franklin, it will be remembered, became convinced that lightning is nothing more than electricity passing from one cloud to another. This hypothesis was suggested to him by a consideration of the many respects in which lightning resembled electricity. Lightning sets things on fire; so does electricity. Lightning melts metal, kills people, causes blindness; so does electricity. Lightning is attracted to pointed bodies, e.g., spires, trees, mountaintops; so is electricity. His famous experiment with the kite was designed to confirm a prediction based on the hypothesis suggested by these many analogies. If lightning is electricity it ought to be possible to get a spark from it and to charge a Leyden jar. So he sent a kite up during a storm. To the end of the kite string he tied a key. To the key he tied a silk ribbon by means of which he controlled the kite. When the string had been dampened by the rain, sparks were drawn from the key, and a Leyden jar was charged by being attached to the key. Franklin thus believed his hypothesis to be confirmed.

2. Columbus had arrived at the hypothesis that there was land to the west, long before he made his first voyage. This hypothesis accounted for a wide range of facts which were almost enigmatical on any other hypothesis. The earth was known to be spherical, and two-thirds of its surface had been explored. The remaining third lay between the west coast of Europe and the east coast of Asia. Many geographers, both ancient and modern claimed a westward passage to India was a genuine possibility. Columbus knew that a Portuguese navigator, sailing some 450 leagues west of Cape St. Vincent, had picked up a piece of carved wood which had not been worked with any metal instrument. As the wind had drifted it from the west, there was a chance that it came from land to the west. He knew, also, that reeds of an immense size had floated to the island of Porto Santo, from the west; and that those reeds were unlike any European flora. He knew, too, that a westerly wind had deposited on the shores of the Azores Islands trunks of huge pine trees of a kind that did not grow on those islands, and the bodies of two dead men whose faces differed from any known race of people. To these facts he was able to add the report of a mariner blown far westward while bound for Ireland, that he had sighted land away to the west which he had taken to be some extreme part of Tartary, i.e., Asia. Upon these facts, Columbus erected the hypothesis that there was land to the west, that it was attainable, that it was fertile, and that it was inhabited. His voyage confirmed the prediction.

3. In the south of England there are many large shallow ponds, on hilltops, known as "dew-ponds" because it is believed, locally, that they are replenished by dew. This local hypothesis is supported by the belief that a heavy layer of straw, placed under the basin of these ponds when they are being constructed, acts as a non-conductor of heat, thus keeping the basin cooler than the surrounding earth, thus causing dew to be deposited, since dew is only deposited on something which is cooler than the dew itself. In 1911 the Royal Geographical Society sent one of their Fellows to investigate these peculiar ponds. His analysis of the case is interesting and instructive logically, whatever it may be geographically. There were, he reasoned, only three sources from which the water could come, ignoring springs: dew, rain, or some hitherto unascertained source. (1)

The dew hypothesis he eliminated on three counts: The straw rots during the first winter and becomes useless as a non-conductor. The least likely place for a dew deposit would be the surface of the water in the pond, because in water the hottest part always rises to the top and forms the surface; and on a warm summer's night there is not sufficient time for this tepid surface water to fall below the dew point and it could, therefore, receive no dew. The investigator carefully checked the night temperatures of ground, air, and water, and found that the water surface remained the warmest. The maximum rate of dew-fall for all England is one and one-half inches per annum. That quantity would be required every night to compensate for what cattle drink from the pond each day. (2) The rain hypothesis was eliminated by the fact that 1911 was a dry year and practically no rain had fallen. (3) In spite of these facts, the ponds did not dry up. Upon what remaining hypothesis could this fact be accounted for? "It is not until one stays all night by one of these ponds that the explanation is found, namely, that the ponds are replenished by the early morning sea mists which roll up over the hills and saturate their tops." This hypothesis explains "why these self-filling ponds are not to be found in valleys, but only on hilltops," since the mists roll up the hills, never stopping in the valleys. If this hypothesis is true, he proceeded to argue, then the pond water should contain a slight amount of salt, since the sea mists are evaporated sea water and by mechanical action a slight amount of salt would be taken up with the moisture. He analyzed the pond water and found that it did, as a matter of fact, contain a slight amount of salt.

4. William James put forth the hypothesis that bodily changes follow directly the perception of the exciting fact and that our feeling of the same changes as they occur is the emotion—we feel sorry because we cry, we are angry because we strike, we are afraid because we tremble. To begin with, particular perceptions certainly do produce widespread bodily effects by a sort of immediate physical influence, antecedent to the arousal of an emotion or emotional idea. If we abruptly see a dark form in the woods, we catch our breath instantly and before any articulate idea of danger can arise. In listening to poetry, we are often surprised at the cutaneous shiver which like a sudden wave flows over us. In hearing music, the same is even more strikingly true. If the hypothesis that emotions follow internal bodily changes is true, argued James, then a person with pathological visceral disturbances (in whom the bodily changes are constantly taking place) should feel an emotion even though there is no external occasion for that emotion. He found such a patient in an asylum. The patient suffered pathological disturbances of the internal glands and would laugh or cry for no reason at all.

James then reasoned that if his hypothesis were true a person with an anesthetic viscera (i.e., one from which he could get no sensations due to destruction of sensory nerves) should feel no emotions. He found a war veteran whose sensory visceral nerves had been destroyed, and the man claimed that he never felt any emotions.

James further argued that if we fancy some strong emotion and then try to abstract from our consciousness of it all the feelings of its bodily symptoms, we find we have nothing left. If we imagine away every feeling of laughter and of tendency to laugh from our consciousness of the ludicrousness of an object, we cannot imagine that the object would be ludicrous anymore. If the theory is true, then any voluntary arousal of the so-called bodily manifestations of an emotion should give us the emotion itself. Within limits this is true. The faster you flee, the more is your fear increased. The more you sit in a moping posture, sigh, and reply to everything with a dismal voice, the more your melancholy lingers. However, James had a number of actors go through all the bodily motions connected with some specific emotion and asked them whether they felt the emotion—the reply was "no."

Sherrington, a physiologist, severed the spinal cord of a dog, thus preventing any sensations from the body from reaching the brain. He then brought a cat into the room, and the dog showed all the emotions associated with such an occasion.

Dr. Cannon introduced electrodes into the body of a cat which cause the same bodily changes to occur as occur in the case of an emotion. When he turned on the electric current and these bodily changes took place within the cat, the animal showed no emotion but continued to purr complacently.

Finally, the opponents of James' theory argued, if the emotions were merely caused by bodily changes, we should have no basis for distinguishing between fear and anger, for in both these cases the internal body changes are the same.

5. The birth of the concept of the existence of neutrinos is another interesting story. Their existence was predicted and their properties described in 1931, but they were not discovered (observed) for 25 years. The predicament was this: The alpha and gamma rays from a radioactive source were found to be either monoenergetic or to fall in a few groups, each of which is monoenergetic; but not so with beta rays, their energies from a given source varied continuously over a wide range. This did not fit the quantum concept of energy emission from a nucleus made up of discreet energy levels. Furthermore, when a neutron changes into a proton and a beta particle (electron) there is a mass loss which must show up as energy, in this case 750,000 electron volts of energy. This should show up as kinetic energy of the products, but the electron and proton rarely have this much energy. If the law of conservation of energy is not violated, how can the energy difference be explained? W. Pauli suggested that a particle as yet undiscovered was emitted at the same time as the beta particle. This new particle carried energy away and it was the energy of the beta particle plus the energy of this new particle that was being measured in the beta ray energy. Thus it was assumed that the beta rays like the alpha rays and gamma rays, were monoenergetic or into several groups, each of which was monoenergetic. Thus we write equations to include the neutrino:

$$n \rightarrow + p + \beta + \text{neutrino}$$
$$\text{neutrino} + = \beta + n \rightarrow + p$$

Because of the mass and charge balance in n, p, and ∞, the neutrino must have zero charge and practically no mass (and, for reasons not explained due to space limitations, the neutrinos must have ½ a quantum unit of spin and obey Fermi statistics). Pauli describes his reasoning about the assumption of the existence of neutrinos as follows:

The difficulty arising from the existence of the continuous ∞ ray spectrum resides, as one knows, in the fact that average life of the nuclei which emit these rays, as well as that of the nuclei of the resulting radioactive materials have very specific values. One necessarily concludes from this that the state, as well as the energy and the mass of the nucleus left after ∞ particle explusion are also very specific or well defined. I shall not elaborate on the efforts that one might make to escape this conclusion, but I believe, in agreement with the opinion of Mr. Bohr, that one will always be confronted with unsurmountable difficulties in the explaining of the experimental facts.

Along this line of thinking, two interpretations of the experiments present themselves. That which is advocated by N. Bohr admits that the laws governing energy conservation and impulsion are inadequate for the case of a nuclear process in which light particles play an essential role. This hypothesis does not look satisfactory, nor even plausible to me. In the first place, the electric charge is conserved in the process, and I do not see why the charge conservation should be more fundamental than energy and impulsion conservations. Moreover it is very specifically energetic relations which dominate several characteristic properties of beta spectra existence of an upper limit and relation to gamma spectra, Heisenberg's stability criterion —If the conservation laws were not valid, one would be forced to deduce from these relations that a beta disintegration is always accompanied by a loss of energy, but never by a gain; this conclusion implies irreversibility of the processes with respect to time, which does not seem very acceptable to me.

In June 1931, in a seminar discussion at Pasadena, I put forward the following interpretation: the conservation laws remain valid, and the emission of beta particles is accompanied by a very penetrating radiation of neutral particles which have not yet been actually observed. The sum of the energies of the beta particles and the neutral particle (or neutral particles, since one does not know whether there is only one or else several) emitted by the nucleus in a single process will be equal to the energy corresponding to the upper limit of the beta spectrum. It goes without saying that we do not only accept energy conservation, but also the conservation of impulsion, of angular impulsion and of the statistic character in all elementary processes.

As to the properties of these neutral particles, the atomic masses of the radioactive elements teach us, to begin with, that their mass cannot greatly exceed that of the electron. In order to distinguish them from the heavy neutrons, Fermi has offered the term 'neutrino'. It is possible that the real mass of the neutrinos be equal to zero, as a consequence of which they should travel at the speed of light, like photons. However, their penetrating power would greatly exceed that of photons of equal energy. It seem quite acceptable to me that the neutrinos should have a half spin, and that they should respect Fermi's statistic, in spite of the fact that the actual experiments do not give us direct proof of this hypothesis. We know nothing about the interaction of neutrinos with other material particles or with photons: the hypothesis that I once advanced that they have a magnetic moment (Dirac's theory leads to the acceptance of the possible existence of magnetic neutral particles) no longer appears well founded to me.

In this order of ideas, an experimental investigation of the impulsion balance (net charge, mass, energy) in the beta disintegrations represents a problem of paramount importance; one can foresee that the difficulties will be very great because the recoiling nucleus will have very little energy.

Following Pauli's assumption of the existence of neutrinos, Fermi worked out a theory of beta particle emission making use of Pauli's assumption of neutrinos; Fermi named this "little bit of nothingness" *neutrino* meaning "little neutral one" to distinguish it from the neutron which also had no charge but is much heavier. It was not until 1955 that a group of scientists from the Los Alamos Laboratory, working at the Hanford, Washington, Atomic Energy Plant, obtained the first positive observation of a neutrino. In 1962 a group of scientists used a high energy neutrino beam and obtained evidence for the twin of the neutrino—the antineutrino. This is a kind of indirect-direct evidence of the existence of neutrinos.[6]

12.2   ELABORATING AND CONFIRMING HYPOTHESES:

A case history as an example   In order to make perfectly clear the hypothesis schema, let us take another case history, one cited by Carl Hempel in *The Philosophy of Natural Science,* (Prentice Hall, 1970). This will help us to spell out other aspects of this method of reasoning.

Ignaz Semmelweis, a physician of Hungarian birth, was head of the medical staff of the Vienna General Hospital from 1844–1846. He was concerned with a particular problem: that a larger proportion of women delivered of their babies in the First Section of the Maternity Ward died of childbed fever than those delivered in the Second Section. How was one to account for this much higher death rate (e.g., 11.45 percent compared with 2.7 percent)? This then was his problem. The next step was to find some answers. First of all, Semmelweis *ruled out some hypotheses as incompatible with well-established facts.* One such hypothesis was that childbed fever was caused by atmospheric changes. But surely all of Vienna would be affected and not just the women of the First Division Maternity Ward. Second, Semmelweis, like Newton, tested out a group of hypotheses to no avail. He tested hypotheses such as that delivery of women lying on their backs rather than on their side was the cause, or that examination by interns was too rough. The decisive clue for the solution to

---

[6] W. Pauli, "Birth of the Concept of that Neutrinos Must Exist," in *That Flash of Genius*, by Alfred P. Garrett; (New York: D. Van Nostrand Company, 1963) pp. 204–07.

Semmelweis' problem was finally given by the occurrence of an accident. A colleague of his, Kolletschka, received a puncture wound in the finger from the scalpel of a student with whom he was performing an autopsy, and died of an illness strikingly similar to childbed fever. Semmelweis hypothesized that cadaveric matter from the student's scalpel had entered Kolletschka's blood stream and caused the fatal illness. Further, he concluded that he, his colleagues and the medical students had been the carriers of infectious material to the women in the First Division, because they used to come to the wards directly from performing dissections in the autopsy room and examined the women in labor after only superficially washing their hands.

Semmelweis' hypothesis then was: childbed fever was caused by the infectious material adhering to the hands. He put his idea to test. Thus, by drawing out an implication of his hypothesis: If childbed fever was caused by infectious material adhering to the hands, then childbed fever could be prevented by chemically destroying the infectious matter adhering to the hands. He issued an order requiring all doctors and students to wash their hands in a solution of chlorinated lime before making examinations. The mortality from childbed fever promptly began to decrease.

His hypothesis found further support because it could account for other facts. (1) The mortality rate in the Second Division was lower because they were attended by midwives who had nothing to do with autopsies. (2) The mortality rates were lower for women who arrived with babies in arm. They were rarely examined. (3) Victims of childbed fever among newborn babies were those of mothers who had contracted the disease during labor, when the infection could be transmitted to the baby through the common bloodstream of mother and baby.

Considering this test case we see that confirmation and disconfirmation of hypotheses takes the following forms:

If H is true, then so is I.
But, (as evidence shows) I is not true.
H is not true.

For example:

If delivery on back causes childbed fever, then delivery on the side will reduce the mortality rate.
Delivery on the side did not reduce the mortality rate.

∴ The hypothesis is not true.

If H is true, then so is I.
(As the evidence shows) I is true.
H is true.

For example:

> If childbed fever is blood poisoning caused by cadaveric matter, then
>   suitable antiseptic measures will reduce fatalities from the disease.
> Suitable antiseptic measures did reduce fatalities from the disease.
> _____
> ∴ The hypothesis is true.

In considering these two forms, it should be noted that the first form, the
case of disproof of a hypothesis, is an argument *Modus Tollens,* and as noted in
the section on truth-functional statement logic, *deductively valid.* If the premises are true, the hypothesis must indeed be rejected. To see again that this
form is valid, let us take a more everyday example of it as follows:

> If it is true that Mary is three months pregnant, then the doctor should be
>   able to detect a heart beat or note other effects of the baby's presence.
> The doctor cannot detect a heart beat or any effects of the baby's presence.
> _____
> Therefore, Mary is not pregnant.

We can also see that this argument is valid by recalling the discussion of
necessary and sufficient conditions in chapter 9 and noting that in the conditional the antecedent is a sufficient condition for the consequent and the
consequent is a necessary condition for the antecedent. The nature of necessary condition is—if it is absent, if it is not true, then the effect is not present or
true. Thus, if the consequent is false, then p, the antecedent must be false.
And, this is precisely what the argument form *Modus Tollens* says.

Turning to the mode of reasoning used in confirming a hypothesis, we find it
is a form of the *fallacy of affirming the consequent.* It is an invalid argument
form. There is, then, no guarantee that if the premises are true, the conclusion
must be true.

Once again we can see that the form of confirming the consequent is invalid
by a simple example.

> If it rains, the picnic will be cancelled.
> The picnic was cancelled.
> _____
> Therefore it rained.

It should be obvious that the picnic could be cancelled for other reasons
(illness, death, etc.), and thus the fact that it was cancelled does not prove that
it rained. Further, the antecedent, p, is only a sufficient condition. When a
sufficient condition is present, the effect will come about—if it had rained, then
the picnic would have been cancelled. However, other conditions can be
sufficient to produce the same effect—a rock, bat, shoe can shatter a
window—and thus from a shattered window, you cannot conclude with confidence to a rock as the cause.

Indeed, as it later turned out, Semmelweis' hypothesis was discovered not to be true, for it was found that putrid matter from living organisms could also produce childbed fever. Further, even if a hypothesis is confirmed by further test implications, there is no guarantee of the truth of the hypothesis, for the following is still a form of the *fallacy of affirming the consequent:*

If H is true, then so are I_1, I_2, . . .I_n.
(As the evidence shows) I_1, I_2 . . . I_n are all true.

$\therefore H$ is true.

Favorable outcome does not provide conclusive proof of a hypothesis. Confirmation is always only a matter of degree and never conclusive.

This point can be made even clearer if we note that most hypotheses, as generalizations, are cast in universal form. Either it is a primary generalization, 'A is always B,' or a statistical generalization, 'A certain percentage of A is always B,' or a functional generalization, 'A always varies with B,' or a causal generalization, 'A causes B'. If we have studied categorical logic we know, by the Square of Opposition, that the contradictory of an **A** or universal statement is an **O** statement, '*At least one A* is not a B.' We also know that if the **I** statement, 'At least one to many many A's are B's' is true, we do not necessarily know that the universal 'All A's are a B' is true. Logically and practically, if many, many, many, many ravens are observed to be black, we do not know either with certainty or with logical deductive certainty that 'All ravens are black'. All observed ravens have been black, and that is an awful lot of ravens, but still, there may be one that is not black. But then, of course, we might say "It isn't really a raven; it is a 'rattaca'." It has all of the characteristics of a raven, except one—it is not black! Ok, but is it okay? Have we been arbitrary in our search for certainty? All ravens are black, except we have found one or some who are not, but 'Oh, they are not really ravens'. Are we merely repeating the old song 'All swans are white—where did those black ones come from?' Our point is two-fold: (1) All ravens are black is a fairly substantial generalization (hypothesis). It may have exceptions, but to recognize exceptions is not to say it amounts to nothing—nearly all ravens *are* black. (2) We must never be overconfident about our laws or generalizations. Knowledge is an ever-growing thing, and continual openness to the evidence is the important thing. Sir Karl Popper, an eminent philosopher of science and a man who has been continually concerned about scientific spirit seeks falsification rather than confirmation because the former spirit is more critical and open to truth. There is some wisdom to this stance—it may be easy to confirm, especially if we twist things a bit, but to falsify might be more honest, more daring and more illuminating!

Another point about confirming hypotheses is the elaboration and confirmation of hypotheses often involves the use of auxiliary hypotheses. Thus, for example, Semmelweis assumes that chlorinated lime solution will destroy the disease-carrying matter. Thus, a more accurate schematic representation of confirmation is:

If H and A *(B, C, D)* then I.
I
————————————————————————
Then probably H and A *(B, C, D)*.

The involvement of auxiliary hypotheses is especially important in disconfirmation.

If H and A *(B, C, D)*, then I.
$-I$
————————————————————————
So not necessarily H or A or etc.

When disconfirmation occurs, it can be the auxiliary hypotheses that is at fault and not the main hypothesis. Further, it is not always easy to know which are at fault—especially if they are closely interrelated in a theoretic framework. For example, Foucault thought he had necessarily disconfirmed Newton's claim that light is a particle when he deduced from Newton's theory the test implication that light would travel faster in water than in air and then found this implication to be false. But what Foucault had refuted was only a whole body of assumptions necessary to deduce the statement that light travels faster in water than in air. Subsequent research revised the corpuscular theory of Newton by altering some of the auxiliary assumptions, and today the nature of light remains an unresolved dilemma of modern physics.

Another important point to discuss relative to hypotheses is the role that alternative hypotheses can play at a certain point in an investigation. Alternative hypotheses are two hypotheses that can explain the data equally well, and that seem to be equal in other ways such as simplicity. A classical case of alternative hypotheses, indeed of alternative theories, was the case of two contending theories of light in the 19th century—Huygens Wave Theory of Light and Newton's Corpuscular Theory. Both could account equally well for the known behavior of light and for refraction and reflection. How then do we decide? The answer is to perform a *decisive test*, a *crucial experiment* to try to prove one wrong. In the case of the theories of light, it was found that from Newton's theory we could deduce that light would travel faster in water than air and from Huygens theory we could deduce that light would travel faster in air than in water. Foucault set up an experiment whereby he determined that light does travel faster in air than in water and thus concluded that Huygens' theory was right and Newton's was wrong. However, as indicated above, a number of auxiliary hypotheses can accompany the main hypothesis in the following pattern.

If H, and A, B, C, D, etc., then I

$\sim I$

$\overline{}$

So not necessarily H or A or B or C or D

It may be one of the auxiliary hypotheses that are wrong and not the main hypothesis at all. Thus, Newton's theory was not by any means decisively refuted. Rather, one or more of his auxiliary hypotheses may have been wrong. It is, however, important to deal with alternative hypotheses and to try to eliminate one of them. Suppose, for example, in dealing with a plane crash, you have determined that it was caused by high explosives in the baggage compartment. However, in sorting out the question of who was responsible, you have centered on two possibilities, a Jack Brown whose mother was killed in the crash and whose luggage was overweight and Tony Caraza, an airline employee who was angry at the airline and had access to the baggage on the flight. Your two rival or alternative hypotheses are: 'The explosion was caused by dynamite placed in the baggage of Ruby Brown by her son, Jack,' and 'The explosion was caused by dynamite slipped into one of the pieces of baggage by Tony Caraza.' Both these hypotheses cannot be true, and you must go on to confirm or disconfirm one or the other. The obvious step is to seek to collect further evidence to see if one or the other of these hypotheses can be eliminated. And in this process you also are refining and building evidence so that if finally one of the alternative hypotheses is eliminated, the other gains in strength.

There are also obvious rules or criteria by which to judge hypotheses. These rules are no guarantee of the truth of a hypothesis, but they do give us guidance to distinguish good, probably true hypotheses from bad probably false ones.

1. A hypothesis, if about the events of the world about us, should be *physically testable*. Suggested explanations of natural events that go counter to the laws of nature or disregard the fundamental character of material bodies in space and time are hardly useful. For example, childbed fever was caused by evil spirits.

2. A hypothesis *should not be contrary to already available evidence*, for example, that atmospheric changes caused childbed fever.

3. A hypothesis should be so conceived that it entails consequences that can be *tested*; it must be capable of confirmation or falsification.

4. A hypothesis *should be simple and clear*. This does not mean "easy to understand," but rather "involving a minimum of presuppositions or extraneous additions." It should be workable and systematically coherent, drawing together the facts in a clear-cut pattern.

5. A hypothesis should be backed by *quantity, variety and precision of evidence*. Is it substantiated by clear-cut, relevant, and varied evidence

or merely asserted to be the case? Is there any evidence that is negative or tends to disconfirm the hypotheses?

Exercises for § 12.2

A. Which of the following statements do you regard as easiest to verify, and why? How would you go about verifying them? Why are the others difficult to verify? [Shaded items are analyzed on Tape 12, band 3.]

1. The melting point of copper is 1083°C.
2. Caesar conquered Britain in 55 B.C.
3. Honesty is the best policy.
4. Heat expands bodies.
5. There are 65 students in this class.
6. John F. Kennedy was assassinated in 1960.
7. Magic performed the function of upholding optimism in primitive societies.
8. All male human beings suffer from an Oedipus Complex.
9. This magnet will attract this iron nail.
10. Our galaxy is expanding.
11. Love makes the world go round.
12. This substance is radioactive.

B. Discuss the following hypotheses. What facts can you enumerate which converge on or are accounted for by each of these hypotheses? Can you point to any diverging facts which might count against these hypotheses? [The shaded items are discussed on the tape.]

1. The theory of evolution that holds that during countless ages of development, all forms of life originated by descent through gradual or abrupt modifications from earlier forms which trace back to the most rudimentary organisms.
2. That the sun is the center of the solar system.
3. That Edward de Vere, Earl of Oxford, wrote all or some of the plays usually attributed to Shakespeare.
4. That geological changes were gradual transformations, not sudden 'catastrophic' changes.
5. That the fall of the Roman Empire was due to its increased immorality.
6. That Adolph Hitler is really dead.
7. That light waves bend as they pass through the gravitational field of the sun.
8. That there is an unconscious portion of the human mind.
9. That the Pentateuch, the first five books of the Old Testament, were not all written by a single author.

10. That the United States Constitution was framed by a group of economic interests which stood to benefit by its adoption. (Proposed by American historian, Charles Austin Beard.)

C. Analyze the following passages by pointing out the problem or data, the hypotheses offered to explain the data and converging or diverging evidence. Using the five criteria for a good hypothesis, determine how 'good' each of the hypotheses is. [The shaded item is analyzed on Tape 12, band 4.]

1. Excerpts from Pasteur's *Memoirs*.

In the historical part of this Memoir I have already referred to the influence, on the subject with which we are concerned, of Gay-Lussac's celebrated investigation of the air in Appert's preserves, and of the illustrious natural philosopher's interpretation of his experiments. Here are his own words:

"By analyzing the air in bottles in which substances have been well preserved, one can convince oneself that it contains no oxygen and, consequently, that the absence of this gas is a necessary condition for the preservation of animal and vegetable substances."

There can be no doubt that the air from the preserves studied by Gay-Lussac was free of oxygen. However, today it cannot be doubted—even though no one has (as far as I know) repeated exactly these experiments of Gay-Lussac's—that Appert's preserves can contain oxygen, especially when they are newly prepared. From the analyses of air that I have reported elsewhere in this Memoir, it follows that the oxygen of air made inactive by heat, by Schwann's method, combines directly with organic materials, producing carbonic acid [carbon dioxide]. This is a very slow action. Nevertheless, direct oxidation exists: it cannot be denied. This oxidation may be more evident in Appert's preserves when they are being prepared, because of the elevated temperature. In all cases, if the preparation leaves any oxygen in the preserves, this gas will disappear little by little because of the direct oxidation of which I have just spoken. There is a circumstance which must do much to minimize or to reduce to zero the quantity of oxygen remaining in Appert's preserves: this circumstance is the ratio of the volume of air to the volume of organic matter. The preserves always contain very little air and a great deal of organic matter—a circumstance very favorable to the completion of the oxidative process [that is, to the complete exhaustion of the small amount of oxygen available in the container]. But, I repeat, nothing would be easier than the preparation of preserves in which oxygen remained, and there is room to believe that they often contain oxygen. Schwann's experiment leaves no doubt on this point.

This is why Gay-Lussac's interpretation of his analyses—namely, *that the absence of oxygen is requisite for preservation* [of organic materials]—is totally erroneous. Dr. Schwann should justly be regarded as the author of the true theory of Appert's procedures. Appert's preserves remain unspoiled in the presence of heated air: that is his discovery. The secret of their preservation is thus to be found not in the absence of oxygen, but in the destruction by heat of a principle contained in ordinary air.

2. Excerpt from Pasteur's Memoirs.

. . . the partisans of the doctrines of spontaneous generation hasten on to a quite reasonable deduction. If the smallest quantity of ordinary air suffices for the production of organisms in any medium whatsoever, and if these organisms do not originate spontaneously, then it follows necessarily that in this indefinitely small portion of common air there must be the terms of a multitude of different organisms. Finally, if things are thus, then ordinary air must, to use M. Pouchet's expressions, be clogged with organic matter, forming a dense fog.

But, here then is a serious and apparently well-founded difficulty. . . . Is it true, as has been supposed, that there is in the earth's atmosphere a continuity of cause of the generations said to be spontaneous? *Is it certain that the smallest quantity of ordinary air is sufficient to produce organized life in all infusions?* [The translator has italicized Pasteur's statement of the central issue.]

The following experiments answer all these questions.

In a series of flasks of 250-cubic-centimeter capacity I place the same putrescible liquid (yeast water; the same with sugar; urine, etc.), the liquid occupying about a third of the total volume. I taper the necks of the flasks with a glassblowers' lamp, I boil the liquid, and I seal off the tapered ends while the boiling is going on. A vacuum is thus formed in the flasks [since the steam has driven out all the air]. Then I break off the sealed tips of the flasks in a specified location. Ordinary air rushes in violently, carrying with it all the dusts that it holds in suspension and all the known or unknown principles associated with it. Then, barely touching them with a flame, I immediately reseal the flasks, and I place them in an incubator at 25° or 30°—that is to say, at the most favorable temperature for the development of animalcules and Mucors.

Here are the results of these experiments, results inconsistent with the principles generally accepted and, on the contrary, in perfect agreement with the idea of a dissemination of germs.

Generally the liquid changes after a very few days, and a great variety of organisms can be seen growing in the flasks. . . . But, on the other hand, it happens frequently (several times in each series of trials) that the liquid remains absolutely unchanged, however long it is left in the incubator, just as if calcined air had been admitted. . . .[7]

3. Again, from Pasteur's *Memoirs*

We have now to test one of the principal foundations of the doctrine of spontaneous generation as formulated in this country. With this view, I place before my friend and co-inquirer two liquids which have been kept for six months in one of our sealed chambers, exposed to optically pure air. The one is a mineral solution containing in proper proportions all the substances which enter into the composition of bacteria, the other is an infusion of

---

[7] From *The Memoirs* of Louis Pasteur. *Harvard Case Studies in Experimental Science*, vol. 2., Trans. James B. Conant (Cambridge, Mass.: Harvard University Press, 1966), pp. 514–16. Reprinted by permission of Harvard University Press. Copyright © 1953 by the President and Fellows of Harvard College.

turnip—it might be any one of a hundred other infusions, animal or vegetable. Both liquids are as clear as distilled water, and there is no trace of life in either of them. They are, in fact, completely sterilized. A mutton-chop, over which a little water has been poured to keep its juices from drying up, has lain for three days upon a plate in our warm room. It smells offensively. Placing a drop of the fetid mutton-juice under a microscope, it is found swarming with the bacteria of putrefaction. With a speck of the swarming liquid I inoculate the clear mineral solution and the clear turnip infusion, as a surgeon might inoculate an infant with vaccine lymph. In four-and-twenty hours the transparent liquids have become turbid throughout, and instead of being barren as at first, they are teeming with life. The experiment may be repeated a thousand times with the same invariable result. To the naked eye the liquids at the beginning were alike, being both equally muddy. Instead of putrid mutton-juice, we might take as a source of infection any one of a hundred other putrid liquids, animal or vegetable. So long as the liquid contains living bacteria, a speck of it communicated either to the clear mineral solution, or to the clear turnip infusion, produces twenty-four hours the effect here described . . .

We now vary the experiment thus:—Opening the back-door of another closed chamber which has contained for months the pure mineral solution and the pure turnip infusion side by side, I drop into each of them a small pinch of laboratory dust. The effect here is tardier than when the speck of putrid liquid was employed. In three days, however, after its infection with the dust, the turnip infusion is muddy, and swarming as before with bacteria. But what about the mineral solution which, in our first experiment, behaved in a manner undistinguishable from the turnip juice? At the end of three days there is not a bacterium to be found in it. At the end of three weeks it is equally innocent of bacterial life. We may repeat the experiment with the solution and the infusion a hundred times with the same invariable result. Always in the case of the latter the sowing of the atmospheric dust yields a crop of bacteria—never in the former does the dry germinal matter kindle into active life. What is the inference which the reflecting mind must draw from this experiment? Is it not as clear as day that while both liquids are able to feed the bacteria and to enable them to increase and multiply, *after they have been once fully developed,* only one of the liquids is able to develop into active bacteria the germinal dust of the air?

I invite my friend to reflect upon this conclusion; he will, I think, see that there is no escape from it. He may, if he prefers, hold the opinion, which I consider erroneous, that bacteria exist in the air, not as germs but as desiccated organisms. The inference remains, that while the one liquid is able to force the passage from the inactive to the active state, the other is not.

4. Again from Pasteur:

I would ask my eminent colleague what he thinks of this reasoning now? The *datum* is—'A mineral solution exposed to common air does not develop bacteria'; the inference is—'Therefore if a turnip infusion similarly exposed develop bacteria, they must be spontaneously generated.' The inference, on the face of it, is an unwarranted one. But while as matter of logic it is inconclusive, as matter of fact it is chimerical. London air is as surely charged with the germs of bacteria as London chimneys are with smoke. The inference just referred to is completely disposed of by the simple question: Why, when your sterilized organic infusion is exposed to optically pure air, should this generation of life *de novo* utterly cease? Why should I be able to preserve my turnip-juice side by side with your saline solution for the three hundred and sixty-five days of the year, in free connection with the general atmosphere, on the sole condition that the portion of that atmosphere in contact with the juice shall be visibly free from floating dust, while three days' exposure to that dust fills it with bacteria? Am I over-sanguine in hoping that as regards the argument here set forth he who runs may read, and he who reads may understand?[8]

5. Alexander Fleming had long been looking for something that would kill germs without killing white blood cells. In the summer of 1928 a lucky accident set him on his way. He had been cultivating dishes of staphylococci and one cover had accidently been opened thus contaminating the plate, for a speck of mold white and fluffy with a speck of green in the center was growing right on top of a colony of staphylococci. Other scientists would have thrown the contaminated plate away, but Fleming was puzzled by an interesting fact.

Away from the mold, the staphylococci were still growing luxuriantly in moist, buttery little mounds. But around the mold there was a clear zone—*a zone in which the staphylococci were obviously being dissolved!*

Fleming decided to look into this mold. Picking up a platinum wire, he sterilized it in a burner flame, let it cool, deftly touched it to the mold, and transplanted a bit of this to a fresh tube of microbe food. Then, for weeks, he grew and studied it; he transplanted it again and again, sometimes to other tubes and sometimes to bottles of broth.

"In broth," he wrote, "it grows on the surface as a white, fluffy growth; in a few days this becomes a dark-green, felted mass. In a few weeks the broth becomes bright yellow."

Could this yellow color (whatever it was) be the stuff that dissolved the staphylococci? Soon Fleming found that the yellow matter had nothing to do with germ killing.

Mixed with the yellow stuff was something else, a second substance that was also secreted by the mold and that also soaked all through the broth. Fleming poured off some of this broth, mixed it with colonies of staphylococci, and found that it stopped their growth. He tried it on streptococci—and it stopped them, too. It destroyed the microbes of pneumonia, diphtheria, meningitis, and gonorrhea. Against other germs— the microbes of cholera, dysentery, and typhoid—this "mold juice," as Fleming called it, was useless. It was not a complete germ killer. When it did work, however, its power was astounding; even when the mold juice was diluted as much as eight hundred times, it could still destroy microbes. This juice, he calculated, was three times stronger than carbolic acid!

And then the thought, "Anything that strong will be murder to animals or human beings. It will wreck their tissues!"

---

[8] *Harvard Case Studies*, pp. 532–34.

He tried it. He put the mold juice through his test with white blood cells, and found that the white blood cells were unharmed. He injected more than half an ounce of the undiluted juice into a rabbit. The rabbit scarcely batted an eye.

Now Fleming concluded that what he had was a new, mysterious chemical which was sheer murder to microbes but virtually harmless to healthy tissues. After identifying the mold as a member of the Penicillium family, he called the potent but still elusive microbe killer, penicillin.[9]

6. What are the effects of levamisole—a drug used for deworming on immune responses, and what are the possibilities of its use for immunotherapy of cancer? Two main points are known about the mechanism of levamisole. First, it does boost cellular immunity. And second, it has this boosting effect only when all mediated immunity is depressed. It may then restore it to normal but never higher.

Big question—whether its capacity to restore cellular immunity will pay off in therapeutic benefits for patients. According to Alexandro Royas of Angelo H. Roffo Institute de Oncolopia in Argentina, Levamisole therapy increased the survival rates of the patients he had studied for a maximum of time of 39 months and prolonged the time when the patients were free of tumors following radiation therapy. J. M. Debois in Belgium found some improvement in the clinical course of breast cancer treated with levamisole.

On the other hand, J. Leonard Lichtenfeld of Baltimore Carees Research Center and Lashav Hirshauf of Memorial Sloan-Kettering Cancer Clinic could show no effects whatsoever of levamisole on the clinical benefit of cancer patients.[10]

D. Analyze in detail the following discussion by Fred L. Whipple on the different hypotheses about the origin of the solar system. What are these hypotheses? What evidence for and against these hypotheses is offered?

A satisfactory hypothesis for the origin of the solar system must first account for the existence of the planets, satellites and asteroids. It must then explain how they were set moving in the remarkable manner already noted, and must provide the system theoretically with the observed amount of angular momentum. Two types of hypotheses have been suggested. In the first type, the system condensed from a gigantic cloud of glowing gases. In the second, the planets were torn from the sun by an encounter with a passing star. Neither is satisfactory, but both have contributed greatly to astronomy by their impetus to thought.

The hypothesis that was believed for the longest time, excepting the Biblical account, was presented apologetically by the great French mathematician Laplace. According to his Nebular Hypothesis, a rotating and flattened nebula of

[9] Paraphrased and quoted from "Miraculous Accident: Fleming, Florey, and Penicillin" by Milton Silverman in *The Amazing World of Medicine*. Edited by Helen Wright and Samuel Rapport, New York: Harper & Brothers, 1961, pp. 89ff.

[10] Jean L. Marx, "Cancer Immuotherapy: Focus on the Drug Levamisole," *Science* (January 9, 1976), pp. 57.

diffuse material cooled slowly and contracted. In the plane of motion, successive rings of matter were supposed to have split off, to condense into the planets of our present solar system. Most of the matter finally contracted to form the sun. Between the present orbits of Mars and Jupiter, the ring failed to "jell," and produced many asteroids instead of a planet. . . .

The Nebular Hypothesis is untenable for several reasons, particularly because a speed of rotation sufficient to leave nebular rings at the present distances of the planets would provide the nucleus with many times the angular momentum of the rings. The Sun, according to the Hypothesis should have *more* angular momentum than the planets, not one-fiftieth as much. Furthermore, James Clerk Maxwell showed that a fluid ring could not coalesce into large planets but would be transformed into a ring of *planetoids*, such as Saturn's ring or the belt of asteroids.

The collision or encounter theories attempt to avoid the difficulties of angular momentum. If another star collided with the sun or passed very close to it, material would be ejected from its surface and might condense to form the planets. Several variations of the encounter theory have been propounded. In the Planetesimal Theory, proposed early this century by T. C. Chamberlin and F. R. Moulton, the passing star was supposed to have raised gigantic tides on the Sun. An appreciable quantity of matter, several times the present masses of the planets, was then ejected from the Sun's surface, and sent spiraling around it by the passing star. Most of the matter was lost or fell back into the Sun, but part remained, with a highly elliptical motion. The gases then condensed into small fragments, the planetesimals, and as time progressed the larger fragments swept up the smaller, to form the planets. The rapid motion of the passing star provided the angular momentum for the orbital motions of the planets, their rotations and the satellite systems. Within twenty million years after the encounter the formation of the planets would have been essentially complete.

Sir James Jeans and Harold Jeffreys have proposed an alternative version of such an encounter. They argue, in their Tidal Theory, that a long tidal filament was drawn out of the Sun by the passing star. The inner part of the filament returned to the Sun while the outer portions escaped into space. A central portion coalesced into a string of beadlike condensations, the embryo planets.

Jeffreys has more recently abandoned the Tidal Theory as untenable, and has substituted a collisional hypothesis in which the approaching star brushed by the Sun in actual contact. The subsequent phenomena of the filament and planet formation follow essentially the same plan as in the original Tidal Theory. R. A. Lyttleton of Cambridge, England, has proposed that the Sun was a double star at the time of the collision. Its companion star was gravitationally torn away by a third star which closely approached the Sun. H. N. Russell had suggested previously that a companion star was struck, and that the planets evolved from its debris.

A number of serious objections have been raised against all of these encounter hypotheses. In particular, when mathematical analysis is applied, the observed distribution of angular momentum in the solar system has not yet been explained. A basic objection of another kind has more recently been presented.

Lyman Spitzer, while at the Harvard Observatory, proved by a physical and mathematical demonstration that the planets cannot be formed by a direct condensation of material taken forcibly from the Sun's surface or interior. Any star such as the Sun consists entirely of superheated gases. At a depth above which there is sufficient material to form the planets, either by a tidal or collisional process, the temperature is approximately 18,000,000° F. These tremendously hot gases would expand and escape except for the enormous pressure of the overlying layers, which are forced down by the sun's great surface gravity. A tidal or collisional ejection, however, would remove the pressure and enable the gases to expand immediately. During a collision, two stars would remain in contact for only an hour or two, and the ejection would occur at velocities of hundreds of miles per second. Spitzer has shown that within a few minutes after their release, the gases would literally explode, long before they could cool by radiation. Even the internal gravitational attraction of a mass twice that of Jupiter would not hold the gases and permit them to condense. Hence planets cannot be formed directly out of matter that is removed catastrophically from the sun.

We are left, apparently, with some form of the planetesimal hypothesis as the least objectionable explanation for the origin of the planetary system. Spitzer's arguments have not been applied mathematically to the formation of the small planetesimals, but certainly it is true that only a minute fraction of the gases ejected from the Sun would ever be available for forming the planets. Moreover, a stellar collision, rather than an encounter, is required. . . .

So far, our new approach to the problem of origin and evolution has not led to a complete solution. Nevertheless, considerable progress has been made. These conclusions are fairly certain. (1) The planets were once very hot, far above the temperature of melting rock. Even Pluto, now cold enough to hold helium and hydrogen, must have been sufficiently hot to lose the ordinary gases of the Earth's atmosphere. (2) The planets, therefore, grew from a fairly rapid condensation of material, not from a slow accretion process. (3) The planets developed probably from the Sun or possibly from another star. This third conclusion is based largely upon similitudes of chemical composition, but is strengthened by the first two conclusions. Interstellar material, the only alternative to stellar material for planet building, is, within our present knowledge, diffuse. Only an accretion process could produce the planets from diffuse material.

The problem of the possible existence of planets about other stars is still unsolved. If a stellar collision is required to produce planets, there will be only a few systems such as ours among millions of stars. If a single star, unaided, can generate a system of planets, then the number of planets may be enormous. . . .[11]

12.3   THE PROBLEMS OF CONFIRMATION

In conclusion, we shall briefly discuss the special problems of assessing evidence that are faced by the historian and by the courts of law. The historian wants to establish the truth of statements about past events. In trying to do this he or she usually is concerned with confirming, with gathering evidence for

[11] Fred L. Whipple, "The Solar System and Its Origin," in *Reading in the Physical Sciences,* ed. by Shapley, Wright and Rapport (New York: Appleton-Century-Crofts, Inc., 1948), pp. 101–112.

three different kinds of statements: (1) statements about specific events (e.g., Napoleon surrendered at Waterloo); (2) causal statements seeking to explain important events (e.g., the fundamental causes of the Civil War were such and such); and (3) general law statements of history (such as the Marxist notion that economic causes are responsible for all that happens in history, or the law such as of supply and demand). We shall discuss historical explanation and the possibility of historical laws and causality in history in chapter 11. Here we are concerned merely to point out some of the kinds of evidence with which the historian deals in seeking to confirm these various kinds of statements.

In gathering evidence, the historian first uses observation of certain tangible remains of the past—such as monuments, inscriptions, art objects, pottery, weapons. Second, the historian relies on the writings of men and women who either were witnesses to past events or who report about these events. Several kinds of problems arise for the historian in his or her dealing with writings and records of the past. The first major problem is to establish whether the document is genuine—was it written at the time claimed and by the person purported to have written it? Maybe it is completely spurious, as some important documents of the past have been discovered to be. Is it really the diary of Milton or the peace treaty signed by Japan and Russia? The second question concerning any writings of the past is about the competence and reliability of the writer. Was the writer a direct witness to the events reported, or is the report heresay? Might the writer have special biases that would distort judgment and make the report less reliable? For example, the historical reports of Abraham Lincoln's decision to enter into the Civil War vary considerably, depending on the source of the reports. How, for example, might the story of the Potsdam Conference differ if written by a Britisher and by a Russian? Note also how American history books in the past have ignored the role played in American history by Negroes. Does the writer seek to give an objective account with specific details, or is it vague, emotional and subjective? To what extent do we find independent and substantially similar accounts of the same events? The historian, thus, must seek to piece together as much evidence from as many independent sources as possible.

Problems similar to those of the historian occur also in courts of law. In the courts, it is usually proper to distinguish between *circumstantial evidence* and the *testimony* of witnesses. Circumstantial evidence is evidence associating an individual with the crime (e.g., fingerprints, footprints, tire marks, stolen money, motive). Anyone who is familiar with detective stories and/or police work knows very well that although circumstantial evidence can never yield more than probability of varying degrees, circumstantial evidence can lead to the conviction of an innocent person. For example, suppose a prominent businessman is robbed and murdered outside his home at 2 A.M. as he returns home from a party. The police believe that a certain man is the robber and murderer for the following reasons: (1) A .32 caliber revolver of the type with which the man was killed was found in the suspect's room; (2) he was seen at a diner near the scene of the crime about 15 minutes before the murder occurred: (3) the businessman had been responsible for the suspect's losing a great deal of money; (4) a button found near the murdered man's body was similar to those of a coat found in the suspect's room; (5) the coat showed evidence of a button being recently sewed on; (6) the suspect lied about his presence in the diner on the morning of the murder; (7) the suspect paid off a substantial debt four days after the murder; (8) the suspect claimed he had won the money in a poker game, but no evidence could be found that such a game ever occurred. The circumstantial evidence in this case is very good and seems to establish with a fairly high probability that the suspected man is guilty of the crime. However, it is still *possible* that the man is innocent, even though all the facts cited may be true.

In dealing with circumstantial evidence then, we should keep three things in mind: (1) this evidence is always only probable and never certain; (2) the gathering of this evidence is done by investigators, and they can make mistakes; (3) evidence can be planted in order to convict an innocent person.

Turning to testimonial evidence, here too we only find probabilities and never certainties. Witnesses can be honestly mistaken, and they can deliberately lie. Even testimony of 'experts' can be faulty, because experts can disagree, as did the psychiatrists in the Patti Hearst case. Even confessions can be suspect. Innocent persons can confess in order to shield others; and there are those people who always rush to police headquarters to confess to sensational crimes.

In courts of law, then, when you are called on to serve on a jury, weigh and balance all evidence very carefully, ask: How significant is the piece of evidence presented? How does it fit into the total pattern of evidence? Are there any facts that have not been accounted for or checked out? Has the defendant had every opportunity to prove his innocence? Finally, however, you will need to make a decision and, in criminal cases, you must decide whether the person has been proven guilty *"beyond a reasonable doubt."*

Exercises for § 12.3

A. The following are based on two examples cited by Lionel Ruby in his *Logic: An Introduction* [Chicago: J. P. Lippincott Company, 1950].

1. *The Sacco-Vanzetti Case:* This case was a sensation in the 1920s during the so-called period of "Red Hysteria." Two anarchists, Sacco and Vanzetti, were accused and convicted of murdering two men, Parmenter and Berardelli, in a payroll robbery. One of the crucial pieces of evidence was the testimony of a Mary Splaine who, along with four other witnesses, identified Sacco as in the car or on the spot of the murder. Following are excerpts from her testimony. Discuss the reliability of her testimony. Look up the facts of this case in *The Case of Sacco and Vanzetti* by Felix Frankfurter.[12] Decide what conclusion you would draw about the guilt or innocence of Sacco and Vanzetti.

---

[12] Little, Brown and Co., 1927.

The character of the testimony of the five witnesses who definitely identified Sacco as in the car or on the spot of the murder demands critical attention.

Splaine and Devlin were working together on the second floor of the Slater and Morrill factory, with windows opening onto the railroad crossing. Both heard the shot, ran to the window, and saw an automobile crossing the tracks. Splaine's identification of Sacco, as one of the occupants of this escaping car, was one of the chief arguments of the prosecution. Splaine, viewing the scene from a distance of from sixty to eighty feet saw a man previously unknown to her, in a car traveling at the rate of from fifteen to eighteen miles per hour. She saw him only for a distance of about thirty feet, that is to say, for from one and a half to three seconds; and yet she testified:

> "The man that appeared between the back of the front seat and the back seat was a man slightly taller than the witness. He weighed possibly from 140 to 145 pounds. He was muscular, an active looking man. His left hand was a good sized hand, a hand that denoted strength."

Q: "So that the hand you said you saw where;"

A: "The left hand, that was placed on the back of the front seat, on the back of the front seat. He had a gray, what I thought was a shirt,—had a grayish, like navy color, and the face was, what we would call a clear-cut, clean-cut face. Though here (indicating) was a little narrow, just a little narrow. The forehead was high. The hair was brushed back and it was between, I should think, two inches and two and one-half inches in length and had dark eyebrows, but the complexion was a white, peculiar white that looked greenish."

Q: Is that the same man you saw at Brockton?

A: It is.

Q: Are you sure?

A: Positive.

The startling acuity of Splaine's vision was in fact the product of a year's reflection. Immediately after Sacco's arrest the police, in violation of approved police methods for the identification of suspects, brought Sacco alone into Splaine's presence. Then followed in about three weeks the preliminary hearing at which Sacco and Vanzetti were bound over for the grand jury. At this hearing Splaine was unable to identify Sacco:

Q: "You don't feel certain enough in your position to say he is the man?"

A: "I don't think my opportunity afforded me the right to say he is the man."

When confronted with this contradiction between her uncertainty forty days after her observation and her certainty more than a year after her observation, she first took refuge in a claim of inaccuracy in the transcript of the stenographer's minutes. This charge she later withdrew and finally maintained:

"From the observation I had of him in the Quincy Court and the comparison of the man I saw in the machine, on reflection I was sure he was the same man."

2. Examine the following: What hypothesis would you suggest as the best explanation for the twistings and turning of the American Communist party

during these years? What evidence would you cite for your hypothesis? Can you suggest a second hypothesis that would also explain the known facts?

A historian, studying the policies of the American Communist Party of the United States, finds the following facts: After the first World War until 1935 the party vigorously attacked American "capitalists" and all other political groups, including liberals, progressives, and non-communist radicals. The moderate Socialists were denounced as "social fascists" and referred to as "Enemy No. 1" as late as 1933–4. In 1933 Hitler came to power in Germany and destroyed the German Communist Party. In 1935 the American Communists decided to collaborate with Socialists and other democratic parties in a "Popular Front" against Nazism and Fascism. The Roman Catholic Church was also invited to join the united front. This policy was coincident with the same policy adopted by the Communist International at its 1935 Congress. On August 23, 1939, the Soviet Union and Nazi Germany signed a nonaggression pact, and the Soviet Union thenceforth gave Germany diplomatic support in its war against the Western powers. The American Communists ceased their campaign against fascism and sought to prevent American aid to Britain and France in their war against Hitler. They denounced as "warmongers" those who wished to aid England and France in what the Communists referred to as the "imperialist war." On June 22, 1941, German armies invaded Russia. Thereafter the Communists denounced fascism and gave their whole hearted support to the American war effort in what they called "the people's war." The leader of the American Communist party, Mr. Earl Browder, now defended American "big business" against criticism from liberal groups, and in his book *Teheran* (International Publishers 1944), he pledged the support of the Communists to the capitalistic system in the United States: "We declare in advance our understanding that the democratic-progressive camp to which we adhere will adopt the defence of 'free enterprise,' that we understand this term as a synonym for capitalism as it exists in our country, and that we will not oppose it nor put forth any counter-slogans."

In 1946 the American Communists attacked the leaders of the United States and its capitalistic system, denouncing them as the enemies of mankind.

B. This exercise is based on the trial of Bruno Richard Hauptmann for the kidnapping and murder of the Lindbergh baby, whose body was found in the woods behind the Lindbergh home after a ransom of $50,000 had been paid. Under the law, Hauptmann is guilty if there is no reasonable doubt that he participated in the kidnapping, even though he may not actually have killed the child himself. You are the foreman of the jury. The following evidence has been introduced by the prosecution.

    a. A wood technologist testified that a ladder found under the nursery window was made by a skilled carpenter (which Hauptmann was).

    b. The lumber used to make the ladder was traced to the National Mill and Lumber Co. where Hauptmann had worked and bought lumber.

    c. The technologist testified further that wood in the ladder was dressed by a plane found in Hauptmann's garage.

    d. He testified further that a piece of wood in the ladder was cut from a board in the floor of Hauptmann's attic.

    e. Another expert testified that nails in the ladder had the same microscopic defects as nails in Hauptmann's garage.

1. Which of the statements in the series above is most significant for the supporting hypothesis that Hauptmann made the ladder?_____

2. Rate the supporting hypothesis that Hauptmann made the ladder. State the criteria you use in rating the hypothesis.

3. Write a hypothesis that explains the facts so far presented, but which leaves Hauptmann innocent.

    Additional evidence introduced by the prosecution includes the following:

    f. Prints of feet wrapped in some kind of cloth were found around the ladder. Hauptmann's feet were small enough to have made these prints.

    g. The footprint of the man who received the ransom was similar to Hauptmann's.

    h. A rung on the ladder was broken.

    i. Marks on the ground indicated that the kidnapper may have injured his leg.

    j. Hauptmann was walking with a cane some weeks after the crime.

4. Write a hypothesis that explains all the evidence so far presented and leaves Hauptmann innocent.

5. On the basis of the evidence so far presented, rate the hypothesis that Hauptmann is guilty.

    As the trial continues, additional evidence is introduced.

    k. Hauptmann had a criminal record in Germany.

    l. The ransom notes were apparently written by a German.

    m. Paper found in Hauptmann's home was identical to the paper used in the ransom note.

n. Handwriting in the ransom notes appeared to be disguised. A sample of Hauptmann's handwriting appeared to be disguised in the same way.

o. The following words misspelled in the ransom notes were similarly misspelled in the diary of Hauptmann: "ouer" for "our," "note" for "not," and "boad" for "boat."

p. Two handwriting experts testified that Hauptmann wrote the ransom notes.

q. A handwriting expert introduced by the defense testified that Hauptmann did not write the ransom notes.

6. Rate the supporting hypothesis that Hauptmann wrote the ransom notes.

7. Write a hypothesis that explains all the evidence presented so far, but which leaves Hauptmann innocent.

8. Rate the hypothesis that Hauptmann is guilty.

Still further evidence was presented:

r. Dr. J. F. Condon, who acted as intermediary, testified that he sat on a bench in a cemetery and talked with a man who presented the baby's nightgown as evidence that he was the kidnapper.

s. Dr. Condon testified that at a later meeting in the cemetery he gave this man $50,000 in bills, the numbers of which were recorded.

t. Dr. Condon testified that Hauptmann was the man he met in the cemetery.

u. A taxi driver testified that Hauptmann was the man who gave him a dollar to deliver a note to Dr. Condon.

v. Lindbergh testified that Hauptmann's voice was that of the man in the cemetery.

w. Dr. Condon testified that he gave his address and a privately listed phone number to the man in the cemetery.

x. This address and phone number were found scribbled on the back of a closet in Hauptmann's house.

y. Hauptmann said he found the address and number in a newspaper ad.

z. The address and number had not been published either in a newspaper or in the telephone directory.

    aa. The baby's nurse committed suicide some weeks after the kidnapping.

    bb. When arrested Hauptmann had $20 of the ransom money, and nearly $14,600 of the ransom money was found under a board in Hauptmann's garage.

    cc. After the ransom money was delivered, Hauptmann lost about $9,000 in the stock market, he bought a new car and he and his wife went on expensive trips. Both quit their jobs.

    dd. Hauptmann testified that a man named Isador Fisch gave him the money just before he left for Europe where he died.

    ee. Hauptmann worked near the Lindbergh home shortly before the kidnapping.

    ff. An automobile seen near the Lindbergh home shortly before the kidnapping was of the same make, color and model as Hauptmann's.

    gg. While on the witness stand Hauptmann seemed reluctant to answer questions and gave such responses as 'Leave me alone.'

    hh. Hauptmann denied his guilt.

9. List the letters of all statements diverging from the hypothesis that Hauptmann is guilty.

10. Which of the statements should be considered true beyond a reasonable doubt?

11. List the letters of the most significant statements coverging on the hypothesis that Hauptmann is guilty.

12. List the letters of the statements that have the least bearing on the hypothesis that Hauptmann is guilty.

13. Write a hypothesis that explains all the evidence, but still leaves Hauptmann innocent.

14. On the basis of the evidence, how would you vote?

Chapter Outline

  A. Hypothesis formulation and testing

    1. Hypotheses are always data and problem oriented, that is they arise out of a problem or some data and must be relevant to and capable of accounting for the problem. They guide and direct inquiry.

2. Hypothesis formulation and testing generally follow six steps:
   a. Clarification of the problem or data
   b. Formulation of relevant tentative hypotheses
   c. Elaboration of the implications of these hypotheses
   d Gathering of more evidence and testing of hypotheses
   e. Elimination and refinement of hypotheses
   f. Confirmation of hypotheses and solution of problem
B. Confirmation and disconfirmation of hypotheses
   1. Confirmation of a hypothesis takes the following form:

   If H is true, then I
   I is true
   _____
   H is true

   This is the *fallacy of affirming the consequent* and thus an invalid argument form. Confirmation, then, is not a guarantee that the hypothesis is true.

   2. Disconfirmation of a hypothesis takes the following form:

   If H is true, then so is I
   I is not true
   _____
   H is not true

   This is *modus tollens* and a valid argument form. That is why many scientists and philosophers of science stress falsification as more important to science than confirmation.

   3. The elaboration and confirmation of hypotheses involves the use of auxiliary hypotheses. If disconfirmation occurs, it may be one or more of the auxiliary hypotheses which are at fault and not the main hypothesis.

   4. Alternative hypotheses are two hypotheses that can explain the data equally well and which seem to be equal in terms of simplicity and testability.

   5. A *crucial experiment* is a test to decide once for all between two alternative hypotheses. A classic example was Foucault's test of the two theories of light.

   6. A crucial experiment may not be decisive because of the role auxiliary hypotheses play in confirmation and disconfirmation.
C. Confirmation in history and the law courts
   1. One of the main sources of evidence that a historian has to work with is the writings of the past. The two main problems the historian has in dealing with these writings are (a) establishing their genuineness and (b) establishing their accuracy and reliability.
   2. In courts of law, two kinds of evidence are distinguished:
      a. *Circumstantial evidence*—evidence associating a person with the crime.
      b. *Testimony of witnesses*—witnesses can be mistaken and they can lie.

13

DECISION MAKING

13.1 THE IMPORTANCE OF ANALYZING DECISION MAKING

Every attempt to analyze decision making in an introductory logic text poses a question that would be humorous if it were not also painful: Should this topic be covered in a *logic* text? This question requires a decision, for, as William James pointed out, some options are forced, not avoidable, and once posed, this one should not be avoided. We have decided to include a short chapter on the problem. We must make decisions. If the principle "avoid all risks" were to be our action-guide, we would never write books, accept job offers, marry, take a bath or do much of anything. There is a more serious reason for even a short discussion of the "logic" of decision making.

Though there are two main reasons for not including it, there are two quite good reasons for doing so. The main objections are (1) that one will likely get caught in what appears to be a deadly quicksand of complexity, i.e., the problem of fact vis-a-vis values, and (2) the claim of some that there just *is* no rationale or logic to decision-making, and that the whole question should be referred to psychologists. The second objection is misguided anyway because psychology is a descriptive study and no matter how exhaustively it describes how people *do* make decisions, it cannot in principle tell us how people *ought* to make decisions.

All the above is instructive for students of logic. It reveals how we may react when facing a problem. The main reasons for studying decision-making are that human beings are decision-making animals, that decision making involves rational processes of thought—and *that* is at the heart of the enterprise of logic—and that contemporary logicians are increasingly concerned to show how processes of clear thinking are involved in everyday life, both personal and collective. Who needs clarity of thought more than, for example, a President of the United States deciding when and where and whether to send our troops outside our borders? Or a parent deciding when, how, or if at all to reprimand a child? Or a person deciding on a job offer or a proposal of marriage? The questions could be multiplied indefinitely as we move from one area of experience to another. What help can the study of logic give?

First is the recognition that decision making, problem solving, and hypothesis formulation and testing are interrelated and in general follow the same type of pattern. This is true because decision making and problem solving follow the hypo-deductive pattern of thinking. What are general precepts for one of these procedures would also be useful for the others. Indeed, decision making and problem solving all begin where hypothesis formulation begins, with a question, *a problem.* As indicated in our discussion of hypothesis formulation in section 12.1, it is crucial to begin with a clear delineation of a question or a problem. Exactly what is the problem? In order to set one on the right path in decision making or problem solving, it is essential that we get a clear picture of the situation posing the problem. Suppose, for example, the problem is: What college should I attend? However, to begin here is far too vague, because presumably attendance at college is a means to some larger or higher end. It may even be an end in itself. To specify this end-means relationship it is necessary to achieve a clearer delineation of the problem. More on "the problem" in a moment.

A second point must be made before we can safely consider the steps in decision making and problem solving. It is the Socratic warning to beware of assumptions or presuppositions. Thus, philosophers in general and logicians in particular, are so committed to the ideal of rational thought and action that they may be accused of falsely assuming that all beliefs and every action must be reason guided and rationally justified. The fact is that many philosophers do not so believe, but the reason for their objection must be clearly stated. A decision, by which we may generally mean the choice or determination to act in a certain way, is the function of the "whole person," not of some special "faculty." Decisions are made not only by reason, as when we say "Quit emoting and use your head—think!" In decision making and problem solving we voluntarily choose, but normally we do so with emotional input as well. The advice to use "cold" reason is misleading if it means that the decision maker ceases to be a person with hopes and fears, loves and hates, and becomes a mere calculating machine. What is required is a decision for which reasons (hopefully good reasons) can be given. Surely, for example, the question whether the United States should drop the atom bomb on Japanese soil was an anguished one—for the scientists who developed the bomb and for President Truman. What we want to know is, what reasons are involved and what reasons are given for the eventual decision? What weight was given pro and con considerations? Were any reasons ignored? The point is this: Although it would be irrational to propose that we make such a momentous decision as that involved in the use of all-out nuclear war on groups of flipping a coin, consulting astrological charts, examining the entrails of animals, and the like, making a rational decision on rational grounds does not mean that our emotions, our total personality is not involved. The more serious the decision or the problem, the more likely it is to be something about which we feel deeply. The analogy is dangerous but also dramatic: Just as love is not blind but involves the total person in a voluntary sharing, so decision making and problem solving usually involves the whole person.

13.2 STEPS IN DECISION MAKING AND PROBLEM SOLVING

When we ask, now about the actual steps to be taken in decision making, that is, about the procedure we ought to follow (which may not be the one we always follow) we should be aware that a parallel question has been the subject of considerable study in a field other than logic, namely, in ethics. Thus, one excellent ethicist, Philip Wheelwright, over a quarter of a century ago analyzed what he called the nature of moral deliberation. He held that it consists of seven steps:

1. A statement of the ethical question (e.g., ought I to have an abortion? Ought I to report a clear case of cheating on an examination?)
2. Identify the possible alternatives.
3. Imaginatively project myself into the situation in the light of each possible alternative.
4. Imaginatively project myself into the position of others who will be affected by the choice I make.
5. Sort out the values (economic, social, moral, etc.) that are involved.
6. Make a decision in light of the above.
7. Act.

Although Wheelright's pattern is cast in terms of moral deliberation, and includes the last step, action (as decision making and problem solving do not) it is instructive because in other respects it is very similar to the analysis we seek. The similarity is helpful to study because all the steps, somewhat differently stated, are involved in the process of decision making. Here, however, we are eager to show how decision making and problem solving in *logic*, as for example in *all the sciences*, is similar to and also different from decision making and problem solving in life generally and in ethics in particular. Let us attempt to provide that analysis. To save a confusing multiplication of examples, keep in mind the case of choosing a college or deciding to marry a particular person. The steps may be stated as follows.

Identify or formulate the problem or the question   Three points become immediately clear. First, John Dewey can be thanked for pointing out that most (he said all) thinking starts with a problem, a question, a block in the normal biological, psychological, social life of a person. Thus, we don't normally think about our stomach until we get a stomach ache. Only a child *thinks* about tying his or her shoe; adults do it without thinking unless the string breaks or is lost. We start thinking about our bank account when it does not balance or if we are told that the account is overdrawn. Much, and a cynic would say nearly all, of our existence from morning to night is habitual or day-dreaming. Thinking begins when a question has to be answered, when a problem needs to be solved. Where did I leave my car keys? Can I afford to make this trip, buy this car, run a mile in three minutes?

Second, defining the problem is sometimes easy—or at first seems to be—but usually it is difficult and often very complex. Because they start with a problem, decisions depend on a correct identification and formulation of the problem. Lawyers, clergy, doctors, and psychological counselors spend much of their time and energy trying to help people fix on precisely what problem is to be solved. President Truman's decision to drop the atom bombs on Nagasaki and Hiroshima was a response to an enormously complex question. It was not merely the simple question, will this action quickly end the war? Of course it would do that.

Third, defining the problem is often a matter of degree. That is, it may be apparently very limited and specifiable, as in mathematics or chemistry, but more often it involves a judgement as to how wide a context is to be taken into account in its statement. A referendum recently appeared on many state election sheets asking voters to decide whether the state should allow the construction of additional nuclear power plants. The trouble with this question is not merely that a thoughtful citizen finds it very difficult to decide and respond with a simple "Yes" or "No". What is worse is that it is difficult to define the problem clearly.

Generate explanatory hypotheses, formulate proposed solutions, state possible solutions   In scientific inquiry hypotheses, as we have seen, are proposals for solving a problem or explaining a puzzling phenomena. Likewise in decision making we are required to state and examine carefully any proposal for solving any problem. If a marriage is "headed for the rocks," by what means, if any, can it be saved? Another and later question is whether it should be saved. A major airline is headed for bankruptcy. What must be done if it is to be rescued? The "inner cities" of many of our major metropoli are in a state of decay. What is the cause, and what proposal(s) do we have for saving them? In the section on scientific inquiry we discuss in detail the marks or criteria for a good hypothesis, and a reading of that section would be beneficial here. The point is that in decision making in the sciences, the hypothesis or proposal must not only be relevant to the facts and capable of explaining them, but it must also be meaningful and capable of being seriously entertained by the people involved in the decision making process. To the family experiencing serious marriage difficulties, it may not be meaningful to propose that their solution is simply to make the problem a matter of prayer.

Draw out the implications of the hypotheses or the proposals   In the physical sciences this is a clearly and regularly employed step. Thus, "the Leavitt-Shapley law deductively implies sentences of the form: If star *s* is a cepheid with a period of so many days, then its magnitude will be such and such." A more extended example is the following.[1]

"The astronomer Tycho Brahe, whose accurate observations provided the empirical basis for Kepler's laws of planetary motion, rejected the Copernican conception that the earth moves about the sun. He gave the following reason, among others: if the Copernican hypothesis were true, then the direction in which a fixed star would be seen by an observer on the earth at a fixed time of day should gradually change; for in the course of the annual travel of the earth about the sun, the star would be observed from a steadily changing vantage point— just as a child on a merry-go-round observes the face of an onlooker from a changing vantage point and therefore sees it in a constantly changing direction. More specifically, the direction from the observer to the star should vary periodically between two extremes, corresponding to opposite vantage points on the earth's orbit about the sun. The angle subtended by these points is called the annual parallax of the star; the farther the star is from the earth, the smaller will be its parallax. Brahe, who made his observations before the telescope was introduced, searched with his most precise instruments for evidence of such "parallactic motions" of fixed stars—and found none. He therefore rejected the hypothesis of the earth's motion. But the test implication that the fixed stars show observable parallactic motions can be derived from Copernicus' hypothesis only with the help of the auxiliary assumption that the fixed stars are so close to the earth that their parallactic movements are large enough to be detected by means of Brahe's instruments. Brahe was aware of making this auxiliary assumption, and he believed that he had grounds for regarding it as true; hence he felt obliged to reject the Copernican conception. It has since been found that the fixed stars do show parallactic displacements, but that Brahe's auxiliary hypothesis was mistaken: even the nearest fixed stars are vastly more remote than he had assumed, and therefore parallax measurements require powerful telescopes and very precise techniques. The first generally accepted measurement of a stellar parallax was made only in 1838."

---

[1] Carl G. Hempel, *Philosophy of Natural Science* (Englewood Cliffs, N.J.: Prentice-Hall, 1966), pp. 22–24.

Tape Exercises

A. In the social sciences and in everyday life, the drawing out of implications of hypotheses or proposal(s) is a bit more difficult. It often is obscure, but it is no less necessary. What about reporting the classmate who is cheating on an examination? Those who have faced this problem at various times at West Point will be the first to tell us how important and how difficult it is to elaborate the implications of such a hypothesis or proposal. [Try this elaboration yourself, and then consult Tape 13.]

B. What are the implications of the proposal that the cure for unequal educational opportunity is to bus students so that equal quality education is achieved? But one scarcely needs an extended study of the Boston experience to see that there are repercussions in terms of race relations, economic (property and business) shifts, and cultural upheaval that might have been deduced from the original hypothesis had sufficient attention been paid to this step in decision making. [Turn to the tape for discussion of this issue.]

Consider a political example. The problem is whether and how to dramatize the "indestructible monolithic unity" of the international Communist movement in 1976. Soviet Party General Secretary Leonid Brezhnev is no amateur at making crucially important decisions. We would expect him to accurately draw out the implications of the hypothesis or proposal, announced three years earlier, that a conference designed to dramatize unity be held in East Berlin in June, 1976. It would take pages to explore even most of the discernable implications. The point of this part of our analysis of decision making is this: The decision to hold the conference was, as *Time* called it, "a massive miscalculation."[2] The points that are underscored are these: Many problems contain so many variables that the decision maker feels like a juggler who has tossed a dozen Indian clubs into the air and finds them all suddenly falling on his head. Further, the whole decision making process is made in a constantly changing situation, so from day to day the implications change. This means, primarily, that the decision making process is often extremely complex and so calls for precisely the kind of careful analysis strategy we are talking about. First, although complexity is indeed a matter of degree, the complexity plus the number of variables plus the fact of human fallibility make successful decision making extremely difficult, sometimes impossible. Second, one of the essential characteristics of scientific thinking is *prediction*. This is illustrated endlessly in the natural sciences, and for an everyday example, in medical practice or in the insurance business. The method of predicting on the basis of diagnosis or analysis "works"; it is effective when employed logically. But when we turn to the social sciences and to personal and collective problems in daily life, the difficulties we stated above make reliable prediction very difficult. To be

---

[2] *Time* (12 July 76), p. 23.

specific: Brezhnev, we said, proposed the summit conference three years in advance. Now, many factors making for the success or failure (again, a matter of degree) could and surely were predicted by him and his codecision-makers. But other factors were not predictable, at least to a degree sufficient to guarantee success. For instance, there were massive strikes protesting food price hikes in Poland. Railroad tracks there were ripped up so that he could not even travel by train as planned. He could not guess, not predict, what the results of political developments in Italy, France, and Spain—to name but three nations—would be. More dangerous, he could not predict what the mood of communist leaders in those nations would be. As it turned out, these leaders were vastly more independent than Brezhnev expected.

We could cite similar examples from decision making in personal and collective life at every level—the individual, the family, the community, school—but this is not necessary to drive home the point.

13.3 IMAGINATIVELY PROJECT SELF INTO THE SITUATION

There is an old song with many stanzas each of which ends on the refrain "But I didn't want what I got when I got it." This voices a final complication: It is difficult to project oneself and more difficult for a group to project itself into the expected situation. This is true not merely because of the difficulty of identifying the anticipated situation, but also because a person and a group of persons undergo so many unexpected, unpredictable changes over a period of time. Little wonder, for example, that so many senior citizens contemplate with regret or bitterness the rosy promises of the joys of retirement.

We have concentrated on the case of the Summit Conference because it affords an excellent opportunity to examine briefly the role of *ends and means* in decision making. Ends and means is ever present in discussions of the logic of decision making. The importance of ends-means analysis can easily be exaggerated as well as underestimated.

From Aristotle on, philosophers have stressed the distinction between *ends* (Greek, *Telos*) in the sense of aims, goals, or objectives, and *means* in the sense of how we try to attain ends or what actions will predictably produce the ends we desire. So stated, the means-ends distinction fits in with our discussion of cause and effect, though it is not limited to nor identical with this way of thinking. Thus, if a person's end or goal is to lose weight, a good (perhaps the only effective) means is to reduce food consumption. M (less food) is the cause of E, the effect (loss of weight). The soundness of his or her decision is as visible and as testable as are most empirical and scientific statements. To refuse to decrease food consumption is probably (only probably, because other factors could be operative, such as illness) to fail to achieve the aim. This way of analyzing our problems in terms of ends and means is so useful that it can be recommended for the decision-making problems we constantly face.

It is not, however, as simple and trouble free as it appears or as we wish it to be. The trouble it generates can be illustrated as follows. What if a person asks, "*Should* I lose weight or not? Why? If I should, why not enjoy my food and cocktails and lose weight by taking pills or using one of the many advertised quickie means to that end?" Now a practical and an axiological question (i.e., the question of values) has been raised. This calls for a quite different decision making process. As for the means, clearly there are many means to a single end—weight loss or almost any other end. If I have a headache, I can take an aspirin or a sleeping pill. If a roommate hits me over the head with the heel of a shoe or a hammer, the headache will not bother me until I regain consciousness. At the level of practicality, therefore, the question is: Which of all possible means is the most effective, speedy, least expensive means to my desired end? Convict Willie Sutton's reasoning was simple: My goal is to have a lot of money; there is plenty of money in the bank, so I'll rob banks and achieve my goal. And he did, until he was caught, convicted, and jailed.

The still more troublesome problem, however, concerns the ethical and valuational judgement of ends and means. So, when the question is posed, should I lose weight, stop heavy smoking or stop drinking, sacrifice for my children, save money rather than spend it, lie to the intruder about the whereabouts of my money or my child, tell my wife or husband that recovery from a operation is unlikely—in all such cases a problem more significant and quite different from mere "How to . . ." has been raised. Plainly, the answer to these questions involve value judgements. This is the area in which logic and ethics overlap. Ethical judgements, moral evaluations, statements of value and of good or evil—these are not solely empirical, though they involve and are influenced by facts. Further, they are not verified or falsified as are matters of sheer fact. The statement, water boils at 212 degrees Fahrenheit at sea level, is factual. "A person ought never to tell a lie" is an ethical statement. Anyone *answering* the question what end ought I to seek, and by what means, does so in light of some value or set of values. Here there is no universal agreement, no scientifically or logically available way of justifying the answer that is given. The question is can value judgements be justified, and if so, on what grounds? This question is extremely difficult and carries us into a field of philosophy known as *axiology.* There are two points to be made for our present purposes. First, all such judgments depend on our ultimate commitments. Second, these ultimate commitments cannot be determined on purely logical grounds though their expression (for example in the form of political, religious and other "creeds") is subject to logical analysis.

Not all philosophers would interpret the problems of ethics and values as we have stated them. Kant, for instance, argued that ethical maxims or principles could be defended on grounds of reason alone, not on grounds of the consequences of our acts, our desires, or the like. He also said that ends and means are integrally related. The end never "justifies the means", e.g., we are never justified in using an evil means on the ground that the end is good. We encourage you to think these issues through on your own, preferably in a solid course in ethics.

13.4 TESTING AND ELIMINATING HYPOTHESES AND PROPOSALS

We have come to the next to the last of the suggested steps in decision-making and now a major difference between decision-making in the sciences and in non-scientific thinking appears. It is this: in the sciences we can test and eliminate hypotheses and proposals; in non-scientific areas we cannot. For example, if the hypothesis concerns the nature of light (Is it wave or particle?), if it concerns sentient life on Mars, if it concerns the cure of cancer—in all these cases we decide which, if any, hypothesis should be favored on grounds of the possibility of controlled tests and experimentation. But we cannot do that with questions concerning persons, groups of persons, and proposals concerning the ends-and-means of their action. Often, and even in the sciences for that matter, two hypotheses or proposals may appear equally meritorious in the eyes of the most careful and critical decision-maker. Alas, refinement and clarification can be carried only so far, then a decision must be made—in the absence of demonstration of truth or falsity.

13.5 DECISION, AND TESTING THE DECISION

This is the final step in decision making. Again, an important difference appears between scientific and nonscientific thinking. In the former the decision is made and can be tested, as we have explained in another section, on grounds of its explanatory capacity, its usefulness, its reliability in predicting, and the like. But in nonscientific contexts decision and action are in most cases inextricably related.

Tape Exercises

A. Should we buy a new car or repair the one we have? All the familiar patterns of analysis are logically appropriate—estimating the amount of money required, the likelihood that the repair job will be satisfactory and fairly permanent, the pride in ownership of a new car versus the possible dissatisfaction with the old one, and so on and on. But we can only imaginatively project most of the answers and tentatively predict some of the answers. Eventually we have to make a decision that we can dignify with the word "rational" if we have taken all the relevant means and end questions into consideration. There is no proof in advance that our decision will be correct.

B. Finally consider William James' famous example of the man who is engaged to the woman of his choice but who postpones his decision assuming that thereby he is avoiding making the wrong decision. One week he is nearly convinced that she is an angel, the embodiment of his dreams of a life partner. The next week, after an encounter with his potential mother-in-law, he recoils in fear: This is not what I want. This continues for years; he is engaged to but he never marries the woman. William James makes two important points. First, the man has deceived himself into thinking that he has avoided a decision. For the practical effect of his indecision is a negative answer. He never marries. He would have been better off (as surely the girl would have been) had he said "Yes" or "No" after a shorter period of reasonable deliberation. Second, his "decision" exhibits a false scientific caution because he can never be proved to be right or wrong. Maybe his marriage would have been the best ever, maybe it would have proved to be a disaster. He will never know. What does reason require in this decision process? [Turn to Tape 13, for a brief analysis of these two questions.]

Exercises for § 13.5

A. In each of the following, what decision would you make, if any? How would you justify or defend the decision you made?

1. To participate (e.g., you, or your children) in busing to another school district.

2. To use "the pill" or not.

3. To have an abortion for a pregnancy caused by a rape.

4. To take a lucrative job upon graduation from high school rather than go to college.

5. To take a lucrative job upon graduation from college rather than enter on a graduate program leading to a Ph.D.

6. To agree with Madam Sadat, wife of the head-of-government of Egypt, that no man or woman should be allowed to have more than two children. (After two, either should be sterilized. This is a separate, subsidiary question.)

7. You are a young, ambitious district attorney who is prosecuting a case of serious theft by a person with a criminal record, but in the process of the trial you come upon evidence, known only to you, that the defendant could not be guilty. What do you decide to do?

8. You are in charge of the United States nuclear defense commission. You must decide whether to maintain capacity to deter or destroy any power that strikes us first or threatens to do so. What do you recommend, and why?

9. John and Mary both want a wholesome family and academic careers. John has his Ph.D. and a position, without tenure, in an accredited college or university. John now wants a family, but Mary argues, "No, I have a right to my profession which requires a Ph.D." If you are John, what do you do?

10. The public utilities argue that nuclear power generators have been in use for over a decade without a failure or catastrophe and that they alone can produce the energy the state needs; the environmentalist committee argues that the nuclear power plant is a potential generator of disasters and that the waste is extremely dangerous. You are the Governor and find yourself in the position of having to decide whether or not to permit the nuclear power plant to be built. What do you decide? Why?

11. Do you think you can rationally decide to commit suicide? Why or why not? Can your decision, regardless of what it is, be justified?

12. You are nineteen years old, unmarried, unengaged, three weeks pregnant and not in love with the man by whom you became pregnant. Do you have an abortion (in a state in which it is legal)?

13. Your seventeen-year-old daughter is a freshman in college and dependent upon you for support. You are her only living parent. She says she plans to drive across country with her boyfriend this summer even though you disapprove and threaten to stop her support.

14. You are the manager of a small business and catch an employee stealing valuable merchandise. The owner says, "Fire that person or I'll fire you!"

15. Your doctor says, "Stop smoking or you will have serious lung trouble and may be dead before you are fifty."

16. You hold the deciding vote on a jury, all other jury members are voting for aquittal, but you, though doubtful, are not fully convinced of the alleged murderer's guilt-as-charged.

17. You are the executor of your life-long friend's will, which gives half-a-million dollars to his only son at twenty-one. The son is a potential alcoholic and has shown no responsibility (the father told you to act as you saw best).

18. You are thirty-five years old, divorced and you are offered half interest in a promising business if you work full-time, nine to five, Monday through Friday and put your two-year-old daughter in nursery school.

19. You are ready to finish your last two years of college and are offered (take it or leave it) a very lucrative job as assistant manager of a franchise business store.

20. You are forty-eight years old, female, and your hair is turning grey; do you use a color rinse or dye?

21. You are driving a car at 2:00 A.M. in a deserted section of town, and the light turns red as you hurry home. There's no traffic to be seen, do you ignore the light?

22. You are asked by your employer to "perform a public service to win goodwill for the business" but you don't approve of the charity or project to which she wants you to contribute.

Chapter Outline

A. Decision-making involves rational processes of thought, and that is at the heart of logic.
B. An analysis of decision-making furnishes one more example of the practical value of logic.
C. Decision-making is related to hypothesis formation, and it involves the entire person—thinking, feeling, and willing.
D. There are specific steps in decision-making, namely:
   1. Identify or formulate the problem or the question.
   2. Formulate a proposed solution; generate an explanatory hypothesis.
   3. Draw out the implications of the proposed solution.

4. Imaginatively project one's self into the situation in light of the possible alternatives.
5. Test and eliminate hypotheses and proposals.
6. Decide and test the decision.

E. We must always remember William James' warning! In dealing with "living" and "forced" options, we cannot postpone decision-making indefinitely. No decision is often the same as a negative decision.

14

PROBABILITY

14.1   DEDUCTION AND INDUCTION

We have discussed various kinds of argument in two preceding chapters. In chapter 6, we examined deduction in detail as ideally exhibited in syllogistic reasoning, and in chapter 10, induction and scientific method. The time has come for a careful statement of the relation between deduction and induction because this is one more point at which logic is used in everday life as well as in scientific research. We shall try to avoid superficiality on the one hand and the highly technical discussion that belongs in philosophy of science on the other hand.

Recall the distinction between validity and truth (See 1.8 and 1.9). We have stressed the fact that validity or invalidity characterized an *argument*, whereas truth or falsity may be ascribed to a *statement* or *proposition*. Further, it was made clear, we hope, that even a valid deductive, syllogistic argument may consist of three propositions every one of which are false. We studied deductive reasoning before examining inductive for two reasons. First, because historically logic began with deductive inference and, in fact, for almost 2,000 years logic was equated with Aristotelian, deductive inference. The second reason is psychological: Deductive reasoning, especially as embodied in the syllogism, has a ring of clarity, specificity, and finality about it. These qualities appeal to beginning students in logic, just as the seeming absence of them often proves to be disturbing because of its lack of finality.

The second point is an issue that affects our attitudes and thought patterns in almost every field. It is this: we should never fall for the false alternative or choice that says, in effect, "Either we have certainty (we know absolute truths or principles, as allegedly in ethics) or we are left with relativism (the notion that one person's opinion is as true or false as another person's)." One of the very important lessons for any college student to learn is to avoid that fallacy. As John Dewey argued so vigorously, the quest for certainty is misguided. The only certainty we have is in the field of logic and mathematics, both of which are *formal*. Thus, as Plato long ago demonstrated when he refuted the Sophists (who claimed that we do not really know anything), no one in his or her right mind would argue about what number is next in the following series:

$$
\begin{array}{cccccc}
1 & 2 & 3 & 4 & 5 & 6 \\
2 & 4 & 8 & 16 & 32 & 64
\end{array}
$$

Again, who would seriously debate the conclusion of the time-worn syllogism

All men are mortal
Socrates is a man
_____

Hence, Socrates is mortal.

In both these areas the conclusion follows (notice, it validly follows) from what is given. But look more closely at these examples so that we can take the next major step. In mathematics the elements are given *by definition*—numbers, triangles—and the rules of deduction are discovered in logic. What about the second example. How does it stand on the criteria of validity and of truth? Well, it is clearly valid for reasons that should be clear to us by now. But the truth of the conclusion depends on the truth of the premises. No one is likely to argue about the minor premise: Socrates is (was) a man. But is it true that "All men (human beings) are mortal"? To know *with certainty* that this is a true or false statement, we would need to know every possible case or instance of men (i.e., human beings). But we do not and cannot know that. An infinite intelligence, surveying all time and all existence, might be presumed to know whether it is true or false. On the other hand, given a limited number of instances, and with finite intelligence, we do not and will not know. These kinds of considerations have lead us to conclude that any deductive argument, such as that stated above, is worth no more or less than its major premise *so far as its truth-value is concerned*. Thus, *if* it is true that all men are mortal, *then* it is true that Socrates, being a man, is mortal.

Finally we come to the heart of the matter: probability. Because we simply cannot know all of the instances of any category of complex objects, events, or processes, all inductive reasoning must be expressed in terms of probability. More accurately, the conclusion must be stated in terms of degrees of probability. And here is a point of crucial importance with reference to the fallacy discussed above: There are *degrees of probability,* and these vary from pure chance (fifty fifty) to a degree of probability that approaches, but never reaches, certainty. So the choice is not between certainty and mere "relative" opinion; it is between pure chance at one end of the spectrum and a very, very high degree of probability at the other end. Consider two examples from every day life. We shall soon discover that if we toss a coin the possibilities are precisely one half ("one" referring to the single coin and single toss and "two" to the possibilities, which are heads or tails). Consider the statement, "The sun rises in the east and sets in the west." Because of the uniform order of events in nature, a uniformity that makes applied science possible, we would call that person a fool, a jokester, or drunk who, upon rising at daylight said, "I wonder where I should look for the sun this morning, south, north, west, or east?" Based on all prior experience, we say that the likelihood of the "sun rising in the east and setting in the west" is 99.999. . . . But it is not 100 percent, for there is always that remotest of possibilities, namely, an interstellar cataclysm or the like such that the "normal" relation of the earth to the sun is suddenly altered. In sum, our claims about anything in the space-time universe vary from very low to very high probability.

14.2 THE MEANING OF PROBABILITY STATEMENTS

There are three basic notions of probability: the classical concept, the relative frequency interpretation, and the logical concept of inductive probability. Each of these attempt to specify what probability statements mean. The classical conception, formulated by LaPlace and Keynes, interprets probability statements as statements or assertions of a mathematical ratio of the number of favorable possibilities available to the total number of possible alternatives. Thus, for example, if one has a bowl full of 1,000 balls and we know that 600 of them are white, the probability of drawing a white ball on the first draw is 600/1,000, or 600 favorable possibilities to 1,000 total possibilities. The determining of a probability ratio is dependent on three conditions: (1) We must know the *favorable alternatives*, that is, the possible ways in which the desired result can be produced; (2) We must know the *total* number of possible alternatives; and (3) We must know that the particular alternatives are *equally possible*. For example, any face of the die has just as much chance of turning up as any other. The other condition is stated in the *Principle of Indifference*, namely, "If there is no known reason for predicating of our subject one rather than another of several alternatives, then relative to such knowledge the assertion of each of these alternatives has equal probability."

Operating as it does with the notion of equipossible events, the classical theory is an *a priori* theory. That is, it is a purely theoretical approach which calculates probabilities *before* and *without* use of information about the events whose probabilities are being determined. *No trial run is made.* No actual dice are thrown. All we do is divide the number of ways in which an event can occur by the total number of possible outcomes. Further, the classical notion of probability does not refer to an objective property of an event, but rather it is a measure of the degree of rational belief, that is, the degree to which one rationally believes that the event will occur. Thus, for example, the statement, "The probability of obtaining an ace on the first throw of a die is 1/6" is interpreted to mean that our *rational expectation* that an ace will turn up on the first throw of the die is 1/6. In assigning numerical values to the rational degrees of belief, the number *one* is assigned to those statements having the highest possible degree of belief (i.e., those about which we feel most certain). It is generally assumed that only *logical truths* could have a probability value of one. *Zero* is the numerical value assigned to those statements having the lowest possible degree of belief. Only logical falsehoods are thought to warrant the probability value of zero. All other statements then would have probability values somewhere between zero and one.

To summarize, in the classical theory of probability the probability of an event A occurring can be determined as follows:

$P(A)$: Probability of event A $= m$: number of favorable events whose probability is to be *measured*.
n: number of equally possible events of a certain kind.

Consider a deck of fifty-two bridge cards and the probability of turning up a heart on the first draw. In this case there are fifty-two equally possible events and thirteen possible favorable cases because there are thirteen hearts in a deck of cards. Thus, the probability, in this case, may be expressed as follows:

$P(A) = 13/52$ or $\frac{1}{4}$ or 0.25

A number of objections have been raised against the classical theory of probability. The first objection concerns the Principle of Indifference and the assumption of equiprobable events. First of all, it is difficult in many cases to mark off equiprobable alternatives (e.g., the decay of atoms in radioactive substances). In science and in life we are usually faced with an indefinitely large number of possible events. Second, it just is not true, for example, that even in straight-forward cases like the die that one is dealing with just six possible outcomes. It is always *logically* possible that the die will land on edge or break apart or explode. It is artificial to stipulate just six possible outcomes. It is also objected that the classical theory is inadequate as a probability theory because it neither gives us sufficient reason to expect one possible alternative rather than another nor does it tell us how probability values are to be calculated in cases when we *do* have sufficient reason to favor one alternative rather than another. A third objection to the classical theory is that it just is not correct that the term 'probable' always refers to the degree of rational belief and never to an objective property of events. Thus, for example, it would seem incorrect to interpret the statement "The probability of a thirty year old man living another year is .945" as a statement about rational belief.

A second widely accepted theory of probability is the *frequency theory of probability*, which interprets probability statements as statements about *relative frequencies*, that is, as statements about the relative frequency with which a certain outcome *O* can be expected in a long series of repetitions of some random experiment *R*. A die may be rolled two hundred times and the proportion of cases that an ace turns up is discovered to be 62/200. The relative frequency theory, in contrast to the classical theory, does not make use of the principle of indifference but rather calculates probabilities *empirically*, assuming that the relative frequency of a given result among as yet *unobserved* events of a given kind will be the same as the *observed* relative frequencies for events of that kind. Thus, for example, insurance companies study a certain class of people (for example twenty-five-year-old women) in order to determine what mortality rate they exhibit. Thus, suppose of 1,000 twenty-five-year-old women, 963 are observed to survive another year. So, we have the probability statement, "The probability that a twenty-five year old woman will live another year is .963." Probability in this case, is not defined in terms of rational belief, but rather as the relative frequency with which members of a class exhibit a specific property.

The relative frequency theory, then, calculates probabilities on the basis of observational evidence and, further, it makes use of this evidence and other information to correct its probability statements. For example, in calculating birth rates, additional information would be sought. The information might include the increased use of birth control, the liberalized abortion laws, the decreasing age of parents. If, however, the birth rate of a nation had remained relatively stable over a long period of time and there was no reason to think that factors affecting the birth rate had changed, the relative frequency probability of the past would be calculated as the same for the future. Finally, relative frequency theory assumes that as the number of performances increases, the relative frequencies of each outcome tends to change less and less. In other words, it speaks of ideal probability values or mathematical limits towards which the relative frequencies converge as the number of performances increases indefinitely. Moreover frequency theorists customarily construe the classes involved in their probability hypotheses as being indefinitely large. Objection is sometimes made against the tendency of the frequency theory to deal with long run frequencies and limits on the grounds that in most cases of probability calculation we are dealing primarily with the *short-run* and with *finite* classes. Thus, those people dealing with birth rates are not concerned with the total class of human births past, present, and future, but with the total number of births in a particular country in the next few years.

In sum, then, probability is calculated in Relative Frequency Theory as follows:

$$P(A) = \frac{m \text{ (the actual occurrences of favorable events)}}{n \text{ (the actual number of events)}}$$

Thus, if out of a representative sample of 3,000 twenty-five year old females, thirty die in their 30th year, we have

P(of a 25 year old female dying in her 30th year) = 30/3,000 or 1/1,000

Hence, "the probability of a twenty-five-year-old female dying in her 30th year is 0.01."

A third and final notion of probability is *logical* or *inductive* probability, which interprets *probability* as degree of confirmation. That is, when we say that "Einstein's Theory of Relativity" is highly probable, we are saying in an indirect way "On the basis of the relevant evidence, Einstein's Special Theory of Relativity is highly probable." In this case, we are talking about the probability of a statement or set of statements with respect to a body of statements, each expressing a statement based on the relevant evidence. In other words, this type of probability is concerned with a *logical* connection between statements. A philosopher of science, Rudolf Carnap, in his *Logical Foundations of Probability* (Chicago, 1950) has worked out in detail an inductive probability which seeks to assign numerical values to inductive probabilities. However, we need only be concerned here to note that the degree of inductive probability varies with context and available evidence. For example when the astronomer Ptolemy said "It is probable that the earth is at the center of the solar system," his statement could be taken to mean "It is probable relative to the evidence now available." The statement, "The earth is at the center of the solar system" by itself is, however, either true or false and neither probably nor improbable. Inductive probability, then, is concerned with an objective relation between a statement (the conclusion) and a body of evidence statements (the premises).

Tape Exercises

Consider the following problems. [Check your answers with Tape 14, band 1.]

1. What is the probability that Jane and Tom will both turn up at a party?
2. You are interested in student elections and you have studied fifty cases. You find that in twenty-five of these elections the number of votes separating the winning candidate from the losing candidate has been 270 of the total number of votes. According to the frequency theory of probability, what would be the probability that in all elections the number of votes separating the winning candidate from the losing candidate will be 270 of the total number of votes?

Exercises for § 14.2

A. Using the Classical Theory, determine the following probabilities.
   1. There are nine black marbles and seven red marbles in a bag. What is the probability that the first one drawn will be red; that it will be black?
   2. In tossing an ideal die what is the probability that
      a. an ace turns up.
      b. a number less than 6 turns up.
      c. an even number turns up.
      d. a number greater than 2 but less than 6 turns up.

3. Criticize the following: "I haven't seen Jack's new car, but the probability that it is red is 1/2, because there are only two possibilities, it is red or not-red."
4. You have a pack of fifty-two bridge cards. What is the probability of
   a. drawing a diamond?
   b. drawing an ace?
   c. drawing an ace of diamonds?

B. Using the frequency theory, determine the following.
1. There have been 30 births in your neighborhood this past year and 20 of these have been boys. What is the probability of the first birth in the neighborhood next year being a boy?
2. A survey of juniors and seniors was taken and the sample was a representative one. The results of the survey were:

	Support Student Fees	Do Not Support Student Fees
Juniors	90	10
Seniors	60	40

What is the probability that
   a. A junior supports student fees.
   b. A senior supports student fees.
3. Out of a representative sample of Southern Californians, 30,000 developed skin cancer. What is the probability that Jane Brown, a Southern Californian will develop skin cancer?
4. Joe's used car lot, during the past year sold 900 used cars, of these, 45 were convertibles. What is the probability of Joe selling a convertible next year?

14.3   THE CALCULUS OF PROBABILITY

Probability calculus is a branch of pure mathematics that enables us to calculate the probabilities of complex events given the probabilities of their component events. In this section, an informal account of the basic principles of the probability calculus will be presented.

First of all, we consider pairs of events such that the occurrence of one of them has an *effect* on the occurrence of the other. For example drawing an ace from a deck of cards without putting it back into the deck has an effect on the chances of getting an ace on the next draw. These events are *dependent* on each other. But other pairs of events are such that the occurrence of one has no effect on the other. Thus, for example, if the ace is put back into the deck it has no effect on the chances of getting an ace on the next draw. Events such that the occurrence of one has no effect on the occurrence of the second are said to be *independent events*.

Further, some pairs of events are such that it is *logically possible* for both of them to occur. Thus, a die may land face up on both the first and second throws. But it is not *logically possible* for an ace *and* a douce to land up on a single throw of die. Such a pair are said to be *mutually exclusive events*.

Having spelled out the possible relationship of events, we can now spell out the rules of the probability calculus.

Restricted multiplication rule (the probability of a joint occurrence)   The restricted multiplication rule is: If A and B are independent events, then $P(A + B) = P(A) \times P(B)$. Thus, the probability of the *joint* occurrence (the conjunction) of two independent events is equal to the *product* of the probabilities of the two independent events. For example, the probability of tossing two consecutive heads is calculated by multiplying the probabilities for each independent toss. The probability of tossing a head is 1/2 because there are two possibilities and one is favorable. Thus, the possibility of tossing two consecutive heads is obtained as follows:

$$P(1/4) = P(1/2) \times P(1/2)$$

That this probability is correct can be seen by noting that in tossing the coin twice there are four possible combinations *HH, HT, TH,* and *TT,* only one of which is favorable.

Suppose now that we have a basket containing 6 white and 8 red balls and another basket containing 9 white and 16 red balls. One ball is drawn from each basket. What is the probability that they would both be red? $P(A)$, the probability of drawing a red ball from the basket is 6/8. $P(B)$, the probability of drawing a red ball from the second basket is 9/16. Thus, $P(A + B)$, the probability that they both will be red is

$$6/8 \times 9/16 = 54/128 = 0.43$$

General multiplication rule (conditional probability)   It is also possible to compute the probability of joint occurrences, even if they are not completely independent. Suppose we want to calculate the probability of drawing two spades from a deck of 52 cards in two consecutive draws. But drawing a spade from the deck on the first draw and not replacing it affects the probability of the second draw. Thus, the probability of drawing a spade on the first draw is 13/52 while on the second draw it is 12/51, since there is one less spade and one less card in the deck. Thus, the probability $P(b)$ of drawing the second spade, given the occurrence of a, the drawing of the first spade is 12/51 or 4/17. Thus, the formula in the case of conditional probability is

$$P(A + B) = P(A) = P(B, \text{ if } A)$$

Suppose now you want to calculate the probability of drawing three spades in a row if they are drawn and not replaced in the deck. The probability would be $13/52 \times 12/51 \times 11/50 = 11/850$.

Restricted addition rule (the probability of mutually exclusive events) Events are mutually exclusive if it is impossible for both to occur, (e.g., rolling a five *and* a six on a given throw of a die). The formula to handle the probability of mutually exclusive events is:

$$P(A \text{ or } B) = P(A) + P(B)$$

In other words, we simply add the two probabilities. the probability of getting a five on a given throw of the die is 1/6, and the probability of getting a six on a given throw of the die is 1/6. Thus, the probability of getting either a five or a six on a given throw of the die is:

$$1/6 + 1/6 = 2/6 = 1/3$$

The *addition theorem* for calculating the probabilities of mutually exclusive events and the *product theorem* for computing the probability of the joint occurrence of events can be used together to calculate the probability of even more complex events. Suppose you want to find the probability of being dealt a flush in a poker game. A flush consists of five cards all of the same suit. Here we are dealing first with four exclusive events; that of getting five clubs, that of getting five hearts, that of getting five diamonds and that of getting five spades. Using the product theorem for calculating the probability of getting five clubs on a single deal we get the following result:

$$13/52 \times 12/51 \times 11/50 \times 10/49 \times 9/48 = 33/66,640$$

Drawing five diamonds, five hearts and five spades have the same probability. So using the addition theorem for calculating the probabilities of mutually exclusive events, we find that the probability of getting a flush is:

$$33/66.640 + 33/66.640 + 33/66.640 + 33/66.640 = 33/16.660$$

General addition rule (the probability of non-exclusive events)   A fourth rule of the probability calculus deals with the probabilities of alternative events which are *not* mutually exclusive. Suppose, for example, we want to know the probability of tossing either an odd number or a number greater than three on the throw of the die. The rule for calculating such a probability is as follows: The probability of *A* or *B* and possibly both, *P(A* or *B)* is equal to the probability of *A* plus the probability of *B*, minus the probability of *A* and *B*.

$$P(A \text{ or } B) = P(A) + P(B) - P(A + B)$$

Thus we can solve our problem. The probability that we will toss an odd number is 3/6; the probability that the number will be greater than 3 is also 3/6.

Finally, the probability that the die number is odd and greater than 3, by the general multiplication rule is $1/3 \times 1/2 = 1/6$. Thus our sought after probability is as follows:

$$P(A \text{ or } B) = (3/6 + 3/6) - 1/6 = 5/6 = 0.83$$

The probability of the non-occurrence of events   It is customary in probability calculus to assume that the probability of an event A and the non-occurrence of A, or $\sim A$, occurring is O. That is, the probability of a *contradiction* is: $P(A + \sim A) = O$. The occurrence of either A or its complement $\bar{A}$ has a probability of 1. That is, the *tautology* has a probability as follows:

$$P(A \text{ or } \sim A) = 1$$

Now, because A and $\bar{A}$ are mutually exclusive, the addition rule is applicable, and we have

$$P(A \text{ or } \bar{A}) = P(A) + P(\bar{A})$$

Thus,

$$P(A) = P(\bar{A}) = 1$$

which yields,

$$PA = 1 - P(\bar{A})$$

It can be seen that we can calculate the probability of an event occurring by computing the probability that the event will *not* occur and subtracting that figure from 1. Suppose we want to know the probability of getting at *least one* 6 with the throw of two die. The probability of getting a non-6 is 5/6, and since we are dealing with two die, we compute the probability as $5/6 \times 5/6 = 25/36$. Thus, the probability of getting at least one 6 is

$$1 - 25/36 = 11/36$$

applied to the event of tossing at least one head in two tosses of a coin. We see that the only case in which the event will *not* occur is when the toss results in tails. By the product theorem, then, the probability of the unfavorable case is

$$1/2 \times 1/2 = 1/4$$

Now the probability of getting at least one head in two tosses of the coin is

$$1 - 1/4 = 3/4$$

Tape Exercises

To test your understanding of the basic rules of the probability calculus solve the following. [Turn to tape 14, band 2 for an analysis.] The problem is: What is the probability that the shooter will win?

1. What is the probability of getting tails every time in three tosses of a coin?
2. The dice game craps has the following rules:
   a. The 'shooter' wins if he or she throws a combination totalling 7 or 11 on the first throw, and loses with 2, 3, or 12 on the first throw.
   b. If one of the remaining numbers 4, 5, 6, 8, 9 or 10 turns up on the first roll, the shooter continues to roll the dice until either that same number turns up again or does not, in which case the shooter loses.

Exercises for § 14.4

A. Compute the probabilities of the following:
   1. 4 heads in a row
   2. three 6's in a row
   3. a 4, 5, or 6 with one die
   4. one head in 3 throws.

B. There are two urns—one containing 7 white balls and 15 red balls and the other containing 12 white and 3 red balls. One ball is drawn from each urn. What is the probability that they are both red?

C. Four players have been dealt five cards from a standard pack of cards. What is the probability that the first card you pick up is the ace of diamonds? What is the probability that the first card the player on the left picks up is an ace of diamonds?

D. Five cards are dealt you from a pack of 52. What is the probability that the top card is a heart? You have no ace or 9. What is the probability that the top card is either an ace or 9?

E. Suppose you draw two cards from a standard deck, *not* replacing the first one before drawing the second. What is the probability that you'll get (a) two aces; (b) at least one ace; (c) two spades; (d) two black aces?

F. A player in a draw-poker game is dealt three jacks and two small odd cards. She discards the two odd cards and draws two more. What is the probability that she will improve her hand on the draw either by drawing another jack or a pair?

G. A slot machine has three wheels with 20 characters on each wheel. Only one character on each wheel shows the jackpot symbol. What are your chances of hitting the jackpot if the machine is not rigged?

H. There is a probability of 0.2 that Jack will take the insurance job and a probability of 0.5 that he will go on to graduate school. What is the probability that he will either take the insurance job or go to graduate school?

I. What is the probability that you can toss at least 2 heads with 3 coins? with 4 coins?

J. Half of the logicians in the world play chess and a fourth of them play the piano. What is the probability that a logician either plays chess or plays the piano?

Chapter Outline

A. The three interpretations of the meaning of probability statements are:
1. The classical notion, which interprets probability in terms of a ratio of the number of favorable possibilities to the total number of possibilities.
2. The relative frequency view, which interprets probability in terms of the relative frequency with which a certain outcome O can be expected in a long series of repetitions of some random experiment R.
3. The inductive probability notion, which understands probability as *degree of confirmation*, a logical connection between a statement and the evidence supporting it.

B. 1. Probability is calculated in classical theory according to the formula:

$$P(A) = \frac{m \text{ (the number of favorable events)}}{n \text{ (the number of equally possible events)}}$$

2. Probability is calculated in relative frequency theory according to the formula:

$$P(A) = \frac{m \text{ (actual occurrences of favorable events)}}{n \text{ (actual number of events)}}$$

C. The theorems of probability calculus
1. *Restricted multiplication rule*
$P(A + B) = P(A) + P(B)$
2. *General Multiplication Rule*
$P(A \text{ or } B) = P(A) \times P(B, \text{ if } A)$
3. *Restricted Addition Rule*
$P(A \text{ or } B) = P(A) + P(B)$
4. *General Addition Rule*
$P(A \text{ or } B) = P(A) + P(B) - P(A \text{ or } B)$
5. *Probability via non-occurrence*
$P(A) = 1 - P(\bar{A})$

Part IV
Answers to Exercises

CHAPTER 1

Exercises for § 1.3

A. 1. This is a statement about the authorship of the play "No Exit."
    3. A question.
    5. A statement about the jury's decision.
    7. A statement.
    9. A performative utterance.
    11. A statement.
    13. A request or command.
    15. A command.

B. 1. The speaker finds it incredible that someone or a particular person whom he/she considers very sensible believes in the reality of witches. Implied statement: It is silly [ridiculous] that you believe in witches.
    3. A juror who is convinced of the man's guilt to another juror who believes the man innocent. Implied statement: You are wrong to believe this man innocent.
    5. Argument about Galileo's action. Implied statement: Galileo was a coward for giving in to the Church.
    7. Poem. Implied statement: It is too bad that the world couldn't be like paradise now instead of like a wilderness.
    9. During a long boring meeting. Implied statements: This meeting is too long and too boring. It should end.

Exercises for § 1.5

1. Probably an explanation because it answers the question why. However, it could be put into the following argument form:

Premise I: Tom is on academic probation.
Premise II: Tom wants to stay in school.
_____
Conclusion: Therefore, Tom will not be able to play basketball this season.

3. Argument:

Premise I: The victim's broken watch stopped at 1 A.M.
Premise II: The coroner testified that time of death occurred between 12 and 3 A.M.

Conclusion: Therefore, the murder probably occurred at 1 A.M.

5. A causal explanation.

7. Probably an argument.

Premise I: South Vietnam finally fell into the hands of the Communists.

Therefore: The Vietnam War was a futile tragedy.

9. An argument.

Premise I: Cornelius, a Thebian, made the statememt, 'All Thebians lie.'

Therefore: The statement 'All Thebians lie' cannot be true.

11. Most likely an explanation, it tells us why there is little of excitement occurring at the farm.

13. An argument.

Premise I: Young children learn by imitation of the actions of others.

Therefore: Parents and older children should take care of their behavior and the things they say.

15. Probably an argument.

Premise I: Public T.V. provides better programs than commercial T.V.

Therefore: We ought to abolish commercial T.V.

Could also be construed as a conditional statement: If we abolish commercial T.V., then we would have better programs.

17. If anything, it is probably intended as a causal explanation for increased leukemia and cancer among children.

Exercises for § 1.6

A. 1. Premise I: Most wealthy men have succeeded without a college education.

Missing Conclusion: Therefore a college education does not help one achieve to wealth and success.
Missing Premise I: A college education does not help one achieve to wealth and success.
Missing Premise II: What helps one achieve wealth and success pays.

Therefore: A college education does not pay.

The first conclusion does not necessarily follow from the given premise because in order to draw that conclusion the evidence required is that 'All wealthy men have succeeded without a college education.'

3. Missing Premise I: All persons who are able to vote are citizens.
                        John is able to vote.

                        John is a citizen.

This argument is deductively valid and thus a good argument. If, however, the missing premise is constructed as: 'All citizens are able to vote,' it is invalid and not a good argument because people other than citizens may belong to the class of voters. Thus, the following is an invalid argument of the same form:

All men are mortal.
My dog is mortal.

My dog is a man.

5. Premise I: Humanities subjects are not quantitative.
   Premise II: Humanities are interested in human beings and their creative activities.
   Missing Premise(s):   Computers can't be used with nonquantitative subjects and with subjects interested in human beings and their creative activities.

   Therefore: Computers can't be used in the humanities.

If the premises are true, it is a good argument.

7. Missing Premise: Inability to spell is not a good reason for thinking a person unintelligent.
   Premise: This child does not know how to spell.

   Therefore: There is no [good] reason for thinking he is unintelligent.

Note the addition of the word 'good' in the conclusion. Certainly inability to spell could be one clue to lack of intelligence, though as a single clue it is poor indeed.

9. Missing Premise: All barbers are good conversationalists.
   Premise II: You are a barber.

   Therefore: You are a good conversationalist.

A deductively valid argument.

11. Premise: Nutrition experts urge us to start the day with a good breakfast.
    Missing Premise: One should do what nutrition experts urge.
    Missing Premise: A coffee and a donut is a good breakfast.

    Therefore: I am going to have coffee and a donut every morning.

13. Premise: The power of making a good metaphor is the power of recognizing important resemblances.
    Missing Premise: The power of recognizing important resemblances is the work of genius.

    Therefore: The power of making a good metaphor is the work of genius.

15. Missing Premises: People who generalize too quickly and impulsively don't make good scientists.
                       People with too much imagination don't make good scientists.
    Premise: Mary generalizes too quickly and impulsively.
    Premise: Mary has far too much imagination.

    Therefore: Mary won't make a good scientist.

17. Missing Premise: All true friends are those who supported me in the election.
    Premise: No (they) are those who supported me in the election.

    Therefore: No (they) are true friends.

19. Missing Premise: God made many of those people he loved.
    Premise: He made many plain people.

    Therefore: God must have loved the plain people.

B.   4. Premise 1:   In the past 10 years the American educational system has been wracked by declining student achievement and rampant inflation of grades and overall lowering of academic standards.

Premise 2:   The number of basic classes have been reduced, graduation requirements have been weakened, and electives which are less demanding are emphasized.

Therefore: Academic achievement is losing its meaning.

5. *Argument I*

Premise 1:   If life were sacrosant, then all heroism, martyrdom, would be wrong, to say nothing of carnivorous diet, capital punishment and warfare.

Premise 2:   Heroism, martyrdom, carnivorous diet, capital punishment and
[Implied]   warfare are not wrong.

Conclusion I: Life is not sacrosant.

Argument II

Premise 3:   Death is not always an enemy—it can sometimes be a friend and servant.

Premise 4:   Life is not sacrosant—its sanctity is not intrinsic.
[Conclusion I]

Conclusion II: The sanctity of life is only extrinsic and good by accident according to the situation.

Argument III

Premise 5:   The sanctity of life is extrinsic and good by accident according to
[Conclusion II]   the situation.

Conclusion III: Thus, when life is not good it deserves neither protection nor preservation.

Argument IV

Premise 6:   When life is not good, it deserves neither protection nor
[Conclusion III]   preservation.

Premise 7:   Laws preventing 'elective death' protect and preserve life which
[Implied]   is not good.

Premise 8:   Laws protecting life which is not good are uncivilized.
[Implied]

Conclusion IV: Our present laws about 'elective death' are not civilized.

6. *Argument I*

Premise 1:   Present divorce laws required a man to support a woman after divorce whether or not she is quite able to maintain herself.

Premise 2:   To expect a man to support an able-bodied woman the rest of her life because he kept her for x years of marriage is iniquitous bondage.

Premise 3:   Men have been freed from this iniquitous bondage in three American states.

Premise 4:   This iniquitous bondage is wrong.
[Implied]

Premise 5:   Unless this wrong is put right, the very institution of marriage will be undermined.

Conclusion: Men should become more aware of the present unjust divorce laws [and change them—implied]

C. 5. *Argument I*

Premise 1: Normal persons do not become drinkers to excess.

Conclusion I: Drunkards are pathological.

Argument II

Premise 2: Drunkards are pathological.
[Conclusion I]

Conclusion II: There is always some factor besides the mere drinking of alcoholic liquors which determines drunkedness.

Argument III

Premise 3: Drunkards are pathological.

Premise 4: Pathological restraint is also bad.

Premise 5: Heavy drinkers would otherwise almost certainly be victims of other vices.

Premise 6: There is always some factor besides the mere drinking of alco-
[Conclusion II] holic liquors which determines drunkedness.

Conclusion III: Abstinence from alcohol should not be enforced for drunkards.
[Implied]

Argument IV

Premise 7: Abstinence from alcohol should not be enforced for drunkards.
[Conclusion III]

Premise 8: The D'Abernon Committee and other bodies of experts have found that many benefits come from moderate drinking.

Premise 9: Alcohol is often medicinally useful.

Conclusion IV: Abstinence from alcohol should not be enforced for everyone.

7. *Argument I*

Premise 1: Moral objective laws must be decreed by a being that is all good.

Premise 2: Human beings are not beings who are all good.
[Implied]

Conclusion I: No objective moral law depends merely on human beings.

Argument II

Premise 3: No objective laws depend on human beings.
[Conclusion I]

Premise 4: There are objective moral laws.

Conclusion II: There must be an all-good being who decrees objective moral laws.

Argument III

Premise 5: There must be an all-good being who decrees objective moral
[Conclusion II] laws.

Premise 6: God is an all-good being.
[Implied]

Conclusion: God exists

8. *Argument I*

Premise 1: The percentage of heroin users who have previously used marijuana is much larger than the percentage of nonheroin users who have previously used marijuana.

Conclusion I: So, there is every reason to believe that a casual connection exists between the use of marijuana and the use of heroin.

Argument II

Premise 2: [Conclusion I]	There is every reason to believe that a causal connection exists between the use of marijuana and the use of heroin.
Premise 3:	We can cut down on marijuana use and thus on heroin use by keeping our laws against marijuana.
Premise 4:	Heroin use is intrinsically bad and should be stopped.

Conclusion II: We should keep our laws against marijuana.

Exercises for § 1.7

1. A. Premise 1: Farmer Jones plowed up two plots of ground, applied a coat of lime to one and then planted both with corn.

   Premise 2: The lime plot yielded ten bushels per acre more than the other.

   Conclusion: Probably the extra yield was due to the application of lime.

   B. Inductive—indicated by the word 'Probably.'

   C. Ampliative because it tell us nothing else about the two plots. If one had been overused, it would yield less in spite of the lime and thus weaken the conclusion.

3. A. Premise 1: The Vietnam War was never legally declared a war by the United States.

   Premise 2: The war was more a civil war among the Vietnamese people

   Therefore: The United States was wrong to enter militarily into the Vietnam conflict.

   B. Inductive

   C. Ampliative because the premises do not indicate why the United States was in error or in what sense their action was wrong.

5. A. Premise 1: All the stolen paintings were oils, and oils are never framed under glass.

   Therefore: There was no glass to cause a reflection, and Arthur could not have seen the burglar's reflection.

   Therefore: Arthur lied when he said that he saw the burglar's face in the reflection of the glass over the Renoir.

   B. Deductive because conclusion necessarily follows.

7. A. Premise 1: The trial judge is forced to devote an unduly large proportion of his time and attention to keeping the situation within manageable bounds.

   Premise 2: In a recent case, the judge made no less than ten separate rulings on television coverage during the trial.

   Premise 3: The presence of television cameras and technicians tends to distract and divert witnesses and can have an unpredictable effect on their testimony.

   Conclusion: Televising of criminal trials creates an atmosphere that makes it impossible to conduct a fair trial.

   B & C. This is an inductive argument—it cites specific facts and its conclusion goes beyond the evidence given in the premises.

9. A. Premise 1: At Stanford University not long ago, doctors tried acebutol for a man with a potentially lethal arrhythmia that resisted all the standard anti-arrhythmia drugs and had required electrical shocking of his heart.

   Premise 2: In the eight months he has been on acebutol, he has had no recurrence of arrhythmia.

   Therefore: Acebutol looks excitingly good for dangerous heart rhythms.

B. Inductive

C. Ampliative because general conclusion is based on only one case study.

11. A. Premise 1:   Two contrary psychic tendencies exist universally in the father-son relationship, i.e., from the Oedipus complex.

Premise 2:   Thus, most patriarchal religions also veer between submission to a
(Conclusion I)   paternal figure and rebellion—and every god promises protection on condition of submission.

Conclusion II: Thus, there are many similarities in the manifest picture of compulsive ceremonies and religious rituals due to similarity of the underlying conflicts.

B. It is inductive. It's conclusion is cautious, though it does go beyond its evidence in the premises.

13. A. Premise 1:   The professor was reading a book written in Hebrew which is read from the back to front.

Therefore: He would not have turned the pages with his right hand but with his left.

B. Deductive—if the premises are true, the conclusion necessarily follows.

15. A. Premise 1: Johnson said the buck rose on his forelegs.
Premise 2: A deer gets off the ground hind-end first.

Therefore: Johnson's story was an invention.

B. Deductive

17. A. Premise 1:   The robbers entered the house either from the front or the rear.
Premise 2:   Had they entered the house from the front, the line crews would have seen their car.
Premise 3:   The linemen did not see their car.
Premise 4:   If the robbers entered the house from the rear, they must have arrived by boat.

Conclusion: The robbers came by boat.

B. The argument is deductive. If the premises are true, the conclusion must be true.

Exercises for § 1.9

A. 1. An example of the valid *A* argument form.
    3. An example of the valid *A* argument form.
    5. An example of the invalid *C* argument form.
    7. An example of the invalid *C* argument form.
    9. An example of the invalid *C* argument form.

B. 1, 2, 4, 5, 8 and 9.

C. 1. True
    3. True
    5. False
    7. False
    9. False

D. 1. No
   3. No
   5. True
   7. Valid and Sound
   9. Invalid

E. 1. No dogs are cats.
   3. All patriots are good citizens.
   5. Some pigs are not flyers.
   7. He is a citizen.
   9. No man can perform miracles.

Exercises for § 1.10

A. 1. False
   3. False
   5. False
   7. False
   9. True

B. 1. Premise: John has liked all three philosophy classes he has taken.

   Conclusion: He will also like the fourth.
   Strengthening Premise: The fourth is taught by the same instructor as the first three.
   Weakening Premise: The first three were value-type courses, but the fourth is advanced logic.

   3. Premise: I have picked three winners at the races today.

   Conclusion: I will win in the next four races also.

   Strengthening Premise: I pick winners every time I attend the races.
   Weakening Premise: I picked four losers before getting three winners.

   5. Premise: The political polls predicted that Governor Snorkle will be reelected overwhelmingly.

   Conclusion: I'm not going to bother to cast my vote for his opponent.

   Strengthening Premise: The poll was well conducted by a reliable group.
   Weakening Premise: The poll was taken only in Snorkle's home county.

   7. Premise: Everytime in the past when the interest rates rose, the stock market fell.

   Conclusion: The stock market will fall this time.

   Strengthening Premise: This has occurred 150 times.
   Weakening Premise: It has occurred only twice.

   9. Premise: Our basketball team has won its last five games.

   Conclusion: It should win tonight's game also.

   Strengthening Premise: They are playing the weakest team in the conference.
   Weakening Premise: Our star center will not be playing tonight.

C. 1. Weakens. Other rats would not know the maze.
   3. Strengthens. The rats are sex starved.
   5. Strengthens—variety.
   7. Probably irrelevant unless sex and age are related in rats.
   9. Strengthens—increases sex drive.

CHAPTER 2

Exercises for § 2.2

A. 1. Primarily informative and descriptive.
   3. Expressive of a personal feeling. Maybe an evaluative judgment, depending on the context.
   5. Directive and expressive.
   7. Informative about the action of the companies. The question implies a negative attitude, and thus is expressive. It implies that the companies have not answered the question and thus is informative and it may imply a value judgment about the companies' action.
   9. Expressive of a negative attitude toward Hitler and certainly evaluative in sociological and psychological terms. This is a case of emotive use of language which is both expressive and evocative.
   11. Informative: Descriptive of the plight of endangered species. Emotive and thus both expressive and evocative—seeks to express and evoke a negative attitude toward those who have caused extinction and to direct some positive action to prevent further extinction.
   13. Informative: Certain claims are made about the journalist—he is a grumbler, a censurer, a giver of advice, a regent of sovereigns, a tutor of nations. Further, it is asserted that newspapers can be more powerful than actual weapons.
   Expressive and Evocative: Of a reluctant respect for the power of journalism and the press.
   15. Informative: Asserts that people should not take words as stable and genuine, but rather as counters people play with.
   Expressive: Of a mildly negative attitude toward the value of words.
   17. Informative: Asserts that a countryman between two lawyers is but an easy prey like a fish between two cats.
   Expressive: Expresses a somewhat negative attitude toward lawyers and a humorous attitude toward a countryman.
   19. Informative: Tells us why laws are the bulwarks of liberty.
   Expressive of a very positive attitude toward laws.
   21. Informative: Asserts that money is essential to a nation.
   Expressive: Of a very positive attitude toward money especially in the phrase "life blood."
   23. Informative: Asserts that imagination is the leading faculty of men who rule the world.
   Expressive of a positive attitude toward imagination.
   25. Informative: Asserts that at present war is more productive of good than of evil.
   A fairly neutral statement.
   27. Informative: Asserts that monogamy is based on the notion of private property and not on sexual love.
   Expressive of a negative attitude toward monogamy.
   29. Informative: Asserts that legal subordination of one sex to the other is wrong and hinders human improvements.

B.   1. Moderately to strongly negative.
      3. Neutral.
      5. Strongly positive.
      7. Moderately positive.
      9. Strongly positive.
      11. Moderately negative.
      13. Strongly negative.
      15. Moderately to strongly positive.
      17. Moderately negative.
      19. Neutral to mildly positive.

C.   1. An aesthetic judgment.
      3. Social judgment.
      5. Ethical judgment.
      7. Functional judgment.
      9. Ethical judgment.
      11. Empirical if—then judgment.
      13. Aesthetic judgment.
      15. Report about the views of many Catholics.

Exercises for § 2.3

Not the Man
1. a. 'thorough analyses'—positive, implies that it was scientific and objective.
    b. 'a product of the Pendergast school of boss rule'—implies power politics and corruption.
    c. 'tossed off'—implies he flippantly ignored the report.
    d. 'go slow'—implies hindrance and hush up.
        'move on'—positive and accentuates the 'go slow.'
    e. 'should have disqualified himself'—'judge who believes in vigorous inquiry'—implies Judge Cowan is not honest and doesn't want inquiry.
2. The facts given are:
    a. Curtiss A. Betts is the Post-Dispatcher's state political correspondent.
    b. Judge Cowan has impaneled the state grand jury to investigate.
    c. 12 years ago Judge Reeves held a fraud inquiry.
3. The editorial is very negative toward Judge Cowan.
4. It wants to force Judge Cowan to disqualify himself.

Exercises for § 2.4

A.   1. Disagree in attitude: (a) is negative and (b) is positive toward Truman.
          Disagree in belief: (a) thinks Truman was not a good President; (b) thinks he was. Genuine disagreement.
      3. Agree on the facts but disagree in attitude: (a) is positive toward the government troops and (b) supports the rebels.
          Implies genuine political disagreement.
      5. Disagreement only in attitude: (a) is slightly negative and (b) is moderately negative. Apparent disagreement.
      7. There is disagreement in attitude toward George and in interpretation of his behavior—apparent disagreement because both probably have some of the truth and could talk it out.

9. Some genuine disagreement. Pliny says every book has something of value whereas Brooke implies some books are just bad and should be discarded.

11. Apparent disagreement: Maverick and Tully are saying two different things. Maverick is talking about men of commerce as artists; Tully is asserting that they have no touch of civilization. Maverick also may be speaking of art in a wider sense of skill and thus what he says is even more irrelevant to Tully's statement.

13. Apparent disagreement: Hazlitt asserts that we must use some ceremony toward others; he does not rule out what Bulwer advocates, namely, that 'at times' to dispense with ceremony is to pay a compliment.

15. Some genuine disagreement: Bailey implies that civilization began and has its impetus from man's desire to avoid doing things, whereas Beecher sees man's drive, initiative and control over nature as central to the origin and growth of civilization.

17. Genuine disagreement: The first statement asserts that all men by nature are equal, whereas Vauvenargues asserts that men are unequal by nature.

19. Apparent disagreement: They are making different statements about truth and falsehood which are not contradictory though their attitude is different. Whatley finds half-truths more akin to absolute falsehoods whereas Keith points to the lure of half-truths which lead us into error because there is some truth to tempt us.

21. Genuine disagreement in attitude. Collier values fame and asserts that those who can't reach it undervalue it. Longfellow believes the search for fame is wrong.

23. Agreement on the value of freedom but disagreement about the use of freedom. Rahel believes freedom is necessary for us to obtain a certain character and life, some ought. Mill sees freedom as necessary for the pursuit of our own good in our own way with no ought implied and as long as we do not interfere with others.

25. Apparent disagreement: Both Franklin and Penn believe frugality is good, but Penn qualifies his statement by asserting that frugality is good if joined with liberality. Franklin does not rule out liberality or speak of the relationship between frugality and liberality.

B. 1. Machiavelli and Aristotle are in genuine disagreement because Machiavelli values laws and arms above good rulers whereas, Aristotle believes good rulers are more important. Goethe's statement talks about a different aspect of government and thus does not conflict with the other statements. Channing's statement also does not conflict with the other statements and seems to be in some agreement with Goethe's statement, namely, both imply less governmental power.

3. Augustine, Fichte, Beecher and Hamerton all agree that there is a connection between happiness and ethical character. They would be in disagreement with Lawson if his statement implies that happiness alone without relationship to character is the object of life. Van Dyke's statement does not specifically speak of happiness but rather implies that we often desire the wrong things. It also counsels contentment with what we have. It thus doesn't conflict with the other statements.

C. 1. The disagreement is over the word 'freedom.' Mill defines 'freedom' in terms of individual liberty—the right to pursue one's own ends in one's own way as long as it does not interfere with others' freedom.
Mabie defines freedom in terms of society and progress—it is mastery of conditions. Because each uses adjectives such as 'only' and 'real'—they see their definitions as the only ones and thus there is genuine disagreement. Otherwise both kinds of freedom could be sought and are not necessarily incompatible.

3. There is disagreement over the word 'good.' a defines 'good' in terms of efficiency and time-saving. b, however, defines good in ethical terms. These are different senses of

'good' and thus it is a verbal dispute. Further, b agrees with a that the computer is useful.

5. Intelligence is being defined in two different ways: a defines it in terms of I.Q. and b in terms of produced work. It is an apparent verbal disagreement.

7. The dispute is over the question of 'wealth.' a defines it in terms of friendships, b in terms of money. It might be a genuine disagreement over criteria for wealth.

9. The dispute is over the meaning of the term 'creative scholar.' a believes 'creative scholar' is defined in terms of ideas stimulated in students whereas b holds that it is defined in terms of discoveries or books. It is a genuine disagreement as any academician knows.

CHAPTER 3

Exercises for § 3.3

A. 1. Conventional Sign
   3. Conventional Sign
   5. Conventional Sign
   7. Conventional Sign
   9. Conventional Sign

B. 1. Term
   3. Term
   5. Sentence
   7. Sentence
   9. Sentence
   11. Sentence
   13. Term
   15. Term

C. 1. Thing, organic substance, animal, mammal, four-legged mammal, dog, bulldog, Boston bulldog.
   3. Liquid, beverage, alcoholic beverage, wine, white wine, light white wine, Chablis.
   5. Class, college class, philosophy class, Logic class.

D. 1. denoted
      connoted
      denoted
      connoted
      denoted
      connoted
   3. connoted
      connoted
      denoted
      connoted
      denoted
   5. connoted
      connoted

denoted
connoted

E. 1. a. objective
      b. subjective
      c. objective
      d. subjective
      e. subjective
   3. a. subjective
      b. subjective
      c. objective
      d. objective
      e. subjective
   5. a. objective
      b. objective
      c. objective
      d. objective
      e. subjective

F. 1. sound— healthy
             waves traveling through air
             noise
   3. good—   morally good
             useful—functional
             aesthetically good
   5. free—   no cost or charge
             not restrained
             open and frank

G. 1. 'public use,' 'without just compensation'
   3. 'excessive bail,' 'excessive fines,' 'cruel and unusual punishment'
   5. 'levying war,' 'adhering to their enemies,' 'giving them aid and comfort'

Exercises for § 3.4

A. 1. Operational
   3. Synonymous
   5. Precising
   7. Stipulative
   9. Operational

B. 1. Other things may have the same function, e.g., a perforated knife.
   3. If you don't know the meaning of the synonym, the definition fails. Nuances of meaning may be missed.
   5. A precising definition may be too precise or not precise enough—this is too narrow.
   7. If you know more of these men, you have not learned much about Existentialists. Further, the examples can mislead because all of these men have different philosophies.

C. 1. Philosopher—a person who studies or is learned in philosophy.
              —a person who thinks or lives according to a system of philosophy.
      This definition takes us in circles—requires us to look up 'philosophy.'

3. Lower class—the social class below the middle class; the working class.
   This definition doesn't tell one anymore than would already be known. Need to know further characteristics of the class.
5. Mind—memory, recollection or remembrance.
   This is a very narrow definition of mind. A better one is listed 5th: the conscious and unconscious together.

Exercises for § 3.5

A. 1. Skyscraper—a very tall building such as the Empire State Building and the World Trade Center in New York City.
   3. Bird—warm-blooded, egg-laying vertebrate with feathers and wings such as sparrow, robbin, dove, pigeon.
   5. City—a large center of population such as New York, Chicago, Los Angeles, London, Tokyo.

B. 1. genus—opening [for admitting light and air]
      differentia—usually having panes of glass, generally movable for opening or shutting
   3. genus—building
      differentia—for human beings to live in
   5. genus—vehicle
      1st differentia —two wheels, one behind the other, equipped with handle-bars and a saddle-like seat—could be a genus
      2nd differentia—propelled by the feet
   7. genus—institution of higher learning
      differentia—qualified to award Ph.D. degree
   9. genus—false statement
      differentia—made with the intent to deceive

Exercises for § 3.6

A. 1. Too broad—there are other unconscious states.
      Doesn't state all the essential characteristics, e.g., normal, refurbishing state.
   3. Too narrow—acts of adultery have been committed in daylight.
      Doesn't state essential characteristics, e.g., illegal sexual relations with married person.
      Violates rule of clarity because it uses humor rather than precision.
   5. Uses humor rather than precision and thus violates the rule of clarity.
      Too narrow—man is much more than an ape.
      Non-essential characteristics stated.
   7. Violates the rule of circularity and indirectly, the rule of essential characteristics.
   9. Primarily violates the rules of clarity and neutrality—it is humorous and sarcastic rather than precise and it does not state any essential characteristics of a conservative.
   11. This definition is both humorous and persuasive and thus violates the rules of clarity, neutrality and essential characteristics.
   13. This definition is too narrow because competition occurs in areas other than economics.
      It is persuasive because it makes value judgments about the outcome of the competition.
   15. This poem as definition is too broad—many animals have tail, teeth and four legs. It violates the rule of essential characteristics because it does not distinguish dogs from cats. It also is persuasive because it judges dogs to be man's best friend.

17. This definition is too broad because there are many forms of government and it doesn't state essential differentia. It also is persuasive.

19. This definition is too broad because divorce is legal separation of people who do not wish to respect and honor; it violates the rule of essential characteristics and it is persuasive.

B.   1.   A.   Premise 1:   The study of the airmen
                Therefore: Religious people who are drawn to the mystical qualities of life are the safest drivers.
                Therefore: The non-religious type had higher scores because of a general tendency to be less conventional, psychologically more complex and conflicted, and more ready to resort to complex defense operations as a protection against anxiety.

      B.   Definition 1:   "The religious man is one who is concerned with the supernatural meaning of an existence and particularly his place in it."
                          This does not state the essential characteristics of a religious person and it is too narrow because not all religions deal with the supernatural.
              Definition 2:   The non-religious type (the Theoretical and Aesthetic)
                          Violates non-essential and is too narrow; it is also unclear because many might not know what theoretical aesthetic meant.
              Definition 3:   Religious people—are those who are drawn to the mystical qualities of life.
                          Too narrow because not all religions have a mystical element and thus it also is nonessential.

     3.   A.   *Argument I*
                Premise 1:   Medicare is socialized medicine and has brought nothing but disillusionment to the patients and headaches to the doctors.
                Premise 2:   Socialism is the takeover by the government of everything traditionally reserved for the individual.
                Premise 3:   To talk about medical care which is free is a contradiction in terms because freedom means no control, no regulation and no restraint.
                Premise 4:   Socialized medicine is against democracy.
                Therefore: Socialized medicine is a completely wrong thing.
                Therefore: We should vote down this bill which proposed socialized medical care in the U.S.

      B.   Definition 1:   Medicare is socialized medicine.
                          Too narrow, nonessential and persuasive.
              Definition 2:   Socialism is the takeover by the government of everything traditionally reserved for the individual.
                          Not neutral.
              Definition 3:   Freedom means no control, no regulation, no restraint.
                          Negative. Too narrow. Persuasive.
              Definition 4:   Democracy is the control of everything by the people.
                          Nonessential, too broad—this would be a good definition of communism.

5. A. Premise 1:   Science fiction is a form of fantasy and the type of reader who enjoys science fiction is really the type of person who believes in the fantastic rather than science anyhow.

   Therefore: There is nothing wrong in including fantasy stories in a collection labeled *Science Fiction*.

   B. Definition: Science fiction is a form of fantasy.
   Too broad and nonessential because it does not distinguish science fiction from other types of fantasy.

Exercises for § 3.7

1. In classifying vehicles one might pick the following principles of division:

   I. air-land-sea
   II. type of propulsion
   III. passenger-carrying cargo

   or

   IV. leisure-work
   V. way constructed, e.g., bicycle-motorcycle.

3. In classifying horses one might try the following principles of division:

   I. male-female   young-old
      fixed-unfixed   breeds-palamino

5. In classifying vegetable one principle of division used has to do with what part of the plant is edible., e.g.,

   root   — a carrot
   tuber   — a potato
   seed   — a pea
   fruit   — a tomato
   stem   — celery
   leaf   — lettuce

7. Books obviously can be classified by reference to subject matter—fiction-nonfiction, and level of reading ability required.

9. Religions can be classified by reference to:

   a. region in which originated—eastern, western.
   b. broad doctrinal beliefs—Hinduism, Buddhism, Islam, Christianity.
   c. more specific doctrinal beliefs—Catholic, Protestant, Orthodox.

CHAPTER 4

Exercises for § 4.2

A. 1. There is an inconsistency in arguing that government should manage all your affairs so that you can enjoy liberty—presumably you would have no liberty.
   3. Can one be prejudiced in an unbiased way? Prejudice, after all, implies bias.
   5. To tell teachers what to teach is inconsistent with the notion of academic freedom and free interchange of ideas.

B. 1. Complex Question
   3. Complex Question
   5. Begging the Question
   7. Begging the Question
   9. Begging the Question

Exercises for § 4.3

1. Appeal to ignorance
3. You too. And Appeal to Authority
5. Appeal to People—Fitting Attitudes
7. Against the man: Abusive
9. Appeal to Ignorance
11. Against the Man—You too
13. Appeal to People—Fitting Attitudes
15. Against the Man—Circumstantial
17. Appeal to Pity
19. You too

Exercises for § 4.4

1. Hasty Generalization—draws a conclusion based on one example
3. Black or white
5. Hasty Generalization
7. Beard
9. Hasty Generalization

Exercises for § 4.5

A. 1. Division
   3. Equivocation on the word 'basic'
   5. Amphiboly
   7. Composition
   9. Amphiboly

B. 1. Appeal to Authority
   3. Appeal to Pity
   5. Beard
   7. Appeal to Force
   9. Against the Man, Circumstantial
   11. You too
   13. False Cause
   15. Begging the Question
   17. Appeal to People—Fitting Attitudes
   19. Black or White

C. 1. Complex Question
   3. Appeal to Authority
   5. Equivocation on 'right'
   7. Black or White
   9. You too
   11. Hasty Generalization
   13. Appeal to People
   15. Begging the Question
   17. Against the Man—Abusive

CHAPTER 5

Exercises for § 5.1

1. Some (professors) are (good scholars but terribly boring lecturers.)
3. All (nuclear power plants) are (so constructed that we need not worry about their possible danger to the environment.)
5. Some (pieces of sculpture which have won prizes and sell for a high price) are not (the kind of things I would want in my bathroom.)
7. Some (members of the Senate) are not (persons of unquestioned moral character.)
9. No (term papers, like women's skirts, which are not long enough to cover the subject but short enough to be interesting) are (papers worth grading.)

Exercises for § 5.2

1. All (democracies with a large number of political parties) (D) are (likely to have weak governments.) (U)
3. No (pornography that embodies sadism and violence) (D) is (fit to be circulated.) (D)
5. All (fat people) (D) are (supposed to be happy people.) (U)
7. No (tennis balls used in ten games) (D) are (fit to be played with again.) (D)
9. All (totalitarian regimes) (D) are (likely to suppress one or more of the "four freedoms.") (U)

Exercises for § 5.3

1. All (the mail) is (that which arrived on time.) A
3. All (cases of a whale) is (a case of a mammal.) A
5. All (things that are expensive) are (good.) A
7. All (who hesitate) are (lost.) A
9. All (who deserve the Congressional medal of honor) are (courageous.) A
11. No (person) is (liable.) E
13. No (thing that is a vegetable) is (a mineral.) E
15. No (place he goes) is (a place I will go.) E
17. Some (coeds) are (innocent.) I
19. Some (things that are not gold) are (things that glitter.) O
21. Some (kittens) are (lovable.) I
23. All (students who are not graduate students) may (sing in the choir.) A
    No (graduate students) may (sing in the choir.) E
25. All (who are respected) are (sincere.) A
    No (non-sincere person) is (respected.) E

Exercises for § 5.4

1. *O* Some (love) is not (friendship.)

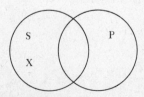

(All love is not friendship.)

3. *A* All (people) are (persons who are familiar with the constant babbling of the small child from babyhood onward.)

5. *A* All (who were denied the rights of citizenship) were (slaves and women.)

E No (non slave or woman) was (denied the rights of citizenship.)

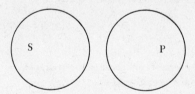

7. *A* All (eligible bachelors) are (scarce people.)

9. *E* No (things, persons, etc.) are (ghosts.)

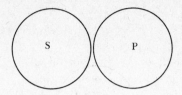

Exercises for § 5.5

A. 1. Subcontraries
    2. Contraries
    3. Contradictories
    4. Alterns
    5. Contraries
    6. Subcontraries

B. 1. unknown; true; unknown
    2. unknown; false; unknown
    3. false; unknown; unknown
    4. false; false; true
    5. true; false; unknown

C. 1. No redheads are hot-tempered.
    2. Some bankers are not dull conversationalists.
    3. All members of the Mafia are good sports.
    4. Some TV shows are not insults to a low-level ape.

D. 1. Some politicians are not dishonest.
    3. Some Marxists are supporters of free elections.

E. 1. Some football players are rough and tough.
    3. Some American-made automobiles are expensive.

Exercises for § 5.6

A. Conversion
    1. **E** to **E**; No (good lieutenant) is (a non-stable person.)
    3. **I** to **I**; Some (snobs) are (wealthy people.)
    Obversion
    1. **E** to **A**; All (unstable persons) are (non-good lieutenants.)
    3. **I** to **O**; Some (wealthy people) are not (non-snobs.)

B. 1. *A* All (non-people who are to be trusted) are (non-honest politicians.)
       or *E* (no contrapositives.)
    3. *A* All (who are eligible) are (union members.)
       to *E* No (non-eligible) are (non union members.)
    5. *E* (yields no contrapositive.)

CHAPTER 6

Exercises for § 6.1

1. All things fattening are things that should be avoided.
    Some cakes are things that are fattening.
    Some cakes are things that should be avoided.

Form: **AII–1**
   Major term = things that should be avoided
   Minor term = cakes are things
   Middle term = things that are fattening

3. All broad education is something indispensable for a writer.
   All studies in the liberal arts and the sciences are part of a broad education.
   All studies in the liberal arts and the sciences are indispensable for a writer.

   Form: **AAA–1**
   Major term = writer
   Minor term = studies in the liberal arts and sciences
   Middle term = broad education

5. All sharks are dangerous.
   Some fish are not sharks.
   Some fish are not dangerous.

   Form: **AOO–1**
   Major term = dangerous
   Minor term = fish
   Middle term = sharks

7. No morals is (leads to) unhappy people.
   Some women do not have morals.
   Some women are unhappy people.

   Form: **EOI–1**
   Major term = unhappy people
   Minor term = women
   Middle term = morals

9. No ghosts are observable things.
   All visible things are observable things.
   No visible things are ghosts.

   Form: **EAE–2**
   Major term = ghosts
   Minor term = visible objects
   Middle term = observable things

Exercises for § 6.2

A.   1. All of the college's cars are Chevrolets.
     All of the cars in the parking lot are Chevrolets.

     All of the cars in the parking lot are the college's cars.
     S = the cars in the parking lot; P = the college's cars; M = Chevrolets.

     All P are M
     All S are M
     ─────────
     All S are P

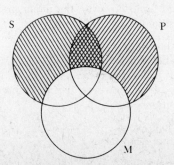

3. No good plan calls for building an outdoor swimming pool in Alaska. This plan calls for building an outdoor swimming pool in Alaska.

   This is not a good plan.

   S = this plan: M = Alaskan pools; P = good plan.

   No P are M.

   All S are M.

   No S are P.

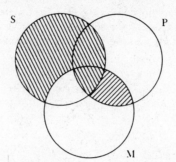

5. All Class A runners are eligible to enter the Olympics.

   No freshmen are Class A runners.

   Some freshmen are not eligible to enter the Olympics.

   S = freshmen; P = eligible to enter the Olympics; M = Class A runners.

   All M are P.

   No S are M.

   Some S are not P.

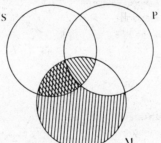

B. If invalid, indicate the rule violation.

   1. All Occidentals are haughty persons.

      Some haughty persons are crooks.

      Some crooks are Occidentals.

      Invalid: Undistributed middle.

   3. All good people are concerned with human welfare.

      All virtuous people are good people.

      All virtuous people are concerned with human welfare.

      Valid: (**AAA**–1)

   5. Some dishes are fragile things.

      No fragile things are iron things.

      Some dishes are not iron things.

      Valid: (For standard form, however, the minor premise should be in the major premise position).

   7. Some athletes are fat persons.

      No fat persons are ballet dancers.

      Some athletes are not ballet dancers.

      Valid: (For standard form, however, the minor premise should be in the major premise position).

   9. No tragic actors are happy men.

      Some comedians are not happy men.

Some comedians are not tragic actors.
Invalid: Exclusive premises.

11. No clowns are poets.
No poets are logicians.
No logicians are clowns.
Invalid: Exclusive premises.

C. Test the validity of each by Venn diagrams.

1. Some *A* is *B*.
All *C* is *B*.
Some *C* is *A*.

IAI=2,
INVALID:

Undistributed middle

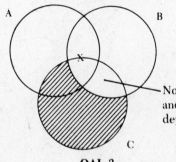

No X in this space,
and conclusion not
depicted in the diagram.

3. Some *A* is not *B*.
All *A* is *C*.
Some *C* is *B*.

OAI–3,
INVALID: Negative

premise, *no*
negative conclusion

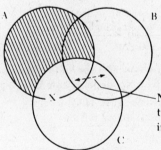

No X in either space. Hence,
the conclusion is not depicted
in the diagram.

5. Some *A* is not *B*.
All *B* is *C*.
Some *C* is not *A*.

OAO–4,
INVALID:

Illicit Major

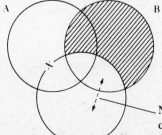

No X in either space. Hence, the
conclusion is not depicted in the
diagram.

7. No *A* is *B*.
   Some *B* is *C*.
   Some *C* is not *A*.

   EIO–4,
   <u>VALID</u>

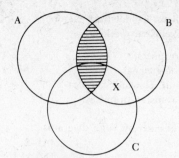

9. All *A* is *B*.
   Some *A* is not *C*.
   Some *C* is not *B*.

   No *X* in either space.
   Hence, the conclusion is . . .

   AOO–3,
   <u>INVALID</u>:

   Illicit major

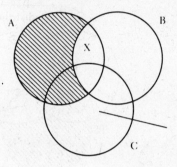

Exercises for § 6.3

1. *S*—cars in the garage; *P*—state cars; *M*—Plymouths
   Substitute: *S*—cats; *P*—dogs; *M*—mammals

All *P* are *M*	All dogs are mammals —True	
<u>All *S* are *M*</u>	<u>All cats are mammals —True</u>	
All *S* are *P*	All cats are dogs	—False

3. *S*—introverts; *P*—good teachers; *M*—shy and retiring persons
   Substitute: *S*—Conservatives; *P*—Republicans; *M*—Democrats

   No shy and retiring persons are good teachers
   <u>Some introverts are shy and retiring persons</u>

   No introverts are good teachers

   No Democrats are Republicans   —True
   <u>Some conservative people are Democrats —True</u>

   No conservative people are Republicans —False

5. *S*—speculative stocks; *P*—dependable investments; *M*—blue chip securities
   Substitute: *S*—mothers; *P*—parents; *M*—fathers

All *M* are *P*	All fathers are parents —True	
<u>No *S* are *M*</u>	<u>No mothers are fathers —True</u>	
No *S* are *P*	No mothers are parents —False	

7. *S*—professors; *P*—vain people; *M*—ignorant people
   Substitute: *S*—dogs; *P*—mammals; *M*—whales

All *M* are *P*	All whales are mammals —True	
<u>No *S* are *M*</u>	<u>No dogs are whales</u>	<u>—True</u>
No *S* are *P*	No dogs are mammals	—False

9. *S*—all those who voted for the new blood and imaginative thinking of John Doe; *P*—people interested in progress; *M*—those who voted the Democratic ticket.
   Substitute: *S*—swimming creatures; *P*—warm-blooded; *M*—whales

All *M* are *P*	All whales are warm-blooded	—True
All *M* are *S*	All whales are swimming creatures	—True
All *S* are *P*	All swimming creatures are warm-blooded	—False

Exercises for § 6.4

A. 1. All responsible beings are rational beings—Missing Premise
      No children are rational beings.

      No children are responsible beings.

   3. All musicians are versatile.
      Some musicians are artistic people.   or   Some artistic people are musicians

      Some artistic people are versatile.

      Both missing premises make valid syllogism because I Proposition converts without loss of meaning

   5. All radicals are crazy
      No sensible people are crazy

      No sensible people are radicals—Missing Conclusion

B. 1. All (determinism) are (philosophies arguing that all events, including human actions, are completely determined by past actions.)
      All (Spinoza's Philosophy) are (philosophies arguing that all events. . . .)

      No valid conclusion can be drawn because the premise do not distribute the middle term and thus a rule is always violated.

   3. No (Sartre) are theistic.
      Some existentialist thinkers are not theistic

      Some existentialist thinkers are not Sartre

      A negative premise requires a negative conclusion, and the S term is not distributed in the premises, so it cannot be distributed in the conclusion, and thus an O proposition is required.

   5. Some philosophers are not those people concerned with ethical judgments.
      Some scientists are those people concerned with ethical judgments.

      No valid conclusion can be drawn because a negative conclusion is required and neither an O or E proposition would produce a valid syllogism because neither the S or P term is distributed in the premises.

   7. No critical thinkers are makers of logical errors.
      All those who read superficially are makers of logical errors.

      No persons who read superficially are makers of logical errors.
                              or
      All persons who read superficially are makers of logical errors.
      No critical thinkers are makers of logical errors.

      No critical thinkers are persons who read superficially.

      A negative universal premise is required and since the E converts without loss of meaning both syllogisms are valid.

C. 1. No things requiring critical thinking are too easy.
   All logical exercise are things requiring critical thinking.

   No logical exercises are too easy.

   3. All deeply reflective people are dissatisfied people
   All sensitive creatures are deeply reflective people.

   All sensitive creatures are dissatisfied people.

   5. All critical thinkers are opposed to dictators.
   All rational men are critical thinkers.

   All rational men are opposed to dictators.

Exercises for § 6.5

1. All those who could have won an acquittal in this case are lawyers as clever as Clarence Darrow.
   All Attorney Jones are those who could have won an acquittal . . .

   All Attorney Jones are (lawyers as clever as Clarence Darrow.)

       d   u
   All *M* are *P*
       d   u
   All *S* are *M*
        d   u
   All *S* are *P*

   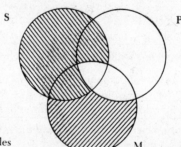

   Valid: Violates No Rules

3. All cases of nations that have lost their moral values are cases of nations that are going to the dogs.
   All (this nation of ours) are cases of nations that are going to the dogs.

   (All) this nation of ours are (cases of nations losing its moral values).

       d   u
   All *P* are *M*
       d   u
   All *S* are *M*
        d   u
   All *S* are *P*

   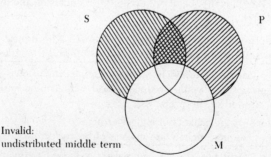

   Invalid:
   undistributed middle term

5. All those who survive are fittest.
   None that are not fit are among those who survive   Invalid—Only two terms

   None who are not fit are among those who survive.

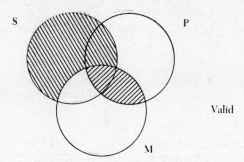

Valid

7. No (case of something that has not been tried) is something that can be said to have failed. All (Christianity) is a case of something that has not been tried.

No (Christianity) is something that can be said to have failed.

    d   u
No *M* are *P*
    d   u
All *S* are *M*
    d   d
No *S* are *P*

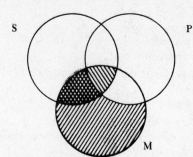

Invalid: Illicit
Major Term

9. All cases of getting a college education are cases of possessing a certain minimum intellectual equipment, habits of work and an interest in getting an education.
No cases of staying in college for four years, having a good time, keeping out of trouble and becoming an alumnus . . . are cases of getting a good college education.

No cases of staying in college for four years, having a good time, keeping out of trouble and becoming an alumnus . . . are cases of possessing a certain minimum intellectual equipment, habits of work and an interest in getting an education.

    d   u
All *M* are *P*
    d   d
No *S* are *M*
    d   d
No *S* are *P*

CHAPTER 7

Exercises for § 7.3

1. Constituent statements: The market does rise.
   We will sell all the Waterville Railway stock.
   Truth-functor: not if-then
   Statement form: If not p, then q.

3. Constituent statements: No treatments are yet in sight for many hereditary diseases;
   Persons with diabetes or hemophilia will still transmit these
   genes to their offspring.
   Truth-functor: and
   Statement form: p and q

5. Constituent statements: You fire the gun too rapidly; it jams.
   Truth functor: If-then
   Statement form: If p, then q

7. Constituent statements: Jane will graduate.
   She passes logic.
   Truth-functor: if and only if
   Statement form: p if and only if q

9. Constituent statements: John was at the party last night.
   Truth-functor: not
   Statement form: not p

11. Constituent statements: We will sell out our oil stock.
    We will invest in some insurance stock.
    Truth-functor: either-or
    Statement form: either p or q

13. Constituent statements: The college will supplement the research funds.
    Outside sources will be sought.
    Truth-functor: either-or
    Statement form: either p or q

15. Constituent statements: Logic involves thought.
    Logic involves practice.
    Truth-functor: and
    Statement form: p and q

Exercises for § 7.6

A. In the following C—"Civil War continues in Lebanon; S—"Syria moves to stop the conflict
in Lebanon; I—Israel remains neutral; U—"The US pledges support to the Christian
Lebanese; R—"Russia pledges support to Lebanese Moslems; and N—"The U.N. steps
into the Lebanese conflict:

1. Statement Form: $C \cdot S$
   Truth Value: $T \cdot T = T$

3. Statement Form $\sim R$
   Truth Value: $\sim F = T$

5. Statement Form: $\sim\sim U$
   Truth Value: $\sim\sim T = F$

7. Statement Form: $\sim(R \cdot U)$
   Truth Value: $\sim(F \cdot F) = \sim F = T$

9. Statement Form: $\sim(C \cdot S)$
   Truth Value: $\sim(T \cdot T) = \sim(T) = F$

B. 1. Conjunction
   3. Simplification

C. 1. $\sim a$

a	$\sim a$
T	F
F	T

3. $\sim S \cdot L$

S	L	$\sim S$	$\sim S \cdot L$
T	T	F	F
T	F	F	F
F	T	T	T
F	F	T	F

5. $\sim(\sim L)$

L	$\sim L$	$\sim(\sim L)$
T	F	T
F	T	F

Exercises for § 7.7

A. 1. $b \vee i$ Invalid
   $\underline{\quad b \quad}$
   $\sim i$

3. $H \vee I$ Invalid
   $\underline{\sim H \quad}$
   $\therefore T$

B. The following symbolizations will hold in this exercise:
   A—The students will approve a student fee.
   N—The college will support the student newspaper.
   O—Outside funds will be raised for the student center.
   V—The students will vote for a college center.
   S—The college opposes student fees.
   L—The college will launch a football team.

1. Statement Form: $A \vee L$
   Truth Value: $T \vee F = T$

3. Statement Form: $V \vee S$
   Truth Value: $F \vee F = F$

5. Statement Form: $(S \cdot L) \vee (A \cdot \sim O)$
   Truth Value: $(F \cdot F) \vee (T \cdot \sim T) =$
                      $\quad F \vee F = F$

7. Statement Form: $\sim[(N \vee O) \cdot (A \vee L)]$
   Truth Value: $\sim[(T \vee T) \cdot (T \vee F)]$
                      $\quad \sim(T \cdot T) = F$

C. 1. $L \vee I$ $L \vee I$
   $\quad \underline{\sim I \quad}$ $\underline{\sim L \quad}$
   $\quad \therefore L$ $\quad I$

3. $F \lor C$ $F \lor C$
      $\sim F$ $\sim C$
      $\therefore C$ $\therefore F$

D. Invalid

Exercises for § 7.8

A.   1. Translates to: If anything is an atom, then it is a system of energy.
Symbolically expressed: $A \supset E$
Negation of a Conjunction: $\sim(A \cdot \sim E)$

      3. Translates to: If the grant is matched by private funds, then the foundation will make a $100,000 grant.
Symbolically expressed: $M \supset F$
Negation of a conjunction: $\sim(M \cdot \sim F)$

      5. Translates to: If the post office is responsible for the package, then it is insured.
Symbolically expressed: $P \supset I$
Negation of a conjunction: $\sim(P \cdot \sim I)$

      7. Translates to: If we permit the student government to carry on without coordinated planning, then the inevitable result is chaos.
Symbolically expressed: $C \supset I$
Negation of a conjunction: $\sim(C \cdot \sim I)$

      9. Translates to: If Brains would help him with math, then Jim agreed to undertake the dangerous mission.
Symbolically expressed: $B \supset J$
Negation of a conjunction: $\sim(B \cdot J)$

B.   1. Statement Form: $M \supset (S \cdot O)$
       Truth Value: $T \supset (T \cdot T) = T$
      3. Statement Form: $\sim M \supset (S \lor P)$
       Truth Value: $\sim T \supset (T \lor F) = \sim T \supset T = F \supset T = T$
      5. Statement Form: $(M \cdot S) \supset \sim B$
       Truth Value: $(T \cdot T) \supset \sim = T \supset T = T$
      7. Statement Form: $S \supset B$
       Truth Value: $T \supset F = F$
      9. Statement Form: $(M \lor S) \supset B$
       Truth Value: $T \lor T \supset F = T \supset F = F$
    11. Statement Form: $S \supset M$
       Truth Value: $T \supset T = T$
    13. Statement Form: $P \lor (\sim M \supset S)$
       Truth Value: $F \lor (\sim T \supset T) = F \lor F = F$
    15. Statement Form: $\sim[M \supset (I \cdot \sim O)]$
       Truth Value: $\sim[T \supset (F \cdot \sim F)] = \sim[T \supset F = \sim F = T]$
    17. Statement Form: $\sim M \supset \sim S$
       Truth Value: $\sim T \supset \sim T = F \supset F = T$
    19. Statement Form: $(B \lor O) \supset S$
       Truth Value: $(F \lor F) \supset T = F \supset T = T$

C.   1. $W \supset P$ Modus Ponens
         W
        $\therefore P$

3. $E \supset D$ Modus Tollens
    $\dfrac{\sim D}{\therefore \sim E}$ Valid

5. $C \supset F$ Invalid: Affirming the Consequent
    $\dfrac{F}{\therefore C}$

7. $S \supset \sim B$ Valid: Modus Tollens
    $\dfrac{B}{\sim S}$

9. $(M \lor Z) \supset F$ Valid: Modus Ponens
    $\dfrac{\sim (M \lor Z)}{\therefore F}$

1. $L \equiv F$
3. $V \equiv D$
5. $R \equiv S$

1. $p \supset q$
    $\therefore \sim p \supset \sim q$

p	q	$p \supset q$	$\sim p$	$\supset$	$\sim q$
T	T	T	F	T	F
T	F	F	F	T	T
F	T	T	T	F	F
F	F	F	T	T	T

—Conclusion false only in this case—Only one that needs to be checked. Invalid because premise is *true* and conclusion false.

3.

p	q	p	$p \lor q$
T	T	T	
T	F	T	
F	T	T	
F	F	F	F

Valid

5.

p	q	r	$p \supset q$	$q \supset r$	$r \supset p$
T	T	T			T
T	T	F			T
T	F	T			T
T	F	F			T
F	T	T	T	T	F
F	T	F			T
F	F	T	T	T	F
F	F	F			T

Invalid rows 5 and 7

7.

p	q	r	~(p · q) v r	~(r · p)	q v	~r	
T	T	T			T	F	
T	T	F			T	T	
T	F	T	F	T	F	F	
T	F	F			T	T	
F	T	T			T	F	
F	T	F			T	T	
F	F	T	T F	T T F	F	F	Invalid row 7
F	F	F			T	T	

9.

p	q	r	p ⊃ (q ⊃ r)	(q ⊃ r)	p ⊃ q	p ⊃ r	
T	T	T				T	
T	T	F	F	F	T	F	Valid
T	F	T				T	
T	F	F		F		F	
F	T	T				T	
F	T	F				T	
F	F	T				T	
F	F	F				T	

11.

p	q	p · (q ⊃ p)	(q ⊃ p)	~p v q	q	
T	T					
T	F	T	T	F	F	Valid
F	T					
F	F	F	T	T	F	

13.

p	q	r	s	p ⊃ (q ⊃ r)	(q ⊃ r)	(q ⊃ r) ⊃ s	p ⊃ s	
T	T	T	T				T	
T	T	T	F			T F	F	Valid
T	T	F	T				T	
T	T	F	F	F	F	F T	F	
T	F	T	T				T	
T	F	T	F			T F	F	
T	F	F	T				T	
T	F	F	F			T F	F	
F	T	T	T				T	
F	T	T	F				T	
F	T	F	T				T	
F	T	F	F				T	
F	F	T	T				T	
F	F	T	F				T	
F	F	F	T				T	
F	F	F	F				T	

15.

p	q	r	p ⊃ (q v r)	(q v r)	(q · r) ⊃ ~p	~p	
T	T	T			T	F	F
T	T	F	T	T	F	T	F	Invalid, rows 2 & 3
T	F	T	T	T	F	T	F
T	F	F	F	F	F	T	F
F	T	T				T	
F	T	F				T	
F	F	T				T	
F	F	F				T	

17.

p	q	r	p ⊃ (q v r)	~q	~r	⊃	~p
T	T	T			F	T	F
T	T	F		F	T	T	F
T	F	T			F	T	F
T	F	F	F F	T	T	T	F
F	T	T			F	T	T
F	T	F			T	T	T
F	F	T			F	T	T
F	F	F			T	T	T

Valid

19.

p	q	r	~p v (q · r)	~q v ~r	~p
T	T	T		F	F
T	T	F	F F	T	F
T	F	T	F F	T	F
T	F	F	F F	T	F
F	T	T			T
F	T	F			T
F	F	T			T
F	F	F			T

Valid

21.

p	q	r	s	p ⊃ (q v r)	(q · r) ⊃ s	p ⊃ s
T	T	T	T			T
T	T	T	F	T	[F]	F
T	T	F	T			T
T	T	F	F	[T] T	F [T]	F
T	F	T	T			T
T	F	T	F	[T] T	F [T]	F
T	F	F	T			T
T	F	F	F	F F	F [T]	F
F	T	T	T			T
F	T	T	F			T
F	T	F	T			T
F	T	F	F			T
F	F	T	T			T
F	F	T	F			T
F	F	F	T			T
F	F	F	F			T

Invalid rows 4 & 6

23.

p	q	r	(p ⊃ q) ⊃ (p ⊃ r)	p ⊃ q	q ⊃ p	p ⊃ r
T	T	T				T
T	T	F	T F F	T	T	F
T	F	T				T
T	F	F		F	T	F
F	T	T				T
F	T	F				T
F	F	T				T
F	F	F				T

Valid

25.

p	q	r	s	(p·q)⊃r	p⊃s	(s·q)⊃r	
T	T	T	T		T	T T	
T	T	T	F		F	F T	
T	T	F	T	T F	T	T F	
T	T	F	F		F	F T	
T	F	T	T		F	F T	
T	F	T	F		F	F T	
T	F	F	T		F	F T	
T	F	F	F		F	F T	
F	T	T	T		T	T T	
F	T	T	F		F	F T	
F	T	F	T	F T	T	T F	Invalid, row 11
F	T	F	F		F	F T	
F	F	T	T		F	F T	
F	F	T	F		F	F T	
F	F	F	T		F	F T	
F	F	F	F		F	F T	

B.

1.

$$S \supset F$$
$$\sim F \lor \sim C$$
$$\therefore \sim(S \cdot C)$$

S	F	C	S⊃F	~F v ~C	~(S·C)	Valid
T	T	T		F	F T	
T	T	F			T F	
T	F	T	F	T	F T	
T	F	F			T F	
F	T	T			T F	
F	T	F			T F	
F	F	T			T F	
F	F	F			T F	

3.

$$\sim G \supset \sim L$$
$$\sim L \supset \sim R$$
$$\therefore \sim G \supset \sim R$$

G	L	R	~G⊃~L	~L⊃~R	~G⊃~R	Valid
T	T	T			T	
T	T	F			T	
T	F	T			T	
T	F	F			T	
F	T	T	F	T	F	
F	T	F			T	
F	F	T		F	F	
F	F	F			T	

5.

$$C \supset (W \lor M)$$
$$W \cdot M$$
$$\therefore C$$

C	W	M	C⊃(W v M)	W·M	C	
T	T	T				
T	T	F				
T	F	T				
T	F	F				
F	T	T	T T	T	F	Invalid, Row 5
F	T	F		F	F	
F	F	T		F	F	
F	F	F		F	F	

7. R ≡ (A · C)
C ⊃ A
∴ R

R	A	C	R ≡ (A · C)	C ⊃ A	R	
T	T	T				
T	T	F				
T	F	T				
T	F	F				
F	T	T	F T	T	F	
F	T	F	T F	T	F	Invalid, rows 6 & 8
F	F	T	T T	F	F	
F	F	F	T F	T	F	

9. (B · I) ⊃ M
~M
∴ ~B ~I

B	I	M	(B · I) ⊃ M	~M	∴ ~B · ~I	
T	T	T		F	F	
T	T	F	T F	T	F	
T	F	T		F	F	
T	F	F	F [T]	T	F	Invalid, row 4
F	T	T		F	F	
F	T	F		T	F	
F	F	T			T	
F	F	F			T	

11. J ⊃ (B ∨ C)
(B · C) ⊃ S

∴ J ⊃ S

J	B	C	S	J ⊃ (B ∨ C)	(B · C) ⊃ S	J ⊃ S	
T	T	T	T			T	
T	T	T	F	T	[F]	F	
T	T	F	T			T	
T	T	F	F	F F	F [T]	F	
T	F	T	T			T	
T	F	T	F	[T] T	F [T]	F	Invalid, row 6
T	F	F	T			T	
T	F	F	F	F F	F [T]	F	
F	T	T	T			T	
F	T	T	F			T	
F	T	F	T			T	
F	T	F	F			T	
F	F	T	T			T	
F	F	T	F			T	
F	F	F	T			T	
F	F	F	F			T	

Exercises for § 7.12

A. **1.** p q (p · q) ⊃ (p ∨ q)   Tautologous

p	q	(p · q)	⊃	(p ∨ q)
T	T	T	T	T
T	F	F	T	T
F	T	F	T	T
F	F	F	T	F

3. $p \quad q \quad (p \cdot q) \cdot (p \supset \sim q)$

p	q	(p·q)	·	(p⊃~q)	
T	T	T	F	F	
T	F	F	F	T	
F	T	F	F	T	
F	F	F	**F**	T	Contradictory

5. $\sim p \quad p \quad (\sim p \cdot p) \cdot (p \supset \sim p)$

~p	p	(~p·p)	·	(p⊃~p)	
F	T	F	F	F	
T	F	F	**F**	T	Contradictory

7. $p \quad q \quad p \supset [p \supset (q \cdot \sim q)]$ Contingent

p	q	p⊃	[p⊃	(q·~q)]
T	T	F	F	F
T	F	F	F	F
F	T	T	T	F
F	F	T	T	F

9. $p \quad q \quad v \quad [p \supset (q \supset p)] \supset [(q \supset q) \supset \sim(v \supset v)]$

p	q	v	[p⊃(q⊃p)]	(q⊃p)	⊃	(q⊃q)	⊃	~	(v⊃v)	
T	T	T	T	T	F	T	F	F	T	
T	T	F	T	T	F	T	F	F	T	
T	F	T	T	T	F	T	F	F	T	
T	F	F	T	T	F	T	F	F	T	
F	T	T	T	F	F	T	F	F	T	
F	T	F	T	F	F	T	F	F	T	
F	F	T	T	T	F	T	F	F	T	
F	F	F	T	T	**F**	T	F	F	T	Contradictory

11. $p \quad q \quad r \quad s \quad \{[(p \supset q) \cdot (r \supset s)] \cdot (q \vee s)\} \supset (p \vee r)$

p	q	r	s	(p⊃q)	·	(r⊃s)	·	(q∨s)	⊃	(p∨r)	
T	T	T	T	T	T	T	T	T	T	T	
T	T	T	F	T	F	F	F	T	T	T	
T	T	F	T	T	T	T	T	T	T	T	
T	T	F	F	T	T	T	T	T	T	T	
T	F	T	T	F	F	T	F	T	T	T	
T	F	T	F	F	F	F	F	F	T	T	
T	F	F	T	F	F	T	F	T	T	T	
T	F	F	F	F	F	T	F	F	T	T	
F	T	T	T	T	T	T	T	T	T	T	
F	T	T	F	T	F	F	F	T	T	T	
F	T	F	T	T	T	T	T	T	T	F	
F	T	F	F	T	T	T	T	T	T	F	
F	F	T	T	T	T	T	T	T	T	T	
F	F	T	F	T	F	F	F	F	T	T	
F	F	F	T	T	T	T	T	T	T	F	
F	F	F	F	T	T	T	F	F	**T**	F	Tautologous

B. **1.** $(L \cdot A) \supset (L \vee A)$ $\quad L \quad A \quad (L \cdot A) \supset (L \vee A)$

L	A	(L·A)	⊃	(L∨A)	
T	T	T	T	T	
T	F	F	T	T	
F	T	F	T	T	
F	F	F	**T**	F	Tautology

3. $J \supset (T \supset J)$

J	T	J⊃(T⊃J)		Tautology
T	T	T	T	
T	F	T	T	
F	T	T	F	
F	F	T	T	

5. $T \quad V \quad \sim\{[(V \cdot \sim(V \lor I)] \supset [I \cdot \sim(I \lor V)]\}$

T	V								
T	T	F	FF	T	T	F	F	T	
T	F	F	FF	T	T	F	F	T	
F	T	F	FF	T	T	F	F	T	
F	F	F	FT	F	T	F	T	F	Contradictory

1. $T \supset J$
 $J \supset S$
 $S \supset \sim T$
 $\therefore \sim T$

T	J	S	[(T ⊃ J)	·	(J ⊃ S)	·	(S ⊃ ~T)]	⊃	~T	
T	T	T	T	T	T	F	F	F	T	F
T	T	F	T	F	F	F	T	F	T	F
T	F	T	F	F	T	F	F	F	T	F
T	F	F	F	F	T	F	T	F	T	F
F	T	T	T	T	T	T	T	T	T	T
F	T	F	T	F	F	F	T	T	T	T
F	F	T	T	T	T	T	T	T	T	T
F	F	F	T	T	T	T	T	T	T	T	Tautology

3. $S \supset A$
 $A \supset S$
 $S \lor A$

S	A	[(S ⊃ A)	·	A ⊃ S)]	⊃	S ∨ A		Valid
T	T	T	T	T	T	T		
T	F	F	F	T	T	T		
F	T	T	F	F	T	T		
F	F	T	T	T	F	F		

5. $T \supset (H \cdot S)$
 $\sim H$
 $\therefore \sim T$

T	H	S	{[T ⊃ (H · S)]	·	~H}	⊃	~ T	
T	T	T	T	T	F	F	T	F
T	T	F	F	F	F	T	T	F
T	F	T	F	F	F	T	T	F
T	F	F	F	F	F	T	T	F
F	T	T	T	T	F	F	T	T
F	T	F	T	F	F	F	T	T
F	F	T	T	F	T	T	T	T
F	F	F	T	F	T	T	T	T	Tautology − Valid

7. A v R
R ⊃ (S · C)
∴ A

A	R	S	C	(A v R)	·	[R ⊃ (S · C)]	(S · C)	⊃	A	
T	T	T	T	T	T	T	T	T	T	
T	T	T	F	T	F	F	F	T	T	
T	T	F	T	T	F	F	F	T	T	
T	T	F	F	T	F	F	F	T	T	
T	F	T	T	T	T	T	T	T	T	
T	F	T	F	T	T	T	F	T	T	
T	F	F	T	T	T	T	F	T	T	
T	F	F	F	T	T	T	F	T	T	
F	T	T	T	T	T	T	T	F	F	Not Tautology
F	T	T	F	T	F	F	F	T	F	Not Valid
F	T	F	T	T	F	F	F	T	F	
F	T	F	F	T	F	F	F	T	F	
F	F	T	T	F	F	T	T	T	F	
F	F	T	F	F	F	T	F	T	F	
F	F	F	T	F	F	T	F	T	F	
F	F	F	F	F	F	T	F	T	F	

9. L ⊃ (G v F)
L
∴ ~G v F

L	G	F	{[L ⊃ (G v F)]	(G v F)	· L}	⊃	(~G v F)	
T	T	T	T	T	T	T	T	
T	T	F	T	T	T	F	F	Rows # 2 & 6—
T	F	T	T	T	T	T	T	Not Tautology—
T	F	F	F	F	F	T	T	Invalid
F	T	T	T	T	F	T	T	
F	T	F	T	T	F	F	F	
F	F	T	T	T	F	T	T	
F	F	F	T	F	F	T	T	

B.

1.

p	q	(p ≡ q)	≡	(q ≡ p)	
T	T	T	T	T	
T	F	F	T	F	
F	T	F	T	F	
F	F	T	T	T	Tautology

3.

p	q	p ≡	[p v	(p · q)]	
T	T	T	T	T	
T	F	T	T	F	
F	T	T	F	F	
F	F	T	F	F	Tautology

5.

p	q	(p ⊃ q)	≡	~	(p · ~q)	
T	T	T	T	T	F	
T	F	F	F	F	T	
F	T	T	T	T	F	
F	F	T	F	F	T	Not Tautologous

7.

p	q	r	[(p ⊃ q) ⊃ r]	≡	[(q ⊃ p) ⊃ r]	
T	T	T	T T T	T	T T	
T	T	F	T F T	T	T F	
T	F	T	F T T	T	T T	
T	F	F	F T F	T	T F	
F	T	T	T T T	F	T	
F	T	F	T F F	F	T	
F	F	T	T T T	T	T	
F	F	F	T F T	T	F	Not tautologous

9.

p	q	(p ⊃ q)	≡	[(p v q)	≡	q]	
T	T	T	T	T	T	T	
T	F	F	T	T	F	F	
F	T	T	T	T	T	T	
F	F	T	T	F	T	F	Tautology

Exercises for § 7.16

1. This illustrates the Law of Contradiction, but is more than likely a Black and White Fallacy because there are degrees of sanity and insanity, and these are dangerous terms to define.
3. This is a misuse of the Law of the Excluded Middle. Every statement is either true or false, but here one probably is not referring to the statement "I am happy," but the condition of being happy which can be referred to in degrees.
5. Once again physical conditions are confused with logical conditions and light does not *simultaneously* appear corpuscular and noncorpuscular.

CHAPTER 8

Exercises for § 8.1

A. 1. Disjunctive Syllogism
    3. Modus Tollens
    5. Addition
    7. Modus Ponens
    9. Constructive Dilemma

B. 1. A
    B
    ─────
    ∴ A · B

    2. A · B
    ─────
    ∴ A

    3. A ⊃ B
    A
    ─────
    ∴ B

    4. (A ⊃ B)
    (B ⊃ C)
    ─────
    ∴ A ⊃ C

  5. $A \vee B$
     $$\frac{\sim B}{\therefore A}$$

  6. $\dfrac{A}{\therefore A \vee B}$

C. 1. Disjunctive Syllogism
   3. Simplification
   5. Constructive Dilemma
   7. Hypothetical Syllogism
   9. Constructive Dilemma
   11. Modus Tollens
   13. Hypothetical Syllogism
   15. Constructive Dilemma
   17. Simplification
   19. Modus Tollens

D. 1. 5. $A \supset C$ 1,2, H.S.
      6. $\sim A$ 5,4, M.T.
      7. $\sim D$ 3,6, D.S.

   3. 4. K 1,3, M.P.
      5. $\sim K$ 2,3, M.P.
      6. $\sim J$ 2,5, M.T.

   5. 5. $M \supset O$ 1,2, H.S.
      6. $(M \supset O) \cdot (P \supset Q)$ 6,3, Conj.
      7. $O \vee Q$ 6,4, C.D.

   7. 4. $A \supset B$ 1. Simp.
      5. $E \supset F$ 2. Simp.
      6. $(A \supset B) \cdot (E \supset F)$ 4,5, Conj.
      7. $B \vee F$ 6,4, C.D.

   9. 5. $M \supset N$ 2,4, M.P.
      6. $(J \supset K) \cdot (M \supset N)$ 1,5, Conj.
      7. $J \vee M$ 3,4, D.S.
      8. $K \vee N$ 6,7, C.D.

E. 1. 1) $(G \vee H) \supset (J \cdot K)$
      2) G $/ \therefore J$
      3) $G \vee H$ 2, Add.
      4) $J \cdot K$ 1,3, M.P.
      5) J 4, Simp.

   3. 1) $A \cdot B$
      2) $(A \vee C) \supset (D \vee E)$ $/ A \cdot (D \vee E)$
      3) A 1, Simp.
      4) $A \vee C$ 3, Add.
      5) $D \vee E$ 2,4, M.P.
      6) $A \cdot (D \vee E)$ 3,5, Conj.

   5. 1) $J \supset K$
      2) $L \supset M$
      3) $\sim N \vee (J \vee L)$
      4) $\sim\sim N$ $/ K \vee M$

5) $(J \supset K) \cdot (L \supset M)$ 1,2, Conj.
6) $J \vee L$ 3,4, D.S.
7) $K \vee M$ 5,6, C.D.

7. 1) $M \supset (B \supset P)$
2) $M \supset (P \supset S)$
3) M $/ \therefore B \supset S$
4) $B \supset P$ 1,3, M.P.
5) $P \supset S$ 2,3, M.P.
6) $B \supset S$ 4,5, H.S.

9. 1. $(A \vee B) \supset C$
2. $(C \vee D) \supset E$
3. $D \vee A$
4. $\sim D$ $/ \therefore E$
5. A 3,4, D.S.
6. $A \vee B$ 5, Add.
7. C 1,6, M.P.
8. $C \vee D$ 7, Add.
9. E 2,8, M.P.

F. 1. 1. $G \supset (S \supset U)$
2. G
3. $\sim U$ $/ \therefore \sim S$
4. $S \supset U$ 1,2, M.P.
5. $\sim S$ 4,3, M.T.

3. 1. $D \supset E$
2. $F \vee \sim E$
3. $\sim F$ $/ \therefore \sim D$
4. $\sim E$ 2,3, D.S.
5. $\sim D$ 1,4, M.T.

5. 1. $L \supset \sim S$
2. $\sim L \supset (H \equiv \sim S)$
3. $(\sim A \vee \sim H) \supset \sim\sim S$
4. $\sim A \vee \sim H$ $/ \therefore H \equiv \sim S$
5. $\sim\sim S$ 3,4, M.P.
6. $\sim L$ 1,5, M.T.
7. $H \equiv \sim S$ 2,6, M.P.

7. 1. $M \supset (\sim R \supset U)$
2. $M \cdot \sim R$ $/ \therefore U$
3. M 2, Simp.
4. $\sim R \supset U$ 1,3, M.P.
5. $\sim R$ 2, Simp.
6. U 4,5, M.P.

9. 1. $(N \vee O) \supset P$
2. $(P \vee Q) \supset R$
3. $Q \vee N$
4. $\sim Q$ $/ \therefore R$
5. N 3,4, D.S.
6. $N \vee O$ 6, Add.
7. P 1,6, M.P.
8. $P \vee Q$ 8, Add.
9. R 2,8, M.P.

Exercises for § 8.2

A. 1. Commutation
    3. Exportation
    5. Absorption
    7. Absorption
    9. Association
   11. Material Equivalence
   13. Material Implication
   15. Transposition
   17. Commutation
   19. Association

B. 1. 3) $\sim\!S$ v $\sim\!R$ 2, Addition
        4) $\sim\!(S \cdot R)$ 3, De Morgan
        5) $(P$ v $M) \supset (S \cdot R)$ 1, Impl.
        6) $\sim\!(P$ v $M)$ 5,4, Modus Tollens
        7) $\sim\!(P$ v $\sim\!M)$ 6, De Morgans
        8) $\sim\!M \cdot \sim\!P$ 7, Comm.
        9) $\sim\!M$ 8, Simpl.
    3. 3) $(\sim\!D$ v $E) \cdot (\sim\!D$ v $\sim\!D)$ 2, Distribution
        4) $(\sim\!D$ v $\sim\!D) \cdot (\sim\!D$ v $E)$ 3, Commut.
        5) $(\sim\!D$ v $\sim\!D)$ 4, Simpl.
        6) $\sim\!D$ 5, Tautology
        7) D v $(\sim\!E$ v $F)$ 1, Association
        8) $\sim\!E$ v F 7,6, Disj. Syllog.
        9) $E \supset F$ 8, Impl.
    5. 2) $(\sim\!P$ v $Q) \supset Q$ 1, Impl.
        3) $\sim\!(\sim\!P$ v $Q)$ v Q 2, Impl.
        4) $(\sim\sim\!P \cdot \sim\!Q)$ v Q 3, De Morgan
        5) $(P \cdot \sim\!Q)$ v Q 4, Double Negation
        6) Q v $(P \cdot \sim\!Q)$ 5, Commut.
        7) $(Q$ v $P) \cdot (Q$ v $\sim\!Q)$ 6, Dist.
        8) Q v P 7, Simpl.
        9) P v Q 8, Commut.
    7. 5) $\sim\!S$ v $\sim\!R$ 4, Addition
        6) $\sim\sim\!Q$ 3,5, Modus Ponens
        7) Q 6, Double Negation
        8) $\sim\!P$ 1,7, Modus Ponens
        9) $Q \supset \sim\!R$ 2,8, Modus Ponens
       10) $\sim\!R$ 9,7, Modus Ponens
    9. 4) J 3, Simpl.
        5) J v K 4, Addition
        6) L 1,4, Modus Ponens
        7) L v K 6, Addition
        8) $J \supset (M \supset N) \cdot (N \supset M)$ 2,7, Modus Ponens
        9) $(M \supset N) \cdot (N \supset M)$ 8,4, Modus Ponens
       10) $M \equiv N$ 7, Material Equiv.

C.   1) $N \supset (P \cdot R)$
        2) $R \supset P$
        3) $\sim\!P$ $/ \therefore \sim\!N$

4) ~R   2,3, Modus Tollens
5) ~R v ~P   4, Addition
6) ~(P · R)   5, De Morgan
7) ~N   1,6, Modus Tollens

3. 1) ~(A v ~B)   / ∴ B
    2) ~(A · ~~B)   1, De Morgan
    3) ~~B · A   2, Commut.
    4) ~~B   3, Simpl.
    5) B   4, Double Negation

5. 1) L v M
    2) ~M   / ∴ ~M · L
    3) L   1,2, Disj. Syll.
    4) L · ~M   3,2, Conj.
    5) ~M · L   4, Commut.

7. 1) (L · E) ⊃ C
    2) (E ⊃ C) ⊃ P
    3) L   / ∴ P
    4) L ⊃ (E ⊃ C)   1, Distribution
    5) E ⊃ C   4,3, Modus Ponens
    6) P   2,5, Modus Ponens

9. 1) A ⊃ B
    2) (~C · ~A)
    3) ~~C   / ∴ ~A
    4) ~(C v A)   2, De Morgan
    5) C ⊃ A   4, Material Impl.
    6) C ⊃ B   1,5, Hyp. Syll.
    7) ~C v B   6, Material Impl.
    8) ~B   7,3, Disj. Syll.
    9) ~A   1,8, Modus Tollens

11. 1) ~E v (~W v ~A)
     2) (W · A) v (~W · ~A)   / ∴ ~E v (~W · ~A)
     3) ~~E ⊃ (~W v ~A)   1, Material Impl.
     4) ~(W · A) ⊃ (~W · ~A)   2, Material Impl.
     5) (~W v ~A) ⊃ (W · ~A)   4, De Morgan on Antecedent
     6) ~~E ⊃ (~W · ~A)   6, Double Negation
     8) ~E v (~W · ~A)   7, Material Impl.

13. 1) (C ⊃ H) · (A ⊃ L)
     2) O ⊃ (~H · L) / ∴ (C ⊃ A) · (H ⊃ M)
     3) O
     4) ~H · L   2,3, Modus Ponens
     5) ~H   4, Simpl.
     6) C ⊃ H   1, Simpl.
     7) ~C   6,5, Modus Tollens
     8) ~C v A   7, Addition
     9) C ⊃ A   8, Material Implication
    10) ~H v M   5, Addition
    11) H ⊃ M   10, Material Implication
    12) (C ⊃ A) · (H ⊃ M)   9,11, Conjunction

15. 1) M ⊃ ~C
     2) ~C ⊃ ~A
     3) D v A   / ∴ ~M v A

4) $M \supset \sim A$	1,2, Hyp. Syllogism
5) $\sim A \supset \sim M$	4, Transposition
6) $\sim\sim A \vee \sim M$	5, Material Implication
7) $\sim M \vee \sim\sim A$	6, Commutation
8) $\sim M \vee A$	7, Double Negation on 2nd Disjunct.

D. 1. 1. $(A \cdot B) \supset C$
     2. $A \quad / \therefore B \supset C$
     3. $A \supset (B \supset C)$ 1, Exportation
     4. $B \supset C$ 3,2, Modus Ponens

   3. 1. $\sim A \supset \sim R$
       2. $R \quad / \therefore A$
       3. $\sim\sim A \vee R$ 1, Impl.
       4. $\sim\sim A$ 3,2, Disj. Syllog.
       5. A 4, Double Neg.

   5. 1. $T \equiv W$
       2. $\sim W \quad / T \supset (E \vee \sim P)$
       3. $(T \supset W) \cdot (W \supset T)$ 2, Material Equivalence
       4. $T \supset W$ 3, Simplification
       5. $\sim T$ 4,2, Modus Tollens

   7. 1. $(R \supset S) \vee T$
       2. $(S \vee T) \quad / \therefore R \vee \sim Q$
       3. $\sim S \cdot \sim T$ 2, De Morgan
       4. $\sim T \cdot \sim S$ 3, Commutation
       5. $\sim T$ 4, Simplification
       6. $\sim(R \supset S)$ 1,5, Disjunctive Syllogism
       7. $(\sim R \vee S)$ 6, Material Impl.
       8. $\sim\sim R \cdot \sim S$ 7, De Morgan
       9. $\sim\sim R$ 8, Simplification
      10. R 9, Double Negation
      11. $R \vee \sim Q$ 10, Addition

   9. 1. $L \supset (P \supset G)$
       2. L
       3. $P \quad / \therefore G$
       4. $P \supset G$ 1,2, Modus Ponens
       5. G 4,3, Modus Ponens

  11. 1. $J \vee (L \cdot A)$
       2. $J \supset W$
       3. $W \supset A \quad / \therefore A$
       4. $J \supset A$ 2,3, Hyp. Syll.
       5. $J \supset (J \cdot A)$ 4. Absorp.
       6. $\sim(J \cdot A) \supset \sim J$ 5. Transp.
       7. $(\sim J \vee \sim H) \supset \sim J$ 6. DeM. Antecedent
       8. $(J \vee L) \cdot (J \vee A)$ 1. Dist.
       9. $(J \vee A) \cdot (J \vee L)$ 8, Commut.
      10. $(J \vee A)$ 9, Simpl.
      11. $(\sim J \vee A) \vee \sim J$ 7, Mat. Impl.
      12. $\sim J$ 10,11, D.S.
      13. A 10,12, D.S.

  13. 1. $(\sim P \cdot A) \supset (B \vee T)$
       2. $\sim P \supset (B \supset S)$
       3. $P \vee (T \supset L)$

4. ~P · A   / ∴ S v L
5. ~P   4, Simp.
6. B ⊃ S   2,5, M.P.
7. T ⊃ L   3,5, D.S.
8. (B ⊃ S) · (T ⊃ L)   6,7, Conj.
9. B v T   1,4, M.P.
10. S v L   8,9, C.D.

Exercises for § 8.3

1. 1) (R ⊃ Q) ⊃ P
    2) T v S
    3) ~(R · T)
    4) ~Q ⊃ ~S   / ∴ P
    5) R   AP
    6) ~R v ~T   3. DeM.
    7) ~T   6.5. D.S.
    8) S   2.7. D.S.
    9) S ⊃ Q   4. Transp.
    10) Q   9.8. M.P.
    11) R ⊃ Q   5-10. C.P.
    12) P   11.1, M.P.

3. On the tapes.

5. 1) A ⊃ B
    2) C v ~A   / ∴ A ⊃ (B · C)
    3) A   AP
    4) B   1.3. M.P.
    5) C   2.3. D.S.
    6) (B · C)   4.5. Conj.
    7) A ⊃ (B · C)   3-6. C.P.

7. 1) F ⊃ (S · L) / ∴ F ⊃ L
    2) F   AP
    3) (S · L)   1.2. M.P.
    4) L   3. Simpl.
    5) F ⊃ L   2-4. C.P.

9. 1) (A v B) ⊃ (C · D)
    2) (D v E) ⊃ F   / ∴ A ⊃ F
    3) A   AP
    4) A v B   3. Add.
    5) (C · D)   1.4. M.P.
    6) D   5. Simpl.
    7) D v E   6. Add.
    8) F   2.7. M.P.
    9) A ⊃ F   3-8. C.P.

Exercises for § 8.4

1. 1) H ⊃ (A ⊃ B)
    2.) ~C ⊃ (H v B)
    3) H ⊃ A   / C v B
    4) ~(C v B)   AP
    5) ~C · ~B   4. DeM.

6) ~C	5. Simpl.
7) H v B	2.6. M.P.
8) ~B	5. Simpl.
9) H	7.8. D.S.
10) A ⊃ B	1. M.P.
11) ~A	10.8. M.T.
12) A	3.9. M.P.
13) A · ~A	11, 12. Reductio Ad Absurdum

3. 1) A ⊃ B
    2) ~(B v C)   / ∴ ~A

3) A	AP
4) B	1.3. M.P.
5) (~B C)	2. DeM.
6) ~B	5. Simpl.
7) ~B · B	6.4. Reductio Ad Absurdum

5. 1) {A ⊃ (B v C)} ⊃ (D ⊃ A)
    2) ~A   / ∴ ~D

3) D	AP
4) ~A v D	2. Add.
5) A ⊃ D	5. Impl.
6) A	5.3. M.P.
7) A · ~A	2.6. Reductio Ad Absurdum

Exercises for § 8.5

1. 1) (S ⊃ C)
    2) C ⊃ (R v O v Y)
    3) R   / ∴ S

    1) F ⊃ T
    2) T ⊃ (T v Fv T)
    3) T   / ∴ F

    Assign: C = T, O = T, R = T, S = F
          Y = T
          or
          RYC = T, Y = T,
          S, O = F

3. 1) P ⊃ Q
    2) R ⊃ S
    3) R v O   / ∴ P v S

    Assign: P, S, R = F
          O = T
          Q = F or T

5. 1) F ⊃ T
    2) T   / ∴ F

    Assign: F = F; T = True

Exercises for § 8.6

1. 1) P ⊃ Q
    2) P · ~Q

3) ~Q	2. Simpl.
4) ~P	1.3. M.T.
5) P	2. Simpl.
6) P · ~P	4.5. Conj.

3. 1) A ≡ B
    2) B · ~A

3) (A ⊃ B) (B · A)	1. Equiv.
4) (B ⊃ A)	3. Simpl.

     5) ~A   2. Simpl.
     6) ~B   4.5. M.T.
     7) B   2. Simpl.
     8) ~B · B   6.7. Conj.

  5. 1) $A \supset (B \vee C)$
      2) $\sim(\sim A \vee C)$
      3) ~B
      4) $(\sim\sim A \cdot \sim C)$ 2. DeM.
      5) ~~A   4. Simpl.
      6) A   5. D.N.
      7) $B \vee C$ 1.6. M.P.
      8) C   7.3. D.S.
      9) ~C   4. Simpl.
     10) ~C · C   9.8. Conj.

  7. 1) $(A \vee B) \supset C$
      2) B · D
      3) $\sim(C \vee \sim A)$
      4) $\sim C \cdot \sim\sim A$ 3. DeM.
      5) ~~A   4. Simpl.
      6) A   5. D.N.
      7) $A \vee B$ 6. Add.
      8) C   1.7. M.P.
      9) ~C   4. Simpl.
     10) C ~C   8.9. Conj.

CHAPTER 9

Exercises for § 9.3

A.   1. $(x) (Sx \supset Rx)$ 11. $(x) (Rx \supset \sim Fx)$
     3. $(x) (Lx \supset Px)$ 13. $(x) (Ox \supset \sim Rx)$
     5. $(x) (Bx \supset Hx)$ 15. $(x) (Sx \cdot Fx)$
     7. $(x) (Px \supset Ax)$ 17. $(x) (Cx \supset Dx)$
     9. $(x) (Cx \supset Dx)$ 19. $(x) (Sx \supset Hx)$

B.   1. $(\exists x) (Wx \sim Mx)$
     3. $(x) (Cx \supset Bx)$

C.   1. $(x) (Dx) \cdot (x) Ex$
     3. $(\exists x) (Bx \cdot Tx) \cdot (\exists x) (Bx \cdot Dx)$
     5. $(x) (Sx \supset \sim Rx)$

D.   1. $Cx \, Dy$—An open sentence.
     3. $(x) \, Cx \supset (\exists x) \, Dx$—A truth-functional compound of quantified statements.
     5. $(\exists x) (Cx \cdot Da)$—Contains an individual constant and existentially quantified state-
           ment.
     7. $(x) (Cy \supset Dx)$—A statement form containing bound and unbound variables.
     9. Dx—An open sentence.

Exercises for § 9.4

1. $(Aa \lor Ba) \lor (Ab \lor Bb)$
3. $(Aa \lor Ab) \cdot (Ba \cdot Bb)$
5. $\{(Aa \cdot Bb) \supset {\sim}Ca\} \cdot \{(Ab \cdot Bb) \supset {\sim}Cb\}$
7. $(Aa \lor Ba) \lor (Ab \lor Bb)$
9. ${\sim}({\sim}Aa \cdot {\sim}Ba) \cdot {\sim}({\sim}Ab \cdot {\sim}Bb)$

Exercises for § 9.5

1. $(x) \{Rx \supset (Gx \cdot Lx \cdot Px)\}$
3. $(x) (Lx\ Sx) \lor (\exists x) (Px \cdot Cx)$
5. $(x) (Bx \supset Lx)$
7. $(x) \{(Bx \cdot Lx \cdot Dx) \supset {\sim}Gx\}$
9. $(\exists x) \{(Px \cdot Hx) \cdot Fx\}$

Exercises for § 9.6

A. 1. On tapes

3. 1) $(\exists x) (Ax \cdot Bx)$
    2) $(x) (Ax \supset Cx)$ $/ \therefore (\exists x) (Cx \cdot Bx)$
    3) $Aa \cdot Ba$ 1. E.I.
    4) $Aa \supset Ca$ 2. U.I.
    5) Aa 3. Simpl.
    6) Ca 4.5. M P.
    7) Ba 3. Simpl.
    8) $Ca \cdot Ba$ 6.7. Conj.
    9) $(\exists x) (Cx \cdot Dx)$ 8. E.G.

5. 1) $(x) (Cx \supset Dx)$
    2) $(\exists x) (Cx \cdot Ex)$ $/ \therefore (\exists x) (Ex \cdot Dx)$
    3) $Ca \cdot Ea$ 2. E.I.
    4) $Ca \supset Da$ 1. U.I.
    5) Ca 3. Simpl.
    6) Da 4.5. M.P.
    7) Ea 3. Simpl.
    8) $Ea \cdot Da$ 6.7. Conj.
    9) $(\exists x) (Ex \cdot Dx)$ 8. E.G.

7. 1) $(\exists x) (Nx \cdot {\sim}Px)$
    2) $(x) (Cx \supset Px)$ $/ \therefore (\exists x) (Nx \cdot {\sim}Cx)$
    3) $Na \cdot {\sim}Pa$ 1. E.I.
    4) $Ca \supset Pa$ 2. U.I.
    5) ${\sim}Pa$ 3. Simpl.
    6) ${\sim}Ca$ 4.5. M.T.
    7) Na 3. Simpl.
    8) $Na \cdot {\sim}Ca$ 7.6. Conj.
    9) $(\exists x) (Nx \cdot {\sim}Cx)$ 8. E.G.

9. 1) $(x) (Wx \supset {\sim}Lx)$
    2) $(x) (Px \supset Wx)$ $/ \therefore (x) (Lx \supset {\sim}Px)$
    3) $Pa \supset Wa$ 2. U.I.
    4) $Wa \supset {\sim}La$ 1,2. U.I.
    5) $Pa \supset {\sim}La$ 3.4. H.S.

6) ∼∼*La* ⊃ ∼*Pa*   5. Transp.
7) *La* ⊃ ∼*Pa*   6. Double Neg.
8) (*x*) (*Lx* ⊃ ∼*Px*)   7. U.G.

B. 1. 1) (*x*) (*Mx* ⊃ *Nx*)
        2) (∃*x*) (*Mx* · *Ox*)   / ∴ (∃*x*) (*Ox* · *Nx*)
        3) *Ma* · *Oa*   2. E.I.
        4) *Ma* ⊃ *Na*   1. U.I.
        5) *Ma*   3. Simpl.
        6) *Na*   4.5. M.P.
        7) *Oa*   3. Simpl.
        8) *Oa* · *Na*   7.6. Conj.
        9) (∃*x*) (*Ox* · *Nx*)   8. E.G.

    3. 1) (*x*) (*Fx* ⊃ *Bx*)
        2) (*x*) (*Bx* ⊃ *Hx*)   / ∴ (*Fx* ⊃ *Hx*)
        3) *Fa* ⊃ *Ba*   1. U.I.
        4) *Ba* ⊃ *Ha*   2. U.I.
        5) *Fa* ⊃ *Ha*   3.5. H.S.
        6) (*x*) (*Fx* ⊃ *Hx*)   5. U.G.

    5. 1) (*x*) (*Tx* ⊃ *Lx*)
        2) (∃*x*) (*Px* · *Tx*)   / ∴ (∃*x*) (*Lx* · *Px*)
        3) *Pa* · *Ta*   2. E.I.
        4) *Ta* ⊃ *La*   1. U.I.
        5) *Ta*   3. Simpl.
        6) *La*   4.5. M.P.
        7) *Pa*   3. Simpl.
        8) *La* · *Pa*   6.7. Conj.
        9) (∃*x*) (*Lx* · *Px*)   8. E.G.

    7. 1) (*x*) (*Px* ⊃ *Ax*)
        2) (∃*x*) (*Wx* · *Px*)   / ∴ (∃*x*) (*Wx* · *Ax*)
        3) *Wa* · *Pa*   2. E.I.
        4) *Pa* ⊃ *Aa*   1. U.I.
        5) *Pa*   3. Simpl.
        6) *Aa*   4.5. M.P.
        7) *Wa*   3. Simpl.
        8) *Wa* · *Aa*   7.6. Conj.
        9) (∃*x*) (*Wx* · *Ax*)   8. E.G.

    9. 1) (*x*) (*Sx* ⊃ *Px*)
        2) (*x*) (*Px* ⊃ *Dx*)   / ∴ (*x*) (*Sx* ⊃ *Dx*)
        3) *Sa* ⊃ *Pa*   1. U.I.
        4) *Pa* ⊃ *Da*   2. U.I.
        5) *Sa* ⊃ *Da*   3.4. H.S.
        6) (*x*) (*Sx* ⊃ *Dx*)   5. U.G.

Exercises for § 9.7

A. 1. 1) (*Ca* ⊃ ∼*Ba*) · (*Cb* ⊃ ∼*Bb*)
        2) (*Ca* · ∼*Da*) v (*Cb* · ∼*Db*)
                / ∴ (*Ba* · ∼*Da*) v (*Bb* · ∼*Db*)
        Ca and *Cb* = True
        Ba, *Bb*, *Da*, and *Db* = False

3. On tapes

5. 1) ~(x) ~Ax or (∃X) Ax
   2) (x) (Bx ⊃ Ax)
   ∴ (∃x) Bx

1. Aa
2. Ba ⊃ Aa   / ∴ Ba
   Aa = True
   Ba = False

7. 1) (Aa · ~Ba) v (Ab · ~ Bb)
   2) (Ba · ~Ca) v (Bb · ~Cb)
   ∴ (Ca · ~Aa) v (Cb · ~ Ab)
   Aa, Ab, Ba = True
   Bb, Ca, Cb = False

9. 1) (Pa · Qa) v (Pb · Qb)
   2) (Ra · Qa) v (Rb · Qb)
   / ∴ (Ra · ~Pa) v (Rb · ~Pb)
   All are = to true

B. 1. 1) (x) (Gx ⊃ ~Sx)
      2) (∃x) (Ix · Gx)
      / ∴ (x) (Ix ⊃ ~Sx)
      1) (Ga ⊃ ~Sa) · (Gb ⊃ ~Sb) · (Gc ⊃ ~Sc)
      2) (Ia · Ga) v (Ib · Gb) v (Ic · Gc)
      ∴ (Ia ⊃ ~Sa) · (Ib ⊃ ~Sb) · (Ic ⊃ ~Sc)
      Gb, Sa, Ia, Ib = True
      Ga, Sb, = False

1. (Ga ⊃ ~Sa) · (Gb ⊃ ~ Sb)
2. Ia · Ga) v (Ib · Gb)
   / ∴ (Ia ⊃ ~ Sa) · (Ib ⊃ ~ Sb)

3. 1) (∃X) (Tx · ~Sx)
   2) (x) (Mx ⊃ Sx)
   ∴ (∃x) (Mx · ~Sx)
   Ta, Tb, Sa = True
   Sb, Ma, Mb = False

1. (Ta · ~Sa) v (Tb · ~Sb)
2. (Ma ⊃ Sa) · (Mb ⊃ Sb)
   ∴ (Ma · ~Sa) v (Mb · ~Sb)

5. 1) (∃x) (Px · Ox)
   2) (∃x) (Ox · ~ Dx)
   ∴ (∃x) (Dx · ~Px)
   Pa, Pb, Oa, Ob = True
   Da, Db = False

1. (Pa · Oa) v (Pb · Ob)
2. (Oa · ~Da) v (Ob · ~Db)
   ∴ (Da · ~Pa) v (Db · ~Pb)

7. 1) (x) (Mx ⊃ Ox)
   2) (x) (Ax ⊃ Mx)
   ∴ (x) (Ox ⊃ Ax)
   Ma, Mb, Oa, Ob = True
   Aa and Ab = False

1. (Ma ⊃ Oa) · (Mb ⊃ Ob)
2. (Aa ⊃ Ma) · (Ab ⊃ Mb)
   / ∴ (Oa ⊃ Aa) · (Ob ⊃ Ab)

9. 1) (x) (Gx ⊃ Bx)
   2) (∃x) (Tx · Bx)
   ∴ (∃x) (Gx · Tx)
   Ba, Bb, Ta, Tb = True
   Ga and Gb = False

1. (Ga ⊃ Ba) · (Gb ⊃ Bb)
2. (Ta · Ba) v (Tb · Bb)
   / ∴ (Ga · Ta) v (Gb · Tb)

Exercises for § 9.8

A. 1. On tape
   3. (∃x) {Px · ~(Fx v Gx)}
   5. On tape

7. $(x)\{(Lx \supset (Wx \cdot Ax)\} \cdot (x)\{(Dx \supset (Wx \cdot Ax)\}$

9. $(x)\{Mx \supset (Tx \cdot Sx) \supset Ax\}$

B. 1. On tape

3. 1) $(x)(Ax \supset Bx)$

    2) $(x)\{(Bx \cdot Ax) \supset Cx\}$ $/ \therefore (x)\{Ax \supset (Ax \cdot Cx)\}$

    3) Ax AP

    4) $Ax \supset Bx$ 1. U.I.

    5) Bx 4.3. M.P.

    6) $\{(Bx \cdot Ax) \supset Cx\}$ 2. U.I.

    7) $(Bx \cdot Ax)$ 5.3. Conj.

    8) Cx 6.7. M.P.

    9) $Ax \cdot Cx$ 3.8. Conj.

   10) $Ax \supset (Ax \cdot Cx)$ 3.9. C.P.

   11) $(x)\{Ax \supset (Ax \cdot Cx)\}$ 10. U.G.

5. 1) $(x)\{Gx \supset (Fx \lor Hx)\}$

    2) $(\exists x)(Gx \cdot \sim Hx)$ $/ \therefore (\exists x)(Fx \cdot Gx)$

    3) $Gx \cdot \sim Hx$ 2. E.I.

    4) $Gx \supset (Fx \lor Hx)$ 1. U.I.

    5) Gx 3. Simpl.

    6) $Fx \lor Hx$ 4.5. E.P.

    7) $\sim Hx$ 3. Simpl.

    8) Fx 6.7. D.S.

    9) $Fx \cdot Gx$ 8.5. Conj.

   10) $(\exists x)(Fx \cdot Gx)$ 9. E.G.

7. 1) $(x)\{(Fx \lor Gx) \supset (Hx \cdot Ix)$ $/ \therefore (x)(Fx \supset Hx)$

    2) Fx A.P.

    3) $(Fx \lor Gx) \supset (Hx \cdot Ix)$ 1. U.I.

    4) $Fx \lor Gx$ 2. Add.

    5) $Hx \cdot Ix$ 3.4. M.P.

    6) Hx 5. Simpl.

    7) $Fx \supset Hx$ 2-6 C.P.

    8) $(x)(Fx \supset Hx)$ 7. U.G.

9. 1) $(x)\{Ax \supset (Bx \cdot Cx)\}$

    2) Aa $/ \therefore Ba$

    3) $Aa \supset (Ba \cdot Ca)$ 1. U.I.

    4) $Ba \cdot Ca$ 3.2. M.P.

    5) Ba 4. Simpl.

C. 1. 1) $(x)(Ax \lor Bx)$

    2) $\sim As$ $/ \therefore Bs$

  or

    1) $(x)(Ax \lor Bx)$

    2) $(x)(Sx \supset \sim Ax)$ $/ \therefore (x)(Sx \supset Bx)$

    3) Sx A.P.

    4) $Sx \supset \sim Ax$ 2. U.I.

    5) $\sim Ax$ 4.3. M.P.

    6) $Ax \lor Bx$ 1. U.I.

    7) Bx 6.5. D.S.

    8) $Sx \supset Bx$ 3-7 C.P.

    9) $(x)(Sx \supset Bx)$ 8. U.G.

3. 1) $(x \{Px \supset (Bx \vee Dx)\}$
    2) $(\exists x) (Px \cdot Dx)$ $/ \therefore (\exists x) (Bx \cdot \sim Dx)$
    3) $Px \cdot \sim Dx)$ 2. E.I.
    4) Px 3. Simpl.
    5) $Px \supset (Bx \vee Dx)$ 1. U.I.
    6) $Bx \vee Dx$ 5.4. M.P.
    7) $\sim Dx$ 3. Simpl.
    8) Bx 6.7. D.S.
    9) $Bx \cdot \sim Dx$ 8.7. Conj.
    10) $(\exists x) (Bx \cdot \sim Dx)$ 9. E.G.

5. On tapes

7. 1) $(x) \{(Nx \cdot Dx) \supset \sim Px$
    2) $Da \cdot Pa$ $/ \therefore \sim Na$
    3) $(Na \cdot Da) \supset \sim Pa$ 1. U.I.
    4) Pa 2. Simpl.
    5) $\sim\sim Pa$ 4. D.N.
    6) $\sim(Na \cdot Da)$ 3.5. M.T.
    7) $\sim Na \vee \sim Da$ 6. DeM
    8) Da 2. Simpl.
    9) $\sim Na$ 7.8. D.S.

9. 1) $(x) \{(Dx \vee Ax) \supset Sx\}$
    2) $(x) \{Sx \supset (Hx \cdot Cx) \vee Mx\}$
    3) $(x) (Mx \supset \sim Fx)$
    4) $(x) (Cx \supset Dx)$
    5) $(x) (Nx \supset Cx)$
    6) $(x) \{Px \supset (Nx \cdot \sim Hx)\}$ $/ \therefore (x) (Px \supset \sim Fx)$
    7) Px A.P.
    8) $Px \supset (Nx \cdot \sim Hx)$ 6. U.I.
    9) $Nx \cdot \sim Hx)$ 8.7. M.P.
    10) Nx 9. Simpl.
    11) $Nx \supset Cx$ 5. U.I.
    12) Cx 11.10. M.P.
    13) $Cx \supset Dx$ 4. U.I.
    14) Dx 13.12. M.P.
    15) $Dx \vee Ax$ 14. Add.
    16) $(Dx \vee Ax) \supset Sx$ 1. U.I.
    17) Sx 16.15. M.P.
    18) $Sx \supset \{(Hx \cdot Cx) \vee Mx\}$ 2. U.I.
    19) $(Hx \cdot Cx) \vee Mx$ 18.17. M.P.
    20) $\sim Hx$ 9. Simpl.
    21) $\sim Hx \vee \sim Cx$ 20. Add.
    22) $\sim(Hx \cdot Cx)$ 21. DeM.
    23) Mx 19.22. D.S.
    24) $Mx \supset \sim Fx$ 3. U.I.
    25) $\sim Fx$ 24.23. M.P.
    26) $Px \supset \sim Fx$ 7-25. C.P.
    27) $(x) (Px \supset \sim Fx)$ 26. U.G.

Exercises for § 9.9

A. 1. $\{(Laa \vee Lab) \vee (Lba \vee Lbb)\}$
    3. $\{(Laa \cdot Lab) \cdot (Lba \cdot Lbb)\}$
    5. $\{(Fa \vee Fb) \cdot (Gxa \cdot Gxb)\}$

B.   1. Something belongs to everyone.
     3. There is something which belongs to no one.
     5. There is no thing which belongs to someone.

C.   1. $(x)\,(Hx \supset Fx)$
     3. $(\exists x)\,(\exists y)\,(Kxy)$
     5. On the tapes
     7. $(\exists x)\,(Mx \cdot Fxd)$
     9. $(\exists x)\,(Bx \cdot Rx)$
    11. $(x)\,\{(Px \cdot Hqx) \supset Hxx\}$ or $(x)\,\{Px \supset (Hqx \equiv Hxx)\}$
    13. On the tapes
    15. $x\,\{Px \cdot (Hx\ Ax)\}$
    17. $(x)\,(y)\,(z)\,\{(Px \cdot My \cdot Fzx) \supset {\sim}Bxyz\}$
    19. $(x)\,(y)\,(Px \cdot Eyx \cdot Lxy) \supset {\sim}(\exists z)\,Sz$

Exercises for § *9.11*

A.   1.   1. $(x)\,(\exists y)\,Lxy$ $/ \therefore (\exists y)\,(\exists x)\,Lxy$
         2. $(\exists y)\,Lxy$ 1. U.I.
         3. Lxy 2. E.I.
         4. $(\exists y)\,Lxy$ 3. E.G.
         5. $(\exists y)\,(\exists x)\,Lxy$ 4. E.G.

     3.   1. $(x)\,(y)\,(Lxy \supset Hxy)$ $/ \therefore (\exists x)\,(y)\,(Lxy) \supset (\exists x)\,(\exists y)\,(Hxy)$
        ▸2. $(\exists x)\,(y)\,(Lxy)$ A.P.
         3. $(y)\,(Lxy)$ 2. E.I.
         4. Lxy 3. U.I.
         5. $(y)\,(Lxy \supset Hxy)$ 1. U.I.
         6. $Lxy \supset Hxy$ 5. U.I.
         7. Hxy 6.4. M.P.
         8. $(\exists y)\,(Hxy)$ 7. E.G.
         9. $(\exists x)\,(\exists y)\,(Hxy)$ 8. E.G.
       10. $(\exists x)\,(y)\,(Lxy) \supset (\exists x)\,(\exists y)\,(Hxy)$ 2-9 C.P.

     5. On tapes.

B.   1. On tapes
     3. On tapes
     5.   1. $(x)\,(Fx \supset Bx)$ $/ \therefore (y)\,(y)\,\{(Fx \cdot Dyx) \supset (\exists z)\,(Bz \cdot Dyz)\}$
        ▸2. $Fx \cdot Dyx$ A.P.
         3. $Fx \supset Bx$ 1. U.I.
         4. Fx 2. Simpl.
         5. Bx 3.4. M.P.
         6. Dyx 2. Simpl.
         7. $Bx \cdot Dyx$ 5.6. Conj.
         8. $(\exists z)\,(Bz \cdot Dyz)$ 7. E.G.
         9. $(Fx \cdot Dyx) \supset (\exists z)\,(Bz \cdot Dyz)$ 2-8. C.P.
       10. $(y)\,\{(Fx \cdot Dyx) \supset (\exists z)\,(Bz \cdot Dyz)\}$ 9. U.G.
       11. $(x)\,(y)\,\{(Fx \cdot Dyx) \supset (\exists z)$ 10. U.G.
            $(Bz \cdot Dyz)\}$

CHAPTER 10

Exercises for § 10.2

A. 1. Primary Generalization
    3. Causal or Functional Generalization
    5. Not a generalization
    7. A Statement—not a Generalization
    9. The conclusion is not a generalization, but application of one.

B. 1. Could be done by complete enumeration.
    3. Could be done by complete enumeration.
    5. Could *not* be done—there may be millions of planets in the universe.
    7. Could be done by complete enumeration.
    9. This could be done by complete enumeration.

C. 1. Young-Middle Aged-Old   Ethnic Groupings   Religious Affiliations
       Urban-Rural   Income Groupings   Different Geographical
       Professional Groupings   Political Affiliations   Areas

    3. Wide Geographical Spread   Occupational Affiliation-Business,
       Political and Religious Affiliation   Labor, Agricultural Scientific,
       Rural-Urban   Housewives
       Income Groups   Young-Middle Aged-Old

    5. Young-Middle Aged-Old   Married-Single-Divorced
       Geographical Distributions   Religious Affiliation
       Occupational Background   Mothers and Non-Mothers

    7. Geographical Distribution-   Large States-Small States
          North, South, East, West   States with Urban Centers and Those
       Political Affiliation   With None

    9. Young, Old, Middle Aged   Occupational Background
       Geographical Distribution   Ethnic Background
       Educational Background   Urban-Rural
       Religious Affiliation

D. 1. The delineation of the population is poor—it does not state what kind—i.e., general
       practitioners, specialists, surgeons, or physicians were interviewed.
       Delineation of the issue is unclear: how was strong opposition to government medical
       insurance determined?—what criteria?—what kinds of questions?
       The number is very weak—only 300 physicians out of a large number of American
       physicians.
       Variety is not good (only one state), and the kinds of physicians is not specified.
       Scope is very broad for the sample given, and thus the generalization is quite poor.

    3. The delineation of the population is biased and poor—"movie goers" is not clearly
       specified (regular, not so regular, etc.)
       Number is not given so the percentages mean nothing.
       Variety is bad because a Foreign Film Theatre would likely attract more educated
       people.
       Scope is too broad for the sample and thus the generalization is quite weak.

    5. Once again the delineation of the issue and the population is not very good—though
       what constitutes a favorite TV program is probably fairly easy to pinpoint. The
       question why it is a favorite, however, would be much more difficult.

Number is not given, and thus the percentage given is meaningless.

Variety is narrow because of the time of day selected—these would likely be house-wives and others at home, and thus the sample is biased because it eliminates most men, the working women, the students and many children.

The scope is very broad because of the lack of variety, and thus it is not a fair picture of the total of America.

E. 1. The generalizations are as follows:
    a. The key to the conduct of many products and services being offered are substan-dard, dangerous and worthless. Statistical
    b. Advertising and personal selling are major sources of guidance for consumers. Primary
    c. Much advertising and personal selling falls short of informing customers faithfully and truthfully about the merits of even a single product. Statistical

Evidence:

No evidence is offered for the first generalization.

Evidence offered for the second and third is:

    a. 8000 advertisements in 1970 appeared untruthful.
    b. 1972—FTC proceeding against manufacturers of eight analgesics—refrain from false advertising.

        a. Delineation of the phrase "falls short of informing" is bad because there is no criteria for knowing at what point they fall short.
            How is consumer defined?
        b. The two pieces of evidence cited reflect a small number and variety in light of the broad scope of the generalizations—much advertising and personal selling.
        c. It is a weak piece indeed.

    3. Generalizations are:
        a. The U.S. is not on the verge of running out of oil, but future output is not likely to increase greatly and over the years it is declining.
            This is probably a functional generalization.
        b. Evidence is:
            a. Decline in oil discovered.
            b. These discoveries were the product of technological advances.
            c. This was the intensive period of research and exploration.
            d. Observed decline not easily accounted for by other factors.
        c. Though this body of evidence does not contain specific numbers and citing of tests, all of the evidence is relevant and significant and thus the generalization is a fairly good one.

    5. Generalizations:
        a. Many scholars find it unbelievable that William Shakespeare wrote the plays—statistical generalization.
        b. DeVere had all the qualities necessary to write the plays of genius whereas Shakespeare did not.

    Evidence:
        a. For generalization a—Shakespeare was of lowly origins and never traveled much. This is attack on the man. Immanuel Kant, a great philosopher never traveled much and wrote extensively on many things. Many men of lowly origins have become great, versatile, erudite.
        b. For generalization b:
            1) DeVere an accomplished poet and his poetry bears similarities to that of Shakespeare—may be only coincidental.

      2) Well educated and a student of the classics—but this does not make him a good playwright.

      3) Associated with plays and actors and wrote some plays in secret poking fun at the court—relevant and fairly good evidence.

      4) Skilled in music and versed in law—not too relevant and what about Shakespeare?

      5) Many of the facts of his personal life in plays—relevant and fairly significant evidence.

      6) The crest and the signing of William's name—fairly good.

    c. The evidence is fairly good, but not enough to say the generalization is true and all of this evidence could be purely coincidental.

7. Generalizations:

    a. The high degree of intellectualization . . . seems to be primary or perhaps statistical.

   Evidence:

    a. Median income of football coach—salary is probably determined according to amount of education the teacher has and thus this is not at all an indicator of bias.

    b. Since education is the university's main business—the major amount to be spent on the library.

    c. Attendance at classes and examinations, once again, is central to education and not fraternity hazing.

    d. Books are more important to education than panty-raids.

All of the evidence is mere assertion and no specific evidence for the statements is cited. It is an extremely biased and poor paragraph.

Exercises for § 10.3

A. 1. a. Strengthen—similarity in age, and young rats are probably more virile.

    b. Strengthen—isolation from all comforts would increase drive.

    c. Difference may weaken because the sexual behavior of grey rats may be quite different from albino rats.

    d. Privation would probably strengthen the drive and thus strengthen the conclusion.

    e. May or may not be relevant—depending on how color affects rat perception.

    f. Would weaken because the scope of the conclusion has been considerably broadened.

3. a. Similarity—strengthen.

    b. Weaken—difference.

    c. Strengthen.

    d. Crucial difference—would weaken. Higher claims, etc.

    e. Probably irrelevant unless it says something about the whole market.

    f. Would weaken if he is buying the company which invests in medical insurance.

B. 1. Probably argumentative.

    Conclusion: The universe could not have been formed out of a fortituous concourse of atoms.

    Premise: This would be like forming an ingenious treatise of philosophy by jumbling the alphabet.

The only properties shared are that they are building blocks for making something. A crucial difference is that atoms are energy points and may be capable of self direction and attraction whereas the alphabet is an arbitrary, man-made thing which cannot form itself.

The argument is quite weak because of this crucial difference between things being compared.

3. a. It probably is an argumentative use of analogy.
   b. Premise: Our Constitution successfully united the thirteen original colonies.
      Conclusion: A United States of Europe will work.
   c. The only similarity which the colonies and the states of Europe would have in common is that they are both disparate units needing unity.
   d. There are many dissimilarities; the colonies had a common purpose, namely freedom from old world domination; the colonies, for the most part, shared a common language. They all were beginning anew. The states of Europe have widely diverse languages, cultures, backgrounds, economic and political structures.
   e. Because of these crucial dissimilarities, the argument is a weak one.

5. a. This is an argumentative use of analogy.
   b. Premises: We, the poor, are the last in the camel train and can only see the camel in front of us.
                  We make this camel the target of our anger.
                  This will solve nothing.
      Conclusion: Nothing is going to happen until we generate our own political and economic power.
   c. The economic classes are being compared to a camel train, each in place in line following the leader, the octopus, i.e., the Washington complex, which is the leader or herder. The government is compared with an octopus because it has many grasping arms—economic, military, educational, etc.
   d. In some senses the powerful and the rich do lead the other economic classes vis-a-vis advertising, influence, the stock market, etc. The government also has many arms.
   e. However, human beings are not camels and need not be blindly led. An octopus' arms are essential to its life—are the military and business that essential to government?
   f. There is some plausibility to Chavez' argument, for men often do act like camels and the government does appear to be an octopus. However, much better and more relevant premises could be found to support Chavez' conclusion.

7. a. This is an argumentative use of analogy.
   b. Premises: College and university teachers are engaged in selling a product.
                  The teacher is the seller and the student is the buyer.
                  Buyers should determine what they want to buy.
      Conclusion: Colleges and Universities should be more concerned with the way they package and market their goods.
   c. Students do pay fees and tuition and in this sense they are buying an education.
   d. However, "education" is not a product, a thing, not even a "service," but a process of learning capabilities and content. The content and the process can perhaps be "packaged" better, but if all that counts is the package, then it is not education.
   e. The argument is highly controversial, very weak.

9. a. This is an argumentative use of analogy.
   b. Premise: Mouse and rabbit blastocysts have been successfully sexed.
      Conclusion: Thus, human blastocysts can be similarly sexed.
   c. There are some physiological similarities between mice, rabbits, and human beings.
   d. There are also some crucial dissimilarities.
   e. The argument thus is weak.

Exercises for § 10.4

1. This is an example of the computer-brain analogy. There are many similarities between a computer and a human brain because man has constructed the computer to perform like a human. However, the computer, as yet, cannot do anything other than that for which it is programmed. A human being presumably does not need to be programmed to act.
   The human brain and the computer may operate in a similar manner, but it is man who has produced this similarity.
3. Here nuclear fission is being compared to the division of a liquid drop.
   This was a highly fruitful analogy in the development of nuclear physics and did not seem to have any misleading aspects.
5. Here the human nervous system and an automatic machine are being compared. They are alike in the following ways:
   a. They both make decisions based on the past.
   b. They both decide between two alternatives.
   c. They both have a special apparatus for making future decisions based on the past.
   d. Both have devices for resisting the increase of entropy.
   Dissimilarities are:
   a. The nervous system is alive; the machine is not.
   b. The nervous system can make creative use of the past—can a machine?
   c. The nervous system can readapt itself if damaged—can a machine?
7. The notion of a container of billiard balls in motion was the foundation model for the kinetic theory of gases. This model worked well in the context of a deterministic, mechanistic, materialistic Newtonian physics. Such a model does not work well in today's context of atomic theory.

CHAPTER 11

Exercises for § 11.4

A. 1. On the tape
   3. Several methods may be employed. (a) This could be explained by physiological deficiency or damage to the brain, especially to areas of the body or brain that help to control memory. If sufficient laws connecting brain and memory functions were available, this could be deductive-nomological explanation, following from certain established physical laws. (b) Freudian psychology would seek to explain this in terms of certain sub-conscious or unconscious defense mechanisms or repressive mechanisms, and this could be considered either a deductive nomological explanation in terms of established psychological laws or a functional explanation in terms of certain functions this memory loss mechanism performs for the self.
   5. This would be a deductive-nomological explanation following necessarily from certain mathematical laws, postulates and definitions.
   7. This would be deductive-nomological explanation following from laws concerning the relationship between the weight of water and bodies floating in water, laws which date back to Archimedes and Greek times.
   9. This would be difficult to explain because of complex psychological and sociological factors which are not easily formulated into casual relationships and laws. Two recent cases of the fact that religious wars do tend to inflame deep hostilities are Northern Ireland and Lebanon. Two possible kinds of explanation that might work are deductive-nomological and functional.

1. on tape
3. on tape
5. The necessary and sufficient conditions are not easily specified, but several possibilities can be cited.
   Necessary conditions: a. Having enough money to invest
                         b. Investing in stocks producing sale price of 1 million plus costs.
   Necessary and sufficient: a. Investing in stocks which produce a million dollars in profit.
7. Again, the conditions are not easily specified, but they do make for interesting discussion and the realization that pinpointing casual relations in many areas of life are very difficult.
   Necessary conditions: a. Being chosen by the selection committee.
                         b. Having competed successfully in one or more of the Olympic sports.
9. If we had the answer to this question, we might be in the White House, but once again it taxes our imaginative and thinking powers to try to find answers.
   Possible: Holding down prices and wages.
             Controlling unfair and monopolistic competition.
             Increasing supply or decreasing demand.

A. 1. Either (i) Concommitant Variation to determine the *amount* or *level* of endurance of (ii) Agreement and Difference to determine whether or not athletes perform with nificant differences at different heights above sea level and at sea level.
   2. Agreement and Difference—in a number of instances the prayer saying should be present and in a number of instances the prayer saying should be absent with all the other circumstances the same.
   3. Agreement and Difference in a number of instances with Vitamin C absent and present and the other circumstances the same.
   4. This illustrates Agreement for there is one common factor, the eating at Immaculate Irene's banquet hall. It should, however, be checked with the Method of Difference to determine the exact food or item at fault.
   5. Agreement—presence of high pitched sounds to determine the effects, Concommitant Variation—to determine whether *level* and length of pitch makes a difference.
   6. Residue—Weigh the truck before and after the delivery.
   7. Agreement and Difference: to determine whether tension was relieved when present and not when absent.
      Concommitant Variation—to determine level and amount of marijuana necessary to relieve tension.
   8. One could try Agreement and Difference by examining divorce rate in the presence and absence of Women's Liberation, but this would be difficult because of the many complex variables involved.

C. 1. On tape.
   3. On tape.

CHAPTER 12

A. 1. This should be done on your own.
   3. There is no right or wrong answer to this question.

5. The problem is the increased pranks and vandalism in upper and middle class neighborhoods.
The solution offered is that the children are neglected by their parents, bored and have been given no sense of property value. Whether this is an accurate or adequate explanation is another question.

B. 1. a. The problem was the nature of lightning.
    b. The hypothesis suggested to Franklin was that lightning was electricity passing from one cloud to another.
    c. Preliminary converging evidence for the hypothesis is the analogical similarities noted by Franklin between lightning and electricity, namely; it sets things on fire, it melts metal, kills people, causes blindness and is attracted to pointed bodies. Franklin then formulates a prediction on the basis of the hypothesis, namely, that one ought to be able to get a spark from lightning to charge a Leyden jar.
    d. Franklin then tests the hypothesis and the prediction with the famous kite experiment. The prediction and the hypothesis were confirmed. As a matter of fact, Franklin went out to formulate a whole theory about the nature and operations of electricity which permitted the development of the lightning rod and the battery.
   3. On tape
   5. a. The first problem was the variation in the energy of beta rays which did not follow the pattern of behavior of the gamma and alpha rays and the concept of energy emission from a nucleus made up of discreet energy levels which was part of the current theory of nuclear energy.
    The second problem was the additional energy produced when a neutron changed into a proton and beta particle—energy which could not be explained in terms of the known elements involved.
    b. W. Pauli formulated the following hypothesis to take care of both problems. That there was an unknown particle, which could be called a neutrino, which was emitted with the beta particle and which had zero charge and practically no mass. Pauli is here using the Method of Residues, postulating an additional cause for the additional energy and energy variation.
    c. Pauli rejects Bohr's hypothesis that the reason the two problems exist is that the laws governing energy conservation and impulsion are inadequate to explain these processes in the case of nuclear energy. He gives several reasons for rejecting Bohr's hypothesis: The most important one is that one would have to conclude that beta disintegration is always accompanied by energy loss, which, in turn, implies irreversibility of the processes with respect to time.
    d. In the Seminar of 1931, Pauli puts forth his hypothesis of neutral particles plus a mathematical formula to account for energy levels in beta particle emission. He also gives a formulation of the possible properties of the neutrino.
    e. Fermi then works out a theory of beta particle emission which uses Pauli's hypotheses.
    f. Finally, in 1955, the existence of the neutrino is confirmed.

Exercises for § 12.2

A. 1. The melting point of copper is easy to verify and as a matter of fact constitutes a defining characteristic of copper.
   3. On the tape
   5. This would be easily verified by a simple process of counting or by checking a class roll sheet.
   7. This would be difficult to verify because we have no easy access to primitive societies and to their thought and behavior processes. It is also difficult to specify the type of

evidence that would be needed to confirm a complex psychological state such as optimism.

9. This would be easily verified by the simple process of trying to attract the nail.

11. Such a vague statement would be very difficult to prove or disprove. In what sense does it make the world "go round"?

B. 1. On tape.

3. On tape.

5. Converging Evidence: One would have to check historical records to find evidence of increased immorality such as increased adultery, increased crime and violence, increased promiscuous sex, increased political corruption and bribery, increased treason and treachery, and then one would have to show that these things led to (a) the breakdown of the family structure so essential to Rome, (b) a decrease in the political rule, (c) an increase in distrust among people and even attempts to overthrow the government; (d) a decrease in military strength and discipline so essential to maintenance of the empire.

Diverging Evidence: One would look for lack of cases of increased morality as well as evidence against any causal relationship between the immorality and Rome's fall.

7. On tape.

9. On tape.

C. 1. The data being discussed is the absence of oxygen in the bottles of preserves.

Pasteur is concerned to disprove Guy Lussac's hypothesis that "the absence of oxygen is a necessary condition for the preservation of animal and vegetable substances" and to offer his own explanation for the absence of oxygen.

The disappearance of oxygen from the preserves is explained by the process of oxidation that occurs when the preserves are heated. Oxidation, however, as Pasteur points out, occurs faster because the preserves contain little oxygen and much organic matter.

Against Guy Lussac, Pasteur cites the fact that preserves do often contain oxygen and postulates that is the destruction by heat of certain elements in the air that is necessary to preservation.

Pasteur's hypothesis is physically possible, is not contrary to the evidence, is testable and seems to fit the evidence. More evidence, of course, is required.

3. Once again, Pasteur is trying to disprove a hypothesis, this time, the hypothesis of spontaneous generation, which argues that bacteria spontaneously generate out of materials in substances. He cites first the two liquids, each containing necessary elements to produce bacteria, but neither of these liquids develop any bacteria. It is only when the solutions are infected with bacteria that they produce additional bacteria. In other words, the bacteria do not spontaneously generate.

Pasteur then cites a second experiment. This time dust is introduced into the solutions. However, only one is able to produce bacteria. Thus, spontaneous generation does not occur and the hypothesis that bacteria exists in the air as desiccated organisms doesn't seem to be confirmed.

5. Fleming's problem was to find something that would kill germs without killing white blood cells. He discovers a possible solution by accident, namely, in the accidental mold growth he notes that around the mold no staphylococci were growing.

He then tries to discover the substance that might possibly inhibit staphylococci growth, believing it might be the mold, then the yellow stuff. However, there seems to be a third stuff which he then tests on staphylococci. It does not stop their growth. Fleming then tests this "mold juice", or streptococci, and the microbes of pneumonia, diphtheria, meningitis, and gonorrhea and it stops their growth. It does not, however, work against the microbes of cholera, meningitis and typhoid.

Fleming's next concern is whether the juice will also kill human tissue. He tests the juice with white blood cells and with a rabbit and discovers no harm is done. Fleming's mysterious hypothesis was discovered by accident and then confirmed by several careful tests. It turned out to be extremely beneficial to all.

D. Attempt this exercise individually, and then check your answers with the instructor.

Exercises for § 12.3

A. 1. Splaine's testimony is obviously very dubious. The identification was not possible immediately after the robbery was witnessed,and memory usually does not improve with passage of time. It is also very doubtful that Splaine could have made such a specific identification given the time and distance involved.

B. 1. Statement c.
   3. Someone wanted to frame Hauptman and used his materials.
   5. Still weak—circumstantial.
   7. Someone framing Hauptman could write notes in German, could know of Hauptman's tendency to misspell and could copy his handwriting.
   9. y, bb, ee.
   11. p, q, r, s, t, u, v, w, x, z, aa.
   13. Someone is framing Hauptman. Maybe Dr. Condon, in cahoots with the baby's nurse.

CHAPTER 13

Exercises for § 13.5

There are no simple true-false answers to the questions in this exercise and chapter. Indeed, in many cases no simple answer can be given; only guidelines can be stated.

1. How much value do you place on racial integration? Does busing improve the quality of education for *all* students involved?—keep in mind that this is a two-way affair. Does busing mix, i.e. homogenize the races and improve their relations? What costs— economic, psychological, sociological, etc. are involved? You may bus your children or not, depending on how you answer these questions.

3. Do you think abortion during the first three months of pregnancy is not taking a *person's* life? Do you think the responsible rearing of a child born of rape is difficult? If considerations of physiological and psychological factors indicates an abortion in this case, you may be justified in having one.

5. Weigh short-term versus long-term advantages; look years ahead to evaluate different life styles involved. What are the job opportunities in your chosen field? What will they be in the decades ahead?

7. Tell the truth and the whole truth.

9. Try to avoid a confrontation; respect each others' rights; if forced to vote on priorities, agree to binding arbitration by a counselor.

11. Consult the evidence very carefully. Your decision depends on your philosophy of life and on the situation, e.g. facing a terminal illness.

13. How are the rights related to the responsibilities in this case? How mature and responsible is (a) your daughter and (b) her boyfriend? Whatever your decision, can you give reasons and be firm?

15. Is smoking more valuable to you than living beyond 50? How about dependents and others affected by your death?

17. Do not give him the money.

19. You should probably continue your **education for this,**involves possible long-term advantages, whereas the job may involve short-term advantages and possible long term risks.
21. Only the strict legalist would sit at the light, if certain that no persons or traffic are around.

CHAPTER 14

Exercises for § 14.2

A. 1. $P(A) = 9/16$—Probability of black.
    $P(A =) 7/16$—Probability of red.
    3. The probability is not 1/2 because there are obviously more than two possibilities, red or not-red. One cannot logically divide color possibilities into one color and not-that-color.

B. 1. $20/30 = 2/3$
    3. Need to know what the total sample was before the probability can be determined.

Exercises for § 14.4

A. 1. $P(A+B+C+D) = P(A) \times P(B) \times P(C) \times P(D) = 1/2 \times 1/2 \times 1/2 \times 1/2 = 1/16$
    2. $1/6 \times 1/6 \times 1/6 = 1/216$
    3. $P(A \vee B \vee C) = P(A) + P(B) + P(C) = 1/6 = 1/6 = 1/6 = 1/18$
    4. $1/18$

C. $1/52 : 1/52$

E. 1. Probability of ace on first draw $= 1/13$
       Probability of ace on second draw $= 3/51$
       Probability of two aces in a row $= 1/13 \times 3/51 = 1/221$
    2. Probability of at least one ace $= 1/13 + 3 \text{ -}51 - 1/221 = 29/221$
    3. Probability of first spade $= 1/4$
       Probability of second spade $= 12/51$
       Probability of two spades $= 1/4 \times 12/51 = 1/17$
    4. Probability of first black ace $= 1/26$
       Probability of second black ace $= 1/51$
       Probability of two black aces $= 1/26 \times 1/51 = 1/1326$

G. $1/20 \times 1/20 \times 1/20 = 1/8000$

I. 1. $1/2 \times 1/2 \times 1/2 = 1/8$
    2. $1/2 \times 1/2 \times 1/2 \times 1/2 = 1/16$

INDEX